Ordeal of the Union

Selected Chapters

ORDEAL
OF THE UNION
Selected Chapters

ALLAN NEVINS

Compiled and Introduced by
E. B. LONG

CHARLES SCRIBNER'S SONS

New York

May 7, 1975

To Allan and Mary Nevins
—The Editor

Contents

Ordeal of the Union
Selected Chapters

Introduction

"No FORM of literature is nobler, more instructive, or more moving than a history of great events greatly related. History sometimes stumbles, but it offers the only sure key we shall ever find to the complex world, the surest guide to judgment and the soundest set of standards." [1]

Thus Allan Nevins expresses at least a part of his philosophy as a historian and humanist. His own master work, the eight-volume *Ordeal of the Union*, more than fulfills these dicta, as he describes and analyzes the mid-nineteenth century in America.

Why did a scholar who spent some sixty years studying the entire sweep of his nation's past, its leaders, its mores, and its culture in so encompassing a manner choose the 1850s and 1860s for such detailed, meticulous, and inclusive treatment? He gives us a portion of the answer: "It was an era of storms and lightning, of fierce passions, of tidal movements of men and ideas, of rascality and debasement, of integrity, heroism, and devotion. Senate, factory, farm, and market; pine-clad mountain, sagebrush plain, fertile prairie, and burning cotton-field; millhand, farmer, preacher, rancher, clerk, and sailor— all felt a surge as of the sea. Part of its pulse should be in every history of the time." [2] Nevins understood that "no volume, no series of volumes, can do justice to the tremendous story of effort, devotion, and valor North and South, in the war which finally vindicated the national unity. A writer can hope but to present a few truthful interpretations of the vast complexity of events and forces." [3] Fully aware of the limitations and frustrations, he undoubtedly did more justice to his epical subject than any previous historian. Few critics, if any, disagree with this appraisal.

In his long career Allan Nevins produced some forty books as author and coauthor, around seventy-five collections and other editings, and so many pamphlets, articles, introductions, speeches, and reviews that he himself has become a part of our history. Often consulted by leading officials in government and education, he served as cultural attaché to the U.S. Embassy in London during World War II, was a cultural ambassador to Australia, and frequently taught and lectured in the British Isles. Among his numerous honors, degrees, and awards were two from Oxford University, including a Doctor of Letters degree in 1965. He worked on various historical committees and was an officer in several scholarly groups. Chairman of the United States Civil War Centennial Commission, he also supervised or edited such major projects as the American Political Leaders series, new Chronicles of America, Nations of the Modern World series, and the Civil War Centennial series. He accomplished all of this without ever receiving a formal Ph.D. degree.

Allan Nevins often called himself "just a country boy from down the 'Q,'" referring directly to his birthplace, the village of Camp Point, Illinois, on the Chicago, Burlington & Quincy Railroad, southwest of Chicago and not far from Quincy on the Mississippi River. Though he left rural Illinois at a young age and moved in ever widening circles, associations, and travels, he remained in the larger sense a "country boy." Even in the years of distinguished recognition he was still, as he put it, a child of the Midwest, of Illinois, of the Mississippi Valley, of the "heartland."

The son of Joseph Allan and Emma Stahl Nevins, Allan Nevins was born on a farm near Camp Point on May 20, 1890. His father, of Scots descent, worked the farm and also sold insurance. Nevins once recounted, "My father had a life of struggle. My grandfather had a life of struggle. They all did. My father—he had been a tenant farmer in Scotland. That's why he had the dream of a better country." [4]

It was on the farm that Nevins became an avid reader. A small but well-chosen home library contained volumes on economics, science, and history. Although he would never be a "collector" of manuscripts or books in an acquisitive sense, books would always provide inspiration for him. He often said that in building a house one should erect the library or study first, furnish it with volumes valued for use and knowledge rather than show, and then, when possible, build the rest of the dwelling around it.

At eighteen, Allan Nevins entered the University of Illinois where he edited the campus daily newspaper and centered his interests on literature and history. When he graduated Phi Beta Kappa in 1912, he was already writing a history of the University of Illinois, which was later published. For another year he remained at Illinois, teaching English and working toward his master's degree. In 1913 he joined the New York *Evening Post* as an editorial writer. By 1914 he had his first book published, *The Life of Robert Rogers,* a biography of a noted colonial frontiersman. During these years he was also writing for *The Nation.* After ten years on the *Post,* he moved to the New York *Sun* as literary editor, and from 1925 to 1931 he wrote editorials under Walter Lippmann for the New York *World.*

During this time he began the steady outpouring of solid, highly regarded books that would be so characteristic of him. The year 1924 marked the appearance of *The American States During and After the Revolution,* considered almost a classic in its field.

In 1927 came *The Emergence of Modern America, 1865–1878,* a sound and revealing economic, social, and cultural history of the Reconstruction years. In this volume he struck a theme that would be continued through the *Ordeal of the Union:* "The new industrialism was only the greatest among a hundred facts and tendencies which were remoulding American life" after the Civil War. The South could count on "an inestimable gain in the fact that, for the first time in history, it was adjusted to the healthful competitive forces, economic and social, of American life." The West was losing its "wildness," and the farmer had taken "the lead in declaring that, if the industrial era had arrived, the excesses of industry must be checked by firm political control." The "vicious tendencies of postwar readjustment were yielding to the idealism and progressivism" typified by various reforms such as civil service. Conscious always of the role of education, the author rejoices that universities had been transformed and that women's and labor movements were rising. "Between the Negro field hand and the Negroes who organized the Fisk University Jubilee Singers, what a gulf! New forces in literature and art caught their color from the quicker, more vital tendencies of the time. The Civil War had marked the end of one great era in American life; the dozen years of reorganization and readjustment which followed it marked the emergence of the new and modern republic." [5] Thus Nevins expanded the period of Reconstruction, a term which he largely avoided in the volume, far beyond the political realm.

In 1928 he turned to biography with *Frémont: The West's Greatest Adventurer,* which he later revised. Indeed, at the time of his death Nevins was working on a major rewrite of the story of the "Pathmarker," one of America's most controversial explorers, soldiers, and politicians.

Still primarily a newspaperman, he joined the history department at Cornell University in 1927. In 1928 he went to Columbia University as Associate Professor of History, and in 1931 that university named him to the DeWitt Clinton Chair in History, a position he held until retirement in 1958. Nevins was to find a spiritual home both in the intellectual milieu of this urban university and in the stimulus of New York City itself. He always remained deeply committed to teaching. Dozens of graduate students, many of them now well advanced in the ranks of historians, can testify to his dedication to them and to teaching. Outside the classroom he counseled historians, writers, and would-be writers, whether formal students of his or not. He felt so strongly about the need for expert teaching that in 1965 he donated a half million dollar fund to Columbia for a chair in economic history.

With his appointment to the chair at Columbia, Nevins's journalism career ended, but only as a main activity. Until his death he was continually writing for the press, often served as special and temporary correspondent at major political conventions, and occasionally was a very knowledgeable radio commentator for special events. Always proud of his career in journalism, he insisted that a good historian was at the same time a good journalist. Current history was not going to pass without his seeing it, commenting on it, and retaining it to weave into the broad fabric of history. It was in current history that Nevins made one of his most valued contributions to historical research by inaugurating the oral history program at Columbia in 1948. Present and future historians and other researchers now have available more than 2,500 taped interviews with contemporary persons. Always a prime advocate of history for the populace, Nevins can also be credited with being the main originator and strongest partisan of *American Heritage* magazine as it is now known. Able men such as James Parton and Bruce Catton were brought in, and the publication flourished, as it still does.

When Nevins left Columbia in 1958, he joined the prestigious Henry E. Huntington Library and Art Gallery in San Marino, California, as senior research associate. There his work continued unabated and, in some respects, it even increased. He traveled at a rapid pace in the Huntington years, and in 1964 he served an unprecedented second term as Harmsworth Professor of American History at Oxford. Death came on March 5, 1971, in Menlo Park, California.

The reading public knows Allan Nevins primarily through his books. Considering only the more prominent volumes, his prolificacy in the 1930s and 1940s was almost dazzling. He frequently worked on several books or editing projects simultaneously. *Grover Cleveland: A Study in Courage* (1932) won for him his first Pulitzer Prize. Four years later he won a second with *Hamilton Fish: The Inner Story of the Grant Administration*, a two-volume biographical study exploring new sources and bringing fresh insight to the Grant presidential years. In his biographical writing, Nevins never obscured his subject's role in the nation. He wrote about the world as well as about the man.

To Nevins the Grant presidency "is a dramatic and richly interesting period," offering many lessons to the careful student. "From the storm of Civil War the North moved into the sunshine of an unrestrained economic boom followed all too soon by panic and depression. From the idealism of tremendous sacrifices on the battlefield and the home front, it moved into the materialism of speculative excess and unscrupulous wealth-getting. The words Reconstruction and Restoration, applied to this period, have an ironic hollowness. Instead of rebuilding the South and regenerating national life, American leadership seemed intent rather on a profligate debasement. Sectional hatred, vindictive persecutions, abusive demagogy, and unprecedented interferences with freedom and justice stained the record of Congress and the executive branches. Dishonesty and sharp practice pervaded half of American business, while corruption seemed inseparable from government in the cities, the States, and the nation. In the long aftermath of war, all society slumped to a lower level of ethics and action. Literature, art, and thought felt the debilitating influences of the environment, and the high aspirations of the early republic seemed for a time almost forgotten." [6]

Believing in the importance of business and economic history, Nevins also wrote about the giants of American business. In 1940 there was the two-volume *John D. Rockefeller: The Heroic Age of American Enterprise*, later revised and published in 1953 as *A Study of John D. Rockefeller, Industrialist and Philanthropist*. Also in the 1940s came his three volumes on *Ford: The Times, The Man, The Company* (written with Frank E. Hill). In all of these he was, in a sense, seeking an objective balance between the muckrakers—who had been holding up the nation's industrialists as stereotyped, economically immoral, grasping, ruthless businessmen—and those who only pointed out their achievements in building up the industrial potential of the nation.

A goodly number of scholars place *The Gateway to History* near the top of Nevins's achievements. First published in 1938, "Gateway" was updated in 1961. It is an exciting, stimulating, and exacting volume on history itself. In his chapter "A Proud Word for History," Nevins calls history "more than a guide for men in their daily round, it is a creator of their future." [7] Almost every aspect of historiography is examined, including the varieties of history, the value of the scientific method in its study, the use of rules of evidence, the problems in writing biography, and the literary qualities necessary to the historian.

Thought-provoking essays may be found in *The Statesmanship of the Civil War* (1953), wherein the statesmanship of that period is compared to other periods in American life and the contrast between the leadership of President Lincoln and the Confederate administrators is painstakingly delineated. In discussing "Lincoln as more than a statesman," Nevins writes, "In this concept that the American Civil War was a struggle for the future of humanity, Lincoln joined hands with the Revolutionary statesmen—Washington, Jefferson, Madison, Adams—who had a vision of the creation of a new and brighter civilization; who believed that they were throwing open the gates to a higher, better future for all men. He became more than a statesman—he was a seer, a prophet, a poet. . . ." [8]

Mention at least should be made of his study of the New York *Post;* of *American Social History Recorded by British Travellers; Abram S. Hewitt: With Some Account of Peter Cooper; America: The Story of a Free People* (with Henry Steele Commager); *The United States in a Chaotic World; The World of Eli Whitney* (with Jeanette Mirsky); *A Century of Cartoons* (with Frank Weitenkampf); *This Is England Today; A Chronicle of International Affairs, 1918–1933; State Universities and Democracy; A Collection of American Press Opinion from Washington to Coolidge;* and biographies of Herbert Lehman and Henry White. Among the volumes edited by Nevins are: *The Diary of John Quincy Adams; Letters of Grover Cleveland; The Diary of James K. Polk; Diary of George Templeton Strong* (with M. H. Thomas); *The Heritage of America* (with Henry Steele Commager).

Thus, Nevins was not exclusively a Civil War historian. While his most ambitious work, *Ordeal of the Union*, belongs in that category, his other writings span the entire breadth of our country's past and even examine its present. In the mid-1940s he announced his plans for a grand epic history in the older style of serious, multivolume studies chronologically covering an entire era. He projected a history of the nation from the Mexican War through the 1850s, the Civil War, and Reconstruction. The original goal was to produce at least ten rather lengthy volumes to be known in their totality as the *Ordeal of the Union*. It eventually became clear that he would not have time to write the last two volumes on Reconstruction. It would all have to end when the war itself ended. Even so, at his death the last two of the eight published volumes were not as he would have wished them. But then, as he said so often, no work of history is ever really completed.

Nevins spanned a wide range of historical methodologies. He wrote and spoke at length on the subject, at the same time teaching himself. Very often he would say, firmly and with no immodesty, that he was "gradually teaching himself something about the Civil War." [9] And what were some of the points, not only about the Civil War, but about history, that he learned?

"History has always been written primarily on a humanistic basis, is today so written, and by every index we can measure will continue to be thus written. . . ." [10] He did have his fears on this point, imbued as he was with the need for humanism and the need for history as literature. He was, of course, in favor of using all old and new tools, but he was concerned about those who wish to "see history become so specialized and scientific that it will lose all relation to literature. It will possess so few of the age-old attractions we have associated with the arts of narration, description, and personal portraiture or characterization, that few people will deem it worth reading. This attitude, if given full rein, would destroy history as art—for it is an art. It would eliminate all the color and drama we have associated with history as *story*—for it is fundamentally a dramatic story. It would reduce historical writing to a narrow set of topics seldom related to any broad framework of meaning." [11]

To Nevins history was filled with a "protean richness," and he felt the "first requirement of the true lover of history is that he shall delight in its endless varieties—that he shall be tolerant of all themes, all approaches, and all styles, so long as the work under examination meets two tests. First, it must be written in a patient search for truth about some phase or segment of the past. Imagination must go into this search, imagination as a literary as well as an historical tool. In the second place, its presentation of truth must be designed to give moral and intellectual nutriment to the spirit of man, just as most ambitious poetry, fiction, and philosophy should be so designed. This is essentially a literary design." [12]

At the same time he wisely questioned the determination of "truth." It was this question, perhaps, that made him rejoice in the belief that the writing of history was never consummated. He himself was not a doctrinaire historian. He was not afraid to alter the shades of his meanings if experience, research, and the passage of more history demanded it. He believed that the important thing was not the views a man held, but how he arrived at them, the depth of his research, the power of his analysis, his integrity as a scholar. "The idea that history can ever be so well written that it does not need rewriting can be held only by those foolish people who think that history can ever ascertain exact truth. It cannot. . . . If history were a photograph of the past it would be flat and uninspiring. Happily, it is a painting; and, like all works of art, it fails of the highest truth unless imagination and ideas are mixed with the paints." [13]

In the same vein, Nevins was long concerned about the stresses between the academic and nonacademic historian. In a memorable address as President of the American Historical Association in December 1959, he said, "If history is to regain its place as instructor of the whole democracy, if it is to communicate with intelligent men as freely as in the year when Prescott and Macaulay died, the academic scholar will have to teach the layman something about precision and depth, while the lay writer will have to teach us a good deal about human warmth and literary form. We can be severe on both sides without animosity or arrogance. . . . We are all amateurs, we are all professionals. Perhaps what we all most need is a dual sense of humility; humility because we know that however we search for Truth we shall not quite find it, humility because we are in the last analysis servants of the democratic public. . . ." [14]

In these brief comments, Nevins touched on many aspects of himself, his work, and of history as it was to him. When he was harsh or cryptic, and it was seldom, he was usually railing against what he regarded as "pedantry." Minutia for its own sake was anathema to him. He was fascinated with and demanded to know the details of a subject, but to know them so as to fold them into the larger view and meaning of history.

Despite his grand designs and tremendous overview, he believed "the great histories are great as much because of what they leave out as what they put in. . . ." [15] Nevins was in reality a master of the economy of words. At the same time, words to him were the building blocks of history or literature, to be used with respect for as much of the truth as could be ascertained. There is a continual sense of fairness throughout his writing, with style never over-riding the facts and conclusions. Sometimes he was criticized for indefiniteness in conclusions, mainly by those with a favorite single point to make. Upon examination of his work, it becomes clear that Nevins was anything but monistic; his grasp was too extensive to be so. To him most events had multitudinous causes, varying in degree of importance, but generally complex.

The "weight of character" in judging the men of history was as vital to him in his work as it was in viewing men of his own day. He was always looking back of the external. After writing an article on Lincoln, for instance, Nevins felt his work defective in "failing to do justice to the spiritual element in Lincoln's attitude toward democracy." [16]

It has been said that Nevins may well have been the last American historian for at least a long time to think and write in the grand comprehensive manner of multivolume scope. The *Ordeal of the Union* was a natural subject for him, and he was not concerned when people mentioned that much had already been written on the causes of the conflict, on the Civil War itself, on the Confederacy and Lincoln. When I interviewed him at his home in August 1969, I asked when he first became interested in the Civil War period. Nevins replied, "Oh, when I was in college I read James Ford Rhodes, and to say that I read him, that doesn't begin to approach it. I read him with fascination. It seemed to me the greatest historical story I had ever read. Nothing like it in ancient history, maybe European history, maybe the Napoleonic Wars, but I had read them very briefly. James Ford Rhodes's story was really an epic in its broad outlines." He pointed out the emphasis that Rhodes, in his volumes covering the Civil War era, brought to the great characters: "He sees these men as the great leaders; how remarkable they were!" Asked, as he was quite often, whether he objected to being called the modern Rhodes, updating, enlarging and improving on the great scholar of the last of the nineteenth century, Nevins would say he did not object, but that it was a "great exaggeration." On the other hand, he admitted with considerable humility and candor that this was his aim.

The *Ordeal of the Union* is marked by certain dominant themes, one of which is the question of the inevitability of the war. "Twice in a century and a half terrible calamities came; twice a failure of statesmanship if not of national character cost the country far more than it could afford to pay. The Civil War and the Second World War should have been avoidable. Because the people and leaders of the United States did not act with determination and sagacity in solving the problems of slavery, sectional irritation, and a right adjustment of races, part of the country was half ruined for generations, and all of it set back by decades. The subsequent failure to consolidate the victory won in the First World War—the refusal to help set up a system of collective security and to play a manly, farsighted part in the world community—imperilled the very existence of the republic. Only colossal effort and the sacrifice of a vast part of the national wealth saved it. Such errors can in time be largely retrieved. But they cannot be forgotten or forgiven, and their lessons should be driven home." [17]

While he wrote in the last volume of one change of view, as will be seen in the text, it was perhaps even more strongly expressed in the interview of August 1969. When I asked if his thinking had really changed in the twenty-two years since publication of the first volume, he answered, "Oh, decidedly. Yes, the war seems now much more what I think of as an evolutionary step in the development of the republic. . . . I feel more and more deeply that it was inevitable, that it was engrained in the American society that had started off in so many wrong ways and remained so immature, so adolescent, so much inclined to the trivial, the exciting, the melodramatic adventure, in its thinking. All the time a deeper issue was simmering. It looks more and more like an inevitable part of our history. Nothing could have averted the Civil War. . . . Walt Whitman wrote this; he thought it a part of the natural evolution that we should come to this terrible disaster and tragedy."

Queried about his present stand on the idea that the Civil War was a breakdown of American democracy, he replied, "Thank God it was not a complete breakdown! The people profited in many ways from it. . . . What a terrible, terrible war it was! How awful, how much suffering and anguish there was. The poor people, North and South, Negroes and whites. . . . I think mankind has to crucify himself from time to time. It certainly has never failed to happen. . . . It is probably a law of life. . . . We have to steel ourselves to it. How that generation did steel itself to do it! You think those poor boys who went into the charges at Cold Harbor and Gettysburg didn't know what they were facing? They knew what they were facing. They knew that they might be stricken down on the battlefield for days and nights in anguish and suffering and despair. But they went ahead. They went ahead on both sides."

But could the nation have achieved the same tendency toward maturity without the Civil War? Nevins answered: "I used to think so, that the whole tragedy might have been averted. Now I don't think so. No. It was part of the inevitable development of the American people, as a nation and as a society." He realized also that "some men were ripened and deepened by the war. How Lincoln grew, under all the terrible difficulties of the office. Jefferson Davis never grew."

Writing some time earlier, Nevins postulated, "Every great war has two sides, the glorious and the terrible. The two aspects do exist side by side." [18] The war "was not a strategic chess game, but a desperate life-and-death contest between two sets of ideas and values, each determined to sway a nation's destiny. It had few ingredients of romance, dash and poetry; instead it was a tremendous national tragedy, full of blood, tears, cruelty, waste and demoralization. . . . The significance of the conflict has thus far been understated. Its full importance to ourselves and to the world remains to be revealed; broad currents flowing down from it have still to be measured. The more we expand our view of its results, the greater will be its inspiration." [19]

Nevins thought of his series primarily as "a narrative history," for "only a careful narrative can lay bare the inner meaning of the crisis, as only an ordered story can do justice to the suspense, drama, and human passion of the era." Of course, he asserted, room would be found, as it was found, for analytical and descriptive elements. He wanted to and did bring the whole civilization of the country under examination. The chapters on social, economic, and cultural life were meant to be integrated and they were. Nevins thought that the sectional issue was essentially misstated when discussed only in terms of North or South. His volumes would "aim at objectivity, and at equal fairness to North and South, East and West. But they aim above all at rendering an impression of the tremendous upheaval of American life, and of its wild variety." [20]

"It seems clear, in the first place, that the conflict of North and South, of slave area and free, was part of a broader movement for the unification of the nation, and for the merging of elements both varied and conflicting into a homogeneous whole." Thus, at the very start, he promulgated a thesis he maintained throughout: "The country felt a strong tendency to organize its energies, knit closer its economic structure, and standardize its moral and social values. Most of the forces created by science, invention, and business technology thrust toward unification. . . . The slavery quarrel and the social differences of North and South were simply the most important of certain disruptive tendencies; but all were gradually being forced to yield to the powerful impulses that were making the United States homogeneous in economic life, political ideals, and social outlook. By 1860 men who gave their patriotism to region, not country, saw the handwriting on the wall. Irresistible factors were making unity triumph over sectionalism, homogeneity over heterogeneity." There was another essential fact to be remembered—that the slavery issue could be readily oversimplified. "The problem offered by the millions of Negroes far transcended slavery. Dominant elements North and South saw all too dimly that the one really difficult problem was that of permanent race-adjustment, that the abolition of slavery would only present it in starker form, and that the united efforts of all sections would be needed to cope with it. Had this truth been clearly grasped, the country might have struggled out of its blind drift toward disaster." Other considerations, more obvious in Nevins's view, included the steady substitution of emotion for reason in prewar years: "Fear fed hatred, and hatred fed fear. The unrealities of passion dominated the hour." Yet, despite the sense of a very real and tragic crisis, the author also grasped the fact that all was not dark in the later 1840s and 1850s. The country was growing, people in a hundred fields were "writing a record of almost unexampled vigor and color. Energy, versatility, progressiveness—these were the traits of the young republic." [21]

After the first four volumes in which he brought the narrative up to 1861 and the war itself, Nevins explained his ideas about the last four books. "Now suddenly the storm changed the atmosphere. The people, both Confederates and Unionists, rose to the most desperate effort of their history. The tenacity with which the North fought on to total victory and the South to almost total ruin vindicated their claim to heroic strength of character, and left the country memories which partially redeem the record of a needless war." [22] Thus in 1959 he was still writing in terms of his original idea of causation.

Nevins treated the plain people as the real heroes and heroines and explored the impact of the war on the national character. "No writer treating the Civil War as a detached unit could fail to give equal emphasis to the Southern and the Northern story. This history, however, has been planned to cover a much longer period, and its emphasis therefore falls on what is permanent in the life of the nation. From this standpoint much of the Confederate effort appears too transitory to require detailed treatment. . . . My regret over the abbreviation of the Confederate story is diminished by the fact that Southern historians have provided several admirable records. In the same way, my regret that tactical military operations are crowded out of a work devoted primarily to political, administrative, economic, and social history, is diminished by the fact that the long list of books of military history is daily swelled by useful additions." [23]

Turning to the heart of the war, Nevins again emphasized developments other than military, although he does not neglect the impact of campaigns and major battles.[24] In fact he did not consider himself a military historian in the sense of investigating extensively the theory of warfare as applied to the Civil War or detailing the minutiae of unit movements. His main treatment of the military was to demonstrate the significance of events, the leadership, and the political, emotional, and social effects of warfare.

The first two of these eight volumes, known specifically as *Ordeal of the Union* when they appeared in 1947, received the Scribners Centenary Prize of $10,000 and the prominent Bancroft Prize. The second two, *The Emergence of Lincoln*, carrying the narrative to 1861, came out in 1950. The following four, entitled *The War for the Union*, were published in 1959 and 1960, and the last two posthumously in 1971. Volumes VII and VIII won the National Book Award for history.

It is hoped that this sampler of some of the more significant chapters from the series will make available the wisdom of this scholar to those who might not otherwise be able to learn from him. Faced with such sweep, flow, and grand design, however, any editor must approach condensation with considerable caution and humility. The eight volumes contain 129 chapters and over 4,000 pages. Roughly a tenth is included herein, largely whole chapters that reflect the author's thinking on special subjects and brief time periods. I have tried to follow his balance as to the military, the Confederacy, the political, social, and economic aspects, keeping in mind the Nevins objectives. The threads of his developing concepts and unique conclusions have been expressed as accurately as condensation allows. Certain subjects, such as lengthy coverage of foreign affairs, have necessarily and regretfully been omitted.

Between each of the thirteen chapters included we have attempted an interstice. These brief passages are written and edited to be as constant as possible to Nevins. They include a sketchy outline of the progress of events to give the reader guidelines not otherwise available in this volume. And, perhaps more important, I have used in these interstices and throughout as many of Nevins's own words as possible, passages taken from chapters that could not be used in their entirety. It has been my aim throughout to keep in mind that this is Nevins's *Ordeal of the Union*. This volume is not intended as, nor can it be, a substitute for the value and pleasure to be gained from reading the full eight volumes.

To Nevins, "History becomes a more formidable subject every year." [25] In providing a key to many great works, he gives an insight into his own: "Why and how are the best historical works written? They are planned because the author has a vision, or an approach to one. The subject takes hold of him, inspires him, and lifts him to a plane where he sees as in a golden dream the volume he intends to write." [26]

E. B. LONG

NOTES

1. Nevins, "The Telling of a Nation's Story," *New York Times Book Review* (Feb. 16, 1958), p. 1.
2. Nevins, *Ordeal of the Union*, Vol. I, *Fruits of Manifest Destiny, 1847–1852* (Charles Scribner's Sons, New York, 1947), Preface, p. viii.
3. Nevins, *The War for the Union*, Vol. II, *War Becomes Revolution, 1862–1863* (Charles Scribner's Sons, New York, 1960), Preface, p. vii.
4. Taped interview with Nevins, made by E. B. Long at the Nevins home, San Marino, California, August 1969. (Hereafter cited as Nevins interview, August 1969.)
5. Nevins, *The Emergence of Modern America, 1865–1878*, A History of American Life series, Vol. VIII (The Macmillan Company, New York, 1927), pp. 405–407.
6. Nevins, *Hamilton Fish: The Inner History of the Grant Administration*, Vol. I (Frederick Ungar Publishing Co., New York, 1957 edition), p. ix.
7. Nevins, *Gateway to History* (Doubleday & Co., Inc., Garden City, New York, 1962 edition), p. 18.
8. Nevins, *The Statesmanship of the Civil War* (The Macmillan Company, New York, 1953), p. 82.
9. Nevins, "The Darkest Hours of the War in the Northwest," address to the Chicago Civil War Round Table, Sept. 11, 1959, taped.
10. Nevins, "The Old History and the New," in *The Art of History*, two lectures by Allan Nevins and Catherine Drinker Bowen (Library of Congress, Washington, 1967), p. 10.
11. *Ibid.*, p. 9.
12. *Ibid.*, pp. 14–15.
13. Nevins, "Should American History Be Rewritten?" *Saturday Review* (Feb. 6, 1954), p. 7.
14. Nevins, "Not Capulets, Not Montagus," *American Historical Review*, Vol. LXV (January, 1960), pp. 268–270.
15. Nevins interview, August 1969.
16. Nevins, "Author's Postscript," to "Lincoln's Idea of Democracy," *WFMT Perspective* (February, 1962), p. 49.
17. Nevins, *Ordeal of the Union*, Vol. I, p. viii.
18. Nevins, "The Glorious and the Terrible," *Saturday Review* (Sept. 2, 1961), p. 9.
19. Nevins, "A Conflict That Was Big with Fate," *New York Times Book Review* (January 29, 1956), pp. 1, 28.
20. Nevins, *Ordeal of the Union*, Vol. I, p. viii.
21. *Ibid.*, pp. viii–x.
22. Nevins, *The War for the Union*, Vol. I, *The Improvised War, 1861–1862* (Charles Scribner's Sons, New York, 1959), p. v.
23. Ibid., pp. v–vi.
24. Nevins, *The War for the Union*, Vol. II, *War Becomes Revolution, 1862–1863* (Charles Scribner's Sons, New York, 1960), p. vii.
25. Nevins, "The Old History and the New," p. 2.
26. *Ibid.*, p. 12.

1.

"To ATTENTIVE hearers the Civil War, if we listen for a deeper chord than its clangor and fanfare, speaks an undying reproach. In part the indictment is simply of man's fate:

> The Sinister Spirit sneered, "It had to be";
> But still the Spirit of Pity whispered, "Why?"
>   (John Masefield)

In greater part it is the indictment of a generation of political leaders, and behind them, of a whole nation, its spirit and civilization." [1]

Allan Nevins begins his search for that "deeper chord" and the substance to the indictment with the "Hour of Victory" in the Mexican War of 1846–1848. The war had created martial ardor, had "excited some unhealthy appetites" as to national expansion, had intensified the question of slavery in the new lands. Beyond this, the military victories of 1847 "neither united the American people nor shed on the Administration the luster which President Polk and his Cabinet coveted." [2]

While the Mexican War had cost comparatively little and gained much, it was far from a popular war in large parts of the Union. And perhaps primarily, "as farsighted men knew, a mere compromise of the Territorial question would not be enough, for it would leave the deeper issues untouched. It would simply afford a foundation on which constructive statesmanship, if the nation had it, might operate to deal with slavery itself, the root of the sectional quarrel. Somehow a way must be found to teach the South that slavery offered simply a temporary and evolutionary status for the Negro; to teach the North that it must shoulder its fair share of the national burden in making the steady evolution of the colored race to this higher status possible." [3]

And yet, despite this underlying problem, in the late 1840s and at least early 1850s "the situation was far from implying an ultimate catastrophe." The young republic had many other aspects to its lineaments. There was a nebulous and diverse emerging culture, a growing mass awareness, a rising "pulse of reform," and a feeling that there "seemed to be no limit to her growth, and no possible check to her rise except internal dissension." [4] In addition, "Every advance in the practical applications of American democracy was eagerly watched by liberals across the seas, where a host of men and women regarded American freedom, egalitarianism, and reform as the brightest hope of mankind." [5]

Throughout much of the period "most citizens were sufficiently well satisfied with their national government to spend little thought on its betterment." Nevertheless no man of outstanding ability had entered the Presidency since Jackson, and the four Presidents before the outbreak of the Civil War in 1861 were "mediocrities," a situation that "can be clearly traced to the torsions which the slavery contest gave to the party system." Congress was clumsily managed and badly divided. With both of these drawbacks, the nation "watched the national crisis grow to a point where even strong leadership could not control it." [6]

As the decade of the fifties began, the danger over admission of new territories and the status of slavery there had been very real. Any abrupt national breach was averted by the Compromise of 1850, arranged primarily through the leadership of Henry Clay, Daniel Webster, Millard Fillmore, and Stephen A. Douglas. Southerners and Northerners acquiesced, but such acquiescence bore conditions and reservations on both sides that ran far deeper than the temporary settlement.

"To most Americans the word slavery calls up as vivid a series of pictures as any noun in the language, each scene tinged with emotional color." [7] It was this emotionalism that arose not only over "the lot of the bondsman" but over the presence of the black. Nevins indicts slavery as "the greatest misery, the greatest wrong, the greatest curse to white and black alike that America has ever known. Its ultimate abolition was an even greater benefit to the Caucasian than to the Negro. But to most Southerners the prospect of so momentous a revolution not merely in the labor system but the social system seemed fraught with incalculable dangers. The South behaved like a man who, afflicted with some horrible growth but fearful of the pain and peril of its excision, hugs it tightly to his bosom and extols it as after all rather a benefit to his health; knowing all the while that he is self-deluded and walking in a nightmare. The South needed compassion and help, not condemnation." [8]

"The most significant fact about the Southern myth of the social and moral superiority of slavery was its fantastic character, its divorce from reality; and it was divorced from reality because the realities were too grim to be frankly faced." [9]

NOTES

1. Nevins, *Ordeal of the Union*, Vol. I, *Fruits of Manifest Destiny, 1847–1852*, p. vii.
2. *Ibid.*, p. 5.
3. *Ibid.*, p. 33.
4. *Ibid.*, p. 74.
5. *Ibid.*, p. 151.
6. *Ibid.*, pp. 186–188.
7. *Ibid.*, p. 412.
8. *Ibid.*, p. 461.
9. *Ibid.*, pp. 496–497.

Slavery, Race-Adjustment, and the Future

THESE IGNORANT black folk, laboring under the overseer's profanity, and wending home at nightfall to the hoe-cake and cabin-pallet—what did they get for all their labor under the sun? Nothing in money; nothing in other material rewards beyond the bare necessities of coarse clothing, primitive food, and crazy furniture; nothing in family security; nothing in hope. They lived rough lives, they encountered a full portion of sorrow and ignominy, and they went to nameless graves.

And yet they were by no means wholly unrequited. They did earn by their toil one bright jewel which their kinsfolk left free in African villages never gained. What they won in the hot cane and cotton of the New World was a brighter heritage for their children. Could they have lifted their gaze from the sordid setting of their drudgery and looked down the generations to come, what would they have seen? Their descendants thronging into schools and colleges; becoming skilled artisans, businessmen, professional workers, and artists; seizing opportunities such as the Negro race in all its errant, thwarted history had never enjoyed; rising to light, laughter, and shining achievement. The hovel and hoe, which seemed to lead to nothing, fell away to a road opening upon wide vistas; and within a hundred years Negro endeavor was flowering into poetry and fiction, song and sculpture, scientific discovery and scholarly achievement. The accomplishments of the Negroes in closing the gap between the white race and themselves have been wonderful, and in one sense those accomplishments have been built upon the foundation laid by the humble slaves.

[I]

Most of the fathers of the republic were sensitively aware of the evils connected with slavery and hopeful of its ultimate abolition. Stern expressions of condemnation are easily culled from their writings. But they perceived that so thorny a problem of race adjustment was involved that emancipation would but dispose of one problem to create others. Franklin, who became head of the

(Ordeal of the Union, Vol. I, Fruits of Manifest Destiny, 1847–1852, Chapter 15.)

Pennsylvania Abolition Society, near the end of his career published an address which described slavery as "an atrocious debasement of human nature." Yet he predicted that "its very extirpation, if not performed with solicitous care, may sometimes open a source of serious evils." On this point Southern leaders naturally felt more strongly still.

Washington, born to a family which had owned slaves for three generations, held them all his mature life, and died possessed of about four hundred Negroes. Never liking slavery, he felt as he grew older an increasing repugnance for it. He wrote Robert Morris in 1786 that no man living wished more sincerely for its abolition, and that his suffrage would never be wanting to support legislative action to that end. Eight years later, addressing Tobias Lear, he expressed an earnest wish "to liberate a certain species of property—which I possess very repugnantly to my own feelings." He spoke elsewhere of his hope that the Virginia legislature might see the wisdom of a gradual abolition. In his will he directed that all slaves held in his own right should be freed on the death of his widow. But he never advocated immediate and general emancipation, for he feared the social dangers of hasty action.

Two more deeply reflective statesmen, Jefferson and Madison, early established their repute as opponents of slavery. But neither believed that abolition should be effected without careful measures for the future disposition of the freedmen. Jefferson suggested that they be transported to a new colony, in Africa or the West Indies, "beyond the reach of mixture." Madison was similarly in favor of segregating the great mass of blacks, but held that the Western country offered the most suitable haven. Both Jefferson and Madison staunchly advocated the diffusion of slavery so long as it existed in America, arguing that its expansion would not add to the whole number of slaves (a very dubious assertion), and would ameliorate the workings of the institution. Both believed also in the principle of state-compensated emancipation, and Madison used spirited language in pointing out that payment of the owners from a national fund would be fair, for the benefits of a general liberation would be national. To the end of his days Madison hoped that farsighted action might be taken. Robert C. Winthrop, visiting Montpelier in 1832, found him elated by the famous speech which James McDowell had just delivered in the legislature. "The recent revolution of opinion in Virginia on the subject of slavery," he exclaimed, "is the most important that had taken place since the Revolution of '76"—adding that almost for the first time he had begun to conceive a confident hope that slavery would yield to a system of gradual emancipation.[1]

---

1 Matthew T. Mellon, *Early American Views on Slavery*. R. C. Winthrop to Rives, June 24, 1856; Rives Papers. As late as 1859 an anonymous Virginian, Vindex, writing in the *National Intelligencer* of February 23, argued for diffusion of slavery as the best means of

Decade by decade many enlightened Southerners continued to regard controlled emancipation as a beneficent goal. But they spoke ever more guardedly.
George Tucker, whose life precisely spanned the years between Bunker Hill and
Fort Sumter, Virginia's greatest economist and the first chairman of her university faculty, wrote of slavery: "We may say of it as of man: the doom of its
death, though we know not the time or the mode, is certain and irrevocable."
But he wrote also that various factors might delay emancipation—westward
migration, the formation of new slaveholding States, a wider use of slaves in
manufacturing, the extension of sugar-growing, or the introduction of such new
industries as silk and wine into the South. In later life, when some of those forces
had become operative, Tucker became discreetly mild on the subject of slavery.
James McDowell, on becoming governor and Congressman, also grew reticent.
Winthrop once told him what Madison had said of his great speech. "Oh, Mr.
Winthrop, do not mention the subject," he burst out. "I should not dare to make
a speech again. It would be burned by the common hangman at the corner of
the streets, if this one has not been so already. I have not changed an opinion
expressed in it, but your abolitionists have now made it a forbidden topic with
us." [2]

Under mighty pressures, the Revolutionary hopes and impulses respecting
Southern emancipation died away. Here and there an intrepid figure, like Petigru
in South Carolina, John Letcher in Virginia, Cave Johnson in Tennessee, Cassius
M. Clay in Kentucky, and Sam Houston in Texas, expressed frank reprobation
of slavery. John P. Kennedy of Maryland, whose picture of the institution in
Swallow Barn seemed superficially mild but was essentially caustic, was unspar-
ing in his private denunciations. Outside the Lower South, he said, slavery was
an unmitigated blight. It was an expensive, unprofitable, and slovenly mode of
tillage; it impoverished the country by suppressing immigration and manufactures; it impeded public improvements; it begot indolence and debased manners.
The sooner it could be thrown off, the better. "Slavery in no community can
ever assume the character of a permanent establishment. It is essentially a transitory condition. Not only sound reason demonstrates this *a priori*, but history
invariably proves it as the condition of the institution in every clime." [3] Nevertheless, hope for early action died away; and the mightiest of the pressures which
killed it was a sense of the frightful difficulties of race-readjustment.

Few careers throw a brighter illumination upon the hopes and fears sur-

---

lifting Negroes in the scale of civilization. He pointed to the analogy of the immigrant.
The alien from Europe remained an alien if he lived in a communty of his fellows; he was
rapidly assimilated to the American type when he dwelt among native-born Americans.

2 Rives Papers, *ut supra;* cf. *Dictionary of American Biography* on McDowell.
3 MS Diary, 1848, pp. 78–80; Kennedy Papers.

rounding this question than that of Edward Coles, a figure who well deserves rescue from his obscurity. Sprung of a prominent Virginia family, Coles was reared in the Albemarle County mansion of his father, a Revolutionary veteran, and often saw at the fireside of "Enniscorthy" such guests as Madison, Jefferson, Patrick Henry, and the Randolphs. Private tutoring, followed by attendance first at Hampden-Sidney and later at William and Mary, gave him an exceptional education. A youth of generous impulses, he found his attention drawn to slavery by college experiences, and after long reading and reflection resolved that he would neither hold slaves nor remain in a slaveholding community. The death of his father in 1808 made him owner of a plantation with gangs of hands, but this merely confirmed his determination. For a time he found difficulty in putting it into effect. Accepting President Madison's invitation to become his private secretary, for six years he acted in that capacity. Soon after peace in 1815 he was sent to Russia on a diplomatic mission, and travelled extensively in western Europe. But meanwhile, unwavering in his purpose, he had decided to settle in the Northwest, which he had briefly explored.[4]

His anti-slavery conviction also led to a correspondence with Jefferson which became celebrated. With idealistic ardor, he urged Jefferson to furnish the country a plan of gradual abolition which might at once be put into operation. "In the calm of your retirement, you might, most beneficially to society and with much addition to your own fame, avail yourself of the love and confidence of your fellow-citizens to put into complete practise those hallowed principles contained in that renowned Declaration of which you were the immortal author." But Jefferson shrank from the task. He was too aged, he declared, to respond to an appeal which was like bidding old Priam to buckle on the armor of Hector. He added that he had outlived that Revolutionary generation in which mutual perils and struggles begat mutual confidence. "This enterprise is for the young, for those who can follow it up and bear it through to its consummation. It shall have all my prayers, and these are the only weapons of an old man." Existing laws, he noted, did not permit men to turn their slaves loose, even if it were for the slaves' good. Jefferson's doctrine was not merely that of gradualism, which was sound, but came near that of drift, which was not. Condemning slavery, he believed that men must wait until its extinction was "brought on either by the generous energy of our own minds, or by the bloody processes of St. Domingo."

At last, in 1819, the year after Illinois was admitted to the Union, Coles was able to make good his long-cherished resolve by removing to that State. He loved Virginia, he had many social ties binding him to the Old Dominion, and

---

4 Cf. E. B. Washburne, *Sketch of Edward Coles, Second Governor of Illinois*, ed. C. W. Alvord; *Illinois Historical Collections*, XV.

he could hope for political eminence if he remained. But he tarried no longer. His slaves, unaware of his wish to liberate them, gladly accepted his announcement of a new home. The whole company embarked at Pittsburgh on two flat-bottomed boats. When well started down the Ohio, Coles marshalled them on deck and in a brief speech told them they were free, and could accompany him or go ashore, as they liked. "The effect on them was electrical," he later wrote. "They stared at me and at each other, as if doubting the accuracy of what they heard. In breathless silence they stood before me, unable to answer a word, but with countenances beaming with an expression . . . which no language can describe. . . . After a pause of intense and unutterable emotion, bathed in tears, and with tremulous voices, they gave vent to their gratitude, and implored the blessings of God on me." They accompanied him to Illinois, where he gave each family a quarter-section of land, and executed for every slave a deed of manumission.

Appointed head of the Land Office at his new home, Edwardsville, Coles soon attained a wide influence in southern Illinois. He found the young State racked by a fierce struggle over slavery. To be sure, the institution was barred from Illinois by both the Ordinance of 1787 and the State Constitution. Yet slavery actually persisted there, the hostility to free Negroes was general, and a large pro-slavery party denied the validity of the Ordinance. How Coles, elected governor, placed himself at the head of the free-soil party, and how after a desperate contest he finally won the victory, is one of the great stories of Illinois history. As the struggle reached its height, the slavery forces invoked methods comparable to those later used in the Kansas struggle. But the scheme for a convention to frame a new pro-slavery Constitution was defeated by a close vote, and rapid immigration from the free States made any renewal of the attempt impossible.

This dramatic story contains much that is instructive. The existence of strong anti-slavery feeling in the Upper South; its essential helplessness as the idealistic impulses of the Revolution spent themselves and new economic conditions appeared; the willingness of many Southerners to make sacrifices to rear their children on free soil; the anti-Negro sentiment common among ignorant folk in the North no less than the South; the existence of an important pro-slavery movement north of the Ohio; its defeat by the combined influences of basic law, climate, immigration, and enlightenment—all this is representative of broad currents in the slavery struggle. Most striking of all is the fact that by 1819 a Southern believer in emancipation had lost all faith in frontal attacks upon slavery, and felt he could achieve his limited personal objects only by evasive action; by removal from the South.

[II]

If the emancipation movement was to revive in the fifties, it would have to be in the border States. Here slavery was numerically weakest and the conviction of its evils strongest. Yet from the Chesapeake to Kentucky, the antislavery movement failed anywhere to attain formidable strength.

In little Delaware, where (as in the Federal District) the number of slaves diminished in every decade after 1820, this failure was partly because freedom seemed gaining an automatic victory. Though at the first census Delaware had 8,887 slaves, by 1850 the number had dropped to 2,290, and was still falling. About two-thirds of the slaves in 1850 were held in the southernmost county, Sussex; and even here many slaveowners believed by 1860 that if left alone, the county would become free soil within a decade. One reason for this conviction was that the underground railroad was easily accessible; through tickets could be had almost for the asking, and it was believed the loss from runaways just about equalled the increment by births. Another reason was that the high prices of slaves induced many holders to sell them outside the State. The late fifties saw speculators roving about, offering from $500 to $1,500 for Negroes, and eager to snap them up. During 1859 a single trader was reported to have sent a hundred slaves out of Sussex, and it was computed that at least six a week or three hundred a year left the county. The institution was thus losing its vitality; gradual emancipation was taking place; and since time would effect the result, no emancipatory law seemed needed.[5]

In Maryland and Kentucky no such automatic solution of the problem was anticipated. Both States kept alive strong movements for gradual abolition, led by such men as Henry Winter Davis and Cassius M. Clay, but in both they were checked by fear of the race-adjustment problem. A slaveholders' convention in Baltimore in June, 1859, debated the best means of regulating the free Negro population. The attendance was large, representative of every part of the State, and determined to repress abolitionist tendencies. It asserted that for the purpose of diminishing "the evils which proceed from the excessive and increasing free negro class," the policy of strict State regulation fixed in 1831 should be reaffirmed, with amendments which "will either prohibit emancipation altogether, or compel the prompt removal from the State of those emancipated. . . ."[6] Kentucky's constitutional convention of 1849 rang the death-knell of all hopes for early steps toward emancipation. Its motives were mixed. Some delegates believed slavery just and profitable, some valued the social dignities it conferred,

5 See survey in N. Y. *Weekly Tribune*, March 3, 1860.
6 N. Y. *Weekly Tribune*, June 18, 1859.

and some felt that hostile action would be a betrayal of the South; but the dominant feeling emphasized the difficulties that would follow abolition.

There were about two hundred thousand slaves in Kentucky, said one delegate; they were valued at sixty-one million dollars; and they produced less than three per cent profit on the capital invested. "That white labor is the cheapest I have no doubt. . . . I have never entertained a doubt that it is the interest of the great slaveholding community of this State, to sell their slaves." [7] But what could be done with the Negroes when liberated? The Kentucky agitation, given the blessing of Henry Clay and Crittenden, and enjoying the leadership of Robert J. Breckinridge, James Speed, and other strong men, rolled on, but achieved nothing whatever.

It was in Missouri that the institution of slavery seemed in most parlous case. The non-slaveholding element was stronger here than in any other slave State except Delaware. Of the 54,438 farms enumerated by the census of 1850, only 8,142 used slaves, while 46,315 did not. Most of the 87,422 slaves were concentrated in the sixteen counties lying along the Missouri River. The steady growth of railroads, manufactures, and cities strengthened the exuberant freesoil sentiment within the State. By 1850 even aristocratic St. Louis, rapidly and healthily expanding, might be called predominantly hostile to the institution. It had nearly six thousand slaves, a few slave auctions, and a sprinkle of slave advertisements, but whenever the auctioneer left his block, the abolitionist could mount it for a much-applauded harangue. Great uneasiness existed among slaveholders, many of whom refused to purchase more hands and advised their children to make no investments in such property. Early in the fifties it was reported that some of the largest planters in Boone, Callaway, Howard, and other counties had sold out and removed to Texas because they felt that a change was overtaking the State, and wanted a safer clime for hands who were currently quoted at twice the Virginia prices. Missouri had too many men from the North, they grumbled, too many foreigners, too many Bentonians, and too many poor whites hostile to slavery. Free labor was clearly more efficient than slave, and according to a common saying in the State, one German worker knocked out three slaves and one Irishman knocked out two.

Were the question of slavery to come up directly in Missouri, trumpeted an observer in 1853, fully three-fourths of the State would vote against the

7 *Debates and Proceedings of the Convention of 1849*, pp. 73–74, statement of S. Turner. James Guthrie, president of the convention, asserted that the Negroes could not be returned to Africa: "Free them, and they will become the Lazaroni of the state. They will crowd to the cities—they will visit the country only on marauding parties—and they will become idle, vicious, and ungovernable. . . . Instead of being productive of wealth, as they are now, they will be destructive of wealth. They will not be advanced in morality, but they will be advanced in crime. They will not be advanced in happiness, but they will be advanced in misery and in degradation." *Idem*, pp. 94–95. Cf. Coleman, *Slavery Times in Kentucky*, 313–325.

institution.[8] No doubt this was true—if getting rid of slavery had meant getting rid of the Negro. But as matters stood, the steady increase in the slaveless population was not accompanied by any marked progress toward emancipation. Though in bustling St. Louis the old 'society' of the city was pro-slavery, the principal businessmen, anxious to outstrip Chicago, were quietly but positively freesoil, and the powerful German-American element felt strongly on the subject. But what could the reformers do? Early in 1857 a resolution was introduced in the legislature declaring that emancipation would be unwise, impolitic, and unjust, and that any movement toward it ought to be discountenanced by good citizens. This passed the Senate 24 to 4, the four St. Louis members voting no; it passed the House 107 to 12, twelve of the fourteen St. Louis representatives opposed. The answer of St. Louis to this demarche was the election of John M. Wimer, heading an emancipationist ticket, as mayor. His inaugural address extolled free labor, denounced the legislative resolutions as intended to bind Missouri to an uneconomic and enterprise-destroying system, and proclaimed: "It is best for the State that it be peopled by white men." The president of the board of aldermen endorsed this principle of "free white labor," and asserted that Missouri would eventually be free. "The heat of the sun does not require an African to stand beneath its rays; none of our agricultural products demands his aid, and certainly our manufactories do not need him." [9]

In fine, these emancipationist city officers were against both slavery and the Negro, and opposed the slave system chiefly because it discouraged white immigration and white labor. The St. Louis *Democrat* and St. Louis *Anzeiger* constantly predicted the eventual extinction of slavery. With the non-slaveholding population increasing thirty per cent every five years, and with the slaveholding population at a virtual standstill, said the *Democrat* in 1857, "Missouri will be a free State during the present generation." But the close of the fifties saw practical measures to effect emancipation seemingly as far distant as when in 1828 a party of about twenty liberal Whig and Democratic leaders in Missouri had met with Benton and Judge Barton to concert plans for a gradual extinction. That lion in the path, race-adjustment, had reared its head then. The bi-party alliance for gradual action had been dropped when Missourians read a highly-colored newspaper story that Arthur Tappan of New York had entertained Negroes at his table and allowed three Negro men to ride out in the same carriage with his daughter! The race-adjustment lion still stood in the road. This fact was advertised to the world when in the winter of 1859–60, following the John Brown raid, a bill passed the legislature by overwhelming majorities to

8 "Letters for the People on the Present Crisis," consisting of letters from an anonymous St. Louis man to a New York friend; pvt., dated October 1, 1853; Huntington Library.
9 *Idem*, Galusha Anderson, *A Border City*, pp. 9–10. N. Y. *Weekly Tribune*, March 7. 1857. *National Intelligencer*, April 14, 1857.

expel all free Negroes from the State. St. Louis had more than a thousand, valued as servants and friends. A thrill of horror ran through the city. For a time the brutal enactment seemed certain to become law—until Governor R. M. Stewart, Bourbon Democrat and pro-slavery man though he was, sagaciously killed it with a pocket veto.[10]

Nowhere, in short, did the emancipationist cause make verifiable and encouraging progress in the slaveholding area between 1840 and 1860. Some liberal men followed Edward Coles's example. Cave Johnson of Tennessee, for example, warmly attached to the sixty-five or seventy colored people whom he had inherited from his or his wife's ancestors, refusing always to sell a Negro except for crime, and never buying one except to unite families, wished late in life to manumit them all. His intention was to buy land for them in Ohio. For this purpose he communicated with Levi Coffin. But the war prevented consummation of his kindly plan. John McDonogh, the wealthy New Orleans merchant who died in 1850, originated a complex scheme by which his slaves purchased their freedom. A determined anti-slavery movement persisted in parts of Virginia. It had the sympathy of more men than dared speak out in its favor. In combination with the pronounced drain of Virginia slaves into the cotton and sugar country, where their labor was far more profitable, it kept alive the dream of emancipation that Jefferson and Madison had cherished. "The causes now in operation," one prominent Virginian wrote in the spring of 1860, "would seem to be sufficient to convert Virginia from a slave State into a free State. The state of *transition* would be a painful one, and might be attended, in *Virginia*, by the irrepressible conflict between free labor and slave labor. . . . The transition has already begun upon the Northern and Northwestern boundaries of the State, and it is a source of surprise to me that it does not go on faster than it seems to do in all parts of the State."

Even in Texas the cause of gradual emancipation had followers. The frontier did not desire slaves. Outspoken and liberal-minded German settlers held a convention at San Antonio in 1854, drew up a broad reform program, and put into it a plank condemning slavery and declaring that if any single State should determine on its abolition, the assistance of the national government might properly be claimed in carrying out the work.[11]

10 *Democrat*, quoted in N. Y. *Weekly Tribune*, March 7, 1857. John Wilson to Thomas Shackelford, January 13, 1866; Slavery MSS, Mo. Hist. Soc., Anderson, *op. cit.*, 12–14; Stewart had been reared in Cortland County, New York. In 1860 St. Louis had a population of 151,780, of which about 1,500 were slaves.

11 W. P. Titus, *Picturesque Clarksville, Past and Present*, 303. W. T. Childs, *John McDonogh, His Life and Work*. John C. Rutherford, Loch Lomond, Va., to W. C. Rives, April 11, 1860; Rives Papers. Cf. G. G. Benjamin, *The Germans in Texas;* R. L. Biesele, *History of the German Settlements in Texas, 1831–1861;* A. M. Hall, *The Texas Germans in State and National Politics, 1850–1865* (U. of Texas thesis).

But where except in St. Louis was a notable victory gained at the polls? When was a strong legislative vote polled for even an exploratory step? Had Delaware boldly abolished her pitiful remnants of slavery, and had Missouri and Maryland both adopted gradual emancipation combined with Negro education, the sharp edge would have been taken off the sectional conflict. Alas that they did not move with the courage which the times demanded! The reasons why they did not could be found in the American tendency to drift, in fear of the effect upon slavery in their sister States farther south, and above all, in the fact that abolition would bring to life a painful race-adjustment problem.

[III]

Precisely what were the anticipated difficulties, and to what extent were they imaginary or real? Many Southerners insisted that only the discipline of slavery could make Negroes work with a steady industry. They argued that in the great districts where Negroes predominated calamitous disorders would follow emancipation. Fallen into barbarian idleness, a prey to agitators, or inspired by hopes of plunder, they would collect in gangs to ravage the countryside. Even if they did not do this, their sporadic robberies and murders would make life unendurable. Doubters were reminded of the massacres of Santo Domingo. It became fashionable for Southerners to say that emancipation would result in a dual struggle; first a contest for political supremacy, and then a life-and-death battle for racial survival.[12]

But above all, Southerners were conscious of a still more formidable possibility. Premature emancipation, wrote a Baltimorean in 1855, would mean that the South would ultimately be peopled by a race of mulattoes. How, in the long run, could a mingling of bloods be avoided? Emancipation meant personal freedom; personal freedom in a democracy means political equality; and political equality is necessarily followed in the end by social equality. The right of blacks to associate with whites on equal terms involved ultimately a deliberate annullment of all distinctions between the two, or an acceptance of the principle that no proper ground for such distinctions ever existed. Once this view was adopted, education of the Negroes would gradually erase all differences in refinement, manners, and intellectual culture.

"What barriers, then, remain to keep those two streams of black and white blood running parallel and level with each other from blending and uniting their currents? They mingle with us in our parlors; why should we exclude them from our chambers? We accept them as partners in the quadrille and the

12 Denman, *Secession Movement in Alabama*, 16ff.

polka; how can our daughters reject their hands for the grand pas-de-deux of matrimony? A well-educated, travelled, refined, accomplished Negro, a Senator in Congress perhaps from emancipated South Carolina (where the Negro vote would be in the majority), and withal, with an income of several thousands a year, would he not be considered a decided 'match' by many a fair-skinned Desdemona in this good time coming of equality and fraternity?" [13]

This might seem an exaggerated apprehension. Yet it struck home to Southerners high and low, gave rise to the ugly label "amalgamationist" for abolitionists, and was not completely met by Lincoln's dictum that it was unnecessary either to degrade the Negro or to marry him; he could just be let alone. The apprehension was founded in part upon the white Southerner's distrust of himself, for abundant evidence existed of a propensity toward one kind of amalgamation. The Southern novelist George W. Cable later wrote a poignant novel, the crux of which lay in a New Orleans quadroon's heroic denial of her own daughter in order that this octoroon might marry a white man; the law forbidding any intermarriage of the races.[14]

In part, the prevalent fear was founded upon the sequels of emancipation in some Latin countries and the British West Indies. It was well known that French and Spanish colonists in the New World intermarried constantly and freely with Negroes. A Bermuda merchant who established himself in Baltimore was quoted as saying that one reason for his migration lay in his disgust over the progress of amalgamation. Negro delegates now represented Negro constituencies in the colonial assembly, and political equality had paved the way for social acceptance. "Instances are not a few where gentlemen moving in the first social circles, particularly Englishmen sent out in the capacity of government officials or agents of commercial houses, have married mulatto or quadroon women, and introduced them and their mongrel children in society." And finally, Southern apprehension was fed by the fact that in various parts of the Southern States themselves certain curious mixtures of blood—Indian, Mexican, French, Spanish, or English with Negro—were already producing some difficult social situations.

Unquestionably not a few mulattoes of very light complexion, decade by decade, passed into the category of white folk and there married. Some States,

---

13 X. Y., Baltimore, November 21, in *National Intelligencer*, November 27, 1855.
14 George W. Cable, *Madame Delphine; National Intelligencer, ut supra*, November 27, 1855. Amalgamation was a word frequently used sneeringly by proslavery men, who attacked abolitionists as amalgamationists. Once when Douglas resorted to the familiar fling, Henry Wilson replied: "This slang about amalgamationist generally proceeds from men who have the odor of amalgamation strong upon them." (Senate, April 21, 1856.) It was a sharp retort but true. Nearly all mulattoes could trace their ancestry back to slaveholding fathers; Southern cities and towns contained many, while one was rarely born in the North. "Mulattoes," caustically observed the N. Y. *Tribune*, "are generally the offspring of lechery on the father's side, and debasement and dependence on the mother's." N. Y. *Weekly Tribune*, April 26, 1856.

notably Kentucky and Virginia, defined a mulatto as any person who had one-fourth or a *larger* fraction of Negro blood; Georgia's definition was *less* than one-fourth. But in no instance did a State law require that a person having a non-perceptible trace of Negro blood should be deemed a mulatto. More drastic laws would have embarrassed white people with a slight tincture, say one-sixteenth, of Negro blood, and would have been difficult to enforce. A perfectly legal migration from the Negro to the white race was possible. But it seems probable that the greater part of the "passing" went on without reference to courts or legal procedure. The scope of the process cannot be measured, for those who "passed" naturally did everything possible to conceal their ancestry. But an indication of the tendency of light-skinned mulattoes to attempt to establish themselves and their children in the white race is found in the repeated instances in which the attempt was detected and legally checkmated. Every-where, meanwhile, mulattoes were likely to become a separate caste. Preference was usually given them as house servants, for they were regarded as neater, handsomer, and brighter than full-blood Negroes; many white fathers treated their mulatto children with special consideration; dark-skinned Negroes then (as today) allowed a certain social superiority to the light-skinned. All this was proof that if emancipation triumphed, then "amalgamation" on a broad scale might ultimately—in the course of generations—be no figment of the imagination.[15]

Obviously, the South raised some needless bogies in facing the question of race-adjustment. Its idea that the Negro would revert to savage indolence was utterly belied by time. Though Southerners liked to quote the very Tory utterances by the London *Times* on the shiftless laziness of Jamaica blacks after emancipation, the real story in that island was creditable to the Negroes' industry. Similarly, the bogey of bloody uprisings and massacres was absurd. Let us remind the Southerner, wrote "Ex-Rebel" in the *Nation* long years afterward, that the Negroes had charge of Southern agriculture during the Civil War, and never shirked their task. "Say to him that during all those dreary days of death and destruction the strong arm of the Negro defended the peace and purity of his home, and he cannot deny it. Recall to him the fact that although our fathers asserted with confidence that the Negro without a master would become such a monster that no society could tolerate his presence . . . the history is that he is as docile as when he wore a chain, and a much more useful inhabitant of the earth than when he was driven to work." [16]

15 James Hugo Johnston, *Race Relations in Virginia and Miscegenation in the South,* 1776–1860, p. 250ff.; U. of Chicago dissertation (1937).

16 For Southern bogies, see John Townsend, *The South Alone Should Govern the South,* pvt., 1860. The London *Times* said: "The freed West Indian slave will not till the soil for wages; the free son of the ex-slave is as obstinate as his sire. He will cultivate lands which he has not bought for his own yams, mangoes, and plantains These satisfy his wants; they

But uncertainty, fear, and dark foreboding were altogether natural. Men of liberal outlook and the highest intellectual distinction accepted this view of the impossibility of incorporating millions of liberated blacks into the tissue of a white civilization. Jefferson had used emphatic language. "Deep-rooted prejudices of the whites, ten thousand recollections of the black of injuries sustained, new provocations, the real distinction Nature had made, and many other circumstances will divide us into parties and produce convulsions which will probably never end but in the extermination of one or the other race." Very similar was De Tocqueville's judgment in 1838. Terming the Negro the most perplexing American problem, he could see but two alternatives: to emancipate and intermingle, or to keep the blacks isolated in a state of slavery as long as possible. "All intermediate measures seem to me likely to terminate, and that shortly, in the most horrible of civil wars, and perhaps in the extirpation of one or the other of the two races." [17]

Just before the Civil War, W. T. Sherman wrote from Louisiana in caustic terms. "All the Congresses on earth can't make the Negro anything else than what he is; he must be subject to the white man, or he must amalgamate or be destroyed. Two such races cannot live in harmony save as master and slave. Mexico shows the result of general equality and amalgamation, and the Indians give a fair illustration of the fate of the negroes if they are released from the control of the whites." [18] The general conclusion of Southerners was stated by the Washington *Union*:

"It is clear that the domestic institution of the South cannot admit of a material change without taking some time to effect it. A precipitate policy would inflict the deepest injury upon the South. It took eight centuries to drive the Moors from Spain. Santo Domingo was ruined by the inconsiderate precipitancy of revolutionary France. Jamaica has been seriously injured by the hasty legislation of Parliament. . . . The white men and slaves could not live happily together, if they were all liberated."

---

do not care for yours. Cotton, and sugar, and coffee, and tobacco—he cares little for them. And what matters it to him, that the Englishman has sunk his thousands and tens of thousands on mills, machinery, etc., which now totter on the languishing estate, that for years have only returned beggary and debts. He eats his yam, and sniggers at 'Buckra.' " *Nation,* April 26, 1888, for "Ex-Rebel."

17　Cf. Ballagh, *History of Slavery in Virginia,* 132. E. G. W. Butler, who married a granddaughter of Mrs. George Washington, compared the lot of the slaves emancipated by George Washington with that of Mrs. Washington's slaves, who remained in servitude: "I speak from my own observations and can appeal to citizens of Fairfax County Virginia for the truth of my assertion, when I affirm that the descendants of the latter, many of whom are in possession of the writer of this, have been and are prosperous, contented and happy; while the former—after a life of vice, dissipation and idleness, may literally be said to have disappeared from the face of the earth." To Gayarré, July 16, 1853; Gayarré Papers.

18　W. T. Sherman, *Home Letters,* 178–179, July 10, 1860. Washington *Union,* May 5, 1850.

[IV]

The one apparent means of effecting a simultaneous solution of the problems of slavery and race adjustment was by removal of the Negro to some other part of the world. A later age was to witness wholesale deportations in Europe and Asia as a rough surgical operation to end the friction between diverse national stocks. It was natural that Americans should consider the same expedient. The glittering chimera of "colonization," a bright delusive dream, floated before the eyes of two generations of benevolent men. Jefferson had advocated the idea as early as 1776, had worked out a plan in his *Notes on Virginia*, and had cherished it to his last days. The American Colonization Society, founded in 1817 with numerous eminent men among its supporters, kept the idea nationally prominent. When it held its annual meeting in Washington in 1852 Henry Clay was president, Webster was vice-president, President Fillmore attended, and numerous Senators, Representatives, and Supreme Court justices applauded a hopeful address by the able Frederick P. Stanton of Tennessee. Various State colonization societies lent their assistance. Money came not merely from philanthropic individuals, but from public bodies. Virginia, for example, passed a law in 1853 appropriating $30,000 annually for five years (which was supplemented by about $10,000 annually from the tax laid on free colored folk) for colonization activities. In New York Governor Hunt devoted a large part of his annual message of 1852 to a glowing account of the Society's work and a plea for State assistance. Lincoln's outspoken belief in colonization was maintained to the end.[19]

The colonization dream, despite the heated opposition of most abolitionists and most free Negroes, gave thousands a comfortable feeling that they were doing something practical to attack the menacing national issue. The stated meetings, with a Bushrod Washington, a Clay, or a John H. B. Latrobe in the chair; the beautifully phrased speeches by Everett or Reverdy Johnson; the pleased editorials by W. W. Seaton or Horace Greeley, all made a pleasant stir. The problem was going to be solved without much pain or trouble to anybody. Churchmen like Bishop J. H. Hopkins of Vermont explained how simple it all was. The value of the slaves in the late fifties might be a thousand million dollars. That was not a quarter of the British national debt. By direct taxes which would never exceed an average of $20 for each taxable inhabitant, and would reach that height only for a few years, the government might buy all the slaves, transport them to Africa, and settle them there. Or the public lands, worth twice as much as the slave property, might be mortgaged for the purpose. And

19 *National Intelligencer*, January 13, 1852. May 14, 1853, January 22, 1855. *Annual Reports* of the American Colonization Society. C. H. Wesley, "Lincoln's Plan for Colonizing the Emancipated Negroes," *Journal of Negro History*, IV, 7ff.

what might not this great work accomplish! National stability, Southern prosperity, a regilding of the republic's fame, the regeneration of Africa, the elevation of the Negro race to its highest level—these would be among the fruits.[20]

And yet justice must be done to the American Colonization Society and its work in Liberia. The true significance of its activities is missed if it is regarded as a fully-developed attempt to solve the problems of slavery and racial antagonism. Men like Webster, Clay, and Latrobe, highly practical all, never dreamed that it could perform so staggering a task. In 1848 the Society sent 129 emigrants to Liberia, in 1849 it sent 422, and in the next three years it transported first 670, then 666, and then 783. The republic of Liberia, brought into existence on June 25, 1847, with a Declaration of Independence, a constitution modelled on that of the United States, and a spirited appeal to Christendom for sympathy, was a pitifully weak and staggering colony, whose first president, the Virginia mulatto Joseph Jenkins Roberts, had to contend against hostile native chiefs, internal factions, and economic disasters.[21] It is easy to sneer at such frail and uncertain achievements. But the real objects of the colonizationists were two. They were to carry out a small-scale demonstration of the practicability of a genuine mass migration, and so pave the way toward governmental action of decisive magnitude. They were also to show the people of Africa that such thriving industries could be based upon sugar, cotton, coffee, palm-oil, and ivory that wars and slave-raids ought to be abandoned as unprofitable.[22]

In short, the colonizationists were conducting an experiment—and they believed it successful. They were showing that white culture and a Christian civilization could be planted on the shores of tropic Africa; that former slaves could build up a stable commonwealth; that even free colored people, rescued from their political and social disadvantages in America, could find a fuller liberty in the new republic; that industries of value to the whole globe could

20 John Henry Hopkins, *The American Citizen, His Rights and Duties* (1857). Yet an important element of Southerners opposed colonization. Calhoun, for example, held that separation of the races would injure the blacks, for they would revert to savagery, and the whites, who would lose economically and socially. Cf. W. G. Bean, "Anti-Jeffersonianism in the Ante-Bellum South," *North Carolina Historical Review*, XII, 103ff.

21 Hunt's message of January 6 in *Messages and Papers of the Governors*. For full statement of the objects of the colonizationists, see *National Intelligencer*, July 17, 1852.

22 R. F. C. Maugham, *The Republic of Liberia*, 33–83. President Roberts wrote an old English friend, G. Ralston, from Government House, Monrovia, July 6, 1853: "A few days since an old chief, who had come down with a large caravan from the interior, some eighty or a hundred miles, called on me, and in the course of conversation remarked that he had felt extremely indignant toward the Liberians for interfering with the slave trade. His grandfather and father, he said, for many, many years had sold slaves, and they were rich, but the Liberians had made him poor; he had therefore never intended to visit Monrovia, or have anything to do with the Americans. He was now convinced, however, that the slave trade was very cruel; that it has produced a great deal of distress and suffering among the country people . . . and he was now very glad that the Liberians had interposed to prevent the foreign slave trade. . . ." *National Intelligencer*, October 8, 1853.

be developed; and that the little nation, together with British Sierra Leone, could destroy the slave trade along an important stretch of the African coast. The hope was that once the scheme proved its worth, the national and State governments would unite in a far grander effort. Nobody thought that individual benevolence and scattered State grants would suffice; the Society was to blaze the way, and the United States, with its immense resources, would carry the transfer of the race to a final consummation.

The undertaking unquestionably had elements of hopefulness. In a highly colored volume issued in 1852 Mrs. Sarah Josepha Hale recited the early achievements of the Liberian settlers, some of them truly heroic. The migrants from America numbered eight thousand; they dominated a land of 200,000 native blacks; they had induced tribes aggregating half a million or more to give up the slave trade; and their progress held out hope that "the time will come when all Central Africa will look to Liberia for protection, for instruction, and for laws, as well as Christianity." President Roberts, visiting Great Britain, gained Queen Victoria's sympathetic ear for his moving story, received from Lord Ashley and other philanthropists a thousand pounds toward purchase of Galinhas, a part of the coast where the slave trade still flourished, and was returned to Monrovia on a British warship.

America sent over missionaries, colored physicians, and shipload after shipload of ordinary freedmen or free Negroes. To see a vessel like the *Elvira Owen* take on colored emigrants at Baltimore, at Hampton Roads, and at Savannah, with hymn-singing, prayers, and rapt ejaculations of praise, was a touching experience. By 1854 the Society had settled in Africa 4,549 freedmen, 3,383 free Negroes, and about 1,000 Negroes rescued from slave-traders at various points. Particularly encouraging was the transit of skilled artisans. In 1853, for example, Montgomery Bell, one of the leading iron-manufacturers of Tennessee, sent over thirty-eight slaves and laid plans for adding eighty more, including hands expert in iron-working; while the same year some free Negroes from Pennsylvania went over with a steam-engine and machinery. Although ten thousand American settlers, two regiments, one armed schooner, twenty-three churches, and fifty-odd schools were but the feeble beginnings of a nation, James Beekman told the New York Senate, they were the acorn from which a splendid oak might rise.[23]

By the end of 1856 materials for a college had been sent out. An academy, a high school, and a Methodist seminary for girls had been set up in Monrovia.

23 S. J. Hale, *Liberia; or, Mr. Peyton's Experiments*. Maugham, *Liberia*, 64. *National Intelligencer*, June 26, 1856, quoting Savannah *Republican* of June 21, April 1, 1854, June 17, 1854. Annual Report of the American Colonization Society, 1853. England in 1853 had regular steam lines from Liverpool and Plymouth to West Africa, furnishing a semi-monthly connection with Liberia. Latrobe's address, Washington *Union*, January 18, 1854.

The first Liberian book, a volume of poems, had been published. Roberts and other Liberians, with support from Latrobe, F. P. Stanton, and others in America, were agitating for a direct steamship line to exploit the West African trade, and compete with the regular British steamship lines from Plymouth and Liverpool.

"And there Liberia stands, and has stood for the last six years," exclaimed the Society's annual report for 1853, "a free and independent nation, a bright gem set upon the dark ground of a vast continent, with some two hundred thousand citizens, exerting an undisputed dominion over some seven hundred miles of seacoast."

Visitors told of hopes for large coffee crops, of prospects for livestock growing, of success in producing tropical fruits. They were particularly optimistic over the prospects of a large palm-oil trade. Inspecting the handsome brick residences of Monrovia and the promising plantations scattered about it, they agreed that only capital, managerial energy, more labor, sugar-grinding machinery, and transportation lines were needed; nothing but that! [24]

But however creditable some of the Colonization Society's achievements, in any broad view the experiment gave a triple demonstration of the impracticability of the general undertaking. It proved that Liberia, its lowlands mainly a densely forested country of tremendous rainfall, trackless and unhealthy, its uplands so difficult to reach that a century after the birth of the republic they still remained half-unexplored, its coast lacking in good harbors, its commercial possibilities even harder to develop than those of neighboring British and French colonies, was unfitted to receive a huge new Negro population. It proved that most Negroes free or slave did not wish to return to Africa, and that the South did not wish to give up their labor. It proved that while a few philanthropists and legislatures would give driblets of cash, large-scale financial support was out of the question.

Virginia under her colonization law of 1850 during three years removed 419 free Negroes or freedmen to Africa at a cost of $5,410, and in the first half-year under the new law of 1853 removed 240 at a cost of $5,800. As the governor remarked, this barely sufficed to prevent any increase in the number of free Negroes.[25] But what could be done to reduce the total of fifty-five thousand free colored people already in the commonwealth? If Virginia, earnestly anxious to send its free Negroes abroad, could get rid of fewer than seven hundred in three and a half years of organized effort, what could the national government accomplish with four million Negroes? The fact was that no part of Africa

---

24 Annual Reports, *National Intelligencer*, May 15, 1855; J. J. Roberts, July 6, 1853, in Buchanan Papers.

25 Governor's message in *National Intelligencer*, December 15, 1853.

then accessible to the United States could absorb any large number of freedmen, and even if fertile South Africa or Australia had been open, still the absorption would necessarily have been by small annual quotas. Housing, transportation, machinery, supplies, and markets would have to be provided concurrently with any wholesale colonization. To settle ten thousand was difficult enough; to settle a hundred thousand a staggering task; to settle a million quite out of the question.

Nearly all free colored people were opposed to colonization, asserting in public meetings year after year that they would never leave America but would fight for their rights. "We intend to plant our own trees on American soil, and to repose in the shade thereof"—so ran the resolution of a national convention of free colored men dominated by Frederick Douglass at Rochester in 1853. They believed that they would gain steadily in strength and power by manumission, the escape of fugitives, and natural increase. Their white friends, including most abolitionists, thought colonization a heartless attempt to get rid of the Negro by taking him to burning deserts and steaming jungles to die. It was only when an increasing number of free States took action to exclude liberated Negroes, while the slave States witnessed a general movement to forbid emancipation except on condition of removal, that a partial change of attitude took place.

Henry Clay stated the dilemma forcibly. If the recent decision of Indiana excluding free Negroes is followed in other areas, he wrote in 1851, what will become of these poor creatures? "In the name of humanity I ask what is to become of them—where are they to go?" James G. Birney dramatically abandoned his twenty years of hostility to colonization. His examination of the Supreme Court decision in *Strader et al. vs. Graham* (1852) concluded with an exhortation to free colored people to remove to Liberia. He declared that the circumstances which had made their presence in the North an encouragement to their enslaved brethren had passed away; pointed to the harsh exclusion laws of various States; and argued that since white superiority would always be asserted to their disadvantage, they should leave. Early in the decade a Liberian Agricultural Association of nearly three hundred Negroes in New York City was actively supporting colonization. Its leader told James W. Beekman that even if he were elected to the State Senate he would have no equality. "When the Senate adjourned, you, sir, would go to Congress Hall, and I, although I have money in my pocket, would go to Dean Street. . . . Here every avenue of distinction is walled up against me, because my skin is dark. I do not choose to submit to this, and for my children's sake I shall go to Liberia." [26]

[26] *National Intelligencer*, July 17, 1852; January 17, 1852 for Clay's letter to Abraham Morrison, September 30, 1851; April 1, 1852 for Beekman's New York Senate speech. N. Y.

Instinctively recoiling from colonization as impracticable, Congress refused to be beguiled into any far-reaching measure of support. Representative Edward Stanly of North Carolina proposed in 1852 that the fourth instalment of the surplus revenue which was to be distributed under the old Jacksonian law, amounting to between nine and ten millions, should be paid the several States with a proviso that interest on it be used to transport free people of color to Liberia. But the bill did not pass. Six years later Representative Frank P. Blair of Missouri urged that a House committee should canvass the possibility of acquiring territory in Central America for colonization, this territory to become a dependency of the United States, with guarantees of the civil and political rights of the inhabitants. Again the proposal gained some support, but came to nothing.[27]

Blair's speech was notable for the emphasis with which he stated the basic problem of race-adjustment. Even faraway Oregon, fearing that problem, had placed its interdict upon the admission of free blacks; while the South, apprehensive that an increase of the free Negro population might bring about slave rebellions, was moving to stop manumission and even to reduce previously manumitted slaves to servitude again. In Virginia during the previous summer and fall, large meetings had petitioned the legislature to authorize a sweeping sale of all free blacks. Both races were vassals to slavery, declared Blair, and both ought to be liberated. The slaveholders were not blamable for the arrest of emancipation. "For, whether as slave or free man, the presence of multitudes of the black race is found to be fatal to the interests of our race; their antagonism is as strong as that of oil and water, and so long as no convenient outlet, through which the manumitted slave can reach a congenial climate and country willing to receive him, is afforded, the institution of slavery stands on compulsion." But suppose Central America were opened to the freedmen? Hundreds of Southerners would instantly send their slaves thither. The border States would

Tribune, July 15, 1853. William Birney, *James G. Birney and His Times*, pp. 377–399; *National Intelligencer*, February 7, 1852. Describing Negro opposition to colonization, Charles Lenox Remond of Salem, Mass., told his audience in a lecture at the Broadway Tabernacle, sponsored by the New York Anti-Slavery Society: "The colored people were, with a few exceptions, opposed to the movement. . . . The American Colonization Society has done more to keep up the cruel and absurd prejudice against color in this country than all the other agencies put together." N. Y. *Tribune*, January 5, 1854.

27 Text of Stanly's bill in *National Intelligencer*, July 17, 1852; on Blair, see *Cong. Globe*, January 14, 1858. Private support of colonization did not fall off; on the contrary, it increased. John Stevens of Maryland gave $36,000 for the building of an emigrant ship in 1856, and the next year this vessel, the *Mary Caroline Stevens*, especially made for the purpose, a comfortable sailing ship of 713 tons, made several trips. In 1867 David Hunt of Mississippi gave the American Colonization Society $45,000. The belief that Central America might be the best scene for large-scale colonization of the Negroes was later held by President Lincoln. Doolittle favored it and said in Congress that he would take Central America "with a friendly hand" and settle the freedmen there to enjoy social and political equality with the natives. *Cong. Globe*, 36th Cong., 1st sess., April 10, 1860.

soon get rid of the Negroes entirely. And what a change for the better all the way from Maryland to Missouri! The chaotic, jangling condition of the four different classes which in these grain-growing States obstructed each other, the masters and slaves mutually dependent, the free Negroes hanging on their skirts, and the white laborers in great measure excluded from employment and farm-ownership, would pass away. As it did so, the broad border region would become a fertile garden of small freeholders, and a throbbing home of varied manufactures.[28]

That under happier circumstances, and with boldly energetic government support, colonization might have achieved considerable results, few can doubt. Liberia was an unfortunate choice for the transplantation. Central America, or Santo Domingo, which had once been populous and was now almost empty, would have proved a more convenient, attractive, and salubrious site. A sustained national effort, financed by tens of millions of dollars, and directed by men as able as those who were building the powerful mid-century railroads and manufactories, might within a generation have planted a state of several hundred thousand self-supporting Negroes. Such a state within another generation might have attracted several hundred thousand more. But the South was neither willing nor able to give up the labor values represented by the Negro; the country was unready to spend the tens of millions required; and the social and governmental structure of the nation had not attained sufficient organization to make such a tremendous enterprise feasible. Moreover, the subtraction of half a million Negroes from the American total would not materially diminish the problem. The country could not escape its home responsibilities so easily.[29]

28 In a letter to the Sycamore, Ill., *Republican*, September 6, 1858, Frank Blair, Jr. (admitting that he owned a few slaves, "most of them purchased by me in order to prevent them from being separated from their families,") wrote that emancipation was urged by some on religious and moral grounds, by some on economic grounds, and by some on political grounds. All had substance. "For my part I have always given greater weight to the objection arising from political considerations, holding as I do that the institution is hostile to all true Democracy, and that its irresistible tendency is to build up an oligarchy and subvert our Republican Government. The idea of liberating the slaves and allowing them to remain in this country, is one that never will be tolerated." It was because the South always raised this objection that he put forward his proposal for colonizing the Negroes in Central America under American protection and guarantees of their civil rights. But Montgomery Blair wrote his father that emancipation was the only cure. Though "full of immediate trouble and perhaps danger," it would so check the increase of the Negroes that "a few generations would extinguish all but those whose industry would render them useful to the state." February 15, 1850; Blair Papers, Princeton Univ.

29 Jacob Dewees of Philadelphia published a 236-page book in 1854 called *The Great Future of Africa and America; an Essay showing our whole duty to the Black Man, consistent with our own safety and glory*. He believed in compensated emancipation, to be paid for by the proceeds of sales of public lands, and transportation of the Negroes to Africa, a process which he thought could not be concluded in less than a century. While he praised the Colonization Society for the limited work it had done, he thought that nothing less than the whole power of the national government could accomplish this huge effort.

[V]

Nothing better illustrated the impasse reached by the country than the harsh and increasingly harsher lot of the free Negro; a lot darkest in the South, but sad enough throughout the North.

In some salient respects more light is cast upon the race problem by Joel Chandler Harris's short story of "Free Joe and the Rest of the World" than by all of *Uncle Tom's Cabin,* for the pathetic tale better illuminates the central difficulty to be met. Free Joe, liberated in a little town of Central Georgia by a wandering speculator who lost all his other property at cards and committed suicide, remains close by the plantation where his wife Lucindy works. At first the humble black man has a jovial time. Lucindy's master is kind, and the two spend much time together. But the master dies, a hard, mean-tempered fellow named "Spite" Calderwood succeeds to Lucindy, and catching Free Joe visiting her one evening, he tears up the pass from the Negro's guardian, and orders him never to set foot on the plantation again. Poor Joe is crushed. But with the aid of his little dog Dan, he presently finds it possible to arrange clandestine meetings with Lucindy at the home of some neighboring poor whites. When Calderwood learns of this through telltale slaves, he sells Lucindy sixty miles away. For months Free Joe hopefully hangs around the plantation without learning what has happened. But the truth leaks out, and Joe, unable to trace or follow his wife, bereft even of his little dog by Calderwood's fierce hounds, homeless, friendless, and hopeless, dies heartbroken at the foot of the tree where he used to wait for Lucindy, the familiar humble smile still on his face. "His clothes were ragged; his hands were rough and callous; his shoes were literally tied together with strings; he was shabby in the extreme. A passerby, glancing at him, could have no idea that such a humble creature had been summoned as a witness before the Lord God of Hosts."

Many a free Negro both North and South might have been summoned in these years as a witness against neglect, oppression, and outrage. The half-million free colored folk who lived in the United States on the eve of the Civil War should theoretically have been happier, more prosperous, and more secure than their kinsfolk in bondage. Actually they occupied a position which was generally forlorn, miserable, and helpless. That they should have been ill-used in the South, where they held an anomalous position, need not astonish us. But the unenlightened and frequently inhuman treatment accorded them in the North, inspiring Greeley to the bitter declaration in 1852 that they had no future in America and should all be settled elsewhere, was a deplorable blot on the country's shield.[30]

30   N. Y. *Tribune,* June 14, 1852.

The free Negroes of the North were kept in menial positions, debarred from the intellectual professions and skilled handicrafts, denied equal educational facilities in many communities, and subjected to legal and political discrimination. They were in fact little better than outcasts. In New York, where they rode only in public conveyances labelled "Colored people allowed in this car," and in some other cities, a Jim Crow line was tightly drawn. The beginning of the decade found them completely or partially disfranchised in Pennsylvania, New York (where Negroes but not whites had to own $350 worth of realty to vote), Connecticut, New Jersey, Ohio, and Wisconsin; and as the years passed they were excluded from the polls in other States. Indeed, when the fifties ended, only three States allowed Negroes to vote on terms of complete parity with white men—Massachusetts, Maine, and New Hampshire, where their numbers were negligible. It was still true that, as De Tocqueville had said in the thirties, race prejudice seemed stronger in States which had got rid of slavery than in those which retained it. A shrewd student of the subject has concluded that in Illinois local antipathy to the Negro increased *pari passu* with the agitation for Southern emancipation.[31]

One State after another stigmatized the free Negroes by excluding them from its borders. When Illinois drew up its new constitution in 1848 an emphatic clause prohibited the entry of such folk, and the legislature five years later not only made it a misdemeanor for any Negro to enter with the purpose of settling, but provided that the offender might be fined and his time sold for a sufficient period to pay the penalty. Iowa in 1851 severely penalized any free Negro who set foot upon her soil. Indiana had a specially creditable body of free colored people about Newport, descendants of slaves liberated by Quakers in North Carolina early in the century and sent north by the North Carolina Yearly Meeting. It was the State of Levi Coffin. It boasted of one of the best travelled lines of the Underground Railroad, Coffin declaring in his classic

31 See Robert Purvis's protest against his children's exclusion from Pennsylvania schools; *Journal of Negro History*, X, 362ff. Gerrit Smith, speech at Peterboro, N. Y., January 23, 1859. N. Y. *Tribune*, January 17, 1852. N. D. Harris, *History of Negro Servitude in Illinois*, 233. A citizen of Jamaica, Long Island, deplored the condition of the free Negroes there: "The most of them are ignorant, superstitious, and in a state of abject servitude, infinitely worse than the subjects of the hardest taskmaster in the South. . . ." N. Y. *Weekly Tribune*, June 21, 1851. The original New York State Constitution allowed Negroes to vote on the same terms as whites. In early years, the fifth ward of New York City, where free Negroes resided in large numbers, was often carried by their votes. In 1821 the Constitution was revised, and the property qualification of whites was lowered, while that of blacks was raised. In 1826 the property qualification of whites was abolished; that of blacks retained.

Between 1804 and 1849 Ohio had several statutes imposing disabilities upon persons of color. One provided that no black or mulatto might give evidence in court, whether in a civil or criminal case, against a white person. A bill to repeal this came up in 1847 and produced a tempestuous debate. Clement L. Vallandigham undertook leadership of the devious maneuverings and engineerings which it was hoped would defeat the bill. See his explanation in *Cong. Globe*, February 8, 1858.

Reminiscences that some 3,300 Negro fugitives passed through the Newport station. And yet when Indiana placed a Negro-exclusion article in her constitution of 1851, the people approved it by the tremendous vote of more than five to one. Oregon adopted a constitution in 1857 stipulating that no free colored people should enter, that those who came should be forcibly removed, and that anybody who harbored or employed them should be punished. It also forbade the Negroes already there to hold real estate, make contracts, or prosecute suits. Proposals for a general expulsion of free blacks were frequent in the border States and by no means unknown farther north.[32]

Worst of all was the general public assumption in the North that Negroes were inferior creatures who naturally fell into degradation and whom it was hopeless to assist. Dr. Leonard Bacon told his New Haven congregation that of nearly a thousand free colored people in the city, a few families were honest, industrious, and sober, but the remainder, branded with ignominy, were in a condition of dreadful degeneracy. Plainly, the Christian citizens of New Haven were doing nothing to assist them. Even the abolitionists did little. Though William Lloyd Garrison lamented that the free colored people were regarded as an inferior caste to whom liberty was a curse, he gave them relatively little attention. When Edward Everett was asked by Peter Cooper to deliver an address at the inauguration of Cooper Union, he noted in his diary that he was inclined to do so on condition that all the proceeds of the ticket sale were placed "at my disposal, to be appropriated to aid poor Charlotte Ashe, my old cook, in purchasing her daughter's freedom. The daughter is a slave in Mississippi, and Charlotte has for years been trying to effect this object." The alacrity of Bostonians in helping Charlotte was plainly remarkable! Governor Washington Hunt unemotionally pointed out to the New York legislature in 1852 that the free Negroes were excluded from most institutions of religion and learning, were shut out from social intercourse, and were condemned to lives of servility and drudgery; a condition which, as he said, crushed the spirit of manhood and made improvement morally impossible. Uttering not a word of reproach to the white people, and recommending not a single reform of a domestic character, he urged simply that the Negroes for their own good be deported to Liberia.[33]

For a time early in the fifties a movement gained popularity to encourage the

32 On Indiana, see J. C. Hurd, *Law of Freedom and Bondage*, 130–131, 217. The vote was 108,413 to 20,951. N. Y. *Weekly Tribune*, August 23, September 13, 1851, In Ohio, a resolution was introduced in the Democratic State Convention in 1859 advocating the exclusion of free Negroes. Senator Pugh successfully opposed its passage, arguing that public sentiment was not yet ripe for it. He said that annually a thousand slaves were brought into Hamilton County to be liberated. N. Y. *Weekly Tribune*, June 11, 1859.
33 *Life of William Lloyd Garrison* by his children, I, 253–254. B. B. Munford, *Virginia's Attitude Toward Slavery and Secession*, Chs. 23–24. Everett, MS Diary, June 22, 1857; Everett Papers. N. Y. *Weekly Tribune*, January 10, 1852.

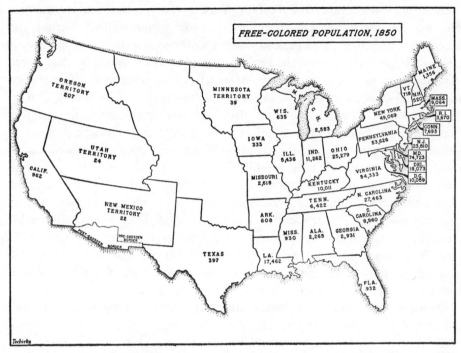

FREE-COLORED POPULATION, 1850

Free Negroes, writes U. B. Phillips, were commonly "industrious, well-mannered, and respected members of society"; and "each locality was likely to have some outstanding figure." But in many areas manumissions decreased and repressive laws grew.

free Negroes (by words, not money) to colonize themselves in detached and self-sufficing communities in the West. It being costly and inconvenient to help these poor people as members of white communities, why should they not look after themselves? A convention of the colored folk of Ohio held at Cincinnati early in 1852 received kindly admonitions from Senator Ben Wade and Representative L. D. Campbell. Did these radical freesoil leaders promise assistance at home? Not at all. Wade exhorted them to withdraw from all menial employments, form their own communities, and by farming, carpentering, blacksmithing, and other crafts attain a sturdy independence, thus overcoming the prejudice against their race. Campbell encouragingly remarked that he thought the existing condition of free colored people "infinitely worse" than it had been ten years earlier, and that he saw nothing hopeful in their immediate prospects. They should prepare to meet an intensified hostility, and he urged them to do so by becoming useful, industrious citizens, setting up their own workshops and their own schools.[34]

34 The convention was held January 15, 1852; New York and Cincinnati press, January 6-20, 1852.

Similar counsel came from the New York *Tribune,* which scolded the free Negroes for their lack of enterprise, dependence on white assistance for executing any project, and general acceptance of a dependent and parasitical position. If, separating from the rest of the nation as the Mormons had done, various Negro groups would set up independent and progressive communities, they would thus do more to advance themselves (urged the editors) than in any other way. Where? Anywhere that land was procurable; a township in New Jersey, a county in the West; just obtain it, settle it, manage it, and improve it. By establishing their own teachers, lawyers, doctors, justices, craftsmen, and expert farmers, they would stride forward as they never could while they insisted on living intermingled with a more powerful, numerous, and ambitious race who repelled them as inferiors.[35] This advice was easy to give, involved no reflection on the chill, aloof whites, required no expenditure by national, State, or local governments, and did not even include a gift of public land. It no more faced the realities of race-adjustment than the abolitionists' demand for immediate emancipation, or the colonizationists' ecstasies over a tiny struggling state in an impossible corner of Africa.

With so little practical assistance given, particularly in the basic economic aid of full employment opportunities, it is not strange that the free Negroes made slow and slight improvement. Here and there exceptional individuals and groups did well. The Negroes of Cincinnati, for example, boasted in 1853 of $800,000 worth of property; of prosperous carpenters, cabinetmakers, barbers, and hotelkeepers; and even of a landscape artist who had been sent to Rome to perfect himself. By 1859 the taxed real estate owned by Negroes in New York City amounted to $1,400,000. The Negro newspapers of New York State, headed by Frederick Douglass' *North Star* (called after 1851 *Fred Douglass's Paper*), were creditable. But the general situation was bad. British readers of Olmsted's pages were shocked by his description of the hard lot of the free colored people of Washington, who constituted one-fifth of the population. Two dozen colored men arrested in the spring of 1855 for holding a private meeting asserted that they had gathered for purely benevolent purposes. Among the objects found when they were searched were a Bible, a copy of Seneca's *Morals,* the constitution of a burial-society, and a subscription-paper for buying the freedom of a young woman. Yet the magistrate ordered one prisoner flogged, sent four others to the workhouse, and mulcted the remainder $111 in fines and costs.[36]

And Edward Dicey, visiting the North in 1861, found his heart wrung by

35 N. Y. *Weekly Tribune,* September 6, 1851, February 7, 1852.
36 N. Y. *Weekly Tribune,* July 15, 1853, on Negroes of Cincinnati. *Idem,* March 22, 1865, for Greeley's long article on the neglect and squalor of Washington Negroes.

the sad lot of the Negroes. Shabby, ragged, downcast, they faced general white antipathy, and seldom gained a post of responsibility. A shrewd, kindly old Ohio farmer, after dilating on the wealth and beauty of his State, concluded: "There is but one thing, sir, that we want here, and that is to get rid of the niggers." He complained of their indolence, illiteracy, and criminality. For such complaints Dicey found some basis of truth, for in every Northern city the free Negroes seemed the poorest, most thriftless, and perhaps most troublesome part of the population. But explained Dicey, if a dog is given a bad name and systematically whipped, he will generally deserve his disrepute. When a resident of Jamaica, L. I., complained that nine-tenths of the free Negroes of that old town, descendants of slaves of the early Dutch settlers, were worthless and dissolute, an illuminating response promptly came from the blacks. Denying the charge, they indignantly retorted that they were refused chances of employment, and their children opportunities of education.[37]

The best excuse which Northerners could make was that their unjust statutes and harsh social attitudes were the work of the baser part of the population, who wished to have somebody to look down upon and feared the competition of the Negroes. In 1854 a mulatto named Allen, announcing that he intended to marry a white girl, was hounded out of up-State New York, finally taking refuge in England. "All such outrages," complained the *Tribune*, "have been the work of the lowest and meanest class of whites, who are . . . particularly furious against 'amalgamation.' "[38] Every loafer, vagabond, and rowdy was indeed violently opposed to any action which would raise the black man toward equality. They had to have somebody to despise, and finding little but the color of their skins to justify a distinction, made the most of that. But it is unlikely that even the most liberal and enlightened people of the North understood how discreditable was their section's callous indifference to the Negroes, and how much doubt it cast upon the sincerity of the anti-slavery movement. Abolition was irrational without some well-studied plan of race-adjustment; yet instead of offering an example of harmony and progress, the North made no real effort to prove that healthy adjustment was even possible!

Southerners were far from blind to this fact. They made much of John Sherman's statement that so far as his observation extended, the relations of blacks and whites were often kindlier in the South than the North. Lucy Stone, traversing a considerable area of the Lower South, found that slaveholders were scornful of such Northern Negrophobes as John Mitchel. Their lips curled with contempt when they spoke of the harsh treatment of free Negroes in

37 N. Y. *Weekly Tribune*, June 14, 28, 1851; Edward Dicey, *Six Months in the Federal States*, I, 65–82.
38 N. Y. *Tribune*, May 13, 1854.

Yankee cities. Even in old Quaker Philadelphia, and in Newport, Ind., she had
not been allowed to lecture in public halls except on condition that all colored
people were debarred. When she told this to Kentucky slaveowners, they
uttered indignant exclamations. In the South, they averred, black people were
not crowded into corners; *they* understood the colored folk and Northerners
did not—a statement that was to go ringing down the decades long after
slavery was dead.[39]

[VI]

In reality, Southern kindliness was chiefly for Negroes in slavery and was
that type of amiability always engendered in superior groups by an immutable
caste system. It seldom extended to free Negroes, who were regarded with
even greater hostility than in the North. Behind this antagonism lay an apprehension of the dangers to the existing order that lurked in the very existence
of any large body of freedmen. If they grew numerous, educated, and
economically secure, they would arouse the envious discontent of the slaves,
become a rallying point against the existing order, and ultimately reduce slavery
to atoms. The South therefore took precautions against their rise to strength.
Most slaveholders would have said with Spite Calderwood: "Don't want no free
niggers 'round here."

For various reasons such Negroes were likely to be of superior type. A good
many, evincing unusual enterprise or belonging to specially kind masters, had
earned enough money to pay for their freedom. At Fort Smith, Ark., lived a
woman, laundress and nurse, who while paying her master ten dollars a month
for her time, earned and saved enough in five years to purchase her freedom
for $1,000. She then saved another $500 to pay for her aged and ailing husband,
and the two continued to prosper pecuniarily. Others had been manumitted;
sometimes out of pure kindliness, particularly to superior house servants, and
sometimes by reason of blood relationship. A high percentage of free persons
of color had white blood. Of the 773 free Negroes in Mississippi just before
the war, for example, more than three-quarters (601) were of mixed ancestry,
while in the general slave population, fewer than one-eleventh were mulattoes.
Not a few slaveholders in signing manumission papers acknowledged their
paternity, and case after case of this kind, involving some legal dispute, came
before the courts. Strong indications can be found that as a body the free
colored people constantly improved their position. This was at any rate true of
Virginia, where as against one family in ten holding taxable property in 1830,
one family in five had property in 1860. But not only did the number of owners

39 *Cong. Globe*, December 8, 1856; N. Y. *Tribune*, January 25, 1854.

double in these thirty years; the value of the property held increased by about three and a half times. Whereas the 9,000 free Negro families of 1830 in the Old Dominion held $253,000 worth of realty in 1830, three decades later the 9,500 such families were credited with $830,000 worth.[40]

But however superior, the free Negro usually led a hard life. Throughout the South the legal assumption was that any Negro was a slave unless proof to the contrary was presented. For this reason all free Negroes were required to obtain and keep proof of their status, and anyone who lost such proof and could not replace it stood in a perilous situation. Even those who held valid papers could be seized, spirited away, and sold into slavery; and all writers who have investigated the subject agree that illegal reduction to servitude was by no means infrequent.[41] Legal reduction was sometimes all too easy. Maryland laws at the beginning of the fifties, for example, provided that a free Negro convicted of his first penal offense should be sold outside the State for a period of years fixed by the court. At every session of court free Negroes were thus sold for two, four, six, or ten years, as the case might be. But they were bought by slave dealers for just as high prices as if sold for life, and many *were* sent out of the State for life—nobody ever seeing them return. A part of the money from the sale went, under the law, to the officer making the arrest. The result was that any Negro who had ever been in the penitentiary was watched with hawk-like eye, and a small theft or a street affray might mean a lifetime of hard plantation toil. This Maryland law evidently had for one object a reduction of the free Negro population—and other Southern laws were not unlike it.

The free Negro of course had no political rights, and might not vote, serve on a jury, or bear witness in criminal cases for or against a white person. He had limited rights to appear as witness in civil suits, and could of course testify in all cases which involved other free colored persons alone. All free Negroes were sternly restricted in their movements. They must have a local white guardian, and could not wander into another county in search of employment without serious risk of being jailed as vagabonds. They were similarly restricted in their occupations. In Mississippi, typical of the lower South, no free Negro could keep a shop except in an incorporated town; none could keep a grocery or sell liquors anywhere; none could operate an inn or tavern, for this might facilitate clandestine meetings and plots; and none could set type in a printing establishment, for this might permit the circulation of seditious publications. Any printer

---

40 Boston *Journal*, Fort Smith letter September 13, 1859, C. S. Sydnor, "The Free Negro in Mississippi," *Am. Hist. Rev.*, XXXII, July, 1927, pp. 769ff. Luther P. Jackson, *Free Negro Labor and Property Holding in Virginia 1830–1860;* U. of Chicago Dissertation, 1937.
41 E. G. R. B. Flanders, "Free Negro in Ante-Bellum Georgia," *North Carolina Historical Review*, IX, 1932, pp. 250ff. "Equal Justice," Baltimore, December 30, 1849 in N. Y. *Tribune*, January 1, 1850.

caught with a colored hand was liable to a fine, while the hand was subject to the death penalty.[42] It need hardly be said that free Negroes found hunting difficult, for the possession of firearms, ammunition, or other weapons was forbidden without a license which was instantly voidable.

For various reasons—to find odd jobs, to engage in the vending prohibited elsewhere, to escape planter and farmer hostility—many free Negroes gravitated toward the cities and towns. In Mississippi, for example, Vicksburg and Natchez always contained a large share of the free colored group. In 1840, considerably more than a fifth resided in these two centers, 278 out of 1,366. Ten years later Natchez alone had 213 free colored persons. Besides taking odd jobs, cultivating market gardens, and operating small farms, free Negroes throughout the South found a variety of occupations. Many were smiths, cobblers, carpenters, barbers, cabinetmakers, shoeblacks, housepainters, or small tradesmen. The New Orleans *Picayune* testified in 1859 that free Negroes supplied the great majority of regular settled masons, bricklayers, builders, carpenters, tailors, and shoemakers; that they counted many excellent musicians, jewellers, goldsmiths, and merchants; and that as a whole they were "a sober, industrious, and moral class, far advanced in education and civilization." Some worked on the river steamboats as roustabouts or deckhands, a life so free that it was carefully hedged about by legal restrictions. Many grew prosperous, acquiring not only realty and other goods, but title to slaves, who might or might not be relatives. One Mississippi Negro in 1830 had seventeen slaves and another sixteen. The 360 colored taxpayers of Charleston in 1860 included no fewer than 130 who owned an aggregate of 390 slaves. Naturally the more enterprising free Negroes found means of giving their children schooling, whatever the law, under white or colored teachers, or both. That many of them were highly respected for their industry, ability, and integrity is attested by a thousand pieces of evidence.[43]

One of the most remarkable men of the ante-bellum South was the free mulatto William T. Johnson of Natchez, whose voluminous diaries and personal and business papers are treasured in the archives of the University of Louisiana.[44] Coming to Natchez in 1830 from Port Gibson, he established a barber-shop, married, and grew prosperous. In time he acquired two other barber-shops and a bath-house in Natchez, bought a plantation in that area, purchased at least one town lot, and established business connections with New Orleans. Bright, affable, energetic, and trustworthy, he became a friend of many planters and businessmen of western Mississippi. He performed small services for them, while if any imbibed too freely, his bath-house was at their disposal till they grew

42 Sydnor, "Free Negro in Miss.," *Am. Hist. Rev.*, XXXII.
43 New Orleans *Picayune* quoted in N. Y. *Weekly Tribune*, August 9, 1859. Sydnor, *op. cit.*, 109ff. Phillips, *American Negro Slavery*, 434. Randall, *Civil War and Reconstruction*, 52.
44 The Johnson collection has 58 bound volumes and 1,304 separate pieces.

sober. They gave him business advice, and he lent money to those who needed it, taking the usual high interest-rates. He thus grew rich. Throughout much of the thirties and forties he kept a diary, occasionally illustrated by his own rough sketches, which both furnishes a detailed commentary upon the events of white society, and portrays the mind and activities of an outstanding representative of the more alert, educated, and enterprising free colored people.

It is clear that he led an enjoyable as well as useful life. Like white men of the region, he liked a good horse-trade. He bought and sold oxen, and traded in corn and potatoes. The management of his barber-shops, each of which often took in six or eight dollars a day, and his plantation, where he rejoiced in good crops, did not keep him too busy to enjoy many diversions. He owned horses and raced them under other men's names. He bet on elections and other events, winning many a wager of a dollar or two. He went to the theatre, chafing under his enforced restriction to the Negro gallery. He fished and hunted. Upon the doings of white folk he bent a more sardonic eye than they suspected. Duels, murders, steamboat explosions, lawsuits, fierce political contests, speeches by such visiting notables as Henry Clay, noteworthy marriages, and auctions all find a place in a chronicle so candid that even today publication would require deletions.

Many white men treated him almost as an equal. "I went out this evening near Mrs. Linton's," he writes on one occasion, "and Shot a Mach with Mr. Jacquemine the 3 best in five for One Barrell of Oysters—I won them with ease." He would go shares with whites in small business deals, as in buying a barrel of pork. Many a small gift came to him, and he made gifts in return. When he proudly grew a forty-three-pound watermelon, he sent it off by steamer to a friend. Now and then a distinguished man treated him like the fellow-gentleman that he was. "General Quitman handed me a letter today that was given him at Jackson for me," runs one note. And he adds with touching emphasis: "He did me proud—he did me proud."

Nevertheless, in his almost helpless legal and social position he suffered many injustices. When paper money was depreciated by half, a debtor took advantage of the situation. "Mr. Blank," writes Johnson, "paid me two hundred dollars that he promised me that he would give me good money for it. Such is the nature of mankind." A "Dutch" family threw a cow of his down the steep bank of a bayou, killed her, and stole the meat. In one unfortunate day a scoundrel knocked out the eye of his mare ("Some Outrageous Rascal—oh if I Knew him"), while "Some infernal Thief" stole his skiff. He makes numerous notes upon a worthless and malevolent country neighbor named Baylor Winn. "B. Winns daughter came down to Hard Scrabble without shoes she had just escaped from Irons that her father had Chained her in to keep her from getting

Married to a Mr. Burk the wood Chopper." The girl made good her marriage. In the late forties he became involved in a suit with Winn and a man named Wade respecting the boundary of their plantations. The controversy was carried to the circuit court, which ordered a survey run, and the disputed land was found to be Johnson's. He thereupon proposed a generous compromise; Winn and Wade were to abandon the land improperly occupied and pay for the wood they had cut, while Johnson was to drop all claim for damages.

The last entries of the diary have a quiet pathos. On May 3, 1851, Wade called to say that they accepted the compromise. On May 16, Johnson's ninth child and fourth son was born. On May 18 he wrote that "Shop below made me $10.25 this week." His crops were doing well, and he took pleasure in inspecting them. On a beautiful day in early June he rode out with his children to gather the plentiful blackberries. The final jotting is for June 14th. The weather was mild and pleasant; business had been dull; he could not find two of his horses, and feared that something was amiss, for it was reported that they had been driven out of Lanieres the previous evening; he had bought some groceries, and had treated himself to fifteen cents' worth of soda and cigars. The ink was hardly dry on this record when he was ambushed and fatally wounded, surviving just long enough to name Winn as his assassin. The bullet had slain one of the most remarkable and interesting of American diarists.

Free Negroes slowly increased in number in the United States, rising from 434,000 in 1850 to 482,000 in 1860. They even increased (more slowly still) in the slave States, which by 1860 had about 250,000. But outside the border area, North Carolina, and Louisiana, the totals remained very small. In Mississippi, Texas, and Arkansas the free colored people actually decreased during the decade, while in Florida the population was stationary.[45] The final decade of slavery was unquestionably a black period for these unoffending Negroes and mulattoes. With sectional tension rising, with world sentiment against slavery increasing, Southerners were filled with fear lest the mere presence of free Negroes should excite discontent and insubordination among their fettered brethren. A tremendously forcible demand for repressive legislation rolled like a tidal wave across the South.

From early times a number of States had taken drastic steps to make sure that any increase in this unwanted population would be slow, difficult, and carefully guarded. The favorite measures had been the placing of sharp limits upon manumission, and the stern prohibition of any immigration of free Negroes. Georgia, for example, had halted manumission by deed of gift as early as 1801. In 1818 it forbade manumission by last will and testament, thus forbidding any Georgian to follow Washington's example. For a time slaves

45 Cf. table in Randall, *op. cit.,* 51.

were permitted to purchase their freedom. But kindly masters who permitted Negroes to hire their time and keep the marginal earnings until they had accumulated enough for self-purchase came to be regarded as a menace. They were not only adding to the number of free Negroes but creating a new class of nominal slaves, neither bond nor free, who might conceivably make trouble. Laws were passed to halt the process. The only method of liberating a slave that remained was by special legislative enactment, which was extremely difficult. In some respects Georgia's laws restricting free colored people were more severe than Mississippi's or South Carolina's. They were debarred from certain occupations; they could not hold title to slaves or real estate in their own names; they were never to be taught to read and write; and they might be compelled to labor on public works for twenty days every year. Any free Negro convicted of idleness or immorality might have his labor sold for one year, while the penalty for a second offense was slavery for life. It is not astonishing that Georgia had only 3,500 free Negroes in the year of Lincoln's election, and that their material and cultural progress was pitifully slow.[46]

Yet as if such Lacedemonian laws were not enough, an outcry arose for compelling free Negroes to choose between exile and reduction to slavery. Two legislatures in the midst of the Kansas crisis, when excitement ran high, bowed to this demand. Arkansas in February, 1859, enacted that all free persons of color must sell their belongings and remove from the State by New Year's Day of 1860. If they did not go, sheriffs were to seize them and hire them out for one year to the highest bidder, using the net proceeds of their labor to enable them to leave. Such as wished to remain might choose masters, who under a Pecksniffian clause were to pay half their appraised value into the common school fund. Two months after the law went into effect the Little Rock *True Democrat* rubbed approving hands over its workings, saying that many free Negroes had returned to slavery, and the disposition of the slaves had improved! Yet the idea that Arkansas had been pestiferously overrun by free Negroes, as another newspaper asserted, withers under the test of census figures. In 1850 only 608 had been enumerated! So fearful was Arkansas of being tainted that another law of 1859 forbade steamboats navigating her waters to employ free Negroes.[47]

---

46 R. B. Flanders, *op. cit.*; Hurd, *op. cit.*
47 Little Rock *True Democrat*, March 7, 1860. Fort Smith *Times*, June 9, 1859. E. L. Harvin, "Arkansas and the Crisis of 1860–1861," MS thesis, U. of Texas. Arkansas Historical Association Pubs. III, 179ff. The Arkansas press carried pathetic advertisements by Negroes trying to sell their property. Henry King of Little Rock, for example, advertised two houses and three lots in that city, with fruit trees, smoke-house, and other appurtenances. The Little Rock *Gazette and Democrat* called attention to this advertisement with the remark that King had been respected since boyhood and that any community to which he removed would be blessed with that noblest work of God, an honest man. February 19, 1859.

Louisiana followed in March, 1859, with legislation which gave all free persons of color not born in the State, upon warning to leave, a choice of exile, a penitentiary term followed by exile, or slavery for life under some self-chosen master or mistress. Its provisions were so complicated that even the native-born were not completely safe. The panic and sorrow among the eighteen thousand free Negroes of the State were indescribable. Newspapers blossomed out with items describing how this or that Negro, giving up well-paid work and independent homes, had selected an owner. Telling of two steamboat cooks, one earning $75 a month and one $100, who did this, the New Orleans *Crescent* added: "From what we hear at present, a great many free negroes, not born in this State, will pick out their masters and become slaves sooner than leave the population and the climate which pleases them so well." Coolly phrased! Behind this smooth, unruffled language, what anxieties, what terror, what agony, as men and women prepared to sell their poor belongings and move northward, or sought for some master whose kindness they could trust! And Louisiana passed another law, under pressure from white stevedores and longshoremen, prohibiting the temporary introduction of free men of color by any ship arriving at the port of New Orleans.[48]

Everywhere in the slave area the feverish excitement of the period and the sense that slavery was on the defensive produced a suspicious and hostile attitude toward Free Joe. Delegates in the Kentucky convention of 1849 murmured against him, saying that vicious whites corrupted him and made him steal, that he was a bad example to slaves, and that he was better off in slavery. In North Carolina his position had long been specially happy. He had once been pronounced a citizen, his right to vote had not been taken away until 1835, he had managed to acquire some education and establish a fairly satisfactory community life, and he practised a wide variety of occupations in the economic system. Yet racial antagonism deepened until in many places it grew intense. Efforts by philanthropic persons to educate the ten thousand free colored people in the District of Columbia meanwhile provoked sharp resistance. They were being instructed far beyond their political and social condition, ran one complaint of 1857; free schools would attract an inundating flood from the surrounding region; and the true course was to prohibit immigration and encourage removals. Tennessee, which until 1834 allowed free Negroes the ballot, hardened its heart; the legislature debated bills late in the fifties to banish these poor folk, and passed a law permitting them to enslave themselves.

48 New Orleans *Daily Crescent*, September 1, 1859, quoted in N. Y. *Weekly Tribune*, September 10, 1859. See Mobile *Register*, November 27, 1859, quoting N. Y. *Journal of Commerce* to the effect that the Louisiana law prohibiting temporary landings of free men of color caused a good many Northern ships to stop at Mobile rather than New Orleans.

Nor were the sixteen thousand slaveholders of Maryland less irritable and apprehensive. They viewed the eighty thousand free Negroes, a body almost as numerous as the slaves, with jaundiced gaze. Many of these black folk had acquired property and standing. Rightly or wrongly, they were connected with the brisk operations of the Underground Railroad running into the very heart of the State. The slaveholders of the Eastern Shore, gathering in convention at Cambridge in the fall of 1858, first blackened the character of Free Joe by accusation of "vicious habits," "refusal to labor," "incapacity for self-government," and then proposed a statewide convention to bring pressure upon the legislature. The proper policy, they declared, was to give all free colored people the choice of leaving Maryland or going into slavery.[49]

Everywhere, North and South, the free Negro offered a demonstration of the fact that the racial problem underlay the slavery problem, and that abrupt action in dealing with the 'peculiar institution' might well complicate the task of race-adjustment. Everywhere, too, the free Negro showed that the colored man's position in American society would be more largely fixed by economic facts, social forces, and inherited attitudes regarding color caste than by laws.

A Southern pamphleteer, Ellwood Fisher, roundly asserted in 1849 that emancipation would fail, because it would leave the Negro's real position largely unchanged. Would the emancipated slave really work as hard as was necessary for competition with the white man, and if he did, would the white laborer welcome such competition? Pointing to the North, Fisher noted some of the rough facts that abolitionists were wont to ignore. Of nearly twelve thousand colored people in the city of New York in 1845, barely a hundred had satisfied the $250 qualification for voting. Throughout the North, despite augmentation by manumissions and escapes, the free Negroes increased more slowly than the slaves of the South. Of all the free persons of color, nearly half preferred to remain in the slave area. The number of Negroes in Boston, the very center of sympathy and agitation for the slaves, had actually decreased during the previous twenty years, while in Massachusetts the percentage of colored persons

49 Debates and Proceedings of the Kentucky Convention, 73ff. John Hope Franklin, *The Free Negro in North Carolina, 1790–1860. National Intelligencer,* May 7, 1857, gives Walter Lenox's denunciation of Miss Myrtilla Miner's Washington school and its enlargement. Wright, *Free Negro in Maryland.* In 1850 Maryland had 74,723 free Negroes; in 1860, it had 83,942. See the Baltimore *American,* November 5, 6, 1858; N. Y. *Weekly Tribune,* November 13, 1858, on the convention at Cambridge. Another Maryland slaveholders' convention met in Baltimore on June 8, 1859. A few members wished to prohibit emancipation and pass laws for the gradual extinction of "Free Negroism." But by an almost unanimous vote, the convention took a more humane view. It adopted resolutions declaring any measure for the general removal of free blacks from Maryland impolitic, inexpedient, and unnecessary, and asserting that for the purpose of diminishing "the evils which proceed from the excessive and increasing free negro class," the policy of the State fixed in 1831 should be reaffirmed with amendments which "will either prohibit emancipation altogether, or compel the prompt removal from the State of those emancipated. . . ." N. Y. *Weekly Tribune,* June 18, 1859.

in the penitentiary was ten times the percentage of whites. The pamphleteer was wrong in concluding that emancipation would be a mistake. But he was right in his demonstration that emancipation would be but one part, and a small part, of a task far heavier and more complex than men realized.[50]

[VII]

With the emancipationist impulse of the fathers dead, with colonization impracticable, with the position of the free Negro tragic in the North and almost intolerable in parts of the South, what was the solution of the great problem? A rising Southern chorus chanted its answer: slavery must be accepted as beneficent, immutable, and eternal. Northerners for the most part held that slavery was a temporary system to be maintained until it could safely yield to gradual emancipation. The abolitionists of course demanded immediate and unconditional liberation. But as they remained a relatively small and uninfluential group, the substantial choice lay between slavery as an immutable discipline, and slavery as an institution evolving toward freedom.

It is a law of history that whenever peaceful evolution fails to effect a needed set of changes, some revolutionary agency steps in and does so. Change and growth are so indispensable in human affairs that whenever an effort is made to erect an immovable dam, the force of the piling waters finally becomes absolutely irresistible. The calamitous error of Southern leadership lay in its refusal to treat slavery as a dynamic institution. By statesmanlike effort reforms could have been introduced (as Robert Toombs advocated in his famous lecture on slavery) to safeguard marriage and the family life of the bondsmen; to give all Negroes fitted for it some education, and to allow those who displayed exceptional enterprise, intelligence, and industry to escape from servitude— in short, to make slavery an educative and transitional labor-system, thus laying the groundwork for a rational permanent adjustment between the races. To be sure, all this would have demanded sacrifice and would have imposed risks. But neither would have been comparable with those incurred when the waters finally broke through with destructive roar.

The great concurrent error of the North was that it did nothing of a practical nature to assist in racial adjustment on a new basis. Merely to rail at the Southerners for holding slaves and to demand instant emancipation was a deplorably barren policy. Why did none of these Northern abolitionists who could easily raise considerable sums of money send agents southward, buy up slaves, and bring them North for settlement? Those who fled from their

50 Ellwood Fisher, "The North and the South" (Lecture, pvt., Richmond, 1849; Huntington Library).

masters were welcomed, but practically nothing was done to purchase any from their owners. Doubtless one reason was that such a course would have raised slave-prices, encouraged slave-breeding, and done little to solve the problem. But another and larger reason was that Northern workers would not have permitted this solution, even had it been valid, for they disliked colored neighbors and colored rivalry. Abolitionists wished to liberate the slaves to compete with the small farmers and workmen of the South; they did not wish to bring them North to compete with farmers, mechanics, and laborers of the free areas. Wealthy Gerrit Smith did distribute an inhospitable tract of land in northern New York among free and escaped Negroes, but that inadequate effort stood alone, cost little in money or care, and demanded no Northern effort at social readjustment. Why did Northern leaders not rally about Webster's proposal that the proceeds of the public lands be used for gradual compensated emancipation, perhaps with some systematic Northern resettlement? Tough-minded men asked these questions. Said the New York *Journal of Commerce* in 1850 of the slaves:

The North first made property of them, and owe much of their gains to them. How many *hundreds* did they ever liberate? On the contrary, when a single individual at the South first liberated sixty, worth as property then at least $30,000, it was found difficult, nay impossible, to raise at the North $3,000 to send them to Africa; and a large proportion of that insignificant sum was contributed from the South. Where is the Northern man, old or young, living or dying, that leaves any bequest of any kind to liberate and restore these people, whom their fathers or themselves have plundered and robbed from Africa, to their homes? [51]

The consequence of these two refusals—the refusal of Southerners to treat slavery as a progressive and evolutionary system, leading by regular gradations to freedom, and the refusal of Northerners to acknowledge that in equity they must share the heavy burdens of racial readjustment—was to place slavery in a position where it became more and more perilous to the body politic. It had to be moved toward a new position, but neither side was willing to move it by gradual plan. Year by year a violent solution of the problem became more probable. The North was quite as much at fault as the South.

Each side could easily rationalize its attitude. Northerners could assert that

51 O. B. Frothingham, *Gerrit Smith*, 235. N. Y. *Journal of Commerce* quoted in Washington *Union*, May 5, 1850. A Southerner, in a letter in the *National Intelligencer*, August 20,1857, sardonically congratulated a National Emancipation Convention shortly to meet in Cleveland for adopting, at last, "a practical direction." It intended to seek a way to abolish slavery and remunerate slave-owners. He proposed that it consider the cost of purchasing slaves who steadily would grow more valuable as their number was decreased by manumissions, the costs of the cotton and sugar estates which would be ruined, the losses of Northern cotton mills, labor, ships when raw goods no longer came to market, and so on.

as the South had for two centuries profited from the unrequited labor of the slave, so now it should meet all the difficulties of assimilating them to its own society. They could also declare that no important problem existed, for the Negro possessed such high intellectual and moral characteristics that he could rapidly and painlessly be lifted to equality with the whites. This sentimental exaggeration of the Negro's immediate potentialities (something very different from his ultimate capacities) was particularly common among abolitionists who knew little of the slave at first hand, and who by an easy process of generalization fancied nearly every field hand a Robert Purvis or Frederick Douglass. Southerners meanwhile rationalized their attitude by so exaggerating the dangers and difficulties of change as to pronounce it utterly impossible. More importantly, as we have seen, they could contrast the worst side of industrialism with the best side of slavery. And most fortifying of all to the Southern spirit, they could consciously or unconsciously take the view that the Negro had never been fit for any position but that of bondsman, and never would be. This became a traditional conviction bulwarked by habit, indolence, timidity, and the desire for security.

The assertion that the Negro was an inferior creation, a being of natural incapacity, lent itself to a thought-pattern which opposed all change in slavery. Cultural, democratic, and humanitarian assumptions applied only to man, not brutes, and the Negro was nearer brute than man—so the implicit syllogism ran. The Negro was a creature of great physical strength, of limited intellectual power (scientifically explained by contracted cranial capacity, early closing of the frontal skull-sutures, and special characteristics of the brain-cells), of natural indolence, conquerable only by stern driving, of powerful sexual impulses, dangerous unless rigidly restrained, of innate superstition, and of constant readiness to revert to savagery.[52]

"We recognize the fact of the inferiority stamped upon the race of men by the Creator," said Jefferson Davis in the Senate, "and from the cradle to the grave, our government as a civil institution, marks that inferiority." [53]

52 Cf. John Dollard, *Caste and Class in a Southern Town.* The idea that the Negro was congenitally thriftless and lazy was sharply condemned in the first report of the Virginia Commissioner of Agriculture (1877). The Commissioner, Dr. Pollard, declared white supervision unnecessary. Speaking from his own experience as a farmer under both the slave regime and the free regime, he declared that "the negro, if promptly paid and fairly dealt by, is as good a laborer as he ever was," and that while some would not work, "the majority of them, and enough to till the lands" would. How much work would they do? As much as white men, he thought. He cited the report of Charles L. Flint, secretary of the Massachusetts Board of Agriculture, on the time consumed by labor in performing various farm tasks. "At the time of reading the report we made a calculation, in connection with another farmer, of how long it would take to accomplish the work here in Virginia, and came to the conclusion that our negro hands would do more work per day than the white laborers of Massachusetts." Cited in the *Nation,* February 14, 1878.
53 Davis in *Cong. Globe,* February 29, 1860. Cf. Dollard, Cason, W. J. Cash, *et aliis.*

This supposed biological inferiority, stated by science and the Bible, condemned the Negro to permanent servility. Convenient instances were selected from the mass of evidence at hand to support the defensive generalization. As Cuffy was stupid, and Meg unchaste, so all Negroes were stupid and unchaste; it being forgotten that Joe was very bright and Sally a model of wifely constancy. Beliefs in the mendacity, thievishness, emotional instability, and laziness of Negroes were thus systematically cultivated in order to build up a defensive pattern supporting the slavery relationship—and behind it a fixed caste relation.

Such rationalizations, with clashing economic interests and general divergences of culture, created a greater and greater gulf of misunderstanding. As the two sections faced each other across the chasm, with rising excitement and growing antipathy, each side gave way more and more to irrational emotion; each seemed to catch the far-off note of throbbing drums and sounding bugles.

[VIII]

But it was not the white men alone, North and South, who were to settle the slavery question. The Negro was always a factor, and as the decades passed a more and more active factor. The Southern contention that the Negroes were what "Vindex," writing in 1858, called a debased race of inordinate animality and little intellect,[54] was refuted by the colored folk themselves. The dictum that their condition was and must remain static was being contradicted by steady advances. Slavery, and still more the general contact of whites and blacks whether inside or outside slavery, were steadily if slowly and unevenly raising the Negro toward the cultural level of the more highly developed race. For in one aspect slavery was a school, a channel of education. From the moment they were landed in America, the Negroes in some fashion, and usually in many, were under the tuition of the dominant race. They learned something of a new, more flexible, and more exacting language, of a nobler religion, of a routine of steady industry, of moral principles, and of complex skills.

Unquestionably a primary step in the education of many Negroes was the inculcation of habits of steady settled industry. While the indigenous culture of various Negro peoples in Africa had been on a much higher level than most Americans of 1850 realized, it was not the product of labor as steady and intense as that of contemporaneous white civilizations. We have the testimony of such sympathetic observers as Albert Schweitzer that certain basic conditions of life among the primitive peoples of Africa—the enervating climate, the ease with which a sufficiency of food, clothing, and shelter may be obtained, the lack of incentive for large accumulations of property—tended to make labor casual and intermittent.[55] But slavery taught the Negro to work without excessive intermissions and with genuine application and method. For some of the most superior slaves brought from Africa such a lesson was superfluous, but for the great majority it meant a valuable toughening of character. Learning that while mere subsistence is possible on a casual labor basis, wealth in volume can be created only by an uninterrupted routine of hard toil, the Southern Negro by 1860 was in countless instances ready to work when he did not please, and for larger ends than mere living.

In the process of working, the Negro acquired valuable new skills. To be sure, very impressive types of craftmanship had existed in Africa. So coolheaded an observer as Sir Harry Johnston calls "wonderful" the culture of one area in metalworking, weaving, pottery, and carving. The Dahomey brasswork, the Benin bronzes, the Ashanti textiles, the iron and basketry of all the peoples, were remarkable. In some districts, as on the lower Congo, a certain differentiation of occupations had grown up; one village devoting itself to fishing, another to palm wine, another to work in iron and copper, and a fourth to trade and brokerage among the rest.[56] But the evidence seems conclusive that the great majority of the black folk brought to America were accustomed to a low stage of endeavor in agriculture, in household management and cookery, in blacksmithing and the mechanic arts, and in the fabrication of clothes and furniture. They grew accustomed to the sight of a much more elaborate and finished set of arts, and to an increasing degree shared in their practice.

Many slaves, to be sure, knew little except the use of the hoe, mattock, and axe. They were constantly and steadily driven up to their work, and the stupid, plodding, machine-like manner in which they labored was painful to witness. So wrote Olmsted of the Old Southwest, and his view that a meaningless drudgery was the lot of most field hands was commonly accepted. But even on the larger plantations of the cotton belt a considerable variety of occupations prevailed. Slaves had to plow, hoe, replant, and pick cotton; to repair fences, houses, and barns, keep plantation equipment in shape, clean wells, and trim trees; to clear new ground, burn brush, and make rails; to manufacture charcoal and bricks; and to look after plantation animals. Most plantations gave some attention to corn, peas, and potatoes. Ginning, baling, and road-repairing all took effort. And then there were the mechanic trades: any ordinary plantation would have a carpenter, blacksmith, shoemaker, shingle-maker, and weaver, or indeed

55 Schweitzer, *On the Edge of the Primeval Forest*, ch. 7; Friedrich Ratzel, *History of Mankind*, II, 380ff.
56 Sir Harry Johnston, *Opening Up of Africa*, 125; cf. Melville J. Herskovits, "Social History of the Negro" in *Handbook of Social Psychology*, ed. C. Marchison, 221–224; W. E. B. Du Bois, *The Negro*, 117, quoting Bucher.

several of each category. A larger plantation would be likely to have a wheel-wright and wagonmaker, with seamstresses, cooks, midwife, and nurses. Crippled Negroes unfit for hard field work would be put to labor in the "loom house" or the cobbler's shop; a boy of great manual skill would be apprenticed to the smith; a lad with a keen eye would be set to laying out the levels for hillside ditches. Of partial Negro self-government on large plantations there were interesting and increasingly numerous examples.[57]

On the smaller plantations and farms the slaves of course had to be master of as many rough crafts as the owner himself; the men carried on all the operations of the place, from breeding livestock and breaking colts to erecting farm buildings and planting orchards; the women spun, wove, sewed, mended, cooked, and cleaned. Plantations or farms which fronted on river or bay offered various water occupations, while those recently cleared from the forest furnished logging and lumbering. In short, it was not merely possible, but indispensable, for hosts of Negroes to acquire nearly as varied a list of skills as those of the frontier or semi-frontier farmer in America, the most resourceful and versatile agricultural worker in the world. One ingenious Maryland slave in 1852 formally applied for a patent on a useful agricultural machine.[58]

The town Negro, it was generally observed, was demarcated from the rural black by superior liveliness and intelligence, but also by a more dubious morality and a slighter sense of duty and responsibility. Both his intellectual superiority and moral inferiority were natural, for while he saw more of life and had fuller opportunities to acquire special training, he was frequently hired out to men who gave his conduct outside working hours no supervision. Town slaves might do almost anything. They might be mechanics, hostlers, carpenters, or shoe-makers. They might work as assistants to white barbers, house-builders, harness-makers, blacksmiths, or wagon-makers. They could be employed in foundries, textile mills, tanneries, brick-making establishments, sawmills, or metal-working shops. Considerable numbers worked in building railroads or as brakemen and firemen, while at least one slave was a locomotive engineer. Others were firemen, roustabouts, cooks, and stewards on river steamboats. Still others labored in gangs to cut down the firewood which the steamboats burned. Negro janitors for offices and shops were numerous, while most larger hotels and taverns kept Negro servants, sometimes quick, alert, and highly useful, sometimes stupid and inefficient. A number of Negroes even learned such crafts as cigar-making. As

57 Olmsted, *Journey in the Back Country*, 81–82. Sydnor, *Slavery in Mississippi*, 9–11. Woodson, *Education of the Negro Prior to 1861*, p. 210. At the famous sale of Pierce Butler's 436 slaves at Savannah early in 1859, coming from a rice plantation near Darien and a cotton plantation on St. Simon's Island, a number of very passable mechanics were included. "There were coopers, carpenters, shoemakers, and blacksmiths, each one equal in his various craft to the ordinary requirements of a plantation." N. Y. *Weekly Tribune*, March 12, 1859.
58 N. Y. *Weekly Tribune*, December 25, 1858.

for the women, they found employment as seamstresses, cooks, and laundry-women.[59]

Cotton factories, slowly increasing in number, found that white labor was more satisfactory than that of Negroes, and one conspicuous South Carolina mill which depended upon the use of black operatives was soon forced into bankruptcy. Nevertheless, by 1850 the South had abundant proof that the Negro possessed the innate capacity to make not merely a capable mill-hand, but a proficient artisan. Indeed, ten years earlier Savannah had 107 Negroes (slave and free) listed as mechanics, and more who were butchers, barbers, engineers, or pilots. The success of Negroes in handicraft occupations was so great that the Georgia legislature passed a law in 1845 to prohibit colored mechanics or masons, whether slave or free, from making contracts to erect or repair buildings.[60]

White mechanics in Mississippi, as in other States, frequently opposed the training of slaves in their occupations as a degradation of the calling, and a source of competition. When one Mississippi artisan was offered the help of three slaves for half a dozen years on condition that he teach them his craft, he angrily rejected the offer. Wide attention was attracted in 1851 to a memorial by the Mechanics' Association of Portsmouth, Va., protesting against the teaching of crafts and trades to slaves. A convention of four or five hundred delegates which met that same summer in Atlanta, Ga., to consider means of advancing the mechanic arts, proposed among other steps the entire stoppage of the instruction of Negroes in skilled trades. It argued that the admission of blacks to various crafts not only limited the opportunities open to white men, but sharpened their wits, made them restless, encouraged them to run away to the North, and gave them a generally unsettled character. They became ambitious to read and write, mastered these arts in clandestine fashion, and then aroused the discontent of other slaves. "A few Negro mechanics in towns and cities," stated the resolutions of the convention, "have done and can do more practical injury to the institution of slavery and its permanent security, than all the ultra abolitionists of

59 Sydnor, *Slavery in Mississippi*, 5–8; P. A. Bruce, *Plantation Negro as a Freeman*. The New Orleans *Picayune*, quoted in the N. Y. *Weekly Tribune*, August 6, 1859, asserted: "Some of our best mechanics and artisans are to be found among the free colored men. They form the great majority of our regular settled masons, bricklayers, builders, carpenters, tailors, shoemakers, etc. . . . while we count among them in no small numbers excellent musicians, jewelers, goldsmiths, tradesmen, and merchants."

60 Phillips, *American Negro Slavery*, 379. Flanders, *Slavery in Georgia*, 204–205. The Selma, Ala., *Sentinel*, quoted in the *National Intelligencer*, October 30, 1858, described the successful use of slaves in the Scottsville, Alabama, mills. The first profits of the mills—$2,200, paid in 1841—were used to purchase a family of Negroes for work in the factory. "This family has so increased that the company values them at $10,000, and most of them are now working in the factory, and are very useful. The company have made several purchases of Negroes with the profits of the factory, and Negro labor is much employed by them."

the country." No better testimony to the capacity and ambition of the Negro could be found; and the fact that the Georgians attached such importance to the matter suggests that the trained Negro mechanics were becoming numerous.[61]

Everywhere, in towns, on the farms, and on great plantations, the slaves had ample opportunity to acquaint themselves with the tastes, ways, and achievements of the white race. Negroes often went hunting and fishing with the whites; they attended court-days, camp meetings, and carnivals with them; they flocked to look at barbecues and fairs. In the border States and even the Deep South, the white sons played with the children of the slave cabins. James Lane Allen has noted the companionship which a Kentucky youngster, graduating from the lap of his Negro mammy, found among the little ragged black imps of the cabins. He stole away to the duck-pond with them to learn to swim; he and they raced up and down the lane on blooded alder-stalk horses; they told him where the guinea-hen had hidden her nest. "To them he showed his first Barlow knife; for them he blew his first home-made whistle. He is their petty tyrant today; tomorrow he will be their repentant friend, dividing with them his marbles, and proposing a game of hop-scotch." He and they laid upon each other the ineffaceable impression of their different forms of speech, their likes and dislikes, their whole character.[62]

How much of the folklore of the Negroes some youngsters absorbed, the country first realized when Joel Chandler Harris published his tales of Uncle Remus; and simultaneously the Negro children unconsciously picked up nursery rhymes, bits of fairy tales, crude notions of national heroes, and all the folklore of the whites. Thousands of Negroes learned to read with white children—or their white elders. Negro women working in the big houses acquired the tastes of their mistresses in dress and furniture, and white skills in cookery. The author of *The Southwest by a Yankee* reported a conversation between the coachman and footman on a large plantation. "You know dat nigger they gwine to sell, George?" "No, he field nigger; I nebber has no 'quaintance wid dat class." "Well, nor no oder gentlemens would." Amusing as a revelation of class feeling among slaves, the dialogue indicates that these household Negroes felt themselves half white men. And well they might; for in many a planter's house the servants had the same food, clothing (at second hand), and conveniences as the white folk, and took pride in the same dignity and good manners. Visitors to Cuba remarked

61 Olmsted, *Back Country*, 180–181. N. Y. *Weekly Tribune*, July 12, 26, 1851.
62 Allen, *Blue Grass Region*, pp. 61–62. Reuben Davis in *Recollections of Mississippi* describes the pleasure with which Negroes attended political barbecues—nay, presided over the roasting of the meat—happier in them than the whites. The music and songs of the slaves early attracted attention; New Yorkers flocked to hear the "Negro Minstrels" in the 1840's. By 1887 the best collection of Negro songs was a volume called "Slave Songs of the United States." In that year Oliver Ditson & Co. published a volume of words and music called "Jubilee and Plantation Songs."

that American slaves were vastly superior to those of the island, and pointed to the closer communion of the two races on American soil as the principal reason.[63]

The religious activities of the Negro, transferred directly from the practices of the whites, were a powerful though uneven educational influence. In frontier or semi-frontier communities, especially in the border States, church minutes reveal large numbers of slave members, who sat separately (often in the gallery, if one existed), but on whom were enforced as high standards of conduct as on the whites. Evidently the slaveowners frequently used the church as a disciplinary instrument, and greatly valued its influence in checking thievery, lying, impudence, and other offenses.[64] Mason Crum in his delightful book on the sea-island Negroes entitled *Gullah* presents the testimony of one ante-bellum planter after another that churchgoing weakened vicious habits, created cheerfulness, and made the slaves more obedient.

Epecially in towns and cities the slaves often had congregations of their own. In Natchez, Miss., in the middle fifties, three Presbyterian preachers of Northern birth and good education preached to Negroes alone; one of them visiting congregations in Louisiana, one ministering to a large body of colored people in Natchez and to neighboring plantations, and the third ranging the countryside for ten or fifteen miles. In Charleston, S. C., the efforts of the Presbyterian and Episcopal Churches to furnish religious instruction to Negroes aroused in 1849 a bitter discussion. A mob attempted to tear down the Calvary Episcopal Church then in course of erection for colored parishioners. Responsible citizens intervened, and James L. Petigru, rushing from his office, made an impassioned plea to the crowd. Let them deliberate on the issue, he urged, and give it careful study. A committee of fifty was appointed to collect information throughout the South. At a meeting in the city hall in the spring of 1850 it reported that the movement for systematic Christianization of the Negroes deserved support. Petigru made a vigorous supporting speech, and the auditors enthusiastically agreed. The question of a separate church for Charleston Negroes was thus definitely settled.[65]

How much the Negroes valued the right of religious assemblage was repeatedly demonstrated. In a revision of the Mississippi statutes, for example, a provision was introduced into the slave code which made the gathering of any considerable number of slaves for religious exercises, without the presence of an ordained white minister, an unlawful assemblage. The colored folk were in-

63 Woodson, *op. cit.*, 119-120. J. H. Ingraham, *The Southwest by a Yankee*, II, 30. Sydnor, *Slavery in Mississippi*, 4. *National Intelligencer*, January 4, 1859. For an admirable statement of modern Southern attitudes see the expert essays gathered in Edgar T. Thompson, ed., *Race Relations and the Race Problem* (1939).

64 W. W. Sweet, *Religion on the American Frontier*, Vol. I, *The Baptists, 1783-1830*.

65 Sydnor, *op. cit.*, 59-60. Carson, *Petigru*, 280-281. MS Schirmer Diary, July 14, 1849ff; Charleston Hist. Soc.

dignant. One of them went to the Methodist clergyman William Winans, a minister of striking personality and forensic power. Winans was a large, muscular man, a fervent exhorter, a Jacksonian Democrat, and in other respects a notable frontier type. In his manuscript autobiography, a remarkable picture of an itinerant preacher's career kept in the Mississippi archives, he tells how the colored protests touched him. He saw that the law prevented white men from

LIBERTY LINE.
NEW ARRANGEMENT---NIGHT AND DAY.

The improved and splendid Locomotives, Clarkson and Lundy, with their trains fitted up in the best style of accommodation for passengers, will run their regular trips during the present season, between the borders of the Patriarchal Dominion and Libertyville, Upper Canada. Gentlemen and Ladies, who may wish to improve their health or circumstances, by a northern tour; are respectfully invited to give us their patronage.

SEATS FREE, *irrespective of color*.

Necessary Clothing furnished gratuitously to such as have "*fallen among thieves*."

"Hide the outcasts—let the oppressed go free."—*Bible.*

☞For seats apply at any of the trap doors, or to the conductor of the train.

J. CROSS, *Proprietor.*

N. B. For the special benefit of Pro-Slavery Police Officers, an extra heavy wagon for Texas, will be furnished, whenever it may be necessary, in which they will be forwarded as dead freight, to the "Valley of Rascals," always at the risk of the owners.

☞Extra Overcoats provided for such of them as are afflicted with protracted *chilly-phobia*.

Advertisement of the Underground Railroad.
The Western Citizen, July 13, 1844.

praying with their slaves, and slaves from holding informal prayer meetings. Finding that the author of the statute, George Poindexter, was a candidate for Congress, he resolved to make his wrath felt. "My position, as presiding elder of a district embracing a large portion of voters, rendered my opposition more conspicuous than that of any other individual." He brought about the defeat of Poindexter, much to that man's mortification, and the law was modified at an early session of the legislature. Talking with a friend, Poindexter said: "I was not beaten by Rankin, but by an old black man named Winter, belonging to Parson Winans!"

The exact number of Negro church-members in the slave area it is impossible to state, but it was clearly large. Some estimates ran up to 300,000 or 400,000. A more conservative authority in 1854 placed it at about 270,000, of whom the Methodists were credited with 147,000, the Baptists with 100,000, the Episcopalians 10,000, and the Presbyterians 7,000. White leaders in all the important sects constantly urged the importance of attending to the spiritual welfare of slaves, and of carrying out broad missionary programs. All masters, exhorted the *Southern Churchman*, should see that slaves were taught the elements of Christianity, that they were regularly allowed to hear a portion of the Bible, that they were required to attend public worship, and that their children were baptized. Baptists were urged by their principal church organ to set up Sunday schools for the oral instruction of slaves old and young. Special material was prepared for the Negroes, their catechisms and lessons often inculcating duty to the owner no less than to God!

It was unquestionably true that, as white observers often pointed out, the sermons of some Negro preachers were mere burlesques on religion, and had the auditors been less simple and fervent, would have tended to bring it into ridicule. But it was also true that the heartfelt piety of many colored congregations might well have put the cold intellectuality of some white services to shame. Not a few elementary lessons in self-government were learned by these colored congregations. Their deacons or elders, regularly elected in many churches by the members, exercised powers of direction, oversight, admonition, and advice that were quite apostolic in nature and scope. A careful and highly intelligent Southern leader, bearing testimony after the war that the Negroes were deeply imbued with Christianity, attributed to this the fact that they were more orderly and moral than the same class in any other country.[66]

[IX]

The problems of slavery and race-adjustment thus presented an equation in which three main elements, the opinions and wishes of the white South, the views of the white North, and the desires of the colored people, slowly but steadily evolving toward a better status, had to be considered. The third group in the triangle must not be ignored. With every upward step the Negro proved

66 *Southern Episcopalian*, June, 1854, pp. 119–123, article by Paul Trapier, a missionary. The Rev. R. G. Curley estimated 300,000 Negro church-members; *National Intelligencer*, November 1, 1853. *Southern Baptist*, December 16, 1856. "Religious Life of the Negro Slave," *Harper's Monthly Magazine*, 1863, XXVII, pp. 479ff., 676ff., 817ff. W. L. Trenholm, "The South: An Address," April 7, 1869 (pvt., Charleston Society Library), in the course of which he said: "These four million descendants of savages were more orderly and moral than the same class in any other civilized country, and they remain so up to the present moment, notwithstanding the temptations and privations of the war, the license of sudden freedom, and the bad advice of political agitators. They were deeply imbued with the principles of Christianity, so much so that since emancipation they have cheerfully devoted their scanty earnings to the building and maintenance of churches and schools, and the establishment of charitable societies; their intellectual powers were stimulated and improved so far as they could be in a condition of slavery, and were sufficiently developed to furnish a stimulus for continued effort, and to constitute the basis of their future self-improvement."

that slavery could not be held a frozen, changeless institution. Every time a Fanny Kemble or Thomas L. Dabney taught a group of slaves to read, the seed of change was sown. Every time a Frederick Douglass lifted himself like Plautus from bondage to the pursuit of culture and letters, proving the possession not merely of talents but of a rare magnanimity, a seed germinated. How could men speak of colored folk as unfit for freedom when they had before their eyes such examples of distinction as James Wormley, who, beginning his career as steward for the Metropolitan Club in Washington, shortly before the war opened a hotel and catering establishment which soon became the best in the national capital? How speak of them as unworthy when the race produced a hero like Bob Butt, who during the terrible yellow fever pestilence which scourged Portsmouth, Va., in 1855, served as gravedigger for eleven hundred and fifty-nine persons, laboring devotedly from morn till dark to give sepulture to the dead, and often making the grave his resting-place.[67]

As the advancing slave learned to know his own worth, he refused to accept the doctrine of an immutable slave system. The old assumption that the vast majority of bondsmen were contented with their lot, or at least passively accepted it, is open to sharp question. Any really penetrating investigation of the institution in the fifties discloses evidence of sharp tension in the Negro-white relation, with indications that countless thousands of colored folk were constantly "fighting back." Some sought to break down the system by insurrection. The list of plots, sporadic outbreaks, and revolts during the decade is long, and it is perhaps significant that the election years of 1856 and 1860, with their pervasive excitement, brought reports of widely-ramified conspiracies. Other slaves resisted servitude by flight, many thousands running away. Still others resorted to economic weapons. Their supposed laziness was frequently a type of passive resistance, while direct sabotage through the destruction of property or maiming of livestock was far from unknown. Slaves who were hard pressed by brutal masters might assert their personalities by impudent language or physical assault. Meanwhile, the colored folk maintained their morale by various devices; by prayer, by hymns and spirituals which emphasized the idea of freedom, by their own interpretation of the Bible, and by clandestine meetings and grapevine communication.[68]

More and more, too, the slaves acquired information about the anti-slavery movement. For example, a mulatto named Sella Martin, who was eighteen in

---

67 *Journal of Negro History*, April 1935, pp. 268–269, January, 1936, pp. 57–59. Report of Portsmouth Relief Assn., 1855, saying Butt "performed duty beyond all price."
68 Herbert Aptheker, *American Negro Slave Revolts*, esp. chs. 6 and 14; R. A. and A. H. Bauer, "Day to Day Resistance to Slavery," *Journal of Negro History*, XXVII, 388–419. J. H. Johnston, "Race Relations in Virginia," gives 82 instances of slaves condemned to death in Virginia. 1786–1845, for murder of masters or overseers.

1850 and worked as errand boy for gamblers and others in a hotel at Columbus, Ga., learned to read. It was not long, as he later recounted in *Good Words* (May 1, 1867), before the other slaves of the town found this out. One day a knot of them invited him to go to the woods to gather wild grapes. When out of sight one took from his bosom a newspaper and handed it to the youth, saying: "Dere, read dat ar, an' tell us whut him say 'bout de bobbolishinus!" Martin read them an account of Clay's doctrines on emancipation. Thousands of similar occurrences doubtless took place, and helped inspire the growing strictness of laws against Negro literacy and Negro assemblages.

Conflict between North and South; conflict among groups and parties within both sections; conflict between whites jealous of their supremacy and the free Negro; increasing conflict between the bondsman and his master—this was the situation which darkened all the prospects of the nation in the fifties. Nowhere did compromise on any essential issue seem to be gaining ground. The South became more stubbornly determined to maintain the existing status, the North more stubbornly denunciatory, the Negro more stubbornly discontented. The conflict of selfish interests, the provocations of sectional pride, the dull weight of inertia, blocked every hopeful change. With every passing year the pent-up forces were growing more powerful and the dangers of an explosion more appalling.

2.

PRESIDENT FRANKLIN PIERCE, inaugurated in 1853, was a pleasant man, but he "unhesitatingly took the weaker and more convenient" of two lines of policy. He could have shown that the Compromise of 1850 was irrevocable as a settlement of the slavery issue, or he could try to placate and conciliate all factions and sections. He chose the easier second course. "A man of sterner temper and keener perception than Pierce would have seen that party unity is never bought by offices and smiles, but only by a determined fight for principle, and that something greater than party harmony was at stake—the safety of the nation." [1]

The national situation at the end of 1853 seemed fairly calm to most Americans, but the storm soon erupted. The crust of the Compromise of 1850 was proving quite thin. The immediate cause of renewed open crisis was the quarrel over a measure, sponsored by Senator Stephen A. Douglas of Illinois, that would create what became the territories of Kansas and Nebraska. The debate became acrimonious, due largely to the question of slavery expansion. The only way to pass the measure was with the help of the South, and to obtain that Douglas had to agree to repeal of the Missouri Compromise. Douglas defended his bill on the ground of popular sovereignty, his belief that the people of a territory should decide on slavery or no slavery. The Kansas-Nebraska Act thus set up the doctrine of nonintervention by Congress in the territories.

Agreement to repeal the Missouri Compromise brought down upon Douglas the wrath of abolitionists and antislavery leaders. Congress approved the measure in 1854, but "within three weeks after Douglas' final bill had been reported, what a change in the whole national scene! Dark stormclouds hung over it, and livid lightning shook a portentous finger across the recently smiling landscape." Douglas, according to Nevins, had opened old wounds, split the Democratic party, completed destruction of the Whigs, set the scene for a new sectional party, and "unleashed forces which no man knew how to control." [2]

The most immediate open result was the desperate struggle now waged over the slavery issue in Kansas. Nevins argues that the sectional competition now focused on Kansas cannot be understood without studying the impact of economic and social forces.[3] Land represented the principal wealth most Americans could obtain in a nation still dominantly agricultural. But there were forces whose impetus was not to be denied. In the wake of the Northwestern surge, and even alongside it, came the railroads. A "web of transport" was being woven that was slowly binding the developing West and the more industrial East. While the question of the Union faced politicians, the question facing business leaders was whether national utilization of resources could be achieved.[4] The years were dark for the labor of the masses but bright for burgeoning industry, particularly in the North.

As the country expanded, "conflict on Kansas soil was inevitable."[5] The Kansas-Nebraska Act crystallized the political parties into new forms. The Whig party died and the Republican party was born. The Know-Nothings or Native American party, while short-lived, added to the confusion. "It was a season of political effervescence and change; new impulses, prejudices, and principles were making the currents of American thought boil and spout; and under all the giddy, foaming surface eddies lay a profound disturbance —the upheaval caused by the collision between the old force of nationalism and the new force of sectionalism."[6]

The years 1855–1856 saw the Kansas troubles between North and South deepen into "a smoulder of civil war" that flared "into a crackling blaze."[7] As spring of 1856 came on, it was clear that the Pierce administration "represented a collapse of American statesmanship, for which President and Congress shared the responsibility. . . . It was sad that a nation which had so many exigent tasks of internal development should spend all its energies during this campaign in a barren debate upon slavery. It was sadder that the debate should be carried on by bodies of such completely antipathetic views that it would tend to accentuate rather than heal the sectional breach."[8]

Two major parties contended for the Presidency in 1856—one the brash, trouble-born Republican party with Pathmarker John Charles Frémont at its head, the other the embattled Democrats with James Buchanan as their candidate. Millard Fillmore ran for the Know-Nothings and Whig remnants. It was a wild and stormy campaign, especially in the North. Southern Democrats threatened disunion if Frémont won. Frémont did not win, but it was close. Although Buchanan was the new President, it appeared that in the next election the North might go entirely Republican. In 1856 the Republican party won eleven of the sixteen free states. Sectional antagonism was clearly deepening.

NOTES

1. Nevins, *Ordeal of the Union*, Vol. II, *A House Dividing, 1852–1857*, p. 43.
2. *Ibid.*, p. 121.
3. *Ibid.*, p. 159.
4. *Ibid.*, p. 242.
5. *Ibid.*, p. 306.
6. *Ibid.*, p. 328.
7. *Ibid.*, p. 380.
8. *Ibid.*, p. 451.

Contrast of Cultures

JUDICIOUS Americans, turning the leaves of their newspapers, listening to street-corner orators, gazing at shop-window caricatures, picking up the pamphlets that littered the land, were grieved by the explosive denunciations that filled the air in the closing phases of the campaign of 1856; fusillades of canister with which each section peppered the other. Ordinarily the angry objurgations of the last bitter days of a presidential canvass are subject to a heavy discount, and October defiances turn into December handshakings. But this time the accusations and counter-charges denoted a searing passion of sectional hatred. It was not a quick fire of leaves and grass; it was a forest conflagration taking hold with sullen roar. The London *Times*, noting the painful impression which the campaign made upon British lovers of America, remarked that no sneering exponent of Old World ideas had ever written or said one tithe the evil against the citizens of the republic which they were now uttering against themselves.[1]

In the North such men as Henry Wilson had made the characterization of Southerners as "lords of the lash" familiar to everybody.[2] Sumner, welcomed back to Boston with imposing honors on November 3, talked of the satanic carnival that slaveholders planned in the Territories, predicted that Cuba would be seized and the slave trade reopened with all its crime, woe, and shame, and declared that the whole country was trodden down by a brutal, domineering despotism. Greeley's *Tribune*, seeking the origin of the barbarism it found stamped upon Kansas and Washington, found it in a fundamental Southern trait. "It is the spirit of Privilege, of Caste . . . that has instigated all these crimes, which the civilized world regards with every just abhorrence."[3]

Meanwhile, the New Orleans *Delta* was not content with hailing slavery as the most conservative element in republican institutions. "In the Northern States," it continued, "free society has proved a failure. It is rotten to the core."[4]

1 October 28, 1856.
2 See Wilson's Tabernacle speech, October 4, 1856.
3 October 30, 1856.
4 Quoted in N. Y. *Weekly Tribune*, November 8, 1856.

(*Ordeal of the Union*, Vol. II, *A House Dividing, 1852–1857*, Chapter 15.)

The Richmond *Enquirer* agreed that free society was "unnatural, immoral, un-christian," that its evils were in the long run "insufferable," and that it must give way to the slavery regime, "a social system as old as the world, universal as man." [5] Scores of Southern sheets were using language like the Muscogee (Ala.) *Herald*, which venomously remarked that Northern wage-earners and farmers were hardly fit to sit with the body-servant of a Southern gentleman. "Free society! We sicken at the name! What is it but a conglomeration of greasy mechanics, filthy operatives, smallfisted farmers, and moonstruck theorists?" [6]

[I]

The general restoration of peace in Kansas, accompanied by the subsidence of campaign rhetoric, furnished a delusive gleam of hope that the Buchanan Administration would be ushered into office under harmonious auspices. Governor Geary, delighted that he had put an end to riot and bloodshed, appointed a day of general thanksgiving. The first issues of the revived *Herald of Freedom* gave an encouraging sketch of the situation, showing that property in Lawrence had maintained its value despite all the recent storms, that two substantial churches had been erected, that houses were going up, and that freesoil settlers continued to arrive in gratifying numbers. When an inoffensive Free-State citizen was slain, Judge Lecompte had the effrontery to let the murderer run free on bail, with Marshal Donaldson as surety. But Geary indignantly had him rearrested, a step which immensely enhanced the governor's moral prestige. It was further strengthened when he went on to suspend Lecompte, whose unjudicial attitude in the Kansas troubles had really grown insufferable, and forced Donaldson's resignation. Unawed by the governor's sudden attack, Lecompte issued a writ citing him to appear in court at Lecompton to answer for illegal interference with the judiciary.[7] But Geary, holding his ground, appealed to the President; and it was clear that if Pierce sustained him, a far better day was dawning in Kansas.

For a few happy weeks, in fact, Americans ceased to think of slavery, feuding settlers, and disunionist plots. They turned their attention to Cyrus W. Field's announcement that he had his cable almost ready to be laid. They bent a rather cynical eye upon Walker's struggle in Nicaragua against increasing odds, for Commodore Vanderbilt was egging on the other Central American states to drive out the invader.[8] They shuddered over the disaster to the French steamer *Lyonnais*, which smashed into a Yankee bark off Nantucket, and sank

5　Quoted in London *Times,* October 28, 1856.
6　*Ibid.*
7　Lawrence correspondence in N. Y. *Weekly Tribune,* December 6, 1856.
8　Greene, *The Filibuster,* 263ff.

with the loss of more than a hundred lives. They talked of the new books, including two entertaining volumes of Webster's private correspondence.

But the dream of continued peace was harshly shattered when, in the opening December days of the new session of Congress, the clerks of the two chambers stood up to read Franklin Pierce's last annual message. House attendance was unusually large, for a new compensation law had brought in many who might have delayed at home. Only one really important piece of public business was anticipated in the short session, an attempt by the Democrats to carry some measure, probably based on the Toombs Bill, for the admission of Kansas. It now seemed plain that with a freesoil majority among the settlers, no rough legislation to make Kansas a slave State would be tolerated by many Northern Democrats. Some way must be found to bring her in as a free State without utterly estranging the South, and the quicker this was done the better.[9] Few expected Pierce's message to refer to any highly controversial points. But to the amazement of all and the horror of many, he tore the bandages from the half-healed wounds of sectional passion, and threw salt into the raw and bleeding flesh.

The petulance of a small man, repudiated and sorely humiliated, breathed in every paragraph. Half of the message was devoted to an arrogant, rancorous, and excited arraignment of the Republican Party, couched in terms much better suited to a stump speech than a state document. The recent election, he said, was essentially a condemnation of mere geographical parties. The considered sense of the nation had rejected a movement fraught with incalculable mischief, which would never have gained ground but for sinister misrepresentations acting upon a fevered state of the public mind, induced by causes temporary in character, and (it was to be hoped) transient in influence.

Ordinarily, said Pierce, the American scheme of government allowed perfect liberty of discussion. But how this had been abused! Under shelter of such freedom, organizations had been formed which pretended only to seek exclusion of slavery from the Territories, but really wished to destroy it in the States. To gain their end, they undertook the odious task of undermining the government, and of calumniating with wild invective not only all slaveholders but all who rejected their assaults upon the Constitution. They knew well that emancipation could be obtained only at the cost of burning cities, ravaged fields, and slaughtered populations, in a wild complication of foreign, civil, and servile wars. Nevertheless, they were endeavoring to lead the country into precisely this furnace of strife; they were appealing to sectional prejudices, and teaching Americans to stand face to face as enemies. Extremes had begotten extremes. Violent attacks from the North had been answered by proud defiance from the

9 Cf. N. Y. *Tribune* editorial December 3, 1856.

South. Thus the country had reached the fell consummation now so pointedly rebuked, the attempt of a sectional movement to usurp control of the nation's government.

This abusive condemnation of a party which had just polled one and a quarter million votes exasperated the Republicans to fury, and opened the gates to a violent new debate. It was a political blunder so damaging to national concord that in literal truth it was worse than a crime.

It was not difficult for a Republican cohort, springing to their feet, to repel Pierce's accusations. They roundly denied that their party sought the abolition of slavery; no plank of the platform, no public meeting, no authorized spokesman, had called for abolition; and the majorities given the party in eleven States testified to a faith in its sincerity. What had really aroused the sectional agitation? It was the repeal of the Missouri Compromise. "Burning cities!" exclaimed John Sherman. "Why, sir, I know of none except Lawrence and Osawatomie. I know of no ravaged fields or slaughtered populations except on the plains of Kansas." Who had labored to deprive the Constitution and laws of their moral authority? The men who, abetted by Administration officers, had robbed settlers of their franchises, had committed murder and arson, had laid waste towns, and had invented the crime of constructive treason. And when had the indoctrination of Americans in mutual hatred begun? In Douglas's famous report, with a new lesson in every act of the President since that time.[10]

The worst effect of the message was that once more, the North and South, through their newspapers and Congressional champions, were assailing each other hammer and tongs. All the billingsgate of the campaign was brought into use again. Mason of Virginia declared that he regarded Garrisonian abolitionists and Black Republicans as equally obnoxious. Rusk of Texas described the Frémonters as a rapacious set of politicians determined to take possession of the patronage of the government, and trample underfoot the sacred compact binding the nation together. Joshua Giddings talked of the infamous crimes of slavery; of masters scourging their servants into submission, and of white men who subjected Negro women to their pollutions and then sold their own offspring. "I want the member from Ohio," rasped Bennett of Mississippi, "to draw the distinction between the slaveholder bringing his slave into subjection by the lash, and the Northerners bringing their poor people into subjection by starvation." [11]

A new apple of discord, moreover, was tossed into the field as the old year closed and 1857 began. Few ideas were more repugnant to most sober Americans than the reopening of the slave trade. The traffic had been so sternly condemned

10 *Cong. Globe,* December 8, 1856.
11 *Idem,* December 4, 5, 1856; N. Y. *Weekly Tribune,* December 6, 1856.

by the united voice of Christendom that a nation which reverted to it would seemingly place itself outside the pale of civilization. Some three years earlier the Charleston *Standard* had proposed the step; and although numerous Southern journals condemned the suggestion, and others treated it with silent disdain, the Richmond *Examiner* and Charleston *Mercury* indicated their acquiescence. After Buchanan's victory the *Standard* spiritedly reopened its crusade. It was joined by the New Orleans *Delta*, which advocated a double Southern policy: acquisition of Cuba, northeastern Mexico, and other territories, and importation of enough black men to let every Southerner acquire one or two, and take them wherever opportunity beckoned to enterprise.

Most astounding of all, Governor J. H. Adams of South Carolina in his annual message called for reviving the traffic. Thus alone, he argued, could the South regain its old equality of power, and let the blessings of slavery be properly diffused. To many Northerners there was a nightmarish ring about his statement that slavery "has exalted the white race itself to higher hopes and purposes, and it is perhaps of the most sacred obligation that we should give it the means of expansion, and that we should press it forward to a perpetuity of progress." [12]

The South, fearing Kansas lost, felt a menacing pressure from the North. The North, despite the refusal of the South Carolina legislature to endorse Adams's hardy proposal, felt that menacing new pressures were being loosed in the cotton domain. It was understood that Pierre Soulé, visiting Walker in Nicaragua, had helped persuade him to decree the establishment of slavery. Free-soil observers envisaged a fierce thrust for the conquest of the Caribbean crescent, accompanied by a demand for the licit or illicit revival of colonization from Africa to fill these areas. The early weeks of 1857 found sectional animosity burning as redly as ever. [13]

In little over a decade, what 'bitter change of fierce extremes, extremes by change more fierce'! Only thirteen years earlier a Southern President, with a Cabinet largely of Southern men, had journeyed to Boston to attend a national celebration of the completion of Bunker Hill monument, and hear Webster deliver one of his noblest orations to forty thousand people. In the course of that visit an eminent South Carolinian, Hugh Swinton Legaré, fell ill. He was deeply admired by many a Massachusetts man. Not because he was Attorney-General, but because he was an old friend, known from student days in Edinburgh, George Tickner took him into his house. Only forty-seven, Legaré expired in

12 Quotations from the *Standard* and *Delta* are in N. Y. *Weekly Tribune*, November 8, 1856; Adams's message, November 21, 1856, was printed in pamphlet form; T. D. Jervey, *The Slave Trade*, 114–116.

13 W. J. Carnathan, "The Proposal to Reopen the Slave Trade," *South Atlantic Quarterly*, XXV, 410–430; New York *Evening Post, Tribune*, December, 1856.

Ticknor's arms. Our city, wrote the Boston scholar, is filled with consternation and sorrow. "He was a man of genius, full of refinement and poetry, and one of the best scholars in the country; but, more than this, he was of a most warm and affectionate spirit." To this South Carolinian, continued Ticknor, the country with great unanimity was beginning to look as a future President, with a perfect confidence in his talents, his principles, and his honor.[14] But by 1857, what faith would citizens of Massachusetts place in the most brilliant South Carolinian, and what confidence would South Carolinians have in the ablest New Englander?

Obviously, the political events of these thirteen years had much to do with the change. The Liberty Party, Texas, the Mexican War, Wilmot, the Fugitive Slave Act, the Nebraska Bill, Ostend, had all widened the chasm. But the fundamental causes of the cleavage lay deeper. Different standards, ideas, aims, outlooks, ideals; a different color of life and throb of pulse; different glories and different shames; different precedents and traditions; different fears and elations, had come to characterize the two sections, which, in a word, were by this time lapped in two divergent cultures. Was the ultimate story to be that of England and Ireland, Holland and Belgium, separating because too much divided by sentiment, or were North and South, like Saxon and Scot, Gascon and Norman, after all to submerge their differences in a larger unity? Men in 1857 found this an urgent question.

[II]

Culture is a word hard to define, and of course many of the highest manifestations of culture simply ignored sectional lines. Science, art, and the purer works of literature knew no North or South, or very little of either. The best achievements in these fields had a national quality, and touched a great many patriotic chords. At the very least, they lifted men's eyes above sectional quarrels, and gave the nation a common stock in which it could take pride.

Take science, for example, which with literature was one of the two fields in which Americans attained enough distinction to attract admiring notice from the Old World. It was national and even international in spirit. The American Philosophical Society had been founded in colonial days to give the savants of the continent an opportunity of pooling their energies; and our science had been cosmopolitan in tone ever since Alexander Garden had corresponded with Linnaeus, Franklin had been honored by French and British students, and Benjamin Thompson, Count Rumford, had left his footprints all over Europe. The American Association for the Advancement of Science, which after its found-

14 *Life, Letters, and Journals*, II, 212, 213.

ing in 1848 quickly rose to a preëminent position, was a younger sister of the British Association. Its annual meetings, which became a notable feature of American intellectual life, were national affairs, attracting scientists from Georgia to Maine, open to the public, and given generous space in the press.

As for the central arsenal of American science, the Smithsonian Institution, it was a national agency founded by a British benefaction. The country well remembered how the clipper *Mediator* had delivered in Philadelphia £104,960 in gold sovereigns as James Smithson's gift for the increase and diffusion of knowledge among men. Though some members of Congress stubbornly opposed acceptance of the gift, the enlightened opinions of John Quincy Adams and others had prevailed; and Joseph Henry, brought from Princeton in 1846 to be secretary, had made the Institution a powerful auxiliary to almost every department of American research.[15]

Scientific journals, which had gained a secure footing, were also thoroughly national in content and spirit. Since the elder Benjamin Silliman set up the *American Journal of Sciences and Arts* in 1818, its publication had never been interrupted. His vigorous editorship, bringing it many original papers of value, with incisive reviews of European books and news of scientific developments everywhere, took no note of States or regions. His son, Benjamin Silliman, Jr., and his son-in-law, James Dwight Dana, succeeding to the conduct of the magazine, maintained its standards. Another important journal, *Science*, which had sprung up in connection with the American Association, was equally catholic in tone. These periodicals and the monographs of learned societies made Europe familiar with the beadroll of notable American investigators—Joseph Henry, Matthew Fontaine Maury, Elisha Mitchell, Henry R. Schoolcraft, Asa Gray, and A. D. Bache, national figures all.[16]

Few men, until a time later than this, thought of Mitchell and Maury as Southerners, Schoolcraft and Henry as Northerners, for their work had no such connotations.[17] Maury's activities, which specially touched the imagination of Americans, enlisted a very general pride. The main reasons for the appeal of his work were that it could be popularly understood, that its utility to navigation and commerce commended it to all practical men, that his eminence at foreign gatherings gave him unusual prestige, and that, touching the great

15 The *Memorial of Joseph Henry*, published by Congressional order in 1880, contains much on Smithsonian history; cf. W. J. Rhees, *Smithson and His Bequest*; N. S. Shaler, *United States*, III, 1040–1041.

16 J. G. Crowther, *Famous American Men of Science*; E. S. Dana et al., *A Century of Science in America*.

17 The adjective pseudo-scientific would best characterize the work of the ethnologist Josiah C. Nott of Alabama, whose seven-hundred-page volume *Types of Mankind*, published in 1854 in collaboration with G. R. Gliddon, comforted Southerners with the absurd doctrine that each of the various races of man was a fixed type "permanent through all recorded time."

mysterious seas, his writings had a poetic quality. Nobody had better reason than Yankee shipmasters for remembering how he had conceived the idea that science would benefit if mariners entered in their logbooks accurate records of ocean currents, depths, and temperatures; how little by little he gathered the data he needed, comparing it with that taken from older logs; how finally he announced his first noteworthy discovery, an improved sailing route to Rio de Janeiro; and how a skipper who consented to try it reached the equator in twenty-four days instead of the usual forty-one. "Navigators now for the first time," he had written, "appeared to comprehend what it was that I wanted them to do, *and why*." His next service had been in shortening the voyage to California by directions that cut the time by weeks. Every informed citizen knew that he had been the central figure of a remarkable international conference which sat at Brussels in 1853, as war clouds lowered darkly over Europe; a conference which arranged for a systematic collection of facts about winds, currents, temperatures, and tides, for the benefit of commerce everywhere.[18]

And Maury's fascinating book of 1855, *Physical Geography of the Sea*, was a national achievement, making scientists as well as general public familiar with striking new generalizations. By a happy phrase he called the Gulf Stream a river in the ocean; a warm-water stream whose fountain was the Gulf of Mexico, whose mouth was in the Arctic, and whose banks and bottom were cold water; its speed greater than that of the Mississippi or Amazon, and the demarcation between it and the ocean clearly visible to the eye as far north as the Carolina coast. He remarked that it was not to be regarded merely as a three-thousand-mile current, but as a balance-wheel, a part of the grand mechanism by which the earth was adapted to the well-being of its inhabitants. And not the water-ocean alone, but the air-ocean as well, fell within Maury's view. Showered with honors by foreign governments, he was better pleased by the thanks of the honest seamen for the charts upon which he had indicated the usual time and place of storms, fogs, rains, and calms.[19]

Next to Maury in popular eminence, and equally a national and international figure, ranked that adopted American, Jean Louis Rodolphe Agassiz, who on accepting his chair in the Lawrence Scientific School had no difficulty in taking leadership in the study of natural history in the United States. A very true

---

18 For Maury's foreign fame see the article on him in *Revue des Deux Mondes*, March, 1858; Lord Wrottesley's speech in House of Lords, April 26, 1853; John W. Wayland, *Pathfinder of the Seas*, chs. 13, 14.

19 The *National Intelligencer*, July 17, 1855, has a long review. Humboldt in 1855 announced to Maury that the King of Prussia had given him the gold medal designed for useful scientific work; *National Intelligencer*, February 3, April 19, 1855. For similar honors from France see M. Vattemare's correspondence with Maury, *National Intelligencer*, March 8, 1856. Napoleon III exclaimed: "Is it possible that such a work could have been undertaken and executed by one man?"

American he quickly became. When in 1857 the French Minister of Public Instruction offered him a post at the Museum of Natural History, he replied that he "could not sever abruptly the ties which for a number of years I have been accustomed to consider as binding me for the remainder of my days to the United States." [20] His home in Cambridge, humming with industry and glowing with enthusiasm, was a center of inspiration for naturalists and scholars from all parts of the republic. Like Maury, he planned a work of ambitious pitch and scope, a ten-volume study which he announced in 1855 under the title of *Contributions to the Natural History of the United States.* His prospectus, widely reprinted in the press, created a flutter. For more than eight years, he wrote, he had been investigating those classes of the animal kingdom which American naturalists had least touched, the time had come to publish his most important results, and he needed subscriptions for the ten quarto volumes at twelve dollars each. "Every man in the country who has the means," R. C. Winthrop told the novelist Kennedy, "ought to subscribe for a copy"—and Agassiz did receive some two thousand five hundred orders. But only four volumes were ever completed.[21]

The nature of his self-defined duties made Joseph Henry's work at the Smithsonian as wide as the nation, and almost as wide as science itself. As much an organizer as investigator, he seemed intent on making the Institution the incubator of American scientific effort in unentered areas. Though his own experiments in electro-magnetism resulted in discoveries of high value for the magnetic telegraph and the future electric-power industry, he would be best remembered for inspiring the work of others. At the end of the first decade he recapitulated the Smithsonian's labors. It had published seventy-one pieces of original investigations filling eight large quarto volumes. It had set up laboratories in terrestrial magnetism and chemistry, had sponsored a regular winter series of popular lectures, and boasted of a growing library, a museum, and an art gallery of sorts. As secretary, Henry corresponded widely to make the Smithsonian a national clearing-house of scientific information. "It is regrettable," he wrote with dry humor, "that so many minds of power and originality in our country should, from defective scientific training, be suffered to diverge so widely from the narrow path which alone leads to real advance in positive knowledge. Providence, however, seems in some measure to vindicate the equality of its distributions by assigning to such a double measure of hope and self-esteem, which serves them instead of success and reputation." [22]

Henry had adopted what he called the system of active operations, by which

20　Letter to M. Rouland, September 25, 1857, in *National Intelligencer,* October 8, 1857.
21　Winthrop, June 20, 1855, in Kennedy Papers; Elizabeth Cary Agassiz, *Louis Agassiz, His Life and Correspondence.*
22　*Tenth Annual Report,* 1855.

he meant pioneering investigation along a broad front. He was adamant in rejecting the proposal frequently urged upon the trustees, that a large part of the income be devoted to spreading knowledge of some branch of the practical arts; and though he feared that the timidity of some associates might permit such encroachments, his own policy steadily gained favor. The variety of the Smithsonian's activities was remarkable. In a typical year (1852) it made a preliminary exploration of the Bad Lands, publishing a description of them; furnished scientific instruments and other aids to an astronomical and geographical expedition to Chile; published results of botanical searches in Texas, New Mexico, and California; issued an illustrated memoir on the sea-plants of the North American coast; collected and published the statistics of American libraries; brought out a volume on the Dakota language; directed attention to American antiquities; and printed a variety of scientific papers. This plan of "active operations" stimulated investigation in many fields, made the exploration and settlement of the West contributory to science, and gave intelligent direction to the government's previously chaotic scientific work.[23]

For Washington in these years was displaying a keen interest in varied types of scientific research, exploration being naturally the most prominent. This was the period of the two so-called United States-Grinnell Expeditions in search of Sir John Franklin's men and a possible open polar sea; enterprises supported partly by the nation, partly by Henry Grinnell, which enabled the young naval surgeon Elisha Kent Kane to lift himself to fame. Kane's modest, graphic account of his tireless labors and frightful hardships, *Arctic Explorations* (1856) "lay for a decade with the Bible on almost literally every parlor table in America." He died at thirty-seven in Havana; and his funeral journey was a national pageant, the body lying in state in New Orleans, Louisville, Columbus, and Baltimore before it reached his native Philadelphia.[24]

In the midst of the presidential campaign of 1856 the North Pacific Survey-

23 The Smithsonian in 1885 published two volumes of the *Scientific Writings of Joseph Henry;* but a modern biography is needed. Quarrels over the policy of the Smithsonian were continuous. Henry earnestly but unsuccessfully opposed putting $200,000 of funds into the "Norman castle" which housed the institution. An important group, well represented among the Regents, regarded the accumulation of a great scientific library as properly the main purpose of the Smithsonian. A so-called compromise was adopted by which the income was divided between the library and museum on one side, the research, publications, and lectures on the other. In 1855 the quarrel broke into the Congressional debates; see Meacham's speech in the House, March 3, 1855.
24 The biography of Kane by William Elder is the subject of an interesting four-column article in the N. Y. *Weekly Tribune* of January 30, 1858. See *National Intelligencer,* September 27, 1856, for an estimate of Kane. Said the House Library Committee in a report of April 16, 1856, on Kane's work in the Arctic and Wilkes's in the Antarctic: "By the noble fruits of these voyages to opposite points of the globe, our country takes rank at once among the learned nations of Europe in the high departments of distant scientific discovery."

ing and Exploring Expedition commanded by Captain John Rodgers returned to the United States. It had surveyed parts of the almost unknown Japanese coasts, had examined Behring Sea, had explored various Pacific archipelagoes, and had brought back rich collections of plants and animals. Its best historian, Lieutenant A. W. Habersham, published next year a volume on the cruise which was compared with Melville. "We did what I suppose no vessel ever did before," he wrote, "we sounded around the world." Maury and John P. Kennedy, Secretary of the Navy when it was outfitted, had helped lay its plans.[25] In another direction lay the before-mentioned Chilean Expedition of 1849–52 under Lieutenant J. M. Gillies of the navy, and the expedition of 1853–56 to the countries bordering on the River Plate.[26] At home the work of exploring and mapping the American domain went steadily on. The commissioners who in 1850–53 had to run the new boundary with Mexico covered nearly five thousand miles of rough terrain. John Russell Bartlett, who began as merchant and amateur scientist, and lived to become a noted librarian, produced two fat volumes of "incidents" of adventure encountered in Sonora, Chihuahua, and New Mexico.[27] In the middle fifties an exploring expedition sent by the War Department to the Upper Missouri visited the Sioux, Rees, Mandans, Gros Ventres, Crows, and other tribes, and brought back from the Yellowstone Valley and Black Hills large collections of minerals, fossils, and biological specimens. Its commander was assisted by a young geologist, F. V. Hayden, who would later gain fame in government employ.[28] Meanwhile, a survey of Lake Superior was being pushed, and included a detailed mapping of the shores as well as careful soundings.

When Congress directed the Secretary of War to collect materials illustrating the history, condition, and prospects of the Indians, the importance of assigning the indefatigable Henry R. Schoolcraft to the task was generally recognized. "Go where he will, whether it be among Sacs and Foxes, or Sioux or Winnebagoes," wrote one who knew him well, "and so long as the 'good medicine' chooses to remain his person is safe from attack and his property from peril, while every man among his entertainers is anxious to do most to propitiate and gratify the guest. . . . He can set a broken limb, extract a ball or splinter, bleed at the arm and prescribe in cases of slight sickness, or he can repair an Indian's gunlock, solder up his broken kettle, and teach him to do the

25 Tuckerman, *Kennedy*, 217ff.
26 The results of the La Plata expedition were embodied in a large octavo by Thomas J. Page, U.S.N., called *La Plata, the Argentine Confederation, and Paraguay,* issued by Harpers. The exposition had some political and commercial objects, while it made no inconsiderable additions to knowledge of the geography, natural history, and customs of Paraguay.
27 Appletons, 1853–54.
28 *National Intelligencer*, December 6, 1856.

same. . . . Honest, kind, simple, and truthful, he wins his way to the hearts of those blunt, hardy men." [29] In 1851 the government published the first of Schoolcraft's six volumes of *Historical and Statistical Information* on the Indians, a work interestingly illustrated by Captain Seth Eastman of the army. This was the crowning achievement of an adventurous writer who had made trip after trip into the Indian country for thirty-five years, had written book after book since his work on the Ozarks in 1819, and had lent an especially strong impulse to ethnological study in his two volumes of *Algic Researches* (1839). Though his "great national work" [30] had its shortcomings, it proved full of indispensable information.

Science, it is clear, would have had frugal fare without government patronage. Maury of the Naval Observatory, Henry of the Smithsonian, A. D. Bache as superintendent of the Coast Survey, Schoolcraft, and Kane all held government posts or enjoyed indispensable Federal assistance. Even Agassiz, whose first important scientific trip was on a Coast Guard steamer as guest of the government, received some important aids. Joseph LeConte, after Maury perhaps the most eminent of Southern scientists, supported himself by teaching first at the University of Georgia, and then at the College of South Carolina. Silliman and the chemist Wolcott Gibbs, Elisha Mitchell of botanical and geological fame, and Benjamin Peirce, the mathematician and astronomer, all found academic havens, though Peirce was also connected with the Coast Survey. But the vigorous Federal interest in science contributed to make it national (so far as it was not international) in spirit. Men who gathered for meetings of the American Association naturally felt themselves citizens of a realm of culture which could only be weakened by sectional division. At the tenth session held in Albany in 1856, for example, all the scientists just mentioned gathered to hear Peirce discuss mathematical problems, Henry the principles of acoustics, and Bache the formulation of tide tables; Mitchell shaking hands with Silliman, Gibbs with Maury, as fellows in the same grand labors.

[III]

The best of American art, too, had no offensive sectional coloration. Few people thought of North or South in viewing the sculptures of Crawford and Powers, or the painting of Henry Inman or Eastman Johnson. A great part of

29 This sketch, probably by W. W. Seaton, is in the *National Intelligencer* of April 1, 1854. Schoolcraft had served the government in various official relations with the Indians, had negotiated treaties with the Chippewa by which the United States gained title to great tracts, had founded a society for the study of the aborigines, and had projected an ambitious Indian encyclopaedia.

30 The phrase used by the *National Intelligencer*, April 1, 1854. Eastman, another enthusiastic ethnologist, had a long acquaintance with the Indian tribes.

the country's limited artistic energy, in fact, went into the celebration of themes that were distinctly national and patriotic.

If the republic had no painters of genius, it certainly had some of high talent. To the late eighteenth-century school of portraitists headed by Gilbert Stuart had succeeded a variety of groups; notably the poets of landscape, with Thomas Cole (who died in 1848), Asher B. Durand, and the panoramic but neatly accurate John F. Kensett at their head; a number of technically dexterous men showing strong English or Dutch influence, such as Chester Harding, Henry Inman, and that sympathetic painter of rural scenes, Eastman Johnson; and a dashing coterie who transferred to America the romanticism of Düsseldorf (an unfortunate influence), among them William Hart and Emanuel Leutze. An incisive genre school, relating anecdotes of native flavor, had also arisen. Year by year a good many interesting and competent canvases were being finished. In New York the annual displays of the National Academy of Design, of which S. F. B. Morse had been the principal founder, might show one of Frederick E. Church's overdramatized and distantly Turneresque canvases—his erupting "Cotopaxi" of 1854 struck a new note of the grandiose; or a graphic illustration of homely life by William S. Mount, such as "Turning the Grindstone" or "Bargaining for a Horse." Boston had painters who remembered the tradition of Copley, Philadelphia its men inspired by the remarkable Peale family, and Charleston a few artists proud of Washington Allston, of the less famous Charles Fraser, who among other achievements had given Thomas Sully his first lessons, and of the gifted school of miniaturists once ensconced in the little city.[31]

It could justly be said, of course, that the nation's roll of distinguished artists was brief, its stock of artistic treasures small, and its fund of taste still slight. No public art gallery of importance yet rose in any city. To be sure, certain societies which purchased and exhibited works of art could be found scattered along the coast. The Redwood Library in Newport and the Charleston Museum, both of colonial origin, had a number of respectable paintings, while the Boston Athenaeum, the New York Historical Society, the Pennsylvania Academy, and the Maryland Institute all placed canvases and sculptures on view. In New York the art dealer had found secure foothold, Goupil of Paris having set up a branch establishment in the forties, while the Düsseldorf Gallery offered examples of the German method of transferring legend and literature into picture-frames.[32] "The builders of houses begin to look for something to cover their walls," wrote Evert Duyckinck after attending a winter auction at high prices in 1852. At first they had bought European copies of old masters; "now, within a very

31 Charles H. Caffin, *The Story of American Painting*, 46–121; Eugen Neuhaus, *History and Ideals of American Art*, 82ff.
32 F. J. Mather, Jr., "Painting" in *The American Spirit in Art*, 16.

few years, a desire to possess the original works of modern, and latterly (greatly through the Art Union) of American works, has sprung up." [33] In Washington the banker W. W. Corcoran had acquired a large collection and in 1859 began the construction of the Corcoran Gallery. In Baltimore, Granville S. Oldfield, making repeated trips to Europe, had spent about $70,000 for some six hundred and fifty pieces which were worth far more when he sold them at auction in 1855.[34] August Belmont in New York helped set a fashion of art-collecting, his intelligent purchases extending to fine porcelains and textiles.

A special service was done the country by several connoisseurs who, though hardly endowed with long purses, used learning, discrimination, and experience in buying European treasures for transfer to their bare if shining land. In 1853 Thomas J. Bryan, whose activities were in Edith Wharton's mind when she wrote *False Dawn*, imported with other paintings a group of about thirty examples of early Italian masters, later (1867) presented to the New York Historical Society. Bryan, testifies Gabriel Manigault of Charleston, was regarded as the most expert buyer among Americans abroad. Though he had no high-priced paintings, "there were nevertheless among the several hundred which he exhibited in Broadway in 1853 after his return enough to give a good idea of the history of European art, and of the styles of the different schools." Manigault himself was a collector of taste and assiduity, whose enthusiasm for art was first fully awakened by a visit to the Louvre in 1847, and who found that the auction rooms of the Rue Drouet sold admirable pieces. Already the European picture trade had swollen into an important branch of business, rich Britons were buying lavishly, and fakes abounded; but he obtained a number of canvases which South Carolinians flocked to see.[35]

The prince of collectors, however, was James Jackson Jarves, the Boston-born son of a glass manufacturer who took up his residence in Florence in the fifties and used his considerable means to satisfy an inborn love of art. He began buying early Italian painting while interest in them was as yet not widespread, and when fine specimens could be picked up, often for low sums, in out-of-the-way places.

"My adventures in this pursuit," he later wrote, "were often curious and instructive. They involved an inquisition into the intricacies of numberless villas, palaces, convents, churches, and household dens, all over this portion of Italy; the employment of many agents to scent out my prey; many fatiguing journeyings; miles upon miles of wearisome staircases; dusty explorations of dark retreats; dirt, disappointment, fraud, lies, and money often fruitlessly spent;

33 MS Diary, December 16, 1852, NYPL. This sale was attended by Corcoran, the Van Buren brothers, and the shipbuilder Webb.
34 *National Intelligencer*, April 24, 1855.
35 See Manigault's undated paper of reminiscences in the Charleston Historical Society.

all compensated, however, by the gradual accumulation of a valuable gallery."
He found a fine Perugino, smoked and dirty, discarded in the lumber-room of
a famous convent; he discovered a splendid full-length portrait of a Spanish
grandee by Velasquez, cut from its frame and crusted with dirt, but underneath
in fine preservation, among the rubbish of a disorderly villa. Jarves's collection,
a total of 145 pictures, was brought over in 1860 to be exhibited in the new
marble gallery of the Institute of Fine Arts at 625 Broadway. It had been well
advertised by enthusiastic letters from Americans and Britons, including T. A.
Trollope, in the *Crayon*, since 1854 the country's leading art magazine; for
though it contained no great commanding masterpiece, it finely represented
three centuries of Tuscan painting. But popular interest in New York and
Boston proved slight, only a few men, notably Charles Eliot Norton, appreciat-
ing what the country had gained.[36]

But from the point of view of nationalism, the American spirit was best
expressed by the genre painters, reproductions of whose genial scenes were
scattered broadcast by such commercial organizations as the American Art
Union. A typical figure was George Caleb Bingham, whose work so capitally
illustrates some picturesque phases of American life. His was the commonplace
story of hard beginnings in an unfavorable setting: Virginia birth, the Missouri
frontier at eight, painting with home-made pigments, a struggle for study first
at the Pennsylvania Academy and then in Europe, and mature residence in Missouri. A keen interest in politics, viewed on its homely institutional side, animated much of his work. His first painting to achieve any reclame was "The
Jolly Flatboatmen," selected by the American Art Union in 1846 as its annual
engraving. A succession of spirited works followed: "Raftsmen Playing Cards,"
"Canvassing for a Vote," "Emigration of Daniel Boone," "County Elections,"
"Stump Speaking," and "Verdict of the People," all popular in the fifties.
Authentic study of manners, and the democratic spirit of the frontier, characterized his work. He knew firsthand the explorers, fur-traders, emigrants, river-
men, politicians, farmers, teamsters, and other figures that he presents, and while
his work was faulty in technique, it showed realism, humor, and a keen eye for
characteristic scenes.[37]

The public character of much of the sculpture of the time gave it greater
popular prominence than painting, and lent it no little influence in instilling
patriotic feeling. If frequency of mention in the press be a test, Americans took
a livelier interest in the work of Crawford, Powers, Joel T. Hart, Story, Palmer,
and Clark Mills than in any similar group of painters. These men made Italy

36 *Letters Relating to a Collection of Pictures Made by Mr. James Jackson Jarves*
(privately printed, 1859); and see Jarves's numerous books, especially *Art Thoughts: The
Experiences and Observations of an American Amateur in Europe.*
37 Albert Christ-Janer, *George Caleb Bingham of Missouri.*

their headquarters. In Story's letters, in Hawthorne's *Italian Notebooks*, and in the life of Crawford which Thomas Hicks wrote soon after that artist's death, we catch rich glimpses of the American colony in the Roman ilex shade or silhouetted against the tawny Arno. The castles, churches, and ancient and medieval masterpieces of sculpture; the romantic villas which American dollars stretched so far in hiring; the almond-eyed children, the cleanly-dressed girls crowned with white-peaked *tovaglia*, the peasants selling squash-seeds, fruit, and pigs stuffed whole; the bright-colored crowds of the cities; the eager talk with Britons, Frenchmen, and Germans—all this was an inspiration. Women crossed the ocean too. Harriet Hosmer, daughter of a country physician in Massachusetts, a small, quick, gifted girl who, burning with ambition, went to Rome in 1852 to work under the English sculptor John Gibson and became a great pet of the Brownings, was but the most eminent of a sisterhood who, in Henry James's words, settled upon the hills in a white, marmorean flock. As James adds, the odd phenomenon of their practically simultaneous appearance has its significance "in any study of the growth of birth and taste in the simmering society that produced them." [38]

Public demand and the public purse channeled much of the energy of the principal sculptors toward national themes and heroes; and people read eagerly of the progress of Hart, Crawford, and Erastus D. Palmer on their chosen subjects.

All three had risen by hard struggle. Born near Winchester, Ky., Hart had, like Lincoln, educated himself by reading at the evening fire; had become a stone-mason; and meeting the sculptor S. V. Clevenger in Lexington at the beginning of the forties, had taken fire from his fame. His career began when a few years later a patriotic women's organization in Richmond asked him to execute a life-sized marble statue of Henry Clay for $5,000; and when Louisville offered $10,000 and New Orleans $14,000 for monuments to the same statesman, he was able to take up residence in Florence.[39] Crawford as a boy in New York had taken drawing-lessons, worked with a wood-carver, and finally become an apprentice to the leading monument-makers of the city, toiling meanwhile on marble busts and studying at the National Academy of Design. Going to Italy, he had first done sculptural work at a laborer's wage, but by the fifties was one of the best-paid artists in the world. The beginning of the decade found him commissioned to produce a grand equestrian statue of Washington for Richmond, to furnish the marble pediment of the Senate in Washington, and to chisel the figure of "Armed Liberty" surmounting the Capitol dome. Palmer, of rural New York origin, who graduated from wood-carving and

38 Henry James, *W. W. Story*, I, 257.
39 See *National Intelligencer*, November 17, 1857, for the New Orleans commission.

carpentry into mosaic-cutting, and thence into sculpture, exhibited his first important work, the "Infant Ceres," in the 1850 showing of the National Academy, and similarly enjoyed a national fame in the days of Buchanan's presidency.

In a land where statuary was rare, the influence of the commemorative pieces which these men scattered over the country was tremendous. As Italian workmen labored in the Capitol grounds on Crawford's huge pedimental work, "The Past and Present of America," the press teemed with descriptions of it. America, with laurel wreath and arrows, stood proudly in the center; about her finely-draped figure were disposed the conquered redskin, the pioneer hunter, the settler with his axe, the soldier, merchant, mechanic, and teacher. While the separate figures had power, the group as a whole breathed the American qualities of confidence and idealism. When Crawford's bronze statue of Washington was brought up the James by a Dutch brig in 1857, Richmond greeted it with jubilation—though saddening news arrived by the same ship that the artist's eager strivings had been ended at forty-four by cancer of the brain. A great crowd assembled to watch the heavy bronze, cast in Munich, slowly brought ashore; the Armory Band played patriotic airs; and at a formal luncheon the governor and leading citizens exchanged toasts.[40] When Hart came back to America in 1859 for the unveiling of his Clay in Richmond, he was handsomely feted. And so the tale ran with other men. Even the failures had a certain influence. When Palmer in 1857 completed his model for a group that he vainly hoped would occupy the House pediment in Washington—the landing of the Pilgrims, with the venerable Brewster, praying with upturned face, the central figure—the press spread vivid descriptions of it over the country.[41]

Story, settling in the Barberini Palace, began in 1852 his statue of his eminent father, and three years later Bostonians poured into the Athenaeum to see the figure of the benignant jurist, seated on the bench in judicial gown, one hand holding a book and the other raised in characteristic gesture. Behind Story lay years of law practise in Boston and the publication of legal texts; before him stretched a long career as sculptor, poet, and miscellaneous writer. He conspicuously illustrated the growing tendency among Americans of means to turn from practical to artistic pursuits. Though he lacked genius, with its all-compelling call, though he had been eminently successful at the bar, where

---

40 Crawford's statues of Jefferson and Patrick Henry for his Washington monument had reached Richmond in 1855. They were at once set up on the west side of the capitol with a railing to hold back the crowds. "They are universally admired as the creations of genius," wrote George B. Munford to Crawford; August 30, 1855, Governors' Letterbooks, No. 26, pp. 301, 302. Virginia was training her own sculptor at the time, Edward Virginius Valentine, who by 1857 had made several portrait busts and next year went to Paris.

41 *National Intelligencer*, April 16, 1857.

his mother wished him to continue, and though he knew that his aesthetic work wanted intensity and high inspiration, he had long loved painting, modelling, and music, and boldly took his leap in the dark. His range was wide, and it was his "Cleopatra" that Hawthorne immortalized in *The Marble Faun*, but he was destined in due time to give the country dignified statues of such sons as John Marshall, Joseph Henry, and George Peabody. His friend the loquacious Hiram Powers, who could talk of everything—of his humble beginnings in Ohio as tavern boy, bill collector, clockmaker, and waxwork modeller, his later struggles in Washington, his Italian friends—had a busy studio in Florence through all these years. His international fame dated from the furor caused by his "Greek Slave" at the Crystal Palace Exhibition in London, but his best work was his long series of portrait busts of Jackson, Marshall, Webster, Calhoun, and others. His full-length statue of the orator placed before the Massachusetts State House in 1859 struck Hawthorne as "very grand, very Webster." [42]

A good part of the artistic effort of the country, in short, went toward creating a national mythology. Leutze's historical rhetoric had begun in the forties with "Columbus Before the Council at Salamanca," and he, S. F. B. Morse (as in his really magnificent picture of the House in session in Monroe's time in its old hall), Daniel Huntington, and others enlarged the work that Trumbull, by his Revolutionary canvases, had begun in creating mementos of the national past. Robert W. Weir was paid $8,000 by the government for his painting of "The Embarkation of the Pilgrims" to hang in the Capitol. "We are about producing in steel after a large painting by Huntington," wrote the publisher C. L. Derby to John P. Kennedy in 1860,[43] "a great national picture entitled 'Washington Irving and his Contemporaries.'" He wished to make sure that F. O. C. Darley, the engraver, furnished a really accurate likeness of Kennedy. His word "national" is worth noting. The steel engravings of J. C. Buttré, whose studio was in New York, became famous, and he specialized in portraits of American leaders. Public men were glad to encourage young sculptors with money and praise, as the Preston brothers encouraged Powers, and as Douglas helped young Leonard W. Volk—who returned from Europe in time to make studies of both Lincoln and Douglas, as he saw them in the debates of 1858. But the new American mythology was by no means wholly

---

42 Late in 1841 Edward Everett, sitting to Powers for a bust, heard him express a wish to execute a statue of a Grecian slave-girl carried captive to Constantinople. Four years later the work was creating a minor sensation in London, with everyone from Prince Albert down coming to see it; the major sensation came later. Frothingham, *Everett*, 182, 252. For an account of the orders which poured in on Powers, see the *National Intelligencer*, May 3, 1855. "Since Thorwaldsen's death," one traveller wrote, "no one hesitates to award him the highest rank in his art."

43 October 5, 1860; Kennedy Papers.

romantic. The realism that went into the genre painting of the day stripped the toga from Washington and gave him a Continental uniform.[44]

[IV]

The theatre, too, was in a very real sense a nationalizing influence, for plays of patriotic theme were numerous, while theatrical productions, as given in all parts of the Union, tended to establish common standards of speech, dress, and manners. The chief events of the Revolution, from Bunker Hill to Yorktown, were celebrated in literally scores of plays; a dozen dramas dealt with the War of 1812; and the titles of such pieces as *The Yankee in Tripoli, The Siege of Monterey*, and *Oregon, or The Disputed Boundary*, speak for themselves. In many a play of contemporary social life a patriotic *motif* was sharply introduced. And the stage was always reaching out its hands to the masses, touching a vein of common emotion in Bowery roughs, Southern gentlemen, and frontier farmers. When at the close of the fifties Joe Jefferson reworked three old versions of *Rip Van Winkle* into an improved play, and gave his inimitable depiction of both the insouciant young Rip, tossing off his dram among his cronies, and the old Rip, returning to his village in beard, tatters, and wonderment, he touched a chord of true Americanism.

No view could be more mistaken than that which regards the theatre of this period in metropolitan terms. All the rising cities of the West had their theatres; no New York house was more admirably built or appointed than the famous St. Charles of New Orleans; and in all States touring performers of the most brilliant type were well known—the second and third Joseph Jefferson, Tyrone Power, George P. Farren and his wife, Edwin Forrest, the finely cultured Macready, and, a little later, John McCullough and Lawrence Barrett. The West produced its own capable actors; for example, Joshua Silsbee, who first appeared in a theatre at Natchez, and who portrayed rural types to perfection. Even California had a gleaming figure, the child-actress Lotta Crabtree,

44 When Clark Mills found from measurements that Jackson had been anything but a well-proportioned man, he wrote the Jackson Monument Committee in Washington for instructions. They replied that they wanted "Jackson, and nothing but Jackson"—and Colonels Haynes, Hampton, Gadsden, and other old comrades in arms found the likeness perfect. Charleston *Courier*, March 8, 1848. John A. Dix, serving on a committee to receive designs for a statue of Washington, was pleased by what he saw in the Italian studios. He had always thought togas a gross anachronism. "Crawford has boldly departed from this prevalent usage, and I think with complete success." To Peter Force, December 8, 1844; Dix Papers, N. Y. Hist. Soc. The country had thrilled responsively to Henry A. Wise's declaration in the House, when Horatio Greenough's statue of a half-nude Washington had been delivered at the Washington Navy-yard: "The man does not live, and never did live, who ever saw Washington without his shirt."

the chief prodigy among the troupers of the gold-coast, who in the later fifties became the pet and pride of her section.

Vivid sketches of the life of travelling performers of the time are to be found in the memoirs of Mrs. Anna Cora Mowatt, and the charmingly humorous autobiography of the youngest and greatest of the three Joseph Jeffersons. A steamboat frozen in at a wild point on the Ohio; stage journeys over frontier roads in bitter midwinter; outbreaks of epidemics; playing of parts when desperately ill to avoid disappointing an audience; ludicrous or tragic accidents—this is the stuff of Mrs. Mowatt's best chapters. Jefferson, after shaking up dusty rat-traps of theatres in Wilmington and Savannah, played Mobile with the lively Julia Dean for six dollars a week apiece. For this reward they changed their politics, their religion, and their costumes at the will of the stage-manager. As Catholics they massacred the Huguenots, and as Pilgrims bade sad adieux to England; they were brigands, gentle shepherds, and revolutionaries by turns. Jefferson tells of the innumerable mischances that befell hastily-mustered companies on improvised stages; the balcony scene in *Romeo and Juliet*, for example, enacted before an audience exploding with laughter because the cornerstone of the Veronese edifice was a box advertising thirty pounds of short sixes. Edwin Booth made his first great impression in America by performances in Baltimore and a tour of the South in 1856. And while prominent figures gave the profitable areas of the West and South an opportunity to see them, scores of minor road companies barnstormed through heat and cold in raw new States and Territories, following the paths that Sol Smith, the great central actor of the frontier stage, had blazed. For Smith, down to his retirement in 1853, had often played in hamlets where it seemed impossible to obtain a respectable audience. The people, as he writes, "seemed to come out of the woods." [45]

The stage, in short, was a living force not only in cities and towns, but in remote areas; it left its imprint on rural society as well as urban; Lincoln, a young lawyer in Springfield, according to Joe Jefferson, defended the elder Jeffersons against an exorbitant tax imposed by church folk, enabling their company to spend a season in entertaining and educating the legislature; and the "floating theatre" of the Chapman family, with like showboat ventures by imitators, reached river hamlets all the way from Pittsburgh to New Orleans. A considerable part of the fare given by roving troupes and stock companies was of high literary quality. The comedies of Goldsmith, Sheridan, and Colman were perennial favorites; historical American pieces were popular; and dramatizations of Dickens and Scott had tremendous vogue. Charlotte Cush-

---

45 Anna Cora Mowatt's *Autobiography of an Actress* was published in 1853; *The Autobiography of Joseph Jefferson* in 1889–90. See Sol Smith, *Theatrical Management in the West and South for Thirty Years*.

man, greatest of American actresses in these years, was renowned for her acting as Nancy Sykes in *Oliver Twist* ("a tigress," wrote the English actor George Vandenhoff, "with a touch, and but one, of woman's almost deadened nature, blotted and trampled underfoot by man's cruelty and sin"),[46] and as Meg Merrilies in *Guy Mannering,* darkly, luridly, picturesquely impressive. Home's *Douglas,* Kotzebue's *Pizarro,* and Lytton's *Lady of Lyons* delighted multitudes. But Shakespeare was the staple and backbone of the American stage, and Mark Twain was faithful to reality when he made his two drunken, thievish, dilapidated old actors, floating down the Mississippi, try to pass themselves off as pupils of Kean and Garrick in Shakespearean rôles.

Nothing better illustrated the public importance of the stage than the veritable worship accorded to Edwin Forrest, an idol about whom surged turbulent nationalist passions. Making his debut in his native Philadelphia at fourteen as Young Norval, he went west for training; and Sol Smith, seeing him in *The Soldier's Daughter* in Cincinnati, prophesied his future greatness. By 1848 he was established as foremost among those actors who tear a passion to tatters, and his energy, audacity, vanity, and bumptious patriotism had installed him in the hearts of plain Americans everywhere. Powerfully built, aggressive in temper, full of animal spirits, he had been equal to anything, whether wandering the wild border country, playing to fiercely applauding Bowery audiences, making two runs in London, or touring all the large American cities. He liked turbulent characters, using his stalwart physique, sonorous voice, and impetuous manner to make them at times thrillingly effective, at times pathetically cheap: Richard III, Macbeth, Spartacus, Pizarro, the Indian chief Metamora. Men either liked or disliked him tremendously. His fits of passion made enemies on every hand. Wayward and irresponsible, he turned his marital difficulties into a public scandal, and when he assaulted N. P. Willis in June, 1856, for defending Mrs. Forrest, laid himself open to widespread censure.

But to the crowd he was not only America's representative tragedian, but an embodiment of the national spirit; the same spirit that flowed into the oratory of Clay and Douglas, the manifestoes of Young America, and the poetry of Whitman. His visits to London were regarded as an American challenge to the motherland. On his second tour he brought himself into collision (1854) with Macready, the lord of the Shakespearean stage. Forrest, choosing without warrant to believe that Macready had inspired the adverse criticisms of John Forster and others, intimated that the English actor (a highminded gentleman) had joined in a conspiracy against him. Attending one of Macready's performances in Edinburgh, he took a front seat and at an opportune moment

---

46 Vandenhoff, *Leaves from an Actor's Notebook.*

hissed! As Joseph Jefferson put it: "The eagle of the American stage was in a frenzy; his plumage had been ruffled by the British lion. So giving that intolerant animal one tremendous peck, he spread his wings and sailed away." The sequel was the bloody Astor Place riot of May 10, 1847, when Macready's appearance in *Macbeth* was the signal for an outburst by New York rowdies and Anglophobes. A stormy section of the audience howled down Macready's lines, a still angrier crowd assaulted the door with clubs and stones, and when soldiers appeared, seventeen persons were killed and many wounded. Deplorable as the riot was, it showed that Americans regarded the stage and its principal personages with great seriousness.[47]

It cannot be denied that there was something peculiarly American in Forrest; in his dauntless pride, his vigor, his democracy, and his preference for rough-and-ready effects. He was best in portraying such elemental, strong-willed rebels as Spartacus and Coriolanus; and a critic has remarked that he was himself an elemental, driving personality in perhaps unconscious revolt against the tamely idealized classical drama. Something of the rude force of pioneer America appeared in the man, so that Bowery boys and rough-fisted westerners saw in him a natural antagonist of Old World elegance, cultivation, and caste. His worst side was shown in the Edinburgh affront to a great fellow-actor, and in the caning of innocent Willis. He revealed his best side in his genuine concern for an American drama. It was his offer of a prize of $500 which inspired the writing of the first successful drama on an Indian theme, John A. Stone's *Metamora, The Pride of the Wampanoags*, with a rôle full of the heroics that he loved. His special tastes did much to inspire the dramatic writings of James Montgomery Bird in the thirties, and of Robert T. Conrad, the Philadelphia author of *Jack Cade*. With George H. Miles, whose *De Soto* was produced in 1852, these men prepared the way for the most important of American dramatists in the period, George Henry Boker.[48]

Science, art, the stage, all had their nationalizing influences, and so of course did literature. It was Bryant who sang "The Song of Marion's Men," and Whitman who, in "Starting from Paumanok," identified himself equally with Pennsylvanian and Arkansian, with every part of his "far breath'd land! Arctic braced! Mexican breezed!" Of the messages of congratulation which Irving received on his life of Washington the most prized came from Charlottesville, Va., written by his old travelling companion William C. Preston. In his letters Longfellow might express strong party feeling, but his verse carried no note

47 Walter Prichard Eaton, *The Actor's Heritage*, 119ff., has an appreciative chapter on Macready; his own account of the riot is in his *Reminiscences and Diaries*, 586ff. Montrose J. Moses has treated *The Fabulous Forrest*.
48 Arthur Hobson Quinn, *The American Drama From the Beginning to the Civil War*, 337ff.

really discordant with his lines of 1849 on that Ship of State which bore the brightest promise of humanity:

> Our hearts, our hopes, our prayers, our tears,
> Our faith triumphant o'er our fears,
> Are all with thee,—are all with thee!

But powerful currents in American culture (using the word in a somewhat broader sense) bore in a divisive if not actually disruptive direction. Great sections of cultural life were particularistic in character, and other sections were on a plane where they were quickly affected by partisan and polemic influences. It was impossible for Americans to be always harking back to 1776; they had to be thinking of 1848 and 1856. Not much of the country's life could really be thought of in the generalized terms which Emerson used in *The American Scholar*. The Lowell who wrote on commanding abstractions like democracy was a good deal less interesting and impressive than Lowell paying tribute to Wendell Phillips, and reviewing Mexican War issues in the *Biglow Papers*. Audiences sauntered in respectable numbers to see *Blanche of Brandywine*, but they rushed in eager hordes to *Uncle Tom's Cabin*. From 1846 to 1861 the main precipitants in letters, journalism, political oratory, and popular art were no longer national—they were sectional.

[V]

They were sectional because two distinct cultures, Northern and Southern, each shading off toward the West in newer and not dissimilar forms, but nevertheless on the whole sharply differentiated, had come into existence. In two areas the sectional characteristics were intensified. Van Wyck Brooks has spoken of the "peculiar flavor of that old New England culture, so dry, so crisp, so dogmatic, so irritating," [49] and though the word stimulating should be added, the qualifications are accurate. At the opposite pole was the culture of the Lower South, genial, elegant, so old-fashioned that it was sometimes antique, and though alert enough in political directions, otherwise largely sterile. Boston and Charleston were now preoccupied with sectional stereotypes and antipathies, and as Garrisonian abolitionism colored all the thought of one city, so Calhounian nullification tinged all the ideas of the other. As Whittier's "Expostulation" was an arraignment of Southern society and its cultural ideals, so Grayson's "The Hireling and the Slave" was an indictment of the Northern economic and social order. New England and the Lower South had become

49 *America's Coming of Age*, 73.

almost incapable of understanding each other, and the Potomac and Ohio separated areas of wide mutual incomprehension.

No one dominant fact explains the special characteristics of Southern culture, which was a complex result of intricate causes. The idea of white domination, which has been called the "central theme" of the section's life, was certainly of fundamental importance.[50] The race question set a ritual for the Southern people which was followed long after slavery was dead. Other students have varied the formula. They have said that Southern culture was stamped above all by a conservatism based upon class stratification and the absence of competitive struggle, engendering an aristocratic, leisurely ideal of life, with much pride of family, scope for learning, and attachment to outdoor pursuits. It is certainly true that agrarian traits marked the South. In contrast with the more and more urbanized, industrialized North, its life was rural—so rural that Augustus Baldwin Longstreet hesitated to accept the presidency of the College of South Carolina because he thought it unwise to subject students to the temptations of a metropolis like Columbia, with its six thousand people.[51] Southerners themselves liked to explain their special culture in terms of ideals. Instead of being restless, unstable, and ruthlessly progressive, they said, they put their surplus energy into the life of the mind, and cultivated the greatest of all arts, the art of living.

In this art of living the tournaments, dinners, and balls of Virginia, the fox-hunting of the Shenandoah, the race-week of Charleston, the theatres and carnivals of New Orleans, were less important than the peaceful pursuits of plantations where the owner (like Jefferson Davis) divided his time among business, politics, and study. The Southern ideal, according to this view, approximated closely to the ideals of eighteenth-century English life. It is easy to romanticize the old South, and a myth-making process which unduly minimizes the importance of middle-class elements and ignores the squalor of the disinherited has gained much too wide an acceptance. Nevertheless, the elements emphasized by Basil L. Gildersleeve—pride of State and lineage, love of classical erudition, courtesy, reverence for the traditions of a static order, ambition to cultivate the graces of existence—did throw a charm over rather limited groups.[52]

A distinctive economic and social pattern, which was basic, became inter-meshed with a specialized body of ideas and customs. The South, completely committed to agriculture, and in great degree to the plantation system; to a labor force which had to be kept ignorant and unenterprising; to a patriarchal

50 Ulrich B. Phillips, "The Central Theme of Southern History," *Am Hist. Rev.*, XXIV, 30ff.
51 Wade, *Longstreet*, 315, 316.
52 *The Creed of the Old South, 1865–1915.*

ideal of social organization; to such limited production of wealth that great bodies of illiterate, shambling, badly-nourished whites became accepted as natural; to a soil-and-labor exploitation which gave one or two classes the means of elegance, learning, and leadership; to the mental conservatism which is bred by isolation—this land had peculiar defects and special virtues. In the Revolutionary period the South had produced more citizens of the world and thinkers of international repute than any other section. Mount Vernon, Monticello, Gunston Hall, Montpelier, had thrown a long shadow across the map. By 1846 the South was more largely withdrawn from the general movement of Western civilization than any other sizable area peopled by an English-speaking stock. Even its code of ethics, its conscience, had been immobilized; by Jefferson's standards, had been moved backward.[53]

The South liked to think of itself as having a warmly human civilization while that of the North was bookish and mechanical. In Yankeeland the long, dreary winters, the business appurtenances of society, the hard drive of the towns, and (said Southerners) the absence of social sympathies, led to the incessant production of technological devices and books. Below the Potomac the open air, bland climate, and agreeable society tempted men to blither pursuits. Southerners read for personal enjoyment and cultivation; Northerners read to invent or write. "The best thing which could happen for the New England literary mind," wrote one observer, "would be the banishment of all books from the studies of her foremost men." [54] The South, according to her sons, fostered conversational talent, while her platform oratory stimulated political thought more forcibly than the newspaper articles of the North. Where was better talk to be heard than at the table of well-educated Virginia planters, or in Natchez drawing-rooms, or at Russell's bookshop on busy King Street in Charleston, where seats were placed for the literary men of the town— William Gilmore Simms, Paul H. Hayne, J. L. Petigru, William J. Grayson, Alfred Huger, Mitchell King, and others? The rural Southerner, going to church, lounging at the crossroads store, and attending muster, barbecues, and co't day, equally loved talk.[55] Visiting Northerners, it was agreed in Richmond and Mobile, never equalled the clear, bold, graceful expression of their hosts. And the topics on which Yankees conversed were inferior; however well-informed and earnest on business subjects, they were at a loss whenever abstract ideas came up.

It was another staple belief of Southerners that their conservatism was wise

53 In Book I of *The Mind of the South*, W. J. Cash discusses the origin and development of the special Southern psychology.
54 *North and South: Impressions of Northern Society Upon a Southerner* (pvt, 1853).
55 Guion G. Johnson, *A Social History of North Carolina 1800-1860*, engagingly sketches the comradely aspects of Southern rural life.

and healthy. The North was swept by the Kossuth craze, but the South stood by the old principle of non-intervention in foreign quarrels. The North was full of Millerism, Shakerism, Spiritualism, Mormonism, and what not; the South clung to its pure and ancient religion. Northern politics was flawed by fads, theories, and unpredictable innovations, but Southern voters held the principles of the fathers. While the Southerner was heartily philanthropic and generous, the Yankees strangely compounded charity with cant, and mercy with malevolence. So ran the generalizations, all open to endless unprofitable argument, but all advanced with a force which went far toward proving that the South *was* different.

[VI]

It is necessary to pierce behind these rather meaningless generalizations to discrete matters of fact. Asked just where, in detail, the differences of the South lay, we can answer under numerous headings.

The white population of the South was far more largely Anglo-Saxon than that of the North, for despite its numerous Germans, its hundred thousand Irish folk by 1860, its French Huguenots, and others, it was one of the purest British stocks in the world. Its dominant attitudes, particularly as to the color line, were Anglo-Saxon.[56] Its life was not merely rural, but rural after a special pattern; for the section was dotted over with large holdings representing great capital values and employing large bodies of slaves. It was a land of simple dogmatism in religion; of Protestant solidarity, of people who believed every word of the Bible, and of faith frequently refreshed by emotional revivalism. Its churches provided an emphasis on broadly social values contrasting with the intellectualization of morals to be found in the North.[57] In the South the yoke of law and government rested more lightly upon the individual than in other sections. Counties, often sprawling in extent, were the chief units of local administration; the States followed the rule that the best government was the least government; and the nation was held at arm's length.

The South drew from its economic position a special set of tenets, naturally accepting Francis Wayland's condemnation of protection as a violation of morality and common sense.[58] With equal inevitability, it drew from its minority position in the political fabric another special set of doctrines. It was a country in which romantic and hedonistic impulses, born of the opulence

56 And remained so; David L. Cohn, *Saturday Review of Literature*, February 22, 1941.
57 Cason, *90° in the Shade*, 66.
58 Mrs. McCord published in 1848, through Putnam's, a translation of Bastiat's *Sophism of the Protective Policy*, while another translation of the same work appeared in instalments in *Russell's Magazine*.

of nature, had freer rein than in the North. The phrases "the merry South," "the sunny South," connoted a great deal. Genuine gusto went into William Elliot's *Carolina Sports by Land and Water*, describing thrilling adventures with devil-fishes in Port Royal Sound, and with wildcats and bears in upland Carolina woods; real delight colored the portrayal of plantation festivities in Caroline H. Gilman's *Recollections of a Southern Matron*, a bit of reality thinly garbed in fiction. The remote quality attaching to much Southern life, which made some travellers feel they had dropped into another world, and the sharp contrast of races, added to the atmosphere of romance.

To a far greater degree than the North, the South was a land of class stratification and vestigial feudalism. Various explanations were given for this fact. One was later repeated by N. S. Shaler when he remarked that Southerners were descendants of that portion of the English who were least modernized, and who "still retained a large element of the feudal notion." [59] It is now known that no such distinction existed between Northern and Southern colonists, for honest middle-class folk, not feudal-minded cavaliers, made up the bulk of Virginia as of Massachusetts settlers.[60] Slavery, the large plantation, and the agrarian cast of life, with some traditional inheritances from colonial days, accounted for the class structure. "Slavery helped feudalism," correctly remarked a Southern writer,[61] "and feudalism helped slavery, and the Southern people were largely the outcome of the interaction of these two formative principles."

The great colonial plantations, established along the South Atlantic seaboard and in Louisiana in days when tobacco, rice, and sugar reigned without thought of a new monarch named cotton, had possessed much the atmosphere and influence of the English manors. Even North Carolina had its first families, the Winstons, Taylors, and Byrds of the Tidewater.[62] The planters enjoyed the social dignities and political leadership of the English squires. They revered the old order, dispensed hospitality, and benignly guided their inferiors in Sir Roger de Coverley style. As a rigorous code of personal honor was enforced by the duel rather than by law, and gentlefolk deemed themselves highly sensitive to slights, they developed a punctilious courtesy. Yet the ideal Southern gentleman seldom appeared in perfection; politeness, gallantry, and dignity had often to be reconciled with the sudden passion of a Preston Brooks, and, as James Branch Cabell has mentioned, a weakness for miscegenation.[63] A planter who entertained much, thought much of the good old times, and

59 "The Peculiarities of the South," *North American Review*, October, 1890.
60 T. J. Wertenbaker, *Patrician and Plebeian in Virginia*.
61 W. P. Trent, *William Gilmore Simms*, 31.
62 Cf. *It's a Far Cry*, by Robert W. Winston (1937).
63 Quoted in Edwin Mims, *The Advancing South*, 214.

handed down his home acres to his oldest son even when primogeniture was no more, naturally made much of family ties. Kinship was counted to remote cousinhood, the penniless spinster who bore the family name had a welcome place in the household, and summer visitings from State to State, across many hundreds of miles, were common. Family did much to knit the South together.

Yet class lines can easily be overemphasized, for they were subject to powerful solvents. The fact that many a poor farmer and rich planter looked back to a common ancestor was one; wealth in such instances usually bowed before relationship. The fact that all white men had a sense of solidarity as against the Negro, and as against the encroaching North, also tended to reduce class stratification. As sectional tensions increased, the political elite of the South were more and more drawn from non-aristocratic levels. It cannot too often be emphasized that such men as Yancey, Wigfall, Reagan, Jefferson Davis, and A. H. Stephens in no wise represented the old aristocracy. Among the wealthy planters a large place was always taken by the *nouveaux riches,* and in the South no less than the North the transition from poverty to opulence and back to poverty, three generations from shirtsleeves to shirtsleeves, was not uncommon. It should be said, too, that the egalitarian theories of Thomas Jefferson (despite all the uneasy effort by various leaders to prove them outworn) made a real impression on thoughtful Southerners.

As in the North the advancing frontier was an unquestionable force for democracy, in the South it at least modified the features of aristocracy. The opening of the old Southwest had furnished a field in which the ambitious, energetic, and able pushed rapidly to the front. Combining cheap land and labor, they built up rich estates. It was not the old Tidewater aristocracy which took possession of the wealth of the western reaches, but younger and more aggressive elements. Of course the new aristocracy modelled its social order broadly after the coastal pattern. But comparatively few of the patrician names of Virginia, Carolina, and Louisiana—not more than five hundred all told—figured in the new beadroll of gentility.[64] Many a rich planter, like the Hairstons, was conscious of his humble origin, felt best at home in associating with the commonalty, and was ready himself to work in the fields. Across the Mississippi in Texas and Arkansas the atmosphere grew more democratic still.

But taken as a section, stretching from the Atlantic to the Father of Waters and from the Ohio to the Gulf, the South had a life of far more aristocratic tone than the North.[65] Both the central weakness of the South, and the main

64 This is the estimate of W. J. Cash in *Mind of the South,* ch. 1; "maybe not more than half that figure."
65 The tenacity of caste in the South is illustrated in John Dollard's *Caste and Class in a Southern Town.* The parvenues of the Mississippi Valley whom Olmsted describes so caustically, and the Cotton Snobs assailed by Daniel R. Hundley in *Social Relations in Our Southern States* (1860), had aristocratic—and autocratic—traits hardly to be matched in any equally large group in the North.

flaw in American social homogeneity, lay in the want of a great predominant body of intelligent, independent, thoughtful, and educated farmers in the slave States to match the similar body at the North. The nation had always drawn most of its sturdy common sense and integrity of character from its farmers. A really strong Southern yeomanry could have clasped hands with Northern tillers of the soil. But the plantation system was inimical to any such body. Whether developing or declining, it wasted soil and toil, reduced the mass of blacks and whites to poverty, kept them in ignorance, and destroyed their hopes. It was not a preparation for the appearance of an independent, industrious farmer class, but a "preface to peasantry." It gave the South the "forgotten man" that Walter Hines Page described in his memorable address at Greensboro a generation later; men too poor, ignorant, and politician-beguiled to be discontented with their poverty, ignorance, and docility.[66]

With all its natural gaiety, simplicity, and love of olden ways the South combined a trait common in countries with unhappy institutions, like Spain, and in lands left behind by modern progress, like Ireland; the trait of uneasy defensiveness. At the beginning of the century most Southerners had believed that Virginia would keep her primacy among the States in wealth, population, and influence, that their whole section would grow faster than the chilly North, and that their grasp on the national tiller would be unshaken. That belief had withered before the Mexican War. Clear-eyed men realized that in nearly all material elements of civilization the North had far outstripped them; and they knew that slavery stood indicted not merely as a moral wrong, but as responsible for this painful lag in progress. In the Southern mind a defensive mechanism clicked into operation. Slavery? It was a blessing. The Negro? They best understood him. "Whatever defects may belong to our system, it certainly has the merit of preserving the Negro and improving his situation. Look at the moderating influences. Look their own advance in health, comfort, virtue, and numbers." [67] Progress? No sane man wanted the "calculating avarice" that, as Calhoun said, marked the factory owner driving his wage slaves.[68]

Hand in hand with this defensive attitude, as all observers noted, went a passionate Southern pride. The Charlestonian loved to descant on St. Michael's, the Society Library, the Broad Street Theatre, the statue of Pitt. If you hinted that his college was but an academy, he spoke of the hospital, the St. Cecilia Society, and the three newspapers. If a visitor suggested that the city needed a good market, men described the ample shipments that came down to every gentleman from his plantation.[69] An aristocratic society is always proud, and

---

66 Arthur F. Raper's *Preface to Peasantry* (1936) is an antidote for some of the agrarian doctrines expressed in Allen Tate and others, *I'll Take My Stand*.
67 *North and South: Impressions of Northern Society Upon a Southerner.*
68 Quoted by Van Wyck Brooks, *The World of Washington Irving*, 230.
69 Trent, *Simms*, 224.

we might trace far back into colonial times the Southern conviction of superiority to Northern and British shilling-grabbers. Many slaveholders liked to talk, at first confidentially but later in speeches frankly addressed to Northern ears, of the defects of shirtsleeves democracy, Yankee industrialism, and the vomit of European slums. More and more, this pride was related to that inferiority complex which is so often a mark of superior peoples set amid unfavorable environments. The pride of the ruling class was bulwarked by an intellectual factor, the influence of the old writers—Hobbes in government, Dryden in poetry, Clarendon in history—who regarded aristocracy as the best form of social control.

In none of its varied manifestations was sectional pride more dangerous than in its constant assertions of superior fighting power. "If it comes to blows between the North and the South," a Yankee heard William Gilmore Simms exclaim, "we shall crush you as I would crush an egg." John B. Gordon heard a judge remark that in the event of war, the South could "whip the Yankees with children's pop-guns." [70] The well-born Southerner was convinced that he was a man of far more spirit and resource than the Northern counter-jumper. Nothing struck William H. Russell more forcibly, in his travels over the South just before the Civil War, than the widespread conviction that the free States would never fight, or if they did would be quickly put in their places.[71] A later writer on "the fighting South" has ascribed its militancy to the old habit of living dangerously, and to a depth of conviction, a 'totality of purehearted affirmation' natural in a simple society.[72] Perhaps more important were the conditions of Southern life, with much hunting, general use of horses, and frequent marksmanship contests; the existence of two fine schools of war, the Virginia Military Institute at Lexington, and the South Carolina Military Academy or "Citadel" at Charleston; and the memory of Southern prowess in the Mexican War.[73] The leading officers, Scott, Taylor, Quitman, Twiggs, and Davis, were all Southrons—if one forgot Kearny or Worth. Indeed, in what war had not Southern commanders stood foremost?

[VII]

Had Southern and Northern ideals of education been alike they would have done much to erase sectional lines, but they differed sharply. Education for utility was steadily gaining ground in the North; education for character

70 *Reminiscences of the Civil War,* 7.
71 "A love of military display is very different indeed from a true soldierly spirit"; Russell, *North and South,* ch. 33.
72 John Temple Graves, *The Fighting South.*
73 Richard Taylor, *Destruction and Reconstruction,* 20.

and grace held sway in the South—and the scope of education was far from identical.

The relatively high development of colleges in the South, and the comparatively low provision of common schools, perfectly fitted a semi-aristocratic society sparsely scattered over an area which had all too little of a prosperous yeoman class. The Southern college was in general decently supported, decently staffed, and well attended. In 1860 Virginia had twenty-three colleges enrolling 2,824 students, as against New York's seventeen colleges listing 2,970 students; and Georgia's thirty-two colleges with 3,302 students nominally overshadowed the eight Massachusetts colleges with 1,733 registrants.[74] To raise the question of standards would have been risky, for all States had too much glass to afford stone-throwing. Virginia spent annually some fifty thousand more than Massachusetts on colleges, and a large proportion of her population were college-trained. In 1856 the enrolment of 558 at the University of Virginia was far above Harvard's roll of 361 students.[75] To be sure, some Southern institutions, such as the University of Georgia, Transylvania, William and Mary, and South Carolina College, were sadly deliquescent. But others were advancing, and one hopeful institution, Bishop Leonidas Polk's University of the South at Sewanee, Tenn., for which an endowment of $500,000 had been collected or pledged, was born in 1859.[76] The South boasted that it had not only established the first State universities, but had cherished the ideal of a college-trained leadership more fixedly than the North.

Higher education appeared at its Southern best in the great university which Jefferson had founded, and which by the middle fifties already counted sons— Robert Toombs, A. H. H. Stuart, Henry Winter Davis—of distinction. The six

74 *Eighth Census, Mortality and Misc. Statistics,* 505.
75 Clement Eaton, *Freedom of Thought in the Old South,* 196. W. E. Dodd declares that in 1850–60 "practically every college and university in the South doubled its attendance"; *Cotton Kingdom,* 111. But Professor Eaton's excellent treatment of the curse of Southern illiteracy is not to be ignored. The Harvard figure does not include the professional schools.
76 Polk had long cherished a plan for a great Southern university, for he believed that south of Virginia the section had no institution worthy of that name. He regarded the University of North Carolina and the University of Mississippi as hardly more than colleges, while other "universities" were simply high schools. He wished to set up an Oxford or Göttingen for the South. His plan was to obtain a great landed domain, erect stately buildings, draw a faculty of distinction from all parts of the world, and build up a community of intellectual eminence which would attract distinguished writers. Strong inducements were to be offered planters and other men of wealth to make their summer homes near the university, which he wished placed somewhere in the mountain region surrounding Chattanooga. The Episcopal Church should sponsor the university, and an endowment of not less than three millions should be collected. An organizational meeting was held July 4, 1857, on Lookout Mountain, with a procession in which a Revolutionary veteran bore the flag, a band playing spirited airs, and an oration by Bishop Otey. It was an auspicious start. Nobody could foresee that within a few years the mountain would be wreathed in cannon-smoke. *University of the South Papers,* I: W. M. Polk, *Leonidas Polk,* I, 219ff.

schools of the collegiate course (ancient languages, modern languages, mathematics, natural philosophy, chemistry, and moral philosophy) were each headed
by a professor who received $3,000 a year, a house, and appurtenant privileges,
and who occupied a position of dignity in Southern esteem. Schools of medicine,
surgery, anatomy, and law completed the university. "The entire establishment,"
wrote a visitor in 1854, "is on a liberal and enlightened scale." He was impressed by the wide geographic range of the 466 students of that year, who
came from seventeen States and the Federal District; by the evident culture of
the faculty; by the scholarship system under which the University educated
thirty-two students at public expense; and by the searching final examination
of each candidate, partly oral and partly written, conducted by a faculty committee. He liked, too, the genial atmosphere; "in passing through these extended
arcades on a warm sunny morning we found the young men emerging from
their rooms and pursuing their studies in the open and shaded air." [77] Other
observers praised the honor system. Even Harvard treated students as unruly
boys, but Virginia made them self-respecting gentlemen under a discipline
which inculcated principle.

Both North and South, colleges still made the ancient classics and mathematics the core of their curricula, still let learned teachers occupy whole settees
rather than chairs (Longstreet at Mississippi, teaching rhetoric, evidences of
Christianity, logic, political economy, and philosophy while serving as president
more than equalled the versatile Nairne at Columbia), and still neglected
science. In 1855 F. A. P. Barnard, then teaching mathematics at Mississippi,
wrote a brochure on the improvement practicable in the nation's colleges.
Describing the chief objects of education as discipline and intellectual development, he declared that the courses should first of all require enough of the
disciplinary studies for a thorough intellectual training. Once this was secured,
the curriculum could then be expanded to cover studies valuable as subjects
of knowledge. But how could room be found for the sciences? In two ways,
he answered; by raising the exactions for admission, or by increasing the length
of the college year. He was in favor of both. But if such steps proved impossible, he would dispense with the utilitarian and scientific subjects and continue to stress classical discipline. [78]

This old-fashioned view remained largely dominant in both sections. The
newer view that dead languages should be ruthlessly thrust aside for science,
history, and government was forcibly asserted in the South by Maury, President
Philip Lindsley of the University of Nashville, and T. S. Grimké of Charleston.
Nor was science utterly neglected, as Virginia's courses in chemistry and natural

77 *National Intelligencer*, September 7, 1854.
78 *Improvements Practicable in American Colleges*, Hartford, 1856.

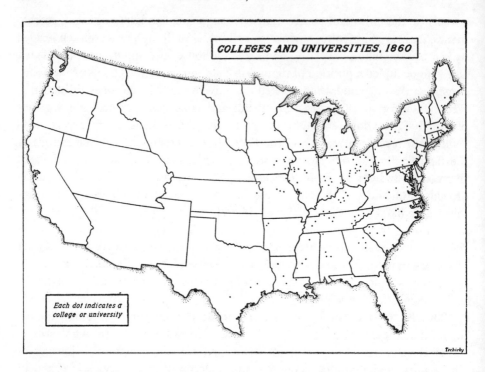

COLLEGES AND UNIVERSITIES, 1860

Each dot indicates a
college or university

Tschirky

philosophy proved. The University of North Carolina early in the fifties
established professorships of civil engineering and agricultural chemistry.[79]

Secondary education, too, fared not too ill in the South. In both sections
this was the era of the academy, a transitional type of school which was in
general privately endowed but sometimes under semi-public control, and which
offered a steadily broadening curriculum. The nation by 1850 had just over
six thousand academies, of which the very respectable number of 2,640 were
in the Southern States.[80] Estimates of the section's enrolment in these schools
ran as high as two hundred thousand. One State, Kentucky, had passed a law
to endow an academy in every county seat with six thousand acres of land;
and numerous academies resulted, though the land was often sold before it
gained real value. Of the nation's public high schools the South had only a

79 Of the 466 students at the University of Virginia in 1853–54, the books showed 220
studying chemistry and 106 natural philosophy. Students at North Carolina interested in
civil engineering and agricultural chemistry could enter one or both courses at the end of
the first senior term, with a view to remaining a year after obtaining the degree of B.A.
President David L. Swain, a shrewd executive who rapidly built up the university, wrote
Barnard that he favored meeting the demand for a practical education, for while Jefferson's
conception of a university was admirable, south of Virginia "there is too little wealth and
learned leisure in the country to afford the requisite patronage for such an institution."
August 23, 1854; Swain Papers, N. C. Hist. Commission Library.
80 A. J. Inglis, *Principles of Secondary Education*, ch. 5.

handful—about thirty out of the 321 listed in 1860.[81] But the academies, practically all of them private institutions, many of them denomination-controlled, and most numerous in the piedmont areas (for rich lowlands and impoverished mountain country were equally uncongenial), were numerous enough to give a host of boys good grammar-school training. Such academies as Waddell's in South Carolina and Liberty Hall in Virginia had a national repute.[82]

Yet in the elementary field the broad humanitarian ideals of Jefferson failed. The South was for the most part a land without free public schools—a land where the poor man's son was likely to go untaught, and the workingman or small farmer to be ignorant if not illiterate. Here lay one of the great gulfs separating North from South. Said C. G. Memminger of the situation in South Carolina: "The mechanic and moving elements of society—those who work the actual machinery of the body politic and are its stay and support—these exhibit few of the results of education." [83] If this was true of Calhoun's own land, what was the situation elsewhere?

The question is easily answered. In Georgia by 1860 only one county had established a free school system. Though Arkansas had passed a general school law in 1843, it was estimated eleven years later that only one-fourth the children of school age were in any form of school. In Mississippi the cities were authorized to organize public school systems, but outside their limits little progress was made; for no local school tax could be laid without the consent of a majority of the heads of families. A public school system existed in Tennessee after 1830, and Andrew Johnson obtained a tax on both property and polls to support it, but it had little real vigor down to 1861. Alabama passed its first general law in 1854, but its system did not take firm root till twenty years later. Louisiana was proud that in 1851 about half her children were attending public schools. And so the story went. By far the best record was made by North Carolina, where the foundations of an elementary school system had been laid in 1839, and where after 1853 an able and devoted superintendent, Calvin H. Stowe—"the first campaigner for schools in the South"—labored to give it strength.[84]

The sharpest indictment of the general neglect of primary education came from Southerners themselves. W. H. Trescot, remarking that slavery was a great blessing, added that it had its inexorable requirements. Foremost among them was the elevation of free labor, for the white race must preserve its

81 *Report U. S. Commr. of Ed.*, 1904, II, 1782ff.
82 R. S. Cotterill, *The Old South*, 283, 284.
83 Charleston *Courier*, January 12, 1857.
84 See summaries in Cubberley, *Public Education in the U. S.*, 247–250; Charles W. Dabney, *Universal Education in the South From the Beginnings to 1900.*

superiority by making its work intellectual as well as manual; every white laborer should possess enough education to lift him high above the black.[85] Memminger bitterly indicted the charity schools of Charleston. Children avoided them as a badge of inferiority. When forced into them, they gave irregular attendance, learned without spirit, and left before they acquired the basic rudiments of knowledge. He confessed that when he saw the wretched buildings, and when he heard one youngster say that four plus four made four, and another state that the capital of England was Scotland, his heart sank.[86] Governor Henry A. Wise of Virginia passionately arraigned the school system of the Old Dominion. Pride, he wrote, "withholds thousands of our poor people from the *charity* of schools, even for the fifty-three days of time per annum, and for the pittance of the cost of $2.57 per capita for the fifty-three days of time; whilst a sound republican *community* of instruction among children of all classes would make all equally beneficiaries of public aid to education." Out of about 200,000 persons over seven and under twenty-one in the State, the middle fifties saw fewer than 42,000 getting "a morsel of mental food" at public cost.[87]

But while Northern education was steadily growing more democratic, the old Southern ideal remained aristocratic. Moncure D. Conway might protest that no real antipathy existed between slavery and free public education, and might argue that Virginia had an opportunity to set up the most perfect school system on earth. He was sharply contradicted by that Southern champion Ellwood Fisher, who declared that the conditions bred by slavery—the great size of agricultural units, sparsity of population, and so on—made schools of the Northern type impossible. "But Virginia has a system of oral instruction which compensates for her want of schools, and that is her social intercourse. The social intercourse of the South is probably much greater than that of any people that ever existed." [88] And a sharper opposition to public schools was often expressed, as by a friend of A. H. Stephens's whose letter indicated how much more education was needed: [89]

"You are aware that the people at the North are all *educated* by government, and where educated they expect to *live* upon government, either town, county, city, state, or national, and *they will do it.* . . . This idea of educating *everybody* is taking root in the South, our people are beginning to demand taxes for the education of the masses, there is to be no more ignorant after this generation

85 Quoted in "The Free School System of South Carolina," *Southern Quarterly Review,* November, 1856.
86 Charleston *Courier,* January 12, 1857.
87 Wise to D. W. A. Smith, December 9, 1856; Governors' Letter-Books.
88 Conway in *Addresses and Reprints,* 1–56; Fisher in *The North and the South,* pvt, 1849.
89 M. J. Crawford, April 8, 1860; Stephens Papers, LC.

according to the new philosophy, upon the idea that its easier to build school-houses than jails and colleges than state prisons, but there never was a greater error upon earth, we can build the latter much cheaper and they are decidedly more useful. . . .

"I am not sure but that you may educate two or three generations and about the third they will go crazy, as for instance in New England they are fanatical and foolish."

[VIII]

If Southern reading differed markedly from that of the North, it was because it was confined to narrower, more aristocratic, and more old-fashioned circles. Fewer people bought books, and they kept less abreast of modern thought. Those with means sometimes formed large and select libraries (though even Simms's ten thousand volumes at his plantation Woodlands by no means challenged such collections as Everett's or Ticknor's), and the cultivated few probably read less ephemera and more standard works than the Northern public. The before-mentioned library of Muscoe Garnett, who shut up his Virginia house and went into the Civil War never to return, was a model collection in almost everything except contemporaneous politics, sociology, and economics. It contained a fine collection in the English classics, history ancient and modern, theology, Greek and Latin literature, and books in French, Italian, and other European languages. A shelf of dictionaries in various tongues affirmed the studious taste of Garnett, who was commencing Sanscrit when the bugles called him; and his heirs found a pile of the *Revue des Deux Mondes* the last numbers dating a few months after his death.[90] Such scholar-planters were the adornment of the South.

Even in a semi-frontier region like Texas literary taste could be austerely conservative. The diary of William Pitt Ballinger, an attorney in busy practise in Austin, reveals a strong taste for historical and political works. Among the books he read in 1860 were Brougham's address on his installation as chancellor of the University of Edinburgh, orations by Everett and G. T. Curtis, Hammond's discourse on Calhoun, a critique of Macaulay on Claverhouse, and Burke's *Reflections on the French Revolution*, which he pronounced a work of "wonderful genius." This was in addition to *The Marble Faun*, the *Tale of Two Cities*, and *The Mill on the Floss*. He subscribed to *Harper's Monthly* and kept abreast of political writing. "I have read the debates between Douglas and Lincoln all through with much interest," he notes after buying the book in St. Louis. "Douglas is far more practised, artful, and unscrupulous—Lincoln

90 Garnett Collection, University of Virginia. Dorfman, *Economic Mind*, II, 890–895.

is the fairer franker man of the two and improves greatly in the course of the debate." [91]

Even the rather stiff, dry R. M. T. Hunter was wont to say, "Books are a necessity to us," and he took his classics so seriously that he used to remark with emphasis: "I would not have written Macaulay's essay upon Chatham for an earldom." He read all the English historians from Clarendon and Hume to Milman and Carlyle; was familiar with Niebuhr and Mommsen; admired Prescott and Thiers; and was well versed in Thucydides, Diodorus, Polybius, and above all, his favorite Tacitus. Like most Southerners of culture, he had a warm reverence for the English giants—Shakespeare, Milton, Dryden, Johnson; he read and re-read Fielding and Smollett; but Scott was his favorite, and to the *Antiquary* he returned at intervals all his life with passionate delight.[92] His sister Martha Hunter has left a fragmentary diary for 1849–50 which describes her own wide reading. It embraced Neander, Macaulay, Thiers, Sir Humphrey Davy, Wiseman, and Mrs. Gaskell, with much in French and German.[93] Most cultivated Southerners read the British reviews. It is significant of the old-fashioned taste of the South that Longstreet, author, teacher, and president of two learned institutions, had a library rich in all the English classics "through Addison," and that he believed the New England writers too puerile for consideration.[94]

[IX]

The cultivation of literature in the South was so sorely handicapped by social and economic factors that the effort to create a sectional literature terminated in total failure. The North summed up the reason for this failure in the word slavery. But a more complex explanation is required. The writers recognized that they worked in a highly unfavorable milieu. They needed one or several great cities, with capital and enterprise, where the attrition of intellects would sharpen the general mind; a larger middle-class, accustomed to buying books and magazines; and some prosperous, well-circulated periodicals. They needed at least one real publisher; not a printer or bookseller, but a firmly-established house like Harper's, Appleton's, or Little, Brown, issuing volumes week after week—ten or twenty a month—and therefore provided with facilities to advertise them, get them into a thousand bookstores, and sell them by mail. They needed the thousand bookshops. And finally, they needed a broader, stronger tradition of literary craftsmanship.[95]

91 Diary of W. P. Ballinger, Univ. of Texas Archives.
92 Unidentified MS memoir of Hunter in Va. State Library.
93 Hunter Papers, Univ. of Va.
94 Wade, *Longstreet*, 298ff.
95 Cf. "Literary Prospects of the South," *Russell's Magazine*, June, 1858.

Southern magazines operated under the same disabilities. The *Southern Review*, founded in 1828, published some able contributions by Legaré, Thomas Cooper, Stephen Elliott, and others, but perished within five years. The *Southern Literary Messenger*, begun in 1834, had two editors of ability, Poe and John R. Thompson. In quality it possibly compared with the *Knickerbocker* or *Graham's*, but not with the *Atlantic* or *Putnam's*. And whatever its quality, it made little appeal to Southerners themselves. The Charleston *Courier* remarked in 1849 that a copy was occasionally seen on the shelves of very literary gentlemen, but among the great mass of readers very rarely.[96] "I must say to you," wrote Thompson to C. R. Lanman in 1850, "that the highest rate of compensation that I allow for articles in the *Messenger* is $2 per page"— and most writers got seventy-five cents or a dollar.[97] By a brave effort in the spring of 1857, a little Charleston group launched *Russell's Magazine* as a rival to the *Atlantic*. The genial inspiration of Simms and his two literary disciples, Paul H. Hayne and Timrod, gave afflatus to the sails while the money of John Russell, proprietor of the well-known bookshop, helped keep it afloat. Though it contained the best interpretation of Southern thought and feeling, its life was to be short, and at no time did it come within sight of its scudding Northern antagonist.[98] The *Southern Quarterly Review* was printing three thousand copies in 1854, but it labored under heavy pecuniary embarrassments, and though its editor J. D. B. De Bow wrote that it represented "the last attempt to establish and build up Southern Literature,"[99] its influence was slight.

The trait which most heavily stamped Southern literature, whether in books or magazines, was its polemic or defensive quality. Literary expression in the

96 October 23, 1849. According to the *Courier*, in Montgomery, Ala., only one copy of the *Southern Quarterly Review* was being taken.
97 Many of Thompson's letters, scattered through various collections, are pathetic. He wrote Edwin De Leon in 1848 that only five copies went to Columbia, S. C., where De Leon was an active journalist. Could not De Leon obtain ten or fifteen new subscribers, keep the money, and in return write at the rate of one dollar a page? In 1851 he sent word that he was going south on a canvassing trip. "This step is most reluctantly taken and is assuredly disagreeable enough, but the *Messenger*, entre nous, is in dire need of accessions and it must be done. Surely, the Southern people will not suffer their only literary magazine to go down at the present juncture of affairs!" October 31, 1848, January 30, 1851; De Leon Papers, South Caroliniana Library.
  Again, he wrote John P. Kennedy in 1860: "The *Messenger*, which I took in better days, has proved a dead loss to me—ever so much money actually sunk, and twelve years of early manhood spent unprofitably in maintaining it." He was then turning to newspaper work. March 25, 1860; Kennedy Papers.
98 Among other excellent articles, *Russell's Magazine* published during its brief career an extremely able criticism of Bancroft's history; a sound analysis of the character of Poe; Dr. Lieber's introductory lecture to his course on politics in Columbia College; and a valuable account of the rupture in 1830 between Jackson and Calhoun. Much of its matter was in defense of slavery. "The Dual Form of Labor" (October, 1859) is an exhaustive and skilful marshalling of all the justifications and palliations of the institution.
99 September 12, 1854; Claiborne Papers, Miss. Dept. Archives and Hist.

North showed sporadic sectional rancor; in the South this was a preoccupation which became painful. The section felt that with stormclouds lowering over it, every intellect was needed in the war for the defense of her institutions. Simms, finding his romances neglected, said goodbye to them and took up work instead that fostered Southern regard. From the moment of the Wilmot Proviso, his too-abundant literary productions fell into two channels, one of romantic dreams, the other of doctrinaire nightmares.[100] As much could be said for many another writer. With one pen Simms wrote his *Surrey*, and with the other assailed Lorenzo Sabine, a Yankee, for criticizing South Carolina's rôle in the Revolution. With one pen W. J. Grayson wrote his pleasant poetry, and with another a virulent article on "The Edinburgh Reviewer Reviewed." By 1859 Simms was exclaiming on behalf of all Southern writers: "We know but the South, and the South in danger!" [101]

[X]

Altogether, South and North by 1857 were rapidly becoming separate peoples. The major Protestant denominations had broken in twain; one major party, the Whigs, had first split in half and then disappeared; press, pulpit, and education all showed a deepening cleavage. With every passing year, the fundamental assumptions, tastes, and cultural aims of the two sections became more divergent. As tension grew, militant elements on both sides resented the presence of "outsiders"; Southerners were exposed to insult at Northern resorts, while Yankees in the South were compelled to explain their business to a more and more suspicious population.

The Southerners loved the Union, for their forefathers had helped build it, and the gravestones of their patriot soldiers strewed the land. But they wanted a Union in which they could preserve their peculiar institutions, ancient customs, and well-loved ways of life and thought. They knew that all the main forces of modern society were pressing to create a more closely unified nation, and to make institutions homogeneous even if not absolutely uniform. Against this they recoiled; they wanted a hegemony, a loose confederacy, not a unified nation and a standardized civilization. They regarded the Union as an association of sovereign States and an alliance of regions that possessed national attributes. The North wishes to dictate to us on the slavery question, wrote Simms in 1852.[102] "But we are a people, *a nation*, with arms in our hands, and in sufficient

100   These are the phrases of W. P. Trent in his *Simms*, ch. 6.
101   *Op. cit.*, 249. As another evidence of the diversion of letters into political channels, note that in Wade's *Longstreet* the eighth chapter deals with "General Literary Effort in Georgia"; the twelfth with "Ecclesiastical Controversy Over Slavery."
102   Trent, *Simms*, 174; italics mine.

numbers to compel the respect of *other nations;* and we shall never submit the case to the judgment of *another people,* until they show themselves of superior virtue and intellect."

This schism in culture struck into the very substance of national life. Differences of thought, taste, and ideals gravely accentuated the misunderstandings caused by the basic economic and social differences; the differences between a free labor system and a slave labor system, between a semi-industrialized economy of high productiveness and an agrarian economy of low productiveness. An atmosphere was created in which emotions grew feverish; in which every episode became a crisis, every jar a shock.

The sands were running out. A few years more remained in which the national fabric might be reknit stronger than ever—if statesmanship were adequate to the task. But Congress had become an arena of constant sectional strife. Pierce had let the Presidency be drawn into the vortex of passion. And in the first weeks of 1857 brief warning items about the case of one Dred Scott began to appear in the press; a case on which the Supreme Court was soon to make a momentous pronouncement. Through the clash and clangor of the times men seemed to hear an ominous note of the future:

"So fierce you whirr and pound you drums—so shrill you bugles blow."

3.

EXPECTATIONS WERE that President Buchanan would uphold national unity, but party unity was another matter. Nevins characterizes Buchanan as being endowed with industry, capacity, and tact, but at the same time he was irresolute, timid, pliable, and self-seeking.[1] He dreaded the thought of secession. His largely Southern cabinet used him, he did not use it.[2]

In March of 1857 the Supreme Court held that a slave, Dred Scott, had no constitutional rights to sue in Federal courts for his freedom, despite the fact that he had resided for a time in free states. Chief Justice Roger Taney held that under the Constitution slaves were not citizens, and therefore Congress had no power either to enact the Missouri Compromise setting a geographical limitation to slavery or to exclude slavery from the territories.

Abolitionists, free-soilers, and most Republicans were aghast, and this "antagonism to the judgment of the Court never subsided. It soon crystallized, for Republicans and Douglas Democrats alike, in a simple refusal to accept the decision as binding upon anyone save the poor black man whose plea had evoked it." [3] Also, it gave the more extreme elements in the South a judicial basis for protection of slavery.

Political skies were more than cloudy, and quite suddenly the panic of 1857 was upon the land. While it was among the lesser financial convulsions, "it may be doubted whether any other, in its implications and consequences, was so fateful." [4] The most telling results were perhaps psychological, though social and political consequences were certainly important. Discontent, radical agitation, and lack of prestige in the administration were all present, as was the increased self-confidence of the South with its belief that its products were indispensable to the world. The depression exacerbated the deepening North-South chasm.

At the same time the issue of slavery in Kansas created a distinct break between Senator Douglas on the one hand and Buchanan and the South on the other. Douglas was now standing firm on popular sovereignty, though it won him the animosity of a large segment of his party. To Nevins, Douglas "had been a great Democratic chieftain; now he was to be a great American leader." [5] While Kansas remained, after all the struggle in that state, largely free, the crisis "left a sinister general heritage in the enhancement of sectional ill-will, and a specific legacy of evil in the Democratic schism." The issue also brought to the forefront the fact that, although the West was generally unsuited to slavery, "its future could not be assured until the contest over slavery was settled." [6]

During these years of crisis the general attitude of the people, the changes in its leadership, the pulse of the nation must be observed to understand the 1850s.

NOTES

1. Nevins, *The Emergence of Lincoln,* Vol. I, *Douglas, Buchanan, and Party Chaos, 1857–1859,* pp. 62–63.
2. *Ibid.,* p. 79.
3. *Ibid.,* p. 115.
4. *Ibid.,* p. 176.
5. *Ibid.,* p. 249.
6. *Ibid.,* pp. 303–304.

Moods, Attitudes, and Leaders

WHEN AN explorer on an unknown river finds the current quickening under his boat, hears a faint but increasing roar, and sees above the farthest treetops a mist of spray, he knows that he is nearing a cataract. Yet if he is bold, if his craft is strong, and if on a prosperous voyage he has already shot other foaming rapids with success, he may push blithely into the unknown, confident that he can override all dangers.

A bold temperament, a blithe outlook—these we can better understand if we glance at the exuberant American nation in the mid-century.

Few decades in our history are more easily misinterpreted than that between the Compromise of 1850 and the election of Lincoln. An excessive emphasis on politics has led most observers to regard the period too exclusively as one of turmoil and uncertainty. It is true that the mounting antislavery agitation and the problems left by the Mexican War had brought the republic into white waters of political peril. Yet, in any broad view, the period stands conspicuous for a peaceful growth and prosperity greater than any that Americans had previously seen. All the territorial gains of the past decade were being consolidated. The dazzled nation, when the fifties began, was just beginning to realize that it held a permanent frontage on the Pacific and was neighbor to the Orient. By 1860, California had become one of the wealthiest of the States; Oregon had fixed her star in the flag; a frenzied horde of miners (with sober settlers on their heels) had made the name of Colorado familiar. From Montana glaciers to New Mexican deserts, sharp-eyed prospectors were scattering into a thousand mountain pockets. Minnesota, her wheatfields waving red, had pushed into the Union; while the farmers of Kansas were knocking at the door. The industrial revolution was gaining momentum in the North. The South exulted in the apparently insatiable demand of the world for its staples.

This was a more restless period than any before known. The energy of the fast-growing population channeled itself into countless outlets—business, trade, politics, reform, religion, letters, art. But the thrust was strongest toward materialistic objects. Already lusty and opulent, the nation instinctively reached for

(*The Emergence of Lincoln*, Vol. I, *Douglas, Buchanan and Party Chaos, 1857–1859*, Chapter 1.)

greater strength and greater riches. Walt Whitman was soon to define in *Democratic Vistas* the two grand preparation stages of America, and to emphasize the fact that the country was in the midst of the second. The first had been "the planning and putting on record the political foundation rights of immense masses of people;" the second (in which these masses were now healthfully immersed) was the creation of "material prosperity, wealth, produce, labor-saving machines, iron, cotton, local, State, and continental railways, intercommunication and trade with all lands, steamships, mining, general employment, organization of great cities, cheap appliances for comfort, numberless technical schools, books, newspapers. . . ."

Critics complained that the land was much too materialistic, too intent on selfish aggrandizement. "We speculate how to get rich; we build railroads and ships, to increase our stores; we spy out the neighboring lands which promise us luxurious harvests hereafter"—so exclaimed a writer in *Putnam's Magazine* in the fall of 1855.[1] Once men had dreamed of a high destiny for the young land, fresh and unpolluted from the hand of its Creator; now, he wrote, the spirit of Timour-Mammon was in the ascendent. But such reflections, however natural to a cultivated New Yorker, did not occur to citizens of St. Paul and Sacramento, which had not existed when the Mexican War ended and were thriving towns in 1860; they did not occur to hustlers who lifted Michigan during the decade to third place in iron ore production; they did not occur to the speculators and toilers who created a new industry in Pennsylvania petroleum. These men were too busy to worry about Timour-Mammon. No such reflections occurred to the Southerners who knew the arguments of David Christy's *Cotton Is King* without reading the book, and who agreed that the $200,000,000 cotton crop of 1858–59 was an indispensable pillar of world economy. "Take from New York, or Boston, or Philadelphia, for one month, Southern exports and Southern trade, and widespread ruin and disaster would follow." [2]

The sunshine of economic prosperity bathed the country throughout the decade, as indeed it bathed the whole Western World. If one brief panic occurred, it was little more than the reaction against too reckless an advance. Great Britain, with her middle classes established in full power, her technological revolution almost completed, and the Peel-Russell system of free trade benefiting manufacturers, merchants, and consumers alike, was enjoying one of the golden ages of her history. Her wealth and prestige had never been greater. Louis Napoleon, proclaiming at Bordeaux in 1852, "L'Empire, c'est la paix," was developing railways, canals, and harbors, half-rebuilding Paris and other cities, encouraging iron mills and textile factories, and by other ostentatious activities assuring

1 *Putnam's Magazine*, "The Kansas Question," October, 1855.
2 New Orleans *Picayune*, September 10, 1859.

employment to artisans and shopkeepers. Prussia and Bavaria, which witnessed an astonishing multiplication of business corporations in this decade, were beginning the creation of industrial Germany. Gold from California and Australia helped force the draught of economic activity. Even the brief wars in which Napoleon, Cavour, and Victor Emmanuel so blithely embarked did something to stimulate production and trade in America.

Vast numbers of people in the Western nations were acquiring wealth; and, in Europe and the United States alike, prosperity bred self-confidence, and egotism engendered an aggressive temper. It was not difficult to measure the arrogance of the British ruling classes which, under the leadership of Palmerston, supported war in the Crimea, applauded Lord Elgin's capture of Peking, and avenged the Sepoy Mutiny, while the arrogance of the French bourgeoisie and the gilt-and-tinsel nobility of the Second Empire was written large in Napoleon's exploits at Magenta and Solferino. Plenty of arrogance was always latent in Prussia. Nor was there any lack of self-assurance and arrogance in the United States. Many Northern businessmen, politicians, and lawyers—the Caleb Cushings, Ben Wades, and Zack Chandlers—after pushing to success in highly competitive fields, deemed themselves capable of solving any problem whatsoever. Their bumptiousness impressed foreign travelers; they were ready to teach the world.[3] Slaveholding planters and politicians meanwhile assured their section that it possessed a superior culture and gentility. Such men as John Slidell, Howell Cobb, and Robert Toombs believed the South the main support of the world's economy. Southerners took pride in Senator James H. Hammond's "Cotton is King" speech—a speech summarized in his boast in 1859 that they were "at this moment unquestionably the most prosperous people on earth, realizing ten to twenty per cent on their capital with every prospect of doing as well for a long time to come;"[4] and their consciousness of material success made them stubbornly insistent on having their own way.

In a period of expansion and explosion, this hardening of temper, this strutting egotism of the self-made and newly rich, carried distinct dangers. Both North and South, large bodies of pushing, successful men were more ready to bluff their way, spurn compromises, and trust to luck than if times had been sterner and failure more frequent. The principal reason why a different outlook was needed lay in the dangerous divisions of the land.

---

3 Hear D. W. Mitchell on the Northerner: "His mind is always at work, engaged seriously on something useful or profitable; and he wears himself out with unceasing anxious thought about gaining and saving. . . . The most serious faults in his character are too much thought of his own personal independence and dignity, too much jealousy of any superiority, and an unduly excited pride and ambition." *Ten Years in the United States* (1862), pp. 194, 195.

4 James Hammond to W. G. Simms, April 22, 1859, Hammond Papers, LC.

[I]

Silently and irresistibly, the ferments released by the materialistic forces of the time were emphasizing the differences among the three great American sections, the East, Northwest, and South. The industrial revolution was well advanced in the East. From the Penobscot to the Potomac, railroads were scarring the fields, factories banking the streams, streets of offices replacing village lanes. A proletariat, largely immigrant, was being created. The sensational cheap press, the ward boss, the rooming houses and parochial schools, the saloon, the labor union, the baseball nine, the slum, all furnished tokens of a novel culture. Radical leaders, especially after the panic of 1857, were lifting demands for new economic rights, the freedoms earlier preached by William Leggett, George Henry Evans, and Elizur Wright. In New England and the North Atlantic States, the great middle class of yeomen farmers, village artisans and storekeepers, and small professional men was still solidly in control of affairs; but this body was increasingly conscious of the growing number of unpropertied, unrooted, and restless wage earners.

While Atlantic coastal communities were yielding to urbanization and the mill whistle, the sway of the frontier in other parts of the half-empty continent was being extended. The great West, a beckoning terrain in which freemen might plant their farms and shops, was in many essential traits precisely what the West had been since colonial days. It was a region of plentiful opportunity and general prosperity, with unrestrained individual energy, much speculative optimism, faith in the common man (and woman), stubborn insistence on political and social equality, and strong national loyalties. Yet the West was changing. It developed primary and even secondary industries with astonishing rapidity, so that by 1860 many communities from Milwaukee to Cincinnati, from Quincy to Ashtabula, were becoming fairly homogeneous with the factory cities of Pennsylvania and Massachusetts. The second or third generation farmer in the West was much more conscious than his father of the importance of foreign markets. Farming for profit, not subsistence, he was more of a businessman and more alert to see his margin of profit defended. Railways, speedy mails, cheap periodicals, and lyceums placed the Hoosier township in the heart of progressive nineteenth century culture.

The egalitarian radicalism of the frontier had always possessed a strong kinship with the radicalism of the town-bred worker. A highly democratic temper marked the farm and village population of the upper Mississippi Valley in these years. This body of Americans was not at all revolutionary-minded; rather it was distinctly moderate on economic and political issues. Yet it felt itself in the

forefront of an advancing western civilization, it disliked aristocratic stratifica-
tions, and it was impatient with outworn and obsolescent ideas. The *Prairie
Farmer* of John S. Wright well expressed the temper of the Northwest. It carried
on incessant campaigns against land speculation, dishonest produce grading, and
poor roads. It demanded crop diversification, soil analysis, and better farm implements. It proclaimed its belief in a democratic population of small landholders
busy making the most creative use possible of their acres. Farmers of the Middle
West might indict slavery mildly as Wright did, or attack it sternly as his fellow
leader Jonathan B. Turner did; but all were instinctively hostile to the great
planters of the South.[5]

Though the South was by no means static in any absolute sense, it seemed so
by comparison with the North and West. The basic elements of its economic
life were merely soil, climate, and low-skilled labor. While large bodies of
farmers in the border regions and uplands closely resembled their Northwestern
brethren, in plantation areas the way of life was hostile to variegation and
progress. The ruling class of Southerners (and it was a *class*) clung to the aristocratic and conservative ideals which the North and West instinctively disliked.
As Northern capital, technology, and labor-saving machinery forced the pace
of industry, the gulf between the sections grew deeper. Those who crossed the
Potomac felt they were entering a foreign land. According to his predilections,
the traveler might pronounce one side or the other superior; he might agree or
disagree with De Tocqueville, who had found the Kentucky bank of the Ohio
River ill-populated and half-tilled, while the Northern shore was marked by
abundant harvests, elegant dwellings, and the confused hum of industry;[6] he
might discover more taste and charm among the slaveholders; but the essential
fact was the difference. It grew from year to year. Like the differences between
the industrial and rural areas of England depicted in Mrs. Gaskell's *North and
South*, it created two sharply divergent populations; the people (when the
novelists came to discover them) of Thomas Nelson Page and George W. Cable
on one side, and of Howells and Hamlin Garland on the other.

Numerous exceptions to the rule of sectional contrast, and many cross-
currents in the broad flow of tendencies, could of course be noted.

Democratic change was by no means wholly victorious in the North, where

5 "I know, and you know, that a revolution has begun. Twenty Senators and a hundred
Representatives proclaim in Congress today, sentiments and opinions, and principles of freedom, which hardly so many men, even in this free State, dared to utter in their homes
twenty years ago. While the Government of the United States has been all that time sur-
rendering one plain and castle after another to slavery, the people of the United States have
been no less steadily and perseveringly gathering together all the forces with which to
recover back again all the fields, and all the castles, which have been lost." Seward's
Rochester speech, 1858 (*Works*, II, 352).

6 De Tocqueville, *Democracy*, Part 1, Ch. 18.

powerful conservative and aristocratic elements could be found. A landed gentry flourished in the valleys of the Hudson, Genesee, and Susquehanna. In Boston, New York, and Philadelphia the merchant groups were inveterately cautious. From these, and from the new founders of industrial dynasties, millionaires were emerging. Already proud mansions were numerous in the Northern cities. Meanwhile, moderate public men of the type of Edward Everett, Rufus Choate, Hamilton Fish, and John A. Dix strove to prevent the new wine from splitting the old bottles. The North had important elements which preferred the good old ways and the aristocratic approach, which tacitly disliked egalitarianism and the consent-of-the-governed theory, and which took a chilly attitude toward talk of reforms and rights.

Again, in parts of the South, frontier radicalism was as strong as on the borders of Iowa and Wisconsin. Albert Gallatin Brown championed the small farmers of southern and eastern Mississippi against the planting interest of the river country. Reform had its intrepid champions like Daniel R. Goodloe of North Carolina, Cassius M. Clay of Kentucky, and "Parson" Brownlow of Tennessee, while the non-slaveholding whites found numerous voices for their discontent—Hinton Rowan Helper's was only the loudest.

The political and social psychology of the city masses in the North, and especially the Irish and Germans who fell naturally into the Democratic Party, offered an interesting field for study. The followers of Fernando Wood in New York, for example, tenement dwellers without culture or capital, toilers given a reckless temper by their harsh struggle for bread, immigrants resentful of the airs and ease of the richer classes, tended to align themselves against the conservative forces of the North. Yet, just because they hated many features of their environment, they were ready to join hands with aristocratic Southern leaders. Rejecting one form of privilege, they accepted alliance with another.

While confusion, conflict, and incongruity were to be found in every section, and while it would be a fatal error to personify North, South, and West with any idea that they represented unified and unchanging entities, the gulf between free-labor and slave-labor societies was real and deep. What Turner has said of the frontier West was true of the South; it was "a form of society rather than an area." Its special psychology, traditions, and principles ran far back into history. The doctrines of the Virginia school on State Rights and strict construction, crystallized by Madison and Jefferson in the Resolutions of 1798–99, continued to find a wide acceptance. The Richmond *South* affirmed in 1857 that these tenets were still as popular in theory as when first expounded, though in practice they commanded less observance; and the hostile *National Intelligencer* agreed that this was so. Many Southerners felt a deep-seated injury in the "centralizing" tendencies of the national government, and in a long succession of measures enacted since Hamilton had prepared his *Report on Manufactures*.[7] Calhoun's literary executor, R. K. Crallé, and ex-Governor Hammond in 1857 stirred up the Southern Rights Associations of the various slaveholding States to lay before Congress a detailed list of the acts which had operated injuriously on the interests and security of the section; and it was with Hamilton that they began.[8] Aggrieved elements in the South, conscious of their peculiar character and interests, had considered radical action in 1798, more radical action in 1832, and still more radical action in 1850. A belief that consolidated power spelt danger had become deeply ingrained.

North and South had always, from early colonial days, found difficulty in understanding each other. William Byrd of Virginia and John Winthrop of Massachusetts Bay had approached life from totally different points of view. By 1830 the divergent psychologies of the two sections presented the most serious obstacles to mutual comprehension. What an Alabamian meant by "liberty" and "democracy" was something very different from what a New Yorker meant by those terms. The Southerner's liberty was more restricted, and his democracy had to be reconciled with a more patrician leadership. "Self-government" had connotations in the Illinois of Lincoln and Douglas quite unlike those it carried in the South Carolina of Calhoun and Pickens.

Perhaps the word "Union," which a European might have supposed could have but one meaning, best illustrated the differences in state of mind. The Yankee and the Westerner thought of the Union with the high emotional fervor which they had learned from Daniel Webster. They thrilled to the term with an intense spirit of nationality, a passionate attachment to the republic as a whole, a conviction that the people must stand as a unit in defense of national honor and freedom. If Union died, liberty died with it. Jackson, Webster, Benton, and Clay had inculcated an ideal of the Union which imparted a grand devotion to the uprising of the North in 1861. The dominant elements of the Lower South held quite a different conception. Their Union had to be yoked with State Rights; it was, next to their sectional liberties, most dear. As a Southern publicist put it, they clung to Calhoun's definition of the Union: "a peculiar association in which sovereign States were held by high considerations of good faith; by the exchanges of equity and comity; by the noble attractions of social order; by the enthused sympathies of a common destiny of power, honor, and renown." [9]

Naturally, the South thought of itself more and more as a separate nation. By 1857 it *was* in many ways a separate nation. Had secession been crowned with success, historians would have said what John Adams wrote of American

7 Richmond *South*, quoted in *National Intelligencer*, April 30, 1857.
8 R. K. Crallé, Columbia, S. C., to Hammond, December 4, 1857; Hammond Papers, LC.
9 Edward A. Pollard, *The Lost Cause*, 52, 53.

withdrawal from the Empire, that separation was a fact before fighting began. Many Northerners wished to recognize the separation. "So perish all compromises with tyranny!" exclaimed Garrison as at Framingham on July 4, 1854, he burned a copy of the Constitution; and he ceaselessly proclaimed in the *Liberator* that but one honest course was open—"The Union must be dissolved!" Southern radicals talked of the South as if it were another Holland under the Spaniards, another Lombardy under the Austrians. "Ireland *would* be free and independent, if she *could*," wrote one of Senator Hammond's Charleston friends; "the South *could* be, if she *would*. It is because of this opinion, that I would urge the straight and open policy of Disunion, and on its general merits. I only want a pretext to announce and enter upon it—such would be the election of an Abolitionist or protectionist." [10]

The extent to which the South cherished the ideal of separate nationality was demonstrated in the resolutions of the Southern Commercial Convention which met at Savannah in the month following Buchanan's election. Not merely did this body call for direct trade with Europe in place of the "triangular trade" which had enriched New York, and for the construction by the Southern States and Territories of a railroad from the Mississippi by way of El Paso to the Pacific; not merely did it urge the Kentucky legislature to build the final Louisville-Cumberland Gap link in the railroads connecting the Potomac and Mississippi: the Convention went far beyond such measures. It wanted Southern ships built in Southern yards, and Southern seamen trained in large numbers by Southern States. It created a committee of Southern scholars, including William Holmes McGuffey, Augustus Baldwin Longstreet, the historian Gayarré, and the scientist Joseph LeConte, to prepare a series of distinctively Southern texts in every department of study, which Southern legislatures might then order used in the schools. It asked for the encouragement of Southern periodicals, books, and institutions of learning. It exhorted the States to see to the establishment of foundries for casting artillery and arsenals for the manufacture of arms—for the South was to be armed as a separate nation. In the same spirit, it directed Southern Representatives in Congress to inquire whether their States had received due quotas of arms, and to see to it that Southern ports were amply equipped for defense.[11]

Gradually, upon many Southern eyes, had dawned the splendid vision of a republic stretching from Cape Hatteras to the Gulf of California, a nation with a future boundless as the hopes of its people. The South that had produced Washington, Jefferson, and Marshall, whose sons had generally held the Presidency, the chief justiceship, and the control of the Senate, would surely con-

10 John Cuningham to Hammond, Charleston, April 18, 1859; Hammond Papers, LC.
11 *Proceedings*, December, 1856; pamphlet, 48 pp.

tinue to exhibit a rich political genius. This new republic would have a historical tradition, a culture, and an economy all its own. Under the bright sun of independence its dormant gifts would quicken into life. Its harbors would nourish a vigorous commerce, its capital would make laws suiting its peculiar conditions, and its wealth would go to developing its own resources. Architects greater than Latrobe, sculptors more talented than Clark Mills, authors more original than Poe and Simms, orators transcending Henry and Calhoun would arise to express its spiritual greatness. Let the latent energies of the South find outlets under the spur of nationalism—let it show what a defiant people could accomplish. A record equalling that of Greece under Pericles and England under Elizabeth might be written by the free and happy people whose domain embraced the plantations of Virginia and South Carolina, the pine-shaded savannahs of Georgia, the bluegrass farms of Kentucky, the mountains and waterfalls of Tennessee, the iron and coal mines of Alabama, the sugar-cane fields of Louisiana, and the cattle-dotted plains of Texas. Their past role in the political and military annals of America was ample guarantee for accomplishment in the future.

While the South had the dream, the North and West had realities. They had the steady growth of industrial power, which meant wealth and higher living standards; more immigration, and a faster increase in population; the wider areas suited to their free-labor system. The spirit of the modern world was reinforcing their demand for the containment of slavery, which was sure to be followed by demands for its regulation or gradual elimination. For the nation as a whole, irresistible economic pressures were strengthening free society. Resist it as the South might, the movement for tariffs, free homesteads, agricultural education, internal improvements, and a better banking system could not long be withstood; halt the thrust one year, and the next it had enhanced force. By 1860 it was plain that if the country held together, every forward step would strengthen the free society as against the slave society.

[II]

Among the manifold causes of division or divergence of interest—tariffs, public lands, ship subsidies, internal improvements, immigration, the Pacific railroad, Federal powers—the issue of slavery remained fundamental. Could the problems of the labor system and racial adjustment in the South have been solved, all other discords might have proved transient. Year by year the slavery question intensified the conflict, increased the misunderstanding, and heightened the prejudice. By the eighteen-fifties the aura of emotion which surrounded it was so dense that no one could view it without distortion. The emotion was compounded of many elements—suspicion, contempt, anger, but above all fear. In many quarters both North and South it had generated a mass hysteria. No comprehension of the later fifties is possible unless we realize that this emotional tension, this hysteria, magnified every incident to portentous size.

Each side, according to its convictions, was right. The South thought slavery a positive good—and in one sense it *was* a positive good. The Negro was better off on a well-managed Southern holding than anywhere else on earth; better off than in Africa, the West Indies, Brazil, or (arguably) some free-Negro settlements of the North. "Oh, dey ain't no place in de worl' like Ole Virginny for niggers, massa," an intelligent sailor-slave told Olmsted.[12] The North thought slavery a positive evil—and except as a transitional status, it *was* a positive evil. The essence of the dispute between the two sections may be found in Robert Toombs's statement of 1856 in Tremont Temple, Boston. "The white is the superior race," said Toombs, "and the black the inferior; and subordination, with or without law, will be the status of the African in this mixed society; and, therefore, it is in the interests of both, and especially of the black race, and of the whole society, that this status should be fixed, controlled, and protected by law." [13] Most Southerners regarded this as unanswerable logic. Most Northerners would have declared that the moment the major premise, the assumption of racial inferiority, was disproved, the argument collapsed; and even accepting the premise, the question was, *what* status? A fixed status, or an evolutionary status? The latter alone was tolerable.

Logic counted for little, however, in the prevalent hysteria. A deep sense of crisis now pervaded the air. Emotion not merely magnified every collision; it made recurrent collisions inevitable. The Brooks-Sumner assault, the Lecompton battle, the John Brown raid were essentially symptoms, not detached realities. To fasten attention primarily upon them would be as erroneous as to fancy that the rocks in the bed of the Niagara rapids, throwing spray into the air, are the primary force rather than the weight of water pouring torrentially down the gorge. Fundamental loyalties are always a matter of emotion; and these were now so challenged as to create in both North and South a sharp sense of fear— fear among Northerners that slavery would be made universal, fear among Southerners that four million slaves would be suddenly freed amid such scenes of violence and rapine as Haiti had witnessed.

The slaveholding States, a Southern woman resident in Philadelphia wrote in 1851, were slumbering upon a volcano. "It is a truth; every day's information, every paper you take up, teems with the same news—the constant warfare

---

12 F. L. Olmsted, *A Journey through the Seaboard Slave States*, 107.
13 W. W. Brewton, *The Son of Thunder*, gives the entire lecture of Toombs on slavery, 218–249.

against us from North, East, West; and all the haters, too, they are sending their
inflamed missiles against us; all, all about slavery and the slave bill. What are we
to do if the South goes on sleeping?" Five years later, even though Buchanan had
just been elected, Governor James H. Adams of South Carolina anticipated
Seward by declaring the conflict irrepressible:

> Slavery and Freesoilism can never be reconciled. Our enemies have been
> defeated—not vanquished. A majority of the free States have declared war
> against the South, upon a purely sectional issue, and in the remainder of them,
> formidable minorities fiercely contended for victory under the same banner.
> The triumph of this geographical party must dissolve the confederacy, unless
> we are prepared to sink down into a state of acknowledged inferiority. We will
> act wisely to employ the interval of repose afforded by the late election, in
> earnest preparation for the inevitable conflict. The Southern States have never
> demanded more than equality and security. They cannot submit to less, and
> remain in the Union, without dishonor and ultimate ruin.[14]

The violence of 1856 in Washington and in Kansas propagated a feeling that
violence might soon become general. That common-sense Yankee, Henry
Wilson, telling a friend early the next year of the constant threats offered him,
said he never left his lodging to go to his Senate seat without wondering whether
his papers were arranged as he should wish if he were never to return alive.[15]
Wendell Phillips had thought just after the passage of the Kansas-Nebraska Act
that the aggressive Slave Power was now in full control of the government. It
would seize Cuba within a year or two, annex Mexico within five, and attempt
to reopen the slave trade. Indeed, the future unfolded a vast slave empire united
with Brazil and darkening the whole Western Hemisphere. Only one remedy
existed—disunion: "it is now with nine-tenths only a question of time."[16]
Theodore Parker was soon to tell Bostonians that the time had gone by when
the great American question of the nineteenth century could be settled without
bloodshed, while Thomas Wentworth Higginson was to ask concerning slavery:
"Is it destined, as it began in blood, so to end? Seriously and solemnly I say, it
seems as if it were."[17] The continuous intensification of fear and hatred came out
horrifyingly in the letters exchanged by Lydia Maria Child and Governor Henry
A. Wise just after John Brown's raid in 1859. Mrs. Child wrote scathingly of
the "slave oligarchy" and its "continual success in aggression," while Wise
assured her that he would not let Virginians insult even a woman "who whetted
knives of butchery for our mothers, sisters, daughters, and babes."[18]

14 James H. Adams, *Governor's Message*, November 24, 1856.
15 *Letters of Lydia Maria Child*, 88, 89.
16 F. J. and W. P. Garrison, *Wm. Lloyd Garrison*, III, 410–412.
17 *Ibid.*, 472; T. W. Higginson, May 11, 1858; Theodore Parker, May 26, 1858.
18 *Letters of Lydia Maria Child*, 103–116.

The Slave Power, the Freesoil Power—each feared the other, and each mistook defensive postures for aggression. The question of the ultimate source of political power was obviously involved, and it presented a fundamental issue. Edmund Ruffin spoke for a multitude of apprehensive slaveholders when in the spring of 1857 he predicted that Kansas would soon come in free, that other Territories would hold the same complexion, and that, probably within twenty years, three-fourths of the States would be freesoil. Slavery would then be extinguished either directly or indirectly. The North had no such apprehension that increasing population and wealth would make its enemies irresistible. Its fear was that the South, already holding undisputed possession of the official strongholds of government, directing the Executive, managing the Legislative, and keeping in reserve the Judicial department, would continue to rule by intimidation and manipulation—and would use its power in reckless territorial expansion. Charles Francis Adams, a man as moderate as he was shrewd, told the South in 1855 just why his section was deeply worried:

This slave power consists, in fact, of about three hundred and fifty thousand active men, spreading over a large territorial surface, commanding the political resources of fifteen States directly, and, through their connections, materially affecting those of five or six more. These persons, and all their numerous friends and dependents, in and out of the slaveholding region, are held together in interest by a common bond, in the sum of two thousand million dollars worth of what they consider property. For the sake of protecting this against the prevailing tendencies of the age, and the effect of public sentiment created by a large body of their own countrymen, it is impossible that they should escape adopting a system of policy aggressive upon the rights of the freemen. They become, in their action, to all intents and purposes, men of one idea. This idea necessarily includes the extension of their own power, whether they are sensible of its influence in that direction or not. They throw into the public councils their allotted portion of representatives, all equally pledged to be faithful to it, whatever they may think upon other subjects. The unity of policy thus secured for all the time spreads its influence far beyond the limits of its own circle. It is always at hand to wield an umpirage in its own favor, between the contending factions and the rival aspirations of prominent statesmen of the free states. It never relaxes in its vigilance over public events. It never is turned aside by the temptation of an incidental pursuit. The sense of danger overrides every other consideration. Around it have been arrayed, for its protection, alike the conservative and the destructive elements of society in the free States—the richest and the poorest class, the best citizens and the worst: the former from an instinctive dread of anything that looks like an attack upon prescriptive rights to property; the latter from an adhesion to the superiority of caste, the more tenacious by reason of the sense of self-degradation in every other particular.

In addition to all this, it must be admitted that the best abilities of the people in the slaveholding region are enlisted in the defence of their rights. There is no path to distinction but that of public life, and that path leads but one way.

Literature, science, and mechanical invention lag far behind, relatively to the progress they make elsewhere. Commerce and navigation are managed by the citizens of the free States; agriculture, by the slaves. With slaveholders, the mind must either lie fallow in sensuality and indolence, or it must seek its exercise in politics directed to one end—the support of slavery. As a consequence, the representation of the slave power in the federal councils becomes one of more than average capacity, of trained experience, of substantial harmony in the adaptation of means to ends, and last, but not least, of quite flexible public morality.[19]

That Adams's arguments possessed force was admitted by some Southerners. A Louisiana planter who contributed to *De Bow's Review* in 1856 an article deprecating the "artificial" Southern passion of fear and excitement, denied, in correspondence with De Bow, that all the aggression was on the other side. "Well—admit the two millions interested in slavery—shall they give the law to the other twenty-odd millions? Are not the rights of majorities as sacred as those of minorities?"[20] This planter represented the capitalist and conservative groups which, in both sections, were ready to resist terroristic movements and confess that the great issue had two sides. But as the years slipped by, the issue of ultimate political authority grew more burning. In the final paroxysm of 1860–61, large bodies of Southerners were filled with frenzy at the idea that a hostile Freesoil Power, already seizing control of Presidency and House, might soon gain the Senate, the Judiciary, and a sufficient number of States to pass constitutional amendments. Large bodies of Northerners were grimly implacable in resisting the idea that a compact Slave Power could continue to nullify their numerical majority, and could retain the opportunity of expanding their institutions over wide Caribbean domains. Fear was largely the product of ignorance, and ignorance—or misinformation—largely the product of propaganda.

Two stereotypes were created. Readers of even moderate Northern newspapers found them full of articles on Southern aggressions in Kansas, Southern filibustering enterprises against Cuba and Nicaragua, Southern domination in Washington, and Southern cruelties to slaves. Readers of even moderate journals in the South found them full of items about Northern slums and poverty, Northern exploitations of immigrant labor, Northern incitations to slave revolts, Northern aggressions in Washington and Kansas, and Northern desire to reduce the South to a fiefdom. Little thinking of the time was a process of reasoning from fact-buttressed premises to logical conclusions. Anybody who measures the political conduct of the fifties from such a premise is bound to be as confused as if he were a believer in Ptolemaic astronomy making careful observations of the Copernican heavens. The thinking was largely irrational, governed

19 C. F. Adams, "What Makes Slavery a Matter of National Concern?" Lecture in New York, January 30, 1855, pamphlet.
20 R. B. Brashear, February 8, 1856; De Bow Papers, Duke University.

by subconscious memories, frustrated desires, and the distortions of politicians and editors.

When L. W. Spratt reported to the Southern Commercial Convention at Montgomery in 1858 in favor of reopening the slave trade, he argued that the North already had one more State than the South; that it had six million more people; that not only was its native increase far larger, but it gained hundreds of thousands of immigrants each year; and that without some drastic preventive, it would soon control the fortunes of the South. Northern commentators promptly raised their own cries of fear. The South, they said, having won the right by the Nebraska Act and Dred Scott decision to carry Negroes into the Territories, now wished the slave trade so that she might fill the West with Africans and gain a permanent national ascendancy. Each section saw the other as a wanton attacker, itself as an heroic defender.[21]

"Take an extreme case," wrote the editor of the Nashville *Union and American* in 1859. "Take a South Carolina fire-eater who declares himself ready for disunion and the establishing of a Southern Confederacy rather than submit to the unconstitutional wrongs and aggressions of the North, and what is his offence compared with that of the filthy, fanatical abolitionist, who, regardless of all right and justice, is seeking to *usurp* the control of the government, destroy the equality of the States, and trample in the dust the sacred guarantees of the Constitution? The extremist of the South errs upon policy in resisting oppression. The abolitionist in the North violates a principle of right, justice, and the Constitution." With equal sincerity, the editor of the Warsaw (Illinois) *Bulletin* was accusing the South of grasping at Kansas, seeking to seize Cuba, and smuggling in thousands of slaves. "The South is not satisfied with what she is fairly entitled to under the Constitution. She wants more. She aspires to nothing short of absolute supremacy. . . . On behalf of the interests of freedom, the Republicans in self-defense have been compelled to resist; and thus the contest will go on, until one or the other shall have achieved an undisputed supremacy." [22]

These stereotypes were steadily reinforced. Leaders on each side made frantic efforts to propagandize their own people. During the first five months of the Congressional session of 1857–58, with its critical battle over the Kansas constitution, Senators of the free States franked out six hundred and eight thousand speeches, Senators of the slaveholding States one hundred and thirty thousand. And each side paid inadequate attention to the views of the other section. In the North, few men ever saw *Russell's*, *De Bow's*, and other Southern maga-

---

21 Spratt's report is in *De Bow's Review*, June, 1858. On the danger of exaggerating the rational element in human affairs, see Graham Wallas's *Human Nature in Politics* (3rd ed., 1921).
22 *Union and American*, July 31, 1859; *Bulletin*, July 28, 1859.

zines; still fewer had the liberality of outlook which Lincoln showed in sub-scribing for the Charleston *Mercury* and Richmond *Inquirer* to learn their opinions. As for the South, it lay under two great tabus, criticism of slavery and displays of religious heterodoxy being equally debarred.

A considerable freedom of thought existed in the North, where many Demo-crats expounded Southern political ideas and Bishop John H. Hopkins and Charles O'Conor freely defended slavery. Opinion was much more restricted in the South. Illiteracy, political agitation, and the "black terror" or alleged danger of servile insurrection were deterrents to freedom of discussion. In South Carolina, wrote B. F. Perry, Calhoun had "thought for the State and crushed out all independence of thought in those below him." A Southern bishop, H. B. Whipple, declared that illiteracy rendered the masses the "dupes" of designing politicians, the ignorant being obviously more fanatical than the well-read. Most Southern States had laws which made it a penal offense to cir-culate any newspaper, pamphlet, or handbill having a tendency to excite discon-tent among the slaves. Under such a law, even in Maryland a colored minister was sentenced to ten years in prison in 1857 for possessing a copy of *Uncle Tom's Cabin.* Humboldt complained that, while his *Political Essays on the Island of Cuba* was freely read in Madrid, it could not be purchased in the United States except with the deletion of all passages condemnatory of slavery.[23]

No iron curtain separated the two sections. Travel was free. Southerners by tens of thousands read Harriet Beecher Stowe, while Northerners discussed the Southern polemics. But a gauze curtain did exist, more opaque on the Southern side than the Northern, distorting the vision of all who tried to peer through.

Basically, the struggle lay between two radically different assumptions. The Northern freesoilers assumed that slavery was morally, socially, and econom-ically wrong, and must therefore be presently circumscribed and ultimately dis-solved. The Southern majority assumed that slavery was morally right, eco-nomically profitable, and socially indispensable, and must therefore be protected and allowed to expand. Each side defended its assumption with full conviction of right. To many Northerners it seemed monstrous that a great people could believe slaveholding ethical. To many Southerners it seemed equally monstrous that a great people could forget how recently the North had held slaves, over-look the immense benefits the Negro had received on American soil, and ignore the terrible problem of racial readjustment if black men were hastily freed. This last consideration cut very deep, for many Southerners would readily have admitted that slavery was unfortunate if they had known what racial controls

23 Clement Eaton, *Freedom of Thought in the Old South, passim;* N. Y. *Weekly Tribune,* May 22, 1858, for franking of Congressional speeches; *ibid.,* June 5, 1850, for Humboldt's le ter. The Maryland statute under which the minister was sentenced is in *Md. Laws of 18:5,* Ch. 325.

to put in its place. The South in 1860 had a slave population of 3,949,557. The States of Georgia, Alabama, and Mississippi each had between 435,000 and 465,000 slaves. What helpful steps did the North propose to take in assisting the South to release this ignorant, penniless, and perhaps unruly horde? Massachusetts had a white population about twice as great as Georgia's; for how many liberated Negroes would the Bay State offer homes, employment, and cultural facilities? The answer is that no help whatever was either asked or offered.

In this sectional conflict, as Lincoln said, a crisis had to be reached and passed. The danger point of the crisis would be at hand when one side realized that it must break up the Union, or admit that its basic assumption was no longer tenable. By the late eighteen-fifties, all the forces of the time indicated that the South would have to make this fateful choice. The election of a Republican President, sure to come sooner or later, was the crisis that would have to be reached and passed. If the South reconciled itself to the idea of a Republican Administration, it tacitly accepted the idea that slavery must be contained within the existing limits, and methods studied for its gradual supersedence. The ruling system of the South in 1857 was in the position of the ruling system of France in 1785, or Russia in 1910; it had time for a few more decisions, but it had to think fast and think courageously. A failure to make a decision would be as fatal as an error in deciding.

Yet when the situation demanded the utmost seriousness of thought both North and South, the quarrel over slavery, State Rights, and ultimate power was rendered doubly dangerous by an irresponsible levity among politicians and people. Posturing and finessing were never more recklessly used by leaders than in this period. Senator Hammond, looking about Washington in 1859, found few men who thought for a moment of the good of the country, the maintenance of the Constitution, or even of justice. Shams, filibustering, and crass maneuvering for advantage, he wrote, were the order of the day. "We are not rushing so fast to disunion, as we are to utter anarchy—*at once.*" Many a lover of national concord echoed this observation. The genial essayist Donald Grant Mitchell, writing from Connecticut to his Virginia friend, A. Dudley Mann, declared that he would tenfold rather see the country become two distinct nations than continue listening to the mad abuse. "Has it not come to this, that with you a man must villify the North to gain applause and place; and with us, it is equally essential that a politician must depreciate and calumniate the South?" Rufus Choate, Edward Everett, and Hamilton Fish in one section, William Cabell Rives, W. A. Graham, and John Bell in the other, found that a man who undertook to defend conservative positions lost most of his influence. Rives wrote Washington Hunt of New York in 1859 that too many politicians were inflaming public opinion by taking extreme stands on slavery, that the issue was being used to divert attention from flagrant corruptions, and that if this demagogy were not stopped, disaster would ensue. But what could he do? [24]

Levity was equally evident in the popular attitude toward the price of disunion. Americans had never fought a really bloody war. The only conflict which most men recalled, that against Mexico, had furnished drama, heroism, and solid national gains at an absurdly cheap price. As the crisis deepened, both sections indulged the delusion that peace could always be preserved, while if by bad luck it were broken, the struggle would be brief. Northern men thought that slaveholders who talked secession were raising the old cry of Wolf! Wolf! and that the sight of a bayonet would quiet this bluffing. Southern men thought with the editor, J. D. B. De Bow, that the North could not make war for three good reasons: it lived by Southern trade, and would submit to anything rather than lose these profits; it had no means to make war except what it got by preying on the South; and its people were too divided, half of them taking the Southern side. Others believed that the Yankees were cowardly. They accepted Franklin Pierce's private assurances to Jefferson Davis that a Yankee army marching to attack the South would first have to fight a bloody battle with Northern Democrats. Disbelieving in the possibility of war, the two sections drifted into a position that made war unavoidable. But then war itself held no connotations grimmer than those of New Orleans or Palo Alto; a little gallant fighting, and the other side would give in.

In all periods of prolonged peace, the longing of hot-blooded elements for action, adventure, and power is translated into a readiness to spring to war. Not a little jingoism, to use a later term, might have been discerned in America of the fifties. For one evident reason, more of the lust for martial excitement was abroad in the slaveholding area than in the North. The industrial revolution drained off much of the restless demand of Yankee lads for risk and desperate effort. Young men like Rockefeller, Carnegie, Jay Cooke, and Collis P. Huntington had no need to think of the thunder of cannon and shock of charging cavalry. When war came, they were so busy harnessing the industrial forces of the land that it seemed an interruption of larger enterprises. The young blades growing up on Southern plantations and farms, however, found that politics and pioneering by no means occupied all their energies. Having a romantic bent, they romanticized war! Hence it was that Charles Francis Adams, Jr., living with his father in Washington in 1859–61, thought that a good many proud "Southrons"—Keitt, Porcher Miles, and Roger B. Pryor—were

24 Hammond to W. G. Simms, January 21, 1858, Hammond Papers, LC; D. G. Mitchell to Mann, August 15, 1858, Miscellaneous Files, Duke Univ.; Rives to Hunt, May 19, 1859, Rives Papers.

"spoiling for a fight." [25] As he says, they got their bellyful of it—and so did their opponents.

Basically, what light-hearted Northerners and Southerners lacked in regarding the grim face of Janus was imagination. If by some prevision the chief political leaders could have seen the four years of carnage, the million graves, and the devastation of broad States, they would have drawn back in horror. Could they have glimpsed for one minute the reeking field of Chancellorsville or Gettysburg, they would have acted far more responsibly. Hugh McCulloch writes that a Senator who visited the Wilderness at the close of the battle told him: "If that scene had been presented to me before the war commenced, anxious as I was for the preservation of the Union, I should have said, 'The cost is too great; erring sisters, go in peace.'" Secession had to be resisted; but it would never have occurred had Americans realized what a great war meant.

[III]

The divisions of the country bring us to the question of leadership. The sentiment of the American majority had never lain with the extremists. They had proved that fact in 1850 and 1852. They had proved it again in 1856, when all the Presidential candidates professed moderate principles, and Buchanan, Frémont, and Fillmore so divided the vote that the first-named fell far short of a majority. Where could the nation find the moderate and constructive leaders whom it wished to follow?

In the debate on Pierce's provocative final message in December, 1856, two radicals, Wade of Ohio and Mason of Virginia, hurled defiance at each other. The North was determined, said Wade, to confine slavery to the States where it existed, letting it into no Territory whatever. The South, averred Mason, would tolerate no interference with slavery in the Territories any more than in the States; and for that reason it had been ready, if Frémont had won the election, to break up the Union.[26] This exchange defined the immediate ground of difference. What path could possibly be found between these two opposed views, each powerful if not dominant in its section? The answer lay in mollification, reassurance, and delay. Time, however, was running short. "In the next four years is, I think, locked up the fate of the Union," wrote Jefferson Davis on April 9, 1857. "If the issues are boldly and properly met my hope is that the Constitution will prevail; if the attempt is made to postpone them the next Presidential election will probably bring us to the alternative of resistance to oppressive usurpation or the tame surrender of our birthright." [27]

25 C. F. Adams, Jr., *An Autobiography*, 44, 45; R. G. Osterweis, *Romanticism and Nationalism in the Old South*, 90–94.
26 *Cong. Globe*, 34th Cong., 3rd Sess., 16, 26, 27.
27 To E. De Leon, De Leon Papers, LC.

The hope of peaceful adjustment (for, despite fatalistic interpretations of history, in 1857 such a possibility existed) rested on the chance that statesmanlike leaders would suppress immediate rancors, plead for patience, lay bare the immense difficulties of race adjustment which underlay the slavery issue, show that time was needed for dissolving them, and bring into the foreground those economic issues which were genuinely pressing. The enveloping national prosperity, the materialistic preoccupations of the people, and the rush of energy into continental development, would assist such leaders. Race adjustment, even though some bold initial steps were vital, was a task for generations. The Pacific railroad, the best use of public lands, a fair compromise between Hamiltonian and Jeffersonian schools on the tariff, and the promotion of scientific agriculture, were subjects of immediate urgency. Could the statesmanship be found which would trace a patient way between exigent and distant problems, teaching the electorate to take long views?

All government is a process of experimentation, full of errors and blind gropings; and the use of government to help evolve a new social and economic order, first in the border States and then in the Lower South, would have been a peculiarly delicate and dangerous matter. Still, it was conceivably not beyond the power of a nation which had produced the Revolutionary Fathers. The eminent Americans of the fifties offered a great variety of character and talent; to what men, if any, could the country look for a leadership paralleling that of its formative period?

On careful examination it becomes clear that the old-fashioned effort to put the leaders in this crisis into radical, moderate, and conservative groups is misleading. To be sure, in 1857 any astute observer would have said that Charles Sumner, Ben Wade, John P. Hale, and Zack Chandler, in the North, and Slidell, Toombs, Henry A. Wise, and R. B. Rhett, in the South, were radicals. He would have said that Seward, F. P. Blair, Sr., Lyman Trumbull, and Douglas, in the North, with Jefferson Davis, Judah P. Benjamin, R. M. T. Hunter, and Alexander H. Stephens, in the South, were moderates. He might fairly have termed J. J. Crittenden, Hamilton Fish, Lewis Cass, and Edward Bates conservatives. But such categories, subject to constant revision, are unenlightening. The essential questions with respect to any leader were three: Did he have a firm grasp on principles—on fundamental realities? Did he possess both tact and courage in supporting principles? Above all (and this was the supreme test before which nearly all failed) was he able to appeal to the nation's imagination, its idealism, its sense of a great historic mission?

Seward, short, rusty-looking, his face and head insignificant, his dress antiquated and badly cut, his only outward title to distinction his quickness of perception and heady flow of talk, possessed talents of a high order. Many thought him the first statesman of the land. He was beloved by all who knew him well;

those who saw his affectionate and unselfish deportment in his family circle, his genuine, hearty fellowship with his Auburn neighbors, who gathered about him as freely as the Marshfield farmers had collogued with Webster, were much impressed. His grasp of mind was unquestioned. Carl Schurz thought that he gave an impression of abilities never fully used, of possessing "hidden, occult powers which he could bring into play if he would." His courage had sometimes been conspicuous. Modeling his public career on John Quincy Adams, whose life he had written, he could take large views of public affairs, a trait he had shown as a young governor in promoting public education and legal reform, and would show when an old Secretary of State in buying Alaska. He was an astute politician, quick to measure men at their true worth and subtle in using them. A man of magnanimous heart, he never exaggerated party differences, never sulked under failure (even when he lost the Presidential nomination in 1860), and never showed pettiness. When his constant opponent Jefferson Davis was ill, he was an assiduous and affectionate visitor. "Benjamin," Seward said, as the Louisiana Senator finished some vituperative remarks, "give me a cigar, and when your speech is printed send me a copy." [28] He was always full of talk, badinage, and kindly offices to others.[29] E. L. Godkin thought him in 1859 the best constitutional lawyer in the country, the least of a demagogue among public men, and the clearest-headed statesman.[30]

But Seward lacked the cardinal requisite of steady judgment. For one thing, he was deficient in tact, in sense of timing, and in verbal discretion, so that most people thought this wary politician rash, and many believed this moderate leader (who had been slow to leave the Whig Party) an extremist. In the debate on Pierce's final message, Senator Mason reminded him that he had told a crowd in 1848 that slavery "can and must be abolished, and you and I must do it." So he had, and though the occasion, a speech in favor of the slaveholder Zachary Taylor, and the context, which was mild, had to be considered, the sentence was indiscreet. His "higher law" speech in 1850 was not only poor politics but bad statesmanship, and the "irrepressible conflict" address of 1858 was still more unfortunate. While rash in the use of words, Seward was also occasionally too complicated, devious, and crafty in action; at one time the high-minded statesman, he was at others the partner of the sly Thurlow Weed, who made politics pay in crass ways. His best biographer describes him as a Jekyll and Hyde personality.[31] Save in devotion to the Union, he seemed to lack constancy. He was capable of taking a bold position one day and retracting three-quarters of it the

28 Schurz, *Reminiscences*, II, 34; H. B. Stanton, *Random Recollections*, 204
29 W. R. Thayer, *John Hay*, I, 253–255.
30 Rollo Ogden, *Life and Letters of E. L. Godkin*, I, 258.
31 Frederic Bancroft, *Seward*, I, 200, 201; II, 88.

next, and he frankly told Mrs. Jefferson Davis that he often spoke without conviction.[32]

In short, Seward was erratic. Perhaps an excess of imagination contributed to some of his worst blunders, as when in 1861 he suggested provoking a European war in order to bring back the South; perhaps his emotions sometimes overruled his head. His abundant letters and diary notes show an appealing streak of artistry. Whatever the cause of his instability, this brilliant little Welsh wizard was most valuable when he could lean upon a more massive strength, like Lincoln's.

Jefferson Davis, a man of elegant accomplishments and—despite his humble origin—a gentleman to the core, possessed the dignity of manner and the distinction that Seward lacked. This West Pointer, the son of a Revolutionary veteran, had some of the best traits of a soldier, for he was reserved, self-controlled, and punctiliously courteous, yet plainly not to be trifled with. He was a scholar, who had used his plantation leisure to read widely in military history and the British classics. He was a practical politician, steeped in precedents and instances. Not an orator, he spoke with a finish, lucidity, and force which produced an impression of great logical power—and with a haughty, defiant mien, as one who would not brook contradictions.[33] As Secretary of War under Pierce he showed himself a resourceful administrator, enlarging the army, pushing forward the construction of the Capitol, and experimenting with camels in the Southwest. He was brooding in these years over a plan for saving both the South and the Union; a plan for something like dominion status for the fifteen slave States, making their domestic institutions untouchable.[34]

Those who studied him closely, however, discerned a burning intellectual vanity beneath his impassive exterior, and saw that it was the wellspring of two fatal qualities—selfishness and obstinacy. His future wife, Varina Howell, noted at their first meeting his grim, moody temper, and his way of assuming that when he expressed an opinion, everyone would agree to it. She found him "the kind of person I should expect to rescue one from a mad dog at any risk, but to insist upon a stoical indifference to the fright afterwards."[35] In the Senate, he could never bear contradiction or opposition. When Douglas half-humorously told his Southern opponents on what terms he would admit them to the Democratic Party if ever he gained control of that body, Davis leaped to his feet with blazing passion: " I scorn your quarter!"

Men saw, too, that despite his brilliant public record, his attainments were rather of the study than of practical affairs. Aristocratic, fastidious, self-

32 Gamaliel Bradford, *Union Portraits*, 200–209.
33 E. A. Pollard, *Jefferson Davis*, 33.
34 N. W. Stephenson, *Typical Americans and Their Problems*, 51.
35 Allen Tate, *Jefferson Davis*, 74, 75.

preoccupied, he was Byronically aloof. He disliked meeting men in offhand give and take; he lacked the strong common sense, the practical sagacity, of tamer spirits like Polk or Sam Houston; and his constraint sealed the book of human nature to him. Hence when he attained power, he made grotesque errors in estimating lieutenants, overrating Bragg and underrating Joseph E. Johnston. Having none of the homely, earthy quality which the best democratic leader must possess, he was never willing to place his faith, like Jefferson, Jackson, and Lincoln, in the aggregate wisdom of the people. Moreover, on Southern rights his touchiness led him to hold it "a true maxim to meet danger on the frontier in politics as in war." His stiff sectional feeling estopped him from taking truly national views, and hence long views.

As a parliamentary combatant, the most impressive figure in the country was Stephen A. Douglas. A dozen years younger than Seward, five years junior to Davis, he was still in his early forties when Buchanan was inaugurated; yet he was a political veteran, for he had been elected State's attorney in Illinois at twenty-one, and had been in Congress in Tyler's time. No man excelled him in riding the storm. He had been in the thick of the struggle for the Compromise of 1850, had labored ambitiously for the Presidential nomination in 1852 and 1856, and had given the country the most controversial measure of the decade in his Nebraska Bill. Indeed, ever since the day when, an ill-educated stripling of twenty with hardly enough law to write a simple instrument, he had hung up his shingle in the Morgan County courthouse, he had been ceaselessly fighting his way forward. He had two elementary articles of faith: he believed in the growth of the country—believed that, as it had pushed across the Mississippi, the plains, and the Rockies to the Pacific, it must continue to expand, either north or south; and he believed in popular self-government. When he flung himself into battle it was with tigerish ferocity. In an early run for Congress he had so enraged his opponent, the stalwart John T. Stuart, that this Whig candidate tucked Douglas's head under his arm and dragged him around the Springfield square. John Quincy Adams had stared in amazement when the five-foot Illinoisan, roaring out one of his first speeches in the House, had stripped off his cravat, unbuttoned his waistcoat, and with convulsed face and frantic gesticulation had "lashed himself into such a heat that if his body had been made of combustible matter, it would have burnt out." Schurz had watched him send his sentences like cannon balls, crashing and rending, into his opponents' ranks. Few were the Senators who dared stand against him.[36]

Yet Douglas's limitations were as striking as his gifts. His conduct was sometimes deplorably lax. Charles Francis Adams has left a graphic vignette of

36 Allen Johnson, *Stephen A. Douglas*, 43; Adams, *Memoirs*, XI, 510; Schurz, *Reminiscences*, II, 30–35.

the man invading a sleeping car in 1860, whiskey bottle in hand and half drunk, to try to drag Seward out to address a Toledo crowd. One day Douglas might be leading his party in the Senate, the next be found with his arm about the neck of a crony in a Washington saloon.[37] Deeply versed in political history, he was ill-informed in almost all other fields of knowledge. He had read little but lawbooks, debates, and government manuals, and had seldom found time for that deeper type of reflection which produces statesmen. A marvellously effective floor debater, he had no real power of abstract thought, and no ability to present such general ideas as are associated with Hamilton and Jefferson, Calhoun and Webster. He had never produced a genuine state paper. While he grappled friends to him with hooks of steel, he taught them to act on practical expediency rather than far-reaching principle.

Above all, he was an improviser. His whole genius, backed by irresistible personal force, was for meeting practical situations with some rapidly devised measure, taking little thought of ultimate consequences, and trusting to the country's growth for remedying all defects. He had improvised as State's attorney and judge when he knew little law and no jurisprudence. He had improvised as a young Congressman supporting Polk and the Mexican War. He had improvised policies and bills; above all the reckless measure, the worst Pandora's box in our history, for organizing Kansas Territory. As he improvised he battled implacably, for he loved nothing more than political combat. The great weakness of the born improviser is that he oversimplifies the problem he faces and forgets that remote results are often far more important than the immediate effect. The great penalty paid by the born fighter is that he gradually accumulates a phalanx of enemies. Douglas by 1857 was a doughty champion, famous for his power to give and take blows, but he had still to reckon his final bill of profit and loss.

The best trait of Douglas was his faith in the expansive energies of the American people. Europe, he had said, is one vast graveyard. "Here everything is fresh, blooming, expanding, and advancing. We wish a wise, practical policy adapted to our condition and position."[38] He must be credited, too, with a fervent belief in the masses—in democracy. But he had a number of less happy traits. One was his chauvinism, for he constantly inveighed against the "tyranny" and "aggressions" of European nations, and showed no appreciation of our cultural debt to older lands. Another was his readiness in debate to twist logic, darken counsel, and even misstate facts. Still another was his constant exaltation of material considerations and depreciation of moral factors: the slavery question, he said on the eve of the Civil War, is exclusively "one of climate, of

---

37 C. F. Adams, *Autobiography*, 65, 66; cf. Milton, *Eve of Conflict*, 258, 259.
38 *Cong. Globe*, 32nd Cong., Sp. Sess., 273.

political economy, of self-interest." [39] Finally, he often suffered from his head-long impetuosity.

In 1857 the brightest pages of his brilliant career lay before him. His success-ful fight against a proslavery constitution for Kansas was to be one of the most gallant episodes of the time; and in 1860 he was to play a more farsighted and heroic role than any other Presidential candidate. But he lacked the capacity to plan, the patient wisdom, and the conciliatory gifts of a great national chieftain.

So we might run down the beadroll of leaders of the time, some of them exhibiting great gifts. How fine in various ways was Charles Sumner, with his broad cosmopolitan culture, his Alpine elevation, his friendship with Brougham, Grote, Macaulay, Longfellow, Prescott, and Tocqueville; yet how petty he could be, too! When he returned to the Senate in 1860, after four years of illness and partial exile, he had an opportunity to deliver a speech full of mag-nanimity, generosity, and Olympian wisdom. Instead, he poured forth a diatribe on "The Barbarism of Slavery," full of erudite venom and personal abuse. Like Douglas, he was incapable of appealing to the highest instincts of the people whom he apostrophized. How able was Salmon P. Chase, who had taken a leading place at the Ohio bar, written for the *North American Review*, helped pioneer the antislavery movement in Ohio, and served with distinction as Senator and governor! Of majestic stature, fine head, and keen eye, he looked like the statesman he was. Unfortunately, he had a touchy self-importance, he let political ambition warp his outlook, he never learned to make friends of national leaders, partly because he could never subordinate himself to others, and he almost totally lacked the arts of popular appeal.[40] He thirsted for the Presidency, yet could never command a large following. How brilliantly capable was Alexander H. Stephens, and how truly national in outlook! High-minded, devoted to principle, well-read and thoughtful, he was the strongest of the Southern moderates. Yet as one of his admirers admits, he was too quick-tempered, too unwilling to yield on details, too eager to score victories for personal prestige or party credit, to carry through any great purpose; while his invalidism made him a bundle of nerves.[41]

[IV]

Where, then, were leaders equal to the crisis to be found—leaders who united intellectual power, moderation of temper, moral earnestness, and the power of lifting the popular heart? All the men named, and others like Lyman Trumbull, J. J. Crittenden, Robert Toombs, and R. M. T. Hunter, seemed

39 *Cong. Globe*, 36th Cong., 1st Sess., 552–559.
40 A. B. Hart, *Salmon P. Chase*, 415–425.
41 Ulrich B. Phillips in *Dictionary of American Biography*.

statesmen *manqués*. And could a fit leader be found in time? For the hysteria, the mounting hatreds and fears made time all too short.

Here and there a new voice of promise was raised. Nobody in the East and few in the West paid any attention to one which was heard at a Republican banquet in Chicago on December 10, 1856. A lanky attorney from Springfield, known only as a man who had served one term in Congress, who had narrowly missed the nomination for Senator that Trumbull got, and who had received some votes for the latest Vice-Presidential nomination, spoke on Pierce's message. He mentioned contemptuously the President's vaunt that the recent election had vindicated "State equality." Then he went on to appeal to the imagination of his hearers and to their high sense of national destiny:

> All of us who did not vote for Mr. Buchanan, taken together, are a majority of four hundred thousand. But in the late contest we were divided between Frémont and Fillmore. Can we not come together in the future? Let everyone who really believes, and is resolved, that free society is not and shall not be a failure, and who can conscientiously declare that in the past contest he has only done what he thought best, let every such one have charity to believe that every other one can say as much. Thus let bygones be bygones; let past differences as nothing be; and with steady eye on the real issue, let us reinaugurate the good old "central idea" of the republic. We can do it. The human heart is with us; God is with us. We shall again be able not to declare that "all States as States are equal," nor yet that "all citizens as citizens are equal," but to renew the broader, better declaration, including both of these and much more, that "all men are created equal." [42]

If the Union could yet be saved, if the Ship of State was not to go over the cataract whose thunders ahead shook the air, it would be by some leaders, somewhere, who thus reminded Americans that their republic must be kept the last, best hope of mankind. Lincoln appealed to the older faith in America as "a bulwark for the cause of men." That a deep reservoir of idealistic feeling existed in the nation, and that beneath turbid surface eddies the old moral forces still flowed with pomp of waters, unwithstood, was demonstrated, as we shall now see, by the best literary voices of the young republic.

42 *Complete Works* (Nicolay and Hay ed.), I, 225–226.

4.

Many people had hopes that the institution of slavery might be immobilized, that attrition would set in at the margins, that some colonization of blacks might take place, and that a free labor system would be set up. But two groups were aligned against these thoughts. On one side were the abolitionists and Radical Republicans "who wished emancipation attained in a hurry—and many of whom, men of malicious temper, wanted to hurt the South. . . . The other group were the Southern extremists, the fire eaters. . . ." [1]

In Illinois, 1858 was to see Senator Douglas up for reelection. His opponent, Abraham Lincoln, was clearly the outstanding figure of the state Republican party. At the capitol he had delivered the perceptive "House Divided Speech," prophesying that the nation must in time be all free or all slaveholding, the latter unthinkable. Douglas replied, and the heated, momentous campaign was on. A major feature was the commonly labeled "Lincoln-Douglas Debates," which Nevins, sensing the importance of Douglas, terms the "Douglas-Lincoln Debates." Slavery was the consuming subject. To Lincoln the institution was the one great divisive issue threatening the nation. It must be restricted and put on its way to extinction. Douglas stood by his principle of popular sovereignty, "Let the voice of the people rule!" [2] Harmony was possible between free and slave states, he claimed. While the Republicans won a close contest in the popular vote, they did not carry the legislature. Douglas was reelected.

Was the country slipping swiftly toward disunion or even war? The economy was being restored by 1859, but "all the while the sectional quarrel, like a cancer gnawing at the viscera of some outwardly healthy man, furnished constant spasms of pain and fever." [3] Congress was in a state of deadlock and fission, with the Democrats looking to the election of 1860. The rents in the party, however, might be too drastic to repair. Although Douglas was the leading name, Southerners were seeking their own man and Buchanan appeared to be more and more aligned with the radical proslavery men. The split between Douglas and Buchanan grew rapidly. At the same time, the Republicans were gaining consistently, at least in the North.

"Words may excite mankind, but it is the violent act which raises emotions to fever heat." [4] An extraordinary fanatic of iron will, partly self-deluded, and with consuming inner fire furnished that violent act in October 1859, when John Brown and his band invaded Harpers Ferry, Virginia. Brown's attempt at a slave uprising was pitiful in its results, but the raid itself, the trial of Brown, and his execution by hanging deepened the antislavery sentiment of the North. In some quarters Brown was almost canonized. The South was angered and frightened, almost to hysteria. As for the slaves, "It was a bitter irony that Brown's effort to aid them should have made their lot harsher." [5]

The year 1860 opened with the almost violent quarrel over the Speakership of the House of Representatives, another example of mounting sectional antagonism that seemed almost to be a "drifting into destruction" by the Union. Threats of secession increased and sentiment seemed to be hardening rapidly.

In late April 1860 the Democratic Party Convention opened in Charleston, South Carolina. When it ended the delegates of the "cotton kingdom" had walked out of the hall, and no candidate had been named. Douglas's supporters had failed to nominate the Illinois senator. But more than that had happened: "The Democratic Party had been riven asunder, and the stage set for secession and disunion." [6] A vastly different convention met in Chicago in late May.

The delegates of the Republican party gathered in complete confidence of victory and with great exuberance. The story is a familiar one. William H. Seward of New York seemed fairly assured of nomination, but when the excitement died the still youthful Republican party had Abraham Lincoln as its presidential candidate. In the end voters had the choice of four major candidates: Stephen A. Douglas for the Northern Democrats; John C. Breckinridge of Kentucky for the Southern Democrats; John Bell of Tennessee for the Constitutional Union party; and for the Republicans, Lincoln. "By late summer, the question was no longer of Lincoln's election but of the results of his impending victory. . . ." [7] In the campaign "the country had the sensation of watching one of the old double dramas of the Elizabethan stage, a play within a play; the outer drama determining whether Lincoln, Breckinridge, or Douglas should gain national leadership, while the far more fateful inner drama decided whether the republic should be torn in twain." [8]

"Men might, as always, dispute the meaning of the election. On the surface it seemed to offer no clean-cut national verdict for anything; certainly not for Lincoln and the Republican tenets. Yet its central import was actually plain. The nation had taken a mighty decision—the decision that slavery must be circumscribed and contained. . . . Dreadfully clear now, to ears attuned to the future, sounded the drums and bugles." From that November election day on, the clamor for secession of the Deep South increased to a roar. "South Carolina was like a bed of charcoal suddenly leaping into flame." [9] The sovereign people of South Carolina broke the bonds of the United States on December 20, 1860, by leaving the Union. Many felt that such secession could be peaceful, but all recognized that the possibility of war was increasing.

Nevins is of the view that in the six weeks after the election great opportunities were lost. The Buchanan administration appeared helpless, and even after its reorganization into a stiffer and more Northern body, it was powerless to halt the march of events. In a blundering and legalistic fashion, Congress tried the previously successful avenue of compromise, but to no avail. A new nation was taking shape in the South, and for the old Union a new President was taking over.

NOTES

1. Nevins, *The Emergence of Lincoln*, Vol. I, *Douglas, Buchanan, and Party Chaos, 1857–1859*, p. 345.
2. *Ibid.*, p. 347.
3. Nevins, *The Emergence of Lincoln*, Vol. II, *Prologue to the Civil War, 1859–1861*, p. 3.
4. *Ibid.*, p. 70.
5. *Ibid.*, p. 109.
6. *Ibid.*, p. 222.
7. *Ibid.*, p. 286.
8. *Ibid.*, p. 272.
9. *Ibid.*, pp. 316–318.

The Rival Republic

WHILE COMPROMISE was grinding to a standstill, the dramatic process of creating a new Southern republic was attracting general attention. It might be viewed with all the eager hope of Yancey or Toombs, with the amused cynicism of W. H. Russell, the British correspondent who travelled to Montgomery to witness its birth, or the scornful hostility of Sumner, Wade, and countless other Northerners. But that it was an event of the first magnitude, none could doubt. It was necessarily built upon the completion of secession in the Lower South.

[I]

Mid-January found Milledgeville, on the Oconee River in central Georgia, filling up with delegates for the State convention. The eyes of most Southerners were fixed on the gathering, for the adherence of Georgia was essential to sectional unity. Jacob Thompson was writing Howell Cobb: "I have all along felt that as goes Georgia, so goes the whole South." The little town, with its capital, its cluster of four substantial churches, and its handsome residences, for it was much liked by wealthy Georgians, was soon crammed to bursting. One visitor, secretly a correspondent for the New York *Tribune*, found himself in such an incessant jostle that he dared take no written notes. On Tuesday the fifteenth, the two camps, the separate secessionists and co-operative secessionists, held caucuses and anxiously counted noses. During the next two days, crowded galleries watched the convention elect officers, give the South Carolina and Alabama commissioners a hearing, and do other preliminary work. Then a seal of secrecy was clapped on the session. Nothing could be picked up, grumbled newspapermen, but a few crumbs moistened by the prevailing whiskey.[1]

The tide of popular feeing in Georgia had been setting steadily toward an early abandonment of the Union. Alexander H. Stephens had written at the

1 N. Y. *Weekly Tribune*, February 2, 1861.

(*The Emergence of Lincoln*, Vol. II, *Prologue to Civil War, 1859–1861*, Chapter 14.)

close of November that while large numbers would sustain his conservative position, the odds were against them. It was all too true, he thought, that most leading Georgians did not wish to remain on any terms. "They do not wish any redress of wrongs; they are disunionists *per se*, and avail themselves of present circumstances to press their objects; and my present conviction is that they will carry the State with them by a large majority." He kept reiterating these despondent statements.[2] Howell Cobb's long argument for secession issued simultaneously with his resignation had much effect; so did Toombs's public letter in the Savannah *Republican* of December 17, and his admonition to Georgians just before Christmas to thunder secession from the ballot box. The two men differed on one point, Cobb wishing secession immediately and Toombs preferring it on March 4; but on the need for a severance they stood together.

The election of delegates on January 2, held as a terrible storm smote Georgia, apparently resulted in a decisive victory for the separate secessionists. Only about two-thirds of the voters went to the polls and their verdict was roughly four to three for immediate action. Stephens, who struggled through the storm to vote and make a speech, believed that the weather had cost his side ten thousand ballots, for it favored the town dwellers and planters who had the best means of getting to the polls. "It really appears as if Providence was on the other side," he ejaculated.[3] As he prepared to leave for the convention, he wrote his brother that he had known for weeks that secession was certain, for the currents of the day were irresistible.

Yet the convention battle between the advocates of immediate and of postponed secession proved closer than had been anticipated. The gathering was one of remarkable ability. The radical leaders included Toombs, T. R. R. Cobb, and Francis S. Bartow, along with Governor Joseph E. Brown and Howell Cobb, who were invited to seats on the floor; the cooperationist leaders were Stephens, his brother Linton, Benjamin H. Hill, and Herschel V. Johnson. The latter group were handicapped by the lack of any preconcerted plan of action, by an old enmity between Stephens and Hill, and by the defeatist temper of Stephens. When the ordinance of secession was offered, Hill offered a substitute plan which Johnson had hurriedly drawn up. This series of resolutions declared the South in danger, proposed a convention of slaveholding

2 Cleveland, *Stephen*, 159, 160; Johnston and Browne, *Stephens*, 369 ff.
3 Johnston and Browne, *op. cit.*, 378, 379. Election figures vary; one set is 50,243 for immediate-action delegates and 37,123 for cooperationists. Pendleton, *Stephens*, 178. It should be noted that group attitudes were complex. The cooperationists included (1) those who wanted immediate secession but only by united State action; (2) those who wished to attempt compromise, and secede only when that failed; (3) those who desired to await an overt act of aggression by Lincoln before seceding; and (4) strict Unionists playing for delay. For a full elucidation see Dumond, *Secession Movement*, 113 ff.

States at Atlanta the next month, suggested some needed amendments to the Constitution, and deferred Georgia's decision until the North could be given an opportunity to reply. The substitute was lost 164 to 133. A change of but sixteen votes in the total of two hundred and ninety-seven would have reversed the result. Hill and others then joined in passing the secession ordinance 208 to 89, and all but half a dozen delegates signed it.[4]

Analysis of the vote showed that, like other Southern States, Georgia divided largely on economic and regional lines. The radical secessionists came from the Savannah River valley, the seacoast, and the tier of counties behind it, extending into southwest Georgia. Here dwelt most of the wealthy planters and large slaveholders. The townspeople, whether in Savannah, Augusta, Columbus, Macon, or Atlanta, were predominantly sympathetic with the planting interest. They included the merchants and factors who handled cotton and merchandise, the professional men who sprang largely from the planter class, and many retired or absentee landholders. It was noteworthy that all fifteen of the delegates from these five cities were immediate secessionists. On the conservative side, the great strongholds were, as we have noted, the pine barrens and the northern hill country. Here lived a population of small farmers, stockmen, and others with a pioneering tradition, whose immediate forebears had conquered the wilderness and fought the Indians. They liked the Union; their instinct was for the doctrines of Jackson, not Calhoun; they had little direct interest in slavery; and their concern for a peculiar Southern culture was slighter still. While exceptions to these generalizations were numerous, the convention decision was broadly a victory of plantation and town over the small farmer.[5]

When secession was announced, Milledgeville sprang into a spasm of illuminations, bonfires, Roman candles, cannon salutes, and speechmaking. Yet many were heavy-hearted. "I never felt so sad before," Herschel Johnson later wrote. "The clustering glories of the past thronged my memory, but they were darkened by the gathering gloom of the lowering future."[6] Georgia's action was widely regarded as decisive for the whole Lower South. With her great production of cotton, wheat, corn, and rice, her flourishing seaport of Savannah, her textile factories, her key railroad system, and her energetic population, the State was vital to a new republic. The step was described then

4 A. D. Candler, ed., *Confed. Records of Ga.*, I, 213 ff.; I. W. Avery, *Hist. Ga.*, 149 ff.; Hill, *Joseph E. Brown*, 44, 45; Pearce, *B. H. Hill*, 49–53.

5 A. J. Cole, "Sentiment in Ga. Toward Secession, 1850–61," MS, Univ. of Ill.

6 Flippin, *Johnson*, 192. Johnson always thought that "a fair and energetic canvass" would have shown a large majority of Georgians against secession; he always believed that ambitious Southern leaders wanted disunion as a means of establishing their personal power. *Idem.* 168–170.

and thereafter as one that electrified the cotton kingdom and determined the revolution; and while this is an overstatement, it is certain that it cleared up a great area of doubt and hesitation.

The Lower South was now swiftly completing its withdrawal from the Union. Already, on January 9, the Mississippi convention, sitting at Jackson, had passed its secession ordinance 84 to 15. On the tenth, Florida had followed, 62 to 7. On the eleventh the Alabama convention, its temper fired by Yancey, the Patrick Henry of the new cause, had decided upon withdrawal by a vote of 61 to 39. The Louisiana convention passed its secession ordinance on January 26 by a vote of 113 to 17, and on February 1 Texas took the same step, 166 to 8. Seven States were not as many as Ruffin and Yancey had hoped for, but they were regarded as sufficient for a viable new confederation.

[II]

On their face, the heavy convention majorities for secession seemed to point to an overwhelming disunionist strength. Actually, however, in every State the division of opinion ran deep, the forces opposing immediate secession were formidable, and, while the question defies settlement, perhaps a majority of citizens were Union men in the sense that they opposed secession altogether, or wished it deferred until other remedies had been exhausted, or hoped for a reconstruction of the nation on better terms within a few years. Certainly in the fifteen slave States taken as a whole, a heavy majority were against a permanent severance of ties. The apparently crushing victory of the immediate secessionists in the Lower South was accomplished by skillful use of the advantages before enumerated; their driving energy, superior organization, success in making action so rapid that the opposition could not mobilize, effective use of shibboleths and epithets, and capitalization on the demand for moral unity. They were aided in some States by favorable apportionment systems, and in nearly all by the excessive influence wielded by the planting class and its various allies.[7]

Public opinion in every such crisis necessarily moves like a great pendulum, gathering momentum. It was inevitable that the bright vision of a Southern republic should catch the imagination of multitudes of men and women. The spirit of nationalism, with its heady, volatile appeals—to traditionalism, to ancestral reverence, to folklore, to pieties of hearth and home, to the ideal of sacrifice—and its demand that the individual lose himself in a mass solidarity,

7 On this insoluble problem of the real sentiment of Southerners toward secession, see Potter, *Lincoln and Secession Crisis*, 208 ff.; Rhodes, *United States*, III, 273 ff.; Dumond, *Secession Movement*, Ch. X.

had already made impressive progress. As volunteer companies marched to the "Southern Marseillaise," as crowds began singing "The Bonnie Blue Flag," as slogans of freedom and justice ran through the press, a kindling sense of sectional patriotism swung even the dubious from their old allegiances. To join the new movement seemed (especially to youth) an affirmative, progressive, heroic act; to resist it seemed negative and timid. Every day, militancy grew. And as one step after another was taken, more doubters yielded to State loyalty, and to their feeling that the hard-pressed Southern people must at all hazards stand together.

All the standard agencies for moulding opinion were brought to bear upon conservatives. In Mississippi, for example, the Jackson *Mississippian*, Vicksburg *Sun*, and Natchez *Free Trader*, with other newspapers, spoke of moderation as a policy of imbecility, of delay as abject submission, and of Union men as enemies of the South. Many churches throughout the cotton kingdom preached resistance. The Thanksgiving sermons of the Rev. B. M. Palmer, head of the largest Presbyterian church in New Orleans, and the Rev. W. T. Leacock, his Episcopal colleague, two stirring exhortations to secession which were scattered broadcast in pamphlet form, were long remembered. "I warn my countrymen the historic moment once passed never returns," rumbled Palmer. "Sapped, circumvented, undermined, the institutions of your soil will be overthrown; and within five and twenty years the history of San Domingo will be the record of Louisiana." [8] The official journal of the powerful Baptist denomination in Mississippi urged citizens to insist upon their full rights within the old nation, or win them outside in a new. [9]

Plangent effects were produced by a steady reiteration of inflammatory news items from Washington and other centers. The Congressional leaders of secession had long been in close touch with the Washington correspondents of Southern newspapers, and many of the fire-eaters knew the art of manufacturing and coloring press intelligence. Many Southern editors, for their part, made a one-sided selection of the news. "Every morning for the past three or four weeks," complained A. H. Arthur of Vicksburg on January 10 to Joseph Holt,

---

8 The two sermons were printed together in "The Rights of the South Defended in the Pulpits," and were notable for their violent tone. Palmer declared that it was the South's duty under God "to conserve and perpetuate the institution of domestic slavery as now existing," and that "the abolition spirit is undeniably atheistic." Leacock was even fiercer. Who could hesitate, he asked, "when we consider the treatment we have received from the hands of our enemies; our character they have defamed; our feelings they have lacerated; our rights they have invaded; our property they have stolen; our power they have defied; our existence they have threatened? Murderers and robbers have been let loose upon us, stimulated by weak or designing or infidel preachers, armed by fanatics, and sustaind by a band of assassins out of the very wealth which they have accumulated by their connection with us."

9 *Mississippi Baptist*, cited in Rainwater, *Mississippi*, 173, 174.

"we have been inundated with fresh dispatches from your region to keep up the courage of the leaders at home, and still further inflame the public mind." A week later another of Holt's correspondents, J. O. Harrison of New Orleans, wrote that the South was flooded with dispatches describing the unjust and coercive policy of the government. Censorship and intimidation meanwhile suppressed much news favorable to the cause of compromise and the Union. One Southerner after another, hearing indirectly of Andrew Johnson's great Union speech but unable to find any of it in the press, wrote him for copies, and spoke bitterly of the suppression of facts and opinion.

The companies of minute men, too, placing graybeards alongside striplings, were active propagandist agencies. State flags and badges helped win the wavering. When in Eufaula, Alabama, an enthusiastic lady flung from her window a banner of fifteen stars and fifteen stripes, the Eufaula Rifles promptly paraded and fired a fifteen-volley salute.[10] Such incidents were incessant and they had a cumulative effect.

In some areas, the secessionists frankly capitalized upon the illiteracy or apathy of the many voters who, as Helper and others had noted, knew all too little of public measures. In South Carolina, one radical exulted that ignorance played into the hands of his party. Secession had to be achieved by a select minority, he wrote. "I do not believe that the common people understand it; in fact I know that they do not understand it. . . . We must make the move and force them to follow." [11] The use of threats was not infrequent. Senator Iverson set a bad example when he suggested that the loyal Sam Houston was a Caesar who might yet find his Brutus. A Georgia secessionist, speaking of such men as the Stephens brothers, growled: "When the State goes out and we are on our own hook, those fellows will have to walk straight and keep quiet." The Savannah correspondent of the New York *Tribune* wrote in December that conservatives did not dare express their views with any force and warmth. A wealthy planter had confessed that he would be ejected from the State if he spoke his mind. "For," he said, "when a man once falls under the hand of the mob, though they only threaten him today, they will doubtless return tomorrow and burn his property, and the next day they will bring a rope with them." [12]

The extremists have taken our positions by storm, lamented one conservative of the Lower South. Nevertheless, Stephens was unjust in asserting that the people had run mad, and were "wild with passion and frenzy, doing they know not what." [13] The number who struggled to the last for delay, or yielded

10 Denman, *Secession in Alabama*, 89.
11 A. P. Aldrich, November 25, 1860; Hammond Papers.
12 *Weekly Tribune*, January 19, 1861.
13 Johnston and Browne, *Stephens*, 369, 370.

in the hope that the Union could yet be rebuilt, was formidable. Just how equivocal the character of the decision really was in some States will become evident from a brief examination of the secession struggle.

. . .

[IV]

All in all, we may wonder if the result in the Lower South would not have been different if South Carolina had not acted in such haste; if there and in Louisiana the governmental system had not been weighted heavily on the side of the wealthy planting interest; if in Georgia men like Stephens had exerted themselves more vigorously and the election had been held in sunny weather; if conservative Alabamians had been given more time to rally their forces in the northern counties and Mobile; and if a fair and calm election of delegates had been held in Texas. The amount of thick-and-thin Union sentiment in this section was not impressive. But the sentiment for delay and cooperative action might well have won the day; and a deliberative Southern convention, offering reasonable conditions to the North, might well then have furnished a solid foundation for compromise.

It will be seen that certain common features stamped the action of these seven States on secession. No really effective plebiscite on immediate as against cooperative action was held in any of them. In all except Georgia, the period allowed for discussing the issues and selecting delegates was deplorably short; usually but three or four weeks, and in Florida less than three. In all of them the vote for convention delegates fell surprisingly short of that just cast in the presidential election, being less by two-fifths, one-third, or one quarter. In a number of States (though not in Mississippi), the slaveholding aristocracy and its allies profited by advantages running even beyond those written into laws and constitutions. In Louisiana, for example, much of the slaveless population was too unstable in residence to qualify for voting, even if it cared to vote; in 1859, scarcely seven percent of the whites of New Orleans were registered voters, and immigrants among them were subject to intimidation at the polls.[41] In all these States, too, observers agree on the emotional power and kinetic force of the spirit of Southern solidarity, speaking of it as a torrential current, an irresistible wind, carrying all before it.

It will also be noted that in their formal declaration of the reasons for secession, the seven States almost completely ignored any questions but those which pertained to slavery. Even South Carolina, in the clearheaded, dignified "Declar-

41 Shugg, *Class Struggle*, 130.

ation of Immediate Causes" written by Memminger, made no mention of tariffs or other economic grievances. In Georgia, both the hot secessionist Toombs and the reluctant secessionist Stephens were old-time Whigs who had believed in the justice of moderate tariffs. The ablest statement of Alabama's reasons for secession, made by E. S. Dargan of Mobile, rested the action squarely on fear of emancipation. The South, he argued, had more than four million slaves; the removal of such a host was impossible; and if they were liberated without restraint, the result would be utter disaster. "They would either be destroyed by our own hands, the hands to which they look, and look with confidence, for protection, or we ourselves would become demoralized and degraded." [42]

All the seceding States held for a time an anomalous position. They were in their own eyes independent republics, yet they patently lacked the full governmental equipment of republics. Were the Federal laws dead within the States? Was the national coinage still valid? Should the national government continue to deliver mails? A. P. Calhoun told the South Carolina convention that having pulled down a temple which it had taken three-quarters of a century to erect, they must clear away the rubbish and erect another. "We are now houseless and homeless, and we must secure ourselves against storms." [43] The simple method of meeting the situation was to adopt the whole body of United States laws, and take over the whole corps of postmasters. In various States, as the conventions continued to sit and pass ordinances, a murmur arose against the doctrine that all powers were now lodged in a revolutionary group brought together under circumstances of intense excitement. Much fluttering of the pages of old histories for Revolutionary precedents took place in the weeks while men waited for a new Southern Confederacy to replace the United States with an indispensable central authority.

Meanwhile, the problem of relations with the Upper South and borderland raised anxious questions. Many hotheads of the cotton kingdom would have preferred to create a new nation without including the border States. The small number of men eager to reopen slave importations, and the much larger number intent upon establishing a free-trade republic, knew that Marylanders, Virginians, and Missourians would obstruct their aims. In Charleston, Savannah, and parts of Alabama and Mississippi in particular, a cotton republic thus seemed desirable. "We must beware lest the Border Slave States overslaugh us," William Gilmore Simms wrote Porcher Miles. "Their destiny involves more rapid

---

42 Smith, *Hist. and Debates*, 93, 94.
43 N. Y. *Tribune*, December 20, 1860. Although Governor Pickens of South Carolina assumed charge of postal affairs and appointed a head of the postal department, Postmaster Alfred Huger of Charleston informed Joseph Holt that he would continue to account to Washington for the finances of his office; Holt Papers.

changes than ours. . . . They will become manufacturing." [44] Moreover—and this is important—radical leaders were well aware that the Upper South and border would probably quit the Union (if at all) only with the expectation of reconstructing it. That seemed to be the dominant sentiment in North Carolina, Virginia, and Tennessee as well as in the slaveholding areas north of them. Hostile to any such policy, and taking "once out, always out," as their motto, many of the fire-eaters wanted nothing to do with States which hoped to reknit the old ligaments. Not a few of them denounced the border men as fainthearts, Laodiceans, and skulkers.

The more sober view, however, which all cooperationists strongly preached, was that the Lower South was bound both by duty and self-interest to gain the adherence of other slaveholding States. The erection of a mere cotton republic would do great wrong to the borderland, and irreparable injury to the institution of slavery. It was the Upper South which suffered most from Northern injuries and abolitionist propaganda; and could this region be left alone in resisting Yankee encroachment? Already, Northern writers were computing that for a little over ninety million dollars every slave in Maryland, Delaware, and Missouri could be purchased at the generous average price of five hundred dollars a head, and set free. For the Lower South to maintain its separate republic, many urged, would be a base and cowardly desertion of slaveholders in the sister States. Nor was this all. A cotton republic would not be strong enough to conquer Cuba or overrun Mexico in the teeth of European hostility. Slavery there, confined within narrow bounds, faced with world reprobation, and, as the blacks multiplied, operating to "Africanize" large districts, would in Seward's image eventually sting itself to death.[45]

In the chaotic situation which had developed by the beginning of February, many Gulf State men clearly perceived a terrible dilemma. They could probably not gain the accession of the Upper South, which they required, without striking a blow, and to strike a blow would precipitate all the horrors of a fratricidal war. Meanwhile, opinion in the great region from North Carolina and Virginia to Missouri was racked and torn by a thousand currents and countercurrents; and the idea that this populous area might soon be dragged into war by the impulsive cotton kingdom, while pleasing some, gave others the deepest anguish.

[V]

In Washington, the hope of compromise still existed. Charles Sumner saw Buchanan on February 2. "What, Mr. President," he inquired, "can Massachu-

---

44 February 26, 1861; Porcher Miles Papers, Univ. of N. C.
45 N. Y. *Weekly Tribune*, February 2, 1861; Rainwater, *Mississippi*, 182–185.

setts do for the good of the country?" "Much," responded Buchanan, "no State more." "What is that?" "Adopt the Crittenden proposition," said the President.

"Is that necessary?" asked Sumner. "Yes." The Senator made an emphatic gesture. "Mr. President, Massachusetts has not yet spoken directly on these propositions. But I feel authorized to say—at least I give it as my opinion—that such are the unalterable convictions of the people, they would see their State sunk below the sea and become a sandbank before they would adopt these propositions."

Such an explosive statement was to be expected of Sumner, who, according to Edward Everett, was laboring under a morbid excitement which approached insanity. He had a magnificent project for acquiring Canada, and gladly accepting the secession of such slaveholding States as would not live in the Union under the tenets of the Republican platform.[46] But while the Crittenden Compromise was dead, other schemes of conciliation were not. Seward and Charles Francis Adams, whose opinions were fairly in unison, believed that by concessions on every point but territorial extension, they might yet save the Union. Both believed that the slavery issue had been substantially settled by the election. Both believed that to let this settlement be followed by a dissolution of the Union would be a terrible blunder as well as a catastrophe. Seward had written Lincoln on January 27 that a generous and hopeful attitude was indispensable; that the new Administration must collect the revenues and regain the forts; but that "every thought that we think ought to be conciliatory forbearing and patient, and so open the way for the rising of a Union Party in the seceding States which will bring them back into the Union." [47] Adams wrote to R. H. Dana in much the same terms. The first duty of the government, he thought, was to reestablish confidence by conciliatory language, to encourage the loyal Southerners, and to deprive the conspirators of the materials with which they had worked. Men in the Upper South were plucking up hope, the efforts to reject secession were growing more systematic, and if a fair understanding could only be reached in Congress or the question postponed until after Lincoln came in, "I think we shall have won the day." [48]

---

46 Sumner stood at one extreme as Howell Cobb stood at another. On January 10, Cobb had written Porcher Miles that all the threat of coercion was attributable to the false position of Southern men talking of adjustment in Washington. "We ought to let it be distinctly understood, that we will accept no settlement—and if that position had been firmly taken at Washington from the beginning, the trouble would now be all over, and the country engaged in the discharge of the only remaining duty to be performed and that is, the terms of a *peaceable* and *perpetual* separation." Miles Papers, Univ. of N. C. Sumner narrates his talk with Buchanan in a letter of February 3, 1861, to John A. Andrew; Andrew Papers, MHS.

47 Robert Todd Lincoln Papers.

48 February 9, 1861; Dana Papers.

It was assuredly of good omen that neither the firing on the *Star of the West* nor the seizure of scattered forts and arsenals had enraged Northern opinion. While few Northerners were ready to admit that every outgoing State was entitled to all the national property within her limits, to be taken whenever a revolutionary agency chose, these "aggressive acts" had been accepted calmly. Even Horace Greeley spoke of them merely as highhanded.[49] The forbearance of Major Anderson in not returning the fire of the Charleston batteries on the Federal vessel was generally applauded, and Secretary Holt sent him the formal commendation of the President.[50]

Of calming psychological effect, too, in these last weeks of the Buchanan Administration, was the quasi-truce respecting Fort Sumter reached at Charleston between Major Anderson and Governor Pickens, and that respecting Fort Pickens at Pensacola arranged between various Southern Senators and President Buchanan. The attorney-general of South Carolina and one of Anderson's officers travelled jointly to Washington to initiate negotiations for determining the status of Sumter. The resulting parley came to nothing. South Carolina again demanded the surrender of the fort; the Administration again sharply refused it.[51] Secretary Holt delivered a grave warning to the State. "If with all the multiplied proofs which exist of the President's anxiety for peace and of the earnestness with which he has pursued it," he wrote, "the authorities of that State shall assault Fort Sumter, and peril the lives of the handful of brave and loyal men shut up within its walls, and thus plunge our common country into the horrors of civil war, then upon them, and those they represent, must rest the responsibility." This was a just anticipation of the verdict of history. An unwritten understanding continued, however, that the United States would not reinforce the fort without notice, and that South Carolina would meanwhile not yet attack it; an understanding the easier to respect because Anderson did not want reinforcements. Secretary Holt had told Anderson, nevertheless, that whenever he needed supplies or men, a prompt and vigorous effort to forward them would follow.[52]

The Fort Pickens truce was ampler and stronger. It was agreed that the government might provision the post but not disembark troops, and that in return the Florida authorities would make no attack. Buchanan gave firm orders through Holt to the provisioning force, which included a small body of troops: "The *Brooklyn* and other vessels of war on the station will remain and you will

49   Signed article, N. Y. *Tribune*, January 8, 1861.
50   January 11; *Official Records*, Series I, Vol. I, 140.
51   Buchanan, *Administration*, 194 ff.; Curtis, *Buchanan*, II, 452; Crawford, *Sumter*, 222 ff.
52   *Official Records*, I, I, 134–190.

exercise the utmost vigilance and be prepared at a moment's warning to land the company at Fort Pickens and you and they will instantly repel any attack on the Fort." This was a display of proper vigor. He was anxious to maintain the truce while the Peace Convention under ex-President Tyler labored, and while other efforts at reconciliation were being made. But he was emphatic that the national forces should be ready to meet an attack on Pickens or preparations for an attack. "In either event, the *Brooklyn* and other vessels will act promptly." Had such a clear truce been made respecting Sumter, worry over the future would have been greatly lessened.

[VI]

Three days after the secession of Texas, and on the very day that the Peace Convention opened in Washington, February 4, delegates from six States met in Montgomery to launch their hopeful new Southern republic. South Carolina had proposed the gathering a month earlier. Delegates had in general been chosen by the various State conventions, in proportion to the number of electors each State possessed under the Constitution. They made up a distinguished body of men. Alexander H. Stephens asserts, indeed, that he was never associated with one of more ability; that nobody in it failed to rank above the average of the House in any of the sixteen Congresses in which he had served; and that several of the delegates might justly be placed among the first of the land.[53] Jefferson Davis, Yancey, Slidell, and Judah P. Benjamin were not present. But Toombs, the two Cobbs, Rhett, Memminger, Reagan, J. L. M. Curry, and Benjamin H. Hill were. The spirit in which they met was one of high enthusiasm and optimism. A patriotic harmony prevailed, and many of the wisest believed that their future was one of assured peace.

With Howell Cobb as presiding officer, and with each State given one vote, the convention moved with great celerity. Only four days after assembling, it adopted a Constitution for the provisional government of the Confederate States of America; and on the fifth day it elected Jefferson Davis as provisional President. The choice necessarily had to be conservative in character, for while Rhett and Yancey were both highly receptive, their elevation to the leadership of the new nation would have frightened Virginia and the other hesitant States. At the outset, it was the general impression that the palm would be awarded to Toombs, who in the eyes of Stephens seemed far better equipped for the place than any rival. Davis would have preferred a high military post for himself. Unfortunately for Toombs, the Georgia delegation was divided, some members

53 Stephens, *War Between the States*, II, 325.

supporting him, some Howell Cobb; the veteran Democrats in the convention distrusted him as an old-time Whig; Yancey, when forced to withdraw, did so in favor of Davis; and after a good deal of complicated maneuvering, the Georgia Senator himself agreed to the austere Mississippian. Some small part may have been played in the rejection of Toombs by his well-known weakness for drink. By another unanimous vote, Stephens was selected for Vice President.[54]

No stronger pair of men could have been selected. Here were one representative of the older South, and one of the new frontier South; one of the old-time Whigs and one of the old-time Democrats; one of the Breckinridge men, and one of the Douglas men. Both were capable orators and parliamentarians. Davis had shown his skill and energy as an administrator in one of the most difficult of the government departments. Their election pleased cautious elements in the borderland; and the fact did not escape the North that, while the convention professed to be adamantine in spurning the old Union forever, both Davis and Stephens had followed a policy which made them seem not totally averse to its reconstruction.

The provisional Constitution had been drawn up by a committee of two from each State, with Memminger its chairman; and by general consent the Federal instrument was accepted as its basis. Within a few weeks a permanent Constitution was drafted. It differed from the old national model chiefly in its emphasis on State Rights, its careful guarantee of slavery (which it named without any cimcumlocution), and a number of interesting reform provisions. The general welfare clauses were omitted. Any Confederate official acting within the limits of a State might be impeached by the State legislature, though the Constitution, laws made under it, and treaties were declared "the supreme law of the land." The central government was forbidden to pass any law denying the right of property in slaves, and although the African slave trade was prohibited, the interstate rights of slaveholders were safeguard. Provision was made for a judicial system like that of the United States, including a Supreme Court. The restrictions upon the States followed in general the old pattern; they might not coin money, make alliances, form compacts with other States, or grant titles of nobility.

The most remarkable features of the new instrument sprang from the purifying and reforming zeal of the delegates, who hoped to create a more guarded and virtuous government than that of Washington.[55] The President was to hold

---

54 See *So. Hist. Assn. Pubs.*, XI, 163 ff.; Johnston and Browne, *Stephens*, 389–391.
55 We speak here of the permanent Constitution, adopted early in March. Texts of the Confederate and Federal Constitutions are given in parallel columns in Davis, *Rise and Fall*, I, 640–675.

office six years, and be ineligible for reelection. Expenditures were to be limited by a variety of careful provisions, and the President was given a budgetary control over appropriations which Congress could break only by a two-thirds vote. Subordinate employees were protected against the forays of the spoils system. No bounties were ever to be paid out of the Treasury, no protective tariff was to be passed, and no post office deficit was to be permitted. The electoral college system was retained, but as a far-reaching innovation, Cabinet members were given seats in Congress for the discussion of departmental affairs. Some of these changes were unmistakable improvements, and the spirit behind all of them was an earnest desire to make government more honest and efficient. The process of ratifying the new Constitution by the people of the respective States was destined to be slow; and the permanent government of the Confederacy was not to be inaugurated until Washington's birthday in 1862. Meanwhile, the provisional Administration served with all the authority that its leaders could give it.

On the evening of February 16, Jefferson Davis arrived in Montgomery, to be met with a storm of cheers as his erect figure was discerned emerging from the train. To the crowd at the station, he spoke a few sentences. "Our separation from the old Union is complete," he declared. "No compromise and no reconstruction can now be entertained." Two companies of Georgia militia, with a committee of the Confederate Congress and a deputation representing the city, escorted him to the Exchange Hotel, where a greater crowd awaited him. Their exultant shouts soon brought him out upon the balcony. Prominent among the distinguished men who surrounded him was William L. Yancey. He stepped forward, gesturing for silence that he might introduce Davis, and his voice rang out with clarion vibrance: "The man and the hour have met!"

Lincoln Takes the Helm

AS THE President-elect left Springfield for Washington on February 11, it was evident that the national crisis was gathering itself to some mighty climax; but no man could say what that climax would be. A complex web of intertwined and fateful questions would have to be decided within the next ten weeks.

Lincoln had as yet fully determined upon only two members of his Cabinet. Though compromise by the Missouri line was dead, lesser concessions to the South hung in balance in Washington; the House did not receive the report and proposals of the Committee of Thirty-three until three days after Lincoln's departure, while, for that matter, the Senate still had to take its final vote on the Crittenden scheme. Major Anderson had not determined when his garrison would need provisions and other stores, the South Carolina authorities marked time while the *Mercury* exhorted them to take the forts, and the new Confederate government remained without a policy as to Sumter and Pickens. The people of the border States still anxiously debated their future, and although Stephens told a Montgomery audience that the new nation might soon have more stars than the thirteen of the original Union, the battle of conservatives and radicals continued to rage in North Carolina and Virginia, in Kentucky and Tennessee. Seward believed the general excitement was abating, but Seward was always optimistic. To most people, the public bewilderment, apprehension, and irritability seemed as great as ever.

So great was the uncertainty that Lincoln was vastly relieved to learn at Columbus, Ohio, on the evening of the thirteenth, that the counting of the electoral votes had been safely completed in Washington that day. The country shared his feeling. Circumstantial stories of plans for a Virginia attack had been afloat. Joseph Medill had written Lincoln on New Year's Eve that the disunionists expected to have an army in the capital within five weeks.[1] Elihu B. Washburne had informed the President-elect on February 3 that a wide and powerful conspiracy to seize Washington undoubtedly existed. But Winfield Scott had

1   Robert Todd Lincoln Papers.

(*The Emergence of Lincoln*, Vol. II, *Prologue to Civil War, 1859–1861*, Chapter 15.)

gathered troops and taken precautions. "I have said," he thundered to a New England visitor, "that any man who attempted by force or unparliamentary disorder to obstruct or interfere with the lawful count of the electoral vote should be lashed to the muzzle of a twelve-pounder and fired out of a window of the Capitol. I would manure the hills of Arlington with his body!" The New York attorney and civic leader, George Templeton Strong, noted in his diary that the metropolis was glad to have the critical day passed. "A foray of Virginia gents with Governor Wise at their head and Governor Floyd at their tail could have done infinite mischief by destroying the legal evidence of Lincoln's election (after they had killed and beaten General Scott and his Flying Artillery, that is)." [2]

[I]

The man who was journeying east to grapple with the crisis possessed more qualifications than men dreamed, but great public prestige he sadly lacked. Douglas had told a New Orleans audience, just after the election, that Lincoln, faced with hostile majorities in Congress, was entitled to commiseration rather than envy. While the adverse majorities were now melting away, the question of his power to push through such a thickening jungle of difficulties remained. Outside Illinois he was generally regarded as a secondary leader of commonplace gifts. A typical verdict of the hour characterized him as a fair Western lawyer, a good stump-speaker, and an adroit hand at electioneering, but a politician and not a statesman. C. H. Ray, who knew him well, wrote Governor Andrew that one reason for getting Chase into the Cabinet was that Chase's "great ability in affairs will give the force to Mr. Lincoln which nature has denied him." [3] The men who interviewed him during the winter—Weed, Chase, Cameron, Duff Green—had struck no note of pleased surprise over unexpected talents. His task was made harder by the general supposition that, like the four Presidents preceding him, he would be controlled by his intimate advisers.

But his Illinois intimates knew that he had plenty of backbone. C. H. Ray of the Chicago *Tribune*, stationed in Springfield, assured Elihu Washburne on January 7 that the Party leaders might trust Old Abe implicitly. "He is rising every day in the estimation of all who know him best. He is wiser and more sagacious than I thought he would prove to be. Our cause is dearer to him than anything else; and he will make no mistakes. Depend on that." And Horace White bore the same testimony: "There is no backdown in Old Abe, nor any toleration of that element in others."

2 L. E. Chittenden, *Recs. of President Lincoln*, 38; Strong MS Diary, Columbia Univ.
3 John Rutherfoord, December 19, 1860, Rutherfoord Papers, Duke Univ.; Ray, January 17, 1861, Andrew Papers, MHS.

Since election, he had been incessantly busy seeing politicians, answering letters, discussing Cabinet selections, paying a short visit to Chicago and conferring with Hannibal Hamlin there, tidying his personal affairs, and preparing his inaugural address. He had named John G. Nicolay, a Bavarian-born newspaperman of twenty-eight, frail-looking, wispy-bearded, and ceaselessly industrious, as secretary. Nicolay, overwhelmed with work, had presently suggested that John Hay—an active, brilliant young man from western Illinois, a Brown graduate of literary tastes—be retained as well, and Lincoln, after humorously demurring that he couldn't take the whole State to Washington, had consented.[4] Under the remorseless attack of job-hunters, Lincoln told Herndon that he was sick of his office before he got into it.

It is impossible to overemphasize the fact that his twin tasks of Cabinet-building and policy-making were inextricably entangled; that the stark battle being waged in Washington between the Seward-Adams moderates, who wished to show a conciliatory front toward the South in the hope of holding the border States and eventually rebuilding the Union, and the Sumner-Wade-Chandler implacables, who agreed with Greeley that the very word concession was hateful, was directly connected with efforts to manipulate the new President in the choice of his official family. The struggle on both these closely-linked fronts was to continue until the hour he entered the White House.

As Lincoln moved on toward Cleveland, Buffalo, and New York, Charles Francis Adams wrote Richard H. Dana that the negotiation between North and South was complicated by difficulties growing out of rival approaches to the new chief. "It is not to be disguised that two distinct lines of policy advocated by opposing parties within our ranks are developed. The index of one of them is Mr. Seward. That of the other [is] Mr. Chase. As yet there is no evidence before the public which will be adopted. Until it appears, there will be no firmness here. As yet I can form no opinion of the character of the chief. His speeches have fallen like a wet blanket here. They put to flight all notions of greatness. But he may yet prove true and honest and energetic, which will cover a multitude of minor difficulties."[5]

Antagonism between the moderate and the "iron-back" wings of the party, long jealous and suspicious, grew more bitter as each reached for power. Sumner was now ranting about Sewardism as a fatal policy of cowardice. To Congressional friends he orated, declaimed, and issued ukases after his wont, saying that the path of duty was plain as Washington Monument. Adams set him down as "crazy—actually frantic." He said he would give up nothing, not even the Personal Liberty law of Massachusetts. Characteristically, he denounced Seward

4 Thayer, *Hay*, I, 87; Helen Nicolay, *John G. Nicolay*, 1–65.
5 February 18, 1861; Dana Papers.

to his face. Just before the New Yorker made his great Senate speech on conciliation, Sumner went to his house, heard it read, and angrily protested. "I pleaded with him," he told friends, "for the sake of the cause, the country, and his own good name, to abandon all his propositions and simply declare that Mr. Lincoln would be inaugurated on the 4th March President of the United States, and to rally the country to his support." [6] Seward, laughing at Sumner as he seemed to laugh at everybody, was aware that he faced one of the most desperate battles of his life. For all his effervescent show of cheeriness, he looked thin, worn, and older than the previous summer. "The majority of those around me are determined to pull the house down," he said, "and I am determined not to let them." He was willing to risk his reputation in various ways to save the country. Not merely did he preach compromise where it was unpopular; he kept in close touch with Dix, Holt, and Stanton, encouraging and advising them as they managed the Administration.

Next to Weed, the ablest and most loyal of Seward's helpers was Charles Francis Adams, who possessed a weight of character that Weed lacked. The old family friendship of Seward and the Adamses had been reinforced the previous summer, when they stumped the Northwest together. The Senator hoped that Adams would be New England's representative in the Cabinet. Adams, for his part, believed that the destiny of the nation rested with the New Yorker. "All depends upon Lincoln *and the power of Seward in influencing his policy*," he wrote.[7] Like many others, Adams was annoyed by what he deemed the vacillating course of the President-elect, believing that he had begun well but failed to carry his policy through. Lincoln, thought Adams, should be like Seward—firm on the principle of non-extension of slavery, but conciliatory on other points, and suave in avoiding talk of coercion.

[II]

Lincoln's initial steps in forming his Cabinet had been taken before differences over policy could develop. The day after election, smitten with a crushing sense of the burden he was to take up, he made a tentative Cabinet slate. "It was almost the same that I finally appointed," he said later. But the problem was too difficult to be rapidly solved. His guiding principle, from which he never deviated, was to give places to the major leaders of the party, thus forming a ministry of all the talents—what Seward called "a compound Cabinet"—and reducing the danger of factional revolt against himself. If it could be kept in harmony, it would harmonize the party. Leaders and groups held such divergent

6 So he wrote Andrew, January 17, 1861; Andrew Papers.
7 February 28, 1861, Dana Papers; my italics.

views, however, that at times he despaired of realizing his object. An additional complication lay in the commitments his managers had made at the Chicago convention.

With the basic initial selection, that of Seward, we have already dealt. His position as the foremost leader of the party, his preeminent abilities, his long experience, and his genial personal qualities combined to make his appointment to the first position in the Cabinet almost imperative. With great friendliness toward the man, Lincoln could not be completely happy about the choice. He knew that Seward's undeserved reputation for radicalism made the South suspicious of him, that many Republicans disliked him for his real moderation, and that the Weed machine association was a handicap. Nevertheless, on the whole Seward's acceptance greatly strengthened his position. Another selection, that of Edward Bates as Attorney-General, was made without hesitation or difficulty. Not only was the Missourian fully equipped for this post by his legal erudition, fidelity to constitutional principles, and assuasive temper, but his appointment would gratify Union men in the border area. In December, Lincoln paid him the compliment of proposing to call on him in St. Louis. "I thought I saw an unfitness in *his coming to me*," writes Bates, "and that I *ought to go to him*." When they talked in Springfield on the fifteenth, Lincoln, discussing his whole Cabinet problem with candor, remarked that he thought Bates's participation in its work essential to his complete success. There was no refusing such an invitation.[8]

It was a weirdly unhappy comedy of errors which brought the wily Simon Cameron into a position where (though his appointment was still undecided when Lincoln left for the capital) a Cabinet assignment seemed almost a necessity. This drama, at times almost farce but in the end almost tragedy, began when David Davis and Swett promised Cameron's followers at the Chicago convention that he would be given a Cabinet seat. It was an unauthorized and disreputable bargain, but David Davis insisted that it be honored. So did Cameron's loyal Pennsylvania clansmen, and a number of old-time opponents, like David Wilmot, who had an eye on his senatorship. Seward was distinctly favorable to Cameron, and went so far as to urge Weed—unsuccessfully—to make a special trip to Springfield to press the nomination. Cameron himself, while protesting to various men that he did not want a post, left no wire unpulled and no stone unturned, until by extracting from Swett an invitation to visit Springfield, he was able late in December to push himself into Lincoln's presence. He faced a deeply troubled President-elect.[9]

Precisely what passed at this interview we do not know, and some have sur-

---

8 *Diary of Edward Bates,* 164–167; Nicolay and Hay, *Lincoln,* III, 351, 352.
9 Gideon Welles states that Swett's invitation was unauthorized; *Diary,* II, 390.

mised that the unwilling Lincoln let himself be browbeaten into offering an appointment. Cameron's own statement, now available in the papers of S. W. Crawford, would indicate that this is not true—that Lincoln had already yielded to Davis and others. Cameron writes:

> At that interview a tender of the Secship of the Treasury was made by the President to Genl C. who replied that he was then in the Senate of the U. S. and satisfied with that position and that he was not seeking any other. But it was repeated by the President, who considered as arranged and then said "Now what am I to do with Chase." Why not offer him the War Dept. said Genl C. it is the most important department now as there is no doubt that a war is imminent. Will you take the War Dept. yourself, said Mr. Lincoln. I offer it to you. But I am not seeking for any position replied Genl C. and I would not decline of course what I had recommended to another. Genl C. returned at once to Harrisburg having remained but one day in Springfield. . . .[10]

It is unnecessary to accept this memorandum at face value. What is certain is that Cameron received from Lincoln a letter dated December 31, 1860, stating that "by your permission I shall at the proper time nominate you to the United States Senate for confirmation as Secretary of the Treasury or as Secretary of War—which of the two I have not yet definitely decided." Even if the President-elect did not believe that the unholy compact at Chicago had to be redeemed, he must have felt that to rebuff Cameron and the powerful Pennsylvania machine behind him would be politically dangerous.

The vituperative resources of the English language are large, but they were almost exhausted by the storm of condemnation which beat upon this selection as soon as it was suspected or known. William Cullen Bryant wrote Lincoln on January 3 that all observers of Cameron's career felt "an utter ancient and deep seated distrust of his integrity—whether financial or political." [11] Thaddeus Stevens went further; he pronounced Cameron "a man destitute of honor and honesty." [12] Matthew Carey informed the President-elect that Cameron stood charged in the courts of Pennsylvania with serious crime, that most good citizens "look upon him as the very incarnation of corruption," and that his appointment would be "a signal to all the vultures of the Union to flock around the Treasury." The fact that Cameron on January 21 made a conciliatory speech in the Senate, saying that Pennsylvania would do anything consistent with honor to save the Union, deepened the antagonism of the "iron-backs." [13] Governor Andrew G. Curtin and his faction expressed violent opposition, the State Chairman in Pennsylvania, A. K. McClure, telegraphing that the appointment

10 Undated memorandum in S. W. Crawford Papers, Ill. State Hist. Lib.
11 Robert Todd Lincoln Papers.
12 To E. B. Washburne, January 19, 1861; *Ibid.*
13 L. F. Crippen, *Cameron*, 229, 230.

would mean the destruction of the Party in that State. Lincoln, taken aback, summoned McClure to Springfield and listened to a circumstantial account of all Cameron's derelictions. The chairman bore letters from various men supporting his charge that, in view of "the notorious incompetency and public and private villainy" of the Pennsylvania boss, the selection would disgrace the republic.[14]

Lincoln now saw that he had acted prematurely. His proper course would doubtless have been to revoke his offer, drop Cameron completely, and keep him dropped. Instead, he followed a hesitant policy. First, he wrote the Senator on January 3 an abrupt letter, saying that "things have developed which make it impossible for me to take you into the Cabinet"; that this was partly because of McClure's interposition but more largely because of "a matter wholly outside Pennsylvania"; and that he wished Cameron to yield tacit assent by sending him a telegram reading, "All right." Unfortunately, McClure at the same time returned to Pennsylvania with loud and positive statements that no final decision had been reached on any Cabinet appointment for that State. This put Cameron, who had talked boastfully of Lincoln's offer, in an impossible predicament. If he sent the President-elect the desired telegram and kept quiet, the public would believe that he had lied about his selection, and that, after his lie, McClure had summarily put him in his place. He refused to budge.[15]

Not only that, but he employed all his varied political resources to bring fresh pressure upon Lincoln. Springfield was deluged with letters, telegrams, and signed memorials in Cameron's behalf. The Pennsylvania legislature passed resolutions of eulogy and endorsement. A stream of emissaries, including Senator-elect Edgar Cowan, was hurried to Springfield to expostulate. David Davis and Swett were rallied to return to the charge. Various Pennsylvania newspapers, led by the Philadelphia *Inquirer*, gave Cameron their support, some because they were allied with his machine, and some because they saw in him a pillar of protection. Under this bombardment, Lincoln wavered—for, after all, the allegations against the Senator were mainly vague, and McClure, when asked to document them, had declined to do so. The endorsements of Cameron soon outnumbered the protests three to one, and Lincoln was able to declare that "he is more amply recommended for a place in the Cabinet than any other man."[16]

In vain did various men, East and West, strive to resist this pressure. Horace White, declaring that Cameron's appointment would be positively

14 McClure, *Lincoln and Men of War-Times*, 41, 42, 141–143.
15 Burton J. Hendrick, *Lincoln's War Cabinet*, 108 ff.; Carman and Luthin, *Lincoln and the Patronage*, 39, 40.
16 To Lyman Trumbull; Tracy, *Uncollected Letters of Lincoln*, 173, 174.

awful, did so. So did C. H. Ray. So did Elihu Washburne. From New York came a deputation of three, George Opdyke, Hiram Barney, and Judge Hogeboom, supported by Greeley's *Tribune* and Byrant's *Post,* who in a three-hour interview told Lincoln what they thought were plain home truths. "If this goes on, and Thurlow Weed and Cameron get the reins," they declared, "no course will be left but a disgraceful compromise with the South. After that, the Administration will forfeit the confidence of the country, and the Democratic Party will regain its strength in all the free States." Some Springfield men hoped that the trio had given Lincoln an eye-opener; but Old Abe had a way of making up his own mind.

The upshot was that Lincoln sent Cameron a gentler letter, contritely disclaiming any intention of giving offense, or any doubt as to the Senator's ability and fidelity in a Cabinet post. He stuck to the withdrawal of his offer. At the same time, he made it clear that he was still considering Cameron's name. "If I should make a Cabinet appointment for Pennsylvania before I reach Washington," he wrote, "I will not do so without consulting you, and giving all the weight to your views and wishes which I consistently can." David Davis remained certain that Cameron would get a place, and assured him of the fact. Moreover, strong economic interests entered the contest in the Senator's behalf. The iron and coal men of Pennsylvania, hungry for tariffs, set to work and persuaded Curtin and McClure to withdraw their opposition. As Lincoln passed through Philadelphia, they had a spokesman there, the ironmaster James Milliken, to tell the President-elect that practically all elements wished Cameron appointed to the Treasury. The astute and tireless boss had succeeded! The New York *Times* on February 25 declared that although one of the bitterest political fights in all American history had been waged against him, he had won a complete victory, and it was a settled fact that he was to represent Pennsylvania in the Administration.[17]

One other promissory note of the Chicago convention was presented for payment, and in the end was met. Davis and Swett had pledged a Cabinet position to Caleb Blood Smith in return for Indiana delegates that Smith did not really control. This lawyer, politician, newspaper owner, and promoter of railways and canals, a commonplace contriver of Whig antecedents, had seconded Lincoln's nomination and spoken industriously during the campaign. It seemed important that Indiana receive some reward; Smith's interest in internal improvements suggested that he might do for the Interior Department; and Lincoln, after hesitating between him and Colfax, took the older man. You "are sure of a bright future in any event," he wrote Colfax; "with Smith it is now or

17 Crippen, *Cameron,* 239–242; Baringer, *op. cit.,* 288–291. He was to get the War post.

never." Corwin praised Smith as industrious, well-informed, and firm—but he was to prove firm in some wrong directions.[18]

[III]

As Adams remarked, the two opposed poles in the Party leadership were represented by Seward and Chase. Each man had followers in Lincoln's immediate entourage. While such moderate Illinoisans as David Davis heartily liked Seward and his policies, radicals like Norman B. Judd and the editors of the Chicago *Tribune* espoused Chase. Lincoln's choice of Seward for the State Department had no sooner been disclosed than the milk-of-the-word Republicans, the true-blue implacables, rallied for their own champion. "We," wrote C. H. Ray of the *Tribune* (meaning radical Chicagoans), "are doing what we can to get Mr. Chase into the Cabinet as a counterbalance to the schemers who hang upon the skirts of Mr. Seward." [19] To men like Sumner, Preston King, Wilmot, and Zack Chandler, the idea that Seward would dominate the Administration was horrible; just as to Weed, Charles Francis Adams, and Cameron, the idea of domination by Chase was ghastly.[20]

The drive to make certain that Chase would be offered one of the best Cabinet positions and would accept it (for as a newly-elected Senator he might prove coy) was entirely successful. By invitation, he visited Springfield on January 3. As in other interviews of the sort, Lincoln was candor itself. He first inquired if Chase would accept the Treasury if it proved possible for him to offer it; and then, as his visitor hesitated, explained that Seward was to be Secretary of State (for Chase could hardly stand second to any less important man), and that if Seward had declined, Chase would have been his second choice. This statement largely disarmed the touchy Ohioan of any pique. He felt a little offended that Lincoln did not approach him with the same prompt definiteness as Seward, but he could not deny that the New Yorker had superior claims to first place. The two separated with a quasi-understanding. While Lincoln, his fingers just badly burnt in the Cameron fire, did not quite commit himself to an

18 Corwin to Lincoln, January 18, 1861, Robert Todd Lincoln Papers. One aspirant for the Interior Department, Norman B. Judd, was pushed aside. Mrs. Lincoln, who was in Washington in mid-January, wrote David Davis on the 17th asking him to warn Lincoln against that appointment. She had heard people at a neighboring table that morning laughing at the idea of Judd for the place. "Judd would cause trouble and dissatisfaction, and if Wall Street testifies correctly, his business transactions have not always borne inspection." David Davis Papers, Ill. State Hist. Lib. The letter is interesting as evidence of Mrs. Lincoln's participation in political affairs.
19 January 17, 1861; Andrew Papers, MHS.
20 For Lincoln's own early ideas of Cabinet-making, see Welles, *Diary*, I, 82.

offer, he almost did so; and while Chase said he must consult friends, he almost promised to accept.[21]

At once, Chase and his friends bestirred themselves to give firmer outline to this understanding. It is impossible to detect an iota of hesitation in Chase's attitude. He wanted the Treasury because it was more important than a senatorship, because it would put him as a low-tariff man in a place that might otherwise go to the high-tariff Cameron, and above all, because it would enable him to checkmate Seward. He wrote a number of friends, hinting to George Opdyke of New York that he would like a deputation to visit Lincoln and press his nomination, and plainly telling J. S. Pike that the support of Greeley and Dana would be much appreciated. He probably wrote to Bryant, for that editor shortly sent a highly significant letter to the President-elect. It was important to nominate Chase to the Treasury Department, he stated, as a man of wisdom, rigid integrity, and force of character—"not to speak of the need of his presence as a counterpoise to another member who, to commanding talents, joins a flexible and indulgent temper, and unsafe associations." It was also important to hurry his nomination, for it was nearly certain that he would not take the place "unless it were offered him early." [22] Sumner was hot to see Chase safe in the Cabinet; "it is our only chance," he exclaimed.

As Congress labored throughout February, Seward and Adams still cherished the idea of conciliation, while Chase and Sumner steadily opposed all compromise. One of Chase's phrases gained wide currency: "Inauguration first, adjustment afterward"—by which he meant that unconditional submission by the South must precede any concessions. Seward, who believed it imperative to hold Virginia and the borderland and to build a groundwork of fraternal feeling for ultimate reconstruction, regarded such an attitude as calamitous. He had been intensely worried lest a secessionist victory in Virginia, which held elections for her convention on February 4, might precipitate an attack by Governor Wise upon Washington and open a war. The victory of the Union men heartened him enormously, for it seemed to indicate that his policy might well succeed. When the middle of February came without disturbance, he was still more relieved. Every day, he believed, was bringing the people nearer the tone, temper, and ideas that he hoped would prevail. Knowing that Lincoln was at work on his inaugural, he had written him a long letter in the hope of influencing its tenor:

21 R. B. Warden, *Chase*, 365 ff.; Schuckers, *Chase*, 201–203. Chase wrote Elihu Washburne on January 14: "Should he conclude it is desirable that I take the position, he will let me know; and then I shall decide with just as little reference to personal considerations as possible." Washburne Papers.
22 January 22, 1861; Robert Todd Lincoln Papers.

The appeals from the Union men in the Border states for something of concession or compromise are very painful since they say that without it those
states must go with the tide. . . . In any case, you are to meet a hostile armed
Confederacy when you commence. You must reduce it by force or conciliation.
The resort to force would very soon be denounced by the North, although so
many are anxious for the fray. The North will not consent to a long civil war.
. . . For my own part I think that we must collect the revenues, regain the
ports in the gulf, and if need be maintain ourselves here. But that every thought
that we think ought to be conciliatory, forbearing, and patient, and so open the
way for the rising of a Union Party in the seceding states which will bring
them back into the Union.

It will be very important that your Inaugural Address be wise and winning.[23]

With every passing week the antagonism of the two factions became more
acidulous, and more threatening to the harmony of the new Administration.
Early in February, Greeley opened all the *Tribune* batteries upon Seward. He
had reserved his fire for a time, merely because a severe struggle was raging at
Albany for the senatorial seat soon to be vacated. The Seward-Weed forces had
united behind the brilliant young William M. Evarts; the opposition, rallying
against Weed with the cry, "Down with the dictator!", had divided its votes
between Greeley and Ira Harris. The outcome left Greeley half-elated, half-
frustrated. When Weed, sitting in the executive chamber nervously smoking,
learned that Greeley was leading and Evarts was about to be overwhelmed, he
suddenly transferred his votes to Harris, thus robbing the editor of the prize.
Nothing was now too harsh for Greeley to say about the humiliating surrender
of Seward to the compromise spirit. "Mr. Seward Renounces the Republican
Party," ran one of the *Tribune* headlines. Bryant's *Evening Post* was equally
virulent, for neither man could reconcile himself to the prospect of four years
of government by what Samuel Bowles called "the New Yorker with his Illinois attachment." [24]

[IV]

The policies of the new President were as yet but adumbrations projected
against two jutting principles, as rising mist might cling to two mountain crags.
One principle was inflexibility on the territorial question. "I am for no compromise," Lincoln had written Seward, "which *asserts* or *permits* the extension
of the institution on soil owned by the nation. And any trick, by which the
nation is to acquire territory, and then allow some local authority to spread slavery over it, is as noxious as any other." The other principle was an anxious desire

23 January 27, 1861; Robert Todd Lincoln Papers. Punctuation slightly altered.
24 N. Y. *Weekly Tribune*, February 9, 1861; Merriam, *Bowles*, I, 318.

to maintain peace, first by taking no aggressive step, and second by making concessions on all points but that of new slaveholding territory. "As to fugitive slaves, District of Columbia, slave trade among the slave States, and whatever springs of necessity, from the fact that the institution is among us, I care but little; so that whatever is done be comely, and not altogether outrageous. Nor do I care much about New Mexico, if further extension be hedged against." [25]

One evidence of his desire to woo the South lay in his effort to find a Southern leader who could and would enter his Cabinet. Various men suggested that he retain, as head of the War Department, the capable Joseph Holt, who was not merely a native of Kentucky but a former resident of Mississippi. The Lower South, however, now hated Holt. Seward sat down on Christmas Day to propose Randall Hunt of Louisiana, and John A. Gilmer and Kenneth Raynor of North Carolina, while he later added Robert E. Scott of Virginia to the list.[26] Of these, Gilmer, a strong antagonist of secession and advocate of compromise, seemed the most promising. On Lincoln's authorization, the Senator wrote Gilmer (they were warm friends), inquiring as to his willingness to serve, but received only a hesitant, evasive answer. Lincoln himself had meanwhile invited him to come to Springfield; and he could not have been pleased when Gilmer not merely declined the visit, but called upon the President-elect to restate his policy toward the South in more satisfactory terms. When Seward talked with Scott of Virginia late in January, it appeared that he too would not do; he was too exacting in his demands on behalf of the slave States.

The fact was that, as even Seward was compelled to admit, such men as Gilmer, Scott, and W. C. Rives were now halfway secessionists, holding that their States could and should depart unless the government executed sweeping guarantees—guarantees that the North would find abhorrent. Lincoln's early belief that no really able and influential Southerner could be found except on terms that would mean hopeless future friction thus appeared justified, and the quest was abandoned.

In one respect the pathway ahead of the incoming President seemed to grow clearer. The departure of many Southern members from Congress gave a coalition of Republicans and Northern Democrats an opportunity to carry through some long-thwarted measures. On January 21, in a scene which thoughtful men found affecting, Senators Yulee and Mallory of Florida, Clay and Fitzpatrick of Alabama, and Davis of Mississippi had formally withdrawn from the Senate. All of them reproached the North, Clay's speech being a bitter indictment; all, and particularly Yulee, defended secession as springing from a profound sense

25 Seward, *Seward*, II, 504.
26 Senator Doolittle suggested Major Anderson, a Kentuckian, for the War Department; January 10, 1861, Robert Todd Lincoln Papers.

of duty to the Southern people and to posterity; and all voiced their regret at leaving old friends. Mallory spoke with horror of civil war—"imbrue your hands in our blood, and the rains of a century will not wash from them the stain"; but Davis expressed a magnanimous good will toward the North—"I wish you well; and such, I am sure, is the feeling of the people I represent towards those whom you represent." [27] Other members from seceding States, at appropriate times, uttered their farewells.

On the very day the five Senators departed, the bill to admit Kansas passed the Senate 36 to 16, with nine Northern Democrats joining the Republicans in its support. Much the same alliance carried legislation organizing the Territories of Dakota, Colorado, and Nevada. In accordance with the Republican platform statement that the normal condition of all Territories was that of freedom, it was assumed that no explicit exclusion of slavery was necessary. Since Lincoln would appoint the territorial officers, and since no sane Southerner would carry a slave into such regions, the assumption was quite sound. Nevertheless, Douglas did not miss his opportunity to point out that the organizing acts left slavery in the three Territories, so far as Congressional interference was concerned, precisely where his law of 1854 had left slavery in Kansas; that the Wilmot Proviso was relegated to oblivion.[28] His taunt did not disturb his opponents, who knew that the three Territories in 1861 stood in a very different position from that in which Kansas had stood when Pierce was in the Executive Mansion, and when Missouri was full of men eager to carry slavery into the valley of the Kaw.

The mild tariff bill of the preceding session, amended after a fashion which we shall discuss later, was carried through Congress with the aid of Democratic votes from Pennsylvania, New Jersey, and New York, and President Buchanan signed it as one of his last official acts.[29] Once more, the Pacific Railroad died amid unhappy wrangling over routes—but in the certainty of an early resurrection. Impressed by the popular interest in reform, Congress stopped the subsidy for the carriage of mails to the Pacific by steamship, revised the patent laws, and created a Government Printing Office to do the work heretofore farmed out on the scandalous terms exposed in the Covode Report.

27 *Cong. Globe.*, 36th Cong., 2d Sess., 484–487.
28 *Ibid.*, p. 1391. The fact was that Republicans did not need or want positive prohibition in these Territories; and sensible Southerners did not want positive protection of slavery, which would have been useless.
29 Lincoln dealt briefly with the tariff in his speech at Pittsburgh on February 14. Saying that "it is a question of national housekeeping," and that "it is to the government what replenishing the meal-tub is to the family," which was then true, he pledged himself to support the Chicago plank on the tariff; but he admitted that it was subject to varying interpretations, and said frankly that "I have by no means a thoroughly matured judgment upon this subject, especially as to details." N. Y. *Herald, Tribune*, February 15.

Although the cry of sectional legislation might be hurled against some of these enactments, they actually contained little of which the South could legitimately complain. The population in the three Territories obviously needed a governmental machinery near at hand. A higher tariff revenue had become exigent, and the new duties were moderate by any standard. In one field, too, sober Congressional leaders conspicuously avoided any provocative action. Buchanan having asked Congress for increased power to deal with disorders, the House spent days in discussing various proposals to enable the President to use the militia and accept volunteer forces to maintain the peace in Washington and to protect or recover Federal property elsewhere.[30] Among other steps, it set up a committee of five to investigate certain alleged plots, backed by subversive organizations, to prevent Lincoln from taking power. All this pother came to nothing, however, when the Democrats and the cooler Republicans in the House, fearful of offending Virginia and of closing the door to reconciliation elsewhere, refused to help carry any new measure looking to the employment of armed forces. Various leaders, including Charles Francis Adams, were anxious for the Northern States to arm and drill troops, without fuss or undue publicity, for the protection of the national government, and they wrote urgent letters to the State capitals.[31] But no force bill was allowed to pass. Lincoln, after reaching Washington, used his influence against any such measure.

Fort Sumter, where Major Anderson and Captain Abner Doubleday were energetically bossing laborers and soldiers who sweated to strengthen the post, was still the danger point. A host of South Carolinians burned to seize it. Governor Pickens was eager to attack as soon as he felt strong enough. Reports that he was about to strike had led Robert Toombs and ex-President Tyler to beseech him to stay his hand; and as he continued to breathe threats the Confederate Congress, much alarmed, passed a resolution on February 12 taking control of the question of the forts. At once Pickens sent a vehement protest to the president of Congress, Howell Cobb. It was vital, he wrote, to seize Sumter before Buchanan left office, so that the incoming Lincoln Administration would face the

---

30 There were in fact three principal measures. One, reported from the select committee on the President's message of January 8, empowered the President to accept the services of volunteers in protecting or recovering the forts and other national property. A second, from the same committee, gave the President such additional powers in collecting imports as he seemed to need in the port of Charleston. The third, reported from the House Military Affairs Committee, gave the President power to call out the militia in dealing with insurrections against the Federal authority; the existing laws covering only the use of militia against foreign invasions, or when the State governments asked for aid in quelling revolts against their peace and order. *Cong. Globe*, 36th Cong., 2d Sess., January 30–March 1, *passim*.

31 See Adams's letters, Andrew Papers; Medill's letters, Robert Todd Lincoln Papers. The steps which Northern and Southern State governments had been taking will subsequently be covered in detail, as will the situation in Virginia and the border States.

question of a declaration of war separated from any hostile act occurring since it held power! Radicals in Montgomery also wanted bold action. The Confederate Congress therefore made an aggressive move on February 22. It passed a resolution declaring that steps should be taken to obtain Forts Sumter and Pickens, by negotiation or force, as early as possible, and authorizing President Davis to make all necessary military preparations. Davis for his part wrote Pickens on March 1 that he wished to see Sumter in Confederate hands as quickly as possible, but that they must make sure of victory at the first blow; and the same day he ordered Brigadier-General Beauregard to take command at Charleston. In Washington, meanwhile, Acting-Secretary Holt warned Southern leaders again and again that the government could not give up Sumter, that it had as much right to reinforce it as to occupy it, that if Anderson required reinforcements they would be sent, and that any attack on Sumter would mean war. The stage had been set for a grand battle tableau—but still men waited.

[V]

"Lincoln is making little speeches as he wends his way toward Washington," wrote George Templeton Strong in his diary of February 18, "and has said some things that are sound and creditable and raise him in my esteem." It was true that he had said some good things. Standing on the balcony of the Bates House in Indianapolis, with the mayor and Governor Oliver P. Morton beside him, while a crowd of twenty thousand waited in the cold February twilight, he had said that maintenance of the Union depended upon the people. He had said that the word coercion needed definition: "If the United States should merely hold and retake its own forts and other property, and collect the duties on foreign importations," would that be coercion? He had said that the secessionists had a queer idea of the country: "In their view the Union, as a family relation, would seem to be no regular marriage, but rather a sort of free-love arrangement, to be maintained on passional attraction."

In Cincinnati, where he was greeted by an imposing procession and an enthusiastic crowd, he flung a pledge across the river to the Kentuckians: "We mean to treat you, as near as we possibly can, as Washington, Jefferson, and Madison treated you. We mean to leave you alone, and in no way to interfere with your institutions." In Pittsburgh and again in Albany, he had explained that he did not wish to speak prematurely on the issues: first, "I should see everything, hear everything, and have every light that can possibly be brought within my reach." Some of his extempore utterances were less felicitous. His repeated assertions that the crisis was all artificial, and that if tempers were restrained the trouble would soon come to an end, jarred on anxious citizens.

His rather clumsy attempts at wit were inappropriate to the tension of the hour. When at Westfield, New York, he asked for Grace Bedell, the little girl who had written him suggesting a beard, and said, "You see I let these whiskers grow for you, Grace," most people thought the episode undignified; as undignified as his invitation to a coal-heaver at Freedom, Pennsylvania, to clamber up on the train platform and measure heights. He did find private opportunity, however, to tell governors and local leaders that they must all stand firm in defense of the Union. On the nineteenth, he reached New York, where Strong had a glimpse of him:

Lincoln arrived here yesterday afternoon by Hudson River Railroad from Albany. I walked uptown at 3:30. Broadway crowded, though not quite so densely as on the Prince of Wales's Avatar last October. The trottoir well filled by pedestrians (vehicles turned off into side streets) and sidewalks by patient and stationary sightseers. Above Canal Street they were nearly impassable. At St. Thomas's Church I met the illustrious cortege moving slowly down to the Astor House with its escort of mounted policemen and a torrent of ragtag and bobtail rushing and hooraying behind. The great rail-splitter's face was visible to me for an instant and seemed a keen, clear, honest face, not so ugly as his portraits.

Four days later, on Saturday, newsboys at noon were crying extras in all the eastern cities. They told how a plot for Lincoln's assassination had been revealed to him at Harrisburg the previous evening; how he was to have been attacked as he rode from one station to another in Baltimore the next day; and how he thereupon left privily, disguised "in a Scotch cap and long military cloak," and by traveling all night reached Washington early in the morning. Though the alleged conspiracy sounded like a sensational piece of romancing, much evidence upon its reality has been preserved; and Lincoln's reluctant secret journey, made under the pressure of worried advisers, was wise. It was unfortunate that it detracted from the effect of his impressive short address at Independence Hall the previous morning.[32]

The eastward trip had taken eleven days; nine more were to be spent in Washington before the inauguration. Lincoln, housed in the best suite of Willard's Hotel (vacated for the time being by the wealthy William E. Dodge),

[32] The Scotch cap and military cloak were fictions, and despite newspaper gibes, Lincoln's journey was entirely dignified. One element in the situation was distrust of George P. Kane, head of the Baltimore police, later arrested by General Banks and in time a Confederate officer. See Norma B. Cuthbert, *Lincoln and the Baltimore Plot, 1861*, which furnishes evidence from the Pinkerton files; R. W. Rowan, *The Pinkertons*, 82–118; Seward, *Seward*, II, 508–511. The story of the plot was temporarily discredited by W. H. Lamon in his *Life of Lincoln* because Lamon had a spiteful quarrel with Pinkerton; but it may now be regarded as valid. Nevertheless, the midnight journey did not add to Lincoln's prestige. Strong wrote in his diary for February 23: "It's to be hoped that the conspiracy can be proved beyond cavil. If it cannot be made manifest and indisputable, this surreptitious nocturnal dodging or sneaking of the President-elect into his capital city . . . will be used to damage his moral position and throw ridicule on his Administration."

was under the special guidance of Seward, who entertained him at breakfast and dinner the first day, took him to church the second, and escorted him on his visit of courtesy to President Buchanan. But Chase had taken quarters on the same floor of Willard's as Lincoln, and saw as much of him as possible. The President-elect had to receive everyone: the Illinois delegation in Congress headed by Douglas; the chief of the army, Winfield Scott; the Blair family, both father and sons, and an endless round of political callers. On his first Sunday in Washington he gave Seward a copy of his inaugural address, and that very evening the New York Senator indited a list of suggested emendations. Every observer was struck by the worn, haggard, troubled aspect of Lincoln's sensitive face.

About the incoming President, whose primary task was the completion of his Cabinet, swirled deep and murky currents of intrigue. To Seward, a perfect Cabinet would be one which included Charles Francis Adams for New England, Cameron for Pennsylvania, and Henry Winter Davis for Maryland—and which did not include Chase. Weed was in Washington, ably abetting his chieftain. To leaders of the radical wing, an ideal Cabinet would be one which included Gideon Welles for New England, someone like Wilmot for Pennsylvania, and Montgomery Blair for Maryland[33]—and which did not include Seward. Every motion that Lincoln made was watched by the rival forces with hope, dread, and suspicion. Greeley, who had come to the capital to do what he could, was almost frantic with anxiety. He wailed, on February 28, that Seward kept the incoming President perpetually surrounded, and that the compromisers would have full swing. "Old Abe is honest as the sun, and means to be true and faithful; but he is in the web of very cunning spiders and cannot work out if he would. Mrs. Abe is a Kentuckian and enjoys flattery—I mean deference. And God is above us, and all things will be well in the end. Life is not very long, and we shall rest by and by."[34]

But Lincoln intended, come what would, to be master in his own house. He meant to rule by a balance of factions and forces, in which he would hold pivotal authority. From the outset he had been determined, if possible, to have

---

33 Montgomery Blair, and indeed the whole Blair family, were at this moment radical with a fine Jacksonian fervor. They believed that if Buchanan had shown the nerve of Jackson, the Southern movement might have been checked at once. Montgomery wrote Governor Andrew on January 23 that he would not much care to serve in the same Cabinet with Seward and Cameron. "Neither of these gentlemen seem to me to appreciate the crisis or to comprehend what action it demands from the government. Violence is not in my judgment to be met with peace. Men intent on crime are not to be stopped from committing it by the promise of impunity, and it is my deliberate opinion that if such a policy is acted on we shall have a long and bloody war and permanent disunion. The truth is my dear friend that these gentlemen are wholly unfitted by mental and moral qualities for bearing sway in times of difficulty." Andrew Papers, MHS.
34 Greeley Papers, LC.

both Seward and Chase in his Cabinet and to give the direction to neither. He had no intention of yielding on the one side to Seward's objections to a "compound" Cabinet, nor on the other side to the last-minute battle of Chase, Greeley, and other radicals to close the door against Seward's ally in a policy of moderation, Cameron. As his biographers tell us, he listened patiently for a week to the voices of contending leaders, and found his original judgment as to the need for a balanced combination of talents unshaken.[35] He would not let Seward carry out the alleged agreements of a conference at Saratoga with David Davis the previous summer; he would not let the Chase-Sumner group be equally proscriptive on the other side. In the end, he decided to appoint Cameron to a place—which gave deep offence to the radicals or "iron-backs"; but also to appoint Welles and Montgomery Blair—which gave deep offence to Seward and his backers.[36]

By March 2, the heat generated by this battle had become so intense that informed Washingtonians looked for an explosion. Seward, the previous day, had presented an ultimatum: If Blair, Welles, and Chase all went in—and he particularly objected to Chase—he would go out. "There are differences between myself and Chase which make it impossible for us to act in harmony," he said. "The Cabinet ought, as General Jackson said, to be a unit." Lincoln expressed astonishment that at so late a day, after all the pains he had taken, and after all the negotiations that had taken place, he—facing so terrible a national upheaval—should be met with such a demand. He calmly asked Seward to reconsider the matter. Before he would yield, he was ready to part with the temperamental New Yorker. His friend Judd, hearing the gossip that was flying about, burst late one night into Lincoln's suite and asked whether he intended to put Henry Winter Davis in Blair's place as Postmaster-General. "Judd," replied Lincoln, "when that slate breaks again, it will break at the top."[37]

35 Nicolay and Hay, *Lincoln*, III, 368; Welles, *Diary*, II, 391.
36 Young Charles Francis Adams accepted the shelving of his father philosophically. Seward, he wrote R. H. Dana on February 28, had to drop the elder Adams and concentrate his energies on getting Cameron into the Cabinet; otherwise Lincoln would have fallen under the influence of the "iron-backs." To checkmate Chase, so violently pressed by the "ramwells," and to maintain his own peace-seeking policy, "Seward was obliged to abandon his wish to have my father in the Cabinet, and to throw his influence in favor of Cameron as a counterbalancing conservative force." But this was only one facet of the truth. Dana Papers, MHS.
37 Much light purports to be thrown on this Cabinet crisis by the mysterious *Diary of a Public Man*, attributed by Dr. Frank M. Anderson to Samuel Ward; and while its authenticity cannot be completely accepted, it bears some inner marks of veracity. See the editions by F. Lauriston Bullard and Dr. Anderson, with their introductions. Full treatment of all the complexities of the crisis would require much greater space than is here available. See Sandburg, *Lincoln*, I, 140–160; Randall, *Lincoln the President*, I, 256 ff; Nicolay and Hay, III, Ch. XXII; Hendrick, *Lincoln's War Cabinet*, 113–123; Carman and Luthin, *Lincoln and the Patronage*, 11–52; T. Harry Williams, *Lincoln and the Radicals*, 19–23, and the many biographies of Cabinet members.

Lincoln was actually ready to break his slate at the top—or to use the threat of such action to bring Seward to terms. Meeting George G. Fogg, who as secretary of the campaign committee had won his confidence, the morning after Seward's ultimatum, he described the situation. With a humorous twinkle, he remarked: "We must give up both Seward and Chase, I reckon; and I have drawn up here a list of the Cabinet leaving them both out." He showed Fogg a new slate which assigned the State Department to William L. Dayton of New Jersey and the Treasury to a New Yorker hostile to Seward. "I am sending this to Mr. Weed," dryly announced Lincoln.

That same day, Saturday, March 2, a New York deputation headed by Seward's friend Simeon Draper called to protest against Chase. They argued that Seward could never work with him. Lincoln, after listening patiently, remarked that the prime need of the nation was a hearty cooperation of all good men and all sections. At this the delegation pricked up hopeful ears, thinking he might say he would drop Chase. The President-elect drew a paper from a drawer. This, he explained, contained both his careful choice of Cabinet members, and an alternative list—the second list being in his opinion the poorer. As his hearers still radiated hope, he paused dramatically. Then he exploded his stick of dynamite! Mere mortals cannot have everything they like, he moralized. "This being the case, gentlemen, how would it do for us to agree on a change like this? How would it do for Mr. Chase to take the Treasury, and to offer the State Department to Mr. William L. Dayton?" He added that he could make Seward minister to Great Britain. And he bowed the stupefied delegation from the room.

In short, Lincoln made it plain that if Chase went, Seward must go too. And Seward had no mind to let the Administration be dominated by his rivals and enemies. He still hoped that time would justify the editorial prophecy just made by the New York *Herald*: "The destinies of the country are in Mr. Seward's hands. He will be the master spirit of the incoming Administration." He had embodied his oral ultimatum of Friday in a letter of March 2, informing Lincoln that circumstances seemed to make it his duty to withdraw his acceptance of the State Department; perhaps Draper's deputation had carried this with them. But when he heard from both Weed and Draper that if he persisted in his stand he would be shut out in the cold, he prepared to recede. On Sunday, Lincoln told Gideon Welles that although some difficulty still existed, he was satisfied that he could arrange the matter. He knew that his counter-ultimatum, "No Chase, no Seward," would be effective. "I can't afford to let Seward take the first trick," he told Nicolay.

On the morning of Monday, March 4, while the notes of the bands in the assembling procession drifted into the windows at Willard's, Lincoln penned a note, kindly but firm in tone, asking the Senator to countermand his withdrawal. "Please consider and answer by 9 o'clock tomorrow," he wrote. And that afternoon Seward, after a talk with Lincoln, came to terms. The New Yorker admitted to his wife that he had yielded. "The President is determined that he will have a compound Cabinet," he wrote; "and that it shall be peaceful, and even permanent." But even yet Seward did not begin to comprehend Lincoln's strength. After telling of his withdrawal and subsequent consent, he added: "At all events I did not dare to go home, or to England, and to leave the country to chance." Any Cabinet without himself was abandonment of the nation to chance! [38]

On the morning of the 5th Lincoln sent the Senate the names of his department heads. They were Seward as Secretary of State; Chase as Secretary of the Treasury; Cameron as Secretary of War; Gideon Welles as Secretary of the Navy; Caleb B. Smith as Secretary of the Interior; Edward Bates as Attorney-General; and Montgomery Blair as Postmaster-General. Four of the seven had been identified with the Whig Party before becoming Republicans; the other three had once been Democrats. Bates at sixty-seven was the oldest, and Montgomery Blair at forty-seven the youngest. Four members had a large national reputation, and Blair and Welles were quickly to earn one. Radical Republicans rejoiced that Chase had gained a place at Lincoln's right hand.

"Yes," exulted Greeley, "we *did*, by desperate fighting, succeed in getting five honest and noble men into the Cabinet—by a fight that you never saw equalled in intensity and duration. Gov. Chase, the ablest Republican living, who (as Gen. Dix said) was almost indispensable to the Treasury, got it at last, by the determined courage and clearheaded sagacity of Old Abe himself, powerfully backed by Hamlin, who is a jewel." Moderates also rejoiced, for their leader was head of the Cabinet. In reality neither of the two great factions of the party had won; the victory lay with the courage and wisdom of Abraham Lincoln.[39]

Meanwhile, a lesser struggle had been taking place over the contents and tone of the inaugural address. This paper had been written and set in type in Springfield, where David Davis and other intimates had read it. On the way east Lincoln showed it in Indianapolis to Orville H. Browning, who, while thinking it admirable, suggested one change. Lincoln had declared that he intended to *reclaim* the public property and national places lost to the South; Browning

---

38 For this Cabinet struggle, see Seward, *Seward*, II, 518; W. H. Lamon, *Recollections of Lincoln*, 49–51; Baringer, *A House Dividing*, 328, 329; Frank B. Sanborn, *Recollections of Seventy Years*, I, 26, 27; Welles, *Diary*, II, 391, 392; Nicolay and Hay, *Lincoln*, III, 370 ff.; N. Y. *Herald, Tribune, Times*, March 1–5, 1861.

39 March 12, 1861, Greeley Papers, LC. For criticism of the Cabinet, see Parker, *Morrill*, 124.

thought this too much of a threat; and Lincoln struck out the word. The most sensitive question remaining was whether, in addition to condemning secession as unconstitutional and unallowable, he should announce his purpose of protecting the property of the United States, South as well as North, executing all laws, and collecting the revenues. Any such statements will have a coercive look, said many; they will make it impossible for the Union men to hold Virginia, Maryland, Kentucky, North Carolina, and Tennessee; they will throw the border into revolution.

On this main point Lincoln stood his ground. Seward thought that instead of saying flatly that he would hold the forts and other public property, he should take refuge in an ambiguous statement that he would employ "the power confided to me" with efficiency but also with discretion. But Lincoln was adamant. He kept in his message a determined assertion: "The power confided to me will be used to hold, occupy, and possess the property and places belonging to the government, and to collect the duties and imposts." The one important change in content Lincoln made primarily on his own deeper reflection. In his original document he had spoken slightingly of any amendment of the Constitution, writing that he was not much impressed with the belief that it could be improved. Seward proposed a noncommittal statement. But Lincoln rewrote the passage, reversing his position. Stating that he would himself propose no amendments, he recognized the authority of the people over the question of constitutional change, concluding: "and I should, under existing circumstances, favor rather than oppose a fair opportunity being afforded the people to act upon it."

In lesser matters of style and tone, Seward was responsible for some marked improvements. When he objected to references to the Republican Party and Chicago platform, Lincoln, recognizing that they were improperly partisan, left them out. Lincoln elsewhere had written, "The Government will not assail you, unless you first assail it"; on Seward's advice, he omitted the last clause. Particularly did Seward improve the close of the document. Lincoln had ended with a prosaic statement that his oath required him to preserve, protect, and defend the government, and that it was for the secessionists and not himself to answer the question of peace or a sword. Seward, feeling the importance of sounding a higher note, and of concluding with words of affection and confidence, penned two paragraphs, and suggested that the President-elect take his choice. The second was truly inspired. Lincoln seized on it and gave it a perfection which has placed it among the nation's treasures of speech.[40]

40 On the inaugural address, see Browning, Diary, I, 455; Nicolay and Hay, *Lincoln*, III, 318 ff., 327-343; Randall, *Lincoln*, I, 297-310; and the well-informed Washington correspondence of the N. Y. *Herald*, March 2-5, 1861. David M. Potter in *Lincoln and the Secession*

[VI]

As a solemn public pageant, the inauguration ceremonies left nothing to be desired. The early morning was chill and cloudy, with a sharp northwest wind which swirled clouds of dust through the streets; but noon brought calm and a bright, cheerful sun. The usual host of visitors had surged into the capital, but with one sharp difference from previous years—few Southerners had come. Both Buchanan and Lincoln were busy at an early hour: the President signing bills at the Capitol, for the Senate had sat all night, and the President-elect giving a final touch to his address and receiving Bates, Welles, Cameron, Trumbull, David Davis, and other visitors. By nine o'clock crowds were filling the downtown streets, gazing at the volunteer soldiery who had begun to march and counter-march, and listening to the bands play patriotic music. Gradually the throng thickened; gradually the mounted marshals under B. B. French, with blue scarves, white rosettes, and blue-and-gold batons, got the procession into line. By noon double columns of troops flanked Willard's Hotel, and at 12:30 rolling cheers announced Buchanan's arrival in his open carriage.

General Scott had taken full precautions. As the procession to Capitol Hill got under way, riflemen were concealed on the roofs of scattered houses along Pennsylvania Avenue; platoons were stationed every hundred yards; cavalry guarded the side streets; and a guard of honor from the regular army and marines surrounded the presidential carriage so closely that it was often hard to see the occupants. Sharpshooters in the windows of the Capitol bent hawk-like eyes upon the crowd, and a battery of flying artillery was posted just north of that building. But the public saw little of all this. Its gaze was fixed on the fluttering flags and bunting, the gaily-dressed military corps, the pounding bands, and the float of thirty-four pretty girls representing as many States. Lincoln, entering the Capitol through a heavy plank passage-way, found Congress, the Supreme Court, and the diplomatic corps assembled in the Senate chamber. As attendants beat the dust of the avenue from his clothes, a reporter noted that he looked pale, fatigued, and anxious. Well he might, after the incessant conferences, interviews, dinners, receptions, and toils of the past ten days! He shook hands with friends. Then the march to the platform at the east portico began; and he was soon taking his place on that flag-dressed structure, the

---

Crisis holds that in declaring that he would not force unwelcome Federal officers upon any reluctant interior community, that he would exercise his authority "according to circumstances actually existing," and that he looked toward "a peaceful solution of the national troubles and the restoration of fraternal sympathies and affections," Lincoln was laying down both a formula and a plan; 327 ff. The mails would be delivered "unless repelled"; the duties would be collected, if at all, at sea. In short, Lincoln did not contemplate coercion, though he did insist that the Union "will constitutionally defend and maintain itself."

army and navy officers and uniformed diplomats splashing the black-coated groups about him with color.

Observant members of the great crowd (estimated at twenty-five thousand or more) facing the platform and the unfinished dome enjoyed some moments of drama. If we may believe Carl Schurz, Henry Watterson, and the author of *The Diary of a Public Man* (whose recollections, however, are not substantiated by any contemporaneous evidence) they saw Douglas, when Lincoln awkwardly sought a place for his tall hat, seize it and hold it on his knees as a symbolic act. They saw Lincoln's well-loved friend, the English-born Senator from Oregon, E. D. Baker, step forward and introduce the President-elect. They saw Lincoln lay down his manuscript, clap his hands in his pockets, and pull out a pair of steel-bowed spectacles—a surprise to those who knew him only through his pictures. As he read in his clear, shrill voice, which carried well to the outskirts of the assemblage, all listened in a solemn silence, as if moved by a conviction that the hour was big with their own fate and that of the nation. The sun shone down brightly on the gay dresses of the ladies, the uniforms and glittering weapons of the volunteer companies standing at rest on the outskirts, and the waving flags. Lincoln closed amid an intent hush. Then the crowd saw the bent, shrunken Chief Justice Taney, tottering with age and emotion, administer the oath to an incoming President whose views he deeply distrusted.[41]

The inaugural address had been awaited with feverish anxiety throughout the North, where nearly everyone felt that the nation was on the verge of its final decision for peace or war. Bulletins appeared in New York at noon: "Great excitement in Washington. The new President up all night. Great efforts to make him alter his inaugural. The President firm." This was a canard. Extras appeared there and in other cities at two o'clock, announcing that the ceremonies were safely under way; and multitudes of citizens, reading them, fervently exclaimed, "Thank God!" Evening editions carried first half and then all of the address. The comment of George Templeton Strong doubtless represents the first response of countless intelligent men. "I think there's a clank of metal in it," he wrote of the speech. "It's unlike any message or state paper of any class that has appeared in my time, to my knowledge. It is characterized by strong individuality and the absence of conventionalism of

41 The hat episode is also mentioned in J. G. Holland, *Lincoln*, 278 (1866). For a discussion of the authenticity of *The Diary of a Public Man* see James G. Randall in *Amer. Hist. Rev.*, XLI, 277–279. For the organization of volunteer companies in the District of Columbia to ensure the protection of the national capital and an orderly inauguration, see the interesting essay by Colonel Charles P. Stone in *Battles and Leaders of the Civil War*, I, 22, 23. Stone accuses Floyd of treasonable intentions. The N. Y. *Herald*, *Tribune*, and *Times* give full accounts of the inaugural ceremonies.

thought or diction. It doesn't run in the ruts of Public Documents number one to number ten million and one, but seems to introduce one to a *man*, and to dispose one to like him."

There was indeed a clank of metal in the address. Reciting the constitutional and historical arguments for deeming the Union perpetual, Lincoln declared: "It follows from these views that no State, upon its own mere motion, can lawfully get out of the Union; that laws and ordinances to that effect are legally void; and that acts of violence within any State or States against the authority of the United States are insurrectionary or revolutionary, according to circumstances." He proceeded:

I therefore consider that, in view of the Constitution and the laws, the Union is unbroken, and, to the extent of my ability, I shall take care, as the Constitution itself expressly enjoins upon me, that the laws of the Union be faithfully executed in all the States. . . . In doing this there needs to be no bloodshed or violence; and there shall be none, unless it be forced upon the national authority. The power confided to me will be used to hold, occupy, and possess the property and places belonging to the government, and to collect the duties and imposts; but beyond what may be necessary for these objects, there will be no invasion—no using of force against or among the people anywhere.

But the address was also full of expressions of a conciliatory spirit. Lincoln once more, and emphatically, declared that he had no purpose to interfere with slavery in the States where it existed. He asserted that in the matter of reclaiming fugitive slaves, Congress must make good the unanimous oath of its members to support the Constitution. He promised that where hostility to the United States in any interior community should be so great as to prevent resident citizens from holding Federal office, "there will be no attempt to force obnoxious strangers among the people for that object." Asking the nation to take time and think calmly, he appealed directly to the people of the South. "In your hands, my dissatisfied fellow-countrymen, and not in mine, is the momentous issue of civil war. The government will not assail you. You can have no conflict without being yourselves the aggressors. *You* have no oath registered in heaven to destroy the government, while *I* shall have the most solemn one to 'preserve, protect, and defend' it." And he ended, in poetic phrases for which Seward had supplied the framework of ideas:

I am loth to close. We are not enemies, but friends. We must not be enemies. Though passion may have strained, it must not break our bonds of affection. The mystic chords of memory, stretching from every battlefield, and patriot grave, to every living heart and hearthstone, all over this broad land, will yet swell the chorus of the Union, when again touched, as surely they will be, by the better angels of our nature.

I close., We are not we must not be aliens
or enemies but ~~countrym~~ fellow countrymen
and brethren. Although passion has strained
the bonds of affection too hardly they must
not be ~~broken~~ ~~they will not~~, I am
sure they will not be broken, The
mystic chords which proceeding from ~~every~~
to so many battle fields and ~~patriot~~ so
many patriot graves ~~band~~ pass through
all ~~the~~ hearts and ~~hearths~~ all ~~the~~
hearths in this broad continent of ours
will yet ~~harmon~~ again harmonize in
their ~~ancient music~~ when ~~touched as they~~
~~are~~ breathed upon ~~again~~ by the ~~better~~
~~angels~~ guardian angel of the nation

Seward wrote the paragraph above and submitted it for the close of the inaugural address, to read: "I close. We are not we must not be aliens or enemies but fellow countrymen and brethren. Although passion has strained our bonds of affection too hardly they must not, I am sure they will not be broken. The mystic chords which proceeding from so many battle fields and so many patriot graves pass through all the hearts and all the hearths in this broad continent of ours will yet again harmonize in their ancient music when breathed upon by the guardian angel of the nation." Lincoln revised this, shortened, transmuted it into slightly different meaning and a distinctly changed verbal music, adding it to the printer's proof text brought on from Springfield, as below:

You can have no conflict, without being yourselves the aggressors. You have no oath
registered in Heaven to destroy the government, while I shall have the most solemn one
to "preserve, protect and defend" it. ~~...~~

☞ I am loth to close. We are not enemies,
but friends— We must not be enemies. Though passion may
have strained, it must not break our bonds of affection.
The mystic chords of memory, stretching from every battlefield, and patriot grave, to every living heart and hearthstone, all over this broad land, will yet swell the chorus of the Union, when again touched, as surely they will
be, by the better angels of our nature.

It was natural that public response to the inaugural should be governed largely by party lines. The Chicago *Tribune*, the St. Louis *Democrat*, the New York *Evening Post* and *Tribune*, the Springfield *Republican*, all praised it warmly. So did such Republican leaders as Greeley, Sumner, Preston King, Hale, and Trumbull. On the other side, the Philadelphia *Pennsylvanian* called it a weak declaration of war on the South, a tiger's claw concealed under the fur of Sewardism; the Albany *Atlas and Argus* predicted that the attempt to collect revenues must lead to collision and war; and the New York *Herald* condemned it as bearing "marks of indecision, and yet of strong coercion proclivities." In the now all-important border States the secessionists regarded it as warlike, while many Union men seized on its mild phraseology as ground for hope. Thus in Virginia the fire-eating Richmond *Enquirer* declared that peace was now impossible—"Virginia must fight"; yet Governor John Letcher thought that it strengthened the hands of the conservatives. Many North Carolinians attacked it as a war message; but John A. Gilmer held that it offered cheering assurances which justified the South in waiting for the sober second thought of the North. Douglas said in the Senate on March 5 that after a careful analysis he had come to the conclusion that it was a peace and not a war speech; and John Bell declared that the South should accept it as a peace offering until by some act the North proved it otherwise.[42]

In the Lower South, however, it was generally treated as a justification of armed secession. The Charleston *Mercury* denounced Lincoln's "insolence" and "brutality"; Mobile and New Orleans journals grew inflammatory; and dispatches from Montgomery on the 5th universally construed the address as meaning that war was inevitable.

Far more important than the outward pageantry of the day were certain events of which the public knew nothing. On that historic March 4, the outgoing Secretary of War received from Major Anderson a disturbing dispatch, stating that the supplies of Fort Sumter were running low; intimating that he could not hold out much longer without help; and declaring that in his and his officers' opinion it would take at least twenty thousand troops to force their relief.[43] The South Carolinians had so strengthened the surrounding batteries, he wrote, that the fort might easily be reduced at any time. On that March 4, Martin J. Crawford of Georgia, Commissioner of the Confederate States, who had arrived in Washington only the previous day, held eager conferences with

42 Strong's comment on the inaugural is his MS Diary of March 5, 1861. The N. Y. *Herald* of March 5 and 6 contained an excellent resume of editorial opinion; the N. Y. *Times* of March 6 a number of excerpts. Jubal A. Early told the Virginia Convention that Lincoln's words showed he would perform his duty in moderate spirit; Munford, *Virginia's Attitude Toward Slavery and Secession*, 266. For a general survey see Randall, *Lincoln*, I, 303–308.
43 *Official Records*, Series I. Vol. I, 188 ff.

such Southern leaders as remained in the capital; and he mailed to Robert Toombs, Secretary of State in the Confederate Government, a long letter describing the situation. He wrote that Chase and Blair would compose the element in the Cabinet standing for coercion; that John Bell was in Washington, and was urgent in his entreaties to Lincoln not to disturb the Confederate States, but that he would not be heeded if the new Administration believed that it could act vigorously without losing the border States; and that "whatsoever the Republican Party can do without driving out Virginia it will do, and such coercive measures as the new Administration may *with safety* adopt it will most certainly." [43a] Ex-Senator Wigfall telegraphed from Washington that night to Charleston: "Inaugural means war. There is strong ground for belief that reenforcements will be speedily sent. Be vigilant."

Lincoln, as a matter of fact, wished to do everything within the limits of his duty to avoid a collision. When Scott, after studying Anderson's dispatch, reported to him that "evacuation seems inevitable . . . if indeed the wornout garrison be not assaulted and carried in the present week," he calmly instructed the general to give the subject further study. Nevertheless, the situation had become highly inflammable. Edward Everett, reading Lincoln's inaugural address, believed that its conciliatory tone was more than offset by the pledge to hold the forts and to collect the customs. "Either measure," he wrote in his diary, "will result in civil war, which I am compelled to look upon as almost certain." [44] Had he known what Major Anderson was reporting to Washington and what Commissioner Crawford was reporting to Montgomery, his forebodings would have been darker still.

*   *   *   *   *   *   *

Great and complex events have great and complex causes. Burke, in his *Reflections on the Revolution in France,* wrote that "a state without the means

---

43a Robert Toombs Letter-Book, Trescot Papers, South Caroliniana Library. Crawford's letter was dated March 3. His fellow Commissioners, John Forsyth and A. B. Roman, had not yet arrived. Bell, wrote Crawford, had assured Lincoln "that any attempt to reinforce the Forts, collect the revenue, or in any way whatever to interfere with your Government would be the signal for every border State to secede from the Union and join the Southern Confederacy. He advises an *indefinite* truce; the withdrawal of the troops from the Forts (except a sergeant with a nominal force); the flag of the U. S. to be kept floating on the fortifications to satisfy the war party North; in the meantime the Confederate States are to be left alone, to do as they may choose, prepare for war, strengthen defences, in short to do whatever may seem good to them. The advantages to the U. S. being, that the more we may do, looking to independence and safety, the greater will be the amount of taxation upon the people and the sooner will a current of dissatisfaction and discontent set in, resulting at last in a reconstruction upon the most permanent and durable basis." Crawford thought that part of the Administration was receptive to these ideas—but they would not prevail.

44 MS Diary, March 4, 1861.

of some change is without the means of its conservation," and that a constant reconciliation of "the two principles of conservation and correction" is indispensable to healthy national growth. It is safe to say that every such revolutionary era as that on which the United States entered in 1860 finds its genesis in an inadequate adjustment of these two forces. It is also safe to say that when a tragic national failure occurs, it is largely a failure of leadership. "Brains are of three orders," wrote Machiavelli, "those that understand of themselves, those that understand when another shows them, and those that understand neither by themselves nor by the showing of others." Ferment and change must steadily be controlled; the real must, as Bryce said, be kept resting on the ideal; and if disaster is to be avoided, wise leaders must help thoughtless men to understand, and direct the action of invincibly ignorant men. Necessary reforms may be obstructed in various ways; by sheer inertia, by tyranny and class selfishness, or by the application of compromise to basic principles—this last being in Lowell's view the main cause of the Civil War. Ordinarily the obstruction arises from a combination of all these elements. To explain the failure of American leadership in 1846–1861, and the revolution that ensued, is a bafflingly complicated problem.

Looking backward from the verge of war in March, 1861, Americans could survey a series of ill-fated decisions by their chosen agents. One unfortunate decision was embodied in Douglas's Kansas-Nebraska Act of 1854. Had an overwhelming majority of Americans been ready to accept the squatter sovereignty principle, this law might have proved a statesmanlike stroke; but it was so certain that powerful elements North and South would resist it to the last that it accentuated the strife and confusion. Another disastrous decision was made by Taney and his associates in the Dred Scott pronouncement of 1857. Still another was made by Buchanan when he weakly accepted the Lecompton Constitution and tried to force that fraudulent document through Congress. The Northern legislatures which passed Personal Liberty Acts made an unhappy decision. Most irresponsible, wanton, and disastrous of all was the decision of those Southern leaders who in 1858–60 turned to the provocative demand for Congressional protection of slavery in all the Territories of the republic.[45] Still other errors might be named. Obviously, however, it is the forces behind these decisions which demand our study; the waters pouring down the gorge, not the rocks which threw their spray into the air.

At this point we meet a confused clamor of voices as various students

---

45 We stated in an earlier chapter that Southern leaders in 1857 had time for a few more decisions, but they had to think fast and think straight. This slave-code demand represented their most flagrant error. It has been said that Jefferson Davis adopted it because his blatherskite rival A. G. Brown took it up. But a true statesman does not let an irresponsible rival force him into courses he recognizes as unwise.

attempt an explanation of the tragic denouement of 1861. Some writers are as
content with a simple explanation as Lord Clarendon was when he attributed
the English Civil War to the desire of Parliament for an egregious domination
of the government. The bloody conflict, declared James Ford Rhodes, had "a
single cause, slavery." He was but echoing what Henry Wilson and other
early historians had written, that the aggressions of the Slave Power offered the
central explanation. That opinion had been challenged as early as 1861 by the
London *Saturday Review*, which remarked that "slavery is but a surface question in American politics," and by such Southern propagandists as Yancey,
who tried to popularize a commercial theory of the war, emphasizing a supposed Southern revolt against the tariff and other Yankee exactions. A later
school of writers was to find the key to the tragedy in an inexorable conflict
between the business-minded North and the agrarian-minded South, a thrusting industrialism colliding with a rather static agricultural society. Still another
group of writers has accepted the theory that the war resulted from psychological causes. They declare that agitators, propagandists, and alarmists on both
sides, exaggerating the real differences of interest, created a state of mind, a
hysterical excitement, which made armed conflict inevitable.

At the very outset of the war Senator Mason of Virginia, writing to his
daughter, asserted that two systems of society were in conflict; systems, he
implied, as different as those of Carthage and Rome, Protestant Holland and
Catholic Spain. That view, too, was later to be elaborated by a considerable
school of writers. Two separate nations, they declared, had arisen within the
United States in 1861, much as two separate nations had emerged within the
first British Empire by 1776. Contrasting ways of life, rival group consciousness, divergent hopes and fears made a movement for separation logical; and
the minority people, believing its peculiar civilization in danger of suppression,
began a war for independence. We are told, indeed, that two types of nationalism came into conflict: a Northern nationalism which wished to preserve the
unity of the whole republic, and a Southern nationalism intent on creating an
entirely new republic.

It is evident that some of these explanations deal with merely superficial
phenomena, and that others, when taken separately, represent but subsidiary
elements in the play of forces. Slavery was a great fact; the demands of Northern industrialism constituted a great fact; sectional hysteria was a great fact.
But do they not perhaps relate themselves to some profounder underlying
cause? This question has inspired one student to suggest that "the confusion
of a growing state" may offer the fundamental explanation of the drift to war;
an unsatisfactory hypothesis, for westward growth, railroad growth, business
growth, and cultural growth, however much attended with "confusion," were

unifying factors, and it was not the new-made West but old-settled South Carolina which led in the schism.

One fact needs emphatic statement: of all the monistic explanations for the drift to war, that posited upon supposed economic causes is the flimsiest. This theory was sharply rejected at the time by so astute an observer as Alexander H. Stephens. South Carolina, he wrote his brother on New Year's Day, 1861, was seceding from a tariff "which is just what her own Senators and members in Congress made it." As for the charges of consolidation and despotism made by some Carolinians, he thought they arose from peevishness rather than a calm analysis of facts. "The truth is, the South, almost in mass, has voted, I think, for every measure of general legislation that has passed both houses and become law for the last ten years." The South, far from groaning under tyranny, had controlled the government almost from its beginning, and Stephens believed that its only real grievance lay in the Northern refusal to return fugitive slaves and to stop the antislavery agitation. "All other complaints are founded on threatened dangers which may never come, and which I feel very sure would be averted if the South would pursue a judicious and wise course." Stephens was right. It was true that the whole tendency of Federal legislation 1842–1860 was toward free trade; true that the tariff in force when secession began was largely Southern-made; true that it was the lowest tariff the country had known since 1816; true that it cost a nation of thirty million people but sixty million dollars in indirect revenue; true that without secession no new tariff law, obnoxious to the Democratic Party, could have passed before 1863—if then.

In the official explanations which one Southern State after another published for its secession, economic grievances are either omitted entirely or given minor position. There were few such supposed grievances which the agricultural States of Illinois, Iowa, Indiana, Wisconsin, and Minnesota did not share with the South—and they never threatened to secede. Charles A. Beard finds the tap-root of the war in the resistance of the planter interest to Northern demands enlarging the old Hamilton-Webster policy. The South was adamant in standing for "no high protective tariffs, no ship subsidies, no national banking and currency system; in short, none of the measures which business enterprise deemed essential to its progress." But the Republican platform in 1856 was silent on the tariff; in 1860 it carried a milk-and-water statement on the subject which Western Republicans took, mild as it was, with a wry face; the incoming President was little interested in the tariff; and any harsh legislation was impossible. Ship subsidies were not an issue in the campaign of 1860. Neither were a national banking system and a national currency system. They were not mentioned in the Republican platform nor discussed by party debaters. The Pacific Railroad was advocated both by the Douglas Democrats and the Republicans; and it is noteworthy that Seward and Douglas were for building both a Northern and a Southern line. In short, the divisive economic issues are easily exaggerated. At the same time, the unifying economic factors were both numerous and powerful. North and South had economies which were largely complementary. It was no misfortune to the South that Massachusetts cotton mills wanted its staple, and that New York ironmasters like Hewitt were eager to sell rails dirt-cheap to Southern railway builders; and sober businessmen on both sides, merchants, bankers, and manufacturers, were the men most anxious to keep the peace and hold the Union together.[46]

We must seek further for an explanation; and in so doing, we must give special weight to the observations of penetrating leaders of the time, who knew at firsthand the spirit of the people. Henry J. Raymond, moderate editor of the New York *Times,* a sagacious man who disliked Northern abolitionists and Southern radicals, wrote in January, 1860, an analysis of the impending conflict which attributed it to a competition for power:

In every country there must be a just and equal balance of powers in the government, an equal distribution of the national forces. Each section and each interest must exercise its due share of influence and control. It is always more or less difficult to preserve their just equipoise, and the larger the country, and the more varied its great interests, the more difficult does the task become, and the greater the shock and disturbance caused by an attempt to adjust it when once disturbed. I believe I state only what is generally conceded to be a fact, when I say that the growth of the Northern States in population, in wealth, in all the elements of political influence and control, has been out of proportion to their political influence in the Federal Councils. While the Southern States have less than a third of the aggregate population of the Union, their interests have influenced the policy of the government far more than the interests of the Northern States. . . . Now the North has made rapid advances within the last five years, and it naturally claims a proportionate share of influence and power in the affairs of the Confederacy.

It is inevitable that this claim should be put forward, and it is also inevitable that it should be conceded. No party can long resist it; it overrides all parties, and makes them the mere instruments of its will. It is quite as strong today in the heart of the Democratic party of the North as in the Republican ranks; and any party which ignores it will lose its hold on the public mind.

Why does the South resist this claim? Not because it is unjust in itself,

46 South Carolina's Declaration of immediate causes of secession ignored economic issues, and concentrated upon slavery. Rhett's Address to the other slaveholding States did charge the North with gross injustice in tariff legislation; but the whole body of South Carolina's Representatives and Senators had voted for the existing tariff of 1857, and Rhett in defending his Address declared that to win the sympathy of Britain and France, a protest against protective tariffs would be more useful than a protest grounded on the slavery question. McPherson, *Political History,* 12–20.

but because it has become involved with the question of slavery, and has drawn so much of its vigor and vitality from that quarter, that it is almost merged in that issue. The North bases its demand for increased power, in a very great degree, on the action of the government in regard to slavery—and the just and rightful ascendency of the North in the Federal councils comes thus to be regarded as an element of danger to the institutions of the Southern States.

In brief, Raymond, who held that slavery was a moral wrong, that its economic and social tendencies were vicious, and that the time had come to halt its growth with a view to its final eradication, believed that the contest was primarily one for power, and for the application of that power to the slave system. With this opinion Alexander H. Stephens agreed. The Georgian said he believed slavery both morally and politically right. In his letter to Lincoln on December 30, 1860, he declared that the South did not fear that the new Republican Administration would interfere directly and immediately with slavery in the States. What Southerners did fear was the ultimate result of the shift of power which had just occurred—in its application to slavery:

Now this subject, which is confessedly on all sides outside of the constitutional action of the Government, so far as the States are concerned, is made the 'central idea' in the platform of principles announced by the triumphant party. The leading object seems to be simply, and wantonly, if you please, to put the institutions of nearly half the States under the ban of public opinion and national condemnation. This, upon general principles, is quite enough of itself to arouse a spirit not only of general indignation, but of revolt on the part of the proscribed. Let me illustrate. It is generally conceded by the Republicans even, that Congress cannot interfere with slavery in the States. It is equally conceded that Congress cannot establish any form of religious worship. Now suppose that any one of the present Christian churches or sects prevailed in all the Southern States, but had no existence in any one of the Northern States,—under such circumstances suppose the people of the Northern States should organize a political party, not upon a foreign or domestic policy, but with one leading idea of condemnation of the doctrines and tenets of that particular church, and with an avowed object of preventing its extension into the common Territories, even after the highest judicial tribunal of the land had decided they had no such constitutional power. And suppose that a party so organized should carry a Presidential election. Is it not apparent that a general feeling of resistance to the success, aims, and objects of such a party would necessarily and rightfully ensue?

Raymond and Stephens agreed that the two sections were competing for power; that a momentous transfer of power had just occurred; and that it held fateful consequences because it was involved with the issue of slavery, taking authority from a section which believed slavery moral and healthy, and giving it to a section which held slavery immoral and pernicious. To Stephens this transfer was ground for resuming the ultimate sovereignty of the States. Here we find a somewhat more complex statement of James Ford Rhodes's thesis that the central cause of the Civil War lay in slavery. Here, too, we revert to the assertions of Yancey and Lincoln that the vital conflict was between those who thought slavery right and those who thought it wrong. But this definition we can accept only if we probe a little deeper for a concept which both modifies and enlarges the basic source of perplexity and quarrel.

The main root of the conflict (and there were minor roots) was the problem of slavery *with its complementary problem of race-adjustment;* the main source of the tragedy was the refusal of either section to face these conjoined problems squarely and pay the heavy costs of a peaceful settlement. Had it not been for the difference in race, the slavery issue would have presented no great difficulties. But as the racial gulf existed, the South inarticulately but clearly perceived that elimination of this issue would still leave it the terrible problem of the Negro. Those historians who write that if slavery had simply been left alone it would soon have withered overlook this heavy impediment. The South as a whole in 1846–61 was not moving toward emancipation, but away from it. It was not relaxing the laws which guarded the system, but reinforcing them. It was not ameliorating slavery, but making it harsher and more implacable. The South was further from a just solution of the slavery problem in 1830 than it had been in 1789. It was further from a tenable solution in 1860 than it had been in 1830. Why was it going from bad to worse? Because Southern leaders refused to nerve their people to pay the heavy price of race-adjustment. These leaders never made up their mind to deal with the problem as the progressive temper of civilization demanded. They would not adopt the new outlook which the upward march of mankind required because they saw that the gradual abolition of slavery would bring a measure of political privilege; that political privilege would usher in a measure of economic equality; that on the heels of economic equality would come a rising social status for the Negro. Southern leadership dared not ask the people to pay this price.

A heavy responsibility for the failure of America in this period rests with this Southern leadership, which lacked imagination, ability, and courage. But the North was by no means without its full share, for the North equally refused to give a constructive examination to the central question of slavery as linked with race adjustment. This was because of two principal reasons. Most abolitionists and many other sentimental-minded Northerners simply denied that the problem existed. Regarding all Negroes as white men with dark skins, whom a few years of schooling would bring abreast of the dominant race, they thought that no difficult adjustment was required. A much more numerous body of Northerners would have granted that a great and terrible task of race adjustment existed—but they were reluctant to help shoulder any part of it. Take a million or two million Negroes into the Northern States? Indiana, Illinois, and even Kansas were unwilling to take a single additional person of color. Pay tens of millions to help educate and elevate the colored population? Take even a first step by offering to pay the Southern slaveholders some recompense for a gradual liberation of their human property? No Northern politician dared ask his constituents to make so unpopular a sacrifice. The North, like the South, found it easier to drift blindly toward disaster.

The hope of solving the slavery problem without a civil war rested upon several interrelated factors, of which one merits special emphasis. We have said that the South as a whole was laboring to bolster and stiffen slavery—which was much to its discredit. But it is nevertheless true that slavery was dying all around the edges of its domain; it was steadily decaying in Delaware, Maryland, western Virginia, parts of Kentucky, and Missouri. Much of the harshness of Southern legislation in the period sprang from a sense that slavery was in danger from *internal* weaknesses. In no great time Delaware, Maryland, and Missouri were likely to enter the column of free States; and if they did, reducing the roster to twelve, the doom of the institution would be clearly written. Allied with this factor was the rapid comparative increase of Northern strength, and the steady knitting of economic, social, and moral ties between the North and West, leaving the South in a position of manifest inferiority. A Southern Confederacy had a fair fighting chance in 1861; by 1880 it would have had very little. If secession could have been postponed by two decades, natural forces might well have placed a solution full in sight. Then, too, the growing pressure of world sentiment must in time have produced its effect. But to point out these considerations is not to suggest that in 1861 a policy of procrastination and appeasement would have done anything but harm. All hope of bringing Southern majority sentiment to a better attitude would have been lost if Lincoln and his party had flinched on the basic issue of the restriction of slavery; for by the seventh decade of nineteenth century history, the time had come when that demand had to be maintained.

While in indicting leadership we obviously indict the public behind the leaders, we must also lay some blame upon a political environment which gave leadership a poor chance. American parties, under the pressure of sectional feeling, worked badly. The government suffered greatly, moreover, from the lack of any adequate planning agency. Congress was not a truly deliberative body, and its committees had not yet learned to do long-range planning. The President might have formulated plans, but he never did. For one reason, no President between Polk and Lincoln had either the ability or the prestige required; for another reason, Fillmore, Pierce, and Buchanan all held that their duty was merely to execute the laws, not to initiate legislation. Had the country possessed a ministerial form of government, the Cabinet in leading the legislature would have been compelled to lay down a program of real scope concerning slavery. As it was, leadership in Washington was supplied only spasmodically by men like Clay, Douglas, and Crittenden.

And as we have noted, the rigidity of the American system was at this time a grave handicap. Twice, in the fall of 1854 and of 1858, the elections gave a stunning rebuke to the Administration. Under a ministerial system, the old government would probably have gone out and a new one have come in. In 1854, however, Pierce continued to carry on the old policies, and in 1858 Buchanan remained the drearily inept helmsman of the republic. Never in our history were bold, quick planning and a flexible administration of policy more needed; never was the failure to supply them more complete.

Still another element in the tragic chronicle of the time must be mentioned. Much that happens in human affairs is accidental. When a country is guided by true statesmen the role of accident is minimized; when it is not, unforeseen occurrences are numerous and dangerous. In the summer and fall of 1858, as we have seen, the revival of a conservative opposition party in the upper South, devoted to the Union, furnished a real gleam of hope. If this opposition had been given unity and determined leadership, if moderate Southerners had stood firm against the plot of Yancey and others to disrupt the Democratic Party, if Floyd had been vigilant enough to read the warning letter about John Brown and act on it, the situation might even then have been saved. Instead, John Brown's mad raid fell on public opinion like a thunderstroke, exasperating men everywhere and dividing North and South more tragically than ever. The last chance of persuading the South to submit to an essential step, the containment of slavery, was gone.

The war, when it came, was not primarily a conflict over State Rights, although that issue had become involved in it. It was not primarily a war born of economic grievances, although many Southerners had been led to think that they were suffering, or would soon suffer, economic wrongs. It was not a war created by politicians and publicists who fomented hysteric excitement; for while hysteria was important, we have always to ask what basic reasons made possible the propaganda which aroused it. It was not primarily a war about slavery alone, although that institution seemed to many the grand cause. It was a war over slavery *and* the future position of the Negro race in North America. Was the Negro to be allowed, as a result of the shift of power signalized by Lincoln's election, to take the first step toward an ultimate position of general economic, political, and social equality with the white man? Or was he to be held immobile in a degraded, servile position, unchanging for the next hundred years as it had remained essentially unchanged for the hundred years past? These questions were implicit in Lincoln's demand that slavery be placed in a position where the public mind could rest assured of its ultimate extinction.

Evasion by the South, evasion by the North, were no longer possible. The alternatives faced were an unpopular but curative adjustment of the situation by the opposed parties, or a war that would force an adjustment upon the loser. For Americans in 1861, as for many other peoples throughout history, war was easier than wisdom and courage.

5.

WHEN IT CAME, "the Civil War, fought by every element in the Northern and Southern population, was a people's war, a *Volkskrieg*, in a fuller sense than any earlier conflict of modern time. On both sides the resourcefulness, stubborn courage, and devotion to high aims, the disorderliness, theatricality, and impatience, were alike popular traits. Behind the uprising after Sumter lay the demagogy, selfishness, and blindness of the period since Winfield Scott had occupied Mexico City; years of yeasty growth, leavened by little political honesty or wisdom. . . ." [1]

In Nevins's last four volumes, covering the conflict itself, a central theme is that the people were the heroes of the war and that it was their national character that was being altered. "Their thesis, insofar as a single idea can be applied to a struggle so many-sided, is that the war measurably transformed an inchoate nation, individualistic in temper and wedded to improvisation, into a shaped and disciplined nation, increasingly aware of the importance of plan and control. The improvised war of 1861–1862 became the organized war of 1863–1864. The invertebrate country of Bull Run days, goaded by necessity, gathered its energies together, submitted to system, and became the partially-structured country which heard the news of Five Forks. Northern manufacturing enterprises that had been unicellular became complex and organic; primitive transportation lines became parts of a fast-growing network; mercantile undertakings, professional groups, and cultural enterprises, gelatinous in 1861, became muscular enough to bear their share of the burden. To organize armies, to organize the production of arms, munitions, clothing, and food, to organize medical services and finance, to organize public sentiment—all this required unprecedented attention to plan, and an unprecedented amount of cooperative effort. The resultant alteration in the national character was one of the central results of the gigantic struggle." [2] Although the people were "Hero" in the Civil War, they could have accomplished little without leadership. "Well it was for the republic that out of such a political milieu rose a Chief Executive who combined the noblest qualities of the heart with a singularly lucid intellect and a piercing vision." [3]

In 1861, while there were men who could still recall the nation as it had been under Washington, America stood convulsed and divided. Liberal currents ran under the "superficial ice of reaction" in Europe. "Never might the example and encouragement of a free, united, progressive America have been more effective. For three generations, in a world of fitful political progress and frequent relapse, the Western republic had represented to uncounted millions a sober, steady hope. It was the brightest governmental and social experiment ever made." Now the question was whether this republic would endure. And if it failed would its failure "prove that only a centralized autocracy could govern wide areas and large populations with efficiency? . . . The whole future of the American nation, as the chief exponent and shield of liberal democracy, was thus placed in doubt by a struggle concerning an institution which the moral impulses of the age pronounced a blot on the national shield, and concerning the constitutional ideas involved in this contest. Sensitive leaders felt keenly the tragic bearing of the convulsion on world affairs. Many Southerners winced at the renunciation of Jeffersonian principles by their hotheads. Many Union men saw that the meaning of the American dream to mankind was being put to the test." [4]

NOTES

1. Nevins. *The War for the Union*, Vol. I, *The Improvised War, 1861–1862*, p. v.
2. *Ibid.*
3. *Ibid.*, p. vi.
4. *Ibid.*, pp. 8–11.

Peace or War?

"GOD GRANT that the Constitution and the Union shall be perpetual," exclaimed Buchanan to the crowd when he reached his Lancaster home just after Lincoln's inauguration. Most Americans still believed a sectional adjustment possible without bloodshed. They were naturally optimists; they had discounted radical threats for so many years that they could not now take them at face value, and the idea of a brothers' war was too monstrous to seem credible. A reporter of the New York *Tribune* speculated on the use to be made of the extra troops in Washington when the capital "resumes its wonted quiet." Rebellion had asserted itself, but civil war had not begun.

As yet, only seven States had left the Union. In at least three, Georgia, Alabama, and Louisiana, strong evidence existed that a really fair plebiscite might have shown a majority for the national tie, while in the four others, Mississippi, Texas, South Carolina, and Florida, vigorous minorities had opposed secession. Southerners could not point to a single right except that of the prompt return of fugitive slaves which was being abridged or directly threatened, and some of the Northern States with personal liberty laws were repealing or amending them. While half a dozen Republican governors, led by E. D. Morgan of New York, Richard Yates of Illinois, and N. P. Banks of Massachusetts, recommended that such laws be wiped from the books, Rhode Island, Massachusetts, and Vermont took appropriate action.[1] If the South had no concrete grievances of importance, many asked, why should it revolt? Had not Congress just submitted, by two-thirds vote in each chamber, a constitutional amendment forbidding any change in the organic law which

---

1 On this subject see Appleton's *Annual Cyclopaedia*, 1861, pp. 436, 452, 556, 576 ff., 634; McPherson, *Pol. Hist. of the Rebellion*, 44; Rhodes, *Hist. U. S. from the Compromise of 1850*, III, 253; Randall, *Civil War and Reconstruction*, 229. Ohio had no law, but Governor Dennison urged conditional repeal in other States. The governors of Maine and Michigan opposed repeal. The total number of cases arising under personal liberty laws was probably small; see W. B. Hesseltine, *Lincoln and the War Governors*, 103 ff., 124 ff. Lincoln said that if the laws were as bad as Southerners asserted (he had never read one), they should be repealed.

(*The War for the Union*, Vol. I, *The Improvised War, 1861–1862*, Chapter 2.)

would enable the government to interfere with slavery inside a State? [2] Was it not certain that this amendment, if needed to save the Union, would be quickly ratified?

In the wide border area, when Lincoln entered the White House, the situation appeared hopeful. The Delaware legislature, after hearing a secessionist agent from Mississippi, had voted down his proposals—the house unanimously. Governor Thomas H. Hicks of Maryland, though asserting that the State sympathized with the South and hoped to see it given new guarantees, had stubbornly refused to call an extra legislative session as a first step toward rebellion, and had been overwhelmingly supported by the people. In Kentucky the senate, appealing to the South to recede, voted more than two to one against a State convention. Arkansas chose a convention with a decidedly conservative majority, and Missouri elected one which did not include a single advocate of immediate secession. In Virginia, the house in January had voted down a secessionist resolution. The Unionists had carried the elections for a convention, and from the moment that this body met in mid-February, it had been under the sway of astute conservatives. North Carolina, in a popular election, defeated the call for a convention, and at the same time chose eighty-two conservatives as against thirty-eight secessionists to sit in that body if it ever met. The people of Tennessee likewise voted decisively against a convention, and still more decisively for a Unionist majority of delegates.

"Here are eight of the fifteen States," rejoiced the New York *Tribune*, "declaring that they wish and mean to stay in the Union, and not follow the defeated and bankrupt officeholders into the abyss of secession, treason, and civil war." The borderland, lamented the Charleston *Mercury*, was ready to accept much less than the proposed Crittenden compromise, which would have restored the Missouri Compromise line across the Federal Territories and protected slavery south of it.[3] Many Union men, believing that the cotton States had been thrown into revolt by a temporary emotional reaction following Lincoln's election, thought that a counter-reaction might soon hurl the fire-eaters into oblivion.

Lincoln shared this hope. Three days after the inauguration, Representative T. A. R. Nelson of Tennessee, a strong unionist of the American Party, obtained an interview at the White House. Lincoln said that he was anxious to maintain peace, and believed that the Federal revenues should not be col-

---

2 This passed the House Feb. 28 by 133 to 65; the Senate March 2 by 24 to 12; *Cong. Globe*, 36th Cong., 2d Sess., 1285, 1403.

3 N. Y. *Tribune* March 7, 1861; Charleston *Mercury* Feb. 14, 1861. For action of the border States see *Ann. Cyc.* 1861, pp. 256, 257; 395; 442–444; 677–679; 729–731.

lected in the seceded States until men had time for reflection. As he still regarded Southerners as members of the national family, he was not inclined to deny them mail facilities. Congress was equally hopeful and still more anxious for peace. Up to the end of its session on March 3, it had been careful not to give the South needless offense. No Republican Senator made any effort to press the bill outlawing slavery in the old Territories which the House had passed in the first session of the 36th Congress. It was not necessary (New Mexico after ten years of slavery protection had only twenty-two slaves, ten of them transients), and not politic.[4]

Nor did the Republican majority, passing bills to organize the new Territories of Dakota, Colorado, and Nevada, include any formal prohibition of slavery. It was a basic Republican doctrine that the natural state of any Territory was one of freedom, and that action was hence unnecessary; but the party leaders also wished to avoid any provocative act. Nor did Congress pass any measure giving the President military weapons to meet the crisis. Two bills for this purpose—"force bills," in Southern parlance—were introduced in the House, but not carried.

All but a few extremists hoped for peace, but on what terms? The answer was clear. To men of the North and the borderland, with a restoration of the Union; to men of the cotton kingdom, with a peaceable separation. All efforts at an arrangement had thus far proved abortive. The Crittenden compromise, which Lincoln opposed, had been defeated by a substitute resolution affirming that no need existed for amendment of the Constitution. Though this resolution passed, 25 to 23, only when six senators from the lower South refused to vote, the Republicans were mainly responsible for it. They had three main reasons for defeating Crittenden's plan. The first was that, protecting slavery south of 36° 30', it might stimulate Southern annexationist schemes in Mexico, Central America, and Cuba. The second was that it nominally handed over to slavery a region nearly as large as the original thirteen States, which had come to the United States as free soil, without a single slave when annexed; and it did this at a time when the party, declaring its solemn conviction that the government had no power to plant slavery on soil previously free, had just elected Lincoln on a platform forbidding slavery extension. The third reason, comprehending the other two, lay in Lincoln's moral imperative: the South must agree that slavery was temporary.

Meanwhile, the Peace Convention, with its eminent delegates from twenty-one States, had foundered in floods of oratory. The shrewd Adams-Seward

---

4 Representative Nelson describes his interesting interview with Lincoln in the Knoxville *Whig*, March 19, 1861. For slavery in New Mexico see the speech by C. F. Adams in *Cong. Globe,* 36th Cong., 2d Sess., Appendix, 124–127.

plan for putting an end to quarrels over slavery in the Territories by immediately admitting the whole Southwest (the present area of New Mexico, Arizona, Nevada, and Utah) as one State had been rejected by Southerners, for that State would obviously come in free.[5]

Yet most men still believed that peace would be preserved. They calculated, on the basis of the vote for Lincoln, Douglas, and the Bell-Everett ticket, that a decisive majority of Americans wished for peace, moderation, and compromise. Those who, like Zachariah Chandler of Michigan and Barnwell Rhett of South Carolina, wanted "a little bloodletting," were a small minority.[6]

[I]

Southern expectation of peace was based on the idea that the North would yield. Secessionist leaders hoped that the Lincoln Administration would let the new cotton republic go its way without hindrance. Many in the deep South cherished an illusion that Yankees were interested only in money-grubbing. Utterly materialistic, secessionists told themselves, Northerners lacked the fine sense of honor and fighting spirit which characterized the best "Southrons." Moreover, according to the Dixie view, these New Englanders or Ohioans, aware that they would soon be worsted, shrank from conflict. Had not all the great American generals, Washington, Andrew Jackson, Winfield Scott, Zachary Taylor, been Southerners? Had not the Mexican War been won mainly by Southern troops? Did not military schools, military parades, and military adventures appeal to the South, while Northerners kept their noses in ledgers? This confidence was buttressed by Northern talk of peace, the anti-war fulminations of Northern Democrats, a faith in border State protection, and a feeling that the South was irresistible.

Secessionist leaders had taken note of Franklin Pierce's irresponsible assertion that before any Northern army reached the South it would have to fight organized forces in its own section. Unfortunately, they heard many similar Northern voices.

Douglas, telling the Senate on January 3 that peace was the only sane course, declared that if war began, reunion would be impossible. The alternatives were subjugation and extermination on one hand, and separation on the other; and since extermination was unthinkable, he felt convinced that war would mean "final, irrevocable, eternal separation." His follower Senator

5 Nevins, *Emergence of Lincoln,* II, 397 ff., details measures and efforts in Congress and elsewhere for peace; see also Randall, *Civil War and Reconstruction,* 200 ff. The Adams-Seward plan is best followed in the manuscript diary of C. F. Adams.
6 The phrase is Zack Chandler's; Nevins, *Emergence of Lincoln,* II, 411, 412.

George Pugh of Ohio found the idea of coercing the South "utterly revolt-ing." John A. Logan of Illinois echoed them, saying that war would not only fill the land with widows and orphans, but result in "disunion forever." Henry M. Rice of Minnesota assured the Senate that it must never expect the North-western States to vote a man or a dollar for war. Numerous journals spoke in like terms. The Detroit *Free Press* had the effrontery to predict that if a conflict came, *"that war will be fought at the North,"* and to threaten that in Michigan 65,000 men would interpose between any Union army and the Southern people. The Cincinnati *Enquirer* warned coercionists that if Ohio troops were called out, they might march against the government, not for it.[7]

Southerners could not believe that the North was capable of war when they read that citizens in southern Ohio, Indiana, and Illinois, assuming that dis-union would be permanent, proposed taking the lower part of these States into the Confederacy. This was a very real movement. "I believe, upon my soul," the editor of the Chicago *Tribune* had written Senator Lyman Trum-bull in January, "that if the Union is divided on the line of the Ohio, we shall be compelled to struggle to maintain the territorial integrity of this State." Samuel Medary, former territorial governor of Kansas and Minnesota, had just established a journal in Columbus, Ohio, which pledged obstruction to the use of force. Similar fulminations came from the Chicago *Times and Herald*, controlled by Cyrus H. McCormick, the New York *Day Book*, and the Boston *Courier*. No paper was blunter than the New York *Express:*

> If the people of one section madly proposes to itself the task of trying to whip the other, the hope of reconciliation is extinguished forever. . . . There is a chance that fraternal relations, though temporarily ruptured, may one day be restored, if peace is preserved.

When the municipal elections this spring, from Cleveland to Chicago, re-vealed a shift in favor of the Democrats, hope that this party might prevent coercive action increased in the South. Buchanan later denounced the politi-cians and editors who assured the Confederacy it would have powerful allies. "This, with the persistent inaction of Congress and General Scott's 'views,' induced the leaders of the Cotton States to believe there was but little danger of Civil War."[8]

7 Pierce fruitlessly wrote the other ex-Presidents (Tyler, Fillmore, Van Buren, Buchanan, a singularly uninspiring lot) proposing a meeting to suggest remedial measures. Douglas' speech is in *Cong. Globe*, 36th Cong., 2d Sess., Appendix, 35–42; Pugh's *Ib.* 29–35; Logan's *Ib.* 178–181. Pugh spoke Dec. 20, 1860; Logan, Feb. 5, 1861. Vallandigham called coercion "atrocious and fruitless"; O. C. Hooper, *The Crisis and the Man*, 7. Rice's speech is in *Cong. Globe*, 36th Cong., 2d Sess., 1373. Cf. Wood Gray, *The Hidden Civil War*, 45 ff.

8 C. H. Ray quoted in Wood Gray, *op. cit.*, 45; O. C. Hooper, *op. cit.*, 1–35; A. C. Cole, *Era of the Civil War*, 253–257; N. Y. *Express* (controlled by Benjamin and Fernando Wood), Jan. 16, 1861; Buchanan, July 1, 1863, to Royal Phelps, in Miscellaneous Presidents'

Still greater was the Southern faith in a protective borderland shield. If this area was against secession, it was equally adamant against coercion.

Hicks of Maryland declared that his State would make common cause with its sisters in resistance to tyranny if need arose. Even Unionists in Kentucky asserted that they would desert the government if it used force. The Virginia house with but five dissenting votes denounced any thought of coercive action. In Nashville the legislature served notice that if any Union force were sent south, Tennesseeans would join as one man in repelling the invaders. These declarations had fervent conviction behind them. The great majority in the border region, Southern in origin, tastes, and sympathies, would feel a blow against Southern culture as one which smote themselves. Devoted as they were to the Union, they shrank from the idea of saving it by blood. And behind their antagonism to force lay a hope that if time were allowed for reflection, the two sections would find reason overcoming passion, and agree on a reasonable compromise.

The feeling of the cotton States that war was impossible because they were unconquerable was partly braggadocio, for the region was rich in Captain Bobadils. It sprang more rationally, however, from the military preparations they were making, and the deep hold taken by the doctrine that King Cotton ruled Britain and France.

The new republic, against countless handicaps, was trying to establish forces able to face the Northern regulars and militia. Its Congress had passed legislation creating a provisional regular army of 10,500 officers and men, including 4 brigadier generals and 9 colonels. P. G. T. Beauregard, resigning from the Union army, had been appointed brigadier and hurried to the command at Charleston. An act of February 28 authorized the President to receive State forces if tendered, or volunteers with State consent. Southerners hoped that their troops, under the new flag of 3 stripes, red, white, and blue, with a union of 7 stars, would soon number 50,000. Meanwhile, the States were filling their ranks. Mississippi in January had authorized the formation of a division of infantry and was sending a force to Pensacola. Its volunteers came in more rapidly than they could be equipped, officered, and drilled. In Louisiana the secession convention established 2 standing regiments, 1 infantry and 1 artillery, while by mid-February the State had issued arms to 28 volunteer companies with a strength of 1765. A similar story could be told of the other cotton States. On March 9, under a law passed

---

File, NYPL. Buchanan laid the blame for "go in peace" utterances on certain Republicans, but Democratic leaders were of course much the more numerous and flagrant offenders. "My voice was unheeded," he wrote, "though I often warned them [the secessionists] that the first gun fired at Charleston would unite all parties."

three days earlier authorizing the President to ask for any number of volunteers up to 100,000, Secretary of War L. P. Walker called on all the seceded States to furnish quotas, chiefly for garrisoning forts; and he stood ready to issue a further call at any time.[9]

Meanwhile, the Montgomery government was blithely taking over a great part of the arms and munitions lodged in old Federal repositories. It deeply galled the North to read of large stores thus "stolen" from the United States. New Orleans on March 6 gave an imposing ovation to General David E. Twiggs, fresh from his surrender (still in national uniform, and before passage of the State ordinance of secession) of nineteen army posts in Texas. Bands pounded along Canal Street, which was dressed in pelican bunting and palmetto flags; oratory resounded, cheers echoed; and Twiggs, his large bald head uncovered, bowed right and left from his barouche with General Braxton Bragg, heading files of troops. Early in the year Southern forces had taken over Fort Pulaski at Savannah, Fort Morgan at Mobile, and Fort Barrancas at Pensacola, with their contents. The head of the navy department, S. R. Mallory, was busy recruiting sailors.[10]

Even if peace reigned, it seemed probable that the Confederacy might be more of a military nation than the United States. At first it would use its armed power to deter the North from attack. Then its ardors might turn elsewhere. Vice-President Alexander H. Stephens, after predicting to an Atlanta audience that Sumter would be surrendered, the North would accept the situation, and the border States would eventually join their sisters, spoke in Columbus, Georgia, of martial conquests. The Confederacy, acting on the principle that slavery must be extended and perpetuated, might in time acquire Cuba and parts of Mexico and Central America.[11]

Altogether, the cotton kingdom flexed its muscles with a sense of exuberant strength. Its leaders had cherished the forecast of Langdon Cheves at the Nashville Convention: "Unite and you shall form one of the most splendid empires on which the sun ever shone." And never for a moment did the Deep South forget what Senator James H. Hammond and others said of its power to rally European support. A threat to the cotton kingdom would be a stroke at the jugular vein of the greatest naval powers of the globe.

"The first demonstration of blockade of the southern ports," prophesied Major W. H. Chase of Florida in the January issue of *De Bow's Review*,

9 J. D. Bragg, *Louisiana in the Confederacy*, 53–55; *Statutes at Large. Provisional Govt. CSA*, 43–52; O. R. I, iv, pt. 1, 135; N. Y. *Tribune*, March 19, 1861.
10 Moore, *Rebellion Record*, I, 7 ff.; Twiggs, a Georgian by birth, was soon made a major general in the Confederate army, but was too old for active service.
11 Columbus *Sun*, quoted in N. Y. *Tribune*, March 19, 1861; Johnston and Browne, *Alexander H. Stephens*, 356, 363, 396. Slavery was the cornerstone, said Stephens.

"would be swept away by English fleets of observation hovering on the Southern coasts, to protect English commerce and especially the free flow of cotton to English and French factories. The flow of cotton must not cease for a day, because the enormous sum of £150,000,000 is annually devoted to the elaboration of raw cotton; and because five millions of people annually derive their daily and immediate support therefrom in England alone, and every interest in the kingdom is connected therewith. Nor must the cotton states be invaded by land, for it would interrupt the cultivation of the great staple." Even the Northwest, he continued, would act to protect the free ports and markets of the South.[12]

Cotton would maintain peace, for cotton ruled the world.

[II]

Most Northerners expected peace to prevail for a quite different set of reasons. They thought that the seven cotton States had no vital grievances and would soon come to their senses, that the new republic was too weak to be viable, and that the border area would offer persuasive arguments for a return. They had seen so many other crises—1820, 1833, 1850—disappear that they gave rein to cheering hopes. "I guess we'll keep house," said Lincoln. They had heard so much gasconade that they lumped most secessionists with the fire-eaters. "I incline to believe," wrote Charles Eliot Norton on March 5, "that they will not try violence, and that their course as an independent Confederacy is nearly at an end." In a let-them-cool-down mood the *Atlantic* published a resigned quatrain:

> Go then, our rash sister! afar and aloof—
> Run wild in the sunshine away from our roof;
> But when your heart aches and your feet have grown sore,
> Remember the pathway that leads to our door!

On the absence of substantial Southern hurts, Douglas was emphatic. He argued that the South had gained more than if the line of 36° 30′ had been revived by the Crittenden amendment. "There stands your slave code in New Mexico protecting slavery up to the thirty-seventh degree as effectually as laws can be made to protect it. . . . The South has all below the thirty-seventh parallel, while Congress has not prohibited slavery even north of it." It was true that slavery had a legal right to spread farther than for climatic and economic reasons it might actually go. What a Southern historian was later to call the natural limits of slavery had perhaps been reached. Charles Francis

---

12 *De Bow's Review*, vol. 30, January, 1861; Chase, an ardent secessionist, argued that the potency of cotton made Southern armies and fleets superfluous.

Adams was equally derisive as to Southern grievances. To complain of personal liberty laws which had never freed a single slave, of exclusion from territory which slavery could never hope to occupy, and of fear of Federal interference with slavery in the States, against which the North was now willing to erect a solemn bar—this was puerile. Adams called upon the Southerners to recover from what he called "panic, pure panic." [13]

Adams, like Seward and many others, was certain the Confederacy must soon collapse from inner weakness. It could never be more than a secondary power, he declared; never a maritime state. It labored under the necessity of keeping eight millions of its population to watch four millions. If independent, it would have to guard several thousand miles of frontier against the flight of slaves to territory where they could never be reclaimed. "The experiment will ignominiously fail." So thought John W. Forney, writing his Philadelphia *Press* from Washington that anybody who talked with secessionists could see that they lacked heart in their enterprise, and looked forward to the speedy collapse of their whole conspiracy. Douglas, who never faltered in his hope that inner weakness would undo the new nation, announced late in March: "Division and discontent are beginning to appear in the revolting Southern Confederacy." [14]

Always bold and imaginative, Douglas was revolving a plan of which he spoke to William H. Russell of the London *Times* and others; a plan for a North American customs union embracing Canada, Mexico, and the United States, which he hoped would pave the way to reunion. Like others, he believed in the healing power of delay. He wished to fix a conciliatory character upon Administration policy, and, as he told friends, to "tomahawk" the Administration if it took a belligerent line. On March 6 he therefore gave the Senate an elaborate misinterpretation of Lincoln's inaugural as a pacific manifesto. He was delighted, he said, to find Lincoln so conservative in temper, for the Union could never be cemented by blood. The President had promised to abstain from any offensive acts, had let clear Federal rights lie dormant, had suggested that the Constitution be amended, and had promised to allow the people to devise such changes as they desired. Furthermore, he had declared that in every exigency he would lean to friendly solutions.[15] Douglas went on, in a pernicious warping of Lincoln's words:

13 Sandburg, *Lincoln: The War Years*, I, 120 ff.; C. E. Norton, *Letters*, I, 219; Adams in *Cong. Globe*, 36th Cong., 2d Sess., *Appendix*, 127 (Jan. 31, 1861); Douglas, *Cong. Globe*, 36th Cong., 2d Sess. (March 25, 1861), p. 1504; *Atlantic*, May, 1861.

14 Adams, *ut sup.*; Forney is quoted in Springfield *Republican*, March 19, 1861, Douglas in Chicago *Morning Post*, March 27, 1861.

15 Russell, *My Diary North and South*, April 4, 1861, for Douglas' plan; *Cong. Globe*, 36th Cong., 2d Sess. (March 6, 1861), pp. 1436-1439. But Douglas frankly told Welles that he had no influence. The Democratic party had broken up; the Republican party had no use for him; nobody would follow him. *Diary*, I, 34, 35.

In other words, if the collection of the revenue leads to a peaceful solution, it is to be collected; if the recapture of Fort Moultrie would tend to a peaceful solution, he stands pledged to recapture it; if the recapture would tend to violence and war, he is pledged not to recapture it; if the enforcement of the laws in the seceding States would tend to facilitate a peaceful solution, he is pledged to their enforcement; if the omission to enforce these laws would best facilitate peace, he is pledged to omit to enforce them; if maintaining possession of Fort Sumter would facilitate peace, he stands pledged to retain its possession; if, on the contrary, the abandonment of Fort Sumter and the withdrawal of the troops would facilitate a peaceful solution, he is pledged to abandon the fort and withdraw the troops.

Of far greater importance, in this crisis, was Seward's belief in peace. The veteran New York politician, who for a dozen stormy years in the Senate had closely observed Southern friends and enemies, and who as a man of tortuous expedients believed that expediency ruled human conduct, was certain that war could be avoided. As Gideon Welles put it later, Seward had no doubt that he could set to work immediately the new Administration came in, reconcile the main differences, and within ninety days restore harmony to the nation. *He* was head of the Republican party, and *he* would be the real power behind the weak railsplitter. During the brief month of William Henry Harrison's Administration he had dominated that President; during Zachary Taylor's sixteen months he had again swayed the scepter; now he would be Grand Vizier once more. Thrusting Lincoln aside, he would rely on time, forbearance, and patience to bring the cotton States back.

"I learned early from Jefferson," Seward had told the Senate, "that in political affairs we cannot always do what seems to us absolutely best." He would like to see all the Territories organized at once into two States, one Southwestern, one Northwestern, reserving the right later to subdivide them into several convenient new States; but such a reservation was constitutionally impossible, and he believed that the embarrassments resulting from the hasty incorporation of two areas of such vast extent and various characteristics and interests would outweigh the immediate advantages of halting the slavery quarrel. To admit one great Southwestern State was as far as he would go. Meanwhile, he would trust to cool second thoughts:

When the eccentric movements of secession and disunion shall have ended, in whatever form that end may come, and the angry excitements of the hour shall have subsided, then, and not until then,—one, two, or three years hence— I should cheerfully advise a convention of the people, to be assembled in pursuance of the Constitution, to consider and decide whether any and what amendments of the organizational law ought to be made.[16]

16 Welles, Nov. 27, 1872, to I. N. Arnold, Arnold Papers, Chicago Hist. Soc.; *Cong. Globe*, 36th Cong., 2d Sess., Jan. 12, 1861.

Seward, thin and worn, said just before Lincoln came in: "The majority of those around me are determined to pull the house down, and I am determined not to let them." [17] He had written Lincoln on February 24 that he knew the real peril much better than his Republican colleagues in Washington, and that only the soothing words which he had spoken "have saved us and carried us along thus far." A man of ripe political experience, he could show impressive astuteness, and had a fine capacity for persuasive public speech. Yet he revealed at times superficial thinking, erratic judgment, and a devious, impetuous temper, which were the more dangerous because he was cockily self-confident. He had immense vanity; in fact, remarked the British minister, so much more vanity, personal and national, than tact, that he seldom made a favorable impression at first. [18] Now he was sure that he could restore the Union with one great if—if Lincoln would let him take the helm.

Justice John A. Campbell of the Supreme Court, a mild, sagacious Alabama unionist, attended a dinner party which Douglas gave shortly before the inauguration and which Seward dominated as the great power-to-be. When asked for a toast, Seward proposed: "Away with all parties, all platforms, all persons committed to whatever else will stand in the way of the American Union." After dinner, Campbell told the company that slavery was a transitory institution, which though yet strong in the deep South was steadily dying in the border area. Once the Constitution was amended to protect slavery in the States from any national interference, the only question would be that of New Mexico, which was unsuited to slavery anyhow. "How, Mr. Seward," he asked, "can you fail to effect an adjustment?" The Senator replied: "I have a telegram from Springfield today in which I am told that Senator Cameron will not be Secretary of the Treasury, and that Salmon P. Chase will be; that it is not certain that Cameron will have a place in the Cabinet; and that my own position is not fully assured. What can I do?" He had hoped that Simon Cameron might abet his conservative labors for peace.

What he did was to make a last-minute movement to keep Chase, whom he feared as a radical, out of the Cabinet. When this failed, he nevertheless took the State Department, confident that he could manipulate Lincoln and so save national peace. [19]

Horace Greeley likewise believed a rapid readjustment possible. His suggestion that the erring sisters go in peace was qualified by his insistence that they should first prove that a majority of their people wished to go, for he was

17 C. F. Adams to R. H. Dana, Jr., Feb. 28, 1861; Dana Papers, MHS.
18 Newton, *Lord Lyons*, I, 117; Nicolay and Hay, *Abraham Lincoln: A History*, III, 319, 320.
19 Campbell, undated memorandum "Relative to the Secession Movement," Confederate Museum; Nevins, *Emergence of Lincoln*, II, 452-455; N. Y. *Weekly Tribune*, April 30, 1861.

confident that in Florida, Alabama, and Louisiana no such majority existed. Even late in the spring he told a Cooper Union audience that the Southern people were at heart for the old ties. "I believe that the tide makes for the Union, and not against it; that secession is exhausting itself as a fever; and if it can be judiciously handled for a few months, it will burn out." S. F. B. Morse proposed an amicable temporary separation pending negotiations for a new and better Union. The two peoples should conclude an immediate alliance, divide the national property, and sever the flag (the blue union diagonally, the stripes horizontally) until such date as their junction should again make the banner one.[20]

This faith that if Lincoln's Administration accepted the status quo, vigorously waving a palm branch, the cotton domain would come back, was shared by that old Jacksonian Democrat George Bancroft. He assured an English historian that Southern leaders had seceded only with a view to reconstructing the Union on their own terms, possibly with New England (as Bennett's *Herald* suggested) left outside. John Bell of Tennessee, lingering in Washington after March 4 and repeatedly seeing Lincoln, entreated the President not to molest the Confederacy, for any attempt to reinforce the forts or collect the revenues would result in bloodshed and Border State secession. He advised an indefinite truce. The more the cotton States armed and the heavier the taxation they imposed, the sooner would a wave of popular discontent rise, resulting at last in a friendly reconstruction. Bell might have quoted such voices of discontent as the New Orleans *True Delta*:

The odds and ends of every faction which have combined themselves together to precipitate the cotton states into revolution have shown an audacity which Marat, Danton, or Robespierre might have envied. Special privilege, a rag money aristocracy, and favored classes, will now be fastened upon unfortunate Louisiana; and in return the people will have the consolation derivable from the reflection that one of her greatest domestic interests is destroyed and her importance as a state of the Union dwarfed into a pigmy association with decaying, retrograding, and penniless confederates. The depth of our own degradation for the time distracts the attention of the people from the progress of oligarchical usurpation and tyranny in our sister States, which are made participators with us in a humiliating calamity.[21]

If worst came to worst, in the opinion of some Northern observers, unity could be restored on the basis of Manifest Destiny; that is, on the common ambition of powerful groups North and South to take possession of the whole continent and its islands.

---

20 Morse manifesto, undated, S. F. B. Morse Papers, LC.
21 M. A. DeWolfe Howe, *Bancroft*, II, 135–136; *True Delta*, April 10, 1861. Bell's views are summarized by M. J. Crawford, writing March 3, 1861, to Toombs; Toombs Letterbooks, South Caroliniana Library.

[III]

The realities of the crisis were grimly different from these dreams. Peace, as time proved, was impossible. It was impossible because neither North nor South could now yield. Both were prisoners of the situation created by long years of paltering and evasion.

The Confederacy must stand fast because its goal was not readjustment, but independence. The successful secessionist conspiracy had been a drive, we repeat, to give the people of the Deep South full power to settle their own problems in their own way. Retreat would mean a sacrifice of their constitutional principles, a humiliating blow to their pride, and a definite subordination to the North and Northwest. The heads of the Confederacy were not bluffing, but in deadly earnest. They were determined to maintain their new nation at all hazards and whatever cost.

Certainly every public and private utterance emphasized the permanency of their government. Mrs. Jefferson Davis, who like her husband would have preferred to see the Union kept intact on Southern terms, wrote Buchanan on March 18 that she had found the opposition in Montgomery to reconstruction quite violent. "I fear me greatly, my dear old friend, that you are really the last of an illustrious line." This was the conviction of John Slidell of Louisiana. He wrote S. L. M. Barlow, one of the first great corporation attorneys of New York and an ardent Democrat of conservative views, that reconstruction was a hopeless idea at any time or under any conditions. "At this point there is unanimity of feeling of which you can form no idea without passing some time amongst and mixing freely with our people." We could quote other men at tiresome length. Louis T. Wigfall of Texas in the Senate on March 7 repeated Robert Toombs' statement that the seceded States would never come back under any circumstances. Treat them as independent and the nation could have peace, he vociferated; treat them as part of the Union and it would have war. Wlliam M. Browne, former editor of the Washington *Constitution*, now in the Confederate State Department, was amazed by Northern talk of reconciliation. "Knowing, as we do here," he wrote from Montgomery March 6, "the temper of the people, not the politicians—their hopes, aspirations, resolution, and resources—we look upon union as impossible as the annexation of the Confederate States to Great Britain in their old colonial condition."

The roots of this Southern determination ran deep indeed. Secession, as old Barnwell Rhett said, was not the work of a day, but had been preparing for twenty years.[22]

---

[22] Slidell to Barlow, New Orleans, March 24, 1861, Barlow Papers; Browne to Barlow, March 6, 18, 1861, *Ibid*. Still only in his middle thirties, handsome, wealthy, and cultivated.

Sectional pride, and sensitiveness to sectional honor, had played a large part in crystallizing Confederate resolution. The South was denied equality in the Union, men argued, when it was debarred from taking its slave property into the common Territories. This feeling of sectional jealousy and patriotism more than any other explains the surge of rejoicing that swept across the cotton kingdom as the secession ordinances were adopted. How humiliating now to fall back! But material motives played their part. Convinced that the South was systematically exploited by Northern merchants, brokers, shippers, and bankers, estimating that Yankee harpies bled it of a hundred and fifty millions a year, and resentful of Northern tariffs, coastal trade monopoly, and fishing subsidies, Southern leaders believed they had issued a declaration of economic freedom. They would build a richer agriculture; they would have their own flourishing ports and fleets; they would make New Orleans, Mobile, Charleston, and Savannah opulent seats of finance and industry.

But above all, Southern determination rested on a sense of fear which had grown more acute ever since John Brown's raid; a foreboding that they could never entrust the intertwined problems of slavery and race adjustment (they feared that emancipation would mean eventual amalgamation, a negroid South) to a Northern majority. "A crisis must be met and passed"; but they refused to *pass* it—to take the decision to put slavery on the road to ultimate extinction. They feared Northern clumsiness, precipitancy, and ruthlessness. Henry W. Hilliard of Alabama stated this frankly in a letter to a New England friend. "It is supposed," he wrote, "very generally, that we apprehend some immediate mischief from Mr. Lincoln's administration; some direct and plain interference with our rights; and we are appealed to by our northern friends to await some hostile demonstration on his part; we are reminded that his character is conservative. . . . Now all this may be conceded, and yet if the whole southern mind could be brought to yield implicit faith in these assurances, still the attitude of the southern states would remain unchanged. It is not any apprehension of aggressive action on the part of the incoming administration which rouses the incoming administration to resistance, but it is the demonstration which Mr. Lincoln's election by such overwhelming majorities affords, of the supremacy of a sentiment hostile to slavery in the nonslaveholding states of the union." [23]

The South contained many who felt a repugnance to slavery. Hilliard

---

Barlow belonged to the Buchanan wing of the party. Keitt of South Carolina said, "I have been engaged in this movement ever since I entered political life"; Springfield *Republican*, Jan. 19, 1861. A Northerner interviewed Davis, Toombs, and R. M. T. Hunter in Washington in December and January of the secession winter, and presented his report, "Conversational Opinions of the Leaders of Secession," in the *Atlantic*, Nov., 1862, pp. 613–623. All three regarded secession as final; Toombs and Davis spoke of using force to sustain it.

23 Quoted in Springfield *Republican*, Jan. 1, 1861.

knew that world sentiment was hostile to it. What he meant was that the
Lower South could not commit its fate, in its position of delicacy and peril, to
a sectional majority which might prove heedless and dogmatic. This was the
Hobbesian ultimate of fear, the chief cause of war; the fear of a people that
its way of life would be overthrown by a rival power and creed. The South
could not turn back.

[IV]

Still less could the North yield on the mighty issue of disunion. How
long had its leaders been explicit on that point! "Liberty and Union, now and
forever, one and inseparable"—every schoolboy knew the reply to Hayne.
"Our Federal Union: it must be preserved!"—every Northern youth thrilled to
Jackson's sentiment. Webster had said in his Seventh of March speech that the
idea of peaceable secession was an absurdity. Henry Clay that same year had
declared that if any State put itself in military array against the Union, he was
for trying the strength of the nation. "I am for ascertaining whether we have
a Government or not—practical, efficient, capable of maintaining its authority. . . . Nor, sir, am I to be alarmed or dissuaded from any such course by
intimations of the spilling of blood. If blood is to be spilt, by whose fault is it?"
Thomas Hart Benton had fiercely asserted that the Union must be upheld, if
need be, by arms, and President Taylor had promised cold shot and hempen
rope to traitors. Lincoln but echoed these leaders when he placed in his
inaugural his single veiled threat to Southerners: "In your hands, my dissatisfied fellow-countrymen, and not in mine, is the momentous issue of civil war."

Beyond a sentimental attachment to the idea of Union, beyond old fealties,
loomed irreducible material considerations. Divorce usually means a partition
of property. Men might pause but briefly over the question whether they could
divide the Fourth of July, Yorktown, Lundy's Lane, and Buena Vista; but the
government held title to vast physical possessions. Said the Chicago *Tribune:*
"No party in the North will ever consent to a division of the national territory,
the national armaments, the national archives, or the national treasury." A
President consenting to it would have courted instant impeachment. What
of the Southwest? If peaceable secession were permitted, the Confederacy
would lay claim to part of New Mexico and Arizona, with hope of a frontage
on the Pacific. Confederate sympathizers in Texas, Arkansas, and Missouri
would almost certainly attempt to seize the Indian Territory, a key to the
Southwestern domain. Where would the international border be drawn, and
how would it be policed? Once demarcated, that boundary would certainly
be crossed by numberless runaway slaves—and streams of free Negroes; it

would be invaded by Northern agitators; and new John Browns would raid more Harpers Ferries.[24]

How, asked John Minor Botts of Virginia in a letter to disunionists, are you going to dispose of the Mississippi River? That question stung Northwestern emotion like a poisoned barb. Let the South try to sever the stream, said Douglas, and the men of Illinois would follow its waters inch by inch with the bayonet to the Gulf. The lower part of the great river had been paid for out of the common purse for the common national good. When Northerners read that Mississippi had placed a battery at the Vicksburg bluffs which was halting steamboats bound downstream, their blood boiled. Congressmen and editors spoke in no modulated tones. "We would like to see them help themselves," retorted the Memphis *Evening Argus.* Later the Confederate Congress conceded the full and free navigation of the river, but it made no provision for the landing or transshipment of cargoes. As river boats could not go to Europe nor ocean ships ascend to St. Louis, import and export shipments were thrown under Confederate power. Amos Kendall, the veteran Jacksonian, told an Illinois friend that if he were an editor he would make the nation ring with his protests. He would declare that the West should never submit to such a situation; that its industrial and commercial interests were hanging over an abyss; and that when Southern complaints touching slavery had been removed, the seceding States must reënter the Union—under compulsion if necessary.[25] He knew that compulsion was war.

It was obvious, moreover, that the precedent of Southern secession might be fatal to the entire national future. Winfield Scott in the "Views" he had sent Buchanan had babbled of a land of four capitals, at Albany, Washington, Columbia, S. C., and Alton or Quincy, Illinois. Each of these four new countries would have ports on navigable waters. But what if some interior States were shut out of the new confederations and left landlocked? What if Michigan could at any time join Canada, closing the Soo? For that matter, what if the Confederacy found Texas becoming opposed to slavery, withdrawing from the new bond, and making herself independent again? American stability, credit, prestige, and power would be dealt shattering blows by a principle of withdrawal which held the potentialities of unlimited dissolution—of national suicide. A once great nation might be Balkanized. The idea, abhorrent to all thoughtful Northerners and many Southerners, was abhorrent most of all to those who saw the nation as a beacon-light of stability, moderation, and freedom in a disorderly world.

24 Clay's speech (a reply to Dawson of Georgia) is in *Cong. Globe.* For Benton see *Thirty Years,* II, 200; for Douglas' views, Milton, *Eve of Conflict,* 396; the editorial in the Chicago *Tribune,* Dec. 12, 1860, was repeated more emphatically Dec. 22.
25 Kendall to J. D. Caton, March 14, 1861; Caton Papers, LC.

Farewell, if secession prevailed, to all ideas of American greatness, and of American leadership of the liberal forces of the globe! Instead, the emergence of two jagged, unhappy, mutually resentful fragments, one a slave-mongering nation of oppressor and oppressed, the other a nation compelled to militarize itself and debase its temper and institutions because of an antagonistic neighbor. Farewell to the old fraternalism, optimism, and idealism, now to be replaced by a Peloponnesian atmosphere, a hostility like that of Athens and Sparta, Rome and Carthage!

Northern unwillingness to yield was heightened by the growing conviction that however fervent was the emotion of the cotton States, it had been brought to its climax by a conspiracy as deliberate and selfish as Catiline's. A deep anger burned in many Northerners as they read of this conspiracy. The Nashville *Patriot* during the recent Presidential campaign had arraigned W. L. Yancey, Barnwell Rhett, and Porcher Miles as its leaders. It had related how the conspiracy began with the Southern Convention in Montgomery in May, 1858; how the Southern League, to promote a great Southern party, had been systematically organized; how Yancey had persuaded the Alabama legislature to assert that it would never submit to the domination of a sectional Northern party; and how he had induced the Democratic State convention in Alabama on April 23, 1859, to declare that unless the Federal Government gave slavery positive protection on the high seas and in the Territories, it would use its best endeavors to withdraw from that government. The *Patriot* described how Yancey appeared in Charleston as leader of the disunionists and helped engineer the disruption of the Democratic Party, simply to make sure of Republican victory and subsequent secession.[26] "Then we can excite the South to rise," Yancey had said.

The *National Intelligencer* in Washington took up the conspiracy thread and pursued it further. In that careful, moderate paper a noted Southerner, a former member of Congress, published on January 9, 1861, his *j'accuse*. "I charge," he wrote, "that on last Saturday night a caucus was held in this city by the Southern secession Senators from Florida, Georgia, Alabama, Mississippi, Louisiana, Arkansas, and Texas." They resolved, he went on, to seize all political and military power in the South. They telegraphed orders for the drafting of final plans to seize all forts, arsenals, and custom houses; they sent advice that the secession conventions then or soon to be in session should pass ordinances for immediate withdrawal; and they directed the assembling of a secession convention at Montgomery on February 13. In order to thwart any attempted interference by Washington, they determined that the seceding States

26 Widely republished, South as well as North; for example, in Selma, Ala., *Reporter*, July 26, 1860.

should temporarily keep their members sitting in Congress. "They have possessed themselves of all the avenues of information in the South,—the telegraph, the press, and the general control of the postmasters." [27]

"Have we not known men," Andrew Johnson presently asked the Senate, "to sit at their desks in this chamber, using the government's stationary to write treasonable letters; and while receiving their pay and sworn to support the Constitution and sustain the law, engaging in midnight conclaves to devise ways and means by which the government should be overthrown?" [28] Stephen A. Douglas went further. He believed, with Charles Francis Adams, that the conspiracy embraced a plan to seize the Capitol before Lincoln could be inaugurated there, and to paralyze the government; a plan which only the unexpected strength of the Virginia Unionists in the election of 1860 frustrated.

Because of the tremendous sentimental and moral values attached to the Union, because of the impossibility of dividing its assets and dissevering a land where the greatest river systems and mountain valleys ran athwart sections, because secession meant a chain process of suicide, because the integrity of the republic was the life of world liberalism, and because to most observers it seemed that a squalid conspiracy had turned natural Southern aspirations and apprehensions to unnatural ends, the North could never give way. Certainly Lincoln would not give way; his inaugural address had clearly stated his determination to maintain the Union and hold its property. But in believing that he could do this and still avoid war, he made three errors. First, he temporarily underrated the gravity of the crisis. Second, he overrated the strength of Union sentiment in the South, as he showed in a futile effort to persuade Sam Houston of Texas to rally the nationalist groups. And lastly, as David M. Potter says, he misconceived the conditional character of much Southern Unionism. These were errors of the head, not of the heart, and because of the confused and murky situation were natural enough.[29]

27 This letter was vouched for by the eminent editor W. W. Seaton. Arkansas, not yet seceded when Lincoln took office, stood on the brink.
28 *Cong. Globe,* 37th Cong., 1st Sess. (July 27, 1861), 297.
29 Jefferson Davis wrote later that he knew war was inevitable. He had served long in Washington beside Northern leaders. "With such opportunities of ascertaining the power and sentiments of the Northern people, it would have shown an inexcusable want of perception if I had shared the hopes of men less favored with opportunities for forming correct judgments, in believing with them that secession could be or would be peacefully accomplished." "Lord Wolseley's Mistakes," *North American Review,* vol. 149, Oct., 1889, 475. In his Senate speech Jan. 10, 1861, he had predicted long years of war, terrible devastation, and a final peace between two republics. He wrote to Governor Pickens, Jan. 13: "We are probably soon to be involved in that fiercest of human strife, a civil war." Lincoln would never have written that! Davis knew that *no* Federal Government worthy of the nation could avoid meeting with arms the policy he was helping carry through. Even Buchanan, since the revolution in his Cabinet, was not that feeble! "When Lincoln comes in," wrote Davis to Franklin Pierece, Jan. 20, "he will have but to continue in the path of

[V]

The Confederacy in March faced a vital issue: Should it wait or strike? If it waited, it might gain by finding time to install its government, organize its resources, and import foreign materials. It might also lose by giving Union sentiment in large areas, such as northern Alabama, time to reassert itself once the first fine rapture of independence began to decline. But above all, its attention was centered on border States. If it waited, would they gravitate to the Confederacy, or fix their allegiance yet more firmly in the Union? If it struck, would the shock make them embrace secession or recoil from it?

The best opportunity for a stroke presented itself at Fort Pickens on Pensacola Bay and Fort Sumter in Charleston Harbor, two thorns in Confederate flesh. Pensacola was much the less sensitive spot. Florida was not South Carolina. Here a Yankee lieutenant occupied Pickens, which could be easily reinforced from the sea, with a tiny body of troops under a workable arrangement that he should hold his island fort unharmed while Florida forces occupied the neighboring mainland positions without disturbance.[30] Danger of an explosion was slight, and he had provisions for five months.

Sumter held a different status. Recent events had made it to Northerners a symbol of the maintenance of the Union, and to Confederates a symbol of foreign intrusion. Radical Northerners believed that it must be held, radical Southerners that it must be taken. Under Robert Anderson, a veteran of the Mexican War, it symbolized the choice between acquiescence in secession, or stern resistance to it.

Confederate leaders had forcibly indicated their determination to attack Sumter if it were not quickly evacuated. Judah P. Benjamin wrote S. L. M. Barlow in New York as early as January 17, 1861, that an act of war impended at Sumter or Pickens. "At neither can it be long delayed." When Jefferson Davis was elected President, William Porcher Miles of South Carolina was at hand in Montgomery. He favored an early assault, but urged his State government not to permit it until the Confederate authorities gave the word. Our attack, he wrote, would necessarily plunge the new nation into war with the United States, and that before the six other States were prepared. Davis on March 1 appointed Beauregard to command at Charleston. As he did so he informed the Governor, Francis W. Pickens of South Carolina, that he was anxious to vindicate Southern rights territorial and jurisdictional, and that he

---

his predecessor to inaugurate a civil war." Dunbar Rowland, ed., *Jefferson Davis, Letters, Papers, and Speeches,* V, 36–38. Potter's statement is in *Lincoln and his Party in the Secession Crisis,* 375.

30 On Lieutenant Slemmer and his opponents see O. R., I, i, 333–342.

had discussed with Beauregard the works needful to reduce Sumter most speedily. Confederate authorities hurried a colonel to New Orleans to buy fifteen tons of cannon powder for immediate shipment to Charleston. The moment the governor of Florida read a synopsis of Lincoln's message he telegraphed Pickens in South Carolina: "Will you open at once ¬on Fort Sumter?" [31]

Yet before Lincoln took office, the Buchanan Administration, fortified by the addition of Edwin M. Stanton, Joseph Holt, and John A. Dix to the Cabinet, repeatedly warned the Confederate leaders that an attack on the fort would mean war. Buchanan not only refused to withdraw the troops from Sumter, but declined to promise not to reinforce them. Indeed, as he wrote later, he uniformly declared he would send reinforcements whenever Major Anderson requested them or the safety of the post demanded them. Joseph Holt, as Secretary of War, met South Carolina's demands for evacuation with the stiffest denials. The United States held absolute sovereignty over the fort, he declared; the government possessed no more authority to surrender it than to cede the District of Columbia to Maryland; the small garrison was not a menace, but was maintained to protect South Carolina from foreign foes. If rash leaders assaulted Sumter "and thus plunge our country into civil war, then upon them and those they represent must rest the responsibility." [32]

Charleston throughout March resounded with martial activities, for Beauregard put new energy into preparations for war. He found the harbor already bristling with guns, every point of access from the sea fortified, the channel obstructed, and watch maintained to make sure that not even a small boat reached Fort Sumter. Charlestonians, their State troops drilling day and night, thought they had done everything possible. But Beauregard mobilized a large body of Negro laborers to strengthen the harbor defenses, improved the position of the guns, enlisted more artillerists, and hastened the arming of small vessels to operate in coastal waters. Secretary of War Walker urged him on: "Give but little credit to rumors of an amicable adjustment," he wrote March 15. During battery practice a heavy ball struck the Sumter walls; and though an officer was sent at once to explain that it was a chance shot, Charlestonians guessed that their gunners were fixing the range of the fort. A floating battery was heavily armed to be anchored near Sumter. [33]

31   Barlow Papers; Miles Porcher to F. W. Porcher Feb. 9, 1861, Amer. Art. Assn. Catalogue Feb. 5, 1929, p. 39; Davis to Governor Pickens, A. S. W. Rosenbach Collection; Memminger, Feb. 16, 1861, to Col. M. A. Moore, Memminger Papers South Caroliniana Lib. Gov. W. O. Perry to Gov. Pickens, March 5, 1861, Pickens-Bonham Papers LC.
32   Curtis, *Buchanan*, II, 541 ff.; Holt, Feb. 6, 1861, to Attorney-General J. W. Hayne of S. C., N. Y. *Tribune*, Feb. 9, 1861.
33   O. R. I, i, 275, 276; Charleston correspondence, March 9, 10, in N. Y. *Tribune*, March 13, 16, 1861.

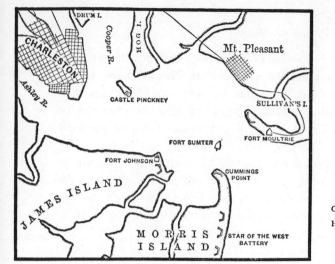

CHARLESTON
HARBOR

Many officers were spoiling for a fight. Beauregard, reporting March 22 that all his batteries would be in full trim in a few days, was able to add that Sumter was nearly out of fuel and provisions. Five days later he expressed hope that the fort would soon surrender, for the uncertainty ought not to last beyond the period when he had completed all his preparations to compel Anderson to surrender.[34]

[VI]

Meanwhile, in Washington, Abraham Lincoln, new to high office, totally untrained in administrative duties, inexperienced in the leadership of Congress and public sentiment, and quite unacquainted with his Cabinet, had to face a multiplicity of problems with scanty assistance and amid constant distractions. For secretarial aid he had only two men, John Hay and John G. Nicolay, both able, but very young, very green, and very provincially Western. The country would have gained had Lincoln brought some capable Republican of more experience, like Horace White of the Chicago *Tribune* staff, who had reported the Lincoln-Douglas debates, to reinforce them. The first week Lincoln had to receive callers in droves, meet the diplomatic corps as it paid its respects, address delegations from six States, handle a swollen mail, and hold his first formal Cabinet meeting (March 9). That week Seward, on whose friendly if contriving advice he could best lean, was ill with lumbago.

In his first days Lincoln had to fill the principal existing vacancies before the Senate adjourned its short special session; to consult with General Scott on the bad position of the army, whose two principal administrative officers, Samuel Cooper as adjutant-general and Joseph E. Johnston as quartermaster-

34 O. R., I, i, 280, 283; Beauregard to Walker, March 22, 27.

general, leaned to the South; and to study the possibility of keeping Maryland, Virginia, Kentucky, and Missouri in the Union. Washington was speculating on antagonisms within the Cabinet, with Seward, Cameron, and Bates understood to be moderate, while Chase, Montgomery Blair, and Welles supposedly held more extreme views.[35] Martin J. Crawford, one of three Confederate commissioners whom Jefferson Davis had just sent to Washington to explore the chances of a treaty of amity, was busily inquiring as to the intentions of the new regime, and reporting to Montgomery on March 6 that Seward and Cameron could be relied on to maintain a peace policy. Another commissioner, John Forsyth, arrived on his heels, and both men began using ex-Senator Gwin of California and Senator R. M. T. Hunter of Virginia in an effort to establish unofficial relations with Seward.

When did Lincoln have time to ponder the one question that mattered: the question what course could best serve the cause of peace and reunion? Not during his first levee, which so jammed the White House that for an hour those who wished to leave had to get out through the windows. And not while he was incessantly besieged by office-hunters and Congressional patronage-dispensers. At first he refused to limit his hours for seeing people. But when he found that he had no time to take a drink of water, he fixed them at ten o'clock till three, and later at ten till one.[36]

Lincoln thought it appalling that while the national house was on fire at one end, he had to be letting out rooms at the other. Sane observers were equally aghast. We have no national policy, no administration plan, one of Greeley's friends lamented near the end of March; while the government crumbles underfoot, the only problem considered is whether some supplicant should be a tide-waiter, a village postmaster, or an Indian agent. But the system existed; the President had no escape.

He was in fact the focal point of pressures which reached out to every town and county with a sizable Republican vote. After filling his Cabinet, he had but one important personal appointment to make—that of Hiram Barney, a capable attorney, to be collector of the port of New York. Barney, a friend of William Cullen Bryant, had extended Lincoln some valued courtesies at the time of the Cooper Union address, and had supported him in the Chicago convention. The President took a certain interest also in sending Charles Francis Adams to London, W. L. Dayton to Paris, Norman Judd to Berlin, and that eccentric egotist Cassius M. Clay to St. Petersburg. In the main, however, his appointments had to be parceled out to clamorously selfish men and groups.[37]

35 Blaine, *Twenty Years*, I, 285, 286.
36 N. Y. *Herald*, March 9, 1861; Helen Nicolay, *Lincoln's Secretary*, 82, 83.
37 The Barney appointment is discussed in Alexander, *Political Hist. N. Y.*, II, 390–396; cf. Wm. Allen Butler (a law partner), *A Retrospect of Forty Years*, 349, 350.

Every Republican in Congress wished to strengthen his political organization; every editor coveted a post-office connection to swell his subscription
list; every jobless politician wanted a salary. The Illinois members, for example,
met in conclave to draw up a slate of appointments to be requested of Lincoln.
After dividing marshalships, district attorneyships, and territorial posts, they
demanded a slice of foreign-service pie. Senator Lyman Trumbull wanted two
consulships, Representative Elihu Washburne one, and Representative W. P.
Kellogg one. Joseph Medill of the Chicago *Tribune,* meanwhile, wished one
of his staff made the new Chicago postmaster. "If Mr. Scripps has it," he explained, "the country postmasters of the Northwest would work to extend
our circulation." And Illinois was but one State! Three-quarters of the March
correspondence of the typical Senator, Representative, or Cabinet member in
this hour of crisis pertained to jobs. A clamor of greed and grumbling filled
the capital.[38]

In this matter Lincoln was the victim not merely of the national system, but
of the special necessities of the Republicans. They did not as yet have a coherent, well-organized party. It had been born some half dozen years earlier as a
patchwork of local organizations; it had fought the campaign of 1856 under a
hastily-chosen nominee as a coalition of new, uncertain State organizations, and
had lost; in the three years after 1856 it had largely disappeared from view as
a national entity. Its enthusiastic rally in 1860, a marvel of improvisation, might
have failed again but for the Democratic schism. Its members included former
Whigs, former Know-Nothings, former Freesoil Democrats, and young men
who were simon-pure Republicans. Now it needed the cement of national office
to make it a unified, well-knit party on a truly national basis. Its chieftains—
governors, Senators, Representatives, editors, State and local committeemen—
were resolved that it should obtain this cement, and anxious to determine its
quality. Lincoln was well aware that parties are essential to democratic government, and that his Administration could not possibly succeed without strong
party support. In the hours he gave to applicants he was not merely dividing
spoils; he was building a foundation.

Throughout March the hotels were jammed. In one, three hundred un-
bathed men slept in the dining room. Anybody could get into the White
House, and nearly everybody did. The physical and psychological pressure on

38 Medill's letter, March 4, 1861, is in the Lyman Trumbull Papers, LC; see also the
Washburne Papers. Among the dissatisfied elements the Constitutional Unionists were
prominent. Edward Everett resentfully noted that in Maryland, Kentucky, and Missouri,
where the Republican vote had been trifling and the Constitutional Union vote tremendous,
Lincoln had bestowed the three great plums on Republicans—Montgomery Blair, Cassius M.
Clay, and Edward Bates. Everett, March 31, 1861, to Sir Henry Holland; Everett Papers,
MHS.

Lincoln was crushing. On March 14 one correspondent shouldered his way through the fragrant throng. "I saw the President this morning, and his whole air was that of not only a worried but an ill man. He would require a fortnight's rest, it seemed to me, to enable him to let off a joke or a jolly backwoods reminiscence." Not until hundreds of appointees had been confirmed, and the special Senate session had ended on March 28, could the Administration give wholehearted attention to the grave national issues.

To add to Lincoln's difficulties, Douglas as the chief Democratic leader spent March indicating that he would harass the Administration mercilessly unless it sacrificed almost everything for peace. He seemed a very different Douglas from the man who had recently talked of hanging traitors. For one reason, he was trying to pull the defeated Democratic party together, and to rally Union forces in the South. For another, he was drinking heavily again, a fact which explained some excesses of language and one bout of fisticuffs on the Senate floor. But when all allowances are made, his attacks were outrageously sharp. He introduced a resolution calling on the Administration to tell the Senate how many forts, arsenals, and navy yards it held inside the seceded States, with what forces, and with what intentions. His object, he stated, was to press the government into a definite avowal of policy. In his opinion, it had but three courses open: It could amend the Constitution to preserve the Union, it could assent to a peaceable division, or it could make war to subjugate the lost States. "The first proposition is the best and the last is the worst," he declared.

If Douglas wished assurances that Lincoln would not wantonly provoke war, he got them. Senator Fessenden, assuring him that the President would use no questionable powers and violate no law in an effort to collect the revenues, obviously spoke for Lincoln. It was not clear that the government had any right to collect customs dues aboard a warship, and it would certainly not do so without explicit mandate from Congress. Yet day by day Douglas kept up his scoriac outbursts, often using bitter personalities. His manner was satanically provoking. Sometimes he exhibited a heavy-handed malignity, sometimes he was patronizingly sarcastic. You state that you mean peace, he said tauntingly, and yet pass laws that cannot be enforced without war. You talk of maintaining the Federal authority, yet you have not a Federal officer, acting by your authority, in the whole secession area. However affronted, his opponents thought it best to bite their lips in silence.[39]

One eloquent foreign voice, in these dark days, was raised to hearten Amer-

---

39 *Cong. Globe,* 36th Cong., 2d Sess., 1436 ff. "I expect to oppose his [Lincoln's] administration with all my energy on those great principles which have separated parties in former times," Douglas said March 6; but on a Constitutional amendment to settle the slavery issue, he would support Lincoln.

ican friends of freedom. Elizabeth Barrett Browning wrote an American acquaintance that some evils were worse than civil conflict. "My serious fear," she declared, "has been, and is, not for the dissolution of the body but the death of the soul—not of a rupture of states and civil war, but of reconciliation and peace at the expense of a deadly compromise of principle. Nothing will destroy the republic but what corrupts its conscience and disturbs its frame— for the stain upon the honor must come off upon the flag. If, on the other hand, the North stands fast on the moral ground no glory will be like your glory." [40] These were the sentiments of millions of lovers of the Union.

Most men on both sides in the sectional struggle felt that they stood upon sound moral ground. It was all-important that the leaders on each side, and especially on the Union side, should act on high principle and not expediency. Would Lincoln, so untried in great responsibilities, yield to the heavy pressures for peace at any price—for delay beyond the point of no return? Or would he stand by his declaration that evasion must stop? Before the answer was given, a quietly desperate struggle between him and Seward had to be decided.

40 N. Y. *Independent,* March 10, 1861.

6.

LINCOLN WAS the head of what may be described as a coalition government, representing as it did groups of diverse origins and principles. Seward, as Secretary of State, had not yet given up the idea that he would be a sort of Prime Minister; Lincoln had to disabuse him of that. At the same time, the question of Fort Sumter was paramount. Major Robert Anderson had reported to Washington that it would take twenty thousand men to reinforce the Charleston post. Nevins feels that early in his administration Lincoln had almost made up his mind to evacuate Sumter as a military necessity. A whole series of official and unofficial moves and of jockeying by the administration, Confederates, and intermediaries was underway, the details and motives of which are still questioned by historians. In the end, Lincoln decided to send an expedition to Sumter with provisions, backed by warships. After all, "he would not tolerate secession, 'the essence of anarchy,' and he would use the power confided to him to hold the property and places belonging to the government, and to collect its revenues." Thus he could not fail to provision Sumter or hold Fort Pickens.[1]

Finally the Sumter expedition was off, and South Carolina was warned of its approach. By April 12 the fleet was off Charleston Bar. The issue was now up to the Confederates: Major Anderson would not surrender and the Union was clearly going to resupply, if not reinforce, Fort Sumter. "The strong current of radical Southern feeling carried Davis along with it." [2] At 4:30 A.M., April 12, 1861, came the dull boom of the Confederate signal shot. Then other guns opened and the war began. On April 13 Fort Sumter surrendered.

"Looking backward, we can now see that a conflict between North and South had been certain when Lincoln was inaugurated. Nothing the government might legitimately have done could have averted it. The seven States of the cotton kingdom were determined to erect a separate republic; the United States was determined to maintain the Union. At some point and some moment battle was certain. . . . The point at which the Civil War could possibly have been averted lay much further back." [3] Although both sides showed a lack of wisdom over Fort Sumter, the "callousness evinced in Montgomery's rush into battle is especially discreditable." While mistakes were undoubtedly made, "the complete integrity of purpose exhibited by Lincoln" was a bright element in the crisis.[4]

The "thunderclap" of Sumter crystallized feelings on both sides. Soon after Lincoln called for troops, four more states—Virginia, Tennessee, Arkansas, and North Carolina—seceded. There was concern in Washington, cut off from the North for a time by the pro-Southerners in Baltimore, but Maryland was to be held fairly firm to the Union. The two nations "lurched" to war; "the ardor of the South after Sumter was as impressive as that of the North—and the lack of hardheaded planning just as remarkable."[5] Both sides underestimated the magnitude of the war before them. "The wonder was that under these circumstances, amid hurry, guesswork, and reckless expedients, in an atmosphere of shortsighted optimism, so much was accomplished."[6]

Conflict intensified in the Mississippi Valley, along the Ohio River, and in the East. The intense struggle in Missouri left wounds that were long in healing. Although that state maintained a Confederate government, often in exile, and fighting was heavy throughout the war, it remained basically Union. Kentucky attempted to remain neutral, despite a geographical position that made such a posture impossible. Both Federals and Confederates jockeyed for the state, but it, too, finally remained largely with the North. Nevins praises Lincoln's actions in handling the situations in Missouri, Kentucky, and Maryland, thus helping to save these vital areas for the Union.[7] "On the whole, the North had achieved a great deal in holding most of the debatable borderland. . . . Strategically, the North held the entrances to the Shenandoah Valley, the Cumberland and Tennessee Rivers, and the lower Mississippi."[8]

While major action did not occur in the early summer of 1861, there were Union victories by George B. McClellan in western Virginia, soon to become West Virginia, and fighting along borderlands in the West. With the Northern masses demanding action, Lincoln tried to organize for war and consolidate his political position; Stephen A. Douglas led Federal support by the War Democrats, but he died that summer in Chicago. Among those who put forth plans for a grand strategy, General-in-Chief Winfield Scott proposed the "Anaconda Plan" calling for a naval blockade and concentric military pressure on the Confederacy. The blockade of the Atlantic and Gulf coasts was begun, but it was far from fully implemented.

On both sides the leaders were amateurs at large war, and the armies were mostly inexperienced. War was still "romance, the muskets and bayonets were for parade, and the nurses were proof of home solicitude, not a portent of wounds and disease. In short, confusion, improvisation, and deficiencies that under a grimmer war test would have been intolerable could be grimacingly endured, while excitement and exaltation fixed the mood of the day." [9] Leadership was being challenged on both sides. Davis had to move his Confederate capital from Montgomery, Alabama, to Virginia and had to contend with much more important things. Lincoln remained to be tested.

NOTES

1. Nevins, *The War for the Union*, Vol. I, *The Improvised War, 1861–1862*, p. 58.
2. *Ibid.*, p. 68.
3. *Ibid.*, p. 71.
4. *Ibid.*, p. 73.
5. *Ibid.*, p. 92.
6. *Ibid.*, pp. 115–116.
7. *Ibid.*, p. 136.
8. *Ibid.*, pp. 146–147.
9. *Ibid.*, p. 178.

The First Test of Strength

BY THE TIME Davis reached Richmond and Beauregard partly organized his command at Manassas, the grand strategy of the Confederacy had taken shape. On land, a generally defensive policy was to be pursued while the new nation awaited aid from cotton-starved Europe. The Confederate Congress declared a defensive attitude by resolution just after Sumter, Jefferson Davis proclaimed it in his message to Congress, and Robert E. Lee as head of the Virginia forces asserted it in special orders: "The policy of the State, at present, is strictly defensive." Since the Confederacy as yet lacked strength to invade the North, the defensive policy, despite Beauregard's protests, was inescapable. It imposed on the South a manifest disadvantage in the loss of the initiative. While the North could choose its point of attack, the Confederacy was like a wary duelist, waiting to parry a lunge or a slash. One countervailing advantage was the ability to use distance for defense, transferring troops by inside lines, so far as transport facilities permitted—for inside lines are useless without traffic arteries—while the Union was making long outside marches. Another advantage was the power of awaiting attack behind entrenchments.

The defensive military policy of the South would have had far greater effectiveness if the section had been buttressed by natural physical barriers. Unhappily for its generals, the Confederacy had no Pyrenees, no Vosges, no Carpathians, while the South found it utterly impossible to gain and hold the Ohio, which might have been a real rampart. West and northwest the section was pierced by great rivers: the Mississippi, the Red, the Tennessee, the Cumberland. From Ohio, the Monongahela led southward; from Pennsylvania the Shenandoah Valley opened a corridor. Eastern Virginia was singularly exposed. The Potomac tributaries and the York, Rappahannock, and James, all admitted hostile armies well within the Old Dominion. From the sea, Wilmington, Charleston, Mobile, and above all New Orleans seemed readily assailable. The Confederates lay in a besieged fortress with many entry-ports open. Nevertheless, the principal Southern leaders believed they could withstand all

(*The War for the Union*, Vol. I, *The Improvised War, 1861–1862*, Chapter 11.)

Union attacks until the Yankees grew tired of the butchery, or Europe intervened.[1]

The energy that the South might have put into a rapid exchange of cotton for arms while the seas remained fairly open went instead into a brisk but essentially futile campaign of privateering.[2] Davis' proclamation (April 17) that all who wished to use privately armed ships to resist Northern aggression might apply for letters of marque sent a spasm of activity through Southern ports. Two days later Lincoln proclaimed that any Southerner molesting American commerce under such authority would be subject to the penalties for piracy; but of course the North could not hang captured privateersmen, for instant retaliation would have followed. Southern leaders being eager to get the "militia of the sea" into action, the rebel Congress passed comprehensive legislation, signed by Davis early in May, which secured to holders of letters of marque and reprisal practically the whole proceeds of their captures. The same law gave Northern merchantmen in Southern ports thirty days to get home, a privilege which the North did not extend to Southern ships. Bounties were offered for the destruction of enemy warships of superior force, and for every naval rating taken prisoner.[3]

The enthusiasm in Southern seaports for the combined opportunity of striking the Yankees and pocketing a neat profit was feverish. Wharves, counting-rooms, and hotel lobbies responded with talk of Drakes to sweep the ocean. The New Orleans *Daily Crescent* dreamed that within 4 months at least 750 swift vessels averaging 4 mighty guns apiece would be crippling the Northern strength. Unhappily for the Confederacy, some of the best Southern ships were seized in Northern harbors. Three fine vessels of the Charleston line, the *South Carolina*, *Massachusetts*, and *James Adger*, with the *Bienville* of the New Orleans line, were soon Northern cruisers. What they might have done for the South is suggested by the feats of the *Nashville*, also of the Charleston line, which served the Confederacy as transport, privateer, and warship. However, despite the Southern lack of good shipyards and mechanics, some busy hornets were soon sent out.

1 On Confederate strategic policy see Davis, *Rise and Fall*, I, Ch. VI; Clifford Dowdey, *The Land They Fought For*, 126; Eaton, *Southern Confederacy*, 124, 125. John M. Daniel in the Richmond *Examiner* inveighed against the "policy of retreat"; see editorials June 12, June 15, July 2, etc., and F. S. Daniel, *The Richmond Examiner During the War*.

2 The exchange of cotton for arms at this date could not have been large, nearly all the 1860 crop having been exported or sent to New England, but it might have been useful. See Owsley, *King Cotton Diplomacy*, 25 ff.; Coulter, *Confederate States*, Ch. X; J. H. Reagan, *Memoirs*, 113; Schwab, *Confederate States*, 13–16, 233, 234.

3 Statutes, Provisional Govt. CSA, 2d Sess., Ch. III; Richardson, *Messages and Papers of the Confederacy*, I, 60–62; Robinson, *The Confederate Privateers*, 17–20, 30 ff.; and on Washington's belated offer to adhere unconditionally to the Declaration of Paris outlawing privateers, 64th Cong., 1st Sess., Senate Doc. 332. For fundamental material on the Confederate privateers see *O. R. Union and Conf. Navies*, Series II, i, 247–249.

New Orleans on May 16 dispatched the little steamer *Calhoun*, which that same evening captured a Maine bark with 3,000 barrels of lime. She was immediately joined by two other New Orleans privateers which began cruising the Gulf. Beauregard had urged Louisiana to fortify the Mississippi below the city, arming Forts Jackson and St. Philip with the heaviest guns to be found, and constructing heavy booms, one of timber and one of barges, across the river. This was delayed, but the privateers delighted Creole hearts. Charleston, meanwhile, had her first privateer active June 2, when the schooner *Savannah*, armed with one 1812-style eighteen-pounder, put to sea on a brief and unfortunate cruise. After capturing a Maine brig laden with Cuban sugar, she was seized by a Union warship. Landed in New York, the small crew were ironed, confined in the Tombs, and tried for piracy, with the death penalty staring them in the face until the jury happily disagreed.[4] Another Charleston privateer named for Jefferson Davis, a brig armed with five English guns of 1801 vintage, went to sea in June, and soon captured a Philadelphia freighter and a Massachusetts schooner. A third, the *Dixie*, sailed in July and within four days placed a prize crew aboard a Yankee bark full of coal.

By this time merchants and shipowners in all North Atlantic ports were clamorous for an immediate intensification of the blockade. Even if the Confederacy could place only a few dozen privateers on the ocean, unless its ports were quickly sealed it would deal Northern commerce a staggering blow. Steamship companies, shippers, and insurance interests demanded that the government put guns and gunners on important steamers like those which brought forty millions in gold from San Francisco to New York every year, furnish convoys on dangerous routes, and station warships in such busy sea lanes as Vineyard Sound.[5]

Even during May, blockading vessels trailed their smoke across the skies outside Charleston, Savannah, Mobile, and New Orleans. But no Yankee ever uttered a frostier understatement than Secretary Welles's remark that the navy was "not as powerful or in numbers as extensive as I wished." When Sumter fell, only forty-two ships, including tenders and storeships, were in commission. Six were in Northern ports, four at Pensacola, one on the Great Lakes, and the others dotted over the globe from the Mediterranean to the East Indies. With authority from Lincoln, Welles instantly ordered the buying or leasing of twenty vessels.[6] He assigned an Atlantic force the task of closing

4 Four of the twelve jurors stood for acquittal; see Robinson, *Privateers,* 135–147, for details.

5 Nineteen New York insurance companies demanded that the navy give immediate protection to commerce; O. R. I, i, 9.

6 Welles established in New York an advisory board of five, including Governor E. D. Morgan, William M. Evarts, and Moses Grinnell, to assist in forwarding men and supplies. His MS diary contains some matter not in the published version.

Confederate ports from the Chesapeake to Key West, and shortly divided it into North Atlantic and South Atlantic squadrons under Louis M. Goldsborough and Samuel F. Du Pont respectively. A Gulf squadron was instructed to shut every port in that area. Blockade runners were soon being captured. The seizure of three British ships off Charleston on May 22 posed a difficult diplomatic question, which was settled when the government, after Seward appealed to Welles, released them.[7]

It was soon evident that no exterior patrol would suffice to shut the Southern ports. Along such an extended coast, with so many inlets, harbors, and bays, it was easy for blockade runners and privateers to slip in and out. Only when some of the major ports had been captured could the movement of ships be brought under control. By July conversations were under way between the army and navy upon an amphibious expedition against Wilmington. Meanwhile, the navy had let contracts for the hurried construction of warships. The sloop *Tuscarora* was launched at Philadelphia on August 22. "Her keel was growing in the forest three months ago," boasted Welles. Vessels of every size and shape were also bought for refitting and arming. "Alas! It is like altering a vest into a shirt to convert a trading steamer into a man of war," lamented Du Pont, but the work went on. Although summer found the blockade still highly ineffective, naval officers could reflect that the war was young.

The South, indeed, by midsummer had a premonition of the days when imports would cease, and shortages become crippling. Northern commercial interests equally felt a foreboding of grave damage to the American merchant marine. Long so proud, it might be swept from the seas or compelled to take refuge under foreign flags.

[I]

On land, meanwhile, the time had come for harder blows. North and South, the clamor for fighting grew ever more strident. In Richmond the rebel war clerk Jones wrote in his diary for June 12: "The vast majority of our people are for 'carrying the war into Africa' without a moment's delay."[8] From Washington a gallant New York soldier, Francis Barlow, destined to become known as the boy general and to have his monument reared at Gettysburg, wrote that the demand for crushing the enemy made a campaign so imperative that if Lincoln objected, he might be replaced by a military dictatorship.[9] "Already the murmurs of discontent are ocean-loud against the slow and cau-

7 West, *Welles*, 117; J. R. Soley, *The Blockade and the Cruisers*, 8, 9.
8 Jones, *Rebel War Clerk's Diary*, I, 51.
9 Francis Barlow had enlisted as a private April 19, married the next day, and left his bride at the church to go to the front. His letter of May 27, 1861, is in the S. L. M. Barlow Papers.

tious courses of the war. I see this in the files of responsible and pervading correspondence which crowd the Secretaries' mails, and I know it from the President himself."

The sight of troops pouring to the front gave people on each side a false impression of strength. When Beauregard left Montgomery for the Virginia front on May 29 his train, according to a Boston-born physician aboard, counted 148 cars, all filled with troops bound for Augusta and points north, and drawn by two locomotives.[10] This may be an exaggeration, but it is true that Southerners who cheered massive troop trains expected a prompt advance. Jefferson Davis explained to Joseph E. Johnston on July 13 that a North Carolinian who accused the government of wantonly holding back 17,000 eager men from his State was writing nonsense. Volunteers swarmed everywhere, but Davis had to tell these eager units: "I have not arms to supply you." [11] In Washington, it was assuredly a mistake to show members of Congress on July 4 an imposing military pageant, some 25,000 troops filling Pennsylvania Avenue like a blue river, while their tread sounded like dull thunder, for the spectacle made many members recklessly impatient. "This was war," wrote one. "We should bring on the battle." [12]

Each side underrated the need for preparation, and undervalued the fighting quality of its opponents. "It was a favorite notion," wrote General Barnard later, "with a large class of Northern politicians (and the people too) that nothing but an imposing display of force was necessary to crush the rebellion." [13] Surely, since pioneers had fought under Andrew Jackson at the wave of a hat, a regiment hardly needed three months' drill! Why wait, when only a thirty-mile march was needed to overwhelm the enemy?

Both the Confederate camp at Manassas and the Union camps before Washington were slovenly. Neither army had properly assembled and organized its baggage trains, tents, food arrangements, or medical supplies. Beauregard could have said precisely what McDowell did say later: "I had no opportunity to test my machinery, to move it around and see whether it would work smoothly or not." Yet each section waved aside reasons for delay. "True enough, you are green," men admitted. "But the enemy is green too—you are all green alike." [14]

The North had a taste of the bloody realities of war on June 10. Ben Butler —urged on by Montgomery Blair, who denounced the "miserable do-nothings" in Washington and expressed confidence that a march to Richmond would be easy—moved that day to capture two Confederate posts, Big and Little Bethel,

10 Dr. Martin McQueen in Syracuse *Journal*, May 27, 1861.
11 O. R. I, ii, 976–977.
12 A. G. Riddle, *Recs. of War Times*, 29.
13 Barnard, *The C. S. A. and the Battle of Bull Run*, 42.
14 Hurlburt, *McClellan and the Conduct of the War*, 103.

a few miles from Fort Monroe. The command was given to an incompetent. He used faulty old maps, sent out two columns on a night march which, instead of joining hands and cooperating, actually fired into each other, and by this tragic mishap gave the alarm to the Confederates at Little Bethel, who fell back on Big Bethel. He then completely botched an attempt to flank this well-chosen position, where the enemy was protected by a swampy creek and a battery of guns. As Butler later wrote, "Everything was mismanaged." The Union forces withdrew just as the Confederate leader, fearing reinforcements from Fort Monroe, himself retreated! The reason which the Northern commander later offered for retiring was that his troops were hungry from long marching. Actually they had covered about eleven miles, and if they had halted to eat lunch from their haversacks, they could have kept the position the enemy was abandoning! [15]

It was evident, meanwhile, that the Northern forces were loose, clumsy, and inharmonious. The aged Scott reigned without actually ruling. He had three armies, Patterson's in the Harpers Ferry area, McDowell's at Alexandria, and Ben Butler's at Fort Monroe, which he failed to coordinate, and whose commanders all distrusted him.[16]

Patterson, who on June 28 had 14,350 men facing Joe Johnston's 10,700, made a series of erratic movements. Elated by his success in driving Johnston from Harpers Ferry, he thought that with Scott's support he could win a brilliant victory; but Scott, with superior insight, disapproved of his plans, and withdrew some of his troops. The result was that the Pennsylvania general believed that he had been checked just as he was on the point of seizing a bright advantage. Had he held Charlestown just south of the Potomac, he would have been in a position to strike at Winchester, intercept Johnston if that general suddenly moved to join Beauregard at Manassas, or himself march rapidly to reinforce McDowell. Instead, he put himself in a remoter position at Martinsburg.[17] Relations between Scott and McDowell continued bad, with Scott petulant and McDowell resentful. By July 16–17, returns for the McDowell-Mansfield command in the Washington-Alexandria area showed

15 On the two Bethels, see *Butler's Book*, 266–270; Swinton, *Army of the Potomac*, 31. The saddest loss at Big Bethel was that of Theodore Winthrop, a more than promising American man of letters.

16 Lossing, *Civil War*, I, 525, 526; Swinton, 33, 34; O. R. I, ii.

17 For Patterson's Shenandoah operations see O. R. I, ii, 156–187, 607, 694; his own *Narrative* is best read in the light of T. L. Livermore's careful paper on the campaign in Military Hist. Soc. of Mass., I, *Campaigns in Virginia 1861–62*. Alonzo H. Quint's *The Second Mass. Infantry* gives an interesting view. Patterson when forced to retreat had to endure silently a great deal of public criticism. "Great injustice is done you and your command here," John Sherman, who had been on his staff, wrote from Washington June 30, "and by persons in the highest military position." When Patterson placed his forces at Martinsburg they were behind Johnston, who was thus free to move to Manassas at any time with Patterson trailing in his rear.

37,321 officers and men present for duty, but McDowell felt that Scott had denied him the staff, equipment, and latitude in training which he needed.

If Patterson and McDowell distrusted the head of the armies, Butler's opinion was scorching. The day he was appointed major-general, May 16, he called on Scott to exchange angry accusations. Scott accused him of running terrible risks in Baltimore, thwarting the government's pacific plans, and show-ing general highhandedness. Butler retorted that Scott knew nothing of the situation, had made dangerous concessions to the disloyal mayor, and should have helped him suppress the murderous plug-uglies. Though Cameron and Chase urged the indigant Butler to stay in the service, and Montgomery Blair assured him he was entirely right, his irritation grew when he found Fort Monroe shockingly ill equipped. It had no horses, no proper water supply, no provisions but hardtack and meat; the seven or eight thousand men he com-manded were insufficient to do more than keep Magruder at bay. The sym-pathetic Blair, who had hoped to see Butler march direct on Richmond, wrote Cameron on June 22 in high dudgeon. Instead of 20,000 men with proper artillery, cavalry, and wagon trains, Butler had less than half that force, no transport, no cavalry, and few guns. Blair added:

My want of confidence in the enterprise of the General-in-Chief grows. Besides, he does not approve our policy and is not heartily with us. He means to play Pacificator. I counsel you to take these matters into your own charge, seeing that you have the responsibility.[18]

The West Virginia campaign furnished new evidence of want of plan and liaison in Washington. McClellan exaggerates the facts when he declares that from first to last he had no "advice, orders, or instructions from Washington or elsewhere," and acted on his own initiative; for actually he got some helpful information from Scott. But he was left altogether too much to his own re-sources. He issued a proclamation to the people of West Virginia of strong political tinge, and an equally political address to his soldiers. When he sent Lincoln copies, with a letter explaining his reasons for the invasion, he got no comment from President, Secretary of War, or General Scott. It was unfor-tunate that Cameron and Scott did not fully and promptly inform McClellan of their plan of action in front of Washington. Had they done so, the troops flushed with victory at Rich Mountain might have marched, as McClellan suggested, toward the Shenandoah to help Patterson pin down Joseph E. Johnston.[19]

18 See *Butler's Book*. Blair in the rough draft of his letter to Cameron included a sentence later deleted: "As our friend Chase even has fallen out with the Genl I hope we will pluck up courage to take our affairs into our own hands." Blair Papers, LC.

19 See McClellan's published *Report*, 15-17, 51, 52; for Scott's advice see O. R. I, ii, 648, 743, etc.

[II]

Like two wrestlers glowering at each other across the ring, McDowell and Beauregard early in July faced each other across twenty miles of broken Virginia countryside. The Union commander, after detaching about 6,000 men to protect his communications, had 30,000 troops with 49 guns; the Confederate general had some 22,000 men with 29 guns. Both might be rapidly reinforced—the Southern army by Johnston's Shenandoah force, which at the beginning of July comprised about 11,000 men with 20 guns, and the army of McDowell by Patterson's larger force.[20] In this matter of reinforcing Beauregard and McDowell the Confederacy held the advantage, partly because Johnston could use the railroad from Winchester to Manassas, while Patterson had no ready means of reaching the area.

The Administration had good reasons for wishing to see McDowell offer battle. One was that the ninety-day men were soon to quit, they hoped to see action before they left, and obviously they ought to be used. Another was that European governments might be impressed by Northern vigor. The most important, however, was that Northern morale must be sustained.

Impatient Congressmen varied their debates by grumbling loudly about procrastination. Wagons and horses were needed? Well, buy them! Regiments had to be organized into brigades and divisions? Well, shove them in! Zack Chandler, who came to the Senate full of plans for seizing rebel property, thought that Scott could avoid hard fighting just by showing a little energy: he could simply surround the scoundrels, make their case hopeless, and compel them to retreat to Richmond. Chandler and others were talking about hanging the worst traitors as soon as they were caught.[21] Half of the press was ringing with demands for hard blows. As an echo of Horace Greeley's suggestions, Fitz-Henry Warren, a Washington correspondent of the *Tribune*, wrote his famous "Forward to Richmond" article; Greeley allowed Charles A. Dana to repeat and reinforce it in subsequent issues; and other newspapers caught it up. "Forward to Richmond! Forward to Richmond! The Rebel Congress must not be allowed to meet there on the 20th of July!"—so from June 26 onward ran the *Tribune*'s daily iteration of "The Nation's Battle-Cry." [22]

20 On numbers see Ropes, I, 127, 128; *Battles and Leaders*, I, 175; O. R. I, ii, 309, 487. A few ninety-day men did quit just before the battle, and the position of the whole body affected Union morale.

21 Chandler to his wife, Washington, June 27, 1861, Chandler Papers, LC; F. W. Banks, Washington, July 9, 1861, to S. L. M. Barlow, Barlow Papers; Washington correspondence dated July 11, 12, in N. Y. *Tribune*, July 13, 1861.

22 Cf. Charles A. Dana, "Greeley as a Journalist," N. Y. *Sun*, Dec. 5, 1872; and Dana's dictated statement to Ida M. Tarbell in Tarbell Papers, Allegheny College. Dana had been with the *Tribune* since 1847 and in some of Greeley's absences had taken full charge.

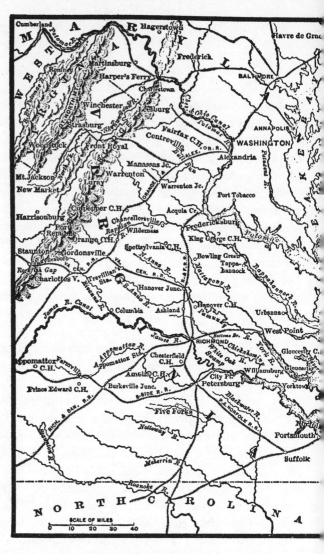

FIELD OF OPERATIONS
IN VIRGINIA

On the Confederate side various prodders, including the Richmond *Examiner*, had made Jefferson Davis nearly as anxious to hazard battle as Beauregard. Davis wrote Johnston July 13 that the one great object was to give the Southern columns capacity to take the offensive and prevent the junction of the enemy's forces.[23]

Nothing could have been more haphazard than the way in which McDowell's forward thrust was determined upon. First, Scott orally asked him to submit a plan of operations against Manassas, with an estimate of the men needed. Second, McDowell sent his plan to Scott, who read and approved it. Third, a council was held June 29 in the East Room of the White House attended by Cabinet members and leading officers. McDowell read his plan,

23 O. R. I, ii, 976, 977.

on which nobody made any comment except Mansfield, commanding in Washington, who said that he had not thought about the matter, knew nothing about it, and was unprepared to speak! The relation of Patterson's army to the movement was discussed, and one participant states that Scott explicitly promised to have it keep the Confederates in the Shenandoah engaged: "I assume the responsibility for having Johnston kept off McDowell's flank." Finally, McDowell submitted his plan to the army engineers, who made no constructive suggestion. In short, no real debate on the wisdom or mode of the attack took place.

Once the plan was accepted, McDowell had great difficulty in implementing it. Some regiments crossed the Potomac late, and a few not till the very day he was to start his army. He set out with no baggage trains, and though he possessed ammunition wagons and ambulances, had no facilities to carry food or tents. The men carried three days' rations in their haversacks. Said the jealous Mansfield, in effect, "I have no transportation to give you." Said Meigs, head of the quartermaster arrangements: "I have transportation, but Mansfield does not want me to supply it until the troops move." Said the overburdened McDowell: "I agree to that, but between you two I get nothing." So he set off, telling Scott he was not really ready to go: "So far as transportation is concerned, I must look to you behind me to send it forward." The egregiously bad marching of his troops McDowell explained by saying that Americans were unused to foot travel. Starting on Tuesday morning, July 16, the army did not reach Centerville until Thursday afternoon, when it camped until the battle advance began Sunday morning the 21st. Why?—partly because its provisions had not come up.[24]

Actually, McDowell's plan was well conceived and well drafted. By defeating Beauregard at Manassas, he would not only dispel the threat to Washington, but seize the important junction between the Orange & Alexandria Railroad and its lateral branch to the Shenandoah. He had the advantage of superior numbers, better ordnance, about 1600 regular soldiers, and the prospect of a timely reinforcement by Patterson. But a sharp check at Blackburn's Ford on the Bull Run July 18 discouraged his men, who wondered whether the Confederate line could really be penetrated. He and the army engineers used the next two days trying to discover the best place for attack. Meanwhile Patterson, whose duty was to hold Joseph E. Johnston, marched in precisely the wrong direction. He had been alarmed by vague reports that he had 30,000 to 40,000 troops before him. In a half-hearted demonstration, he moved toward

---

24 McDowell dates the East Room conference June 29; Montgomery C. Meigs says the beginning of July. See McDowell's testimony, *Comm. on Conduct of the War*, II, 35 ff.; Meigs Papers, Box IV, LC; and O. R. I, ii, *passim*, full of material on the campaign.

Winchester and Johnston on July 16, but then next day retreated to Charlestown, and a little later pulled still farther back to Harpers Ferry. Johnston
no sooner learned that Patterson had fallen back than he exultantly set his
troops in motion, hurrying them on as fast as he could to join Beauregard.

The result was that on July 20 the main body of Johnston's force joined
Beauregard. His intelligence service, for he had Major J. E. B. Stuart's cavalry
to scout for him, was as superb as Patterson's was worthless. While Patterson
was asking Scott for aid at Harpers Ferry, Johnston's command was fraterniz-
ing with the defenders of Manassas. This, said McDowell later, was "the fatal
thing" that decided Bull Run.

Yet it was not the only fatal element. At first the Union advance on the
21st seemed victorious. Pressing against the Confederate left, McDowell's raw
volunteers threw the Southerners back in some disorder. The main fighting
began about ten; at noon the battle was raging heavily beyond Bull Run,
around and on the hill capped by the Henry farmhouse; reports of a disaster
swept Richmond. The gallant James S. Wadsworth of New York thought at
two o'clock that the Union army had won the field. But command liaison on
the Union side was very poor, so that troops moved in piecemeal and raggedly.
Then, soon after three, a new part of Johnston's army, fresh from the trains,
arrived on the scene—the brigade of E. Kirby-Smith. That force, delivering
a severe discharge of musketry, followed it with a hot charge. Some Union
elements stampeded, and as Beauregard ordered an attack along the whole line,
the Union troops were swept back. By five they were in full retreat.

Beauregard had possessed complete warning of the Federal advance, for at
8:00 P.M. on July 16 a sealed letter, brought him by relays from the Confederate spy Mrs. Greenhow in Washington, had announced in cipher that
McDowell had been ordered to move. Early next morning he telegraphed the
news to Jefferson Davis. On the 17th the Richmond authorities had been able
to order Johnston's Army of the Shenandoah to join Beauregard, and T. J.
Jackson's brigade had forthwith led the van in the march to the nearest railroad
station. Scott, meanwhile, had failed to give Patterson positive orders.[25]

Not only were the Southern forces better coordinated, but they had better
officers and showed superior morale. During the battle the Confederate generals kept close under fire. Johnston and Beauregard were in the front lines at
critical moments, Brigadier-General B. E. Bee was mortally wounded, Colonel

---

25 See Col. Alfred Roman's *Beauregard*, I, 71 ff. (practically an autobiography); Johnston's
Narrative, 50 ff.; Gen. James Wadsworth's testimony in Committee on the Conduct of the
War, II; Swinton, *Army of the Potomac*, 58, 59; Ropes, I, 131 ff. Swinton and Ropes empha-
size the defective leadership and uneven fighting on both sides. *Comm. on Conduct of the
War*, II, 103. By Patterson's own statement, he could have held Johnston with 8,000 men;
op. cit., 107. A mass of military dispatches may be found in O. R. I., li, pt. 2.

J. F. Thomas, chief ordnance officer, fell while leading broken troops back into battle, and Jubal Early was equally intrepid. It was while Bee was appealing to his South Carolinians to sustain the honor of their State that he pointed to a brigade of the Army of the Shenandoah standing on the Henry house hilltop awaiting the Northern onslaught: "Look, there is Jackson with his Virginians standing like a stone wall against the enemy." [26] The men responded by a spirited charge. Young Jeb Stuart, leading two companies of cavairy, made his first appearance on a battlefield by a timely onslaught against the Union right flank, sweeping through the supports of two Federal batteries and leaving the guns an easy prey to an advancing regiment of Virginians. Throughout the hottest part of the battle the Confederate morale rose.

The Union troops had the disadvantage of advancing over unknown terrain against a foe of unknown strength. Raw troops fight more steadily when stationary, as most of the Confederate units were; in attacking they become confused and disorganized. Many Northerners entered the fight hot, tired, and thirsty from previous marching. Sights of wounds and agony frightened the green men. General William B. Franklin went forward with the Fifth and Eleventh Massachusetts to try to extricate an exposed battery. The infantrymen could not be brought up to the mark: they would rush forward, deliver a volley, and then, instead of taking hold of the guns, fall back to a safe place to reload. The Union artillery was badly served, and Griffin's expert West Point Battery showed the usual contempt of regulars for volunteers. Early in the combat it tore through the New York Seventy-first at top speed for a front-line position, cutting the regiment in two. Later, it ran out of ammunition. The caissons tore recklessly back for a fresh supply, scattering the units in their path, and men who saw the horses and gunners madly ripping out for the rear, thought all was lost—and ran too.

The Union retreat, at first orderly, quickly became a disgraceful rout. As Beauregard's lines swept forward, the panic grew, and soon men were in headlong flight, amid heat, dust, anguish, and terrific profanity. W. H. Russell, riding forward on horseback, found himself among the first fugitives. "What does this mean?" he demanded, and an exhausted officer gasped: "Why, it means that we are pretty badly whipped." [27]

The scene between Manassas and Alexandria that evening was never to be forgotten. The fields were dotted with fugitives, mounted officers outstripping

26 *Century*, XLVIII, vol. 48 (May, 1894), 155, 156.
27 Russell's vivid description, *My Diary*, Ch. 50, is corroborated by the photographer Mathew Brady, caught in the flight; Representative A. O. Riddle, quoted in S. S. Cox, *Three Decades*, 158; Horace White, *Lyman Trumbull*, 165–168. Trumbull, who had gone to the battle with Senator Grimes and others, wrote: "Literally, three could have chased ten thousand."

BULL RUN
DISPOSITION OF
CONFEDERATE FORCES

privates afoot. Down the Centreville highway poured a river of wagons, ambulances, soldiers belaboring mules, and dirty, disheveled troops. Every vehicle was jammed with men, who threw out even ammunition to make room. The ground was covered with provisions, overcoats, knapsacks, blankets, muskets, canteens, and cartridge boxes. Drivers whipped their teams; reeling soldiers clung to stirrups and wagon gates; and at every interruption of traffic masses of troops yelled frantically with rage: "The cavalry is on us! Get along, get along!" Over the crossroads rose columns of dust, for here, too, masses of troops were fleeing as from some unknown terror. As the flight roared northward, its noise like that of a great river, more and more men fell out from exhaustion. At Centreville some fresh reserve regiments formed line on a good defensive slope, and the fleeing forces might well have considered themselves safe.[28] But when a neighboring battery opened fire, the thud and flash precipitated a fresh panic.

It was the familiar story whose moral Kipling later compressed into three lines:

Ye pushed them raw to the battle as ye plucked them raw from the street,
And what did ye look they should compass? War-craft learned in a breath
Knowledge unto occasion at the first far view of Death?

In Washington that Sunday intense suspense had gripped everyone. Scott, anxious to allay men's anxiety, talked confidently of success and went to

28 A reserve brigade under Miles and a brigade under Richardson, in and just beyond Centreville, had taken no part in the fighting, maintained good order, and served as a dependable rear guard; Ropes, I, 153.

church at eleven. Early in the afternoon the President began receiving telegrams every quarter hour from Fairfax Court House, three or four miles from the battlefront. They at first gave the impression that the Union forces were retiring, and Lincoln, alarmed, went to see Scott, whom he found asleep. The General explained that the noise of battle was often misleading, for the wind made the firing seem first near, then far. Lincoln, returning to the White House, found news that the battle still raged, but that McDowell now seemed to be winning. Pleased by word that the Confederates had been driven back, he went for a ride. His secretary Nicolay records:

At six o'clock . . . Mr. Seward came into the President's room with a terribly excited and frightened look, and said to John [Hay] and I, who were sitting there, "Where is the President?" "Gone to ride," we replied.
"Have you any late news?" said he.
I began reading Hanscom's dispatch to him.
Said he: "Tell no one. That is not so. The battle is lost. The telegraph says that McDowell is in full retreat, and calls on General Scott to save the capital, etc. Find the President and tell him immediately to come to General Scott's." [29]

[III]

The Confederates made no real pursuit. By a determined thrust from either the east or west, they might have turned the small reserve force at Centreville. Some regiments on the Confederate left did ford Bull Run and set out to follow the fleeing troops, but were recalled by a staff command given in error. That night President Davis and the principal Confederate generals held a battlefield conference.[30] Davis was at first willing to send the freshest units, the brigades of Ewell, D. R. Jones, and Longstreet, in pursuit, but because doubts were thrown upon a major's report that he had seen a wild flight, with abandoned wagons and choked roads, he finally decided against the step. Johnston believed that his raw troops, poorly supplied with food and ammunition, could not execute forced marches and attack the fortified lines before Washington. He thought his troops more disorganized by victory, indeed, than the Union forces by defeat. Beauregard also opposed an attempt at pursuit. Previously hot to take the offensive and advance on Washington, he now declared that the prostration of the men, the shortage of supplies—the Manassas army had never possessed food for more than two days, and sometimes no rations at all, while it now held only enough ammunition for half a battle—and the general confusion, forbade a forward thrust.

29 Nicolay to his wife, July 27, 1861; Nicolay Papers, LC.
30 Davis had reached the battlefield just in time to witness the rout of the Union forces, and at once exultantly telegraphed his War Department that 15,000 Confederates had defeated 35,000 Federal troops. Roman, *Beauregard*, I, 111.

This decision deeply disappointed both Richmond and the many Southern sympathizers in Washington. Mrs. Greenhow, who had repeatedly assured Beauregard that the Union works south of the Potomac had been barely commenced and mounted few guns, and that a Confederate advance was greatly dreaded in the capital, ended more than one dispatch after Manassas: "Come on! Why do you not come?" But Johnston and Beauregard made a correct decision. By an implacable pursuit, flogging on their tired soldiers, the Confederates could have taken more prisoners and stores, making the defeat still more humiliating. But as they approached Washington they would have met the reserves from Centreville, the divisions of Mansfield and Runyon, some 11,000 Pennsylvania troops who arrived on Monday, and perhaps Patterson's force. Beyond the fortifications lay the Potomac. The night after the battle a dull, drenching rain began which continued all next day, turning the roads into mud. The railroad bridge across Bull Run had been destroyed. And the Confederates were hungry. Their commissary service, in the hands of the ill-tempered, inept Colonel Lucius B. Northrop, who had refused to let Beauregard sweep the area south of Washington clean of provisions, was distressingly inefficient.[31]

Even without pursuit, the Confederates claimed fully 1200 prisoners; 28 fieldpieces of good quality, 8 of them rifled, with more than 100 rounds for each gun; some 500 muskets and 500,000 rounds of ammunition; and horses, wagons, caissons, and ambulances. Losses on both sides have been variously computed, but the best source places the Union killed at 481, the Confederate at 387.[32]

The exultation of part of the Southern press and public was not only unrestrained, but tinged with an arrogant tone. "The breakdown of the Yankee race, their unfitness for empire," declared the Richmond *Whig*, "forces dominion on the South. We are compelled to take the sceptre of power. We must adapt ourselves to our new destiny. We must elevate our race, every man of it, breed them up to arms, to command, to empire." [33] The Louisville *Courier-Journal* was equally insolent. The South, remarked the editor, had until a few

31 "The want of food and transportation has made us lose all the fruits or our victory," wrote Beauregard, July 29. "We ought at this moment to be in or about Washington, but we are perfectly anchored here, and God only knows when we will be able to advance; without these means we can neither advance nor retreat." Roman, *op. cit.*, 121, 122. George Cary Eggleston in *A Rebel's Recollections* emphatically states the view of those who thought the army should have pursued. Jubal Early in his reminiscences emphatically agrees that advance was impracticable and impolitic; *Narrative*, 43–46.

32 O. R. I, ii, 327, gives Union killed 481, wounded 1011, and missing 1216; the Confederate killed at 387, wounded at 1582.

33 July 23, 1861. One able Southerner, the engineer R. H. Lucas, said he would not give ten cents on the dollar for New York property; Manigault, MS Recollections, Univ. of N. C., 326, 327.

weeks since governed the North as its Norman ancestors had governed the Saxon churls. The Yankee revolt would not last long, for, "dastards in fight and incapable of self-government, they will inevitably fall under the control of a superior race. A few more Bull Run thrashings will bring most of them once more under the yoke, as docile as the most loyal of our Ethiopian chattels." [34] *DeBow's Review*, picturing the North as divided and half-prostrated, predicted that the battle would confirm the independence of the South.[35]

Needless to say, responsible men like Davis and Lee knew that the test had only begun.

34 Quoted in Rossiter Johnson, *War of Secession*, 70.
35 September, 1861.

7.

"The effect of Bull Run at the North, as its meaning sank in, was as stimulating as a whiplash. It blew away illusions like rags of fog in a northwest gale. . . . The defeat brought Northern dissidents to better support of the war, and stimulated every State to intensified effort. . . . A second Northern uprising was at once evident. . . ." [1]

Union command in Virginia had to be reorganized. General McClellan was brought in from West Virginia to replace the beaten McDowell. The western Virginia campaign had appeared brilliant and all credit went, perhaps erroneously, to "Little Mac." "McClellan's handsome, soldierly presence, kind, modest manners, and evident care for his troops, made a happy impression." [2] McClellan, not yet 35, "struck everyone by his air of energy, confidence, and address." [3] Organization was his strong point. As Nevins puts it, McClellan's "splendid gifts were mated with terrible handicaps," a martyr complex, perfectionism, timidity, a tendency to find scapegoats, over-caution, and self-distrust. [4]

It was becoming clear that the holiday war was over and "grim war had begun." [5] In the West in August Federal arms were defeated at Wilson's Creek, and General John Charles Frémont's controversial reign in St. Louis came to an end when he was replaced by Henry Wager Halleck in November. There were important Federal successes on the Atlantic Ocean at Cape Hatteras, Roanoke Island, and farther south at Port Royal. Some of these coastal incursions enabled the Union to establish coaling stations for blockaders and to pose threats to the interior of the South. In November McClellan replaced the aging Scott as general-in-chief, but there was no grand march advancing out of Washington during the fine fall days. Despite a much superior force, the Federal army in Virginia failed to move against Joseph E. Johnston, now Confederate commander in the state. People were asking when, and grumbling became louder.

Lincoln's problems were increasing, with concern over Kentucky and then over Frémont's unauthorized emancipation proclamation which the President had to disavow. "The vigor with which Lincoln rejected the concept of a war fought not only to save the Union but to destroy slavery reflected his concern over a growing public radicalism. He believed in evolution, not revolution; he wished to shorten the conflict, not lengthen it." [6] Lincoln believed first that it was a war for a grand national idea, but now powerful elements were regarding it as a grand humanitarian ideal. Then came the capture of the British mail steamer *Trent* and seizure of Confederate commissioners to Europe, Mason and Slidell. A worrisome embroglio with Britain followed until near year's end when the commissioners were released from prison and sent on their way. Early in 1862 the President would have to ease Secretary of War Cameron out of office and replace him with the prominent Democrat Edwin M. Stanton.

On first glance there seemed to have been more Union failure than achievement in 1861. Crisis followed crisis and military action had not even come close to winning the war. "It had been a year of improvisation, and of the errors inseparable from haste, amateurishness, and disorganization. . . . Yet on careful view the Northern achievement seemed more impressive." [7] Despite many vexations, ineptitudes, and confusion, recruits for the Union rolled in from farm, forge, factory, store counter, and professional desk.[8] A large army had been formed, trained, and supplied. "The gathering of the huge volunteer forces in and about Washington was an inspiring sight, which gave many who witnessed it an exultant confidence." [9] "Many believed that the new army was a formidable human machine that would soon roll inexorably and victoriously southward." [10] Naval squadrons were in operation, with more coming. Northern hosts were pointed toward the South.

Thus, early in 1862, "the North could feel a greater firmness and confidence; the tub was being strengthened. . . . The central view was that Lincoln, on whom all the fortunes of the Union depended, had begun to lead firmly. In his early months he had shown sagacity, moderation, poise—but not a strong captaincy." There was now developing "the firmness of a strong leader, a chieftain who grew with the demands laid upon him. . . . The President was beginning to feel his strength, to ride in the tempest, and direct the storm." [11] "Like a tocsin awakening a lethargic giant, the war had brought into play unsuspected powers of mobilization and administration. . . . Amid the confusion, blundering, and selfishness patriots could also find cheer in the unanticipated resourcefulness of the State governments. . . . The war had shown that the North was still underdeveloped industrially; but it had demonstrated that the Union had a wide advantage over the South." [12]

NOTES

1. Nevins, *The War for the Union*, Vol. I, *The Improvised War, 1861–1862*, p. 223.
2. *Ibid.*, p. 225.
3. *Ibid.*, p. 269.
4. *Ibid.*, p. 273.
5. *Ibid.*, p. 227.
6. *Ibid.*, p. 339.
7. *Ibid.*, p. 414.
8. *Ibid.*, p. 235.
9. *Ibid.*, p. 237.
10. *Ibid.*, p. 239.
11. *Ibid.*, pp. 412–413.
12. *Ibid.*, pp. 415–416.

Giant in Swaddling Clothes

ANXIOUS though the people were to get on with the war, the late summer lull had at least this important effect: It gave North and South a pause to assess their situation. They began to comprehend that they were locked in a life-and-death grapple. Ex-Senator John Slidell of Louisiana wrote S. L. M. Barlow just before Bull Run that in all the South he did not know a solitary man who would reëstablish the Union on any terms. "You can scarcely hope to subjugate us. We *know* that you cannot, and if your views prevail, there can be no other termination of the war than by the mutual exhaustion of both parties." [1] The idea bit deep that the war must be fought to a devastating conclusion. Assistant-Secretary of War P. H. Watson told McClellan that the rebels would persist to the death gasp. [2] Though great numbers on both sides still looked forward to 1862 as the year of victory, most men of sense knew that the contest might be protracted, that it would test the people to the utmost, and that it would produce a new America.

Lincoln sat daily for long hours in his office on the south side of the White House; the kind of office that a county judge or prosperous doctor might be expected to have. Its furnishings were a large cloth-covered table for Cabinet meetings, a smaller table where the President usually wrote, a high wall desk with pigeonholes for papers, two horsehair sofas, an armchair, and some straight-backed chairs. Over the marble mantel of the brass-fendered fireplace hung a faded steel engraving of Jackson. Elsewhere on the wall were a photograph of John Bright, and a number of framed military maps. His secretaries, Nicolay and Hay, gave him efficient help, and a young Illinois newspaperman, W. O. Stoddard, went through the mail to sort out trivial or offensive letters. Other assistants he had none except an occasional clerk lent from some department. The offices of Cabinet members were equally primitive. They had changed little since 1800. The same wooden tables, desks, pigeonholes, and ledger-size copybooks as in John Adams' day, the same quill pens and scuffed carpets,

1 July 20, 1861, Barlow Papers.
2 Chase, *Diary and Corr.*, 50, 51; this talk was Nov. 11, 1861.

(*The War for the Union*, Vol. I, *The Improvised War, 1861–1862*, Chapter 13.)

and the same anemic staffs docketing papers, surrounded Chase, Welles, Cameron as they struggled with visitors.[3]

These executives looked out on a nation which seemed as vertebrate as a jellyfish. They could ask for aid from individuals, but not from capable associations or societies, which hardly existed. The war necessarily had to be a vast social and economic as well as military effort. But where were the leaders trained in social and economic organization? The nation had only small managerial groups and little skill in cooperative effort. Of the 8,200,000 people whose occupations were noted by the recent census, 3,300,000 were farmers, planters, and farm laborers, and many more were indirectly connected with agriculture. A shrewd observer, Sir Morton Peto, shortly estimated that seven-eighths of the population was engaged in tillage or the callings materially dependent thereon; an understandable exaggeration.

This agricultural country, just passing through a transportation revolution, was fairly well organized for farming and for all kinds of communication—by railways, canals, telegraphs, and express systems. The manufacture of farm machinery, the handling of farm products, the milling of grain, the packing of meats, the sending of a new host of settlers westward every year, and the supply of this host with consumption goods, were all competently done. As yet, however, they did not carry the country far from the old order of small enterprises, local outlooks, and unrestricted individualism.

A war machine can be built quickly and efficiently only if many components already exist. The Department in 1861 had no difficulty in making decisions. It soon found that the half-million volunteers embodied under the July legislation would wear out shoes in two months and uniforms in four; they therefore needed 3,000,000 pairs of shoes and 1,500,000 uniforms a year. It was easy to decide that they must have mountains of arms, a hundred miles of wagons, great base hospitals, and incredible miscellaneous supplies. The difficulty lay in implementing the decisions.

Problems of selection became acute; which firm could really fill the orders? Problems of scheduling were even more perplexing; how could everybody down the line of supply be told just what was needed, and when, and where? Industrial discipline was as important as military discipline; factories, contractors, and agents had to be held to rigid performance. And nobody knew the indispensable facts! Figures of industrial capacity, lists of companies, data on car supply, information on the ability of heads of firms—all this was beyond the reach of the tiny Washington departments. Such terms as "coordination," "priorities," "allocation of materials," and "flow of supplies" lay far in the future; the idea of "production management" was beyond human

3 Leonard D. White, *The Jacksonians*, 548.

ken. The realities which such words represented could no more exist in America of 1861 than the roof of an unbuilt house could float in mid-air, for no supporting structure existed.

The government which was now girding itself for war labored under the sharpest limitations. It had always been a government of noninterference, made for the freedom of the individual; of calculated inaction, to give State and local agencies the fullest scope; of economy, passivity, and short views.

No national banking system existed. Washington paid no real attention to agriculture; a weakly supported, feebly administered bureau in the new Interior Department represented the only Federal provision for the fundamental industry of the land. So important a subject as public health had never engaged the attention of any national bureau, or for that matter, of any State. In Europe the English sanitarian Edwin Chadwick, the French pathologists, and the new school of medical statisticians had spurred the leading governments into at least elementary attention to public sanitation. But Americans were stone deaf to their one eminent figure in the field, Lemuel Shattuck, whose report on conditions in Massachusetts (1850) had met blank indifference.[4] So, too, the transportation revolution which was remolding America proceeded without any attention in Washington save for land-grant legislation and a few Far Western surveys. Any proposal that government guidance should accompany government subsidies would have met a hostile wall.

One significant index of the weakness of the central government was the deficiency of trustworthy statistical data. The national censuses were ample in numerical facts, decently accurate, and issued with really useful interpretation. A few cities and one State, Massachusetts, had systems of vital registration; New York took an efficient census of its own in 1855. As yet, however, the country was without the great mass of trustworthy data later to be gathered continuously by numerous Federal agencies.[5]

Statistics are a function of complexity in government as of society, for whenever new problems demand new solutions it becomes necessary to probe into exact conditions and measure precise results. For want of an apparatus of consistent fact-finding, Americans groped in the dark in meeting the crisis of 1861. When armies had to be raised, for example, it was important to know the ages of the male population. The census merely furnished facts on the population, male and female, in each five-year bracket to the age of twenty, and each ten-year bracket thereafter; all this set down by counties.

4 John Koren, *History of Statistics;* and see the article on statistical needs by ABC in *National Intelligencer,* May 29, 1856.
5 Such as the Bureau of Agricultural Economics, Interstate Commerce Commission, Bureau of Foreign and Domestic Commerce, Bureau of Labor Statistics, and Bureau of Internal Revenue, to name but a few.

Hence in the fifteen–nineteen age bracket, the government did not know how many were boys of fifteen, and how many young men of nineteen. In the succeeding age bracket, it did not know how many were twenty, and how many were twenty-nine. Yet by the date of the Civil War, all important European nations but Switzerland had permanent statistical bureaus under proficient management. The proposals for such a bureau in Washington, made by S. B. Ruggles and others, had met stubborn opposition from state-rights quarters.

In short, Lincoln presided over a weak government which suddenly had to be made strong. And behind the government lay a largely inchoate society; a society which believed in accomplishing the impossible, but whose libertarian bent made accomplishment terribly difficult. A tremendous gulf separated the unformed nation of the Civil War from the nation that in the next great conflict was to mobilize its energies so massively under the Council of National Defense. Where were the technicians in 1861? Where were the efficient business administrators? Where were the thousand organizations, industrial, commercial, financial, professional, to lend them support? Where were the principles and precedents?

If we briefly examine this society, we shall see that Great Britain in the first throes of the Napoleonic struggle had been better adapted to wage war than the shambling, uncertain American giant of 1861. "Organization" is a key word, and from one point of view the transformation of an unorganized land into an organized nation was the key process of the Civil War.

[I]

The country we have called invertebrate, and this invertebracy reflected a deeply ingrained spirit. "In the United States," wrote August Laugel during the conflict, "there is a horror of all trammels, systems, and uniformity." [6] Americans were hostile to discipline and jealous of every encroachment on personal freedom. As autumn leaves fell on drilling soldiers and thickening lines of factory hands, some observers saw that old ways were falling too. "The Great Rebellion a Great Revolution"—so ran the title of a *Herald* editorial on November 24, 1861. Our manufactories have been revolutionized, said the paper, our mode of living has been changed, and "everything the finger of war touches is revolutionized." A few discerning men saw the essence of this revolution. It was the conversion of a loose, inchoate, uncrystallized society into one organized for a mighty and many-sided effort.

6 Laugel, *The United States During the War*. The roots of individualism ran deep into frontier experience, and deep also into the Protestant emphasis on individual interpretation of truth and the individual will; deep too into Nonconformist tradition, Lockean and Jeffersonian ideas of the right of revolution, and egalitarian principles.

Crèvecœur in delineating the American had emphasized his love of independence and impatience of control. Cooper and Melville depicted a population of unfettered, self-assertive character. "Call me Ishmael!"—even that was better than repression. Emerson's chapter on "Solidarity" in *English Traits* contrasted British unity—"marching in phalanx, lock-step, foot after foot, file after file of heroes, ten thousand deep"—with American separatism. Thoreau, living on a patch of ground, experimenting with civil disobedience, and giving up his little pencil factory to preach an ideal society of noble villagers, and Cooper crying, "God protect the country that has nothing but commercial towns for capitals," [7] appealed in different ways to deep American instincts.

Most people instinctively veered away from strong social and economic combinations just as they veered away from strong government. John Taylor of Caroline, sharing Jefferson's idealism, inveighed against "monopoly and incorporation," and argued that capitalist combinations went arm-in-arm with a powerful centralized government, both fostering caste rule, the exploitation of farmers and laborers, and social injustice. Such doctrine, like the appeals of William Leggett and George Henry Evans to radical workmen, harmonized with the natural attitude of millions. Horace Greeley, anxious to better both the farmers and city wage earners, and striving to democratize the land system, was too wise to attack industry. Like a good Whig, he wished to see it grow. But he never lost his suspicion of the larger forms of business organization. In the midst of war the *Tribune* published long indictments of corporations: their profiteering, mismanagement, nepotism, and the tyrannies of their agents and officers. They were "heartless," wrote Greeley.[8]

Reared in an ungirt, unplanned society, Americans since the seventeenth century had been busy improvising. The first demand of the frontier, farm, and small shop was for such improvisations as the log cabin, the long rifle, the hand-hewn chest, the Conestoga wagon, and the overshot water wheel. The term "homemade" had a wider application in America than elsewhere. An ingenious people not only respected the amateur but belittled the expert. Peter Cooper building his engine *Tom Thumb*, Lincoln patenting his device for lifting boats over shoals, Goodyear spilling his rubber on a stove, Ezra Cornell wrecking his pipe-laying machine so that he could string his telegraph on poles, all believed that an amateur could do anything, and many concluded that organization would inhibit the gifted amateur. Generations later, Henry Ford reflected this attitude by shunning organizational charts, destroying business forms, and refusing to assign fixed duties to officers of the huge Rouge plant.

7 Cooper, *Correspondence*, II, 404.
8 See, for example, the long editorial April 3, 1863, entitled "Manufacturing Mismanagement."

Even in old Eastern cities, experts commanded little regard. Young James B. Angell, entering the office of the Chief Engineer of Boston in 1851, found that the staff had worked their way up from rodmen's jobs by rule-of-thumb methods. Work was under way on the Cochituate water system. It turned out that Angell was the only man in the whole office who had studied calculus and could deal with the involved formulae for water problems. This went to prove the force of Francis Wayland's argument that it was high time American colleges dealt less in theology, and more in science and technology.[9]

The nation was full of good craftsmen and husbandmen, able to work alone or in small groups. Company B of the Tenth Massachusetts, a Berkshire regiment, contained a typical array: 23 farmers, 3 merchants, 2 teamsters, 2 shoemakers, 2 hostlers, 2 carpenters, a seaman, laborer, clerk, bookkeeper, painter, peddler, blacksmith, calico printer, cloth manufacturer, and cheese-factory superintendent.[10] Such men, facing ordinary problems, could improvise with happy dexterity. But war presents innumerable large-scale problems, which demand experts supported by large-scale organizations. In time both the experts and the organizations were to appear—and with them would emerge a new nation.

As they appeared, the country lost a certain freshness and bucolic charm, and the strength which it gained was a coarser strength; but the gain was greater than the loss. The dynamism of national life, with population moving westward, new towns shooting up, and immigration combining with a high birth rate to stimulate growth, had kept life plastic and full of picturesque novelty. Successive frontiers had meant successive rerootings, seldom deep or strong. American life was to remain dynamic, but it would soon be dynamic in a different way, with larger elements of a disciplined, hardened kind. Its roots were to go deeper, and the plastic freshness was to be exchanged for well-planted power.

Much of the lack of organization was basically immaturity. The nation had no standard time, so that New York, Philadelphia, Washington, and Pittsburgh kept what time each city or its railroads liked. Only two American cities in 1860 had paid fire departments; all the others—New York until 1865, Philadelphia until 1870—depended on volunteers. All New England in 1860 had only three hospitals; the entire South had one in Charleston, one in Savannah, one in Mobile, "perhaps one" in Richmond, and one in New Orleans renowned for its wretchedness.[11]

Only an immature country would have endured the wretched postal facilities against which New York and Boston committees had protested in 1856. James Harper, Peter Cooper, and others that year pleaded for a uniform

9   Angell, *Reminiscences*, 78; Wayland, *Thoughts on the Present Collegiate System* (1842).
10 J. K. Newell, *The Tenth Mass. Volunteers.*
11 E. W. Martin, *The Standard of Living in 1860*, 233–236.

two-cent rate on letters, for in all large cities private carriers profitably distributed mail at that rate, and in New York about ten million letters were privately carried as against a million sent by post. The committees asked for compulsory prepayment by stamps, and free letter delivery in all large towns. In Europe dead letters were returned to senders; in the United States they were simply burned—four to five millions yearly. Though some reforms were adopted, the situation continued wretched. Although in 1860 the American population materially exceeded the British, the number of letters posted in the United States was only 184,000,000, one-third the 564,000,000 posted in Britain. The post office had three regular rates on letters, five surcharges, and forty-nine rates on papers and periodicals. Drop letters in New York numbered 1,500,000 in 1860; in London, 63,200,000.[12] "We are now enduring a postal system," remarked *Putnam's Magazine*, "which worries government, vexes and injures the public, demoralizes the officials, and pleases nobody." Bryant's *Evening Post* asserted that a barrel of flour could be sent by an express company from New York to New Orleans more quickly than the government could transport a letter over the same ground.[13]

The horror of all trammels, system, and uniformity, to use Laugel's phrase, prevented farmers from associating in production or marketing. Rural co-operation had taken firm root on the European continent immediately after the Napoleonic wars, and by 1860 was gaining maturity in Denmark, Germany, Switzerland, and other lands. New Zealand was soon to show how strong it could become in a pioneer community. The large size of American farms, mobility of the population, and individualistic temper of rural areas prevented any similar growth in the United States; nor did the government offer the slightest encouragement. Similarly, national labor unions as yet counted for almost nothing. In 1857 nine or ten such unions had been gaining vigorous stature when the panic felled all but three, the typographers', the hat finishers', and the journeymen stonecutters'. Before Sumter a few others, including the iron-molders' union under the indomitable William H. Sylvis, emerged. None had much vigor, for a half-dozen environing forces were unfavorable: the steady immigration of unskilled labor, lingering public hostility toward "conspiracy" in the labor market, the adolescent character of the factory system, the ruthlessness or paternalism of employers, and again the strong individualism of native Americans.[14]

12 Representative Hutchins of Ohio in 1862 vigorously attacked the postal abuses in Congress; see editorial, N. Y. *Tribune*, June 25, 1862.
13 Dec. 13, 1855; and still true in 1860. The government had issued its first stamps in 1847.
14 Commons, *et al.*, I, 335-453, gives the history of unions destroyed in the panic of 1857, and of the revival down to the war; see also George R. Taylor, *The Transportation Revolution*, 252 ff., 283 ff.

Thus neither agriculture nor labor when the war began was able to speak with united voice, furnish the government trained administrative talent, or lend any organized assistance to the war effort. Business and finance of course offered more resources, for they could not exist without some degree of organization. Nevertheless, it was a rudimentary degree, with short-comings more conspicuous than strength; as we shall see if we examine even the best-developed field, that of transportation.

[II]

Transportation could be expected to make comparatively rapid progress in systematization, for it was nurtured by the vast American distances, the irresistible westward movement, and the general American restlessness. The development of the West had seemed the nation's great primary task. The building of turnpikes, canals, and railroads to carry people across mountains, prairies, and plains, the shipment of crops eastward and a thousand varieties of commodities westward, and the necessity for extending the commercial and cultural interchanges of new and old states, had required careful planning and administration of communications.

The east-west railroads, particularly north of the Ohio, were in 1860 the country's most imposing business creations, their securities the very core of the investment market. National expansion had required an increasing con-solidation of railway controls. The Pennsylvania, for example, had attained a more extensive dominion than most people realized. Its main Philadelphia-Pittsburgh line, with branches and leased strips, covered 423 miles, of which 250 were double-tracked. This, however, was but the beginning. In 1856, three lines westward, in Ohio, Indiana, and northern Illinois, had merged as the Pittsburgh, Fort Wayne and Chicago. The Pennsylvania, which had in-vested substantial sums in building the three lines, received nearly $770,000 in stock. Thomas A. Scott, the Pennsylvania's vice-president and general super-intendent, was appointed to the board of the new company; George W. Cass, a director of the Pennsylvania, was made president. For all practical purposes the Pennsylvania thereafter controlled an additional 465 miles of railroad in the Middle West. Before 1860, the Pennsylvania had come to dominate about 165 miles of railroad reaching to the Ohio River and through southern Ohio, and about 200 miles running northwest from Pittsburgh to Cleveland. Thomas A. Scott again appeared on the boards of the tributary roads.[15]

The same process which gave the Pennsylvania an imperial system could

15 H. V. Poor, *History of the Railroads and Canals of the U. S.*, I, 470 ff.; H. W. Schotter, *Pennsylvania Railroad Company, 1846–1926*.

be traced in the development of the New York Central. At the outbreak of the war, this line from Albany to Buffalo, and the connecting Lake Shore and Michigan Southern, gave a group headed by Erastus Corning control over 650 miles of continuous rail into Chicago. The Erie, a hill-and-valley line from New York (Piermont) to Dunkirk on the lakes, was as yet still seeking a westward extension. But the Baltimore and Ohio, which ran to Parkersburg, made connections there to Cincinnati, and thence extended to St. Louis by a controlling arrangement with the Ohio and Mississippi, was very powerful indeed, and thirty-eight year-old John W. Garrett, its recently elected head, was a man of wide influence. Paralleling the early boundary between the Union and Confederacy, the B. & O. was to play an important role in the conflict. It was a source of great strength to the North by 1861 that three strong trunk lines, obviously soon to be joined by a fourth, connected the northern seaboard with the midwest.[16]

Other remarkable achievements in organization were the anthracite railroads, with their docks, freight yards, and coal trestles. Of the north-south lines the Illinois Central, as yet terminating at Cairo, and the Louisville & Nashville, a 185-mile road completed on the eve of conflict, had great importance. In the South the Memphis & Charleston, finished in 1857 on a line through Atlanta, cherished dreams of a grandeur it was never to attain.[17] Since every isolated community longed for the scream of a locomotive, ideas of growth animated the whole railroad world. Superintendent J. G. Kennedy of the Census, announcing that the railways of the nation had hauled 26,000,000 tons on their 30,800 miles of track in 1860, declared that three-quarters of this bulk had been created in the previous decade.

Yet from the standpoints of management and equipment, the railroads had a rudimentary aspect. The British expert S. F. Van Oss, writing much later, remarked on their adolescent traits. "Englishmen live in a country which has arrived at maturity; America still is in its teens." [18] Slow wood-burning locomotives ran all too often over rickety tracks on erratic schedules. The existence of at least eight different gauges required frequent loading and unloading. Most railway heads were less interested in methodical organization and progress than in slapdash policies and quick returns. Management tended to be autocratic, one man or a small clique controlling lines large or small. Speculation exulted in almost unchecked license. Few large roads had arrived at a scientific allocation of functions among their officers; the B. & O. was in fact conspicuous

16 Festus P. Summers, *The Baltimore and Ohio in the Civil War.*
17 A Confederate quartermaster officer testified that Southern railroad managers showed "the best business talent" in the South; O. R. IV, ii, 882.
18 Van Oss, *American Railroads as Investments*, 10.

for its well-planned departmentalization.[19] Still fewer lines had heads of pre-eminent ability. The two strongest executives were Garrett, trained in his father's commission house, and J. Edgar Thomson of the Pennsylvania, a proficient engineer who had studied railroad practice in Europe. The mere promoter was much more common.

The rule of small business salaries applied to railroads as to other establishments. In 1856 the Illinois Central cast about for a chief engineer. As its officers had seen George Brinton McClellan's report on his survey of a railway route across the Cascade Mountains, they selected him. His captain's pay had totaled $1,326 a year. President W. H. Osborn offered him $3,000 a year for three years. He showed marked administrative enterprise. Before long he was in general charge of railroad operation in Illinois, and by the end of 1857 was vice-president. He helped meet the depression that winter by harvesting Lake Michigan ice to be sold by the carload all the way to Cairo when summer became torrid. Early in 1858 he contracted with a group of steamboat owners to establish an Illinois Central line of packets to New Orleans, thus for the first time linking Chicago and the Gulf by scheduled year-round transportation. Yet his salary remained $3,000,—a proof of the low esteem for managerial talent.[20]

The fact was that the transportation revolution presented some remarkable feats in organization alongside glaring gaps and failures. No pageantry of the time excelled that of the western rivers. The mile-long line of boats smoking and throbbing at the St. Louis levee, surpassed by a still longer line at New Orleans; the floods of pork, tobacco, corn and cotton that the Ohio, the Cumberland, the Arkansas, and the Red poured into the central Mississippi stream; the motley passengers—fur traders, immigrants, Indians, soldiers, cotton planters, land speculators, gamblers, politicians, British tourists; the inter-city rivalries, the desperate races—these made the steamboat world a tremendous spectacle. The 1600 steamboats which plied the Mississippi before the war had cost perhaps $60,000,000; the 900 steamboats, barges, and flatboats which

19 As early as 1848 it had a master of transportation, a master of the road, a master of machinery, and a general superintendent, along with division superintendents; Hungerford, *The Baltimore & Ohio.* Centralized purchasing by large roads, even the B. & O., was unknown; each large department purchased for itself.

20 33rd Cong., 1st Sess., House Exec. Doc. 129; C. J. Corliss, *Main Line of America*, 90, 91. It need not be said that the broad foundation of all transport in the republic was the ox, mule, and horse, the cart and wagon. Between 1850 and 1860 the number of horses rose from 4,337,000 to 6,249,000, giving an average of one horse to each family of five. The number of asses and mules rose from 559,000 to 1,151,000, predominating in the South; a panegyric of the mule may be found in the census volume on Agriculture, p. cxiii. It is significant of the survival of primitive rural conditions that the number of working oxen rose from 1,701,000 to 2,255,000, the South having 858,500 and the Middle West 820,000. *Ibid.*, cviii–cxv.

plied the Ohio carried an annual Cincinnati-Louisville commerce valued at $35,000,000. This traffic on the great water highways, creating cities wealthier than Venice or Shanghai, represented no inconsiderable planning and organizing. Packet owners made various attempts at combination, but they were loose and abortive. During the war, the immense flotillas were to prove invaluable to the Northern armies. But the railroads already threatened them, the conflict strengthened the railroad lines, and before long the gaudy steamboat commerce was to prove as evanescent as the caravel.

In maritime commerce, meanwhile, defects of American planning and enterprise cost shipowners dear. The beautiful clipper ships, the transatlantic packets flying the Black Ball flag, and the coastal vessels had written proud pages in the American record. But on the Atlantic, the British-owned Cunarders showed better organization and safer management than their Yankee rivals operated by Edward Knight Collins, naval architect and shipping merchant. In twenty-six transoceanic passages in 1852 the Collins ships made much the faster time; but a strain of American recklessness appeared in the exclamation of Captain Asa Eldridge of the *Pacific*, "If I don't beat the *Persia*, I will send the *Pacific* to the bottom." Successive misfortunes, including the loss of the *Arctic* in 1854 with more than 300 dead, the foundering of the *Pacific*, and the withdrawal of the government subsidy, were too disastrous to be survived. Meanwhile, American shipbuilders clung tenaciously to wooden vessels propelled by sails or paddle-wheels, though British builders were turning to iron ships and screw propellers. Even the boasted *Vanderbilt* was a wooden ship with two walking-beam engines and two great paddle-wheels forty-two feet in diameter. The emigrant business began passing to British vessels. In the summer of 1857 the *National Intelligencer* carried a significant article, "Losing Our Carrying Trade." It pointed to reports that the better organized British yards were building 300 oceangoing steamboats: [21]

What are to become of sailing vessels when these 300 ocean steamers, or even one-half of them, shall be navigating the Atlantic Ocean? Already sailing vessels have to content themselves with the most bulky and least profitable freight; passengers, specie, light and costly goods, and so on being carried almost exclusively by steamers. The mode of travel and transportation upon the ocean is undergoing the same change that has already taken place on land; the old slow coach or vessel is being cast aside for the rapid rail-car and the storm-defying steamer. England, seeing this inevitable change, has, with the sagacity, prescience, and bold energy which characterize her, thrown her-

21 Louis C. Hunter's admirable *Steamboats on the Western Rivers*, 237–240, 308–357, covers organization and disorganization in the river steamboat business in careful detail. On Atlantic shipping see R. G. Albion, *The Rise of New York Port, 1815–60;* George W. Sheldon, "Old Shipping Merchants of New York," *Harper's Monthly*, vol. 84 (Feb., 1892), 457–471; *National Intelligencer*, July 25, 1857.

self forward in this revolution, and has covered, and is covering, the great highways of commerce with her steamers, and taking from all other nations, and especially from us, the most profitable portion of the carrying trade of the world.

New England might have been expected to organize large-scale transportation with special acumen. Instead, the section conspicuously failed in farsighted organization. The Boston & Worcester was completed in 1835, and the Western, from Worcester to the Hudson opposite Albany, in 1842. But down to the war the two railroads had not been united, though of course through trains were run over them. Moreover, Boston had no connecting railroad across upper New York to the lakes. The Boston-Albany line was fifty miles longer then the rival New York-Albany line, and had to traverse the rough Berkshires, while New York City offered a much better port and a far more magnetic shipping center. Hence, as C. F. Adams, Jr., pointed out, New York railroads, merely by intersecting any line that Boston tried to build across New York State, could draw down its traffic to the metropolis.

Meanwhile, in southern New England unification proved equally unattainable. The Hartford & New Haven was completed during Van Buren's Presidency, and the New York & New Haven was finished in Taylor's, but it was not until a decade after Sumter that they were consolidated. Thus the regime of small affairs continued dominant on the New England railroad scene even while J. M. Forbes was mobilizing Boston capital to help build the Michigan Central, the future Chicago, Burlington & Quincy, and the Hannibal & St. Joseph.[22]

Unevenness—ragged, sporadic action in a desert of individualism—was the keynote of the country's organizational activity. That handmaiden of transport, the telegraph system, was in its way astonishing. From a swarm of small companies a number of large concerns was presently born; and then by a program of consolidation carried out in the fall of 1857, the American Telegraph Company became dominant in the East, while the Western Union held a similar primacy in the West. The American, when Lincoln was elected, had nearly 300 offices and 13,500 miles of wire, controlling the business from Halifax to New Orleans. Over it and all the remaining companies the North American Telegraph Association held a loose control.

The country, which had long suffered from a jumble of little precarious companies, hoped for a reign of order. That might indeed have been the result but for the covert mutual enmity between the American and the Western Union. While the former wished to support Cyrus W. Field's Atlantic cable

22 C. E. Kirkland, *Men, Cities, and Transportation*, I, 127 ff., II, 72 ff.; Van Oss, *American Railroads*.

project, the latter was much more interested in a telegraph line to California. They were rivals in absorbing the surviving independents, and they quarreled violently over relations with the Associated Press, which the Western Union befriended and the American attacked as a dangerous news-gathering monopoly. The telegraph war which loomed up in 1860 showed that organization had gone far, but not far enough.[23]

That other handmaiden of transport, the express system, a uniquely American growth, had been somewhat more completely organized. So efficient were the various express companies that a Boston gentleman who wished to give a dinner party with Western buffalo hump, Ozark wild turkey, New Orleans shrimp, Minnesota wild rice, Georgia scuppernongs, and Shenandoah apples could command them all. The large sums the government used throughout the country were safely handled by express; all the long-distance financial exchanges of the country were conducted in the same way. Consolidation had been nearly as important in this industry as in the telegraph business. A union of two older companies had given birth in 1850 to the American Express, guided by Henry Wells and William G. Fargo, and this in turn soon organized Wells, Fargo to carry on the Western business, and the United States Express Company as an Eastern subsidiary. Various smaller concerns survived. In monetary terms the business was small; but the speed, economy, safety, and responsibility with which the agencies delivered letters, money, and parcels all over the continent made them invaluable to the country, and illustrated organizational enterprise at its best.[24]

The trunk-line railroads, steamboat interests, and telegraph and express companies were well enough organized to serve the Northern war effort effectively. But could as much be said of the equally important manufacturing industries?

[III]

Any reader of the massive report on manufactures in the census of 1860 is struck by the smallness of the units listed. Generally speaking, production rested on a multiplicity of petty establishments. The nation's pig iron came from 286 furnaces, with an average invested capital of about $14,000 each, and an average annual product much below that figure. Pennsylvania, the most

23 Robert L. Thompson, *Wiring a Continent*, 310–342.
24 Alvin S. Harlow, *Old Wayvills, passim.* Henry Wells published in the N. Y. *Tribune*, Feb. 20, 1864, a complete account of his and his companies' achievements. The earliest important line had been W. F. Harnden's Boston-New York package express; Wells had been the first to suggest and execute an express business to Buffalo, then Chicago, and ultimately the Far West. Total operating costs of the three corporations in 1864 were only about ten millions.

important iron State, had an industry of small furnaces widely scattered. In the Lehigh Valley gangs of smoke-grimed, hard-muscled men operated about twenty anthracite furnaces, in the Schuylkill Valley as many more, and in the Susquehanna Valley twenty-five. A westward drift had spawned iron-making centers in the Juniata, Johnstown, and Lewisburg districts, but they too were small; the four furnaces of the noted Cambria works could not average 10,000 tons apiece.

And the manufactories which took the iron? The firearms of the country came in 1860 from 239 establishments, with an average invested capital of less than $11,000. Connecticut, thanks to the Colt, Winchester, and other plants, was the main seat of fabrication, yet the 9 factories at work there employed fewer than 900 people in 1860, and the value of their product fell below $1,200,000. Smallness was equally characteristic of the sewing-machine industry, based upon American ingenuity and readily adapted to war work. Isaac M. Singer had founded his company only in 1851, and was still working hard to effect a pooling of patents and a union of enterprises. The census reported sewing machines made by 74 companies in a dozen States; and the 5 factories of Connecticut, which held the lead, divided an output of some 24,000 machines valued at just over a million.

Some industries of wide fame worked on a surprisingly modest scale. Though John A. Roebling was already well known for his wire-rope and suspension bridges, his Trenton factory had a capital of only $100,000, and its 70 hands made rope worth only $70,000 annually. And though Richard M. Hoe had revolutionized the printing of large newspapers by his rotary presses, the country had 14 press manufacturers, all small, with an aggregate yearly product of less than a million dollars.[25]

Surely, it would be said, the manufacturers who supplied agriculture and transportation had organized large enterprises; and it was true that important foundations had been laid. The largest manufacturer of locomotives, at Paterson, N. J., however, employed only 720 men in 1860 to build 90 engines. The largest car-wheel factory in the country, at Wilmington, Delaware, employed only 200 hands to cast 30,000 car wheels annually. One of the best-known industries in the land was the shovel factory of Oliver Ames & Sons in Massachusetts; running 26 tilt-hammers in 4 plants, it made 250 dozen spades and shovels a day, still rather a small-scale operation. Yet more famous was Cyrus H. McCormick's factory in Chicago, which produced 4,131 reapers and mowers in 1860. To meet varying regional needs, farm-implement manufacturing was widely distributed. In this field several corporations were achieving an impressive capital and a fairly complex organization. Nevertheless, the

25 Census of 1860, *Manufactures;* see the long introduction.

rule of smallness still had general validity. In the single county of which Canton, Ohio, was seat, the aggregate product of fifteen firms or individuals was worth more than twice as much as McCormick's whole output.[26]

New York City and its vicinity had a variety of machine shops which had sprung up principally to furnish iron forgings and castings, together with marine engines, to shipbuilders. They included the Fulton, the Allaire, the Neptune, the Morgan, the Delamater, and the Novelty iron works, with several more in Brooklyn. The works of the Stevens family in Hoboken and the Continental Iron Works at Greenpoint, Long Island, fell into the same category. Nearly all were destined to become important during the war. The Allaire establishment, successor to Robert Fulton's Jersey City shop, dated back to 1816, the Novelty Works to 1830, and the Morgan Works to 1838. At Cold Springs on the Hudson the West Point Foundry also had vigorous engineering facilities, and later planted branch machine shops in New York City. Other sturdy engine-building plants were found on Western waters, at Pittsburgh, Steubenville, Cincinnati, and Louisville. Undertakings of considerable size did not daunt the major shops. The Novelty Works had cast a sixty-ton bedplate for the engine of Collins's ship *Arctic,* the Corliss Engine Works at Providence turned out flywheels 25 feet in diameter, and a Philadelphia machine shop bored castings 18 feet long and 16 feet in diameter.

Yet these machine shops, however ambitious some of their undertakings, were small compared with British works and primitive in organization. They were obviously expansible, but when war demands came nobody knew how fast or effectively they could expand. Although they were becoming more specialized, they offered no products comparable with the finer parts of the reaper or sewing machine.[27]

Of all American manufactures, none had grown so strikingly during the previous half-century as textiles. The first complete textile factory, the Boston Manufacturing Company at Waltham, had been born of war in Madison's day. It had paved the way for the larger factories in the Merrimac Valley, and demand had grown so heavily that the country now had 1,091 cotton factories alone, more than half of them in New England. Massachusetts alone

26 The manufacture of labor-saving farm machinery, naturally one of the greatest branches of American endeavor, had given some men and firms nation-wide renown. S. M. Osborne & Co. in Auburn, N. Y., Adrian Platt & Co. in Poughkeepsie, R. L. Howard in Buffalo, and C. Aultman & Co. in Canton had a general fame. H. & C. Studebaker had begun their wagon business at South Bend in 1852. Already in 1860 a machine bound grain by wire. The census report stated that four-horse harvesters with two men to bind and two to shock could harvest twenty acres of grain a day; "we shall soon have machines that will cut, gather, and bind up the grain in one operation." *Manufactures,* cciv et seq.

27 For the machine shops see N. Y. *Tribune,* Feb. 7, 1863, an informative article; Clark, *History of Manufactures,* 107 ff.; Bishop, *History of American Manufactures,* III, 112.

counted 217 cotton factories; New England employed nearly three-fourths of the capital and made two-thirds of the product in the cotton industry. Some mills, like those of the Sprague family in Rhode Island, were imposing. It was in woolens, however, that the highest degree of concentration had been effected. Worsted manufacture was conducted mainly by three establishments, the Pacific Mills at Lawrence, Massachusetts, the Manchester Print Works at Manchester, New Hampshire, and the Hamilton Woolen Company works at Southbridge, Massachusetts. These three organizations loomed up as giants on the flat American scene with their total of 3,400 hands. The largest, the Manchester mill owned by the Merrimac Mills Corporation, which also made cotton prints in large quantities, was one of the few industrial wonders of the land. At Lawrence a fourth enterprise, the Bay State Mills, had become the world's leading makers of cashmeres, shawls, and other fine woolens. The census commented on the completeness and order of the large New England woolen factories.

A nation needing mountains of uniforms could take encouragement from the vigor of the ready-made clothing industry. It had grown up with democratic mass demand, cheap cloth, and the sewing machine until 3,800 firms with a capital of nearly $25,000,000 were engaged in it. A silent revolution was merging many small shops into large wholesale establishments. The average product was largest in the Middle Atlantic and Yankee shops, approaching $25,000 a year. East of the Alleghenies female hands were giving way to men. The principal cutters and salesmen in the bigger shops were often former merchant tailors, glad to invest their capital and influence in the large units. Thus, "with all the advantages of large capital and machinery," remarked the census, they could "supply every town and village with ready-made clothing at the lowest prices." [28]

Though in a hundred areas industry was forming larger units, even the biggest were still usually ill organized and amateurishly administered. One-man supervision predominated, and managerial problems were solved by trial and error. The McCormick factory was managed by Leander McCormick, Cyrus's brother, and four foremen. The Cooper & Hewitt iron works at Trenton were directed by Abram S. Hewitt, with advice from Peter Cooper and assistance from Edward Cooper. Erastus B. Bigelow, founder of a thriving carpet business, a determined enemy of corporate as distinguished from individual management in manufactures, published in 1858 a testy pamphlet on

---

28 Census, *Manufactures*, xxxii, lx, etc. The making of boots and shoes had grown into a large industry in Massachusetts, which by the State census of 1855 turned out nearly 12,-000,000 pairs of boots and some 17,000,000 pairs of shoes. The whole number of shops in the country making boots and shoes in 1860 was 2,439. But as yet the industry was poised between the domestic and factory systems.

the subject.[29] Businesses should not be controlled from commercial and financial centers, he argued, but on the spot; for unity of purpose, one head was worth far more than the divided responsibilities of a large corporate organization. Isaac Singer, Samuel Colt, and Oakes Ames would have agreed. So long as the controlling brain was as keen as McCormick's, Hewitt's, or Bigelow's, it might well be superior to group management. Some industries were specially adapted to one-man control, and some business geniuses had to rule alone.

The most typical American manufactory in 1860 was the property of a man or family who had founded it, ownership passing from father to sons. This was true even of the older houses. The varied enterprises of Phelps, Dodge & Company, for example, were carried on by a close-knit group, members of the Dodge, Phelps, Stokes, and James families. Five men in 1860, of whom "the Christian merchant" William E. Dodge was the best-known, held total ownership and direction. From their Cliff Street offices in New York they managed the largest metals business in the country, a New Jersey bank, railroad interests, wide tracts of timber, iron, and coal lands about Scranton, and other undertakings with quiet efficiency.[30] But incompetents could wreck a business as easily as talented creators could make it. No New England textile mill was more noted than that of the Middlesex Company in Lowell, but its heads lost the entire capital by appalling "mistakes and irregularities." [31] And the trend of the times was toward multiple ownership and management.

As concentration gave birth to larger units, control by individuals and families declined. To reduce costs by standardization of product and improvement of methods; to stimulate or seize upon changes in market demand; to hold orders by prompt delivery of excellent goods—this, no less than growth in size and capital, required a more elaborate managerial organization. Larger buildings, larger stocks of materials, larger working forces, and more complex machinery meant expert planning and supervision. This fact was being illustrated by the shoe industry on the eve of the war. Amid a multitude of domestic producers and tiny cobbler shops, factories of real size had emerged primarily because customers had to be sought, materials purchased cheaply, labor supervised vigilantly, and innovations rapidly adopted. By 1860 steam power was being introduced into the larger manufactories, making the hand power of small shops seem pitifully slow.[32] Lyman Blake's machine for stitching uppers to soles had been invented, and would at once accelerate the tendency toward big and complex shops, with more and more elaborate staffs.

29 Entitled "Depressed Condition of Manufactures in Massachusetts."
30 R. G. Cleland, *Phelps-Dodge 1834–1950*, Ch. III. The Connecticut shops of the Ansonia Brass and Copper Company made a wide variety of products.
31 Crowley, *History of Lowell.*
32 Blanche E. Hazard, *Origin of the Boot and Shoe Industry in Mass.*, 123 ff.

This change in corporate administration, however, was in 1860 still slow and gradual. After all, in most areas the shift from small to large units had to wait on the progress of railroad facilities, and the consequent rise of regional or national markets. State impediments to large-scale organization were formidable. Without notable exception, State laws forbade corporations to hold property in other States, or stock in other companies, except under special charter. It was with great difficulty that legislators grasped the fact that it might serve the general good to encourage companies to undertake broad interstate activities. General incorporation laws were themselves recent, the Connecticut statute of 1837 being the first of broad character. Chief Justice Lemuel Shaw of Massachusetts did an important work 1830–60 in adapting the law of partnerships to corporations, and sheer economic necessity widened the influence of his decisions.

Until after the war, however, joint stock corporations were restricted mainly to railroads, banks, and insurance companies; State and railroad securities remained the staple of the stock exchanges. Manufacturing was not to adopt the corporate form on a broad scale until after Appomattox, and not to own interstate properties until still later. One reason for the formation of the Standard Oil trust as late as 1881 was that State laws blocked such interstate ownership.[33]

[IV]

Of the great range of organized activity among the churches, the educational bodies, the professional groups, the publishers, the writers, the social service societies, and lesser participants in voluntarism, how much was likely to aid a government at war? How much of this activity encouraged the principle of cooperative effort? Very little.

All the powerful church organizations, with two exceptions, had split in two on the sectional issue. The Catholics, an ecumenical body under foreign governance, remained ostensibly united. So, formally, did the Episcopalians, for even after communicants in the Confederacy established a separate church, the General Convention called the roll of the Southern dioceses. The other denominations rallied with fervor to the conflict. Quoting "The Lord thy God is a God of war," Southern Presbyterians, Baptists, and Methodists, as sects, as earnestly aligned themselves with their chosen cause as Northerners of the same churches supported the Union. Probably most Americans gained their

33 F. H. Chase, *Lemuel Shaw;* Arthur H. Dean, *William Nelson Cromwell,* 18. New York by an act of 1811 had permitted incorporation by general law rather than by special enactment, but the authority had strict limits.

first lessons in organization and cooperation from their church bodies. These great agencies enrolled millions who knew no society, club, or company, they enlisted men in active continuous work to an extent never equalled even by the political parties, and they touched life at more points than any other body. For women they furnished the one great means of organized expression.

But although the churches were in fact multifariously useful for the war, they were dismayingly limited in their usefulness. North and South, they undertook a great variety of labors. They supplied chaplains for the armies; they distributed Bibles, devotional books, and tracts; they supported revivals in camp; they helped meet problems of poverty and home relief behind the lines. Northern church leaders formed societies to assist the freedmen, inspired the Christian Commission, sent leaders (rather unsuccessfully) to occupy pulpits in conquered areas, and furnished spokesmen to plead the Northern cause abroad. Yet the central purpose of the churches debarred them from intensely practical activity. Their primary concern was with the other world, not with this. After an immemorial concentration upon extramundane activities one day out of seven, they could not give full weekly labor to mundane concerns.

Nor had the concept of social Christianity, as preached in England by Kingsley and Maurice, in France by Lamennais and Buchez, yet reached America. In 1857 the Y. M. C. A. in New York had been torn apart by a secession of nearly 200 members, including prominent clergymen, who asserted that political and social topics, including slavery, were too much discussed, and that the society had wandered from its original objects.[34] This small but significant event emphasized the doctrine that the central business of the church was to save souls and quicken the spiritual life of the people. Any wide departure from that path—beyond, say, raising the $2,500,000 collected by the Christian Commission—would have aroused condemnation.

As for education, it had a far more uneven and precarious organization than religion. When Henry Barnard established his *American Journal of Education* at Hartford in 1855, the principle of a unified system of public schools under State control was fairly well rooted in the North. To implant it had required a long battle against penny-pinching enemies of public expenditures, religious bodies which wished to fractionize the educational system, and fossil obstructionists of "book learning." Associations of teachers and friends of education, fighting this battle, had founded numerous societies all over the East and Middle West.

Yet the results were so uneven and new that no powerful educational bodies useful for war work yet existed. New York and Illinois had not gained separate State superintendents on a permanent basis until 1854, and Pennsyl-

34 *National Intelligencer*, April 30, 1857.

vania until 1857. In 1861 a belt of States reaching from Maine and New Jersey to the far borders of Kansas had permanent State school officers, but only nine, including California and Alabama, possessed regularly organized combinations of State and county administrators.[35] Teachers' organizations had narrow scope and slight vigor. The one important national agency, the American Association for the Advancement of Education, was ten years old; but however commendable, it was unable to rally the nation's teachers in united effort.

Significantly, no educator made an effort to form classes in army camps, convalescent hospitals, or prison camps. The Northern volunteer regiments were full of youths torn from academy or college, of semi-illiterates, and of half-Americanized aliens, apt material for teaching. But no body capable of implementing an educational plan, had one been broached, existed.

The medical profession, like the ministers and teachers, had the aid of schools, journals, and societies in fostering its special aims. But standards of training were so low, quacks and charlatans were so abundant, and public interest in medical advancement was so slight, that the profession lacked organized power.[36] In Great Britain and Europe, S. Weir Mitchell later wrote, medicine by 1861 held places of trust in the government, but in America it was neglected. "Our great struggle found it, as a calling, with little of the national regard. It found it more or less humble, with reason enough to be so." [37] General medical societies had a history running back into colonial days, and before 1861 State-wide societies overspread the whole map east of the Mississippi, save in Louisiana, which left the field to a New Orleans association.

Most early medical societies, however, both State and local, were primarily social organizations of scant authority or prestige. For a time some State governments clothed specified societies with power to license physicians, regulate fees, and punish malpractice. Such authority was in general ill exercised, and the State tended to turn instead to special medical boards. Several close-knit, well-led urban societies gained more repute and influence than the loose State associations. In Philadelphia the College of Physicians, dating from 1789, in Boston the Society for Medical Improvement, from 1838, and in New York the Academy of Medicine, from 1846, all had a distinguished membership, listened to papers of merit, and commanded public respect. Societies in Cincinnati, St. Louis, and one or two Southern cities had dignity. The membership, however, was always smaller than it should have been. Their interest in medical education did not lead in the best direction, and when much later university medical schools of adequate standards came into existence, it

35 Cubberley, *Public Education in the U. S.*, 122 ff., 246 ff.; Cubberley and Elliott, *State and County School Administration Source Book*, 283 ff.
36 H. B. Shafer, *The American Medical Profession, 1783–1850*, pp. 169–173.
37 *In War Time*, Ch. IV.

was from other impulses and indeed against the opposition of some leading medical organizations.[38]

On the initiative of New York physicians, the American Medical Association was founded in 1846. Its committee on education did effective work to improve medical training within the old pattern, urging lengthened terms of study, the use of hospitals for clinical teaching, higher admission requirements, and stricter examinations. It labored also to improve. American drugs, inculcate higher ethical principles, and stimulate original research and writing. Holding annual conventions in different cities, it enlisted adherents in each, until by 1856 it had more than 3,000 members.[39]

But on the whole, medical organization when the war broke was in its groping initial stages. Most societies were social or amateurish, and not one had produced a great administrator or initiator. They held banquets, combated quacks, and passed resolutions, but they did much more to promote *esprit de corps* than to increase medical knowledge or influence public opinion. Hampered by financial difficulties, languid interest, factional squabbles, and lack of professional dignity, many of them kept up but an intermittently active existence. The American Medical Association was as yet so narrowly professional, deficient in broad social interests, and fluctuating in strength, that it was of slender general value. Medical education would have to be revitalized before medical associations could grow powerful.[40] No society was able to give the government important aid during the conflict. The chief wartime organizers of medicine, surgery, and nursing were to be a clergyman, a landscape architect, a frontier army doctor, an attorney, and a woman clerk in the Patent Office.[41]

Of all the great professions, that most glaringly deficient in organization was the bar. When the nation sprang to arms, no legal society worth mentioning existed North or South. Although Philadelphia laid claim to a city association founded in 1802, it was nothing more than a lawyers' social club. Even New York City had no bar association until Samuel J. Tilden, under stress of a dire civic emergency in Tweed days, led the way in founding one, and the American Bar Association did not arise till some years later. The earliest State association seems to have been one which led a precarious life in Iowa for some years after 1874. Lawyers with an instinct for leadership or a cause to

38 W. F. Norwood, *Early History of American Medical Societies*, CIBA Symposia, 1947, No. 9.
39 Shafer, 232 ff.; John Shaw Billings, "Literature and Institutions," in E. H. Clarke, *et al.*
40 F. R. Packard, *History of Medicine in the U. S.*; W. D. Postell, *The American Medical Association*, CIBA Symposia, 1947, No. 9; F. C. Stewart, *On the Medical Schools and the Conditions of the Medical Profession in the USA* (1856), 116.
41 Bellows, Olmsted, Hammond, George T. Strong, and Clara Barton; but mention might also be made of three physicians, Drs. Tripler, Van Buren, and Agnew, and a scientist, Wolcott Gibbs.

promote turned naturally to political parties. For improvements in the efficiency and ethics of the bar they looked to legislatures, the State attorneys-general, and the courts.[42] If any officer of the national government wished legal advice—in making appointments to the bench, in drafting legislation, in searching for precedents, in dealing with questions of constitutionality—he could apply to individuals; but help from associations he could not get.

One of the greatest indirect contributions to the war strength of the nation was made by the press, both daily and periodical. It kept the people informed, it more than any other agency molded public sentiment, and despite shrill dissident voices and conflicting policies, it crystallized a spirit of national unity. Daily journalism was competitive in the extreme. In New York City the coarse, fickle *Herald*, the enterprising, solidly informative, and socially radical *Tribune*, the eloquent and cultivated *Evening Post*, and the moderate, judicious *Times* contended for leadership. While their daily circulation was almost wholly metropolitan, by weekly and semi-weekly editions they reached the entire North. Every city had its daily, almost every county seat its weekly.

The country was full of newspapers, read more voraciously, perhaps, than in any other land. New York State had more dailies than all Great Britain. A current story told of a minister who preached hell-fire without effect; but his announcement that the godless went to a land without newspapers made his congregation turn pale and profess conversion.[43]

While outwardly newspapers seemed to illustrate the essence of individualism, actually they possessed a remarkable solidarity. The practice of exchanging subscriptions was universal. A country editor might get twenty or fifty exchanges from all parts of America; he produced a better journal by swift use of the scissors than by laborious employment of the pen, with the result that the content of many newspapers was much the same. The government subsidized this system of exchanges by special postal concessions. A remarkably telling editorial by Greeley, Bryant, or Raymond, by Samuel Bowles or John W. Forney, was certain in the end to appear in many journals. A striking piece of special correspondence in the Chicago *Tribune* or Springfield *Republican* would be widely clipped. The Associated Press, originally a combination of New York dailies to collect news, had by 1860 taken almost complete control of news-gathering in the United States and Canada. Though bitterly assailed as a ruthless monopoly after it defeated the effort of the telegraph companies to establish separate news services, it did its work efficiently and cheaply.[44]

42 Charles Warren, *History of the American Bar;* M. Louise Rutherford, *Influence of the American Bar Assn.*

43 D. Macrae, *The Americans at Home,* Ch. 31.

44 Victor Rosewater, *History of Cooperative News-gathering in the U. S.;* Oliver Gramling, *The A. P.*

Indeed, the diffusion of intelligence was one of the best-organized branches of national endeavor. The New York *Tribune* or *Herald* published every night 55,000 copies, with each department—European correspondence, Washington, Albany, and metropolitan news, editorials, Wall Street article, agricultural column, produce and shipping news, letters to the editor—copiously filled; it dealt systematically with advertisements, legal printing, and birth, marriage, and death notices; it provided for paper supply, street sales, local deliveries, and subscriptions—all through carefully coordinated activity. This was possible because each journal had a body of trained employees, an eye to system, and an instinct for the latest inventions. Stereotyping, for example, developed by Charles Craske of New York, came into use just in time for the large war editions. The *Tribune* boasted that in the spring of 1862 its weekly edition circulated more than 150,000 copies, and its semi-weekly 18,000; its consolidated circulation of more than 220,000 copies was, it declared, much the largest in the world.[45] Altogether, it reached fully one-twentieth of the whole newspaper-reading public of the North. Such a feat was impossible without careful organization.[46]

The publication of books and magazines was likewise a vigorous department of American life, for mass education meant mass reading. The Scottish publisher William Chambers, looking primarily at New England, wrote that every American bought and read books—a gross exaggeration; Anthony Trollope declared that Americans were the greatest consumers of literature on earth, taking 10,000 copies of a book where Englishmen took one.[47] Although the invention of electrotyping ten years before the war had reduced costs, during the 1850's the annual dollar value of books trebled. Harper Brothers just before the panic of 1857 turned out 3,000,000 volumes in a single year. To be sure, the purchase of books hardly averaged a dollar a year for adults, but the market well repaid the largest firms. The houses of Appleton, Lippincott, Harper, Ticknor & Fields, Putnam's, and Scribner's flourished while they honorably allied their names with the best literature. *Harper's Monthly Magazine* before the war attained a circulation of more than 100,000; farm journals, religious journals, and women's magazines like *Godey's Lady's Book* were widely read; Robert Bonner's New York *Ledger* was reputed to sell 400,000 copies a week; and the two important illustrated journals, *Harper's Weekly* and *Frank Leslie's*, overcoming their initial crudities, were reaching and instructing great bodies of readers.[48]

45 N. Y. *Tribune*, April 10, 1862.
46 The census reported that in 1860 the nation had 383 daily newspapers, and more than 3250 weekly or semi-weekly newspapers. The totals were steadily growing.
47 Chambers, 219; Trollope, *North America* (1862), I, 271.
48 Martin, *Standard of Living in 1860*, 324, 325.

The largest book-and-magazine houses, like Harper's and Ticknor & Fields, were organized on a sturdy scale. But book-publishing in general was as much decentralized as most manufacturing, for prosperous firms were found all the way from Albany and Richmond to St. Louis and Nashville. Equally noteworthy was the wide diffusion of bookshops; just before the panic at least three thousand shops dealt exclusively in books and periodicals, while nearly seven thousand more sold them in connection with other wares. The book trade was not efficiently managed or systematized, for it perhaps never can be. The American Publishers' Association had recently been founded to bring publishers and booksellers into better relations, and its weekly organ, the *Publishers' Circular*, carried full information on the trade. But as of newspapers, it could be said that the seemingly chaotic book business had more internal solidarity and coordination than men supposed. It was well arranged to stimulate literature, and to keep the nation fairly informed upon events and forces.

While in a narrow view the manysided publishing activities of the North were of limited value to the war effort, in any broad view they were of priceless utility. The press kept the country informed of every phase of government activity, offered a free forum of discussion which was indispensable to the healthy workings of democracy, and through its best journals gave the nation encouragement and inspiration. "We cannot too often repeat that the first duty of the citizen at this juncture is to give the President a generous, confiding, and cordial support," said *Harper's Weekly* just after Bull Run,[49] and most publishers took a similar view in dark hours. One influential pamphlet on the nation's resources, scattered broadcast late in the conflict, was worth a small army.[50] It was unfortunate that in some other areas the national energies were not equally well organized.

[V]

The lack of associative elements, the plastic state of society, and the prevalent individualism, had their compensation. They fostered self-reliance, enterprise, and ingenuity. Blessed with great natural wealth, and aided by capital accumulations, energetic Americans wrought great achievements. "The period following California gold," writes one historian of technology, "developed an apex of individualism perhaps never before and certainly never since attained in the world's history." [51] The ingenuity was as striking as the energy.

49 August 3, 1861 (V, 482).
50 "Our Burden and our Strength," by David A. Wells (1864).
51 Roger Burlingame, *March of the Iron Men*, 312, 313.

Repeatedly a lonely experimenter who knew little of the general state of the arts would devise some memorable improvement. John Deere thus produced his self-scouring plough, Robert L. Stevens his T-rail, Linus Yale, Jr., his famous pin-tumbler cylinder hook, and Crawford W. Long, in an isolated Georgia village, his anaesthetic. Elias Howe thus solved the problem of devising a needle which, working from the top plane only of a piece of cloth, would stitch both its top and bottom.

Herman Haupt, a young Pennsylvania West Pointer, who went into railway construction, was suddenly faced twenty years before the war with the necessity of finding the laws by which the transmission of strains in a trussed bridge was governed. He sat down in a country town in Pennsylvania without books of reference or scientific apparatus, and by experiments on the resistance of timbers, and his own methods of obtaining mathematical formulae, met the exigent requirements of the York & Wrightsville Railroad. He did more; he arrived at some valuable new principles of bridge building. Just before the war, helping direct the boring of the Hoosac Tunnel, and confronted with the task of piercing strange rock strata, he devised drilling machinery comparable with that used in piercing Mont Cenis. In short, without supporting organizations, he repeatedly displayed a triumphant inventiveness. Brought into the army in 1862, Haupt showed his ingenuity in building bridges of novel materials (beanpoles and cornstalks, said Lincoln), making implements for twisting and straightening rails, devising torpedoes, and so on; while his skill in helping several generals move troops and meet fast-changing strategic situations was equally notable.[52]

But were these empiric methods good enough? A significant contrast might be drawn between Charles Goodyear in America and Charles Mackintosh in Scotland. While the Connecticut experimenter, without scientific training or advice, hit on the vulcanization of rubber by stubborn plodding and luck, the systematic Glasgow manufacturer arrived at great results by well-considered steps. He obtained the guidance of the brilliant chemist-surgeon James Syme of Edinburgh, dissolved raw rubber in coal-tar naphtha, and applied the solution as a varnish to cloth. While Goodyear sank into debt, Mackintosh became rich. It was only when well-organized groups placed themselves behind Goodyear's discovery that American rubber products far outstripped the British goods. There could be no question in 1860 that the inexorable process of business consolidation, the steady growth of industrial undertakings in size, and the new scientific knowledge, demanded group activity in place of individual enterprise; but individualism still reigned supreme.

52 See Haupt's pamphlet, "Hints of Bridge Construction," 1841; Frank A. Flower's useful preface to Haupt's *Reminiscences*.

Very different was the situation in England. John Stuart Mill, commenting on the intellectual progress of the working classes, remarked that their advance in the habit of cooperation was equally surprising. "At what period were the operations of productive industry carried on upon anything like their present scale? Were so many hands ever before employed at the same time, upon the same work, as now in all the principal departments of manufactures and commerce? To how enormous an extent is business carried on by joint stock companies. . . . The country is covered by associations." [53]

America was now ready to take wide and rapid strides on the same road. The transportation revolution was creating national markets; they in turn would help create the industrial revolution, with large national agencies of manufacture. Business giants governing huge combinations would soon arise. But as matters stood in 1861, Lincoln never thought of summoning a group of business leaders to assist him in wartime administration; the businessmen had no faculty of cooperation. Except for the Sanitary Commission, the government made practically no use of professional groups in war work; it picked men here and there, but in haphazard fashion. In short, it used little organized machinery, for the machines had never been created. Lincoln might well have found valuable assistance, for example, in a board of transportation. But how was such a board possible in a country where the first through train of freight cars did not pass from the State of New York into the State of Ohio until January 11, 1863? [54]

53 Mill, *Dissertations and Discussions,* I, 196, 197 (Boston, 1864).
54 Edwin A. Pratt, *The Rise of Rail Power in War and Conquest,* 22, 23.

8.

In 1862 and 1863 the American Civil War gradually became a revolution. "The ice-sheet of the War" seemed to congeal most of the normal activities of men and there was no sign of a break or thaw, but "underneath it the currents of change ran with accelerated force. War partly retards, partly stimulates, the factors of growth in a nation. In the South, with its scanty population and weak economy, the record was of retardation. In the North observers were struck by the ability of twenty-odd millions of energetic people to make use, while lustily fighting, of the new opportunities created by war contracts, tariffs, the great release of capital and westward expansion. . . . Improvisation of troops, naval forces, munitions, quartermasters' services, chains of command, and modes of attack necessarily gave way to plan and system, the old individualism yielded in a hundred ways to disciplined association. . . . In short, pressures of war were compelling the amorphous nation of 1860 to acquire form and structure. . . . A modern America was being born." [1]

Much was to happen, however, before this change came about. Lincoln had difficulty getting his generals, McClellan, Buell, and Halleck, to advance early in 1862. But once begun, the invasion of the Confederacy went on apace. Early in the year there were Federal victories in Kentucky, and the defensive wall of the South was pierced when Federal gunboats captured Fort Henry on the Tennessee and when Ulysses S. Grant, new to fame, captured Fort Donelson on the Cumberland. "The results of these river conquests were far-reaching." [2]

By spring Grant's army was deep in Tennessee. Among the blossoming trees, Albert Sidney Johnston's Confederate army attacked at Shiloh or Pittsburg Landing, April 6–7. Sorely pressed, Grant held his ground. Johnston was killed and Beauregard had to pull back to Corinth, Mississippi. Grant was still learning his trade, so that "the lack of bold Union generalship made the battle far less decisive than it might have been." [3]

Elsewhere in the West the river boats, operating in conjunction with the armies, were inroading the South, including the Federal capture of Memphis on the Mississippi. On the Gulf Coast Admiral David Glasgow Farragut's fleet ran past the defending forts at the mouth of the Mississippi to capture the South's largest city, New Orleans, in late April. Along the coast, Federals achieved victories at Fort Pulaski near Savannah, Georgia, at New Bern and Fort Macon, North Carolina. In March they were also successful at Pea Ridge in Arkansas. With the triumphs in the West, the war seemed at its climax. But the chance of overrunning the whole Western theater slipped away because, as Nevins puts it, the top commanders were unable to perceive the opportunity. Those who looked to the future with confidence "little realized how swiftly incompetent generalship and ill fortune could change the scene." [4]

Meanwhile that spring, Lincoln, Stanton, and McClellan were laying their plans. It was finally decided that McClellan's Army of the Potomac would be moved by sea from northern Virginia down to the Peninsula east of Richmond. Before that campaign could get underway, a revolution in naval warfare occurred. The C.S.S. *Virginia*, an ironclad better known as the *Merrimack*, sank two Federal vessels of the traditional type on March 8. The following day the *Merrimack* was challenged by an entirely new vessel, the largely iron ship *Monitor*. While the Hampton Roads fight on March 9 can be said to have been a draw, the *Merrimack* did go back to harbor, never again to emerge.

A condensed narrative such as this precludes giving details of the hard and bloody fighting of the summer of 1862. McClellan, now commanding just his own army, laboriously moved up the Peninsula toward Richmond. He was challenged but not halted by Joseph E. Johnston at Seven Pines or Fair Oaks May 31–June 1. In the Shenandoah Valley Stonewall Jackson carried out his amazing campaign, with which his name would be forever linked, diverting Union attention from McClellan in front of Richmond.

For the South, a new commander, Robert E. Lee, took over what was now known as the Army of Northern Virginia. Of Lee, Nevins writes, "War was in fact a passion with him. . . ." Yet he was "a merciful man" who was "sensitively aware of the suffering which war imposes." But his "energetic nature" rendered conflict a "congenial element," and he drew "special pleasure from swift movement and battles against odds." [5] Joined by Jackson, Lee attacked McClellan's huge force in the Seven Days' Battles, June 25–July 1, pushing McClellan back from Richmond and forcing his retreat to the James River. Richmond had been saved. Great argument raged then, and has raged ever since, over McClellan's failure and who was to blame. For the North "stretched the prospect of a prolonged war." [6] It was now feared that Lee would turn north toward Washington, and he did. He faced a new Federal army, that of John Pope, supposedly to be aided by McClellan's troops. With Jackson in the fore, Lee struck Pope near the battlefield of First Manassas or Bull Run in late August. And like the first clash, it was again a Confederate triumph.

Pope was severely beaten and McClellan took over all the troops in the main Virginia theater. The Federals in the East found themselves on the defensive.

While this immense amount of major fighting was going on, along with hundreds of lesser struggles, Lincoln was wrestling with the political strife. With the Federal advance in the West slowed down, he was experiencing some of the most anxious days of his life.[7] The rising voice of Radicals called for harder fought war and action on emancipation, while the rising voice of war opponents called for armistice and settlement. It is clear that the slavery issue had never been far from the President's mind. He had been trying to push for colonization of freed Negroes, but to no avail, and he had been even more anxious to set up a system of compensated emancipation for freed slaves in Union territory. Apparently ever since mid-July 1862, Lincoln had stood by a decision to issue a proclamation of emancipation which "had become essential as a political measure, to keep the Republican party behind him; a war measure to cripple the South; a foreign policy measure, to align the humanitarian sentiment of the world, and especially Great Britain, with the North; and a measure to lift national morale." [8]

And then, on July 22, shortly after the Federal setback in Virginia, in what Nevins calls the most historic of cabinet meetings, the President announced to the cabinet the draft of an emancipation proclamation. Considerable consternation and discussion followed, with Secretary of State Seward suggesting that this was a poor time for such an announcement, considering numerous reverses on the field of battle. Seeing the wisdom of this view, Lincoln laid the paper aside for an hour of victory. "The general public guessed nothing. But the great decision had been taken; the most revolutionary stroke, in a war which had now become revolution in the broadest sense, hung poised for delivery." [9]

NOTES

1. Nevins, *The War for the Union,* Vol. II, *War Becomes Revolution, 1862–1863,* pp. vii–viii.
2. *Ibid.,* p. 25.
3. *Ibid.,* p. 85.
4. *Ibid.,* p. 108.
5. *Ibid.,* p. 132.
6. *Ibid.,* p. 138.
7. *Ibid.,* p. 139.
8. *Ibid.,* p. 163.
9. *Ibid.,* p. 166.

Antietam and Emancipation

IN THE dark hours before dawn on September 4, Lee's veterans began splashing through the shallow fords of the Potomac midway between Harpers Ferry and Washington. He had chosen a point near the capital so that his invasion of Maryland might menace both Baltimore and Washington, and draw the Union army after him until he could fight it somewhere distant from its base. Thousands of his troops were barefoot, and nearly all tattered, darkly sunburnt, lean, and hungry-looking. Though a Union battery banged away with some effect near Edwards's Ferry, elsewhere they swarmed across with little opposition. D. H. Hill's fresh division had reinforced Lee, giving him in theory nearly 70,000 men, but he took only about 60,000 into Maryland and his ranks continued thinning.[1] On the morning of the 7th the Confederates marched into Frederick, where Lee issued a proclamation declaring that they had come to liberate Maryland, not harm it. As foraging groups scoured the country for livestock, paying partly in greenbacks, partly in Confederate paper, his major forces concentrated about the town. Here he could threaten even Philadelphia, and menace the communications of the capital with the North and West.

A tremor ran through the Union. Boston on the 9th gave a frantic ovation to the Sixth Massachusetts, leaving for the front once more. The New York

[1] John Esten Cooke, himself in the army, writes: "All the roads of northern Virginia were lined with soldiers, comprehensively denominated 'stragglers'; but the great majority of these men had fallen out from the advancing column from physical inability to keep up with it; thousands were not with General Lee because they had no shoes, and their bleeding feet would carry them no farther, or the heavy march without rations had broken them down. This great crowd toiled on painfully in the wake of the army, dragging themselves five or six miles a day; and when they came to the Potomac, near Leesburg, it was only to find that General Lee had swept on, that General McClellan's column was between him and them, and that they could not rejoin their commands." He estimates that 20,000 or 30,000 thus failed to reach the Maryland battlefields. *Stonewall Jackson*, 341. Lee's numbers have been the subject of much dispute. O. R., I, xix, pt. 2, p. 639, gives a field return Sept. 30 of 62,713 present and 52,990 present for duty. Longstreet estimated after the war that the army should have numbered 63,000 at the passage of the Potomac; letter July 15, 1885, to D. H. Hill, Hill Papers, Va. State Library. A careful military critic in the N. Y. *Nation*, Dec. 20, 1894, computed that Lee had 60,000 in the campaign.

(*The War for the Union*, Vol. II, *War Becomes Revolution, 1862–1863*, Chapter 9.)

press declared that the hour of opportunity had at last struck, for Lee might be defeated so decisively as to crush the rebellion. Throughout New England and the Middle States enlistments, lagging again since Pope's defeat, showed tokens of a revival. In Philadelphia, as long troop trains of replacements began passing through the city, the armories were thrown open for volunteering, and green recruits were hastily drilled. In Scranton cannon and bells summoned the adult males for training; in Harrisburg, Governor Curtin conferred with Thomas A. Scott on emergency measures. Deepest of all was the alarm in Baltimore, where merchants, knowing what wholesale seizures of goods the Southern host would make, and Unionists, well aware that the "Secesh" element in the city was growing dangerous, looked to their defenses.

Lee's hazardous movement was not difficult to explain, for politically and militarily it was almost a necessity. His army was so ill equipped and so inferior in numbers to the growing Northern forces that he could not afford to stand still. As he had to move aggressively, he shared the view of most Southern officers and editors that it should fight on enemy soil, and there make the war support itself. Jackson was particularly anxious to invade. Some of the troops told Frederick citizens that to them the movement was a question of food or starvation—for three days they had lived on green corn, apples, and little else. The effort to buy out shops in Frederick and other towns disclosed other necessities. Lee wrote Davis that the army lacked shoes, lacked clothes, lacked transport animals, and lacked "much of the material of war." He knew with Napoleon that an army marches on both its shoe leather and its belly.[2]

The political motives were equally important. A victory beyond the Potomac not only offered the best hope of gaining Anglo-French intervention, but also presented the largest chance of raising Northern war weariness to the point of negotiations for peace. "There is but one method of putting an end to the war," declared the Richmond *Examiner*, "and that is by destroying the Federal credit"; in other words, financial pressures would compel a new attitude.[3] As soon as Southern legions made good their stand on Maryland soil, Colonel J. F. Marshall of South Carolina prophesied to Davis, the North would lose heart. "The tone of the Masses, the Press, and the Legislatures will all

---

2 Lee had information that Washington had already received 60,000 replacements who would soon be embodied in the army. Freeman, *Lee*, II, 350. McClellan actually had a mobile force of nearly 100,000 in addition to the troops about Washington and Harpers Ferry. The North continued to overestimate Southern force in the grossest manner; thus the N. Y. *Herald* on September 9 declared that Lee's army was "at least 150,000 strong."

The sad outward appearance of the Confederates led some observers to form hasty judgments. "They are the dirtiest, lousiest, filthiest, piratical-looking cut-throats white man ever saw," wrote Edward S. Bragg to his wife, Sept. 21, 1862, Bragg Papers; but they were gentlemen compared with some marauding troops under Pope and Grant.

3 July 21, 1862.

change from a thirst for our blood and property to that for peace." [4] And Lee no sooner reached Frederick than he wrote Davis that the time had come for the Confederacy to propose to the North a recognition of its independence, for it would obviously be negotiating from strength, not from weakness.[5]

Because Lee hoped to win both recruits and friends in Maryland, his army behaved with exemplary restraint. No citizen was maltreated, no goods were taken without payment, and no offensive display of Southern sentiment was permitted. General Bradley T. Johnson, the provost-marshal charged with enlisting as many men as possible, rode up to a soldier cheering in the Frederick streets for Davis, and smashed him over the head with his revolver. "There, you damned blankety-blank," he said, "see if you disobey orders again!" [6] The army brought with it a civil commissioner, E. Loring Lowe, a friend of Herschel V. Johnson, with authority from Jefferson Davis as well as General Lee to undertake any political mission for which victory might clear the way. Lee's proclamation in Frederick assured Marylanders that they would once more enjoy their ancient freedoms, and could freely decide their own destiny. One Union officer paid tribute to the conduct of the hungry, dysentery-weakened rebels as they marched through the Maryland towns. Though they looked haggard, their clothes were often mere bundles of rags, and many were so unkempt and unwashed that they stank, yet in discipline they surpassed the well-fed, well-clothed, Union forces.

"No one," wrote this officer, "can point to a single act of vandalism perpetrated by the rebel soldiery during their occupation of Frederick, while even now a countless host of stragglers are crawling after our army devouring, destroying, and wasting all that falls in their devious line of march." [7]

[I]

Lee had to open his campaign with a hazardous blow to maintain his communications. His hope that Marylanders would rally to his banner proved unfounded, for they remained timid or hostile. While Eastern Maryland, which held the great body of Southern sympathizers, was dominated by the Union forces, the invaded heart of the State stood mainly with the North.[8] Although

4 July 11, 1862, Davis Papers, Duke Univ.
5 See O. R., I, xix, pt. 2, p. 600, for evidence that he expected Maryland to rise.
6 Baltimore corr. dated Sept. 11 in N. Y. *Tribune*, Sept. 13, 1862.
7 MS letter of James Gillette, commissary officer, to mother, Sept. 13.
8 As the Barbara Frietchie legend, immortalized by Whittier, suggests. This legend has no basis in fact. Mrs. Frietchie, then ninety-six, waved a Union flag from her porch when Union troops passed through Frederick later, not when the Confederates passed, and she and Jackson never saw each other; *Battles and Leaders*, II, 618, 622. But it possesses poetic truth, for many Maryland women had the defiant valor imputed to Mrs. Frietchie, and Jackson had the chivalry. Cf. Lenoir Chambers, *Stonewall Jackson*, II, 192, 193.

some hundreds of young men did flock in, most of them soon flocked back, explaining that after "seeing and smelling" the rebel host, they had decided to stand aloof. It was a most heroic army, but its life was all too heroically arduous. Realizing that he could not rely for communications on the Leesburg-Manassas line close to Washington, Lee had to make sure of the Shenandoah Valley instead. He had supposed that his penetration of Maryland would compel the Union forces to evacuate Harpers Ferry and Martinsburg, and McClellan in fact urged their removal; but bad policy kept them there. He therefore determined to send Stonewall Jackson to take Harpers Ferry and open the Valley line while the rest of the army continued operating in Maryland.

This division of his tired, ill-equipped force was perilous, as Longstreet pointed out in a protest. But Lee knew McClellan well enough to be sure he would move slowly; he was aware how wretched a commander the North often put at places like Harpers Ferry, and he never forgot that the South had to take desperate chances. Before Little Mac rouses himself to active operations, he told one of his brigadiers, "I hope to be on the Susquehanna." He outlined the proposed operation with care in Special Order No. 191.

If Lee were to succeed—not only dividing his army in the presence of superior enemy forces, but placing a river between the two parts—he required complete secrecy, and he counted on the abysmal inefficiency of McClellan's intelligence service. Fortune, however, betrayed him. At this time his general orders were frequently transmitted by headquarters direct to each division commander; that is, the staff took Lee's instructions, wrote them down, entered one copy in the "confidential book" or held it to be copied later into the general order book, and sent another copy by orderly to the commander addressed. Sometimes the orderly was told to bring back a receipt, sometimes not.[9] This time Jackson, seeing the importance of a clear understanding of Special Order No. 191, wrote out a copy in his own hand and sent it to General D. H. Hill, of his command. It directed that part of the army was to march northwest on the morrow to Hagerstown and Boonesborough. The divisions of McLaws, Anderson, and Walker were to turn south, however, and seize Maryland Heights, Loudoun Heights, and Harpers Ferry, while Jackson by the longest march of all was to recross the Potomac, cut the Baltimore & Ohio, take Martinsburg, and pick up any fugitives from Harpers Ferry. All these detached forces, their mission accomplished, were to rejoin the main army at Hagerstown or Boonesborough.

This vital order some Union troops, entering Frederick on Lee's heels, found

9 Charles Marshall, Nov. 11, 1867, to D. H. Hill on procedure; Hill Papers, Va. State Lib. Lenoir Chambers, *Stonewall Jackson*, II, 188-191, 200-202, supplies details.

wrapped around three cigars in a field outside Frederick, and they sent it to McClellan on September 13! D. H. Hill has usually been held responsible for losing it, for though he later denied culpability, Charles Marshall, Lee's aide and military secretary, holds him to blame.[10] Whatever the circumstances, McClellan had early notice of the division of the Confederate army; the troops of Jackson and Walker had hardly recrossed the Potomac before he knew they were south of the river.

The forces which Lee sent on this daring mission moved with characteristic rapidity. By afternoon of the 13th they had taken Martinsburg and the two eminences overlooking Harpers Ferry, and held the Union garrison there at their mercy. The commander, D. H. Miles, should either have abandoned the trap in time or posted all his troops on one of the strong heights; he did nothing. The Confederate batteries were soon shelling him heavily, and at dawn on the 13th he surrendered his 11,500 men, with 73 guns, 13,000 small arms, 200 wagons, and much camp equipment.

Jackson as usual wasted not a moment. Astride his horse in the early sunlight, he received the Union officer sent to offer unconditional surrender, and penned a dispatch to Lee. Then he rode into Harpers Ferry past dejected Union troops, many of whom uncovered. "Boys," said one, "he's not much for looks, but if we had him we wouldn't have been caught in this trap." [11] Late that afternoon, the 15th, his forces were on their way to rejoin Lee. It was high time, for the main Confederate army by that hour was in a dangerous predicament. Stonewall and his fellow commanders in their brilliant two-day coup had taken a larger army than those of Burgoyne or Cornwallis, well armed, well provisioned, and established near highly defensible heights; as Northern newspapers said, Hull's surrender was nothing to that of Miles.[12] The guns, small arms, and wagons that the Confederates had seized were of inestimable value to them. Nevertheless, the South would have paid too high a price if Lee had been smashed before Jackson could get back to him.

10 Hill's denial is explicit. He declares no such order came to him from Lee, but that an identical one did arrive from Jackson, which he kept; "The Lost Dispatch," in *The Land We Love*, February, 1868. Colonel Marshall could not conjecture just what had happened, but admitted later that the loss of the order might have occurred in many ways. Randolph B. Marcy and S. W. Crawford, in affidavits written May 5 and Aug. 22, 1868, state reasons for believing that the order was found in the tracks of A. P. Hill, not D. H. Hill; D. H. Hill to Marshall, Nov. 11, 1867, Hill Papers. See also Hal Bridges, "A Lee Letter," *Va. Mag. of Hist. and Biog.*, LXVI (April, 1958), 161–166.

D. H. Hill had been accused of losing an important order during the Seven Days, which was recaptured on the person of a Union soldier before it got to headquarters; Fitzgerald Ross, *Cities and Camps*, 45, 46.

11 *Battles and Leaders*, II, 625–627.

12 Miles had been prominent in the Bull Run disaster, and critics demanded why he had been given such an important command; N. Y. *Tribune* editorial, Sept. 20, 1862. A chance shot as the white flag was raised mortally wounded him.

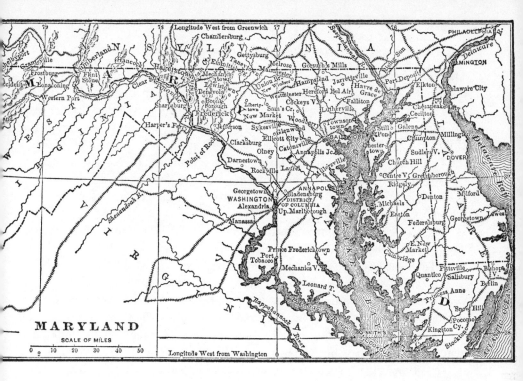

MARYLAND WITH HARPERS FERRY AND ANTIETAM CREEK

Indeed, Lee might have been crushed by the 16th but for McClellan's delays. The statement that he was warned in time that McClellan had obtained the lost order seems untrue. But McClellan had been displaying his characteristic defects and virtues. He had capably reorganized his forces, putting Banks in charge of the Washington fortifications, replacing McDowell (who now disappears from active duty) by Hooker as a corps commander, and keeping Burnside, Sumner, Franklin, and Fitz-John Porter in command of their old corps. But as Lee had anticipated, his movements were dilatory. In the six days from September 7, when he took the field in Maryland, to the 13th, he advanced barely thirty miles. Certain as usual that Lee outnumbered him, on the 11th he demanded reinforcements of 25,000. Halleck shared his nervousness.

Lee was thus able to bring his troops into good defensive position on the eastern slopes of South Mountain, the long irregular range of hills which continues the Blue Ridge into Maryland. Longstreet, Stuart, and D. H. Hill took their stand in the area of Crampton's and Turner's Gaps, passes from 400 to 600 feet high which pierce the thousand-foot ridge. Here on September 14, Confederate officers, peering through field glasses from the heights, descried an advance division of Jacob D. Cox's force on the turnpike to the southeast;

and soon they could see the blue uniforms and glittering bayonets of almost the whole Army of the Potomac swarming down from the far-off Catoctin Ridge near Frederick, and crossing the intervening valley. By noon that hot day the battle was raging violently. Along a wide stretch of South Mountain the Union troops performed astonishing feats in surmounting steep hills, penetrating dense woods, and scrambling over jagged rocks. The Northern artillery outranged the Confederate guns, while superior infantry strength permitted outflanking operations. By five in the afternoon Franklin had pushed his way through Crampton's Gap.

The day's fighting along South Mountain might be called a drawn battle. To be sure, it left the Confederates in a position of great peril. With one gap forced and the other rendered untenable, Longstreet and D. H. Hill at nightfall had to retreat. But the anxious Lee could take pride in the stubborn courage with which 18,000 Southerners had held the front against 30,000 Union troops. While the Northern volunteers displayed steady valor—"not a man fell back or straggled," wrote one reporter—the Confederates had fought with almost unmatchable devotion. And Lee had after all gained what was really important to him—time; time for Jackson to come up. He had in fact gained the whole twenty-four hours beginning at dawn of the 14th. His men fell back in exemplary order. At Keedysville, on the road to Sharpsburg, citizens later testified that the half-starved troops took nothing unless people were willing to sell. One miller, asked to dispose of grain and flour, refused, saying they could have nothing without breaking his lock. "We break no locks, sir," was the reply, and the hungry column marched on.[13] As Lee's forces crossed Antietam Creek he learned by a courier from Jackson that Harpers Ferry had surrendered, and he then disposed his troops on the hills about Sharpsburg.

McClellan next day indulged in exultant boasts. At 8 A.M. he telegraphed Halleck: "I have just learned from General Hooker, in the advance . . . that the enemy is making for Shepherdstown in a perfect panic; and that General Lee last night stated publicly that he must admit that they had been shockingly whipped." Two hours later he reported that the rout had been confirmed. "It is stated that Lee gives his losses as 15,000." [14] Actually Lee's losses had been only 3,400, and his retreat was effected without panic. Moreover, as he formed his lines in the new position near Sharpsburg, he had the comfort of knowing that Jackson was on the way. By a "severe" march after midnight, Stonewall reached Lee's lines early on the 16th.[15]

13   N. Y. *Tribune*, Sept. 19, 1862.
14   O. R., I, xix, pt. 2, pp. 294, 295.
15   Henderson, II, 226, 227; Freeman, *Lee*, II, 381, 382.

[II]

Although the Confederates had escaped a hammer blow while still divided, their position remained dangerous. At Sharpsburg, a hamlet only three miles from the Potomac, they lay behind the crooked Antietam Creek, which wriggles its way down to the river above Harpers Ferry. They had the advantage of holding a low crescent-shaped ridge, their right flank resting on the Antietam, and their left making some use of stone walls, limestone ledges, and thicketed woodlands. Perhaps because they lacked tools, they dug no entrenchments, though they could have strengthened their lines greatly at various points by hasty field works. With but 50,000 men at most, they faced McClellan's well-armed force half again as large. They were more tired, hungry, and ragged than ever, and their spirits had suffered by the retreat from South Mountain while those of the Federal army had risen. "The *morale* of our men is now restored," McClellan informed Halleck.

Lee's daring resolution was never better exhibited than in his decision to stand and fight. Longstreet, always cautious, advised retreat, and some military critics have regarded Lee's choice as a cardinal mistake. But Jackson, when he arrived, approved a decision that for several reasons was almost inevitable. The invasion of Maryland was a desperate effort to end the war at one stroke by laying a foundation for foreign intervention, and spreading discouragement throughout the North; luck, strategy, and heroism could yet win a victory, and if it were half as signal as Second Manassas it might achieve the object. McClellan exaggerated when he wrote later: "One victory lost almost all would have been lost. Lee's army might have marched as it pleased on Washington, Baltimore, Philadelphia, or New York . . . nowhere east of the Alleghenies was there another organized force to avert its march." This was McClellan's self-glorification as the savior of the Union. The Northern forces were now too numerous to be scattered by one blow, and each of the four cities would have remained well defended. Nevertheless, the effect of a Union defeat on foreign opinion and the autumn elections might have been disastrous. With so much to gain, Lee could only play his hand out to the end.

By retreating, Lee would put his army on the defensive for months to come. That no army fighting a defensive campaign with smaller numbers ever wins a decisive battle is a well-tested maxim of war; Hannibal, Marlborough, Frederick, Washington, Napoleon, Wellington, all won their victories when they took the offensive.[16] Moreover, if Lee fell back he could augment his forces but slowly while the Union army would grow rapidly in strength. Under

16 Sir Frederick Maurice, *Lee*, 151, 152.

recent calls, the North was putting 600,000 more men under arms; it was at last manufacturing artillery, small arms, ammunition, and camp supplies in almost adequate quantity; it was finding better brigadiers and colonels. As Herschel V. Johnson was writing A. H. Stephens, a protracted war must close in combatant exhaustion—and the South would be exhausted first.[17] If Lee waited, he would soon find that the North had trained its raw recruits and gained an overwhelming field superiority. McClellan could then enjoy just what he desired; a campaign of movement after full ranks, improved administration, and an overhauled supply system put his army in shape to prosecute the war without intermission to a successful end.

It was a remarkable battlefield that Lee had chosen, so compact that from some vantage points observers could witness the struggle in its entire length and breadth. The crescent-shaped ridge which furnished the main Confederate line was backed by a broad tableland of woods and ravines, offering cover for troops everywhere. Lee had two good highways, the Shepherdstown Road and the Williamsport Road, open at his rear for possible retreat to the Potomac. The sluggish Antietam flowed in front of the Confederate position, too deep for passage by artillery and well guarded at its three stone bridges. But in view of the heavy superiority of the national troops and of the guns which McClellan massed at the center, the Confederates needed every aid they could draw from the terrain.[18]

[III]

McClellan was as usual open to criticism. He had delayed in thrusting his columns forward on September 13 to reach South Mountain before the Confederates could establish themselves on its slopes, and he had then made a faulty use of his forces in attacking the Southern positions on that ridge.[19] He delayed again in pushing forward after the retreating Lee. He knew early on the morning of the 15th, when he telegraphed Halleck, that D. H. Hill and Longstreet had evacuated Turner's Gap, and he declared that "our troops are now advancing in pursuit of them." But they were not advancing.[20] A swift forward movement would have caught Lee off balance before he could con-

17 Johnson to Stephens, Sept. 28, 1862, Johnson Papers, Duke University. At the moment, the disparity in size between the two armies, while great, was not overwhelming. Livermore in *Numbers and Losses*, 92, 93, concludes that at Antietam, Lee had 51,844 men engaged, and McClellan 75,316 effectives.

18 The N. Y. *Tribune* of Sept. 20 has a graphic description sent from Sharpsburg.

19 Cf. Henderson, II, 226.

20 O. R., I, xix, pt. 2, pp. 294, 295. Some Union services were poorly organized, as usual. Lossing writes, II, 476: "There was found to be a lack of ammunition and rations, and these had to be supplied from tardily approaching supply trains."

centrate behind Antietam Creek. Instead, orders to move were inexcusably delayed. Some units, like the Ninth Corps under Cox, did not receive them until late afternoon. A correspondent posted near the Confederate lines wrote the evening of the 15th that Union troops had been slowly coming up all day:

> Sumner arrived about three o'clock and took command, but his troops were mostly far back on the road. Very little artillery came, and altogether the whole movement was unaccountably slow. The road was good, and the ground on both sides favorable for parallel columns, but yet no considerable force arrived until nearly dark. Burnside emerged from the lower gap about five o'clock, but Hooker's own troops were not within a mile of the front at seven o'clock. . . .[21]

The Union army might, as many officers expected, have attacked on the 16th. McClellan, however, spent most of the day reconnoitering Lee's lines, and fixing an exact position for not only every corps, but every division and brigade. This annoyed subordinates. His battle plan, as he explained it, was simple. His right wing under Hooker and Sumner, already partly across the Antietam, would swing around to force the Confederate left back on the center, while cutting off the roads to Hagerstown and Williamsport. His left under Burnside would meanwhile force the Antietam at a stone bridge a mile below the central turnpike, and crumple the Confederate right into Sharpsburg. This would pinch Lee in a vise, and bar his retreat towards the fords of the Potomac. For any emergency, Fitz-John Porter's force at the center would act as a reserve.[22]

At daybreak on the 17th desultory infantry firing began. As the sun rose the musketry deepened to a roar, and before the mists lifted from wood and field Hooker was hotly engaged with the veterans of Stonewall Jackson and Hood. On the Confederate side the story was one of stubborn resistance, varied by one magnificent charge—that of A. P. Hill's division, which, ordered up from Harpers Ferry at dawn, after marching seventeen miles without rest, fell with tigerish ferocity on the Union left. These roadworn troops flung an advancing corps in confusion back down the ridge toward the Antietam. On the Union side equal leadership was displayed by one corps commander, Hooker, whose impetuous vigor fairly earned him his sobriquet of "Fighting Joe"; but two others, Sumner and Burnside, failed to seize opportunities that might have led to complete victory. Here McClellan's overall strategy was chiefly at fault, for he had ordered piecemeal attacks instead of simultaneous assaults along the whole front.[23]

21 N. Y. *Tribune*, Sept. 19, 1862; W. C. Cochran, "Political Experiences of Jacob D. Cox," MS, Western Reserve Hist. Soc., I, 669–671.
22 "Personal Recs. of the War," by a Virginian, *Harper's Magazine*, XXXVI (February, 1868), 281.
23 Ropes believes that if Burnside had attacked early and furiously, he might have gained the victory before A. P. Hill's troops came up; Kenneth P. Williams indicts McClellan's

At Antietam the sun looked down on some of the bloodiest close-order fighting of the war. Where Hooker's men fought with Jackson's in a corn-field smitten by artillery on both sides, the losses were murderous. Thirty acres of grain, reported Hooker, were cut as close as by a scythe, and on the stubble Northern and Southern dead lay in heaps. Later, when two Union brigades struck Hood's Texan command, the blue and gray seemed like duelists who had lashed themselves together. They stood loading, firing, and reloading at fifty to eighty paces, determined to kill before being killed. In another area the slain lay in rows precisely as they had stood in their ranks a few moments before. Francis M. Palfrey commanded the Twentieth Massachusetts when Sumner marched a division into an ambush where ten Confederate brigades took three Union brigades in front, flank, and rear. "Change of front was impossible," wrote Palfrey later.[24] "In less time than it takes to tell it, the ground was strewn with the bodies of the dead and wounded. . . . Nearly two thousand were disabled in a moment."

The day closed on an undecided field. The Confederates had been forced back on their left by more than a mile, and on their right by half that distance. However, they still held a strong continuous line passing through Sharpsburg, and affording about as many natural advantages as that first chosen. On the field lay a multitude of dead and dying, for of the 130,000 men in the two armies, at least 21,000 or 16 per cent had been slain or wounded. "Who can tell, who can even imagine," wrote the colonel of the Twentieth Massachusetts long after, "the horrors of such a night, while the unconscious stars shone down, and the unconscious river went rippling by?" McClellan stated—or more probably understated—the Union loss as 2,010 killed, 9,416 wounded, and 1,043 missing. The Confederate casualties were fully as great; McClellan reported that, after the rebels themselves had buried many, 2,700 were counted and buried by the Northern forces.[25]

Lee and Jackson knew that although the army had fought magnificently, their gamble had failed. Nevertheless, Lee was unwilling to acknowledge defeat. Early that night the Confederate generals rode up, one by one, to report. They found Lee seated on his horse beside the highway. He asked each commander in turn, "What of your part of the line?" Each reported heavy losses, deadly

---

whole management of Burnside and others. Ropes, *Civil War*, II, 373–375; Williams, II, 450–458. A. D. Richardson wrote his managing editor Sept. 27: "The feeling with some of Burnside's staff officers (and I infer, with him also) is very bitter. They swear that Mc-Clellan tried to ruin him in the battle, by putting him where, with the force he had, he was sure to fail. They attribute it to jealousy of Burnside's reputation; Burnside *is* a great favorite with the troops." McClellan knew that Burnside earlier had been offered the command in his place, but we can agree with Richardson that he was above such an act. Gay Papers.

24 Palfrey, *Antietam and Fredericksburg*, 86, 87.
25 See map of the field, *American Conflict*, II, 205; Henderson, II, 261; Palfrey, *op. cit.*

fatigue, and a dismaying Federal superiority in numbers; the consensus favored retreat across the Potomac before daybreak. Even Jackson betrayed discouragement. He had never before met such odds, he said, and many of his best officers were dead. Hood was still more dejected, declaring that he had no men left. "Great God!" exclaimed Lee, "Where is the splendid division you had this morning?" "They are lying on the field where you sent them," responded Hood. "Few have straggled. My division has been almost wiped out."

Lee remained undaunted. He did not say, as a subsequent fable stated, that he was ready to give battle again in the morning; but he was confident that if McClellan delivered an attack, the Confederate lines would bloodily repulse it. At his back he had only one good ford over the Potomac, and in front a much stronger army, much of which McClellan had never used, for he had deliberately declined to throw in his reserves. No matter; with serene determination Lee posted artillery, distributed rations, and sent out guards to collect stragglers. He was ready for any eventuality except immediate retreat.[26]

Why did not McClellan hold a council of *his* lieutenants? Late in the afternoon he had met one of his division commanders, an old and trusted friend, who reported that his troops had done well but were somewhat scattered. "Collect them at once," said McClellan. "Fifteen thousand fresh troops have come up; more will arrive during the night. Tell your men that! We must fight tonight and tomorrow. If we cannot whip the enemy now, we may as well die upon the field. If we succeed we end the war." But he did not stick to this resolution.[27]

Lee counted on the cautious Union commander to lie still next morning—as he did. The long lines of troops faced each other, as the sun rose, with rifles and muskets loaded; the batteries stood unlimbered for instant action; pickets fingered their triggers nervously. While hour after hour ticked by, McClellan made no use of his overwhelming superiority in men and materials. Lee was encouraged by this quiescence to think of delivering an attack, but a brief inquiry showed it out of the question. He reluctantly admitted that it would be folly to attempt, as he momentarily thought of doing, to break the Northern right wing under Hooker. This was the unanimous judgment of his officers. When Jackson bade an able chief of artillery, Colonel Stephen D. Lee, to inspect the Union lines and ascertain positively whether with fifty guns and the available men he could smash the Union position, the report was unequivocal:

26 Henderson, II, 262, 263, Freeman, *Lee*, II, 403, 404. Longstreet wrote General E. A. Carman, Feb. 11, 1897, that the assemblage was not a council of war, but "the usual meeting of leading officers at night after battle to make their reports"; extra-illustrated *Battles and Leaders*, HL.

27 So reports A. D. Richardson, N. Y. *Tribune*, Sept. 29. McClellan also received large supplies of ammunition from Baltimore, while thousands of Pennsylvania militia had reached the Maryland boundary.

"General, it cannot be done." With evident dejection, Robert E. Lee accepted the verdict.[28]

All day September 18 the Confederate army waited in battle array. But its position grew more untenable every hour, for large national reinforcements were coming up. Late in the afternoon Lee decided upon retreat, and that night the Southern units, one by one, moved down to Boteler's Ford, two miles from Sharpsburg, and recrossed the Potomac. McClellan made no effort to molest them. Indeed, not until dawn of September 19 did reconnoitering Union detachments discover that Sharpsburg had been deserted, and by eight that morning the last Confederates were crossing the river.

[IV]

Of all McClellan's errors this failure to pursue was one of the most inexcusable. Had he pushed the national forces forward in a night attack, he might have thrown Lee's army into confusion. Rain fell throughout the night, roads and fields turned into pasty mire, and the single lane which led from the Shepherdstown highway to the ford was dangerously narrow. An enterprising commander would have inflicted heavy losses. As it was, the Union forces took not a single gun or wagon. "We were the conquerors," wrote one Northern reporter, "and yet our property—small arms and accoutrements by the hundred —was the only property thrown away to waste upon the field." [29] When McClellan on the 20th tardily ordered Fitz-John Porter to exploit the enemy retreat, he still had an opportunity to achieve a striking success. Union troops had now taken the ford, so that Porter easily crossed to the south bank:

> The Confederates [writes Henderson] were in no condition to resist an attack in force. The army was not concentrated. The cavalry was absent. No reconnaissances had been made either of lines of march or of positions. The roads were still blocked by the trains. The men were exhausted by their late exertions, and depressed by their retreat, and the straggling was terrible. The only chance of safety lay in driving back the enemy's advanced-guard across the river before it could be reinforced; and the chance was seized without an instant's hesitation.[30]

So before Porter's force, inadequately sustained, could move a mile and a half beyond the Potomac, Jackson struck him and drove him back with a loss of 340 men. McClellan was so easily discouraged that he made no further effort to follow Lee, though he had received the quite fresh divisions of Humphrey

---

28 Henderson, II, 264–267, based on a letter by Gen. Stephen D. Lee; Freeman, *Lee*, II, 405.
29 N. Y. *Tribune*, Sept. 23, 1862.
30 Henderson, II, 269.

and Couch, and Washington made it plain that it expected pursuit and battle. Once more the Union intelligence service proved wretched. When a great cloud of dust had been espied in Virginia on September 18, one Union general demonstrated that it was Confederate reinforcements coming up. The morrow showed that the dust had been stirred by retreating rebel trains. It is very strange, commented one correspondent, that our generals, with their elaborate and expensive detective work, get such poor information. "The enemy outwit us under our very noses." [31] Lee's army, physically exhausted, disorganized by losses, and bereft of some of its ablest officers, was in sad estate. He informed President Davis that his force was too far diminished in numbers, and worse still, too much shaken in fighting spirit, to permit of a renewal of the offensive: "the hazard would be great and a reverse disastrous." [32] It was highly vulnerable to attack, but no attack came.

While Lincoln, Stanton, and the whole North waited for news of rapid movement and repeated blows, McClellan was writing Halleck: "This army is not now in condition to undertake another campaign nor to bring on another battle, unless great advantages are offered by some mistake of the enemy or pressing military exigencies render it necessary." He actually feared "a renewal of the attempt in Maryland"; he demanded every possible reinforcement.[33] The fact was that McClellan, as his letters to his wife show, had no thought of *destroying* Lee, for to check him seemed enough. "I feel some little pride," he wrote, "in having, with a beaten and demoralized army, defeated Lee so utterly and saved the North so completely." And again: "I feel that I have done all that can be asked in twice saving the country." [34] Not to conquer the South, but save the North—this was the object!

Lee's failure in his throw for high stakes was complete. The handful of recruits gained in Maryland did not equal his desertions; the captures of shoes, clothing, and other stores did not offset the loss of material by wear and tear; the gaps torn in Confederate ranks could never be repaired, for the men slain, disabled, and captured were among the best veterans of the army. But at any rate he had exerted himself to the utmost.

No such claim could be made for McClellan. Given a rare opportunity of overwhelming victory by his discovery, from the lost Confederate order, that Lee had divided his army, he had moved his troops at least twelve hours too late. Had he thrown the heavy bulk of his army through Crampton's Gap in South Mountain, he would probably have saved Harpers Ferry and would almost certainly have severed Jackson from Lee. Thereafter he moved so slowly

31 N. P. in N. Y. *Tribune*, Sept. 23, 1862.
32 O. R., I, xix, pt. 2, p. 627; Sept. 25, 1862.
33 *Ibid.*, pt. 1, pp. 70, 71.
34 *Own Story*, 613, 614.

that at Antietam, too, he fought his battle at least a day late—perhaps, says his subordinate Francis W. Palfrey, two days late.[35] Not only that, but his movements the evening before the battle advertised to the enemy his intention of using Hooker's right wing in the initial attack. His subsequent orders were of mediocre quality. He made practically no use at all of two corps, the Fifth and Sixth; permitted Burnside to delay his movement until six or seven hours after he had been ordered to seize a vital bridge and move forward; and failed properly to coordinate the action of the first, ninth, and twelfth corps, which should have moved forward in unison.

Lee, falling back to the area of Winchester and Bunker Hill, where the Shenandoah Valley afforded ample supplies, indulged his troops in much-needed rest while he made every effort to refill his ranks. The Richmond authorities so effectively assisted him that by October he had almost 68,000 officers and men. Though shoes and weapons were at first much needed, the government gradually supplied them. McClellan reoccupied Harpers Ferry as a safe bridgehead on the south side of the Potomac, placing Sumner with two corps in possession of it and the fortified heights. While he had just boasted that "our victory was complete," he was still not quite certain as to Sumner's safety, writing: "I think he will be able to hold his position until reinforcements arrive." His own strength was fully half again as large as Lee's. But believing that the Confederate army still outnumbered his own, he did not think it "safe" to go beyond Harpers Ferry, for it would not do to provoke this overwhelming Confederate host. Not until October 26th did the main national army, 110,665 strong (not counting the corps which was kept at Harpers Ferry under Henry W. Slocum and 4,500 troops guarding the upper Potomac) begin crossing the river.[36]

In the aftermath of the battle a telling illustration of the reliance Americans still placed upon improvisation was furnished by Oliver Wendell Holmes in his long-famous "hunt after the captain"—the captain being the future Justice Holmes. The night after Antietam the Autocrat of the Breakfast Table received from some unknown source a curt telegram: "Capt. Holmes wounded through the neck thought not mortal at Keedysville." He at once set off southward. After two days of travel he reached Frederick, where he heard a rumor that his boy was killed. Hiring a wagon, he began ransacking hospitals in all the towns about Sharpsburg—in Middletown, Boonsborough, Keedysville. It

---

35 Palfrey, who fought on the field, is explicit also in censuring McClellan for not doing more to inspire the troops by his active presence on the field once the battle was joined: "He passed the whole day, till toward the middle of the afternoon, when all the fighting was over, on the high ground near Fry's house, where he had some glasses strapped to a fence. . . ." *Antietam and Fredericksburg*, 119.

36 O. R., I, xix, pt. 1, p. 70; Ropes, *Civil War*, II, 440, 441.

would seem that colonels should have been able to report their dead and wounded; that hospitals could have made up central lists in each town; that nurses could have kept records to show when and where the wounded were forwarded to new destinations. But Holmes groped in the dark for his son. Finally he heard that the captain had set off north, not badly hurt, in a milk cart. Hotly pursuing this scent, at Harrisburg he learned that his son had taken the train to Philadelphia; but then came word that he had not appeared at the house of some Philadelphia friends whom he would naturally seek. Another frantic search of Harrisburg hospitals still disclosed no son. Finally, almost by accident, he lighted on the wounded captain in a train.

How many thousands of parents thus searched for their sons? How many wives waited weeks in anguish for news of a husband's fate? With no proper record of casualties by officers, no proper hospital lists, no burial records or graves registration, a darkness settled down on every great battlefield.

The dreary story of McClellan's complaints, delays, and excuses, which had so long irritated Lincoln and enraged the radicals who insisted on a vigorous war effort, was being resumed. Disappointment in the army itself over McClellan's failure to follow up Antietam was intense. Some soldiers read his excuse of "fatigue and exhaustion" with incredulity. "To us of the Thirteenth [Massachusetts]," wrote one "it seemed just possible that the enemy might be equally tired and a good deal more discomfited. . . . When men are stimulated by success in battle they forget everything but pushing their good fortune to a complete triumph." Many intelligent volunteers agreed with A. D. Richardson: "If McClellan had only attacked again early Thursday morning, we could have driven them into the river or captured them. . . . It was one of the supreme moments when by daring something, the destiny of the nation might have been changed." [37]

The anger of even moderate men in Washington when they saw that no effort was being made to press Lee's forces was emphatic. T. J. Barnett of the Interior Department talked at length on September 23 with both Lincoln and Caleb Smith. "I am convinced," he wrote S. L. M. Barlow, "that the government, if they dared, would supersede Mac." Why did they not dare? Because of apprehension that much of the army would be resentful, fear of a violent reaction in the North, and inability to find anyone to put in his place. But, records Barnett, Lincoln's praise for the victor of Antietam was very chilly: he felt "great confidence" in McClellan, he thought the general "well educated but very cautious," and altogether damned him with faint praise. In high circles, since Lee's escape, Barnett found men again whispering that McClellan was of a

37 C. E. Davis, Jr., *The Thirteenth Mass. Volunteers*, 142, 143; Richardson to S. H. Gay, Sharpsburg, Sept. 19, 1862, Gay Papers.

school and party which wished to exhaust the two sections, with a view to reconstructing the Union along conservative lines. This story had many variations and many believers.[38]

But if Northern discouragement after Antietam was keen, that of many Southern leaders was greater. The defeatism of Herschel V. Johnson and Alexander H. Stephens deepened. Jefferson Davis, subject to alternate waves of optimism and depression, was so hard hit that he again talked of resigning. "Our maximum strength has been mobilized," he told the Secretary of War, "while the enemy is just beginning to put forth his might." [39]

[V]

If McClellan could not use victory to convert the defensive into an offensive, Lincoln could. He had to deal with moral and political forces as powerful for harm as Lee's army, with Democrats hoping to use victory in the fall elections to save the South from utter revolution, selfish moneyed men whining about bankruptcy, and foreign haters of the United States who, encouraged by Confederate agents, hoped to use intervention to cripple the republic. But he knew how to strike promptly and effectively. As he said later, he did not wait for crushing victory; he waited only until Lee was driven from Maryland. That gave him sufficient vantage ground for the offensive he intended to launch.

Lincoln saw it was important, while waiting, to prepare the public mind for his decision to use emancipation as a war measure. Horace Greeley fortunately offered an opportunity. When readers opened the *Tribune* of August 20, 1862, they found the editorial page blazing with an open letter by Greeley headed "The Prayer of Twenty Millions," addressed to Lincoln. The editor

38 Barnett to Barlow, Sept. 23, 1862, Barlow Papers. Judge Thomas M. Key of Cincinnati, an Ohio legislative leader who became aide and acting judge-advocate on McClellan's staff, gave Nathaniel Paige, a well-known Washington lawyer serving as war correspondent of the N. Y. *Tribune*, just three days before Antietam, a remarkable story. "He told me," later stated Paige, "that a plan to countermarch to Washington and intimidate the President had been seriously discussed the night before by the members of McClellan's staff, and his opposition to it [that is, Key's opposition] had, he thought, caused its abandonment." McClellan himself did not know about it. These staff officers wished to make Lincoln abandon his interferences with slavery, in the hope that thus the war could be stopped. Eighteen years later a writer for the Washington *Capitol*, who had known Paige, gave some corroboration. He declared that these staff officers used to call Lincoln, Halleck, and Stanton "the old women at Washington"; that they regarded Lincoln with contempt and Stanton with hatred; that it was their fixed belief that the war was folly, and bound to end in failure; and that they were really fighting for a boundary line, and not for the Union. Paige's statement, clipped from the *Tribune* without date, is in Hay Papers, Ill. State Hist. Library; Washington *Capitol*, March 21, 1880.

39 Edward Younger, *Inside the Confederate Govt.*, 28, 86; Strode, *Davis*, 307 ff.

stated at length what the twenty millions complained of, what they had a right to expect, and what they required.

They demanded, he wrote, that Lincoln execute the laws, and especially the provisions of the new Confiscation Act liberating the slaves of rebels. They insisted that he cease giving undue weight to the counsels of fossil politicians in the Border States, and recognize that whatever fortified slavery in this area also fortified treason. They wished the government to show more energy, opposing force to force in an undaunted spirit. They asked that he give up his mistaken deference to slavery in the South, and called on him to rebuke the army officers, including prominent generals, who showed greater regard for slavery than freedom. Finally, they demanded that he turn to the Negroes for aid. "We cannot conquer Ten Millions of People united in a solid phalanx against us, powerfully aided by Northern sympathizers and European allies. We must have scouts, guides, spies, cooks, teamsters, diggers and choppers. . . ."

This letter, with what Lincoln called its erroneous statements, false inferences, and impatient dictatorial tone, had to be answered. It gave him so perfect an opportunity for an explanation paving the way to his proclamation that Greeley three years later expressed the belief that the President had his statement ready written, and seized the occasion to promulgate it.[40] Lincoln saw that he must make his position entirely clear without prematurely betraying his decision on emancipation, and Greeley gave him a sounding board. He was President of the whole nation, Democrats and Republicans, conservatives, radicals, and moderates; he was not the tool of border reactionaries as Greeley intimated, or of Senate abolitionists as some Democrats said, but his own master, prosecuting the war with a single eye to maintenance of the Union. He sat down to produce one of his most memorable state papers—a paper that, published everywhere within the week, was worth a battle gained:

I would save the Union. I would save it the shortest way under the Constitution. The sooner the national authority can be restored, the nearer the Union will be to "the Union as it was." If there be those who would not save the Union, unless they could at the same time *save* slavery, I do not agree with them. If there be those who would not save the Union unless they could at the same time *destroy* slavery, I do not agree with them. My paramount object in this struggle *is* to save the Union, and is not either to save or to destroy slavery. If I could save the Union without freeing *any* slave I would do it, and if I could save the Union by freeing some and leaving others alone I would also do that. What I do about slavery, and the colored race, I do because I believe it helps to save the Union; and what I forbear, I forbear because I do *not* believe it would help to save the Union. I shall do *less* whenever I shall believe what I am doing hurts the cause, and I shall do *more* whenever I shall believe that doing more

40 Greeley's MS lecture on Lincoln, HL, published in *Century Magazine*, XX (July, 1891), 371 ff.; he was mistaken.

will help the cause. I shall try to correct errors when shown to be errors; and I shall adopt new views so soon as they shall appear to be true views.[41]

The applause given Lincoln's reply in moderate circles far outweighed the dissent from extremists on both sides. Greeley attempted a rebuttal; but Raymond's *Times*, the Douglasite *Morning Post* in Chicago, the Springfield *Republican*, the Cincinnati *Commercial*, and the influential Presbyterian *Observer* agreed on the President's cool sagacity. News was spreading around Washington (for the Cabinet had leaked it) that he had an emancipation proclamation ready, but that Seward and Blair wished it withheld.[42] Reports also spread of a colloquy between Lincoln and a Western delegation, including a couple of Senators, who had called to offer two Negro regiments—which under the new confiscation law he was empowered to accept. The President told them that he was ready to employ Negro teamsters, cooks, pioneers, and the like, but not soldiers. A warm discussion followed, which Lincoln was said to have closed with the words: "Gentlemen, you have my decision. It embodies my best judgment, and if the people are dissatisfied, I will resign and let Mr. Hamlin try it." Such heat had been generated that one caller exclaimed: "I hope, in God's name, Mr. President, you will!" [43]

Lee's retreat across the Potomac brought Lincoln the opening for which he had waited. At noon on Monday, September 21, occurred the famous Cabinet meeting at which he announced his final action. The members, summoned by messenger, were portentously solemn; and Lincoln, who did not like portentous solemnity, broke the spell by taking up a newly received copy of Artemus Ward's latest book, and reading aloud with happy enjoyment the chapter "Hihanded Outrage at Utica." Everybody except Stanton shared his laugh. Then the President also became solemn, and recalled their previous consultation on emancipation. Chase reports his speech:

"I think the time has come now. I wish it were a better time. I wish that we were in a better condition. The action of the army against the rebels has not been quite what I should have best liked. But they have been driven out of

41 Dated Aug. 22 and published in the *Tribune* Aug. 25, 1862; *Works*, V, 388, 389.

42 A few days before Greeley published "The Prayer of Twenty Millions," his reporter Adam S. Hill had written S. H. Gay, the managing editor, that Summer and Gurowski both possessed inside knowledge of the emancipation proclamation, and the fact that it had been temporarily suspended at the suggestion of Seward, Blair, and Thurlow Weed. Hill also wrote Gay that Senator S. C. Pomeroy gave him to understand that Lincoln would issue the proclamation as soon as he had assurance that his colonization project would succeed; Pomeroy being much interested in the Chiriqui plan. Greeley must therefore have known that the proclamation was impending when he brought out his letter of minatory tone. Perhaps he hoped to end all hesitations. See Hill's letters, Aug. 21, 25, 1862, Gay Papers.

43 The Chicago *Morning Post* and Chicago *Tribune*, Aug. 6, 1862, both carry accounts of this scene from their Washington correspondents.

Maryland, and Pennsylvania is no longer in danger of invasion." When they were at Frederick, he said, he had promised himself and God that he would issue his proclamation as soon as they were driven out. "I am going to fulfill that promise. I have got you together to hear what I have written down. I do not wish your advice about the main matter—for that I have determined for myself." But he would be glad to accept suggestions about phraseology or other minor points.

Lincoln added that he knew that various men in this and other transactions would do better than he, and if satisfied that another leader had a fuller measure of public confidence, he would—were it constitutionally possible— yield to him. "But though I believe that I have not so much of the confidence of the people as I had some time since, I do not know that, all things considered, any other person has more. . . . I must do the best I can, and bear the responsibility. . . ."[44]

All the Cabinet members acquiesced. Chase said he would have taken a somewhat different course, Blair reiterated his old fears as to the effect of the proclamation on the border and the army, and Seward suggested some verbal changes, but they were obviously pleased. Executed that day, the proclamation appeared in the morning newspapers September 23. Its essence lay in the third paragraph:

That on the first day of January in the year of our Lord, one thousand eight hundred and sixty-three, all persons held as slaves within any State, or designated part of a State, the people whereof shall then be in rebellion against the United States, shall be then, thenceforward, and forever free; and the executive government of the United States, including the military and naval authority thereof, will recognize and maintain the freedom of such persons, and will do no act or acts to repress such persons, or any of them, in any efforts they may make for their actual freedom.

Lincoln's sagacity did not fail him in the form of the document. It was an exercise of war powers; its main intent was not the liberation of a race (though he was fully conscious of this aspect) but the furtherance of the war effort and the preservation of the Union; and he did well to couch it in cold legal phraseology, direct and deadly as a bullet. Sumner and Greeley regretted the absence of rhetorical flourishes; "a poor document, but a mighty act," was John A. Andrew's verdict. But its moral import spoke for itself, and Lincoln, as Lowell remarked in the *Atlantic*, would have weakened it by an attempt at misplaced eloquence.[45]

44 Donald, ed., *Inside Lincoln's Cabinet*, 149, 150.
45 The proclamation did not embrace Tennessee, but in all of eight other States, and in the greater parts of Virginia and Louisiana, it did proclaim freedom. "We shall drive the conservatives of proslavery hunkerism into the very caves and holes of the earth," wrote Governor Andrew to Col. A. G. Brown, Sept. 23, 1862; Carnegie Bookshop Catalogue, N. Y.

That the proclamation was indeed "a mighty act" nobody could deny; but what were its precise results? To answer this question we must examine two entirely different subjects: first, its direct pragmatic effects in turning slaves into freedmen, and second, its impact upon public sentiment—the sentiment of the North, of the army, of the South, and by no means least, of Britain and the overseas world.

It is quite true that the popular picture of Lincoln using a stroke of the pen to lift the shackles from the limbs of four million slaves is ludicrously false. Since the proclamation was an exercise of the war powers, what its legal effect would be after the war ceased was uncertain. As the President could issue a proclamation, so he, or a successor, could revoke it. It did not apply to those districts which the Union armies held on the date Lincoln designated, January 1, 1863; could not be enforced in those districts which they did not hold; and had no application whatever to the four border slave States. To this extent it is a fact that, as Seward said, the proclamation emancipated slaves where it could not reach them, and left them in bondage where it could have set them free.[46] Lincoln himself continued to believe gradual emancipation better than summary liberation, and to cherish his plan for thus freeing the Negro in loyal areas. His friend David Davis, visiting him two months after the proclamation, found his ideas unchanged. Wrote Davis: "Mr. Lincoln's whole soul is absorbed in his plan of remunerative emancipation and he thinks if Congress don't fail him, that the problem is solved. He believes that if Congress will pass a law authorizing the issuance of bonds for the payment of emancipated negroes in the border States that Delaware, Maryland, Kentucky and Mo. will accept the terms. He takes great encouragement from the vote in Mo." [47]

But the proclamation had three immediate, positive, and visible effects. First, every forward step the Union armies took after January 1, 1863, now became a liberating step. Every county in Mississippi, Alabama, Virginia, and the Carolinas that passed under military control was thenceforth legally a free-soil county, the army bound to "recognize and maintain" emancipation.

In the second place, the percolating news of the proclamation encouraged slaves to escape, bringing them first in trickles and then rivulets within army

---

46   Greeley fiercely attacked Lincoln for not at once decreeing the liberation of all slaves in Louisiana and Tennessee; two States, he wrote, which "have more than One Hundred Thousand of their citizens in arms to destroy the Union." N. Y. *Tribune*, Jan. 3, 1863.

47   Davis found Lincoln weary, careworn, and heavily burdened with preparations for the imminent Congressional session. "It is a good thing he is fond of anecdotes and telling them," commented Davis, "for it relieves his spirits very much." To Leonard Swett, Nov. 26, 1862; David Davis Papers, Ill. State Hist. Lib. Missouri sentiment on slavery was changing fast, largely because of Lincoln's offer of reimbursement. Two months after Davis' letter the legislature was to pass a resolution declaring that $25,000,000 would be needed to carry out emancipation in the State, and asking Congress for that amount. H. A. Trexler, *Slavery in Missouri, 1804–1865*, p. 233 ff.

lines. How did it percolate? By grapevine telegraph, by the overheard discussions of masters, by glimpses of newspapers, by a new tension in the air. The idea that nearly all slaves wished to cling to their masters, a staple of Southern white folklore, did not fit the facts, for whenever escape became feasible, most of them were ready to embrace the opportunity. Edmund Ruffin, prominent among those who defended slavery as a positive good, must have been shocked when after McClellan's invasion nearly the whole work force decamped from his "Marlbourne" plantation in Princess Anne County. A few days later he wrote in his diary: "The fleeing of slaves from this neighborhood, which seemed to have ceased, has begun again. Mr. J. B. Bland lost 17 more a few nights ago, making his whole loss 27—though 5 were recaptured." [48]

The eminent cleric James Freeman Clarke, visiting a contraband camp in Washington early in 1863, asked one Negro just from Virginia whether the slaves down there had heard of the proclamation. "Oh yes, massa! We-all knows about it; only we darsen't let on. We pretends not to know. I said to my ole massa, 'What's this Marse Lincoln is going to do to the poor nigger? I hear he is going to cut 'em up awful bad. How is it, massa?' I just pretended foolish, sort of." [49] In the West the story was the same. The Cairo levees were black with fleeing slaves; Sherman wrote from Memphis that he had a thousand at work on the Memphis fortifications, and could send any number to St. Louis. Peter Cooper reported:

I learn direct from Mr. Dean, the provost-marshal of St. Louis, that the Proclamation of Freedom has done more to weaken the rebellion . . . than any other measure that could have been adopted. On his late visit to my house he informed me that he had brought on a large number of rebel officers and men to be exchanged at Fortress Monroe. During their passage he took the opportunity to ask the officers in a body what effect the President's Proclamation of Freedom had produced in the South. They reply was . . . that "it had played hell with them." Mr. Dean then asked them how that could be possible, since the negroes cannot read. To which one of them replied that one of his negroes had told him of the proclamation five days before he heard it in any other way. Others said their negroes gave them their first information of the proclamation. [50]

And in the third place, the proclamation irrevocably committed the United States, before the gaze of the whole world, to the early eradication of slavery

---

48 Ruffin MS Diary, July, 1862, LC.
49 *Autobiography*, 286.
50 Letter to Horatio Seymour, Sept. 28, 1863, Seymour Papers, LC. Sherman was using about 600 additional Negroes as stevedores, teamsters, cooks, and the like. More Negro men would have fled but for the fact they could not bring wives and children along. Sherman, Aug. 30, 1862, to Capt. Lewis B. Parsons, Parsons Papers. Herbert Aptheker in *Negro Slave Revolts* offers illuminating data on the readiness of slaves to escape.

from those wide regions where it was most deeply rooted; after which, all men knew, it could never survive on the borders. There could be no turning back! The government had dedicated itself to the termination of the inherited anachronism that had so long retarded the nation's progress, and crippled its pretensions to the leadership of the liberal forces of the globe. What was more, Lincoln had converted the war into a struggle for the rights of labor in the broadest sense.

[VI]

The reception given the proclamation ran the gamut from Greeley's paean of joy to Southern denunciations of it as a malignant effort to excite a servile revolt. The radical carping at Lincoln temporarily ceased. He had not merely pledged freedom to four million blacks, wrote Greeley; he was freeing twenty millions of whites from an ancient thralldom. For the moment Wade, Sumner, Chandler, Thad Stevens, Ashley, and their associates were transported. Charles Eliot Norton could scarcely see to pen a letter for his tears. "The President may be a fool," wrote George William Curtis to Frederick Law Olmsted, a stubborn critic. "But see what he has done. He may have no policy. But he has given us one." Among temperate free-soilers a great body undoubtedly took the view indicated by David Davis. "The people," he wrote an Illinois friend, "are fast getting into the belief that as quiet and moderate war measures have accomplished no good, severe measures are now necessary, and if the rebels will not lay down their arms, that is the duty of the Govt. to smite them hip and thigh." [51]

The highest note was struck by those who viewed the proclamation in the light of its liberating power: Whittier, Bryant, Lowell, all using pens tipped with flame. Most eloquently of all rose the voice of Emerson, declaring in the *Atlantic* that the force of the act was its commitment of the republic to justice. Doing this, it proved that the Northern soldiers had not died in vain; it made a victory of the sad defeats; it repaired the health of the nation. It was by no means necessary, he went on, that it should produce any sudden or signal results in the ranks of either the slaves or the slavemasters; indeed, the final redemption of the black race must lie with the blacks. Still, this ill-fated, much injured people would benefit at once. They will "lose somewhat of the dejection sculptured for ages in their bronzed countenances, and uttered in the wailing of their plaintive music"—a race naturally benevolent, joyous, and in-

---

51 Greeley in N. Y. *Tribune*, Sept. 23, 24, 1862; Curtis, Sept. 29, 1862, Olmsted Papers; Davis, Nov. 26, 1862, David Davis Papers.

dustrious, whose very miseries sprang from their talent for usefulness, "which in a more moral age, will not only defend their independence, but will give them a rank among nations." [52]

The jeers of the South were echoed by hisses and groans from the copperhead press of the North. The New York *Express* declared that this foolscap thunder would add 300,000 men to the rebel armies, and bring 30,000 Kentuckians to the side of Bragg. It was grand-scale bunkum, swaggering bravado, which, alas! converted a war for the Constitution into a war against Southern rights and liberties.[53] The Chicago *Times* took the same position. Two chords on which Northern objectors harped were that the proclamation altered the objects of the war, and that its direct result would be a heavy influx of Negroes into the free States. Indiana and Illinois already barred Negro immigrants. S. S. Cox of Ohio, a State which had no bar but repeatedly considered raising one, had already dwelt in his House speeches on Northern fears of a flood of freedmen. Could anyone be sure that Ohio troops would continue fighting if the fruit of their sacrifices was a northward flow of "millions of blacks?" [54] It saddened Lincoln to find his friend Orville H. Browning, his helper in revising the inaugural address, and an able exponent of his Borderland policy, taking the same Negrophobe stand.

In private utterances, few Northern critics were harsher than McClellan, who was aware that Democrats spoke of him as their next Presidential nominee. The ink was hardly dry on the newspaper headlines before he was sounding out the merchant William H. Aspinwall; "I am very anxious to learn how you and the men like you regard the recent Proclamation of the Presdt inaugurating servile war, emancipating the slaves, and at one stroke of the pen changing our free institutions into a despotism—for such I regard as the natural effect of the last Proclamation suspending the habeas corpus throughout the land." [55] His ideas were shared by Fitz-John Porter, who maliciously reported to Manton Marble of the *World*: "The Proclamation was ridiculed in the army—causing disgust, discontent, and expressions of disloyalty to the views of the administration, amounting I have heard, to insubordination, and for this reason—All such bulletins tend only to prolong the war by rousing the bitter feelings of the South—and causing unity of action among them—while the reverse with us. Those who fight the battles of the country are tired of the war and wish to see

52 *Atlantic Monthly*, X (Nov., 1862), 638–642; a forecast of free Ethiopia, Ghana, Liberia, Nigeria, and all the rest. Whittier's "Laus Deo" and Bryant's "The Death of Slavery" in due course fittingly commemorated the great step. "Great is the virtue of the Proclamation," wrote Emerson in his journals. "It works when men are sleeping, when the army goes into winter quarters, when generals are treacherous or imbecile."
53 Oct. 20, 22, 1862.
54 *Cong. Globe*, 37th Cong., 2d Sess., 2501–2503, June 3, 1862.
55 Sept. 26, 1862, extra-illustrated *Battles and Leaders*, HL.

it ended soon and honorably—by a restoration of the union—not merely a suppression of the rebellion." [56]

The question of the real attitude of the troops toward the document is too complex, and the evidence too conflicting, for easy summarization. The army was a reflection of the nation, possessing its radical and conservative wings. But certainly Fitz-John Porter misstated the attitude. The safest generalization is this: that most Northern soldiers approved of the proclamation, but did so not so much from humanitarian motives as because their blood was now up, they wanted to win a decisive victory, and Lincoln's edict seemed to herald a relentless prosecution of the war. The army, Colonel W. H. Blake of the Ninth Indiana wrote Schuyler Colfax, has one central idea, to whip the rebels and dictate peace. It contained little abolitionist sentiment; but "there is a desire to destroy everything that in *aught* gives the rebels strength," "there is a universal desire among the soldiery to take the negro from the secesh master," and so "this army will sustain the emancipation proclamation and enforce it with the bayonet." [57]

But though the plain soldier, like Lincoln, thought of emancipation primarily as a war measure, in countless instances he also rejoiced in its enlargement of human freedom. As the Union troops in marching South studied the worst aspects of slavery, they quickly learned to hate it. When they saw the auction block, the whipping post, the iron gyve, when they glimpsed the field hand cringing under his master's gaze, when the fleeing slave bared his scarred back, or told a tale of young children wrenched from the mother's arms, they resolved that slavery must die.[58]

One result of the proclamation was to turn a potentially harmful convention of Northern governors at Altoona, Pennsylvania, into an innocuous farce. Its prime mover was Andrew G. Curtin of Pennsylvania, who early in September had written Andrew of Massachusetts that the time was ripe to give the war a definite aim, and that the loyal executives should take prompt, united, decisive action. Correspondence among various Northern governors followed. Tod of Ohio, Blair of Michigan, Berry of New Hampshire, Pierrepont of Connecticut, and others were drawn into the movement. It inevitably aroused some pernicious newspaper speculation that it was hostile to Lincoln, that it aimed at the overthrow of McClellan, that it was a maneuver by Andrew and Curtin to get themselves re-elected, and so on. Happily, these two governors had enough sense to go to Lincoln beforehand. He told them of his impending proclamation, and with characteristic considerateness asked if they wished him to defer

56 Sept. 30, 1862, Manton Marble Papers, LC.
57 Glasgow, Ky., Nov. 7, 1862, Colfax Papers, Ind. State Lib.
58 See T. F. Dornblaser, *Sabre Strokes of the Pennsylvania Dragoons*, 120-121, for a vigorous statement.

its issuance until they had requested him to act. They replied that he should by all means bring it out first, and they would follow it with a strong address of commendation.[59] This was done; the conference met on the Allegheny crest September 24, and agreed to a paper written by Andrew. All appended their names but Bradford of Maryland, who, aware how deeply his State was torn, remarked: "Gentlemen, I am with you heart and soul, but I am a poor man, and if I sign that address I may be a ruined one." Misrepresentation of the conference nevertheless persisted, and it had better never been held.

The fact was that some of these governors had been as deeply pained as Stanton and Chase by the reassignment of McClellan to command. John A. Andrew, for one, detested the general. Like many other leaders in this terrible crisis, he became overwrought at times. Once this summer he fell on his knees in his office to pray for emancipation, and made a visitor pray with him! He had written Count Gurowski on September 6: "Besides doing my proper work, I am sadly but firmly trying to help organize some movement, if possible to save the Prest. from the infamy of ruining his country." Curtin, Yates, and Austin Blair felt much the same. But now they knew that Lincoln, after all, had not fallen into reactionary hands or taken a wrong step.

[VII]

Two facts were now abundantly clear: Lincoln was running the war, the reins of power held tightly in his muscular grip; and he was determined to run it so that the North would keep the initiative on all fronts—military, economic, and moral. If McClellan were not a useful implement in maintaining offensive operations, he would discard McClellan. But the Union would relax no pressure and neglect no effort. And no man better grasped the essence of statesmanship, which is the achievement of what is practicable within the limits of what is desirable.

That Lincoln regarded the proclamation not merely as opening a sterner war, but as announcing a revolution, is clear from the message he shortly sent Congress. It *was* revolution, though he hoped to keep it a controlled revolution. When at this very time he made his before-quoted remark to T. J. Barnett about so shaping the tragic conflict that it should always have a peace in its belly, he made it plain that if the South did not yield during the hundred days before the preliminary proclamation gave way to the final document, it must face a mighty socioeconomic upheaval. "What I write," Barnett warned S. L. M. Bar-

59 The Austin Blair and Andrew Papers have full correspondence; see also the statement Curtin gave Rufus Rockwell Wilson in 1881, *Lincoln Herald*. W. B. Hesseltine in *Lincoln and the War Governors, passim*, presents evidence that the governors were anxious to maintain State authority as against Lincoln's growing use of Federal power.

low for the benefit of New York Democrats, "was indicated plainly enough by the President—but I know more of his spirit than his publications imply. The idea is this—From the expiration of the 'days of grace' the character of the war will be changed. It will be one of subjugation and extermination if the North can be coerced and coaxed into it. The South [i.e., the old Southern system] is to be destroyed and replaced by new propositions and ideas." [60]

To those who had eyes, the lineaments of Lincoln's greatness were emerging. His great decision, premature to some, tardy to others, had been taken with his acute instinct for the ripening moment. No journal expressed this fact better than the Springfield *Republican:* "The President's action is timely—neither too soon nor too late. It is thorough—neither defeating itself by halfway measures nor by passionate excess. It is just and magnanimous— doing no wrong to any loyal man, and offering no exasperation to the disloyal. It is practical and effective—attempting neither too little nor too much. And it will be sustained by the great mass of the loyal people, North and South; and thus, by the courage and prudence of the President, the greatest social and political revolution of the age will be triumphantly carried through in the midst of a civil war." [61]

But the most remarkable aspect of Lincoln's stroke was its impact on world opinion—a subject of momentous consequence. . . .

60 Dated "Friday" (Sept. 25, 1862), Barlow Papers.
61 Sept. 24, 1862. Congress had approved of Lincoln's general plan for colonizing freedmen on the Chiriqui coast of Panama in New Granada (Colombia), and in April and June, 1862, had appropriated $600,000 for the settlement there of Negroes liberated under the Confiscation Act and in the District of Columbia. Secretary Usher of the Interior Department was ready to push the undertaking. But Lincoln, seeing that some "political hacks"— Senator S. C. Pomeroy of Kansas was one—hoped to enrich themselves from the contemplated contract, drew back. His hesitancy was shared by Seward, who had become doubtful about the title to the Chiriqui lands and the existence of good coal there. In October, Lincoln bade Usher to tell Pomeroy that the enterprise would be abandoned indefinitely.

9.

Europe, and especially Britain, watched the fighting of 1862 and heard the message of the Emancipation Proclamation. In the late summer of 1862 it is "hardly too much to say that the future of the world as we know it was at stake." No battle of the war "was more important than the contest waged in the diplomatic arena and the forum of public opinion." [1] Permission for the raider *Alabama* to be built and to leave Britain, economic strains, and frequent suggestions about possible mediation and armistice increased tension between the North and Britain. The Emancipation Proclamation dispelled British doubt over the moral issue, while Northern preparations for campaigning in 1863 dispelled doubts about Northern stamina and skill. "The great redeeming feature of the record is the decisive part played by considerations of decency, justice, and humanity as felt by the plain people on both sides of the ocean." [2]

Along the warring fronts the battling continued in the fall of 1862. Raiding, especially in the West, became more and more frequent; guerrilla warfare mounted, principally in Missouri. Confederate General Braxton Bragg launched a fast-moving drive from Chattanooga through central Tennessee and into Kentucky, bypassing Federals under Don Carlos Buell. Finally Buell's army defeated Bragg's army at Perryville, Kentucky, October 8, 1862, and the Confederates moved back to Murfreesboro, Tennessee, below Nashville. In a real sense the invasions by Bragg in Kentucky and by Lee in Maryland "represented the high tide of the Confederate cause." [3] Other fighting at Iuka and Corinth, Mississippi, and along the Mississippi River in the fall resulted in continued Federal threats to the entire valley. Vicksburg, Mississippi, the city on the bluffs guarding the heart of the river, still stood firm. It was obviously going to be the scene of major confrontation before too long, despite preliminary, unsuccessful efforts by the Union to take the city-fortress.

At year's end, Western fighting mounted to a high pitch. "The upheaval of war . . . so racked and brutalized large areas from the Ohio to the Gulf that even if the conflict could then have been halted, the task of reconstruction and regeneration would have been staggering. . . . The decent people of the republic were learning that sad as is the material destruction that accompanies war, the cultural, moral and spiritual losses are far more fearful. And the struggle was not yet half finished!" [4]

In the Eastern theater the lack of follow-up by McClellan after the battle of Antietam caused Lincoln much anxiety. In November he relieved the controversial general. "If Lincoln's removal of the general was questionable . . . it was a decision rendered unavoidable by McClellan's faults. . . ." McClellan was "a victim not of incapacity or inexperience but of his character and temperament." [5] Ambrose E. Burnside replaced the "little Napoleon" and moved the Army of the Potomac toward the central Virginia city of Fredericksburg.

On December 13 Burnside's army charged head-on against the well-posted forces of Lee—a Federal disaster of tragic magnitude and an expertly fought Confederate defensive victory. The military and political repercussions all made for a winter of dissension in Washington. Animosity between Chase of the Treasury and Seward of State provoked a cabinet crisis, causing further discord, although Lincoln dexterously smoothed things over.

On the Federal home front "the liberalization of government policy during the first half of 1862 proved only a prelude to new rigors in the second half. Military failures East and West bred pessimism and distrust, so that disloyalty grew bolder. . . ." [6] The suspension of habeas corpus in some cases, political arrests, and the suppression of some allegedly Copperhead newspapers in 1862 and throughout the war caused considerable opposition, despite administration claims that these civil liberties were violated only to help preserve the Union. The off-year Congressional and state elections went against the administration, to some extent. While the Copperheads never endangered the Union, their raucous voices made them appear more virulent than they really were. But by the spring of 1863 rallies for the war were more prevalent, and there was a definite ebb in the opposition. [7] Dissent remained amorphous.

"It was clear to men in Washington that even amid reverses, Lincoln revealed a steady augmentation of self-confidence and decision. The Emancipation Proclamation had enhanced his prestige. He had fully established his personal and Presidential authority." [8] The Preliminary Emancipation Proclamation of September had been followed, as promised, by the final proclamation of January 1, 1863. The President showed no signs of retreating from his decision.

On January 25, 1863, Lincoln named Joseph Hooker to replace Burnside. Hooker, with great bombast, led the Army of the Potomac up and across the Rappahannock from Fredericksburg, into the Virginia Wilderness, and to an obscure crossroads house known as Chancellorsville. At first it seemed that

Hooker was well beyond Lee's left flank, and then the Federals—or rather Hooker—bogged down. Lee's brilliance in splitting his army and Jackson's successful flank march on May 2 led to a stunning Confederate victory over the Federals. But Confederate cheers were stilled by the mortal wounding of their beloved hero, Stonewall Jackson. Down at Charleston the Federal Navy, too, had failed in its attack on Sumter and Charleston, and the bombardment from land and sea did no lasting damage to the defenders. It seemed that the North took such grave reverses in its stride. Union troops could be replaced; Confederates not always, if at all. The war of attrition was telling.

By mid-1863 the "inevitable outcome of the war was foreshadowed by the fact that while in defeat the North grew stronger, in victory the South became weaker. . . . Unsteadily, sometimes obscurely, but inexorably, forces of internal change by 1863 were transforming American life. The South stood face to face with a socioeconomic revolution from which not even victory could extricate it." [9] "No change in the fortunes of war could now long halt the multiform revolution of the time: the emergence of the North to industrial strength, the replacement of improvisation by plan and organization, the shattering of the slave system." [10] Symbolic of this change were the black soldiers, "chattels no more," marching into battle at Charleston, Vicksburg, and elsewhere.

The war "carried a confusing array of impressions and meanings to the millions, North and South, who were caught in its toils; to the North who felt they were fighting for Emancipation and for Union, two great causes, and to the South who believed they were fighting for Independence. . . . Even while the conflict was producing its heroes, it was becoming more impersonal. It was a war of peoples; of organizations pitted against organizations. . . . The temper of the country was changing. It was becoming tougher, harsher, and coarser; it had cast aside old romanticisms and sentimentalities." [11]

"The North in 1863 held four tremendous advantages: first, its possession of a chief of state who was indisputably the greatest American of his time; second, its ever-growing superiority in manpower, natural resources, all phases of economic life, and money; third, its open ports, largely undamaged rail and river transportation system, and its unoccupied territory; and fourth, the moral superiority that a combatant of slavery could assert over a defender of slavery, although all did not agree on the weight of this. These advantages were sternly impressive, but they were not irresistible. The valor, dash, and tenacity of the South had to be reckoned with. To the end of June in 1863 it had won more tactical victories in the East than had the North, and one of the most striking facts about the war at this period was that these traits, com-

bined with high military leadership, might yet possibly produce a deadlock
—which would mean Confederate success." [12]

NOTES

1. Nevins, *The War for the Union*, Vol. II, *War Becomes Revolution, 1862–1863*, p. 242.
2. *Ibid.*, p. 274.
3. *Ibid.*, p. 289.
4. *Ibid.*, p. 298.
5. *Ibid.*, pp. 331–332.
6. *Ibid.*, pp. 315–316.
7. *Ibid.*, p. 393.
8. *Ibid.*, p. 399.
9. *Ibid.*, pp. 482–483.
10. *Ibid.*, p. 528.
11. Nevins, *The War for the Union*, Vol. III, *The Organized War, 1863–1864*, p. 117.
12. *Ibid.*, p. 45.

Vicksburg: The Organized Victory

THE NATION'S attention was now drawn abruptly to a review of events that had been absorbing the West, and to a study of the prospects immediately at hand in Mississippi. To most Northerners this was a novel scene. Some visitors knew the State as a fertile land of winter greenery, mild breezes in spring and autumn, and mellow winters. Other Northerners had only a vague general knowledge that it was a wide, rich part of the great central Mississippi Valley, and that its growth in population, agricultural production, and river and railroad commerce had made it vital to the life and authority of the battling South. This was an area established upon a unique mingling of slaves and freemen, of whites, blacks and mulattoes, upon a social culture in part cultivated and liberal, and in part ill-educated and marked by decidedly reactionary views, social, economic and political. It stretched from the tawny waters of the Mississippi River on the west, to the low, rolling hills in the central area, white with cotton, and to the piney woods in the north; it stretched from the feudal traditions and principles of Natchez to the bustling, commercial activities and progressive ideas of Meridian and Waynesboro.[1] Its university town, Oxford, was to give birth to one of the greatest men in American letters, William Faulkner, and was long the home of the jurist and courageous thinker, L.Q.C. Lamar, a member of Cleveland's Cabinet. Missis-

---

1. Davis, Reuben, *Recollections of Mississippi and Mississippians,* Heston, 1889, calls attention to the picturesque interest of Mississippi towns in the half-century before the Civil War. It is dedicated by the author to the lawyers of the State, and describes Natchez in the days of the fiery Quitman, Vicksburg in times of the eloquent S.S. Prentiss, and Athens, Corinth, and Aberdeen. This had been a land of duels, and vindictive political feuds, but also a State where many men read as widely as did Jefferson Davis, and prized the arts of conversation and story-telling as much as the people described by the novelist, Stark Young, in his *So Red the Rose,* and by William Alexander Percy in his reminiscent *Lanterns on the Levee.*

Mississippi was primarily, but by no means exclusively, an agricultural state, as J.K. Bettersworth makes plain in *Confederate Mississippi,* Baton Rouge, 1943, 270; Vicksburg was, of course, the commercial metropolis, and Frederick L. Olmsted described its bustling activity in *A Journey in the Back Country,* New York, 1860. This "terraced city of the hills," as it was called, had a public school with 500 children before the war, and a public reading room. The town of Jackson drew vigor from the facts that it held the seat of government in the State, and lay at the junction of the main cross-line State railways, containing numerous people of German, Italian and French origin. Russell, W.H., *My Diary North and South,* London, 1863, *passim.*

(*The War for the Union,* Vol. III, *The Organized War, 1863–1864,* Chapter 2.)

sippi, a part of a great coastal plain widening as it stretched southward, was a muddy land like much of Alabama and Louisiana, given sporadic firmness by the gravel brought down by seasonal floods and by its abundant streams which were productive also of crops of pestiferous mosquitoes.

Mississippi had no mineral deposits comparable to Pennsylvania's, for example, or energy-producing waterfalls equal to those in New England, but students of history were aware of the importance of its strategic position on the Mississippi River, leading up to the Missouri and the Ohio. Mark Twain gives something of the flavor of the place in his *Life on the Mississippi,* including a chapter on the "art of inundation," and describing a town that would "come up to glow in the summer." This State regarded the Civil War with deep and abiding feeling. Mark Twain would later write about the multiplicity of steel-engravings of historic scenes which adorned every Mississippi home in post-war years—scenes that might be entitled: "First Interview Between Lee and Jackson," "Last Interview Between Lee and Jackson," "Jackson Accepting Lee's Invitation to Dinner," "Jackson Declining Lee's Invitation to Dinner," "Jackson Apologizing to Lee for a Heavy Defeat," "Jackson Reporting a Splendid Victory to Lee," and so forth, *ad infinitum.*

[I]

Everyone North and South knew that Vicksburg was of crucial importance. One main object of Confederate leadership in invading the North and fighting at Gettysburg was the hope that this action would compel the Union to halt its operations on the Misssissippi, where a Northern break-through would clearly be decisive. A lesser but allied attempt to divert Union pressure from the great river artery was planned at the same time by the gallant Kirby-Smith, who believed that he might act from west of the Mississippi, with the cooperation of Major-General Theophilus Holmes in Arkansas and Major-General Richard Taylor in West Louisiana. He was encouraged in this enterprise by the success of General John Bankhead Magruder, a West Pointer and veteran of the Seminole and Mexican Wars, who had fought ably in the Seven Days Battles before taking command of the Department of Texas in 1862 (a Department later enlarged to include New Mexico and Arizona). Magruder had cleared Texas of a great part of the Union invaders sent against him.[2]

Kirby-Smith's early prospects seemed bright. He found an able associate in "Dick" Taylor, the son of President Zachary Taylor, who had studied at Edinburgh, Harvard, and Yale, before fighting in the Mexican War and being commissioned Colonel of the 72nd New York. Tall, slender, finely dressed, Taylor was

2. Foote, Shelby, *The Civil War,* New York, 1958, Vol.II, 596-597 describes this ambitious plan.

so proud of his handsome countenance that he refused to wear glasses lest they mar his appearance. His gracious manners and fine courtesy, combined with his descent from Zachary Taylor, won him the complimentary appellation of "Prince Dick." Kirby-Smith himself had many gifts, but unfortunately other officers concerned in the campaign were less distinguished. Holmes proved slow and uncertain. Born late in 1804, he was now elderly, and the fact that he had been a classmate of Jefferson Davis at West Point ceased to count in his favor. He was soon sent to North Carolina to take charge of that State's reserves. The Confederate leader, John S. Marmaduke, a great favorite in Arkansas, made a raid into Missouri in the hope of capturing Helena, but he was repulsed at Cape Girardeau and defeated. Dick Taylor failed in his plans for recapturing New Orleans. Checkmate of the Confederates was to be complete when these two efforts, and Lee's desperate charge at Cemetery Hill, all broke down on July 3rd, the critical day at Gettysburg. On the morning of that day, white flags also blossomed out along the Confederate lines defending Vicksburg.[3]

After Farragut had run past New Orleans, steamed on up the river, and dropped anchor; after Mansfield Lovell had evacuated New Orleans and his retiring Confederates had fired warehouses, cotton, boats, and goods of all kinds along the levees, it was plain that Vicksburg must be the next objective of the Union forces in their drive to cut the Confederacy in two and open a waterway into the middle of the South. This first long stride must be followed by a second. Supplies from the West were plainly indispensable to the Confederacy. Admiral Porter remarked that the shipment of western supplies through Mississippi meant the steady flow of great quantities of hogs and hominy, large contingents of rebel troops, and indeed, of all the resources remaining in the Arkansas and Texas country as well as farther south and west. "Let us get Vicksburg!" Porter exclaimed, "and that country is ours!"

Grant had fully understood from the outset the exigent importance of clearing and sealing the great river. But how should it be done?

This was a war in which every road to success had to be paved with incessant efforts and frequent failures. The background of Grant's undertaking was gloomy. As he approached his great effort, Rosecrans was still recovering from the sickening losses of Murfreesboro, where, beginning with 40,000 effective troops, his brilliantly promising campaign had terminated in a drawn battle. He had moved his Army of the Cumberland out of Nashville just after Christmas Day in 1862 to attack General Bragg's troops near Murfreesboro (alternatively called Stone's River). The battle went on from December 31, 1862 to January 3, 1863. Bragg had been weakened by the despatch of an entire division of his force for the fighting in Mississippi, but he defended himself skillfully. Altogether, Rose-

3. *Ibid.*, II, 596-605.

crans lost 7,543 men wounded, and 1,294 killed. When Bragg evacuated Murfreesboro, Rosecrans's adherents credited him with a victory, yet the Union army was
not able to deliver another blow again for half-a-year.

Several events preceding the Vicksburg campaign influenced the movements
of Grant at this point. After the evacuation of Corinth, General Halleck, who had
gathered an army of 100,000 men, instead of pushing on to pursue the Confederate army, had deliberately divided his forces, adopting a purely passive defense.
Such conduct was, indeed, inexcusable.[4] On October 31, 1862, Halleck went to
Washington to take command of the army, leaving Grant in control of the
Department of Tennessee. Grant was holding the Mobile & Ohio Railroad from
a point 25 miles south of Corinth, with about 75,000 men, divided into four groups,
some of them new levies.

On the Confederate side, Pemberton held a large army—one large body at
Vicksburg, and another at Port Hudson—about 30,000 at the two places. The
rebels had fortified the Port Hudson area from about twenty miles above and
forty miles below the Red River—the Red River being the chief channel of
communication between Arkansas, Louisiana, and Texas. Most of the grain for
Confederate armies came over this Red River route, and the three States named
sent 100,000 troops into the Confederate armies.[5]

If the Union army could gain possession either of Vicksburg or Port Hudson,
it could open the Mississippi to navigation by the superior Union naval power
and thus cut the Confederacy in two.

In the East came defeat at Chancellorsville, May 2-4, 1863, but before this and
other sad and weary news came in from Tennessee and Virginia, Grant and
Porter had been struggling with a series of obstacles, miscalculations, and reverses
that were equally depressing. They held undiscouraged hopes for a time of
opening a new waterway for the Union forces from the Mississippi River to the
upper part of the Yazoo River, which, with many a loop, and with numerous
out-thrown bayous and lakelets, connected with the Mississippi River west of
Vicksburg, and west also of the Walnut Hills bordering the Mississippi.

On January 17, 1863, Grant announced that he would take command in person
of the Union forces against Vicksburg. On January 29 he arrived at Young's Point
near Vicksburg, and on January 30 he assumed command. The problem was to
gain a footing on the dry ground east of the river, so that his troops could move
from this position against Vicksburg. The Mississippi Valley country surrounding the city was a terrain of almost intolerable difficulty, an appalling combination
of hills, wooded valleys with steep sides, superabundant water, deep bayous

---

4. Livermore, William R., *The Military History of Massachusetts*, Vol. XV, 541-585, says an excellent
discussion of the operations before Vicksburg will be found in Major John Bigelow's book, *The
Principles of Strategy*, New York, 1891, 540.

5. Livermore, *op.cit.*, 543; Church, William Conant, *Grant*, New York, 1897, 156.

infested with snakes and alligators, thicket-filled ravines, canebrakes, poisonous shrubs, and boggy paths. The previous winter of 1862-63 had witnessed heavy rains, raising streams, lakes and swamps to unusual levels, and leaving but few stretches of the land sufficiently dry to furnish a road, a camp ground, or even a burial place for dead soldiers. As fighting progressed, and disease and sharp-shooters took a heavy toll, many Northern soldiers had to be interred in the levees adjoining the Yazoo, the Mississippi and other streams. Malarial fever, small-pox and measles broke out among the men. Visitors to the camps told dismal stories of them on returning home, which Northern newspapers relayed back to the soldiers in grossly exaggerated form. Grant wrote of this time in his *Memoirs* that "the real work of the campaign and siege of Vicksburg now began."[6]

The Union leaders found that, for an army to approach Vicksburg from the north, the troops must encounter, as they neared the city, the vast bottomland known as the Yazoo Delta. This difficult stretch of land extends northward along the Mississippi and parallel to its border of Walnut Hills for 175 miles, comprising more than several thousand square miles. Much of the land is soft, very low, and wet. Were it not for the levees built along the Mississippi to hold it back, the Delta would be under water for a large part of the year. A force burdened by heavy guns and wagons would find it an obstacle almost as difficult, and in places impassable, as any large chain of timber-choked hills. If Grant threw an army across the Mississippi and tried to approach Vicksburg on the east of the river from either front or rear, north or south, he would find the approaches equally fraught with difficulties. Troops moving upward toward Vicksburg would have to be supplied by boats, and these boats would have to run the Vicksburg batteries. Hence, Grant's initial effort in November and December of 1862 to beleaguer and seize Vicksburg by a stroke combining land and water operations had been completely checked. He was compelled to keep the Union troops based on the *west* bank of the Mississippi, somewhat upstream from a point opposite the city. While he lay there, making plan after plan to get his troops into position before Vicksburg, seeing one scheme after another fail, he perceived the necessity of engaging the attention of the Confederates by diversionary enterprises. From this perception was born the dramatic raid by Col. Benjamin H. Grierson with a brigade of cavalry, moving swiftly from LaGrange, Tennessee, deep into the South in an effort to cut the Mobile & Ohio Railroad, running east from Vicksburg to Jackson, the capital of Mississippi, and on into the interior. Grierson's diversion prevented the Confederates from dispatching troops from Vicksburg to Port Hudson.

A classic narrative of Grierson's foray, written by S.H.M. Byers, explains how, after Sherman had failed to get across the Mississippi at Vicksburg, Grant

6. Livermore, *op.cit.*, 550-551; Grant, *Memoirs* I, 458.

moved the whole army in the spring of 1863 down the river to begin one of his immortal campaigns.[7] Byers writes that Grant built long stretches of corduroy roads and bridges that ran snake-like for forty miles among the black swamps, canebrakes, and lagoons on the west side of the Mississippi, bivouacking his men on the river shore while Byer's regiment remained above the city as part of a force of possibly 25,000 men holding the Union position there. He describes the momentous passage of Union vessels down the river in terms reflecting the excitement he felt. The sky was black ink, as the Confederates lighted bonfires and opened their guns. The channel became a sheet of flame. The roar of rebel guns from the bluffs, some of them big ten-inch cannon, became thunderous, as cannonballs and shells made some lucky hits, and as Union soldiers and sailors leaped from their craft into the water to escape, "Hell seemed loose." Then suddenly, at dawn came silence. The fleet under Porter had passed the city. Eleven boats had passed the river batteries safely; a twelfth boat was sunk. On the night of April 16 the cheering troops welcomed the advance vessels. Now they felt the campaign could begin in earnest.

Soldiers who had been encamped on the levees up about Milliken's Bend came tramping down through ponds and swamps on little roads, lanes, and paths, to the point where the Union vessels had anchored. The ferrying of additional troops day and night across the river at once began. Byers' force, impressed by the battle-scarred ships of the Union navy, hurried by rapid marches, punctuated by engagements, toward positions in the rear of Vicksburg and Jackson, foraging on farms as they went, and filling their canteens from creeks as they tramped roadways deep in yellow dust. Byers offers a lively description of the assault by McPherson's corps on the Vicksburg lines on the 19th, where he heard Logan's stentorian voice ring over the field, cheering on his troops as they advanced in fearful heat, until their forward ranks lay down in front of the defensive forts.[8]

Grant's intention of crossing at Grand Gulf proved infeasible after a six-hour bombardment failed to silence rebel fire, but on the next day, April 30, he made a completely successful landing on the east shore of the river at Bruinsburg, and was ready to move against the interior beyond Vicksburg. The Union army commenced its march on May 12, and after fighting sharp skirmishes at Raymond and other points, threw Northern forces into Jackson on the afternoon

7. Byers, S.H.M. *With Fire and Sword,* New York, 1911, 54-99. Major Byers of Sherman's staff, a Missourian with bristling moustaches, gives a spirited description of the hot, dusty Union march to Jackson, the long, exhausting siege of that Mississippi capital, and the climactic rebel capitulation. He credits Grant with the plan of attacking Vicksburg from the south, going down the Mississippi to win a firm foothold, and says it had occurred to nobody else. Evidence exists that Frank Blair and Charles A. Dana supported Grant in his plans for a landing at Grand Gulf, treating the possible response of the public to any failure with contempt. Lewis, Lloyd, *Sherman, Fighting Prophet,* New York, 1932, *passim.*

8. Byers, *op.cit., passim.*

of May 14. On May 16, blue-clad troops under McPherson and McClernand came into heavy collision with Confederate forces at Champion's Hill, one of the bloodiest battles of the whole Vicksburg campaign. On the 19th came the tragic assault in which Grant's troops were flung back by Pemberton's army at every point.[9]

On the 22nd Grant mistakenly repeated his assault, for he was anxious to avoid a protracted siege of Vicksburg, which would require him to withdraw needed Union troops from other points. In his second attack, Union casualties were again heavy, and Grant to the end of his days regretted his orders bitterly.[10]

The siege of Vicksburg required more than 70,000 Union troops to conduct it, and at the same time hold the Confederate defensive army under Joseph E. Johnston at bay. The people of the city and the Confederate forces were subjected to a pitiless bombardment, and suffered increasingly from a desperate shortage of food and a lengthening list of casualties from wounds and sickness. By July 3rd, the Confederate officers and men were convinced that the situation was hopeless, and they were ready to discuss terms of surrender.

In the spring of 1863, an observant British officer, Lieutenant-Colonel A.J. Lyon Fremantle, entered the Confederacy by the Matamoros gateway, and after arduous travel across Texas, reached Natchez in mid-May. He found the people of Mississippi fearfully excited and distressed by the conflict raging among them. The capital, Jackson, had just seen the Fifty-ninth Indiana unfurl the Union flag, and watched Grant briefly pace its streets. Then the Northern army had marched westward to cut off John Pemberton's force from that of Joseph E. Johnston. Striking Pemberton two quick, heavy blows, Grant's troops forced him back into Vicksburg. Reaching Jackson soon after Grant evacuated it, Fremantle found factories demolished, houses pillaged, railroads torn up, and piles of stores still burning. The citizens spoke with fury of the outrages they had undergone, and of their hope for a bloody revenge—for retaliation without quarter. But when he joined General Johnston not far from the capital, the Briton heard respectful words upon Union accomplishments. Grant, conceded Johnston, had displayed an astonishing rapidity and energy. On April 30, he had thrown a great part of his army across the river below Vicksburg in a movement of unexampled boldness; on May 14, with an enlarged force well in hand, he had driven the Confederates out of Jackson; and on May 15-19, he had routed them and put an iron investment around the river fortress. It was plain that Johnston did not expect Vicksburg to hold out long. The distant thud and roll of the bombardment was already continuous. Soldiers and civilians alike were highly critical of Pemberton

9. Jones, Jenkin L., *An Artilleryman's Diary*, Madison, 1914, *passim.*, Jones, an eminent Unitarian minister in Chicago, then an artilleryman, told how the Union officers brought up howitzers to the line of caissons before the city.
10. Grant, *Memoirs*, II, 276.

for letting himself be outmanocuvred, and some even doubted the loyalty of the Northern-born Confederate general.

Everywhere, Fremantle found evidence of superior Union strength and a determination to use it with iron resolution. Leonidas Polk told him how heavily the Confederates had been outnumbered at Murfreesboro. Johnston, with a somewhat careless misuse of figures, but no great misrepresentation of the general situation, declared that a garrison of only 20,000 in Vicksburg was besieged by 75,000 troops under Grant; and some of the rebel soldiers, confident despite recent defeats, were clamoring to be led against "only twicet" their own numbers. A brigade, just arrived at Jackson under "States-Rights" Gist, bore good Enfield rifles, but other units were armed only with what they had captured from the enemy. Fremantle heard that Pemberton had lost much of his artillery at Champion's Hill and Edwards' Station; he had, in fact, lost 42 pieces. Johnston was eager to attack, but as he told the Englishman, he was too weak to do any good.

Crossing Mississippi and Alabama eastward, Fremantle saw these States giving up their last sons and ultimate resources in an extremity of anguish. The raid of Grierson's cavalry through nearly the whole length of Mississippi in April, and other Union forays, had left trails of destruction smoking behind them. But the Confederacy was falling into dilapidation anyway. It was painful to hear an old planter gloating over the dead bodies of Northerners in Jackson; to find an officer regretful because a Yankee "surrendered so quick I couldn't kill him"; and to see gentlewomen wild with hatred. At William J. Hardee's headquarters three ladies depressed the Englishman with their innumerable stories of Yankee brutality. Fremantle glowed when General Johnston declared that ninety-nine Southerners in a hundred would rather be subjects of Queen Victoria than return to the Union; but the effect of the statement was spoiled when another officer said they would rather be minions even of His Satanic Majesty! Everywhere he saw misery —combined with resolution.

"We slept at a farmhouse (near Jackson). All the males were absent at the war, and it is impossible to exaggerate the unfortunate condition of the women left behind in the farmhouses; they have scarcely any clothes, and nothing but the coarsest bacon to eat, and are in miserable uncertainty as to the fate of their relations, whom they can hardly ever communicate with. Their slaves, however, generally remain true to them. . . . We breakfasted at another little farmhouse on some unusually tough bacon, and coffee made out of sweet potatoes. The natives, under all their misery, were red-hot in favor of fighting for their independence to the last." The Confederate, he wrote, "has no ambition to imitate the regular soldier at all; he looks the genuine rebel; but in spite of his bare feet, his ragged clothes, his old rug, and tooth-brush stuck like a rose in his button-hole, he has a devil-may-care, reckless, self-confident look, which is decidedly taking."[11]

When Fremantle left the West, Grant's army of some 75,000 effectives had to perform the double task of besieging Vicksburg and fending off Johnston. Pemberton had around 23,000 fit for duty, plus about 5,700 ill, while Johnston had some 28,000 effectives of 36,000 present.[12] If the Confederate armies had been united during the previous three months and strengthened with troops from west of the Mississippi, they would have been a fair match for Grant's army. As it was, their divided forces stood at a hopeless disadvantage. Grant's rear was protected by the Big Black River, winding down to join the Mississippi, and by a maze of hills, minor streams, swamps, and ravines.[13] Johnston telegraphed the Confederate War Department on June 15 that he regarded Vicksburg as good as lost. On the chessboard of war, the Northern forces had been deployed with far more masterly skill than the Southern.

[II]

Two Presidents from the Mississippi Valley led the Union and the Confederacy. Both Lincoln and Davis comprehended the vital importance of holding the Mississippi, but while Davis could not do anything about it, Lincoln could. If Richmond were lost, and Virginia taken, the Confederacy would suffer no vital injury, while if the Mississippi were lost, the back of the Confederacy would be broken. All the men and supplies in the rich area of western Louisiana, Texas, Arkansas, southern Missouri, and the Yazoo district of Mississippi would be sundered from the rest of the country. Great new stores of cotton would fall within the Northern grasp. Scores of thousands of able-bodied Negro men would be turned loose to become soldiers or laborers for the North.[14] The morale of the Northwest would rise to a point at which Copperhead feeling would wither and die; the morale of the lower Valley would sink to a point at which thousands of soldiers would desert to look after their homes.

Why did President Davis, Secretary Seddon, and General Lee fail to take decisive action to protect the Mississippi? Lee, because he thought Virginia more

11. Fremantle, Lieut. Col. A.J.L., *Three Months in the Southern States, April-June, 1863*, New York, 1864, *passim*. Greene, F.V., *The Mississippi*, New York, 1882, 188-190 for numbers. *O.R.* I, xxiv, Pt.3, 452-453, 978; Bearss, Edwin C., *Decision in Mississippi*, Jackson, Miss., 1962, 425, 432. Confederate figures in the Vicksburg Campaign are subject to even more than usual controversy, and it is difficult to be really very definite. Federal figures for troops in the immediate area had increased steadily during the siege.

12. Fremantle, *op.cit.*

13. "The country in this part of Mississippi stands on edge, as it were, the roads running along the ridges except where they occasionally pass from one ridge to another"; *Military History and Reminiscences of the Thirteenth Regiment of Illinois Volunteer Infantry*, Chicago, 1892, 313.

14. *O.R.* I, xxiv, Pt.I, 227. Of the 186,000 Negro troops whom the North enlisted in the South, the Mississippi historian J.S. McNeily states that 24,000 were recruited in Louisiana, 17,800 in Mississippi, and 20,000 in Tennessee: *Mississippi Historical Society Publications, Centenary Series*, II, 174.

important than the great river, knew himself better able to handle a great army than any Confederate general in the West, and supposed the summer climate would be fatal to sustained Union activity about Vicksburg. Seddon, because he was a Virginian, did not understand the logistical advantages which the steamboat gave the Union forces on the Mississippi, and underrated Grant's strength, enterprise, and daring. Moreover, the Confederate government could not manufacture the ironclads and shipping needed. Davis failed to act because he trusted in Lee, and because he still deemed foreign intervention the best hope of victory. To his mind, a victorious invasion of Pennsylvania would be the best means of achieving intervention. All three believed Joseph E. Johnston to be a more dynamic commander than he actually was.

We must repeat that the origins of the Union campaign against Vicksburg, far from being purely military, were in substantial part political. The full conquest of the Mississippi River, always vital in the eyes of the Northwest, had become urgent by the fall of 1862. Since John A. McClernand of Illinois—a veteran Jacksonian who had been elected to four terms in the Legislature and six in the national House, and who as a resident of Springfield since 1856 knew Lincoln well —understood the Northwestern demands, he was busy in Washington in the fall of 1862 crying for energetic action. Three governors, Samuel J. Kirkwood of Iowa, Richard Yates of Illinois, and Oliver P. Morton of Indiana, supported his call for action with a vigor born of their acute apprehension of Copperhead sedition. The Mississippi never eroded its banks more dangerously than dread of the loss of free navigation and control of the river eroded the loyalty of many dwellers in the upper valley. If they ever decided that Washington was indifferent to the great artery, they would react just as Kentuckians had reacted in the days of Aaron Burr and James Wilkinson. Morton believed that an army of 100,000 men could be marched straight down the western bank. McClernand more astutely proposed an attack on the central key to the river system, Vicksburg, by a strong fleet of gunboats and an army of 60,000 men—approximately the force which finally took it.

When Lincoln threw himself behind McClernand's plans, and Stanton equipped him with confidential orders in October to raise or mobilize troops in the Northwest and forward them to Cairo, Memphis, or some other rendezvous so that "an expedition may be organized under General McClernand's command against Vicksburg," the President was not actuated by any particular faith in McClernand's generalship. He knew nothing about it. He was moved by faith in McClernand's political insight, his influence over a powerful array of Jacksonian and Douglasite Democrats in the Middle West, and his energy. The President was also exhibiting a concern for the historic waterway that had no counterpart, unfortunately for the South, in Richmond. "I feel deep interest in the success of the expedition," he endorsed on McClernand's orders, "and desire it to be pushed forward with all possible dispatch, consistently with the other parts of the military service."[15]

Could the South have held the Mississippi if it had centred its main energies upon the task? Probably it could, if a number of posts between Island No. 10 and Port Hudson had been energetically fortified and provisioned; if a powerful mobile army had been kept intact under one bold general; and if this army had been given timely strength by reinforcements from Virginia and from Arkansas. Effective defensive measures could have been taken, but the necessity was not always clear, and in taking such measures the Confederacy would have weakened other areas. The country was full of provisions; it had insufficient transport, to be sure, but determined and resourceful officers, moving in time, could have accumulated enough salt-pork, corn, beans, rice, sugar, and molasses to feed garrisons in Vicksburg, Port Gibson, and Port Hudson for long periods. The river was as much a natural barrier for defense as a natural avenue for invasion. Effectively fortified to prevent the passage of boats—unarmed transports steaming down, slow-moving ironclads struggling upstream—it would have proved a valuable bulwark. The people of the lower valley felt strongly that the defense of New Orleans had been bungled; that it should never have been possible for Farragut to make so easy a conquest. They felt equally outraged that the Confederate flotilla at Memphis should have been so swiftly annihilated.[16]

The North won its triumphs at New Orleans and Memphis by naval power alone, but in the Vicksburg-Port Hudson area such victories were impossible. The Confederacy had critical advantages if it could use them; that is, if they were not nullified by weakness of command. After Grant asserted his primacy, however, the quality of the Northern generalship was as unquestioned as the quality of the Western troops.

Splendid Union armies had been forged in both the East and West, but forged in quite diverse ways. The primary creator of the Eastern army was McClellan, whose masterly skill made it a weapon which an abler strategist might have used to achieve victory. McClellan could not use it with slashing spirit because he was palsied by fear of the defeat that a supposedly superior adversary might inflict upon him. He was succeeded by three generals, Pope, Burnside, Hooker, who failed for different reasons. It was a tribute to the Army of the Potomac that, despite bloody reverses, it never lost the sense of unity which McClellan had instilled into it by careful, methodical drill, and which Hooker strengthened by his dash and pugnacity. The Western armies, meanwhile, had been forged and tempered not by endless drill combined with long avoidance of danger, but by

15. Lincoln, *Collected Works*, V, 468; VI, 230-231; Nicolay and Hay, *Lincoln*, VII, 135-143.
16. June 6, 1862; Greene, F.V., *The Mississippi*, New York, 1882, 14-17.

carly and grim fighting at close-quarters. The Western generals seasoned armies by throwing them into combat without delay. At Belmont, Forts Henry and Donelson, Shiloh, Corinth, and Iuka, the troops of Grant, Sherman, and Buell learned boldness and tenacity from action under heavy fire. Even the green regiments seldom flinched.[17]

In the West, Grant fought on the field with his men. At Belmont he was almost captured; at Donelson he was in the advance line when he learned from an examination of the Confederates' haversacks that they were trying to cut their way out; at Shiloh he risked his life again to help stay the initial rout, and was with his troops when they advanced to the attack on the second day. But McClellan's headquarters were usually so far from the battle-lines that, as a shrewd Scottish-born observer, General Peter S. Michie, says in his biography, "so far as his personal or professional influence was concerned, it may be almost completely ignored in all tactical combinations."[18] At Gaines' Mill his want of direct oversight let almost the whole weight of the Confederate attack fall upon one vastly outnumbered corps; at White Oak Swamp he supplied no effective leadership whatever; and at Malvern Hill he went aboard the gunboat *Galena* when his post of duty was ashore. The close liaison of Western troops and generals contributed to the confidence of the troops; they felt, writes one Ohio corporal under Grant, "strong faith in the sagacity of their leader."[19]

The Western armies differed from the Eastern, again, in that they were largely devoid of political coloration. The humility of Grant—untouched as yet by political ambition, fully aware of the supremacy of the civil authority, and highly deferential to Lincoln and Stanton—contrasted with the hard bright egotism which made McClellan feel himself indispensable to the army and country. McClellan felt bitter hatred for Stanton, and for Lincoln an approach to contempt; Grant held both in high regard. The various corps headquarters of the Army of the Potomac were full of political talk, and the talk in such tents as Fitz-John Porter's was dangerous. If the Western officers talked politics, it was very quietly. They had their prejudices. Some of them said at the beginning of 1863 that they would never serve with Negro regiments. But they surrendered these prejudices; three months later they declared that although Adjutant-General Lorenzo Thomas had erred in encouraging Negro recruiting, they would obey orders nonetheless.[20]

Once the Union leadership gave up the attempt to attack Vicksburg from the north, the blunders of the campaign were nearly all on the Confederate side. For months the Northern and Southern numbers in the campaign were approxi-

17. Except in the shock of the Shiloh surprise.
18. Michie, Peter S., *General McClellan*, New York, 1901, XV.
19. Hopkins, Owen J., *Under the Flag of the Nation*, ed. O.F. Bond, Columbus, Ohio, 1961, 54.
20. C.A. Dana, April 20, 1863, to Stanton, Dana Papers, LC.

mately equal. Moreover, at the beginning, and down to the battle of Port Gibson on May 1, 1863, the forces on each side were about equally scattered. On April 16, Porter's gunboats ran past the Vicksburg batteries. Grant was gathering his forces together on the west side of the river. As soon as he threw part of his army (the Thirteenth corps and one division of the Seventeenth) across the Mississippi to Bruinsburg,[21] confronting 8,000 rebels with 23,000 bluecoats and so making possible the capture of Port Gibson, the superior ability of the Union commanders in concentrating their forces became manifest. This was the greatest amphibious landing in American history before the Second World War. Other Union troops were quickly ferried across the river, and gained hard ground beyond it. The Confederates evacuated Grand Gulf on May 2, the gunboats taking possession next day. But at no time during April and May did Grant have more than 45,000 men available for his approach to Vicksburg.[22] Not until the first half of June, when thousands of reinforcements arrived from the North in response to an urgent plea from Grant, did the Union army outnumber the defending forces. In fact, on June 7, Grant had only 56,000 men in his ranks, while the combined armies of Pemberton and Johnston came to about 60,000. Then in less than a fortnight Grant increased his strength by more than 21,000.[23] In the end, the Federal army gained its victory by superior strength, naval and military; but in the beginning it owed its steady advance to its superior concentration and abler strategy, combined with the indispensable fleet.

And if nearly all the apparent errors, some of them readily explicable, were on the Confederate side, Pemberton was the leader most censurable for them. It was his fate, to be sure, to suffer from the radically conflicting views of his two superiors, Johnston and Davis. The president believed it vital to hold Vicksburg even at the risk of losing a powerful army. He therefore instructed Pemberton to hold the city at all costs. Johnston, knowing that Union warships ranged the river north and south of Vicksburg (which hung by but a fragile thread), thought it far more important to save the well-armed men under Pemberton. If this force were preserved intact it could be united with other troops, and await an opportunity for striking Grant a staggering blow.[24] It can be said for President Davis that he made the most strenuous efforts, by telegraph, to summon assistance for Pemberton from every quarter; from Charleston, from Arkansas, from Tennessee, from the militia and home guard of Alabama.[25] All his exertions failed. His

---

21. As fast as Grant's troops crossed to the West bank, they were collected at a camp about four miles below New Carthage; so wrote Porter. *O.R.N.*, I, 410.

22. Greene, F.V., *The Mississippi, op.cit.*, 136.

23. Bearss, *Decision in Mississippi, op.cit*, 372ff.

24. Johnston, *Narrative, op.cit.*, 178.

25. The telegrams are in Pemberton, John C., *Pemberton, Defender of Vicksburg*, Chapel Hill, 1942, 51-56.

insistence upon the supreme importance of the stronghold meanwhile added to Pemberton's determination to hold it.

The hour of decision for Pemberton struck on May 14. On the previous day Johnston, who was ill and exhausted, had written from Jackson a message intended to bring about an immediate concentration of their forces. Had he not been so weak, he would have gone himself to take command of Pemberton's troops. As it was, his directions were peremptory. He had learned that Sherman, with four divisions, held ground between them at Clinton. If possible, Pemberton should march against the Union rear at once, with all the men he could assemble, and Johnston's troops in Jackson would cooperate in the attack.

Had Pemberton acted instantly on this order, he might have effected a junction with Johnston somewhere near Clinton, and helped preserve the mobility of the joint force. Instead, he called his generals to a council of war, showed them the message, and argued at length against obeying it. A majority of the council voted for accepting the orders; a minority wished to strike at the communications of the advancing Union forces. Pemberton unwillingly adopted the latter plan. Johnston, however, was at this moment forced out of Jackson by Grant's brief occupation of the place, and when he directed Pemberton on the 15th to move directly to Clinton for a junction, his orders were betrayed to Grant.[26]

The Confederates were in fact in a hopeless situation. Their intelligence of the rapid movements of Grant's army, partly because of lack of cavalry, was so poor that they operated half the time in the dark. Even had they been well informed, they would have been fatally crippled by the disagreement between Davis and Pemberton on one side, determined to cling to Vicksburg, and Johnston on the other, insistent on abandoning Vicksburg so as to save the defenders. When Pemberton attempted to cut Grant's supply line, a line really fictitious, for he lived mainly on the country, and on what he had with him, the Confederates failed in the stinging defeat at Champion's Hill. The next certain news that Johnston received was that Pemberton had retreated to the Big Black River Bridge. He must not abandon his base, he explained, and doubtless Confederate sentiment would have held him a traitor had he refused to undergo a siege. In deep alarm, Johnston on May 17 sent Pemberton a final appeal, declaring that Vicksburg was now valueless, and if he were invested he must ultimately surrender. "Under such circumstances, instead of losing both troops and place, we must, if possible, save the troops. If it is not too late, evacuate Vicksburg and its dependencies, and march to the northeast." It was too late. On the evening of the 17th, as the sun sank after a day of stifling heat, the retreating

26. Johnston, *Narrative, op. cit.,* 181; Pemberton, *Pemberton, op.cit.,* XIV.

Confederates moved into the seven-mile line of fortifications about the city, and wave after wave of blue-clad infantrymen closed behind them.

The siege of Vicksburg had begun. "I still conceive it to be the most important point in the Confederacy," Pemberton wrote on the 18th.[27]

It might well have been so considered, so long as it and Port Hudson kept the intervening reach of the river open for ferrying men, livestock, and ammunition from the west shore to the eastern bank. But that era had ended. Warships now ran past the two towns with impunity. The single way left for the transfer of beeves was by smuggling them over at night. Transfers along the lower river had thus been carried on ever since New Orleans fell. Agents of the Confederate commissary bureau would gather hundreds of steers in the Red River valley or southern Arkansas, drive them by night aboard concealed steamboats or barges, and ferry them across. If the lookouts descried smoke from Federal gunboats, the steers would be hastily herded into cover. One agent got 2,250 head of cattle across in eight days.[28] "Pretty good, ain't it?" he demanded of his superiors. The Union patrol, however, an integral part of the blockade of the South, was steadily tightened.

Vicksburg was actually no longer worth defending; but Pemberton had allowed an almost invaluable army to be locked within its earthen walls with only sixty days' provisions and limited ammunition.[29]

With his long miles of trenches and redoubts to fill, Pemberton said he had an effective force of 18,500 men for the work, but he had to keep a mobile reserve of 3,000 to throw into any threatened spot. All thought of a break-out or of a relief expedition by Johnston was folly, for Grant soon had 71,000 men and 248 guns around the city. The situation was entirely different from that in which McClellan had flung his army against Richmond. Then, a strong Confederate army, superbly led and possessing full power of manoeuvre, had faced an army which, timidly led, was caught at a disadvantage in crossing the Chickahominy. Then, the defenders were full of confidence. Now the Union army alone had bold leadership and power of manoeuvre, and all the advantage of morale lay with the Northerners. The only course Pemberton could follow was to lie behind weaker fortifications than the Russians had possessed at Sebastopol, repulse assaults as heroically as they, and, like them, hold out as long as he could. Lack of transport, salt, and energetic aides had made it impossible (so he later said) to accumulate sufficient stores in the city.

---

27. Johnston, *Narrative, op.cit.,* 188; *O.R.* I, xxiv, Pt.I, 241, 272, 273.

28. See Andrew W. McKee, June 13, 16, 1862, to Major W.L. Lauer, Palmer Collection, Western Reserve Hist. Soc.

29. As S. H. Lockett, chief engineer of the Vicksburg defenses, states in "The Defense of Vicksburg" in *Battles and Leaders,* New York, 1887, III, 492, "We had been from the beginning short of ammunition. . ."

[III]

To Grant's admirers his movements seemed Napoleonic in their rapidity and precision. In eighteen days, to march 200 miles; to sunder Pemberton completely from Johnston; to win five fights; and to drive the main Confederate army across the Big Black and into Vicksburg—this was a grand historic feat.[30] Lincoln was delighted. He admitted later to Grant that he had not seen the full possibilities of the situation. He had thought, when Grant first reached the Vicksburg area, that the General should do just what he finally did; march the troops down the west bank, run the batteries with the empty transports, refill them, and thus set the army below. But he believed that thereafter Grant should drop farther down the river and join N.P. Banks to take Port Hudson. So thinking, wrote Lincoln, "when you turned northward, east of the Big Black, I feared it was a mistake." But Grant had been right—"and I was wrong."[31]

The Northern press was as deeply impressed as Lincoln. Greeley's *Tribune* commented a few days after the siege began: "It is hardly possible to praise too highly the extreme rapidity of Grant's operations.[32] It should be added, however, that Grant and Sherman had been exceedingly anxious, during their marches behind Vicksburg, to reach the Yazoo and reëstablish direct communications with the North. "My first anxiety," writes Grant, "was to secure a base of supplies on the Yazoo River above Vicksburg." He and Sherman impatiently accompanied the skirmishers to the point on the Walnut Hills not far from where Sherman had been repulsed the previous December. Gaining the brow, Sherman turned to Grant with the confession that until that moment he had felt no assurance of success, but now he was confident of it.[33] The soldiers were delighted for a different reason. They had missed their crackers and coffee even while feasting on fresh pork, chicken, and eggs, and as Grant came back to the main lines, they set up a chorus of "Hardtack! Hardtack!"[34] It should also be added that, swift and easy as Grant's movements seemed, the swiftness and ease owed much to the river navy, which in turn owed its efficient cooperation to skilled organization. Not numbers, but planning furnished the key to victory.

Grant depended for river transport on a finely educated colonel, later general,

30. Greene, *The Mississippi, op.cit.*, 170; *O.R.* I, xxiv, 273.

31. Lincoln, *Collected Works*, VI, 326, July 13, 1863. It might seem extraordinary that Grant did not inform Lincoln of his bold plan at an early date. But Grant did not determine to move across the river and take Vicksburg in the rear until March 19, 1863; a letter from Halleck then led him to consider sending one corps to cooperate with Banks against Port Hudson; and it was not until May 2 that he finally determined to throw his whole army against Jackson and Vicksburg. Of course, Lincoln did know the general plan was to take Vicksburg. Greene, *The Mississippi, op.cit.*, 139. For more on the campaign to Vicksburg see Nevins, Allan, *The War for the Union: War Becomes Revolution*, 399ff.

32. New York *Tribune*, May 25, 1863.

33. Rear Admiral D.D. Porter and a party of naval officers accompanied Grant, and were greatly impressed by the strength of the Confederate position.

34. Grant, *Memoirs, op.cit.*, I, 528-530.

Lewis B. Parsons, a New Yorker by birth who had lived in Alton, Illinois, and St. Louis before the war, and had been one of the principal executives of the Ohio & Mississippi Railroad. In December, 1861, he had been given charge of all river and rail transportation in the Department of the Mississippi, and after devising regulations for military use of the railways, he devoted his whole attention to the carriage of men and supplies, leaving only what General Peter J. Osterhaus called "gunboat soup" to the naval forces. Few assignments in the West required more ability or experience.

The tasks of river transportation were tremendous, for the boats had to carry men, medical supplies, forage, horses, rations, munitions, cannon, wagons, and an endless list of miscellanies. Parsons had to toil day and night providing all kinds of craft; tugs, barges, hospital boats, transports, mailboats, cargo boats, wood-cutting boats, and snag-removal boats, while lending a hand at times with iron-clads, tinclads, and mortarboats. He was naturally a target for criticism from steamboat owners, army officers, naval officers, and Treasury officers. When Grant expressed a passing disapprobation in hasty terms, the St. Louis quarter-master, General Robert Allen, flew to Parson's defense. "In his zeal to conduct the affairs of the transportation branch of the service with *economy,* he has drawn upon him the whole power of the steamboat interest, and by those representing this interest he has been abused and villified without stint. In this his honest effort to discharge his duty as he understood it, reckless of his personal popularity, is it not hard that he should be rewarded by a sneer from his commanding general?" Grant at once withdrew his censure.[35]

Grant, in fact, repeatedly expressed high esteem for Parsons and his work. He would have been utterly helpless without the naval forces commanded first by Flag-Officer Andrew H. Foote, Charles H. Davis, and later by Rear-Admiral David D. Porter, and the shipping mobilized by Parsons. The warships serving in the Mississippi Squadron in the critical months from the beginning of 1863 to the opening of the siege of Vicksburg numbered 64, of which 5 displaced a thousand tons or more, 12 were ironclads, and nearly all carried guns.[36] The need for a multiplicity of additional vessels large and small never slackened, and their number ran into the hundreds. Grant telegraphed Parsons from his headquarters near Vicksburg on January 30, 1863: "A move may take place at any time requiring the use of all our transports." He demanded so many small boats for his Yazoo Pass operations that he feared enough could not be drawn from the Upper Mississippi, the Cumberland, the Tennessee, and other Western rivers to meet his needs. In March, he wanted the steamboats that were sent from the north

35. Parsons Papers, Illinois State Historical Library; Fox, G.V., Correspondence, Box 6, 1863, New York Historical Society.
36. *O.R.N.*, I, xxiv, 5.

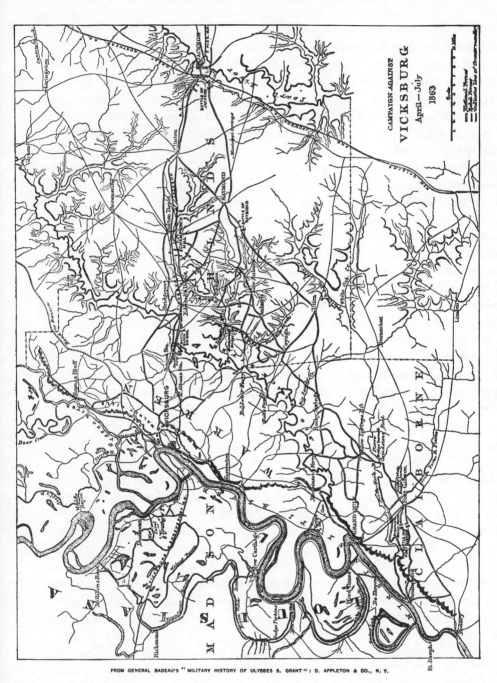

FROM GENERAL BADEAU'S "MILITARY HISTORY OF ULYSSES S. GRANT": D. APPLETON & CO., N. Y.

Map of the Vicksburg Campaign, April–July, 1863

given a double load; subsistence stores and forage below deck, and troops crowding the upper part of the vessels.

At the time when Porter took command on the Mississippi (early in October, 1862; he remained in charge until Vicksburg's fall was assured), the fighting squadron was by modern standards relatively weak. It consisted of fifteen vessels, most of them out of repair, insufficiently protected against shot and shell, and drawing too great a depth of water. Porter immediately sent for a work crew of mechanics and put the ships in efficient trim. He also began buying and arming light-draft steamboats, so that in the next few months he added 54 vessels of 324 guns to his force. The fleet of rams under Col. Alfred Ellet was converted into a marine brigade, manned by 1500 troops, to be used with the gunboats to suppress the guerrillas that had made the river banks a series of hornets' nests.[37] It was under Porter's command that a large fleet of transports had carried Sherman's army of 40,000 troops to his futile attack on the Yazoo River fortifications, and later transported McClernand's successful movement against Arkansas Post. Likewise under his command, perfectly coordinated with Grant's movements, seven gunboats and a group of provision-laden transports ran past Vicksburg on the night of April 16.

This passage of Vicksburg was planned with remarkable efficiency. Pains were taken to get the vessels into line at proper distances from each other, the flagship *Benton* leading the way. Till she was abreast of the forts, no wheel turned except to keep the ships in the four-miles-an-hour current. Even then the vessels "drifted slowly by," as Porter put it, keeping as good order as could be expected in a narrow river amid flame and smoke—so much smoke that the rear vessels had to stop firing to let the pilots see their way clear. Only one empty transport was lost, with some damage to the coal barges, and only 12 men wounded. On the evening of April 22, six more transports were sent past Vicksburg, one being sunk. However, the Union gunboats failed to knock out the Grand Gulf batteries on April 29 after five hours' bombardment. When the time came to move the Union forces from the west to the east bank, Porter was ready. "For 48 hours," he wrote, "the gunboats were employed, in conjunction with the army transports, in carrying over the large army, munitions of war, and transports. Never was there a more rapid or better-planned movement."[38] The placid stretch of waters below Grand Gulf bore a cohort of steamers, the decks covered with bluecoats; beyond the bends above and below, other transports whistled and puffed, their smoke curling over woods and levees. Thickening lines of men marched from the eastern bank toward the rising sun. Those who saw the spectacle thought the army invincible.

37. *O.R.N.*, I, xxiii, 395, 396; the marine brigade was ready for duty March 24, 1863.
38. *O.R.N.*, I, xxiii, 409; 414; xxiv, 553-554.

River-power as mobilized by Parsons, Porter, and Ellet was, in fact, as important as sea-power. It now completed the cordon of the blockade, forging with the Atlantic and Gulf squadrons a ring around the Confederacy. It made possible amphibious operations of an even more telling character than those on the Atlantic. It was not merely invaluable as an auxiliary of the Union armies; the naval elements were equally important as an independent force. Admiral Porter was insistent in his reports that his forces, and not the army's, deserved by far the major share of credit for the capture of Arkansas Post and Grand Gulf. In three hours, he wrote, possibly exaggerating his own role, the gunboats dismounted every gun in the former stronghold with a terrific destruction of men, artillery, and horses. "This has been a naval fight."[39] He agreed with Captain Guild that the Navy alone should be credited with the taking of Grand Gulf. The Army never fired a gun there; and when Grant rode into the place all its guns were out of action and lying at the water's edge, while the sailors were busy dismantling the fortifications. The Confederate forces under Bowen had evacuated Grand Gulf without a fight because of Grant's army to the south marching inland toward Port Gibson, and the Navy did the occupying job.[40] Even when acting in a supporting capacity, the river navy had an enterprise all its own. The suppression of guerrillas was an especially dangerous activity, and required constant alertness. Not only the Mississippi, but all the tributaries had to be kept clear of irregular partisans. "Whenever you hear of a musket fired at a transport," Porter wrote the head of the marine brigade who had been sent to scour the White and the lower Arkansas, "dash in there and clean them out; take every musket you can find . . . The important object is to make continual dashes into the enemy's country, then disappear, to turn up somewhere else. In this way the guerrillas will soon disappear, especially when they find that their style of warfare is not looked upon as civilized."[41]

The lamentations of the Confederates over their difficulties with transportation, among other things, help to illuminate the advantages enjoyed by the Union leaders. General Johnston harped considerably upon this chord. He was bemired while the Federal armies moved with ease. "The whole of the Mississippi Valley is said to be impassable for large wagon trains," he wrote Wigfall from Chattanooga March 4, 1863.[42] When he penned his final report to the Adjutant-General that fall, he declared that he had been completely fettered. Late spring reinforcement, he stated, had brought his army up to about 24,000 infantry and artillerymen, but it had been deficient in guns, ammunition, and above all, in transport.

39. To Fleet Captain A. M. Pennock, Cairo, January 11, 1863; *O.R.N.*, I, xxiv, 114, 115; C.F. Guild to Gustavus V. Fox, Fox Correspondence, Box 6, 1863, NYHS.
40. *O.R.N.*, I, xxiii, 414, 415; *O.R.* I, xxiv, Pt. I, 666.
41. March 26, 1863; *O.R.N.*, I, xxiv, 513, 514.
42. Letters of J.E. Johnston to L.T. Wigfall, and others; copies in Univ. of Texas.

"The draft upon the country had so far reduced the number of horses and mules, that it was not until late in June that draught animals could be obtained from distant points for the artillery and trains. There was no want of commissary supplies in the department, but the limited transportation caused a deficiency for a moving army. . . . The want of field transportation rendered any movement for the relief of Port Hudson impossible, had a march in that direction been admissible."[43]

It was inferior transportation, in the opinion of Johnston, which really made Vicksburg untenable, for sufficient stores could not be collected to hold it. And it was plain to the Confederates as to the Federals that movement by highway or railroad was far less safe than by steamboat. A railway could always be cut by a few lurking men, as Buell had found when he tried to repair the Corinth-Chattanooga line after Shiloh; it could be raided to shut off supplies, as Grant had learned when he tried to march south from Grenada along the Mississippi Central. No river could be cut, and no steamboat derailed. It was true that the stages of water in any stream had to be watched carefully; Grant's advance against Forts Henry and Donelson were necessarily undertaken in a wet season. The Federal Navy did lose three major vessels in the long campaign around Vicksburg, however. The *Cairo* hit a torpedo in the Yazoo, Dec. 12, 1862; the *Cincinnati* was sunk by Vicksburg batteries May 27, 1863; and the *Baron DeKalb* hit a torpedo below Yazoo City in July, 1863. There was also considerable damage to the ironclads in Porter's abortive daylight attack at Grand Gulf, but on the whole the celerity of river transportation was matched by its security.[44]

[IV]

On May 22nd, when the siege of Vicksburg was but four days old, Grant made the most tragic error of the campaign, a foretaste of Cold Harbor. He ordered a frontal attack, launching about 40,000 men over difficult ground against a total garrison 32,000 strong, which held powerful fortifications. He had already been repulsed on the 19th with heavy losses. Now he was almost certain to be repulsed again, although he well knew that if he merely held his lines and continued his bombardment, victory within weeks was certain—an almost bloodless victory.

For this futile and costly assault, he later assigned a number of reasons, all fairly poor. One was that he now held better ground for launching an attack than on the 19th. Although this was to some extent true, on the 19th the Confederate defenders had been largely demoralized, while three days later they had recov-

43. *O.R.*, I, xxiv, Pt.1, 242.
44. *O.R.N.* II, i, 42, 49, 58; a good description of the *DeKalb* in New York *Herald*, July 23, 1863.

ered.[45] Another excuse was that he could not effectively besiege Vicksburg, and at the same time fight off Johnston's army at Canton to the northeast. But Johnston was too weak to save Vicksburg (as he wrote Pemberton on May 29), too weak even to extricate Pemberton unless they made mutually-supporting movements which were infeasible. He was apparently at no time able to interfere with the siege.[46] Grant, too, felt that success then would close the campaign and free his army immediately for further operations. This might have some merit, but was the possible saving of six weeks worth the terrible risk incurred? After all, was the time really lost? As Grant himself says in another connection, "the siege of Vicksburg had drawn from Rosecrans's front so many of the enemy that his chances of victory were much greater than they would be if he waited [to attack] until the siege was over, when these troops could be returned."[47] But Grant's main reason seemed to be that it was the beginning of the hot season, they had won five victories, and "the Army of the Tennessee had come to believe that they could beat their antagonist under any circumstances." He was concerned over the effect on his army of trench life during a siege. He admitted in his *Memoirs* that he regretted two assaults, Cold Harbor in 1864, and that of the 22nd of May, 1863. But he felt there was more justification for the Vicksburg assault, though he admits: "The only benefit we gained—and it was a slight one for so great a sacrifice—was that the men worked cheerfully in the trenches after that, being satisfied with digging the enemy out. Had the assault not been made, I have no doubt that the majority of those engaged in the siege of Vicksburg would have believed that had we assaulted it would have proven successful, and would have saved life, health and comfort." Perhaps some officers and some civilians might have felt so, but would this have been true of the men in the ranks?

"As our troops came in fair view," wrote Sherman later, "the enemy rose behind their parapet and poured a furious fire upon our lines; and, for about two hours, we had a severe and bloody battle, but at every point we were repulsed."[48] The Confederates had dug exterior ditches eight to twelve feet deep, erected ramparts and parapets behind them for their troops, mounted 102 guns, and protected parts of their front by an abattis of felled trees and telegraph-wire

45. In February, 1863, President Davis expressed astonishment that the army was not more efficient in interrupting the Union navigation of the Mississippi; T.C. Reynolds, Jacksonport, June 1, 1863, to Lt.-Gen. T.H. Holmes; Reynolds Papers, LC.

46. Johnston, Joseph E., "Jefferson Davis and the Mississippi Campaign," *Battles and Leaders*, III, 478, 479.

47. Grant, Ulysses S., "Chattanooga," in *Battles and Leaders*, III, 679. Grant, of course, meant that the siege had kept Johnston's army, including troops sent from Bragg, in Mississippi. Moreover, it should be noted that after Vicksburg did surrender, no effective use was made of Grant's released command. By a decision apparently Halleck's, they were "dissipated over other parts of the country," as Grant put it; some going to Banks, some to Schofield, some to Kentucky, some to Natchez. *Battles and Leaders*, III, 680; Grant, *Memoirs*, I, 530-531; II, 276-277.

48. Sherman, William T., *Memoirs of General Sherman*, New York, 1875, I, 326.

entanglements. Three times the Union soldiers poured forward to the assault, and thrice they were thrown back with heavy loss. At two points McClernand's troops crossed the ditches, scaled the ramparts, and planted their colors on the Southern parapets; at one they even seized a detached work, driving out the defenders, and held it—their colonel standing on the parapet and shouting for help—until they were slowly exterminated.[49]

This limited success encouraged McClernand to call for more support. Grant ordered McPherson and Sherman to make new attacks which they did in a somewhat uncoordinated manner. The failure of the assault became a subject of much controversy. McClernand, with the ear of the press and political pipelines to Washington, claimed he had not been supported and had been wrongly condemned. Grant replied that McClernand had misled him as to the degree of his success, so causing much of the afternoon loss. In a rare burst, Grant told Halleck that McClernand "is entirely unfit for the position of corps commander." McClernand said there "appears to be a systematic effort to destroy my usefulness and reputation. . . ." That Grant was responsible for a great needless sacrifice of brave men was clear, but it is probable that all the Union commanders were overly optimistic in view of their recent triumphs. The Confederates estimated that 3,500 men were left dead and wounded between the lines; the records show 3,052 killed and wounded, and 147 missing.[50]

Once more the familiar sequel of battle was enacted. The dead and wounded lay untended on the field as one chill night passed, one hot day, another chill night, and a second hot day. By that time the dead stank, and the living, wrote the chief engineer of the Vicksburg defenses, "were suffering fearful agonies." Not Grant, but Pemberton, proposed a brief truce to succor the Union wounded, and from 6 in the evening until 8:30 a tardy mercy was extended the prostrate men.

Not only was Grant disturbed by what he believed to be McClernand's faults in the assault of May 22; he was further disconcerted by a dispatch of McClernand stating that he had held two of the enemy's forts, and claiming great things for his troops and himself. Charles A. Dana wrote Stanton May 24 that Grant was determined to relieve McClernand at once, but concluded it would be better to

49. Lockett, S.H., *Battles and Leaders,* III, 489.

50. The controversy between McClernand and Grant is so deep and involved that it requires very intensive study to even make a reasoned judgment. For two modern and somewhat opposing opinions, see: Bearss, *Decision in Mississippi, op.cit.* Unfortunately, there is no modern biography of McClernand. For casualties on May 22, see Livermore, *Numbers and Losses in the Civil War,* Boston, 1901, 100. For Grant to Halleck regarding McClernand's ability, *O.R.* I, 37, May 24, 1863. Much material in his own defense will be found in the McClernand Papers, Illinois State Historical Library, including a draft of a letter of McClernand to Grant, June 4, 1863. Also, Grant, *Memoirs,* I, Chap.XXXVIII; Sherman, *Memoirs,* I, 355; New York *Herald,* July 1, 1863. Jones, Jenkin Lloyd, *An Artilleryman's Diary,* Madison, 1914, 91-93.

wait and try to induce him to ask for leave. Dana wrote, "My own judgment is that McClernand has not the qualities necessary for a good commander, even of a regiment." In June, McClernand's orders of congratulation to his troops, a very bombastic statement, found its way into the press. Grant, Sherman, and McPherson were furious, inasmuch as McClernand had not cleared this release with headquarters as required. On June 18, Grant relieved McClernand from command of the Thirteenth Corps and sent him home. E.O.C. Ord, a more stable commander, took over the corps. McClernand, however, would not let things rest. Prior to his dismissal he had written Governor Richard Yates of Illinois, praising his own corps and blaming others. After dismissal, McClernand wrote Lincoln protesting Grant's action: "Is it not hard that I should be dismissed from command and Sherman and McPherson complimented by promotion in the regular army when it will hardly be said that they have done more or better than myself?" He bluntly asked for restoration. He also wrote Stanton and Halleck. This only tended to augment the bitterness.[51]

As the siege continued, the city was given no peace. From the river, hour after hour, came the thud of cannon on the gunboats, and from the western shore the boom of mortars planted on the bank; shells tore through the air with a scream, while bombs rose as black balls in an arc, hung suspended an instant like poised eagles, and then plunged down to fling up earth and debris in an angry roar. Along the waterless valleys and their yellow clay banks the Northern troops pushed their zigzag approaches a little forward every day, every night. Lean, sun-tanned squads, perspiring, grunting, and cursing, flung the dirt to right and left. Where the Union trenches ran close to the Confederate redoubts, hand grenades and shells would be lobbed back and forth, and limbs and bloody lumps of flesh hurled in air. Sometimes quiet would descend and, to the tune of friendly voices, "Time to surrender, Reb!" "Ain't you lost enough men, Yank?", hardtack or bacon, wrapped in paper, would be tossed across in exchange for tobacco. Toiling Union gangs labored stealthily on mines, and Confederates on countermines, men catching the faint clang of enemy picks and spades far underground. Above the river and city hung buzzards awaiting their opportunity, for they could find carrion aplenty if they braved the shot and shell.

Had the Confederate leaders shown more foresight, they would have expelled almost the whole civil population from Vicksburg before its investment. It was no place for women and children, whose extra mouths were a serious problem. By the end of May, the incessant bombardment had forced many civilians into hastily-excavated caves, particularly during especially heavy shelling. Built into

51. Lockett, *ut supra,* 489, 490; Charles A. Dana Papers, LC, Dana to Stanton, May 24, 1863; Catton, Bruce, *Grant Moves South,* Boston, 1960, 466-468; McClernand to Yates, May 28, 1863, McClernand to Lincoln, Aug. 12, 1863, and ms. biography of McPherson, unpublished, McClernand Papers, Illinois State Historical Library.

the terraced hills on which the town sprawled, they were equipped with bedding, clothing, and food; sometimes carpets and fine furniture. One great cavern contained about two hundred people, who lived in fear that a mortar bomb would bury them alive. Even after most houses had been damaged or wrecked, many people clung to them; when church bells rang on Sunday, hardy souls still ventured to the services. It was food which became the insoluble problem. As flour, meal, and bread disappeared, mule-meat became a staple, and some men counted rats the delicacy that the besieged people of Paris would esteem them in 1870-71. However, it is probable that some accounts exaggerated the extent of the lack of food. Pemberton later denied that the garrison was starved out.[52]

"The Federals fought the garrison in part, but the city mainly," one resident records. Nowhere during the war was the heroism of the Southern women more evident. A calm endurance marked the deportment of the poorer women, a wild enthusiasm that of their wealthier sisters. Every man who could bear arms went into the trenches. Some distinguished themselves by daring feats; three, for example, floated down the river on logs to bring back a desperately-needed supply of percussion caps. But, little by little, the hardships and squalor destroyed the morale of garrison and residents alike. After the tenth day, the garrison subsisted on half-rations, later reduced; the people were glad to boil cane-sprouts. Yet a few speculators made the most of the situation, selling flour for $1,000 a barrel, meal for $140 a bushel, and molasses for $12 a gallon. A flow of Confederate deserters kept Grant informed as to conditions inside the city, as did at least one spy.[53]

As the siege continued, the Richmond authorities seemed confused, inert, and hopeless. Secretary Seddon, gaunt, cadaverous, and more toilworn than ever, was now in despair. Like his subordinate Robert Garlick Kean, he felt from the beginning that Vicksburg would fall—probably by the end of June.[54] Although he repeatedly urged Johnston to take more active steps in repelling Grant, he was unable to provide him the forces needed. Davis appealed in vain to governors and generals for help. When Johnston telegraphed on June 4 that his army was far too small to relieve Pemberton, Davis replied: "I regret inability to promise more troops, as we have drained resources even to the danger of several points. You know best concerning General Bragg's army, but I fear to withdraw more. We

---

52. Bell, L. McRae, "A Girl's Experiences in the Siege of Vicksburg," *Harper's Weekly*, June 8, 1912; *O.R.* I, xxiv, Pt.i, 285.

53. Gregory, Edward S., "Fall of Vicksburg," Philadelphia *Weekly Times*, March 9, 1878; Abrams, A.S., *A Full and Detailed History of the Siege of Vicksburg*, Atlanta, 1863, *passim.*; Dana to Stanton, June 20, 1863, Stanton Papers, LC. There are numerous first-hand accounts of the siege both in books and manuscripts. A good collection is Walker, Peter F., *Vicksburg, A People At War, 1860-1865*, Chapel Hill, 1960.

54. Kean, Robert G.H., *Inside the Confederate Government*, op.cit., New York, 1957, 68, 69.

are too far outnumbered in Virginia to spare any. . ."[55] The dispatch reached Johnston in garbled form, leaving him to suppose that the government wished no troops withdrawn from Bragg. Moreover,. he believed that to take a force sufficient to break the siege would involve the surrender of Tennessee. He so telegraphed the War Department June 12-15: "It is for the government to decide between this State and Tennessee."[56] In desperation, Seddon telegraphed the general to attempt the relief of Vicksburg with what force he had; to which Johnston replied that the difficulties were insuperable.[57]

Because of his concern over possible loss of the Mississippi River, Davis had not ordered Vicksburg evacuated. Yet he could find no way really to help either Johnston or Pemberton. After the siege began, he continued to urge Johnston to act, tried to assemble troops for reenforcement, and attempted every possible expedient but to go himself into the field, a course that his health did not permit. If he seemed to fumble the situation, it was because there was little effective that he could do. "The Secretary and President are at their wits' end and seem to have no plan, to be drifting along on the current of events"; so Assistant-Secretary J.A. Campbell in the War Department told Kean.[58] And Kean wrote: "This is characteristic of the President. He is not a comprehensive man. He has no broad policy, either of finance, strategy, or supply." A letter Davis wrote Bragg at Shelbyville, Tennessee, as the siege neared its inexorable climax, certainly revealed him in a state of confused indecision. The assignment of several military departments to a geographical district under Johnston as head had plainly worked badly, for Johnston protested that he could not command in Tennessee while he was absorbed in the Mississippi operations. What suggestions could Bragg make for remedying the situation? Did he have adequate means of communication to direct operations in both Tennessee and Kentucky? How much cooperation could be expected between separate forces without an actual junction? This was the almost despairing letter of a commander-in-chief fumbling in the dark while the Western front fell apart.[59]

Even after Johnston had telegraphed that an attack on Grant would almost certainly fail, that after a repulse the Big Black would cut off his retreat, and that all Mississippi and Alabama would then lie open to attack, Seddon persisted. Convinced of an almost imperative necessity for action, he replied on June 21, he was ready to take the responsibility for the most desperate course the occasion might demand. The eyes and the hopes of the Confederacy were upon Johnston,

55. Johnston, *Narrative, op.cit.*, 233; Rowland, Dunbar, *Jefferson Davis, Constitutionalist*, Jackson, 1923, V, 534 and *passim*.
56. Johnston, *Ibid.*, 247, 248.
57. Kean, *op.cit.*, 74.
58. *Ibid.*, 72.
59. Davis to Bragg, June 19, 1863, Palmer Collection, Western Reserve Hist. Soc.

he continued, and "it is better to fail nobly daring than, through prudence even, to be inactive."[60] Belatedly, for he lacked adequate supplies and transportation, Johnston advanced to the vicinity of Grant's lines on July 1. His troops spent two days in reconnaissances north of the Vicksburg-Jackson railway lines. As scouts had previously reported, no weak spots existed in the Federal position. Attack in that area would mean ghastly and futile losses. Johnston then decided to move on July 5 to the south of the road, where the Union works might be weaker. But it was too late.

Pemberton had queried his four division commanders on the 1st upon the ability of their troops to carry out a successful evacuation, and they in turn consulted brigade and regimental commanders. The unanimous opinion of senior officers was that the troops were physically too exhausted to cut their way out. After day-and-night service in the trenches for nearly a month and a half, now drenched by rains and now roasted by the subtropical sun, ill-fed, denied sleep by the storm of shot and shell, with legs cramped and swollen for lack of free movement, they had grown gaunt and weak. To expect them to march out against an enemy four times their strength, well-fed, well-armed, and full of confidence, would be folly. A petition "From many soldiers" dated June 28, 1863, had warned Pemberton of a crisis. "Our rations have been cut down to one biscuit and a small bit of bacon per day, not enough scarcely to keep soul and body together, much less to stand the hardships we are called upon to stand. . . . If you can't feed us, you had better surrender."[61]

Under a scrawny oak, on a scarred, sun-parched hillside, at three o'clock on the afternoon of July 3, two old comrades of the Mexican War greeted each other with friendly restraint. No one was aware, of course, of what was going on far to the east in Pennsylvania. Pemberton, tall, erect, dignified, his black hair and full black beard adding to the stern effect of his determined features, and Grant, short, of slouching posture, biting a cigar, but of equally resolute mien, stood for some time talking. They strolled a short distance toward the Confederate lines. Disagreeing, they sat down alone while a Northern artist named T.R. Davis remained under the tree to sketch the scene, and while two officers, General A.J. Smith on the Union side and General John S. Bowen on the Confederate, continued the conference. Finally, all agreed that Grant should send a letter with his final terms by ten that night. This he did, offering to parole the entire Southern force, the officers to keep their side-arms and one horse each. These terms seemed to Halleck excessively generous, for he feared the men would break parole and rejoin the army. Grant at the time was a bit reluctant to accept the parole idea, but agreed and later became sincerely convinced it was the right

60. Johnston, *Narrative, op.cit.,* 200, 201.
61. National Archives; *O.R.* I, xxiv, Pt.1, 280-283.

thing. As he later wrote a friend: "I was very glad to give the garrison of Vicksburg the terms I did. There was a cartel in existence at that time which required either party to exchange or parole all prisoners either at Vicksburg or at points on the James River within ten days after capture, or as soon thereafter as practicable. This would have used all the transportation we had for a month. The men had behaved so well that I did not want to humiliate them. I believed that consideration for their feelings would make them less dangerous during the continuance of hostilities, and better citizens after the war was over."[62]

Next day, the 4th, under another burning sun, the hard-faced Union veterans of Frederick Steele's division, with bands playing patriotic airs, swung into the city and garrisoned the principal points. Along the Confederate lines, the defenders filed dejectedly out of their trenches, stacked arms, and then, forming columns, marched with dignity back to their works. Union flags began to go up on buildings. An officer strode into the postoffice to reëstablish Federal postal service. In the center of the city a little group of citizens watched as two men on horseback rode up to the Court House—Pemberton in gray, Grant in blue. They alighted, climbed the steps, and stood at attention. So did the lines of blue troops, bayonets and sabers glittering in the sun, who fronted the building. All saluted while slowly the Confederate banner came down, and the national ensign rose in its stead. The naval forces had been expectantly awaiting this moment; and past the city came gunboat after gunboat, transport after transport, their decks black with men, their flags flying, their bands playing, and their guns firing salutes.[63]

[V]

The North had won its victory primarily by the superior organization of the combined naval and military forces which Admiral Porter and General Grant led, and the superb organization of the supply system for which Lewis B. Parsons was primarily responsible. This was one indispensable element in the success. A secondary but almost equally important element was Grant's generalship: his boldness, decision, and rapidity in executing his plan for flanking Vicksburg from the east.[64] Audacity was never carried further save by Stonewall Jackson in similarly daring and decisive flank movements at Second Manassas and Chancellorsville. Organization gave Grant's army its transportation and supplies up to the point at which both could be partially abandoned; to the time when, once across the river below Grand Gulf, the troops could move by rapid marches over good roads and forage on the countryside for provisions. True to his nature, in his

62. To Gen. Marcus J. Wright, Nov. 30, 1884, Eldridge Collection, HEH.
63. Pemberton, *Pemberton*, 236-239; Grant, *Memoirs*, I, ch. XXXVII; Bell, L. McRae, *Harper's Weekly*, June 8, 1912.
64. Badeau, Adam, *Military History of Ulysses S. Grant*, New York, 1868, I, 222.

dispatches to subordinates he continually emphasized speed, or as he put it in writing to Sherman on May 3, "the overwhelming importance of celerity."[65]

The river flotillas constituted in 1863 perhaps the best-organized branch of the Northern war effort, no whit inferior to the railroad system under Daniel C. McCallum and Herman Haupt. To the very end the Navy, though less conspicuous than the Army, was indispensable in the Vicksburg campaign. Transports brought Grant his indispensable reinforcements and supplies; gunboats shelled the city up to the day that Pemberton rode out to surrender; mortar boats threw their shells into Pemberton's eastern fortifications three miles away. Ellet's patrols suppressed the guerrillas who would otherwise have harassed transports and exploded ammunition boats. On the morrow of the surrender, Sherman wrote Porter a well-earned tribute:

"I can appreciate the intense satisfaction you must feel at lying before the monster that has defied us with such deep and malignant hate, and seeing your once disunited fleet again a unit; and, better still, the chain that made an enclosed sea of a link in the great river broken forever. It is so magnificent a result that I stop not to count who did it. It is done . . . God grant that the harmony and mutual respect that exist between our respective commanders, and is shared by all the true men of the joint service, continue forever, and serve to elevate our national character, threatened with shipwreck."[66]

Four days after Vicksburg, the garrison of Port Hudson surrendered. The siege had actually begun May 24, when Banks's force of possibly about 30,000 at its peak invested Major General Frank Gardner's force of approximately 6,000 at Port Hudson. As we have related previously, Banks's assault of May 27 was a tragic blunder, and, like Grant's at Vicksburg, failed, with Northern losses of 1,842 killed and wounded. The Confederates held an interior line of four to five miles, which necessitated a Federal siege line of seven to eight miles. In mid-June, Banks made some fresh dispositions of his troops, and assaulted again at daybreak on June 14. Although lines were advanced, the Confederates did not break. On July 6, news came of the surrender at Vicksburg. As a result, Port Hudson was formally surrendered July 8. Like Pemberton, Gardner had no way to escape. Also there was no chance that Port Hudson could hold out after Vicksburg was taken. According to eyewitnesses, Port Hudson was not starved out, although rations were substantially reduced.[67]

65. *O.R.*, I, xxiv, Pt.3, 268; Fuller, J.F.C., *The Generalship of Ulysses S. Grant*, New York, 1919, 140ff.

66. Guernsey, Alfred H., and Henry M. Alden, *Harper's History of the Civil War*, Chicago, 1894-1896, 480.

67. *O.R.* I, xxiv, Pt.3, 473. For Port Hudson early stages, see Nevins, *The War for the Union: War Becomes Revolution*, 402-405; Palfrey, John C., "Port Hudson," *Papers of the Military Historical Society of Massachusetts*, Vol. VIII, Boston, 1910, *passim.*; Cunningham, Edward, *The Port Hudson Campaign, 1862-1863*, Baton Rouge, 1963, *passim.*; Wright, Lieut. Howard C., *Port Hudson, Its History from an Interior Point of View*, Baton Rouge, 1861; *Report of the Joint Committee on the Conduct of the War,*

These victories were regarded by some as primarily a marine triumph. On July 16 the steamboat *Imperial* arrived at New Orleans from St. Louis, its path completely clear. A week later, Secretary Chase instructed the customs surveyor in St. Louis to clear boats and cargoes of permissible materials to New Orleans, if desired, taking care not to land goods at intermediate points, except under authorized permits.[68] The cargoes *were* needed. When, early in August, three large steamboats reached New Orleans, beef fell from 40 cents per pound to 25, potatoes from $13.50 per barrel to $3.00, and flour in proportion. Merchants looked forward to a large West-Indian trade. The Vicksburg and Port Hudson levees were lined with steamboats discharging miscellaneous supplies while the owners looked eagerly for cotton to send back by way of Cairo. Sugar and molasses began going upstream. Although Southern planters and shippers complained bitterly of the restrictions placed upon trade by the internal ("infernal") revenue officers, large profits were nevertheless made. The Father of Waters flowed unvexed by guns, but vexed instead by Treasury regulations, and occasional snipers.[69]

[VI]

Deep was the gloom which settled upon Southerners. Yet they were still defiant. "It is strange," wrote one Wisconsin soldier on entering Vicksburg, "to see a people who have suffered so much, spitting forth open defiance to us and uttering such intensified sentiments of hostility to Yankees."[70] The gloom would have been deeper and the defiance perhaps less marked, but for the fact that only high Confederate and Union officers knew the full extent of the calamity which the South had sustained. Not only was the whole trans-Mississippi region largely cut off from the rest of the Confederacy; not only was New Orleans again made a port for the Northwest; not only was Copperheadism in the prairie States dealt a prostrating blow; and not only were the troops of Grant and Sherman now free to operate in Alabama, Tennessee, and Georgia! The immediate losses of the South were staggering. At Vicksburg Grant took 29,500 prisoners, with 172 cannon, over 50,000 small arms (many of them Enfields better than the Union pieces), and much ammunition.[71] At Port Hudson the Confederates lost 6,400

1865, Vol. II, 311-315; *O.R.* IV, 1059. Numbers at Port Hudson are very much in dispute. Cunningham has made a careful study, *ut supra*, 120-124. The letters of the realistic American novelist, John W. DeForest, his fictional sketches, and his book, *A Volunteer's Adventures*, contain much upon the Port Hudson scene, and the fighting thereabouts.

68. "St. Louis During the War," Ms., James O. Broadhead Papers, Missouri Historical Society.

69. New York *Herald*, New Orleans correspondence, August 11, 12, 20, 1863.

70. J. McDonnell, Vicksburg, Aug. 15, 1863, to J.R. Doolittle, Doolittle Papers, State Hist. Soc. of Wisconsin.

71. Grant, *Memoirs*, I, 572; *O.R.*, I, xxiv, Pt.1, 62, *O.R.*, I, xxiv, Pt.2 324-325.

prisoners, 51 guns, and 5,000 small arms, with about 150,000 rounds of ammunition.[72]

Jefferson Davis, plunged into dejection, proclaimed a day of fasting for August 21. Word spread among his intimates that he despaired of success in the struggle. "Oh, for a leader with the calm heroism of a William of Orange!" exclaimed the diarist Kean.[73] A vitriolic exchange of letters between Johnston and Davis did nothing, when it became known, to improve the standing of either in the South, or to further the Confederate war effort.[74] But for Johnston's strong political following and widespread popularity, Davis might have removed him and put D.H. Hill in his place.[75] To a Mississippi friend, Davis confided that the disasters in the State were not only great, but unexpected, for he had thought that the troops at hand made a force sufficient to destroy Grant's army.[76] Yet he had known since mid-June that Johnston believed his force must at least be doubled to save Vicksburg, and that to draw sufficient reinforcements from Bragg would mean the loss of Tennessee.

Rejoicing in the North was matched by that among the friends of the Union overseas who could hail a double victory—the fall of Vicksburg and the coincident defeat of Lee at Gettysburg. "With deep, devout, and grateful joy," declared the London *Star* of July 20, "we publish today the news of victories that are the heralds of a happy peace. . . The glorious Fourth-of-July has indeed received a glorious celebration." The London *Daily News* pointed out that the fall of Vicksburg was a more serious blow to the Confederacy by far than Lee's failure. "All who understand and sympathize with the higher interests and issues of humanity at stake in the great conflict," it added, would join Meade in thanking God for giving victory to "the cause of the just."[77] The *Times* surpassed itself in malignant comment. But John Bright was transported with gratification and relief; the Confederate cotton-loan fell by one-fifth in little more than a week; and the Richmond government, seeing that all hope of British intervention was gone, recalled its unrecognized envoy James Mason from London. As it was now clear that he would never be received, wrote Judah P. Benjamin,[78] it was neither useful nor dignified for him to remain.

Under the stunted oak where Pemberton and Grant shook hands, a tree

72. Harrington, Fred H., *Fighting Politician, Major-General N.P. Banks*, Philadelphia, 1946, 124. Among the prisoners at Port Hudson marched a future chief justice of the United States, Edward D. White. *Report of the Joint Committee on the Conduct of the War*, Washington, 1865, II, 315.
73. Kean, *Inside the Confederate Government, op.cit.*, 86.
74. Davis, Varina, *Jefferson Davis, A Memoir by his Wife*, New York, 1890, Ch.XLII.
75. Kean, *op.cit.*, 83.
76. *O.R.*, IV, ii, 766; Davis to J.M. Howry, August 27, 1863.
77. July 20, 1863.
78. Trevelyan, George M., *The Life of John Bright*, Boston, 1914, 323. Adams, E.D., *Great Britain and the American Civil War*, Gloucester, Mass., 1957, II, 179.

swiftly whittled to shreds by relic-hunters, an imperishable fame was born, although Grant kept the scene undramatic, for no more modest a commander ever lived. "I am afraid Grant will have to be reproved for want of style," Elihu Washburne (as we have noted in *War Becomes Revolution*) had informed Lincoln two months earlier. "On this whole march of five days he has had neither a horse, nor an orderly or servant, a blanket, or overcoat, or clean shirt, or even a sword; that being carried by his boy 13 years old. His entire baggage consists of a toothbrush."[79]

Now, as the country rang with praises, his demeanor was unaltered. Charles A. Dana went back to Washington voluble with admiration. "I tell everybody that he is the most modest, the most disinterested, and the most honest man I have ever known," he wrote. He assured hundreds of this, and more. "To the question they all ask, 'Doesn't he drink?' I have been able from my own knowledge to give a decided negative."[80] Lincoln sent him a letter eloquent with gratitude. And while the taciturn, imperturbable general digested in grim silence the refusal of Halleck to accept his suggestions for effective use of his army, and busied himself in expediting the movement of troops and transports out of Vicksburg, the North made up its mind that at long last it had what it had desperately wanted ever since Sumter—a military hero.

[VII]

The fall of Vicksburg, coinciding with the commencement of Lee's retreat from Gettysburg, caused widespread rejoicing in the North. Predictions that the Confederacy would be crushed within a few months resounded on all sides, and were echoed in England and other countries. But the extreme opponents of Lincoln, and his Reconstruction policies did not share this exultation. They did not wish to see the Confederacy felled immediately, and a rapid peace arranged, for they feared that this would be a peace of delay and compromise, such as that supported by Seward, Montgomery Blair, and Greeley in his New York *Tribune.* The promoters of such policies, they apprehended, might be willing to retain some form of slavery in the South—a type of serfdom with attachment to the land similar to that found among the lower classes in Russia and the Balkans. They believed that such a revised slaveocracy might conceivably challenge the political and economic dominance of the new Northern alliance of freesoilers, Republicans, and industrial progressives. This group now sat safe behind tariff walls, government bond issues, generous land policies and programs for building rail-

79. May 1, 1863; Hay Papers, Illinois State Hist. Library.
80. Dana to E. Washburne, Aug. 29, 1863, Washburne Papers, LC.

roads, canals and colleges, while exploiting to the utmost the natural resources of the land in timber, minerals, oil and agriculture. Charles Sumner declared that the recent victories were more dangerous to the ascendancy of the Republicans which had fostered this new coalition of finance, industry and railroad promotion than defeats would have been.

Sumner (and others) also feared that a compromise peace would do less than full justice to the Negro demands for unslackened progress toward social, political, and eventually economic equality. He lamented the fact that Meade had failed to follow the repulse of the Confederacy at Gettysburg by an onslaught which would have destroyed secessionist and anti-emancipationist forces. Full of abuse for the slavemongers, for the Democrats, for Copperheads and the Tory element in Britain, he violently denounced Seward, and all other Republicans who might insist upon amnesty and restoration of the Union "with no questions asked about slavery." "God save us from such calamity!" he wrote John Bright on July 21, 1864. Before Lee's army was compelled to surrender, he declared that he hoped to see 200,000 Negroes with muskets in their hands.[81] He was in a mood equally dangerous to national concord and to the maintenance of world peace. More upheaval, struggle, oceans of bloodshed, and the loss of many millions in property were as nothing if he could see a vengeance and repression achieved.

Lincoln, who, according to John Hay "was in fine whack," felt more relief than exultation. He believed that the rebel power was at last beginning to crack apart and break into fragments. If the North stood firm, this disintegration would continue, but he wished only to restore the Union, extinguish the doctrine of secession, and continue the work of liberation that he had begun. He did not wish to humiliate the South, or to establish a new dominant truce.[82]

One Illinois Republican had more faith in the President's firmness than some of his associates. Senator Lyman Trumbull awaited the development of events for some light, showing no anxiety lest Lincoln might yield any important ground upon emancipation to please the Southerners and thus hasten a peace. Senator Zach Chandler of Michigan also, to his credit, derided the notion that Lincoln might surrender any vital position. To be sure, Chandler wrote that Seward and Seward's close friend Thurlow Weed were snaky. But he added that the President fortunately had the stubbornness of a mule, and his back was as stiff as ever.[83] Some Republican radicals had become blind with rage at finding themselves helpless in dealing with the President.[84] The President's only positive move was

81. Pierce, Edward L., *Memoir and Letters of Charles Sumner*, Boston, 1877-1893, IV, 143.
82. Dennett, Tyler, *Lincoln and the Civil War in the Diaries and Letters of John Hay*, New York, 1939, 77-78.
83. *Ibid.*
84. Williams, T. Harry, *Lincoln and the Radicals*, Madison, 1941, *passim*.

mild. Lincoln had thought, when he heard that Grant had invested Vicksburg, that the moment had come for General Rosecrans to deliver a crushing blow against Bragg, or to send large reenforcements to Grant's army. But now that Grant had taken Jackson and Vicksburg in rapid succession, he felt more patient. After writing Rosecrans that he was watching what he did with no censorious or unfriendly eye, Lincoln paused to let the General decide on his own course.[85]

85. Dennett, *op.cit.*, 77-78; Staff of the Detroit Freepress, *Life of Zachariah Chandler,* Detroit, 1880, 269ff.

Gettysburg: The Fumbled Victory

[I]

THE VERY leaves on the trees seemed to stop growing (anxious men thought) in sympathy as the country waited during the last June days in 1863 for news of Lee's invasion of the North, and Grant's siege of Vicksburg. That the war was approaching a climax was plain to all. Like spectators in an amphitheatre watching simultaneous performances, people turned their eyes first to the great winding river of the West, and then to the Appalachian valleys in the East. For the moment, all other activities were ignored: the contest between blockaders and blockade runners, the capture of Puebla by the French in Mexico, the deadlock between Bragg and Rosecrans in Tennessee, the bickerings of a constitutional convention in Missouri, and the work of recruiting North and South. Two mighty decisions impended, either of which might determine the outcome of the war.

Of the two centers of suspense, Pennsylvania held the more portentous uncertainty. For one reason, it had become plain to informed observers by early June that Confederate weakness, and Grant's brilliant energy in handling his massive forces, had almost sealed the fate of Vicksburg. The Chattanooga *Rebel* declared on June 7th that many Mississippians deemed the city already lost. For another reason, men knew that even if desperate exertions and some stroke of genius temporarily saved this section of river to the South, the North would simply try again; it was steadily reinforcing Grant. But as Lee crossed the Potomac and swung northwest of Washington, with the laurels of Chancellorsville still fresh on his brow, nobody could predict the event, and all could see that another rebel victory, followed possibly by the seizure of Baltimore or even Washington, might have the most far-reaching consequences at home and abroad.

There had been preliminary moves by part of Lee's army from south of the Rappahannock to near Culpeper Court House. On June 9, Alfred Pleasonton's Federal cavalry corps crossed the Rappahannock in two columns, striking Stuart's Confederate horse in what became the greatest nearly all-cavalry battle

(*The War for the Union,* Vol. III, *The Organized War, 1863–1864,* Chapter 3.)

ever waged on this continent! After vicious, frantic fighting on horseback and on foot, Pleasonton pulled back, content that he had found Lee's army and had punished the great Jeb Stuart rather severely. Brandy Station yielded a small amount of knowledge, rumpled Stuart's exalted plume, and gave the Federal cavalry something to really cheer about. But it was on June 18 that North and South alike were startled by tidings that the Confederate storm had broken the day before upon the high Potomac and the hills beyond. On June 15, powerful forces under Richard S. Ewell had compelled the Union commander at Winchester to cut his way out and retreat to Harper's Ferry with the loss of nearly 4,000 prisoners.[1] The Southern columns had pressed on with all possible speed. By evening of the 15th, other forces of Ewell had crossed the Potomac at Williamsport with cavalry pushing on towards Chambersburg well up the Cumberland Valley of Pennsylvania, so that soon Confederates were threatening Mercersburg to the west, Gettysburg to the east, and Carlisle and Harrisburg to the north. The movement might be a feint. But Lincoln, on that ominous 15th, called out 100,000 militia for six months, half of them from Pennsylvania and the remainder from Ohio, Maryland, and West Virginia. Hooker had shifted north from the Rappahannock, after Lee got away, and was preparing to follow on Lee's heels, keeping between him and Washington.

The campaign entered a more exigent stage when, on June 23-25, the remainder of the Confederate army, following Ewell's corps, crossed the Potomac, and moved up toward Chambersburg. Panicky Washington reports declared it twice as strong as Lee's force at Chancellorsville. Lee and D.H. Hill forded the river at Williamsport and Shepherdstown, united their corps at Hagerstown, and moved along the Cumberland Valley until they entered Chambersburg on the 27th. Ewell in their front meanwhile had pushed ahead deeper into Pennsylvania, reaching Carlisle by June 27.[2] The Southerners drove ahead of them, on all roads, a pell-mell mass of fugitives; farmers in wagons, villagers with their valuables crammed into carts and buggies, bankers and merchants with saddlebags of money, herdsmen with droves of lowing cattle. A wide belt from Baltimore to Pittsburgh was filled with consternation. The militiamen that Lincoln had summoned were slow to appear, Pennsylvania mustering at most 25,000 and Maryland and West Virginia 10,000 more; but New York had taken the alarm and was sending 15,000. Men of Pittsburgh were digging trenches along the Braddock road; men of Harrisburg were drilling with fowling pieces and scythes.

Western Maryland and much of Southern Pennsylvania, indeed, felt abandoned to the foe. Instead of defending the North inch by inch, the government had apparently decided to leave a wide area open to devastation and plunder. As

1. *O.R.* I, xxvii, Pt.2, 313-314, 442ff.
2. *Ibid.*, 443.

the Southern columns advanced, the people despaired. Philip Schaff, a young professor in the theological seminary at Mercersburg, dolefully watched Ewell's infantry and cavalry occupy the town. "We fairly, though reluctantly, belong to the Southern Confederacy," he wrote. He saw that the men, though a motley, roughly-dressed array, were better equipped than in the Antietam campaign. They all had shoes; they carried many Springfield muskets captured at Harper's Ferry the previous autumn; their wagons, some marked "U.S.", were full of supplies taken from Hooker and Milroy. "Uncle Sam has to supply both armies," Schaff ruefully commented. Officers and men, veterans of Stonewall's command, were inured to hardship, in good fighting trim, and proud of the fifteen battles they had fought. Announcing that they would respect private property and pay in Confederate money for seized supplies, they politely ransacked the stores. But a detachment of guerrilla cavalry who came after them, brave, defiant, and bold, took whatever they could use without ceremony or pay.[3]

Marching Confederates in high spirits chaffed the bystanders in Pennsylvania towns. "We got back into the Union at last, you see," they sang out. Few carried knapsacks, a haversack was enough. For blanket-raincoats many used strips of carpet in which they had punched holes for their heads. Young Schaff heard one Confederate general, John D. Imboden, a handsome, commanding man with haughty mien, say bitterly: "Your army destroyed all the fences, burned towns, turned poor women out of house and home, broke pianos, furniture, and old family portraits, and committed every act of vandalism." Southern restraint shone brightly by comparison. As Charles Francis Adams, Jr., remarked, it is doubtful if a force ever operated in an enemy's country leaving behind it less cause for resentment and hatred than Lee's army in these memorable days.[4] But as it pressed on, seizures of property grew, and depredations by stragglers increased. The roads became more crowded. On the right were troops, caissons, and supply wagons; on the left, moving back, droves of cattle and sheep, and farm wagons so heavy with spoils that they frequently used six or eight horses. When rains made the highways muddy, progress became slow, and soldiers who found them impracticable streamed alongside through the fields, to the wrath of farmers. Officers who searched houses for hidden stores meanwhile excited the contumely of irate women.[5]

On and on the Confederates swung. Harrisburg dispatches on June 28 announced that they were within four miles of the city's defensive works, and had burned the Columbia bridge over the Susquehanna twenty miles downstream. Marching into York that day, Ewell demanded food, clothing, and $100,000, and

3. Schaff, Philip, "The Gettysburg Week," *Scribner's Magazine*, XVI, July, 1894, 21-30.
4. "Remarks on Rhodes's History, Vol. V," *Proceedings Massachusetts Historical Society*, XIX, 311-356.
5. Fremantle, J.A.L., *The Fremantle Diary*, ed. Walter Lord, Boston, 1954, 195.

actually obtained not only supplies, but $28,000. "We will occupy the place permanently," threatened Jubal A. Early.[6] The deepest excitement now prevailed in Philadelphia, where workshops and stores shut down or closed early to enable men to drill, the merchants began raising a million dollars for defense, and even clergymen volunteered to handle shovels on the fortifications. By the 29th, Lee had determined to concentrate his army at Cashtown, just east of the Blue Ridge (here called South Mountain), and moving his own troops through a pass toward that village, which was only eight miles from Gettysburg, he sent word to Early at York and Ewell at Carlisle to meet him there. To the puzzlement of some observers, the advance upon Harrisburg abruptly halted on the 29th, but Lee gave as a reason the news that Hooker's army had crossed the Potomac and was approaching South Mountain.

Thus it was that the Confederate columns never quite reached the Pennsylvania capital. In the trenches before Harrisburg a young volunteer named Richard Watson Gilder, later editor and poet, kept an all-night vigil as June closed, quoting bits of verse to a sergeant beside him on the parapet. At last day broke —the day of the 30th; and there in the distance, on the brow of a hill, sat a solitary gray-clad horseman. Though Gilder did not know it until later, this horseman was the cresting drop on the farthest wave of the high tide of the Confederacy.[7]

[II]

Any full rehearsal herein of the details of the Gettysburg campaign would rank high among exercises in futility, for the mountain of books piled upon the battlefield equals in weight the stone and bronze of its serried monuments. Not details but general considerations, attempted answers to the enigmas of the combat, arrest our interest. Who, on the Southern side, made the decision to invade the North, and why? How much clearcut understanding and how much hazy misunderstanding accompanied the decision? For this desperate effort, what tried officers and what numbers and quality of troops could Lee summon into his reorganized army? What were the merits and weaknesses of his plan? In its execution, how much error may be charged to Lee, to Longstreet, to Early, to Jeb Stuart, and to A.P. Hill, and what defects of temper, if any, did they show? How much of the outcome may be attributed to chance, always blindly operative in war?

On the Northern side the questions are equally pregnant. Why was it that the North, with its tremendous superiority in numbers, wealth, and resources, was not able by midsummer of 1863 to muster a weight of men and arms that would

---

6. The New York *Herald*, June 30, 1863, said $150,000. *O.R.* I, xxvii, Pt.2, 307-317, 466.
7. Gilder, Rosamond, *Letters of Richard Watson Gilder*, Boston, 1916, 23-24.

have made all thought of invasion preposterous? What executive mismanagement lay behind the fact that it had to change its commanders just as the crisis broke and the all-important battle loomed imminent? How much of the strategy of the campaign may be attributed to the old commander, how much to the new, and how much to the compulsion of circumstance? In battlefield tactics, was it to Meade, or Hancock, or Gouverneur K. Warren, or John Sedgwick, that the Union owed most? Why was it that a victory won well within Pennsylvania, half a hundred miles from the nearest good crossing of the Potomac, and nigh a hundred from his Staunton base, did not culminate in the total destruction of Lee's army?

The decision to invade the North was Lee's, and he took it under a sense of almost desperate compulsion. Lee reportedly told D.H. Hill that the intention was to "turn back the tide of war, that is now pressing the South." He feared another Northern advance in Virginia during the summer. The Union army might gather all its forces and loose a crushing blow against him in the Fredericks-burg-Culpeper area, or it might establish a base on the James and attack Richmond on McClellan's old front. Lee wrote President Davis on May 30 indicating that he was not confident he could frustrate either move; and either, if not frustrated, could be fatal to the Confederacy.[8] He thought his chances of substituting victory for defeat would be greater if he struck first, hard, and in an unexpected quarter. Even if he won again in northern Virginia, the victory could gain him little. In a war of attrition the South was certain ultimately to lose; already, as he told Davis, he did not receive enough recruits to replace his losses.[9] A daring stroke, such as the capture of Baltimore, offered the only real hope. Knowing how savagely Virginia was being stripped of supplies, he felt the importance of the herds of cattle, the droves of horses, the wagons, shoes, clothing, and arms that Maryland or Pennsylvania might offer.

After the war Lee was said to have stated that "he had never invaded the North with an eye to holding permanently the hostile portions of it. . . . As for Gettysburg—First he did not intend to give general battle in Pa. if he could avoid it—the South was too weak to carry on a *war of invasion,* and his offensive movements against the North were never intended except as part of a defensive system. . . ." Both in his battle report and later, Lee stated that it was impossible to attack Hooker at Fredericksburg so the Federals had to be drawn away, and if practicable, the scene of hostilities transferred north of the Potomac. This

---

8. Lee to Hill, D.H. Hill Papers, Virginia State Library. *O.R.,* I, xxv, Pt.2, 832-833. Among the several shelves of volumes and articles on Gettysburg that might be assembled, there are a goodly number that are significant along with too many that merely repeat the familiar story. Most recent, and most outstanding of all, is Coddington, Edwin B., *The Gettysburg Campaign,* New York, 1968, which proves that new research is possible even on such a well canvassed subject.

9. *O.R.,* I, xxvii, Pt.3, 880-882.

would break up the enemy's summer plans. Of course, the movement was risky, but "everything was risky in our war." Further, Lee said he suggested that Beauregard be brought to Manassas and, with a diversionary force, threaten Washington while Lee went North. But it was never done.

In a momentous debate in Richmond in mid-May, Lee urged these considerations upon a reluctant Davis and a divided Cabinet. A victory on the Northern scene, a seizure of some great Northern city, might deepen Northern discouragement to the breaking point, or even win foreign recognition, although Lee's stated aims were considerably less than this. He carried his plan, but over the opposition of men who believed that he made a cardinal error in not consenting instead to reinforce the West.

President Davis had been specially anxious, as a Mississippian, to hold the Vicksburg-Port Hudson line, and had been fervently pressed for reinforcements by a Mississippi delegation.[10] Secretary of War Seddon had requested Lee to send Pickett's division, which had been serving under Longstreet in the region of Suffolk, Virginia, to Mississippi, but Lee on May 10 had disagreed. Longstreet himself, spending May 8 and 9 in Richmond, had urged a larger strategic plan for the succor of the West. In fact, several Confederates offered plans. Longstreet proposed a grand concentration at Murfreesboro: he himself would take 13,000 men to join Bragg's army, Joseph E. Johnston would bring 25,000 more from Jackson, and Simon Buckner 5,000 from Knoxville. Leading this host of more than 80,000, Longstreet believed that he might defeat Rosecrans's army, and advance into Kentucky to threaten Louisville; he might even compel Grant to withdraw from his position before Vicksburg.[11]

But Lee would not be moved from his purpose. The great thrust would be his, he would keep all the men he could muster under his own command, and he would attack northwest of Washington. His prestige, force of personality, and tenacity in argument compelled Davis to yield. In the Cabinet, Reagan alone, pleading to the last and even forcing a new meeting after the decision had been taken, held out for sending 25,000 or 30,000 men to the West.[12] On the evidence available, it is difficult to believe that Lee either knew or cared much about the Mississippi front. One of his arguments against sending Pickett's division thither was that it could not arrive until the last of May, "and all will then be over, as the climate in June will force the enemy to retire."[13] That statement would have raised a guffaw in Grant's camps! Lee wrote Davis June 2 that he still hoped

10. Strode, Hudson, *Jefferson Davis; Confederate President*, New York, 1959, II, 403. *O.R.*, xxvii, Pt.2, 305, Lee's Report; Col. William Allan's Collection, Univ. of N.C. Library.
11. Alexander, Edward Porter, *Military Memoirs of a Confederate*, New York, 1907, ch. XVI; *O.R.*, xxv, Pt.2, 790.
12. Strode, *op. cit.*, II, 405, 406.
13. *O.R.*, I, xxv, Pt.2, 782.

Johnston would demolish Grant, and save the Mississippi. "The enemy may be withdrawing to the Yazoo for the purpose of reaching their transports and retiring from the contest, which I hope is the case."[14] The Grant who was thus to be demolished had fought Champion's Hill on May 16 and invested Vicksburg on May 18-19. But Lee, seeing the East alone clearly and thinking only of Virginia, believed with the Richmond *Examiner* that the great opportunity of the South had come. "From the first day," said the *Examiner*, "the only reasonable hope of the Confederacy has been the transfer of hostilities to the enemy's territory."[15]

Longstreet unwillingly consented to the thrust. He asked, however, that the tactics be defensive, and that once they entered Pennsylvania they should so operate as to force the enemy to attack them. His impression was that Lee so promised. But this Lee later denied, terming the idea absurd.[16] It should have been plain to both men that, when two great armies were manoeuvring over a vast terrain of hills and streams, all too blind to each other's movements, nobody could predict where, when, or how they would collide. Chance might be the governing factor. The important fact is that, when the movement began, a misunderstanding existed between Lee and his principal lieutenant. It seemed to some observers then (and some shrewd commentators later) that the lethargic but self-confident Longstreet fancied himself Lee's mentor. The part he had played at Williamsburg, Antietam, and Fredericksburg justified his rank of lieutenant-general. But he had been balky, unmanageable, and slow at critical moments in the battle of Fair Oaks and Second Manassas, and had by no means covered himself with glory when he commanded later in the Suffolk area. Far from possessing the decision, dash, and quick intuition of Stonewall, he could sometimes be a dragging impediment.

No one can censure Lee for determining to keep the reins in his own hand and turn his columns toward Pennsylvania. He had just seen that when Longstreet was detached to the lower coast of Virginia he became very detached

14. *Ibid.*, 848-849.

15. May 21, 1863. Of Lee's consummate abilities as a commander, as of his nobility of character, there can be no doubt, but his breadth of view may be seriously questioned. In 1861, he had chosen Virginia in preference to the nation, although this involved a choice also of slavery, which he disliked, and of secession, to which he had been opposed. Now, in 1863, he chose Virginia again in preference to the Western theatre. Much may be said for his belief that at this moment an invasion of Pennsylvania was the most promising military operation. But in a man who had served before the war on the upper Mississippi and in Texas, the notion that summer fighting in the Vicksburg area would be impossible is hard to excuse. And as Joseph E. Johnston throughout May and the first three weeks of June was vigorously telegraphing Seddon in Richmond upon the realities of Grant's strength and his own weakness (*Narrative of Military Operations*, VII), Lee's supposition on June 2 that Grant was retreating to the Yazoo can be explained only on the theory of a preposterous breakdown of communications between Seddon and Lee, or a closed mind on Lee's part.

16. Swinton, William, *Campaigns of the Army of the Potomac*, New York, 1882, 340; Col. William Allan's Conversations with Lee, ms. typescript, Southern Historical Collection, Univ. of N.C. Library.

indeed; he might display the same excessive independence in Tennessee. The welding of a large body of Eastern troops into a new combination in which Johnston, Buckner, and Longstreet were all involved would take time, and time the Confederacy did not have. Lee's demeanor illustrated his sense of desperation, for this was a major occasion on which he exerted himself powerfully to determine Confederate policy, and for a time he remained apprehensive that Davis might interfere with his plans. His decision was logical. It was a mistake, however, not to have made surer of the Western situation, and of the unity of subordinate commanders and the government behind him. The demands of the Richmond press for an offensive suggested the desirability of mobilizing popular support, but he still needed warmer acquiescence in high quarters and more enthusiasm among his principal officers.

He needed them the more because he had just reorganized the Army of Northern Virginia into three corps, a step authorized by Davis and made almost imperative by Jackson's death. Lee had informed Davis on May 20 that the existing two-corps organization was manifestly defective, for 30,000 fighters, the approximate number in each, were too large a body for one commander to direct in the rough Virginia terrain. "They are always beyond the range of his vision, and frequently beyond his reach."[17] He had hesitated to create new corps earlier simply because he had been unable to recommend efficient commanders. Now he kept Longstreet as head of the First Corps, made Ewell (one of Stonewall's most trusted lieutenants) head of the Second, and placed A.P. Hill, who had succeeded Jackson at Chancellorsville, in charge of the newly-created Third.

Two-thirds of Lee's army thus passed under new chieftains; one of them, Hill, with no experience in managing more than one division at a time, though his command had distinguished itself by such celerity of movement that it was called "Hill's Light Division"; the other, Ewell, in poor health and suffering from permanent physical disability. Three of the nine divisions also went under new heads. As for the brigade commanders, the Second Corps in especial had so many new ones that it was thrown into confusion, and Ewell, himself recently absent from the corps for nine months, would find it difficult to coordinate the units. The batteries of the army were meanwhile redistributed, so that their liaison with the infantry was temporarily disrupted. The cavalry was enlarged to include two new brigades, one from western Virginia under John D. Imboden, and one from southern Virginia under A.S. Jenkins. In short, the reorganization, mingling new units with old, breaking old associations, and bringing many veteran regiments under officers unfamiliar with them or with Lee's procedures, meant temporary *dis*organization.[18] To be sure, the Federal side had also under-

17. *O.R.* I, xxv, Pt.2, 810-811.
18. Freeman, Douglas Southall, *R.E. Lee, A Biography*, New York, 1934, III, 14.

gone reorganization, and it had a new commander at the top in Meade.

To succeed in his thrust, Lee needed a well-forged thunderbolt, hurled with speed, force, and accuracy. A reluctant second in command who held a misconception of the fundamental strategy of the movement, believing that it would shift from the offensive to the defensive at the critical moment, and a redisposition of commanders and troops that impaired the army's solidarity, were hardly calculated to forge such a weapon.

[III]

Lee's plan of marching northward up the Shenandoah and Cumberland Valleys offered clear advantages over his previous Antietam invasion. He could keep the Blue Ridge on his eastern flank to shelter and partly screen his troops. While advancing through a high farming country with ripening crops, he could threaten numerous towns and cities in Maryland and Pennsylvania. He could find good roads, and some wagons and horses to haul ammunition and other necessities up from Staunton and Winchester. His movement nevertheless had flagrant weaknesses. He could not move seriously against Baltimore or even Harrisburg without abandoning his Blue Ridge rampart. The farther he penetrated, the more vulnerable his line of supply would become. From Winchester to Harrisburg as the crow flies is nearly 120 miles, and from Staunton to Harrisburg by wagon-road, according to E.P. Alexander's estimate, 200 miles. This long line would be exposed to Union cavalry raids.

When the Confederate columns first lengthened out on their march, Lincoln on June 14 wrote Hooker his famous admonition: "If the head of Lee's army is at Martinsburg, and tail of it on the Plank road between Fredericksburg and Chancellorsville, the animal must be very slim somewhere. Could you not break him?"[19] Hooker did not really try to break Lee, had not really attempted anything since Chancellorsville, and was now forced on the defensive to protect Washington as the Confederate army continued in its northward advance, despite its dependence on precarious lines of communication.

Moreover, as Lee advanced, a growing host of troops, including militia, would rise before him. If he turned westward to strike at Pittsburgh he would have to battle not only distance, but a wilder, hillier country with few roads. If he fought a drawn battle anywhere deep within Pennsylvania, he would have to retreat exhausted, and if he were defeated he would have to retreat precipitately and in badly battered condition. Even if he left ample forces to guard the fords on the Potomac and the river did not rise, he might be in dire peril. It appears that the desperate Lee was never quite certain how much, if anything, he could accom-

19. Lincoln, *Collected Works*, VI, 273.

plish. On the morning that he himself crossed the Potomac, June 25, he had written President Davis on the insufficiency of troops to maintain his communications. "I think," he added, "I can throw General Hooker's army across the Potomac and draw troops from the south, embarrassing their campaign in a measure, if I can do nothing more and have to return."[20] This statement suggests that he was belatedly daunted by difficulties he had not fully measured at the outset. Well would it have been for the Confederacy if he had contented himself with taking prisoners at Winchester, seizing easy booty across the Potomac, frightening the North, and embarrassing whatever plan of campaign the Union leaders had!

Lee's army, as it advanced into Pennsylvania, numbered about 75,000 men and 200 guns.[21] He had called in troops from every available quarter: from South Carolina; from the North Carolina forces of D.H. Hill, who spared him about 8,000 effectives; from the Virginia coast; and from inland Virginia, where recruiting was sternly pressed. He had strengthened Jeb Stuart's cavalry by fresh men and horses. Of course he had to leave Richmond adequately defended. He reassured the anxious Davis on this point, writing that he was doing his best on all exposed fronts: "The question which seems always to be presented is a mere choice of difficulties." It was sufficient, he thought, to keep the local troops and home guard ready for instant service, with advanced commands under General Arnold Elzey north and east of the city equally alert. In an emergency, D.H. Hill's force could be rushed up from North Carolina.

Lee's march was at first ably conducted. His troops found the Pennsylvania extension of the Blue Ridge an even better screen than they had anticipated. It was thickly wooded, the roads across it were narrow and difficult, and the passes could be held by small detachments.[22] The army, exultant over the ejection of the much-hated General R.H. Milroy from Winchester, was further elated by the easy occupation of Chambersburg.[23] Ewell drove with headlong vigor into Carlisle so that he could collect cattle, grain, and stores, although the town lay dangerously far east. With Early of Ewell's corps in York, Brigadier General John

20. *O.R.* I, xxvii, Pt.3, 930-931.

21. Lee's field returns of May 20, 1863, gave him an aggregate of 81,568 officers and men, with 67,567 present for duty. Much troubled by desertions, he asked Seddon to guard the fords across the James. "The deserters usually go in squads, taking their arms and equipment, and sometimes borrowing from their comrades ammunition sufficient to make 100 rounds per man." *O.R.* I, xxv, Pt.2, 814-15, 846;E.P. Alexander in *Memoirs of a Confederate* credits Lee with 76,224 men and 272 guns; the Comte de Paris, after careful study, estimated his battle forces at 68,000 to 69,000 men and 250 guns. (*History of the Civil War in America*, Philadelphia, 1875-1888, III, 692-693); Abner Doubleday gives an estimate of 73,500 men and 190 guns (*Chancellorsville and Gettysburg, Campaigns of the Civil War*, VII, New York, 1882, 123). Frederick Tilburg of the National Park System, in his handbook on the battle, offers the round figure of 75,000. Milroy's defense is in *O.R.*, I, xxvii, Pt.2, 41-52.

22. Hyde, Thomas W., *Following the Greek Cross*, Boston, 1894, 158ff, gives a graphic description.

23. Milroy's brutalities had led the Confederates to put a price on his head; Fremantle, *Diary, op.cit.*, 182, 183. Cf. Lincoln's castigation of Milroy, *Collected Works*, VI, 308, 309.

B. Gordon's brigade was sent on as far as Wrightsville on the Susquehanna. Then, with his forces scattered all too widely, Lee learned on the night of the 28th that Hooker had not only crossed the Potomac in pursuit, but was well north of that river and close to the Confederate rear. At once, the Southern leader scented danger, for part of Hooker's army might thrust west across the Blue Ridge or South Mountain, ensconce itself in the Cumberland Valley across his line of retreat, and seize the initiative. He must concentrate his troops and move them east of Gettysburg, as if closing down on Baltimore, so as to keep Hooker also on the east. On the morning of the 29th he sent hurried orders to Ewell to march from Carlisle directly to Cashtown or Gettysburg, which lie only ten miles apart; ordered Hill to march from Chambersburg toward these two towns; and ordered Longstreet to follow Hill.

Lee supposed at this moment that Gettysburg was free from Union troops. Cashtown, under the very shadow of South Mountain, would have been an excellent concentration point, for there the Confederates could take strong defensive positions and turn east or west as advantages offered. To get involved in a sudden offensive battle at Gettysburg was a different matter. Why was it, we may ask, that Hooker's passage of the Potomac took Lee by surprise? And why was he ignorant of the fact that on the 29th some Federal troops were already in Gettysburg? Because in this critical hour he lacked Jeb Stuart's cavalry or failed to use his other horsemen to bring him essential information.

The fault was primarily Lee's own. In the haste and pressure under which he began his invasion, he had committed the grave error of yielding to Stuart's suggestion that the dashing young cavalryman should sweep into the rear or flank of Hooker's army as it first moved north, and try to find an opening for a swift blow. When John S. Mosby had suggested this raid, Stuart had instantly seen that it might crown him with glory.[24] Lee, at the very least, gave his partial assent in confused and ambiguous orders on June 22 which he confirmed and enlarged the next day: "You will be able to judge whether you can pass around their army without hindrance, doing them all the damage you can, and cross the river east of the mountains. In either case, after crossing the river you must move on and feel the right of Ewell's troops"—that is, of the advance force.[25] Stuart naturally interpreted this grant of discretionary power in his own favor, and plunged forward. Lee's full commands were cloudy, indistinct and permissive, but he seems to have wished Stuart to cross into Maryland, take position on Ewell's right, guard his flank, keep him informed of enemy movements, and collect whatever supplies were available. Instead, Stuart detached himself completely from Ewell, moved into Maryland and Pennsylvania at a wide distance from the

24. Mosby, John S., in Philadelphia *Weekly Times,* December 15, 1877.
25. Lee's important orders are in *O.R.* I, xxvii, Pt.3, 823, 913, 923.

other Confederate columns—the Union forces marching north between him and Ewell—and furnished no information. On June 30, as the armies converged on Gettysburg, he was at Hanover, Pennsylvania, far over to the east. Lee should have realized that this raid could accomplish little of value under any circumstances, and would make Stuart's junction with him in time for a battle unlikely, although Lee did not intend to fight unless attacked by the enemy. When on June 28 Stuart, just across the Potomac, captured a train of 125 wagons at Rockville, Maryland, and halted to rifle them and parole 400 prisoners, the dangers of a miscarriage increased.[26]

Thus Lee was in the dark as to Union movements from the moment he forded the Potomac, and still in the dark when, about two P.M. on July 1, riding eastward from Cashtown, he suddenly came in sight of the action opening on the western and northwestern outskirts of Gettysburg. He had no idea whether he faced the whole Union army or merely a small advance detachment. Stuart had taken with him Wade Hampton and Fitzhugh Lee, who stood hardly second to him as observers and fighters, and whom the army missed sorely. It was as an uninformed commander that Lee had to make his first critical decisions. He had been anxious to avoid a general engagement at least until his whole army was concentrated—until Longstreet's corps had followed Hill's into the area. But when he saw Early's division of Ewell's corps suddenly arrive on the road leading into Gettysburg, he changed his mind, and ordered the troops forward. Under Major-General Jubal A. Early, and Rodes, Heth and Pender, the gray forces swept on. They routed the Union troops on the edge of town, hurled them back to the ridges east and south of it, occupied the streets, and took 5,000 prisoners. "A doubtful morning had ended in a smashing victory."[27] But it was an improvised and hurried victory caught out of fog and mystification, and it was not consolidated by the occupation of Cemetery Ridge beyond the town, which Gordon on the Confederate side and Winfield S. Hancock of the Union army, both on the field, thought would have been easily feasible.[28]

Clearly, in all this Lee was not at his best; not the Lee of Second Manassas and Chancellorsville. Not only had he lost Jackson, a loss that he recognized as irremediable; but the gravity of the Confederate situation, the sense that complete victory or utter ruin might hang in the balance, created an unwonted mental tension in him. Observers spoke of his anxious and excited mien. He was not a well man, for pleurisy and an infection in April had weakened him.[29] The lack

26. Davis, Burke, *Jeb Stuart, the Last Cavalier*, New York, 1957, 327; McClellan, H.B., *The Life and Campaigns of Major-General J.E.B. Stuart*, Boston, 1885, XVII; *O.R.* I, xxvii, Pt.2, 308, 692-697, 823.
27. Freeman, *Lee, op.cit.*, III, 71.
28. Gordon, John B., *Reminiscences of the Civil War*, New York, 1904, 153-156.
29. Eckenrode, H.J., and Bryan Conrad, *James Longstreet, Lee's War Horse*, Chapel Hill, 1936, 173; Freeman, *Lee, op.cit.*, II, 502-504; IV, Appendix 7, 521ff.

of positiveness and decisive clarity in his orders evidenced an inner uncertainty. Prussian officer Justus Scheibert, who accompanied the army, noted that his nervousness infected the men around him with a similar uneasiness.[30] Fretted to exasperation by Stuart's absence and lack of other information on Union movements, he lost his usual confident composure.[31]

[IV]

What, meanwhile, of Hooker and the Union army? Stanton, Halleck, and others in Washington had little or no real faith in Hooker. But the President would not go so far as to remove him until he had firm reasons, partly because the army retained confidence in Hooker, partly because Secretary Chase still championed him, and still more because, after McClellan, Pope and Burnside, a fourth removal would be discouraging to the nation.

As Lee's columns turned north in the Shenandoah, Hooker's first apprehension was that they might strike a sudden blow at Washington. He moved slowly after the Confederates, posting his army at Centreville, Manassas, and Fairfax Court House in such a position as to protect the capital. When Lee forded the Potomac, Hooker determined to cross at once and strike north on an inside line paralleling Lee's and covering the capital and Baltimore. On June 25-26, half a dozen Union corps took up their march through Maryland on a line running northwest from Frederick. Of this Lee knew nothing.

Thus far, in fact, the two armies and the whole country found the campaign mystifying. The North knew that the Confederate array was executing a movement toward Harrisburg, and might seize it, or concentrate against Baltimore, or even lunge toward Philadelphia. Just what would the rebels do?—the entire Northern press agonized over the question. And Hooker's plans were as mysterious as Lee's purpose. He would have done well, Washington thought, to start his pursuit of Lee a few days earlier.[32] Moving into Pennsylvania, he used Pleasonton's cavalry to scout Longstreet's column and make sure the Confederates were closely guarding the Blue Ridge passes. On the 26th he fixed his headquarters at Poolesville, Maryland; on the next day he ordered cavalry sent to Emmitsburg and Gettysburg to discover whether Lee's forces were in the area.[33]

At this moment, with Longstreet in Chambersburg, the high Union command presented an unhappy picture. Halleck nursed his old animosity toward Hooker, dating from California days. Stanton told Lincoln: "I have no confidence

30. Eckenrode and Conrad, *op. cit.*, 191.
31. No "correct intelligence," he later wrote; Lee, R.E. Jr., *Recollections and Letters of General Lee*, New York, 1904, 102.
32. Doubleday, Abner, *op. cit.*, 106.
33. Herbert, Walter E., *Fighting Joe Hooker*, Indianapolis, 1944, 244.

in General Hooker, though his personal courage I do not question."[34] Gideon Welles had lost whatever faith in•the general he had ever possessed; Charles Sumner, who was often in the White House, was dubious or antagonistic. Hooker himself was in an irritated frame of mind, for his recent proposals had met with one rebuff after another. When Lee began to move, Hooker had proposed using his army in a direct attack upon Richmond, but Lincoln had indicated he thought the true object was Lee's army. When on June 16 he had heard that Lee was crossing the Potomac, he had suggested that Pleasonton's cavalry be sent across the river forthwith; but this Lincoln and Halleck again vetoed. It is not strange that he burst out in a telegram to Lincoln:

"You have long been aware, Mr. President, that I have not enjoyed the confidence of the major-general commanding the army, and I can assure you so long as this continues we may look in vain for success . . ." Lincoln replied, "When you say I have long been aware that you do not enjoy the confidence of the major-general commanding, you state the case much too strongly. You do not lack his confidence in any degree to do you any harm. On seeing him, after telegraphing you this morning, I found him more nearly agreeing with you than I was myself. If you and he would use the same frankness to one another, and to me, that I use to both of you, there would be no difficulty. I need and must have the professional skill of both, and yet these suspicions tend to deprive me of both. . . . "[35]

R.E. Schenck, the erratic commander in Baltimore, and Samuel P. Heintzelman, the feeble and timid head of the Washington garrison, both clamoring for protection, added to the confusion. Into the tangle of sometimes contradictory telegrams exchanged on June 16-20 by Hooker, Halleck, Stanton, and Lincoln we need not go. At one moment on the 16th the resentful Hooker informed Lincoln that he was prepared "to move without communication with any place for ten days." In this crisis, there would be no communication between the nation's principal army and Washington! Halleck seemed to many to blow hot and cold. He explicitly assured Hooker: "You are in command of the Army of the Potomac, and will make the particular dispositions as you deem proper. I shall only indicate the objects to be aimed at."[36] Yet Hooker remained fearful that Halleck would not support him with enough troops. Herman Haupt, visiting Hooker's headquarters, found him in a morose temper; he said that all his suggestions having been rejected, he would move only when he got orders, would follow them literally, and if they resulted in failure, would let others bear the blame.[37]

34. Gorham, George C., *Life and Public Services of Edwin M. Stanton,* Boston, 1899, II, 99; precise date uncertain.

35. *O.R.* I, xxvii, Pt.I, 45; June 16, 11 a.m. 1863; Lincoln, *Collected Works,* VI, 281-282.

36. *O.R.* I, xxvii, Pt.I, 47-50.

37. Haupt, Herman, "The Crisis of the Civil War, Gettysburg," *Century Magazine,* XXII, May-Oct., 1892, 794-797.

Chase, visiting the general, did his best to dispel the man's ill humor, and as soon as he got back in Washington on the 20th assured him that he had talked with Lincoln, Chase, and Stanton, and that Hooker might count on their support.

Then Hooker, distrustful, morose, perhaps drinking, suffered three jolts. First, he issued an order to the general commanding at Alexandria. It was not obeyed. When Hooker tried to place the general under arrest, it turned out that Heintzelman had directed him to disregard all orders not coming from Halleck or the War Department.[38] Soon afterward, Hooker ordered a colonel to proceed to Harper's Ferry. The colonel sent a saucy reply that he did not belong to Hooker's command, but Heintzelman's. And third, when Lee's thrust had developed to a point of real peril, and Hooker tried to bring under his direct command the force on Maryland Heights, overlooking Harper's Ferry—some 10,000 men led by General William H. French—he was once more rebuffed.

This rebuff was so important that its story deserves a few details. On the morning of June 27, the anxious Hooker rode into Harper's Ferry and examined the Heights. He quickly saw that French's force was quite useless, for nothing remained at the Ferry worth capturing, and the river, fordable at many other points, could not be blocked. He had telegraphed Halleck the previous evening to ask if there was any reason why the Heights should not be evacuated. His answer was waiting at Harper's Ferry: since Maryland Heights had always been regarded as important, and had been fortified at great expense, it should not be abandoned except under absolute necessity. This disgusted Hooker, and he telegraphed back that the troops ought to be transferred to some point where they would be of real service: "Now they are but a bait for rebels, should they return." He asked that his plea be laid before Lincoln and Stanton.[39] Then, angry and

---

38. *O.R.* I, xxvii, Pt.i, 56-57.
39. *Ibid.*, 60. The question of Harper's Ferry and Hooker's resignation is discussed in the Horatio Woodman Papers, Mass. Hist. Soc., Boston, Document of John Codman Ropes, Boston, Feb. 8, 1870, "Conversation with Edwin M. Stanton." " . . . He said Hooker was never removed, but resigned, and that he resigned most unexpectedly. He was, said he, in Washington consulting with the President, General Halleck and myself, only a week before he resigned. Wednesday I think (24 June 1863) we talked over the matter of Maryland Heights which had been fortified and provisioned and equipped at a vast expense, and it was agreed that they should not be given up, General Hooker concurring without objection—He then went up to the front. Judge then our surprise when a dispatch came in a day or two from General French commanding Maryland Heights, stating that he had been ordered to evacuate the position. We held a brief consultation, and ordered him to hold the position. If Hooker had asked for the evacuation of the Post, he would have been granted to him [sic] to evacuate it, just as Meade had afterwards. But we supposed there might be (as I recollect the conversation) some mistake, and therefore countermanded the order to French until we could communicate with Hooker. But as soon as Hooker learned that his order had been countermanded he resigned." This of course is a bit late and second-hand, and does not take into consideration Hooker's desire to evacuate, received in Washington five minutes before his resignation was received. Halleck to Lieber, Lieber Papers, HEH, Aug 4, 1863:–Halleck stated in this letter that Lincoln "then ordered Gen. H. to report to me & obey my orders. This caused him to be asked to be relieved, which was done instantly. Had he remained in command, we certainly should have been defeated at Gettysburg." Horatio Woodman Papers, Mass. Hist. Soc., Sumner to Woodman of the Boston *Transcript*,

impatient, he waited with his old classmate French for Halleck's response.

At this moment, Hooker mistakenly believed that he was outnumbered. Two Union men who had independently counted Lee's forces on their march through Hagorstown computed them at 91,000 infantry, 6,000 cavalry, and 280 guns. If this count was accurate Lee had about 100,000 men, with more coming; and even including troops drawn from Schenck and Heintzelman, Hooker put his own army at not more than 105,000. He indicated he *must* have French's 10,000. But he did not get them, for a curt telegram from Halleck came directly to French: "Pay no attention to General Hooker's orders." Its contemptuous flavor enraged Hooker. Stepping out of French's headquarters, he encountered an old friend, Andrew T. Reynolds, of the cavalry, who remarked that a battle seemed imminent. "Yes," rejoined Hooker, "but I shall not fight it. Halleck's dispatch severs my connection with the Army of the Potomac."[40] He made good his words by instantly telegraphing Halleck:

"My original instructions require me to cover Harper's Ferry and Washington. I have now imposed on me, in addition, an enemy in my front of more than my number. I beg to be understood, respectfully, but firmly, that I am unable to comply with this condition with the means at my disposal, and earnestly request that I may at once be relieved from the position I occupy."[41]

To this angry dispatch Halleck, only too glad to get rid of a distrusted commander, replied the same day that he had referred the General's request to the President. The same day, for the emergency permitted no delay, Lincoln and Halleck agreed upon the promotion of George Gordon Meade to the command. It was a logical choice. Meade, graduating in the upper half of his West Point class in 1835, had served in both the Seminole and Mexican Wars, had performed engineering and scientific work all over the country, and had been appointed brigadier-general of Pennsylvania volunteers by Governor Curtin after Sumter. He had fought bravely and skillfully in the Seven Days and at Second Manassas, South Mountain, Antietam, and Fredericksburg. His judgment and nerve as major-general, heading the Fifth Corps at Chancellorsville, impelled two other corps leaders, D.N. Couch and John F. Reynolds, both disgusted with Hooker, to urge that he be made head of the Army of the Potomac. Halleck did not know him personally—he asked Heintzelman what kind of a man he was—but recommended him warmly to Lincoln.[42]

Halleck at once selected a tried officer who was in the War Department at

July 1, 1863; "Hooker complained of Halleck & asked to be relieved. I think the change has been taken well. . . . Stanton & Chase did not like it, but since Hooker asked it there was nothing to be said."

40. Herbert, *Hooker, op. cit.*, 245.
41. *O.R.* I, xxvii, Pt.1, 60; received 3 p.m., June 27, 1863.
42. Heintzelman, Samuel P., Ms. *Diary*, June 28, 1863, LC.

the moment, James A. Hardie, to notify Meade of his appointment. Riding a locomotive to Frederick, and wearing civilian clothes lest Stuart's cavalry seize him, Hardie found a driver and buggy, and hurried off on the rough streets, alive with stragglers, many of them drunk, and roads full of crippled army vehicles. It was around three A.M. June 28 when, drawing up in front of Meade's headquarters in the country, he was challenged by a sentry who reluctantly admitted him. The General, emerging in his nightshirt, was astounded and half-dismayed when told he was head of the army.[43] He would have preferred to see the place go to his comrade Reynolds. But modest and self-controlled, he could only accept. A war correspondent saw him a few minutes afterward outside his tent, standing with bowed head and downcast eyes, lost in thought; his slouch hat drawn low, his uniform stained with hard service, his boots dusty.[44] At seven A.M. he telegraphed Halleck that he would move toward the Susquehanna, would keep Washington and Baltimore, as ordered, well covered, and if Lee turned toward Baltimore, would give battle.[45]

In Washington, Meade's promotion afforded general relief, although the supersedence of Hooker shook radical Republicans who had liked his aggressiveness and his sharp criticism of McClellan. Chase, who had tried so hard to assure Hooker of Administration support, first heard of his loss of command when he attended a Cabinet meeting on Sunday, June 28. Chase could hardly believe it. Lincoln cut short his protest: "The acceptance of an army resignation is not a matter for your department." The resentful Secretary wrote his daughter Kate that Halleck, though likable and apparently capable, failed to master the situation, for "he does not *work, work, work* as if he were in earnest."[46]

43. *O.R.* I, xxvii, Pt.3, 369; Nicolay and Hay, *Lincoln, op.cit.,* VII, 226. Meade Papers, July 16, to his wife, Berlin, Md.: "They have refused to relieve me, but insist on my continuing to try to do what I know in advance it is impossible to do.—My army men and animals is exhausted—it wants rest & reorganization—it has been greatly reduced & weakened by recent operations, and no reinforcements of any practical value have been sent—Yet in the face of all these facts, well known to them I am urged, pushed & *spurred* to attempting to pursue & destroy an army nearly equal to my own falling back upon its resources and reinforcements, and increasing its morale daily. This has been the history of all my predecessors, and I clearly saw that in time my fate would be theirs—This was the reason I was dis-inclined to take the command, and it is for this reason I would gladly give it up. . . ." July 18: " . . . I am very worried, and long for rest & quiet—My temperament is not sufficiently phlegmatic for a post of such responsibility as the command of an army, which is really commanded at Washington." This type of comment appears often and is almost without exception left out of the printed version of the letters. "It is impossible to give satisfaction.—If you succeed, they claim the credit, and if anything goes wrong, you are the scape goat even tho you may be strictly carrying out orders. . . ." Aug. 1 to a Mr. Walker: " . . . The whole difficulty lay in the fact that people only looked at the *result* of a *successful* attack, but lost sight of the *consequences* of a *failure*— . . . I however am very well contented with what I have done viz-in less than 30 days defeating Lee & not only compelling him to relinquish his scheme of invasion, but compelling him to evacuate Pa. Maryland-the Valley of the Shenandoah, & return to his line behind the Rapidan. . . ."

44. Coffin, Charles Carleton, *Marching to Victory,* New York, 1889, 189.

45. *O.R.* I, xxvii, Pt.1, 60, 61; Hooker went to Baltimore, as ordered.

46. Schuckers, J.W., *The Life and Public Services of Salmon Portland Chase,* New York, 1874, 469-470.

Meade's first steps were promising. He was not a man to kindle the ardor of his troops. Tall, thin, with a large broad brow, prominent aquiline nose and grizzled beard and mustache, his bent shoulders, nearsighted eyes, and quiet, reserved manner gave him the aspect of a careworn lawyer rather than a soldier. Although his demeanor was usually icy, he frequently gave way to fierce bursts of temper, with vitriolic speeches that made many officers his enemy. He lacked the sense of conscious power, the imperious will, and the spirit of leadership that has nerved great captains from Hannibal to Allenby. It was significant that he found fault with Hooker chiefly for his lack of *caution*. He would clearly be a colorless general—but he began well. He wisely kept Hooker's staff, though he vainly tried to appoint a new chief in place of Butterfield. Harper's Ferry was now under his orders and he took part of the garrison away, but he left a force sufficient to hold Maryland Heights until, influenced by a false report of low supplies at Harper's Ferry, he temporarily evacuated it. His only important deviation from Hooker's plans was to abandon the idea of a stroke against Lee's communications which his predecessor apparently had in mind. Sending his columns forward, by June 30 he had them across the Pennsylvania boundary. His troops, following all the useful roads they could find, with adequate cavalry protection on the flanks, were spread out on a front thirty-miles wide.[47]

Halleck made every effort to assist him. "You will not be hampered by any minute instructions from these Head Quarters," he wrote in a letter accompanying Lincoln's appointment. "Your army is free to act as you may deem proper under the circumstances as they arise." The day after the appointment he thought it probable that Lee would concentrate south of the Susquehanna and so wrote Meade. That same day he exhorted the commander in Harrisburg, Couch, to hold the Confederates in check on the Susquehanna until Meade could give them battle. On July 1, he telegraphed Meade that Lee seemed moving either to turn the Union left, or to press back into Maryland along the South Mountain: "Don't let him draw you too far to the east." That day, of course, the fighting began. At six in the evening Meade had a full budget of news to send Halleck, who doubtless gave it to Lincoln before midnight; two corps had been engaged all day in front of Gettysburg, three more had been moving up, Reynolds had been killed, and Hancock had been sent to assume field command. Meade saw no alternative to hazarding a general battle next day.[48]

Everybody had been taken by surprise. Lee had hoped to give battle, if necessary at all, on the defensive, to Union attackers at or near Cashtown; Meade had hoped to open the combat, on the defensive, somewhere southeast of Gettys-

47. Cleaves, Freeman, *Meade of Gettysburg*, Norman, Okla., 1960, 129ff.; Hunt, Henry J., "The First Day at Gettysburg," *Battles and Leaders*, III, 255ff.; Doubleday, *Chancellorsville and Gettysburg, op. cit.*, 114-115; Meade to Butterfield, Feb. 4, 1864, Meade Papers, Hist. Soc. of Pennsylvania.
48. *O.R.* I, xxvii, Pt.I, 67-72; Halleck Papers, Eldredge Coll., HEH.

burg at works he was preparing near Pipe Creek, Maryland. Lee stood in the more dangerous situation, for his communications must grow increasingly precarious, and his strength must deteriorate. By June 30 it was more urgent for him to grapple with Meade than for Meade to engage Lee. The situation was taking just the form that Longstreet had feared; the Confederates, after assuming the strategic offensive, were being compelled to adopt the tactical offensive as well. The most momentous event on the 30th possessed a significance which nobody appreciated at the time. That morning a Union cavalry division under John Buford had ridden into Gettysburg on a reconnaissance, and posted scouts on the roads leading west and northwest. Pettigrew's Confederate brigade, marching toward Gettysburg for supplies, had seen these scouts and withdrawn, for he had no orders to begin a battle. But Buford, comprehending the importance of the town as a center of nine or ten converging roads, resolved to hold the ridge on the northwest—McPherson's Ridge—and posted his troops there to make a desperate stand.

Pettigrew had done just right; Buford had done just right; and A.P. Hill did what seemed natural and right when at dawn on July 1 he ordered two brigades to march down the Chambersburg road to Gettysburg to ascertain the real Union strength. The battle was thus unexpectedly and abruptly joined in a chance encounter between the forces of subordinate officers at a village of 2400 people, which lay just north of the point where two ridges (soon to be famous) faced each other—Seminary Ridge on the west, and Cemetery Ridge on the east. Near the northern end of Seminary Ridge stood the theological school which gave it its name; opposite, at the northern end of Cemetery Ridge stood the town graveyard on a hill of its own. This was flanked on the east by the higher, rockier eminence of Culp's Hill. The two ridges, with the difficult hills, Little Round Top and Big Round Top, closing the southern end of Cemetery Ridge, would dominate the battle. Had Lee's army been able the first day to push across Cemetery Ridge, holding it and Culp's Hill, he could have flung Meade's army back in retreat. Later, when Schurz arrived to fight the battle at its fiercest, the situation was just as doubtful as he indicated. Lee had held the initial advantage and his men had fought well. His great disadvantage was the persistent, unnerving absence of Stuart, who he had hoped would find and keep a place on Ewell's right in leading the advance of the army, and would be the eyes of his gray host in a strange and much-broken country.

As the forces drew up in battle array, reflective men on both sides could ponder grave errors and shortcomings. Lee's failure to keep Stuart's cavalry in hand was a blunder heavy with misfortune. His tardy concentration of his army at Cashtown was another error for which he would pay heavily. On the Union side, the change of commanders just three days before the battle might have cost the high command a fearful penalty if the conflict had not turned out to be, in the end, a fight in which Northern corps commanders were of much more importance than the chief general. Lincoln should have removed Hooker immediately after Chancellorsville, and given his successor—either Meade or Reynolds—full control of the army before the end of May, when he would have had a golden month to acquaint himself with his forces and their leaders. What if Wellington had been moved up to the chief command of the British army just three days before the battle of Waterloo?

It was a maladroit combination of misunderstandings—with Halleck irritated by Lincoln's direct orders to Hooker, Lincoln disturbed by Halleck's attitude, Hooker angered by the repeated rejection of his proposals, and Halleck and Hooker deeply distrustful of each other—which brought about the latter's request to be relieved. Assuredly these misunderstandings and distrusts should have been terminated long before the campaign in Pennsylvania reached its climax. They endured, however, until June 28, and on July 1, the battle began with an apprehensive, uncertain Meade in charge. We find no real evidence that Meade advocated retreating, despite rumors that he favored withdrawal at a council of war on the evening of the second day. The majority of those present testified that Meade had no idea of pulling out; although other officers, some of them disgruntled with Meade personally or pro-Hooker, received an impression that he was ready to retire from the field. He was abler than Hooker, but he began his work with grave disadvantages.

Saddest of all Union delinquencies, however, was the failure of the government to bring to the field an army decisively superior to Lee's force. Deep in Pennsylvania, close to its capital, the Confederacy marshalled 75,000 men, well-armed, hopeful of still another great victory under their unmatchable leader, and happy in the possession of guns. Such was the army flung forward by an ebbing population of hardly five millions. Against them, so close to the large Northern cities and manufactories, the twenty-odd million people of the North might have been expected to array an overwhelming host. Flanking that host, it might well have placed three or four well-trained army corps in a position to cut off the retreat of the enemy.

Yet what was the fact? Meade, after his army had been strengthened by large contingents drawn from Harper's Ferry and the Washington and Baltimore garrisons, had on the field 84,000 men by one count, 88,000 by another. The two armies were so fairly matched in strength that, had the South defended the ridges and the North attacked, as Longstreet had hoped, the result might well have been different. Such were the fruits of Northern folly in temporarily halting enlistments in the spring of 1862, in letting States recruit many regiments for limited terms, and in delaying operation of a draft until this summer.

Over the errors on each side it was too late to repine—too late, that is, when Heth's and Rode's Confederates struck the first heavy blows on McPherson's Ridge, when Early followed them with a more shattering stroke, and when Hancock, rallying the Union troops on Cemetery Hill, sent word to Meade in the rear that Gettysburg was the place for the battle.

[V]

The story of Gettysburg can neither be justly written in terms of the generals who commanded important posts of the armies at critical times and places, nor in terms of the controversies which instantly arose over the sagacity or ineptness of their movements. To be sure, these controversies are often of compelling interest, and the windrows of conflicting evidence, when impartially examined, offer highly enlightening information upon the bloody three days of fighting. But the heart of the truth about the conflict—does it really lie here?

On the first day, when Heth's division, driving against the Union cavalry picket west of town, found itself hotly embattled with the First Corps of the Army of the Potomac, and, after heavy losses, swept into the central streets and beyond, the stage was set for controversy. The hot sun which shone out after an early drizzle that July 1st saw Reynolds shot dead from his horse as he rallied the Northern line. It saw Abner Doubleday take his place in command, to be quickly superseded by O. O. Howard, and he in turn by Winfield S. Hancock. The Union troops fought a stubborn delaying action until pressed back to a defensive position on Cemetery Hill and Cemetery Ridge. But why did the Confederates in their powerful onslaught, easily the victors of the day, not accomplish more? Why did not Ewell, bringing his corps from the northwest in time to help deliver the first blows and pursue the routed Federals through the town, push on to seize Cemetery Ridge and Culp's Hill while they were still thinly defended? Or were the defenses really thin when he arrived? Could he actually have seized the positions? Endless ink has been expended on these questions, yes and no. The only certainty is that if Ewell had taken Cemetery Ridge and the adjoining heights, the sun that evening would have sunk on a Union army with but one course before it—retreat.

The second day, still hot and clear but for light fleecy clouds, saw both armies curiously quiet all morning except for the early fighting on Culp's Hill. Meade, who had arrived at one A.M., tired and irritable but determined, faced Lee, who had spent part of the night conferring with Longstreet and examining what ground he could by torchlight and moonlight. Why did not Longstreet attack, as Lee expected, in the early hours? Here was the basis for another controversy. Finally, in mid-afternoon an exciting action did open. Longstreet, probing the Union line, found that the Third Corps under Daniel Sickles had pushed forward to a badly exposed position in front of Cemetery Ridge, running out to a sharp salient. The Confederates attacked, hoping to crush Sickles and break the whole Union left. Bloody fighting developed at the Peach Orchard, Devil's Den, and surrounding points, in which Sickles lost a leg, but his command held fast. Had he imperilled Meade's whole army merely in the hope of winning some special glory for himself? Whatever his motives, he had provided materials for another warm dispute. Although the evidence against him seemed clear, the theatrical strutter had never lacked partisans since he had ruthlessly murdered Philip Barton Key for being excessively attentive to his wife.

And still another controversy had meanwhile been born. In their hot thrust forward, Longstreet's troops had all but captured Little Round Top, which if seized and crowned with guns would have enabled them to enfilade the whole Union line. Why did they not take it? Because, some Southern commentators later wrote, one Confederate officer needlessly delayed ten minutes, in defiance of orders, in flinging his troops upon the invaluable height. The only certainty is that credit for the rapid Union thrust which took and fortified the hill in the nick of time belonged to General Gouverneur K. Warren—who might well claim later that his promptness had saved the battle.

Part of the basis for a much larger disputation had been laid as well. Longstreet, depressed by the fact that the Confederate army had been thrust by circumstances into a position where it must fight an offensive battle, and must attack strong positions held by an antagonist superior in numbers and guns, had pleaded with Lee, on the evening of the first day, to break off the engagement and seek new ground. The Southern army was at last well concentrated; it had won the day's fighting and taken thousands of prisoners. Why should Lee not fall back upon its superior marching ability, and manoeuvre for a fresh grapple in a better position? Why should he not swing southeast a few miles around Meade's left flank, thus placing himself between Meade and Washington, and so compel the Union army to do the attacking on ground that Lee himself would select? But to this plan Lee offered emphatic objections. With Stuart still absent, the Confederates lacked cavalry to cover their flanks as they turned, while Meade possessed strong and well led cavalry units under Buford and Kilpatrick. They would be sliced flank and rear with no Stuart to protect them; they would find their communications harried and perhaps cut. No, Lee believed that the best plan would be to attack strongly in front. The difference of opinion was less important in itself than in the indication it gave that Longstreet might, as critics later contended he did, show a lukewarm and reluctant temper throughout the second and third day of the battle—especially the third.

It was indeed true that by the evening of the second day the Confederate outlook was gloomy enough to discourage Lee and daunt Longstreet. Meade had concentrated his forces with a speed and address which astonished the Confederate leaders. Longstreet's blow against Sickles and the Union left, at one time on the verge of success, had been parried. Late in the day, a blow by part of Ewell's corps against Culp's Hill on the Union right had gained a partial and precarious success in taking some of the intrenchments, due to the absence of defenders needed elsewhere. Cemetery Hill near by had repulsed a stroke delivered by the Confederates under Early. It is not strange that Longstreet, seeing his hopes for the avoidance of an offensive lost, and his plan for a flanking movement thrown aside, became ill-tempered and uncooperative, ready to drag his sword. Nor is it strange that when Meade held his council of corps commanders that evening— a council itself the subject of controversy—they helped him maintain a decision to hold his line and strengthen all its parts, from Cemetery Hill along Cemetery Ridge to Little Round Top, against any Confederate assault on the morrow.

The third day opened again hot and fair, with drifting clouds casting shadows on hills and fields. Fighting began at dawn on the Union right, where Confederates tried to increase their hold on Culp's Hill only to meet Federal reinforcements from Slocum's Corps. Why had Ewell's forces not strengthened their ranks and position on the hill? As they had not, they were driven out of what works they held in furious fighting. The retirement depressed them, while the Northern forces felt elated by their recapture of the position, even after terrible slaughter. Then came hours of silence; and afterward, at one in the afternoon, the thunderous Confederate cannonade which heralded Pickett's charge.

We may learn a little about how the battle was directed or misdirected from an examination of the decisions of Lee and Meade—Lee, who was strangely indecisive at times, declining to impose his will firmly upon Ewell, Longstreet, and others; Meade, who counted for less in the conduct of operations than Reynolds, Howard, Hancock, and Warren. We may learn more from studying the reports of the corps commanders on both sides. But the essential character of the struggle can be grasped only when we examine the supreme effort of the troops, the unwavering courage and devotion of the plain soldiers who withstood the fiery ordeal. "A full account of *the battle as it was* will never, can never be made. Who could sketch the changes, the constant shifting of the bloody panorama?" So wrote a young officer, Frank A. Haskell, destined to die within a year at Cold Harbor, whose long letter on the conflict lives as a classic narrative.[49] The participants came nearest catching the Promethean fire of truth from the gun-bursts.

A farm boy of thirteen, picking wild raspberries near Gettysburg when the guns began to boom, gives us a vivid sketch of the foremost Confederate hosts

49. Haskell, Frank A., *The Battle of Gettysburg*, (privately printed twice before the Massachusetts Commandery of the Loyal Legion published it in 1908), 94.

pouring over the hills in clouds of dust. "The first wave swelled into successive waves, gray masses with the glint of steel as the sun struck the gun barrels, filling the highway, spreading out into the fields, and still coming on and on, wave after wave, billow after billow."[50] Reynolds's orderly, Charles H. Veil, wrote that as the General turned to look towards the Seminary "a Minnie Ball struck him in the back of the neck, and he fell from his horse dead. He never spoke a word, or moved a muscle after he was struck. I have seen many men killed in action, but never saw a ball do its work so *instantly* as did the ball which struck General Reynolds, a man who knew not what fear or danger was . . . " The gallant artillery officer Charles S. Wainwright, fighting hard by, also tells us that Reynolds was slain by a Minie ball through the top of the spine, fell from his horse, and expired instantly—that is all.[51] Wainwright then relates how his artillery was pushed off Seminary Hill, although one gun, with an oblique line of fire, cut great gaps in the oncoming lines of the enemy. The streets of the town were a confused mass of Union soldiers, "brigades and divisions pretty well mixed up," and one general drunk, but nobody panic-stricken. Posting his guns on Cemetery Hill, Wainwright fought a sharp artillery duel next day with Confederate artillery on higher ground toward Culp's Hill. Despite losses, he compelled the foe to retire.

"I saw during this artillery duel two instances of the destruction which can be caused by a single twenty-pounder shot," he wrote, "both of which happened within two yards of me . . . One of these shots struck in the center of a line of infantry who were lying down behind the wall. Taking the line lengthways, it literally ploughed up two or three yards of men, killing and wounding a dozen or more. The other was a shell which burst directly under Cooper's left gun, killed one man outright, blew another all to pieces so that he died in half an hour, and wounded the other three . . . The man who was so badly blown to pieces lost his right hand, his left arm at the shoulder, and his ribs so broken open that you could see right into him."

A United States regular with the artillery, Augustus Buell, wrote an excited description of the first day's battle just before the Union line gave way. He states that the Confederate infantry poured volley after volley into the batteries on McPherson's Ridge, while the artillery replied with double canister as fast as men could load. A burly corporal moved among the guns, helping the wounded stagger to the rear and shifting men about to fill gaps; the commanding officer cheered the gunners on with shouts of "Feed it to 'em, God damn 'em! Feed it to 'em!" The very guns took on life; every artilleryman did the work of two or three. "Up and down the line men were reeling and falling; splinters flying from

50. Miers, Earl Schenck, and Richard A. Brown, *Gettysburg*, New Brunswick, N.J., 1948, 50.
51. Wainwright Col. Charles S., *A Diary of Battle 1861-1865*, New York, 1962, 234; Charles H. Veil letter of April 7, 1864, Civil War Institute, Gettysburg College.

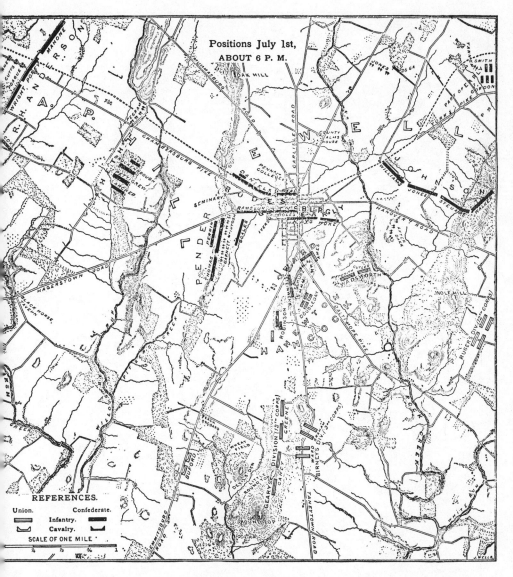

Gettysburg: Map Showing Positions of Union and Confederate Armies on July 1, about 6 P.M.

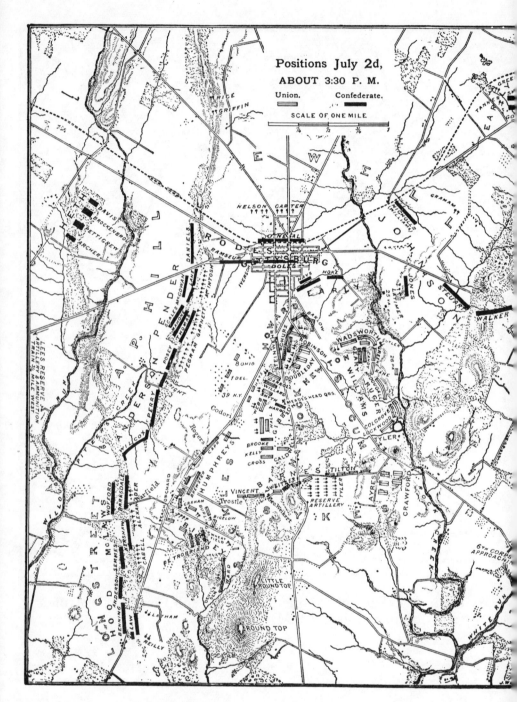

Map of Positions on July 2, about 3:30 P.M.

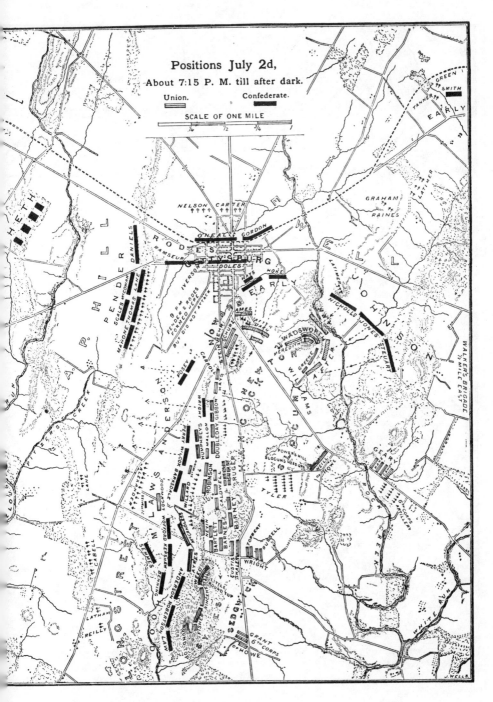

Map of Positions on July 2, from 7:15 P.M. until after dark

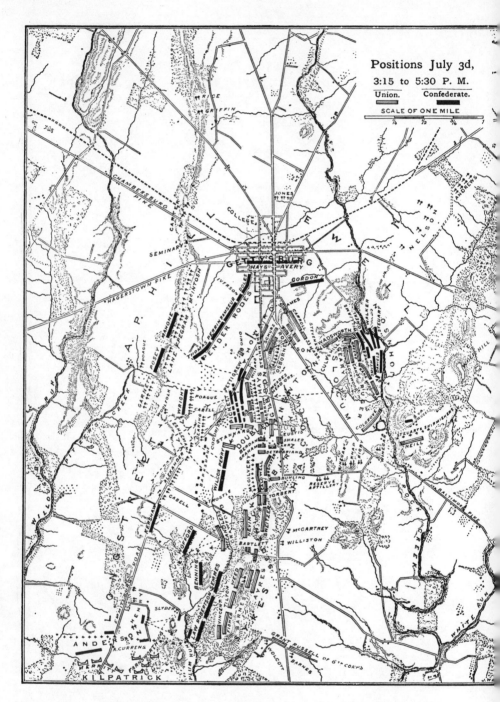

Map of Positions on July 3, from 3:15 to 5:30 P.M.

wheels and axles where bullets hit; in rear, horses tearing and plunging, drivers yelling, shells bursting, shot shrieking overhead, howling about our ears, or throwing up great clouds of dust where they struck; the musketry crashing on three sides of us; bullets hissing, humming, and whistling everywhere; cannon roaring—all crash on crash and peal on peal, smoke, dust, splinters, blood, wreck and carnage indescribable. But not a man or boy flinched or faltered."

The struggle of Union troops to hold Big Round Top, the sugar-loaf hill about 400 feet high at the extreme left of Meade's line, is described by Daniel G. McNamara of the Massachusetts Ninth. On its right, connected by a narrow wooded defile, stands Little Round Top, about 300 feet high. Both were wild, rocky, and full of brush, both had huge boulders scattered over their steep sides, some of them concealing dangerous caverns and pitfalls. Between these two heights and the Devil's Den lies a valley which, after thousands perished in it on the second day, was dubbed the Valley of the Shadow of Death. The colonel of the Ninth formed his battle line on the northeast base of Big Round Top, with a breastwork of rocks laid by the masons of the regiment. "Skirmishers from General Hood's division of Longstreet's corps, on the west side of the hill, assaulted this point at various times during the day intending to capture the hill and flank Little Round Top, but they were always driven back by our rapid infantry fire. The enemy, mostly Hood's Texans, would creep and crawl and stumble through the thickets and underbrush, that grew wild and tangled among the scrubby trees, until they appeared in sight, when the Ninth would open on them."

And Little Round Top? Porter Farley, the historian of the 140th New York, tells how, under direct orders from Warren, his regiment began ascending the wooded, rocky eastern slope of the hill just in time.[52] "As we reached the crest a never-to-be-forgotten scene burst upon us. A great basin lay before us full of smoke and fire, and literally swarming with riderless horses and fighting, fleeing, and pursuing men. The air was saturated with the sulphurous fumes of battle and was ringing with the shouts and groans of the combatants. The wild cries of charging lines, the rattle of musketry, the booming of artillery and the shrieks of the wounded were the orchestral accompaniments of a scene very like hell itself—as terrific as the warring of Milton's fiends in Pandemonium. The whole of Sickles' corps, and many other troops which had been sent to its support in that ill-chosen hollow, were being slaughtered and driven before the impetuous advance of Longstreet." Farley saw that a broad ravine between the two Round Tops led down into the basin filled with this bloody melee. Right up this ravine,

52. Farley, Porter, "Reminiscences of the 140th Regiment New York Volunteers," *Rochester Historical Society Publications*, xxii, Rochester, N.Y., 1944, *passim*. Buell, Augustus, *The Cannoneer*, Washington, 1890, 70; McNamara, Daniel George, *The History of the Ninth Regiment Massachusetts Volunteer Infantry*, Boston, 1899.

the easiest path, was advancing a rebel force which outflanked all the troops in the plain below. The 140th had no time to form a new battle line. With loud shouts they rushed down the rocky slope, their sudden appearance as formidable as if they were carrying fixed bayonets. "Coming abreast of Vincent's brigade, and taking advantage of such shelter as the huge rocks lying about there afforded, the men loaded and fired, and in less time than it takes to write it the onslaught of the rebels was fairly checked, and in a few minutes the woods in front of us were cleared except for the dead and wounded."

The melee in what Farley calls the plain or hollow was the fierce battle in which Longstreet endeavored to crush the impetuous Sickles. Whitelaw Reid of the Cincinnati *Gazette* witnessed the desperate attempt of Massachusetts and Maine batteries to hold a position with Sickles. When a fierce Southern charge put them in dire peril, Captain Bigelow received orders to hold on at every hazard short of total annihilation. He opened with double charges of grape and canister, but could not halt the oncoming line.

"His grape and canister are exhausted, and still, closing grandly up over their slain, on they come. He falls back on spherical case, and pours this in at the shortest range. On, still onward, comes the artillery-defying line, and still he holds his position. They are within six paces of the guns—he fires again. Once more, and he blows devoted soldiers from his very muzzles. And still mindful of that solemn order, he holds his place as they spring upon his carriages, and shoot down his horses! And then, his Yankee artillerists still about him, he seizes the guns by hand, and from the very front of that line drags two of them off . . . That single company, in that half-hour's fight, lost 33 of its men, including every sergeant it had. The captain himself was wounded."

Seldom did a battle of the war entail such hand-to-hand fighting; seldom was so much slaughter endured so bravely by so many companies on both sides. Who could have fought more intrepidly against odds than the South Carolinians in J. B. Kershaw's brigade, sent on the second day to drive the Union troops out of the Peach Orchard? One company went into action with forty men, of whom only four remained unhurt to bury their comrades. His losses exceeded 600 men slain or wounded, or about half the force engaged.[53] How many stories we have like that of the Texas sergeant at Devil's Den who reached a rock in advance of his line and stood erect on its top amid a storm of bullets, firing as fast as wounded men below could hand him loaded guns, until a ball in the right leg brought him down; who then, regaining the top, continued firing until a bullet in the left leg felled him again; and who then once more crawled to the top, fighting on, until

53. See J.B. Kershaw's own account, "Kershaw's Brigade at Gettysburg," in *Battles and Leaders*, III, 331ff. Whitelaw Reid of the Cincinnati *Gazette*, in Greeley, Horace, *The American Conflict*, Hartford, 1867, II, 381.

he received a bullet in the body which prostrated him, weeping because he was helpless. And how many men had the spirit of the officer who, carried through the Thirty-seventh Massachusetts to have his leg amputated, exclaimed, "I don't begrudge it a bit! We drove the graybacks a mile and a half, and it was worth a leg to see them go!"[54]

In one encounter after another, combatants wrote later, the air seemed alive with lead, but troops still rushed to the fray amid the "terrible medley of cries, shouts, cheers, groans, prayers, curses, bursting shells, whizzing rifle bullets, and clanging steel."[55] Hill's corps had numbered about eight thousand effectives when the battle began, and came out of it with fifteen hundred. The 143rd Pennsylvania had 465 men at the outset, and 253 at the end. Of the 150th Pennsylvania, which lost 264 men, the official report ran: "They all fought as if each man felt that upon his own arm hung the fate of . . . the nation."

Most dramatic and memorable of all was the final attack of the Confederates upon the Union center, where Hancock's Second and Third Corps were to bear the brunt of the assault. The Union troops had every advantage of position; a definite ridge topped along most of its crest by a wall of small stones, which they had strengthened with rails and earth to make a fair breastwork for kneeling men.[56] A second line of defenders could fire over the heads of the first. The North had the further advantage of easy reinforcements, for troops could be quickly despatched from left or right to the center. The eighty guns which they had posted along the ridge and on Cemetery Hill could spew out destruction, unless silenced, over the slope and open wheatfield before them. The Confederates had nothing but disadvantages. They nevertheless cherished a hope that by concentrated fire they might smash the Union guns before the infantry charge began, and might send to the top of Cemetery Ridge a greater number of hard-fighting men than the Union army had posted there.

From the moment that he learned of Lee's plan, Longstreet believed that defeat was certain. "It is my opinion," he declared, "that no 15,000 men ever arrayed for battle could take that position." But Lee remained immovable, believing that a heavy bombardment could clear the way. Doubtless he recalled that

---

54. Bowen, James Lorenzo, *History of the Thirty-seventh Regiment Mass. Volunteers*, Holyoke, Mass., 1884, 184; Polley, J.B., *Hood's Texas Brigade*, New York, 1910, 170.

55. Gerrish, Theodore, *Army Life, a Private's Reminiscences of the Civil War*, Portland, Maine, 1882, 154.

56. The inevitable clash of testimony blurs even the picture of these defenses. The correspondent of the Washington *National Republican* (July 9, 1863) stated that the front before Pickett consisted of a line of men behind hastily constructed defenses, partly stone wall, partly rifle pits, and partly natural projections of rock. Whitelaw Reid wrote the Cincinnati *Gazette* (quoted in Greeley, *American Conflict, op. cit.*, II, 386:) "We had some shallow rifle pits, with barricades of rails from the fences." But Abner Doubleday testified before the Committee on the Conduct of the War that his position was "Quite strong, and well strengthened with rails and stones." The correspondent of the Richmond *Enquirer*, writing July 8, termed the Union position "almost impregnable." *O.R.*, I, xxvii, Pt.2, 331.

Napoleon had won Austerlitz by a massive use of artillery; doubtless, also, he thought that the butchery of his own troops at Malvern Hill and Burnside's men at Fredericksburg had little relevance to the coming encounter. He hoped that when Pickett's, Pettigrew's, and Trimble's splendid body of Virginians, North Carolinians, Tennesseeans, and others swept up to the crest they could carry all before them. Longstreet, retiring from their final conference, wrote a discouraged note to artillery officer E. P. Alexander. "Colonel: If the artillery fire does not have the effect to drive off the enemy or greatly demoralize him so as to make our efforts pretty certain, I would prefer that you should not advise General Pickett to make the charge. I shall rely a great deal on your good judgment to determine the matter . . ." But Alexander pointed out that any alternative to the charge should be weighed before the bombardment, not after it, for his artillery had just sufficient ammunition to make this one test.[57]

As noon drew near, perfect silence descended upon Gettysburg. About Culp's Hill the clangor of battle had ceased, and only the groans of the wounded could be heard. Along Cemetery Ridge Hancock's troops lay perfectly quiet. From a bright sky, with a few fleecy clouds casting shadows on the grass, the sun poured burning rays upon muskets stacked in orderly array, and brass and steel artillery in perfect immobility. The wheatfield in front rippled under an occasional breeze and then was still again. The Union soldiers lay silent in the heat, some of them shielding their heads by shelter tents raised on a ramrod. The hum of bees, the noise of army wagons and caissons in the distance, and the far-off echo of commands, mingled in a drowsy murmur, so that some infantrymen went to sleep. General Meade and John Gibbon, with a few other officers, sat down at Gibbon's headquarters in the rear to a meal of stewed chicken, potatoes, buttered toast, tea, and coffee.[58]

On wooded Seminary Ridge a mile to the west the same somnolent quiet reigned. Longstreet had disposed the troops for the charge in two long lines, six brigades of perhaps 10,000 men in the first, and five brigades of 5,000 in the second. Alexander and other officers had posted the guns for the cannonade: 83 of Longstreet's First Corps, 44 of the Second Corps, and 60 of the Third, or 187 in all—but of these 56 stood idle; the whole number used by the Confederates in the battle was 172, and in the attack on Cemetery Ridge 115.[59] As the Southern troops took position in the shelter of the trees, orders came to lie down in line

57. Alexander, *Military Memoirs of a Confederate, op. cit.*, 414ff; Longstreet, James, *From Manassas to Appomattox*, Philadelphia, 1896, XXVIII, *passim.*

58. Meade, George, *The Life and Letters of George Gordon Meade*, New York, 1913, II, 104-105, calls this a hasty breakfast; Meade was busy all morning on various parts of the line, so that every possible enemy movement had been considered, "every contingency anticipated."

59. Alexander, *Military Memoirs, op. cit.*, 418. Alexander writes (p. 416): "Our artillery equipment was usually admitted to be inferior to the enemy's in numbers, calibres, and quality of ammunition."

of battle until, when the bombardment ended, they were to advance and sweep all Yankees from their path. Some composed themselves for a nap; Longstreet himself, up most of the previous night, dismounted and slept briefly.[60]

Suddenly, at one o'clock precisely, the sharp crack of a Confederate gun echoed across the field, and after it, another. Above the crest of Cemetery Ridge suddenly bloomed the smoke of two bursting shells, plainly a signal. Before men could look at each other in surprise, gun after gun rattled a thunderous staccato. From the Southern line streamed a steady bombardment; all along the opposite swell, smoke, dust, and fire traced the exploding shells. A moment more, and the Union artillery awakened in a hoarse roar of reply. Flaky streams of fire spouted from the muzzles of a hundred guns—nearly half of the 220 pieces the Union employed in the battle. Shells began exploding in the Confederate woods. The whole two miles of the Union line, Alexander tells us, was soon blazing like a volcano. The field appeared a playground of giants pelting each other with thunder, flame, and iron.

In this terrible duel Northern officers for a time feared severe losses. Shells exploding over limber-boxes blew up, one by one, eleven caissons. Solid shot struck other Union guns, throwing fragments of wood and iron in all directions. Limbs from the shattered trees fell with a crash. Mangled horses writhed and kicked while others galloped madly over the fields. Wounded men hobbled to the rear, followed by stretcher-parties carrying the more seriously injured. All the while, against the dull roar of the cannon, a horrific din filled the upper air as the various missiles shrieked, hissed, howled, and muttered. Yet the damage actually inflicted was not great. The Southern gunners, once billowing smoke shrouded the area, could aim but blindly; they fired too fast, and made the mistake of cutting their fuses so long that many shells exploded tardily and harmlessly. Doubleday exaggerated when he later testified: "They had our exact range and the destruction was fearful."[61] As General Pleasanton said, the Confederate fire should have been more closely concentrated; or as General T. W. Hyde put it, the whole of their fire directed on the Second Corps would have given their attack a better chance. Union men who were at first frightened became cool. "Let it go on," they told each other. "We are beginning to like it."[62]

Meanwhile the Confederates, as the minutes passed, themselves suffered heavily from the Union riposte, which one captain calls "very effective and deadly."[63] Both commanders came under fire. Meade's headquarters were in the thick of the falling shells, so that he rode to Slocum's safer position on Powers

60. Fremantle, *Three Months in the Southern States,* New York, 1864, 270.
61. *Report of the Joint Committee on the Conduct of the War,* Washington, 1865, Vol.I, "Army of the Potomac," 309.
62. Hyde, *Following the Greek Cross, op.cit.,* 151-154.
63 W. W. Wood in Miers and Brown, *Gettysburg, op.cit.,* 228-232.

Hill.[64] On the opposite ridge, Lee and a single companion suddenly appeared on horseback between the artillery and the troops lying behind the guns. Thrilled but horrified, for the ground was swept by Union missiles, the men shouted to him to retire, and doffing his hat in acknowledgment, he quickened the pace of Traveller to a quieter spot.

At three, Meade's chief of artillery, Henry J. Hunt, anxious to let his guns cool and conserve ammunition, ordered a cease fire. Numerous pieces were limbered up and withdrawn. Alexander on the Confederate side concluded that the Northern artillery was being silenced. He had agreed to give Pickett his signal for the charge; he thought the moment had come. As orders rang out, the gray veterans clambered to their feet, formed ranks, and swung forward. The plan was that some eleven Confederate brigades numbering perhaps 15,000 men, all under Longstreet and led by Pickett, Pettigrew, and Trimble, would attack the center of the Union lines, while other troops were to furnish support and threaten. The idea was that the Union army would be ripped apart, its two wings entirely separated. Many Southerners thought the formation a poor one, with its six brigades in the front line, plus four more in the second, and another echeloned to the right rear. "Both flanks of the assaulting column were in the air;" writes E. P. Alexander, "and the left without any support in the rear."[65] Above all, success depended on the destruction of the Union artillery, and all along Cemetery Ridge Hunt was wheeling up his reserve guns, filling his ammunition boxes, and marshalling his gunners to use shells and solid shot at distance range, shrapnel when the Southerners drew nearer, and finally canister.

"We believed that the battle was practically over," wrote one Confederate officer, "and that we had nothing to do but to march unopposed to Cemetery Heights and occupy them."[66] Pickett's men felt their first moment of dismay when they saw that the supporting columns on the flanks were not moving forward with proper alacrity. In vain did mounted officers dash up and down the line urging greater speed. Still the main advance went on. The men moved to a post-and-rail fence, climbed it, and halted beyond to reform. Just as they started forward again, a cannon shot came from the left, striking down a long line of men. At that instant the breeze lifted the smoke from the ridge in front to reveal the full panoply of Union strength in its terrifying grandeur, a double line of infantry in front, guns frowning beside them, and reserves in thick platoons farther back. The Confederates pressed on undaunted, densely crowded together, battleflags tossing in the breeze, musket barrels and bayonets gleaming in the sun. As the

64. Doubleday, *Chancellorsville and Gettysburg, op.cit.,* 190-191; "a very uncomfortable place," writes Colonel Thomas L. Livermore, *Days and Events, 1860-1866,* Boston, 1920, 260; "the yard later showing a dozen or score of dead horses."
65. Alexander, *op.cit.,* 419.
66. Miers and Brown, *op.cit.,* 231.

15,000 swept over meadow and wheatfield, grimly magnificent in their precision, still hardly a noise broke the silence in front. But had the Confederates halted to listen closely, they might have heard the click of locks as the Union infantry brought their pieces to the ready, the clank of cannon wheels as the guns slid a little forward, and the clatter of ammunition boxes dumped open for eager fingers.

Along the Union line rode steel-cold John Gibbon, speaking with impassive calmness to each platoon: "Don't hurry, men—Don't fire too fast. Let them come up close before you fire, and then aim low and steadily."

Thus came the swift climax, so swift that it was over almost before men comprehended the fact. In a sudden roar, the Union artillery belched forth fire and smoke. As Pickett's line, despite terrible gaps, came on without faltering, the gunners changed from shrapnel to canister. The gaps grew. The right flank of the Confederates, moving farther right than it should when the men saw Doubleday's position defended by five lines, swung close to a Vermont brigade which delivered a withering flank fire. Recoiling nearer the center, the shattered line at once resumed its charge.[67] The gray host was at last well within musket range, and a sheet of flame leaped from the Northern line toward Pickett's and Pettigrew's columns. Stung to a response, the Virginians and North Carolinians halted, fired, reloaded, and fired again. A moment more and Pickett's troops were up to the wall occupied by Alexander S. Webb's brigade of the Second Corps, which had suffered most heavily from the bombardment. A. H. Cushing's battery of regular artillery on the crest had but one serviceable gun left. Though wounded in thighs and body, and bleeding heavily, Cushing—a brother of the naval hero —pushed his piece forward, gasping to Webb, "I will give them one more shot!" As it rang out he called "Good-bye!" and fell dead.

Along the wall the red flags thickened, and the defenders, as the Southern vanguard poured up, wavered. Lewis A. Armistead, who had led his brigade with cap on upraised sword, leaped at the Union line shouting to perhaps a hundred followers, "Give them the cold steel, boys!" He fell dead over the muzzle of Cushing's cannon. One officer, Colonel James Mayo, claimed he had carried enemy intrenchments and, "At this critical juncture when seconds seemed more precious than hours of any former time, many an anxious eye was cast back to the hill from which we came in the hope of seeing supports near at hand and more than once I heard the despairing exclamation, 'Why don't they come!' But no help came." Already Webb's officers were rallying their men, and the Union defense, as reserves came on the run, was being restored. Everywhere the Confederates were falling back. Pettigrew's men had lost all but one of their field officers; they had mustered 2800 strong on the morning of July 1, and at roll call

67. Hyde, *op.cit.*, 156.

on the 4th would number but 835.[68] The rebel yell was heard no more. First the extreme left of the Confederate assault broke, and then the retreat rapidly extended to the right. For Pickett's men in particular, it was soon a case of *sauve qui peut.* Only a third of his division was left unscathed; the rest lay on the field. Trimble's and Wilcox's supporting troops had failed to grapple with the Union line, so that the brave Virginians and North Carolinians in advance were left with no choice but to face about or be overwhelmed. And as the Southern troops fell dejectedly back, fresh musket volleys and shells from newly-fetched guns sped them on their way. To the east of Gettysburg Stuart's cavalry, which arrived the day before, fought the Federal cavalry of David McM. Gregg. Stuart was repulsed in his effort to cut off Meade's communications.

Once more quiet reigned over the Gettysburg terrain. As the sun sank in the West, the sultry evening felt breaths of coolness. Before darkness came both sides had a last look at the fields and valleys. They were scarred with shells and scored with round shot; the fences were levelled, the wheat trodden into the dirt, the trees gashed and rent; the ground was littered with broken weapons, haversacks, canteens, blankets, coats, and muskets; here and there horses weltered in their blood, some dead, some alive. Everywhere lay the slain and wounded, in heaps, in lines, in single dark spots, some seeming to sleep unhurt, some writhing in the pain of frightful mutilations, some stirring slowly. The twilight deepened; the lanterns and torches of ambulance men and doctors flickered here and there; and from the ground rose the terrible symphony of thousands in agony of body and mind.

Pickett's charge, as Longstreet and other Confederate officers saw at the time, was a blunder founded on two miscalculations; first that it was possible for the Confederate guns to silence a greater number of Union cannon, and second, that a charge over a mile of ground against well-entrenched troops, superior in number, could ever succeed. It was not difficult, as the Georgian A. R. Wright wrote, to reach Cemetery Ridge—he himself had briefly penetrated it the second day; the trouble was to hold it, for the convex Union line of defense made it easy to reinforce any point, while the concave Confederate line of attack made it hard to move long enveloping arrays effectively. The Southern army was defeated because, distant from its bases, outnumbered, and limited in ammunition, it had accepted battle where it must not only attack, but attack under a grave disadvantage—the disadvantage of bringing a wide hemispheric line to bear upon a shorter, stronger inner line. Lee might have striven more vigorously to compel Meade to deliver the attack. He might even have endeavored to accomplish this, as Longstreet proposed, by a final flank movement that placed his army between

68. Greeley, *American Conflict, op.cit.*, II, 385; Col. James Mayo to Pickett, unpublished report of battle. George E. Pickett Papers, Duke Univ. Lib.

Meade and Baltimore, for Meade would never have dared to let Lee hold for long an inner position, with roads open even to Washington.

It was a glorious charge, but it was not war. Some thought it glorious that color-bearers of thirty-five regiments were shot down, and that seven Confederate colonels were buried on the battleground after Pickett fell back; glorious that a Union general could write, "I tried to ride over the field, but could not, for the dead and wounded lay too thick to guide a horse through them."[69] Yet futile carnage is never glorious. From any humanitarian point of view such losses were as horrible as they were calamitous from the Confederate standpoint. As the survivors fell back within their original lines, Lee rode toward them, and meeting General Cadmus M. Wilcox, who was on the verge of tears over the frightful losses of his brigade, exclaimed, "Never mind, general, all this has been my fault —it is I that have lost this fight, and you must help me out of it the best way you can."[70] It was a manly statement, and it was true.

[VI]

The figures can give only a most superficial idea of the horrors of any battle, particularly one of the size and length of Gettysburg. But even the figures are stark enough. While estimates and totals vary, it is probable that the official casualty toll for Gettysburg is fairly correct, although the Southern figures are possibly lower than they actually were. For the Union, 23,049 total casualties including 3,155 killed, 13,529 wounded, and 5,365 missing or captured; for the Confederacy, 20,451 total casualties including 2,592 killed, 12,709 wounded and 5,510 missing or captured.

For the first time, a bloody battle found the field medical service of the Union army adequate. Dr. Jonathan Letterman, reorganizer of this service, had proved the value of his ambulance corps and other preparations at Chancellorsville; now he did still better. He had at hand 3,000 drivers and stretchermen equipped with 1,000 ambulances; he had 650 medical officers present for duty. [71] Each night the wounded within the picket lines were picked up by stretcher parties, and carried to waiting teams; surgeons dealt with the more desperate cases on the ground. By noon of July 4th, 14,000 men had received attention. The Southern casualties fared as well as the Northern. When surgeons lifted a soldier to the table, they never stopped to see whether he wore blue trousers or gray; they looked only at his wound. The proximity of the battlefield to large Northern centers made it easy for the Sanitary Commission, Christian Commission, and other associations,

69. Hyde, *op.cit.*, 157.
70. Fremantle, *Diary, op.cit.*, 215.
71. *OR* I, xxvii, Pt.1, 187; Pt.2, 346; Adams, George W., *Doctors in Blue*, New York, 1952, 91.

as well as the surgeon-general's office, to pour in abundant quantities of lint, bandages, chloroform, surgical instruments, garments, bedding, food, and delicacies.[72] From fans to mosquito-bars, from fruit to brandy, everything needed was available.

The field hospitals were fated not to complete their task of caring for the total of about 21,000 wounded, nor the surgeons to cope with such a multitude of exhausted, maimed, and gangrened men. When Lee retreated and Meade began his slow pursuit, another heavy battle seemed imminent. While his immediate task was yet unfinished, therefore, Letterman detached more than 500 of his 650 medical officers for the anticipated emergency farther south. Since at Gettysburg every doctor had about 300 patients, and every operating surgeon about 900 cases, this was a costly blunder. Letterman could plead that he was counting on an influx of additional physicians and surgeons from all over the North, and on the rapid transfer of many of the wounded to Harrisburg, Baltimore, and Washington; but he should have waited until his burden was thus mitigated before dropping it.

To the poignant disappointment of the country and the President, Meade failed to pursue and destroy Lee's army when it seemed that he had repeated opportunities to bring his foe to bay. He can be excused for not ordering a vigorous advance just after the close of Pickett's charge. Lee dreaded it. The Confederate guns had an average of only five rounds left. But the hour was late, most of the Union army was exhausted, worn and severely blooded from long marches and three days' fighting. Meade feared a repulse on Seminary Ridge. Longstreet later declared that an attack by Union forces would have been thrown back. "I had Hood and McLaws, who had not been engaged; I had a heavy force of artillery; I should have liked nothing better than to have been attacked, and have no doubt that I should have given those who tried as bad a reception as Pickett got."[73] Meade was prudent, and prudence counselled inaction. If he had shown the imprudence exhibited by Lee and Jackson at Second Manassas and Chancellorsville he might have routed the Confederates and ended the war; but it is difficult to fault his caution. Far different was the situation later.[74] Lee, on July 4, ordered his trains, with many wounded, to move toward Williamsport, while after dark the army itself was put en route toward the Potomac. A number of wagons and ambulances were captured because of high water, for heavy rains had flooded the Potomac so that it was impassable except by two small ferries. While Ewell's corps did not leave the Gettysburg area until July 5, the Confederate army managed to reach Hagerstown on the 6th and 7th. Except for small

72. Sp.Correspondence of *English Medical Times*, n.d., Hall, Newman, *A Reply to the Pro-Slavery Wail*, London, 1868, *passim*.
73. Swinton, *History of the Army of the Potomac, op.cit.*, 364. Swinton quotes from memory.
74. Cf. Biddle, J.C., "Why Meade Did Not Attack Lee," Philadelphia *Weekly Times*, May 12, 1877; Gen. Alfred Pleasonton, Philadelphia *Weekly Times*, Jan. 19, 1878, censures Meade sharply.

cavalry actions, Lee had no opposition until July 12, when Meade's army approached. Lee then took up a previously selected position covering the Potomac from Williamsport to Falling Waters, remaining there during two days penned up in a highly vulnerable position, where he seemed at the mercy of Meade's advancing army, augmented by powerful reserves. For the first and only time, Alexander says, he found the General visibly anxious. After the war, Lee was quoted as saying that he would have crossed the Potomac at once if he could have done so. "He would not have been sorry if Meade had attacked him there, but he did not stop specially to invite it, but because the river was high. Meade's failure to attack showed how he had suffered." On July 15, Lee wrote his wife that the return to Virginia "is rather sooner than I had originally contemplated but having accomplished what I proposed on leaving the Rappk. (Rappahannock) viz: relieving the valley of the presence of the enemy and drawing his army north of the Potomac, I determined to recross the latter river. . . ."[75] General French, left unemployed with 7,000 Union veterans at Frederick during the battle, had shown enough energy before Lee's arrival to send a cavalry detachment to Williamsport to destroy the bridge there. It was, in fact, one of his few exhibitions of energy. Very fortunately for Lee, Meade's pursuit was preternaturally slow. By nature cautious, new to the responsibilities of chief command, aware how all his predecessors had failed, he made safety his guiding rule. He remained at Gettysburg for two days resting his troops, succoring the wounded, and burying the dead; then, turning southeast of Lee's line, he halted another day at Middletown for fresh supplies and the arrival of his trains. It was not until July 12 that Meade caught up with Lee's army, now fortified on the Potomac for a last stand. He might have attacked that day, but contented himself with a reconnaisance. Only Pleasanton's cavalry showed any spirit in the pursuit. Capturing large trains of wagons and taking many prisoners, it demonstrated that if Meade had begun a rapid march on the 4th or 5th, Lee would probably have found surrender unavoidable.[76]

As Lincoln and Halleck waited in Washington for news of some heavy blow by Meade they were tormented by alternating hopes and fears. "I presume from what the President said this morning," Montgomery Blair wrote his father on July 8, "that the Rebels will not get over the river in safety. He was much discouraged yesterday and seemed to think they would escape from Meade. He did not speak with confidence this morning, but he said he felt better . . ."[77] That same day Halleck wrote Meade that Lee was reported crossing the Potomac. "If

75. Alexander, *op.cit.*, 439; Allan, William, "Conversations with Lee," ms. Southern Historical Collection, Univ. of N.C. Library; to his wife July 15, 1863, from Bunker Hill, Va., R.E. Lee Papers, LC.

76. Pleasonton, *ut supra;* Alexander, *Military Memoirs, op.cit.*, 435.

77. Blair Papers, Princeton University.

Lee's army is so divided by the river, the importance of attacking the part on this side is incalculable. Such an opportunity may not occur again." If, on the contrary, Lee was keeping his army together, Meade should take time to concentrate —but he should still attack. General Benjamin F. Kelley was under orders from Hancock to move to strike the Confederate right; General W. T. H. Brooks was moving from Pittsburgh to reinforce Kelley; troops were being sent from New York and Fort Monroe directly to Harper's Ferry. "You will have forces sufficient to render your victory certain. My only fear now is that the enemy may escape by crossing the river." That same July 8, Meade told Halleck that the army was in high spirits, and ready and willing to push forward. He would move forward the moment he could get different commands together and supplied. However, "I expect to find the enemy in a strong position, well covered with artillery, and I do not desire to imitate his example at Gettysburg, and assault a position where the chances were so greatly against success. I wish in advance to moderate the expectations of those who, in ignorance of the difficulties to be encountered, may expect too much. All that I can do under the circumstances, I pledge this army to do."[78]

The critical hour arrived on Sunday the 12th. Lee issued a rousing address to his army that day, full of boasts and threats that were but a blind; he strengthened his long earthworks near Meade's front, which looked formidable but were merely heaped earth covering a continuous line of piled rails; he had campfires built at night to simulate a strong immobile army even while his regiments were beginning to cross the Potomac—some by a new pontoon bridge, some by rafts and boats which his engineers had constructed of boards from dwellings. That evening Meade summoned his corps commanders to a council at headquarters to determine whether the powerful Union army should attack next morning. Reynolds had been killed, Hancock badly wounded, and Warren slept in exhaustion. The majority of the corps commanders opposed an attack, but a good many other officers seemed to favor it. Meade himself was for fighting, but in such a lukewarm, hesitant mood that he yielded his will. As the war correspondent Noah Brooks wrote, Hooker would probably have listened to the council—and then would have attacked, although one has to remember Hooker's failure to continue his advance at Chancellorsville.[79] "Upon this day (July 13) the soldiers who bore muskets wished to hear the commands, 'Take arms,' and 'Charge,' because they knew, what is conceded now, that it would have captured all the cannon, *materiel*, and men from the enemy, and finished the Rebellion without a hard contest or a large loss of valuable lives. . . ."[80]

78. Halleck Papers, Eldredge Collection, HEH; *O.R.* I, xxvii, Pt.i, 84.
79. Letter dated Boonsborough, Md., July 14, 1863, in Sacramento *Union*.
80. Blake, Henry N., *Three Years in the Army of the Potomac,* Boston, 1865, 229.

Another war correspondent, Theodore C. Wilson of the New York *Herald*, had been taken prisoner by Stuart. On Monday night, the 13th, he and other prisoners were marched to Williamsport. Gray infantrymen were passing at the time, many of them singing gaily. "In the distance, toward Hagerstown, burned a long line of well-lit camp fires, illuminating the sky for miles around; yet little did the Unionists know that these campfires while they helped to deceive them, also helped to light the very path of the retreating rebel army." Southern officers had been very fearful of an attack by Meade until the evening of the 12th. Then Wilson heard them begin to laugh and make derisive remarks. "Yes," said Stuart to Rodes and Fitzhugh Lee, "the Yankees, instead of attacking us, are actually throwing up some kind of entrenchments; and they boast that they are not afraid of us and are pressing on for a fight. Well, they had better come."[81]

Of Lincoln's chagrin, grief, and anger we have abundant records. The most impressive is perhaps the statement his son made years later to a friend. "Entering my father's room right after the battle of Gettysburg," said Robert, "I found him in tears with head bowed upon his arms resting on the table at which he sat. 'Why, what is the matter, father?' I asked. For a brief interval he remained silent, then raised his head, and the explanation of his grief was forthcoming. 'My boy,' he said, 'when I heard that the bridge at Williamsport had been swept away, I sent for General Haupt and asked him how soon he could replace the same. He replied, 'If I were uninterrupted I could build a bridge with the material there within twenty-four hours, and Mr. President, General Lee has engineers as skilful as I am.' Upon hearing this I at once wrote Meade to attack without delay, and if successful to destroy my letter, but in case of failure to preserve it for his vindication. I have just learned that at a council of war of Meade and his generals, it has been determined not to pursue Lee, and now the opportune chance of ending this bitter struggle is lost."[82] The essential, if not literal, truth of this statement we can hardly doubt.

It was at Falling Waters, four miles below Williamsport, that Lee drew in his final lines to cross the river, and as the Federal forces took a threatening position on the 13th, the Confederates began crossing that night, completing the move by early afternoon of the 14th. Dashing cavalrymen under Buford and Kilpatrick seized some 2,000 prisoners here—all they could capture of an army which a general of high courage and consummate skill might have forced to a surrender as complete as that of Bazaine, a little later, at Sedan. Such a surrender would have ended the war. It is impossible not to blame Meade for the failure. But it is also impossible not to ask whether a large responsibility did not rest with the highest

81. New York *Herald*, July 18, 1863.
82. George H. Thatcher of Albany, N.Y., letter in *American Historical Review*, Jan., 1927, Vol. XXXII, No.2, 282-283; see Nicolay and Hay, *op.cit.*, VII, 280-281, for the letter he wrote Meade and suppressed.

Union command—Lincoln, Stanton, Halleck—which had not found a general for the most fateful battle of the war until three days before it began, so that Meade was still nervously uncertain of what his various corps could accomplish;[83] and which had not assembled powerful reserve forces, far surpassing those available, to cooperate with Meade as he followed the retreating rebels, and to join him in the final struggle.

83. The military historian, John Codman Ropes, who spent much time with the Twentieth Massachusetts in the field, told Thomas L. Livermore that "in the first place, General Meade was utterly unacquainted with his command and did not know what it could do"; Livermore, *op.cit.,* 271.

10.

"THE UNION, as we have said, could win the war only by a sufficiently crushing defeat of the main Confederate armies, along with the blockade and dismemberment of the South, to end all resistance East and West. The South, however, might win independence if it held the struggle in such a prolonged deadlock that war weariness numbed the Northern will to fight, and enabled the Peace Democrats to make a successful demand for negotiations to end the slaughter." [1]

Mid-1863 had brought heavy battles and multitudinous problems for both sides. "The majority of Americans were sternly critical of everybody and everything, and swept by gusts of angry self-appraisal. Every leader, and not least Lincoln and Davis, was measured with doubt." [2] People were again asking anxious questions. Draft riots erupted in New York City in July, and other places were not free from opposition to the war and conscription. Drafting manpower for war was the antithesis of American tradition, but both sides had resorted to it, primarily as a stimulus to enlistment. Desertions were increasing throughout each section, although the vast majority of youths did serve honorably.

In Nevins's view it was well that Lincoln was a shrewd politician, that he was a moderate policy maker, and that his prestige was rising, since both parties —and factions within the two main parties—were in a state of flux. Neither "Lincoln's determination to maintain the Union, nor his confidence in the future, founded upon faith in the people, ever flagged despite depressing moments." [3] In the fall elections of 1863 the Republicans and Lincoln candidates swept Ohio, Pennsylvania, Maine, Wisconsin, Massachusetts, Iowa, and other states. Unionists won full control of the House of Representatives.[4]

In central Tennessee slowly and a bit ponderously Rosecrans's Federal Army of the Cumberland moved forward from Murfreesboro June 23. Until early July the Union army marched around Bragg's Army of Tennessee heading toward Chattanooga, in what was known as the Tullahoma Campaign. There were no major battles, no great outpourings of blood. Once started, it was a brilliant campaign, outflanking the Confederates and forcing their retreat. Rosecrans continued his initiative, moving west and south of Chattanooga and then coming through the mountains south of the city and forcing Bragg's Confederates out of the vital center early in September. In the valley of the Chickamauga, southeast of Chattanooga, Bragg counterattacked against Rosecrans in the desperate clash known as Chickamauga, September 19–20. Through untimely mistakes, Rosecrans's army was broken and sent reeling back into Chattanooga. Bragg was held off mainly by the stubborn defense of George H. Thomas. "The Confederates had won a brilliant victory, but nothing more." [5] The South made little strategic gain.

The besieged Federal army held on at Chattanooga under the command of Thomas, who replaced Rosecrans as commander of the Army of the Cumberland. Some of Sherman's troops and two corps from the east came into the Chattanooga area, and Grant himself arrived. After opening the city's supply lines, the Federal army attacked November 23–25 at Lookout Mountain and along Missionary Ridge. On the 25th Grant and Thomas's men were successful in their dramatic charge up the slope of Missionary Ridge, sending Bragg back into Georgia, defeated. Tennessee remained strongly in the Union, but the fall campaign had achieved no climactic victory and had been made at a doleful cost.[6]

In Virginia there had been much marching, much maneuvering, and a little fighting after Gettysburg and during the fall, along the Rappahannock and Rapidan, in the Bristoe Campaign toward Washington, and in the Federal failure at Mine Run. By year's end the armies in Virginia were along the central rivers, and in the West Thomas was poised at Chattanooga.

Nevins pauses now to make a long, detailed, and perceptive analysis of what he terms "The Great Boom in the North," and "The Sweep of Organization." "In almost every field and at every point, the war had laid a profound imprint upon Northern life. . . . The mailed fist of war was smiting the republic hard, but the impact of change on many fronts, economic, cultural, and social, diverted men's attention from the blows." From Maine to Missouri there were no signs of prostration, even of a civilian nature. Military action touched only a small portion of the North.[7] The economic boom came gradually and unevenly, but it came and "was beyond all question real and effective . . . characteristic of all great advances and hopeful changes in American life. . . ." Most people in the North were leading a dual life, "feeling the heart-rending emotions of a nation in the throes of civil conflict, but feeling also the lusty self-confidence of an active people riding the headlong currents of agricultural, industrial, financial, and social growth." [8]

A land primarily agricultural was rapidly being pushed forward by an ir dustrial revolution just now gaining momentum. Manpower was leaving the farm for the city; immigration continued despite the war. There was inflation, luxury, leisure, a higher cost of living, and poverty. But there was also general stability of capital and widespread economic optimism, particularly in and about the West. "From a world view, the most remarkable feature of the war period was the steadily maintained rise in production of great primary commodities, grain, meats, minerals and lumber." [9] While "historians have taken passing looks at the wartime prosperity of the North, few have considered the fact that this was one of the primary factors in the Federal victory." [10] The war demanded a tremendous increase in governmental activities. The war effort was "planned, directed, and organized without concern over whether it was actually violating State, local, or individual rights, though the issue did sometimes demand attention, and was often in the background." [11] Civilian legislation such as the National Banking Act, Morrill Tariff, Morrill Land Grant Act, and the Homestead Act received a good deal of attention.

"The question whether the Civil War advanced or retarded industrialization does not properly invite the pontifical responses it has received. It did both, producing mixed results in a very mixed economy. Unquestionably the war lent direct stimulus to various industries by its flood of contracts, but it was assisted at the same time by the lift which inflation gave market demand and profits, by fresh capital formation and creation of new fortunes, by novel machinery, and by improved technological and commercial methods. . . . The great boom of 1863–1865 was to go down in history as one of the most remarkable phenomena of the nineteenth century. . . ." [12] At the same time it was remembered with mixed feelings. "It was indeed a time of 'guns and butter.' . . . It is not too much to say that no other great nation at that time, or perhaps later, could have enjoyed a similar reign of economic sunshine." [13]

"That the Civil War brought a systematic shift in American society from an unorganized society to a well-organized nation is undoubtedly much too strong a statement. But that the Civil War accentuated and acted as a catalyst to already developing local tendencies toward organization, there can be no doubt. As in so many fields of thought and endeavor, the war changed and stimulated the impulse toward organization, and served as a proving ground or experimental phase for numerous tentative expressions of organization. . . . [This] momentum sprang primarily from necessity or pragmatic impulses, rather than from philosophical devotion to organization for its own sake. That such a pragmatic trend would have occurred without wartime demands is unquestionable, but it certainly would have been different and perhaps slower. The war imposed requirements and opened opportunities. Organization met the demands and grasped many of the opportunities." [14]

This "sprawling country, much of it in the gristle rather than the bone, suddenly had to pull itself together. The unnatural catalyst of war demanded concentration and coordination." [15] "The country did not so much lack business and professional organizations as it lacked those which possessed a national scope and influence." [16] Early organization was fluid because society was versatile and adaptable. "The formless, protoplasmic United States of 1861 emerged from the war four years later eagerly groping toward organization, and much more aware of the paths it must take forward. . . . Multitudes of veterans emerged from the hard lessons of war with this self-confidence born of success, and a pride in duty well done; the spirit of the Greeks after Marathon, and Britons after crushing the Armada. . . . Of all the changes effected by the war, this replacement of an amorphous, spineless society by a national life even partially organized for efficient action—organized first to win the war, and then to develop the continent—was perhaps the most striking, and as vital in effect as the unification of the nation and the renascence of all its liberal impulses and commitments by the abolition of slavery. As the first two years of the struggle might be called the improvised war, the last two could be termed the organized war." [17]

However, for the South it was different. As Nevins puts it, almost throughout "the war, the Confederacy was in a state of siege. Like a medieval fortress, the Southern States had to stand barricaded against the enemy." [18] It was not the ocean blockade, the land blockade, the manpower shortage, the economic weakness, or even military conquest that was the one most important cause of Confederate impotence. All, including the geographical facts of life, must be considered.[19] "The roseate days of strength through victory were passing away, and the iron days of strength through adversity were taking their place. Southerners were learning to substitute grim bravery for bravado, and to remember that this was a war not for military glory, but for national existence." [20] By 1863 war meant for most people almost every conceivable form of endurance. Inflation, shortages of all kinds, war weariness, were taking their toll. Many blamed President Davis. "As the war dragged on, internal dissension increased." [21]

NOTES

1. Nevins, *The War for the Union*, Vol. III, *The Organized War, 1863–1864*, p. 148.
2. *Ibid.*, p. 117.
3. *Ibid.*, p. 148.
4. *Ibid.*, pp. 177–179.
5. *Ibid.*, p. 200.

6. *Ibid.*, p. 211.
7. *Ibid.*, pp. 212–213.
8. *Ibid.*, p. 217.
9. *Ibid.*, p. 245.
10. *Ibid.*, p. 254.
11. *Ibid.*, p. 263.
12. *Ibid.*, p. 268.
13. *Ibid.*, p. 270.
14. *Ibid.*, pp. 272–273.
15. *Ibid.*, p. 277.
16. *Ibid.*, p. 324.
17. *Ibid.*, pp. 329–331.
18. *Ibid.*, p. 332.
19. *Ibid.*, p. 346.
20. *Ibid.*, p. 375.
21. *Ibid.*, p. 406.

Under the Trampling Armies:
The Tragic Lot of the Freedmen

AS UNION troops crossed the borders of the South, tens of thousands for the first time saw slavery face to face. They gazed at it with intense curiosity. Were the Negroes an utterly ignorant folk, unable even to use the English language? Were they, as many Southerners held, a childlike people? Then, too, questions of their history arose. Were evidences of physical maltreatment numerous? Had they suffered heavily from the separation of families? How deeply had they suffered from repression? And how intense was their consequent thirst for freedom? These questions rose in the minds of countless soldiers as black people, roughly garbed, uncouth in manner, and often hardly intelligible, gazed from slave quarters at the marching columns, crowded in shy knots to the camps, or came singly to beg food and give information. The boom of guns, the song of bugles, and the shouts of drill-sergeants brought them into sight as fast as such sounds sent their owners into hiding.

Along the border, slavery showed an outwardly mild face. A Union officer in charge of contrabands at Fortress Monroe found that with one exception these scores of Negroes made no complaint of severe whippings or systematic cruelty. A locust tree in front of Hampton jail had been used as a whipping-post, and they insisted on chopping it down, but only such flagrant offenses as running away had been punished there. Most masters had never gone beyond rough language and chance blows, and many had shown kindness. Complaints of the sundering of families, however, were numerous. "Where is your wife?" "She was sold off two years ago, and I've not heard of her since." As Virginia was a slave-breeding area, a similar answer was often given about children, who were sold at eight years of age or earlier. Evidence of miscegenation appeared on every hand. Many men put to work on the fortifications appeared as white as the sunburnt troops, and many women trailed children who, in color, features and hair, were semi-Cauca-

(*The War for the Union*, Vol. III, *The Organized War, 1863–1864*, Chapter 11.)

sian, sometimes as blonde as the Saxon slaves whom Gregory had met in the Roman markets. All, with great emphasis, wanted freedom: "We want to belong to ourselves."[1]

When opportunity offered, all the way from Virginia to Missouri, they fled in droves within the Union lines. Late in 1862, commissioners appointed to take a census of slaves in King William County, Virginia, reported that while 595 able-bodied males between 18 and 45 remained in the county, 590 had gone to the Yankees, nine-tenths of them able-bodied adult males. "Contrabands in large numbers are fleeing from Missouri into Kansas and especially into Lawrence," a Kansan wrote in the autumn of 1861: "131 came into Lawrence in ten days, yesterday 27 had arrived at two P.M."[2] Not an intelligent slave in Missouri but knew of Lawrence as an ark of freedom, and thousands were determined to get there. Opportunities to escape became easy to find. A Tennessee slave who had suffered from the overseer's cat-o'-nine tails was sent off with a group of others to hunt deer or wild hogs to help the meat shortage. "This was the chance I been wanting, so when we gits to the hunting ground the leader says scatter out."[3] He followed the North Star until he reached Rosecrans's lines, happy amid his hardships, for "I's gwine to the free country, where they ain't no slaves."

Were they ignorant? In the borderland and at favorable points farther south the escaped slaves had learned much from the oratory accompanying Presidential elections, from the talk of their owners, and from a few scattered black men who could read. With rare exceptions, they instantly accepted the Yankees as their friends. When asked if they thought themselves fit for freedom, some answered with rough logic: "Who but the darkies cleared all the land 'round here?" demanded one. "I feed and clothe myself and pay my master $120 a year," responded another. Virginia slaves evinced a general desire to learn to read—a few had been taught clandestinely by white playmates in childhood. They had no monopoly of ignorance, anyway, for of the whites who took the oath of allegiance at Hampton not more than one in fifteen could sign his name. Negroes worked hard on the fortifications there, and faced and dressed the breastworks as well as anybody.[4] John A. Kellogg of the Wisconsin Iron Brigade, escaping from a Charleston prison, was helped on his way by many slaves. "I may be credited with speaking dispassionately," he wrote later, "when I say that in my opinion they were, as a class, better informed of passing events and had a better idea of

1. "The Contrabands at Fortress Monroe," *Atlantic Monthly,* VIII, No. XLIX, November, 1861, 636-637.

2. John B. Wood, Lawrence, Kans., to George L. Stearns, November 19, 1861, Stearns Papers, Kansas Hist. Soc.

3. Botkin, Benjamin A., ed., *Lay My Burden Down: A Folk History of Slavery,* Chicago, 1945, Pt. IV, 198-201.

4. "The Contrabands at Fortress Monroe," *ut supra,* 637.

questions involved in the struggle between North and South than the majority of that class known as the 'poor whites.' "[5]

A future President, campaigning in West Virginia, shared a general opinion that the slaves there would do well in freedom. "These runaways are bright fellows," wrote Rutherford B. Hayes. "As a body they are superior to the uneducated white population of this State."[6] Henry M. Cross of the Forty-eighth Massachusetts thought as highly of the Negroes he encountered at Camp Banks near Baton Rouge early in 1863. "They are smart enough for anyone," he wrote of some casual hands, and he gave a more emphatic verdict on a Negro regiment 1100 strong: "They are not barbarous, or blood-thirsty, but are docile, attentive, and drillable."[7] The first white agents to take charge of Negroes at Hilton Head, S.C., formed a strong impression of "developing manhood." One observer was touched when the refugees there, deciding it was not right for the government to provide free candles, took up a collection to pay for them, and although they earned but pittances, they turned in $2.48. Everywhere the Negroes, when properly supervised, furnished good laborers, stevedores, artisans, bridge-builders, scouts, and guides; the troops often found them responsible and hardworking. "We could never get enough of them," testified Vincent Colyer, in charge of freedmen on Roanoke Island after the fighting early in 1862. They often showed nerve and resourcefulness as spies, but at other times were unreliable. "They frequently went from thirty to three hundred miles within the enemy's lines. . . . bringing back important and reliable information. . . . often on these errands barely escaping with their lives."[8] Southerners learned to fear the scouting capacity of escaped slaves.

Treachery to the Union was practically unknown among the contrabands. "Thousands of soldiers after the war," wrote the historians of the Fifty-fifth Illinois Infantry, "blessed the memory of black men who had given them invaluable aid." If masters tried to frighten them by horrible tales of Yankee cruelty, they were not fooled. Their confidence in "Lincum's sojers" was unshakable. "When, as often happened during the march, information was given by the slaves, it could always be relied upon, and again and again the neighborhood of the enemy was disclosed and the secret hiding places of horses, mules, and forage made known to the great advantage of the army. One day there came into the lines two escaped prisoners bringing with them an aged Negro upon a mule. This freed slave had

---

5. Kellogg, John A., *Capture and Escape*, Madison, Wis., 1908, 147.

6. Hayes, Rutherford B., *Diary and Letters*, ed. Charles R. Williams, Columbus, Ohio, 1922-1926, II, 188.

7. "A Yankee Soldier Looks at the Negro," ed. by William Cullen Bryant II, *Civil War History*, Vol. VII, No. 2, June, 1961, 133ff.

8. Colyer, Vincent, *Report of the Services Rendered by the Freed People to the United States Army, in North Carolina, in the Spring of 1862*, New York, 1864, *passim*.

hidden them in the swamp and fed them for weeks, and in the warmth of their gratitude the men vowed that the benefactor should ride to freedom and be fed on the best of the land for the rest of his life.[9] Undoubtedly this soldier was extreme when stating slave information could "always be relied upon," for in many cases such information was erroneous, or at least distorted and exaggerated.

In the Lower South, and especially on large plantations, the evidences of mistreatment multiplied. Many slaves appeared with backs ridged and livid from floggings: more of them were scarred by cuts or burns; even mutilation was sometimes visible. The London *Times* correspondent, William H. Russell, visiting the plantation of Governor Roman in Louisiana just as the war began, had been struck by the sadness on the faces of the Negroes, convincing him that deep dejection was the prevailing if not universal characteristic of the race.[10] They all looked downcast; even the aged woman who boasted that she had held the governor in her arms when he was a baby, even the attractive yellow girl with fair hair and light eyes whose child was quite white. A soldier of the Eighty-first Ohio, who examined for enlistment a great body of hands fleeing to the Union lines after Iuka and Corinth, was depressed by the evidence of ill usage.

"One gang that I enrolled," he wrote, "sixty in number, had been so terribly abused, beaten, lashed, and branded that they were little better than beasts, and could hardly tell their own names, and not half of them had any idea about their own age, but all referred me to a bright mulatto girl of more than usual intelligence, who had two children with her that looked to me white. As I put down her name I put the usual question, 'Are you married?' and received the answer, 'no!' 'Whose children are these?' 'Them's mine!' 'Who's their father?' 'My master!' As I enrolled this gang of plantation hands and saw the great ugly seams on their backs, and actually great brands on their thighs, fully four inches long, burned so as to leave a deep red scar, and the embruted and pitiable condition of all of them, I thought Mrs. Stowe's Legree a saint compared with the owner of these slaves."[11] Of course many Southerners rejected such evidence. The author of *The Brothers' War*, the cultivated Georgia attorney John C. Reed, testified that among his father's many slaves not one instance of a family separation had occurred before Appomattox, and that, on the contrary, his father had at much expense and inconvenience bought the husband of one slave, and the wife of another, to keep two couples united.[12] Now and then, he admitted, sales which sundered man and wife, or parent and child, were indeed made, but many slaveholders were poor, and sales were declining in proportion to pop-

9. A Committee of the Regiment, *The Story of the Fifty-fifth Regiment, Illinois Volunteer Infantry,* Clinton, Mass., 1887, 401-402.

10. Russell, William Howard, *My Diary North and South,* New York, 1863, Ch. XXXII, 97-100.

11. "Reminiscences of Edwin W. Brown," *Ohio Archeological and Historical Quarterly,* Vol. XLVIII, 304-323.

12. Reid, John C., *The Brothers' War,* Boston, 1905, 166-167.

ulation under pressure of public opinion. He protested earnestly against Lincoln's suggestion that blood was sometimes drawn by the lash, denying this, and forgetting that Lincoln's eloquent utterance was in symbolic, not factual language.[13]

In the Deep South slavery had brutalized some white men as much as their victims. Henry W. Allen, who was elected governor of Louisiana in 1863, had to send officers through the State to halt the stealing of Negroes (especially children from the river parishes) from plantations whose owners had fled; they were seized by so-called guerrillas, taken into Texas, and sold away from their parents and owners. Allen restored about five hundred of these forlorn little wanderers to their families.[14]

It was universally observed that while the Negroes were highly religious, they had limited canons of morality according to Victorian and disciplined white standards. Many had little respect for the Seventh Commandment. It was also universally observed that while they evinced a bustling industry under supervision, they had shown little initiative, morality, or enterprise under slavery. Yet neither their native life in Africa, nor their life as slaves had been conducive to initiative or enterprise in the American sense. Military demands for labor went far toward occupying the contrabands as long as the war lasted, but no longer. As Union forces penetrated deeper into the South and the number of refugees swelled, it was plain that the freed Negroes needed care and supervision. At Yorktown, when the Peninsular campaign began, and later at Memphis, Jackson, and Nashville, they gathered in thousands, forming long lines for rations. Their gratitude for help was touching; they sang, danced, and prayed exultantly. All the way from Tidewater to the Arkansas, as the war progressed, camps of Negroes grew more numerous, active, and troublesome.

Never had America witnessed such scenes. Sometimes the spectacle was merely picturesque. A New York infantryman reached Falmouth on the Rappahannock in April, 1862. "On the day after our arrival," he recorded, "the Negroes came flocking to the guard line, with baskets of eggs, hoe-cakes, and other luxuries, and proved themselves sharp bargainers, doing a lively business." Every squad soon had Negroes as cooks, waiters, foragers for food, and runners of errands.

On occasion, the efforts of freedmen to make a living combined heroism with pathos. At Beaufort, S.C., for example, where several thousand Negroes were quartered outside the town like sheep, volunteers gazed with respect at the shacks where venturesome freedmen sought to attract customers. "Pyes for Sail Here," ran the signs; "Resturent"; "Fresh Bred"; "Soljur's Home"; and "The American

13. *Ibid.*, 169-170.
14. Dorsey, Sarah A., *Recollections of Henry Watkins Allen,* New York, 1866, 244; Mrs. Dorsey herself had three children stolen. Dudley, T., in *The Sable Arm: Negro Troops in the Army, 1861-1865,* New York, 1966, temperately notes this fact.

Hotel." The record continued: "The wild, fervid religious dances, with their accompanying chants, sometimes beginning with Genesis and giving a complete synopsis of the leading points of Bible history from Adam to Peter . . . were the most weirdly exciting yet ludicrous performances imaginable."[15] But pathos was often predominant. The Englishman Edward Dicey, going with Nathaniel Hawthorne to look at Bull Run, was saddened by a group of some dozen runaway slaves huddled upon a flatcar. "There were three men, four women, and half-a-dozen children. Anything more helpless and wretched than their aspect I never saw. Miserably clothed, footsore, and weary, they crouched in the hot sunlight more like animals than men." He overheard one man remarking to a woman, as he munched some white bread he had picked up, "Massa never gave us food like that."[16]

The story of the freedmen in wartime is one of gross mismanagement and neglect. The problem was neither vigilantly foreseen by the government nor dealt with vigorously and promptly by it or by private organizations. Having upset the social system of slaveholding, the North should have acted more generously and promptly to substitute new devices for meeting the old social needs. Almost the whole country was at fault. The abolitionists who had called so long for emancipation should have foreseen that the mere ending of slavery was far from a solution of the stupendous and many-sided problem of creating an efficient and humane social order to meet the exigent new demands. The Lincoln Administration, coping heroically with a multitude of crowding tasks and needs, might ideally have done something more than it did, even if the social, economic, military and governmental standards which then controlled it would have hindered the President from taking such a far-reaching step. Looking back more than a century after emancipation, it might have seemed logical to have urged the creation of a separate government department of Cabinet rank to study, and as far as possible meet, the needs of the freedmen. The government might well have done more than give general support to Grant's plans for succoring the Negroes who flocked into the Army camps, and might have championed more decisively the organization of a Freedmen's Bureau under Brigadier-General John Eaton in March, 1865. Eaton, acting under Grant's orders, had done magnificent work in caring for the physical wants and education of liberated Negroes. In the Department of the Tennessee, including Arkansas, he had set them to work on abandoned plantations, and at cutting wood for the Army and the river steamboats.[17]

All too often squalor, hunger, and disease haunted the refugees, their camps becoming social cancers that were a reproach to the North no less than the South.

15. Mills, John Harrison, *Chronicles of the Twenty-first Regiment, New York State Volunteers*, Buffalo, 1867, 74, 16off.
16. Dicey, Edward, *Six Months in the Federal States*, London, 1863, II, 29-30.
17. Eaton, John and Ethel Osgood Mason, *Grant, Lincoln, and the Freedmen*, New York, 1907, *passim*.

Maria R. Mann, the first woman sent by the Sanitary Commission as agent in a contraband camp, wrote of appalling conditions and often cruel treatment. Deaths were frequent, disease was universal, and the future so bleak that many of the refugees talked of returning to their slave masters, and some did so. Writing of the hospital, she said: "I found the poor creatures in . . . such quarters, void of comfort or decency;—their personal condition so deplorable that any idea of change for the better seems utterly impossible. Many of them seem to come there to die, and they do die very rapidly. . . . The carcasses, filth and decay which 40,000 have scattered over this town, will make the mortality fearful when warm weather comes . . . So much formality attends red tape, and so few friends have the negroes among the Officials . . ." It is impossible to learn whether this camp at Helena, Arkansas, was worse or better than others, but assuredly it was a doleful place. Speaking out sharply, Mrs. Mann charged the Army with "barbarities" against the refugees, while on the other hand admitting, "Our soldiers suffer untold privations here. . . . What is to be done for either class of sufferers under these discouragements I know not. . . ."[18] William Todd of the Seventy-ninth Highlanders described in sad terms the thousands scattered along the river, canal, and roads near Vicksburg just before its capture. The aged, lame, and blind were conspicuous, for most vigorous young men had found some form of army service. One hatless and shoeless old slave wore a blue dress coat with brass buttons; others had little to cover their nakedness but plug hats and old blankets. Some women were decently dressed in coarse plantation homespun or cast-off clothing of the whites; the busts of others were scantily covered with old silk waists. Malnutrition was evident in nearly every place "where the government has been obliged to support destitute contrabands." An aide of General Rufus Saxton at Beaufort reported in midwinter of 1863, that the authorities had issued only such portions of the army ration as were absolutely necessary to support life. He added that intoxication was far rarer than among the white troops. But, the "ill-fed, ill-sheltered, ill-clothed, unmedicined" freedmen were an easy prey of the infectious maladies that swept their poor quarters. "What is to become of them?" asked William Todd.[19]

[I]

What, indeed, was to become of them? The answer was long in coming, and was unsatisfactory when it did come. The story of the freedmen in wartime, as we have already noted, remained one of gross mismanagement and neglect, for the provision made by the government was too little and too late. Washington

---

18. Mann, Maria R., *Letters from the Freedmen's Camp*, Helena, Ark., LC; Todd, William, *The Seventy-Ninth Highlanders, New York Volunteers,* Albany, 1886, 300-301; "To Emancipation League of Boston, Jan. 6, 1863," New York *Tribune,* Jan. 27, 1863.
19. *Ibid.*

failed utterly to foresee the widespread flight of slaves within the Union lines, to assess their needs realistically, and to make considered provision for their future. Lincoln, the War Department, and other agencies, facing a situation completely new in the history of the republic, clung to the usual American policy of delay and improvisation, and manifested the chronic reluctance of government to interfere with personal life. It speaks well for the Army that Ben Butler, David Hunter, N. P. Banks, and above all Grant, showed great sensitivity to the problem, acting with humanity and common sense. But, as we have said, it speaks ill for the Administration not only that it drifted inertly, but that it permitted the care of the freedmen to become in part a football between the Treasury Department and the War Department. Along with Negroes, the Army took possession of much other real and personal property of the rebels, the custody of which properly belonged to the Treasury. To complicate the situation, the Treasury wished to collect the direct tax of 1861 in the seceded States. It therefore legitimately claimed a share in the management of captured Southern property, and Congress recognized the validity of the claim. With foresight and care, a workable adjustment might have been reached, but it was not.

A few officials in Washington, notably William Whiting of the Treasury Department, argued at an early date that the task of caring for refugee slaves and managing abandoned areas demanded a new department of Cabinet rank. It did, indeed. Had such a department been created, and had Lincoln appointed a shrewd and practical head, the new national authority, although it might have suffered terribly from bureaucracy, could have solved some critical wartime problems and smoothed the path of both races into Reconstruction. But Lincoln could not establish a department; Congress alone possessed the power, and for several reasons Congress was unwilling to take farsighted action in behalf of the four million slaves that the war gradually released.

In the first place, most Democrats and the Bell-Everett moderates of the Borderland wished to retard rather than accelerate emancipation. They raised some terrible bogeys: the Negroes would flock northward and flood the labor markets (a fear felt from St. Louis and Cincinnati to Baltimore); they would prove unruly and dangerous; and frightful expenses, necessitating heavy taxes, would be needed to care for the ignorant, helpless, and often ailing refugees. For another reason, many Radical Republicans within and out of Congress believed with Horace Greeley that Negroes were essentially white men with colored skin, who could rapidly learn to care for themselves. Little tutelage or aid would be needed. Turn them loose, lease them vacant lands, and they would quickly become self-supporting, self-respecting citizens, contributing to the wealth of the nation. In short, Radicals seriously underestimated the problem. A third impediment was lack of executive leadership. Lincoln believed at heart in gradual emancipation, and hoped that the white Southerners would show enough wisdom and generosity, once the war ended, to help the freedmen to their feet. He did not wish to see a great bureaucracy ruling the colored people of the South; he hoped to see whites and Negroes ruling themselves, and helping each other.

The strongest impediment of all to well-planned, well-directed action lay in a natural but excessive deference to the military arm. Men believed that the first task was to win the war; nothing must be allowed to interfere with this objective. Officers in the field had expert information and should be entrusted with full responsibility. This belief possessed such great force that many refused to perceive that it did not cover the whole ground; that the inadequacies of government policy injured the Army, the freedmen, and the entire nation in 1864.

[II]

What was government policy, and how was it hammered out on the anvil of war?

Throughout 1861, as we have seen, the Administration adopted no definite program, while the Army wavered between the eagerness of Ben Butler to use refugee slaves, and the determination of John A. Dix in the East and Halleck in Missouri to discourage their reception. The Cabinet, on May 30, upheld Butler's view that, in conquered territory, fugitive Negroes were to be confiscated as contraband of war, and employed by the army. But the final disposition of these contrabands remained uncertain. Meanwhile, until its repeal June 28, 1864, the Fugitive Slave Act remained operative on behalf of *loyal* masters, who could ask Federal marshals to help them reclaim their runaways. When such owners called on Army officers to return fugitives, altercations sometimes ensued. The colonel of the Ninth New York Volunteers gave a Virginia master permission to take home two slaves who had escaped to the Union lines, and he began leading the Negroes through camp by a well-tied rope. As he passed the guard-house a corporal angrily leaped out, cut the rope with his knife, and bade the slaves to run.[20] Some soldiers went much further, attacking and even killing slave-hunters. Actually, an act of March 13, 1862, prohibited military or naval personnel from using force to return fugitives, and by an act of July 17, 1862, no slave escaping into any State from another State could be delivered up except for crime, unless to a loyal owner.

Although the First Confiscation Act, passed in August 1861, applied only to slaves who had been employed against the United States, and Lincoln held Frémont strictly to its letter, Secretary Cameron at once informed Ben Butler that his contraband policy was still valid. In States wholly or partially under insurrectionary control, he wrote, claims to escaped slaves were forfeited by the

20. Graham, Matthew John, *The Ninth Regiment, New York Volunteers*, New York, 1900, 220-221.

treasonable conduct of claimants. In view of the confusion of war, he thought even loyal owners could make few recoveries, and their best course would be to let fugitives be put into the service of the United States with some form of compensation. The Army was not to encourage the flight of slaves, and not to obstruct their "voluntary return" (an absurdity) to loyal citizens.[21] But how could an overworked, harassed officer distinguish between loyal and disloyal masters, or tell whether his troops were quietly encouraging flight or not? Army policy naturally became more and more liberal.

Conservative commanders, apprehensive of Border State anger, nevertheless hung back. Halleck in the Department of Missouri instructed his officers to bar fugitives from their lines.[22] Dix, as head of the Department of Maryland, issued a proclamation to reassure the eastern shore counties of that State and Virginia. "I ordered my colonels to allow no negroes to come within their encampments," he wrote F. P. Blair, Sr., "and I have had no trouble. We have neither stolen negroes, nor caught them for their masters. In a word, we repudiated Genl Butler's whole doctrine of contraband." The government, he foolishly thought, could not undertake to subsist a mass of freedmen while supporting ever-larger armies, for the burden would be too great. Let slavery, now doomed anyway, die a natural death. "The moment you begin to legislate for the emancipation of slaves, you divide the North and consolidate the South."[23] When owners of thirteen fugitive slaves came to Harpers Ferry in the summer of 1861 to demand their property, General Robert Patterson ordered that they be given full assistance, and the runaways were returned. Bull Run was fought within the week, and some of the owners were in the Confederate army![24]

A large part of the Union officers and troops agreed with these conservative attitudes. Many had an instinctive dislike of Negroes, and many shared the views of the Democratic Party on slavery. They turned the Negroes back with contumely. Dissension on the subject persisted until after the Emancipation Proclamation, and never disappeared.

Lincoln continued to support Ben Butler's policy of taking fugitive slaves into the lines and caring for them as contrabands, but it was not at once a national policy. In revising Secretary Cameron's instructions to General Thomas W. Sherman for the Port Royal expedition in October of 1861, Lincoln toned down the orders considerably, directing that Sherman receive fleeing Negroes and put them to work with such compensation to the masters as Congress might sanction. The President eliminated an assurance that the slaves would not again "be reduced to their former condition," and added that they were not to be used as

21. Cameron to Butler, August 8, 1861, War Office Military Book No. 45, National Archives.
22. Meneely, Alexander Howard, *The War Department, 1861*, New York, 1928, 337.
23. Dix to F.P. Blair, Sr., Nov. 27, Dec. 5, 1861 Blair-Lee Papers, Princeton Univ.
24. Quint, Alonzo H., *The Record of the Second Massachusetts Infantry*, Boston, 1867, 39.

soldiers.[25] As temporary army use of contrabands steadily evolved into permanent harborage, and as Halleck, Dix, and other officers who supported the recovery of slaves were more and more angrily denounced by Republican newspapers, pressure upon Congress to take a definite stand increased. Finally, the radical antislavery members forced it to act. On March 13, 1862, the law was approved making any officer who used soldiers or sailors to return fugitive slaves to their owners subject to court-martial and dismissal from the service. Then in midsummer (July 17, 1862) the Second Confiscation Act underlined this policy. Any member of the armed forces who on any pretext whatever presumed to decide on the validity of a claim to a slave, or who gave up a fugitive slave to an owner, should be dismissed. No more slave-catchers in the uniform of the United States!

Under this Second Confiscation Act, the escaped slaves of disloyal masters would be forever free. Fugitives from loyal masters, on the other hand, might be recovered by a Federal marshal or his deputy. The Judge Advocate-General ruled on August 17, 1863, that the Army must follow a line of absolute non-intervention, neither returning fugitives nor preventing civil officers from reclaiming them under the Fugitive Slave Act.[26] But what did this mean? In practical fact, as the armies pushed south *all* masters were regarded as disloyal. Under the new law, Negroes might be hired at $10 a month plus one ration to build entrenchments, perform camp duties, or do any other naval or military work for which they were competent. Officers treated most refugees as captured property, employed many of them, and gave them certificates of liberation. Theoretically, civil officers might appear to estop any certificate, but in war-torn areas they never did.[27] South of the Border States, the armies were thus great mobile machines of emancipation.

In the Borderland alone did the reclamation of fugitives continue, at least until June, 1864. General Curtis wrote from Missouri in the late fall of 1862 that it was still necessary to respect the legal rights of loyal slaveholders.[28] Nearly a year later General Schofield, while urging the enlistment of able-bodied slaves, recommended that the Army give loyal masters a guarantee that they would be returned; and Adjutant General Lorenzo Thomas proposed the same course with respect to Kentucky slaves. As late as the first months of 1864, General Charles J. Paine not only let loyal Kentuckians repossess their slaves, but took steps himself to return them in defiance of the non-intervention rule, because they would be safer and healthier on their plantations than under army care.[29]

25. Meneely, *op. cit.*, 341-342.
26. Holt to Stanton, August 17, 1863, Judge Advocate General Record Book No. 3, National Archives.
27. *Ibid.*
28. Curtis to Loan, Nov. 1, 1862, Dept. of Missouri Letter Book No. 13, 72, National Archives.
29. L. Thomas to G.H. Thomas, Feb. 27, 1864, Thomas Letter Book No. 2, 49ff, National Archives.

It was in the District of Columbia, with its many slaveholders and slaves, numerous free Negroes, and a steady influx of Negro refugees, that controversy simmered most hotly. From Maryland, Northern Virginia, and even greater distances, fugitive slaves slipped into the capital. After the Emancipation Proclamation they flocked in openly. Seward's daughter Fanny wrote in her diary that as they came from church the first Sunday in 1863, the family lighted upon a procession of Virginia slaves trudging toward the contraband camp, a few soldiers escorting them. Each grown man carried a touching little bundle of worldly goods, each woman a baby, and along with them trotted some half-grown children. "In the rear of the procession was a huge wagon, laden with all kinds of possessions, a lively little black face peeping out from the topmost layers."[30] What should be done with the fugitives? They could be put into temporary camps, the almshouse, or in quarters supplied by charitable citizens. The government also rented space for lodging about two hundred.

As they flocked in, the sharp difference of opinion on Army policy between Ben Butler and Dix was paralleled by even sharper differences on District policy between the Federal marshal, Ward H. Lamon, friend of the President, and the oaken-hearted James Wadsworth of Geneseo, N.Y., who became military governor of Washington in the summer of 1862. From 1861 to 1865, Ward Hill Lamon served as marshal of the District Court, one of whose judges was past eighty, and another so disloyal that, as Senator Henry Wilson said, "His heart is sweltering with treason."[31] A Virginian by birth and a hater of abolitionism, the swashbuckling Lamon, a noisy and exhibitionistic figure in Washington life, set himself to enforce both the Fugitive Slave Act and the District stipulation that any slave distant from his master's house without a written pass was subject to arrest. The fact that owners paid an apprehension fee for fugitives encouraged men to lay hands on errant slaves. Many old Washington residents felt a positive hatred for the contrabands. Their care swelled the tax burden, they contributed to local thievery and vice, and their mere presence was a daily reminder that the old era of Southern gentility and arrogance was dying.

When Wadsworth became military governor he found a frightful situation in the District jails, crammed with four times as many inmates as they had been built to hold, and fed on a starvation system that gave Lamon nearly half of the twenty-one cents a day allowed for each prisoner's keep. The previous winter, antislavery Senators had indicted Lamon so fiercely for his arrests and his mistreatment of refugees that Lincoln had been compelled to intervene. He cut through Lamon's protests with an edict in January that the marshal should release all Negroes held on mere suspicion, that he should thereafter imprison no fugi-

30. Fanny Seward ms. diary, Seward Papers, Univ. of Rochester Lib., Jan. 4, 1863.
31. *Congressional Globe,* 37th Cong., 3rd Sess., 1139.

tives except those committed in due legal form, and that he should hold nobody past thirty days.[32] Even so, Wadsworth thought that an undue number of Negroes had been jailed. For those outside the homes that had been improvised for the refugees, many of them ragged, hungry, and wretched, no adequate provision had been made. The callous attitude of many whites was summed up in a statement by T. J. Barnett of the Interior Department: "Among the most disgusting things here is the negro element. They won't work; they infest the town . . ."[33]

Wadsworth gave the weary, helpless runaways more than rations. He found government quarters for them in Duff Green's Row near the Capitol, and he supplied them with clothing, medicines, and other necessities confiscated from blockade runners. He appointed a superintendent to teach them to follow some regular occupation, and find them work. The government used many as laborers at forty cents a day. Wadsworth asserted that of nearly 400 fugitives who arrived during one week in July, employment was found immediately for two-fifths of them. He cooperated with the National Freedmen's Association and other philanthropic bodies in getting schools established and seeing that the Negroes were given instruction in the duties of citizenship.[34] Most important of all, he took a rocklike stand on the rule that no fugitive slave should be restored without a searching inquiry into the master's loyalty. This principle, "the habeas corpus of the contraband," was endorsed by the War Department, and as we have seen, was later incorporated in the Second Confiscation Act.

Altogether, Wadsworth, who returned to field duty after Fredericksburg, stands with Frémont, Ben Butler, and David Hunter as one of the advanced spirits in demanding freedom for escaped slaves, perhaps with less interest in personal and political advancement than Ben Butler, but with Frémont's tinge of impulsive humanitarianism and a little of Stanton's conviction that liberated slaves could be made helpful in winning the war. But the subject remained clouded by equivocal legislation and confused rules. The Fugitive Slave Act was still valid; it was invoked all along the border by owners who protested that they were loyal; Federal marshals and their deputies were subject to heavy fines if they did not execute the law. They had a legal right to search Duff Green's Row, Buell's Louisville, and the army camps of Grant in Kentucky for runaways. Once fugitives were apprehended, it was for civil commissioners, not the military, to decide their fate.[35]

The situation was complicated rather than simplified by the emancipation of slaves in the District of Columbia on April 16, 1862, an act with which Lincoln

32. Pearson, H.G., *James Wadsworth of Geneseo,* New York, 1913, 129ff. Wadsworth returned to field duty in late December, 1862, after Fredericksburg.
33. Barnett, to S.L.M. Barlow, Sept. 23, 1862, Barlow Papers, HEH.
34. Pearson, *Wadsworth, op. cit.,* 133.
35. *Ibid.,* 137-138.

was not in agreement on all details. Anticipating this measure, which Lincoln signed with some reluctance and with personal reflections upon the possible propriety of compensation to the owners, Washington slaveholders had hurried a small army of chattels into Maryland—whence many soon filtered back into the District. Although it was not certain that the Fugitive Slave Act covered these runaways, a deputation of slaveholders obtained from Lincoln what they thought was an intimation that it did. The work of Lamon's deputies in seizing fugitives reached a new intensity, and so did Wadsworth's wrath. When his Negro cook, whose former master he knew to be disloyal, was lodged in the city jail for examination by the civil commissioners, he marched a squad to the prison, took possession, and released all the contrabands inside. Lamon then mustered his own squad of city police at midnight, captured Wadsworth's garrison of two, and held the jail. This conflict of policy continued all summer. The civil authorities of the District, with Southern ideas, tried to enforce the Fugitive Slave Act there; the military authorities under Wadsworth did what they could to nullify it.

This was a conflict which the prompt creation of a strong department for the care and policing of freedmen might have done much to obviate. The Union still had four slaveholding States, wherein the rights of masters had to be protected. The Emancipation Proclamation did not apply to thirteen parishes of Louisiana, the forty-eight counties of West Virginia, or seven counties of Virginia. Here, as everywhere, loyal masters had the right to recover slaves up to the final proclamation. A strong independent agency could have decided which runaways were truly contraband, and which belonged to loyal owners, and could have helped get employment for Negroes arriving in Washington, Cincinnati, Cairo, and other border towns. When Northern speculators tried growing cotton in Kentucky, Missouri, and even Southern Illinois, with Negro hands, an active Bureau might have been of assistance.

Certainly many Negroes, when properly aided, showed a striking capacity for self-help. In Washington, where refugee slaves had increased to perhaps 10,000 by the spring of 1863, with 3,000 more in Alexandria, they were industrious whenever given a real chance. Many men worked as government laborers; the more capable learned crafts, from blacksmithing to shoemaking; and women took positions as cooks and laundresses. A new camp at Arlington, supervised by the Quartermaster's Department, became a well-developed town, with substantial houses, shops, a church, a school and a hospital—the Freedman's Village, quite self-supporting. Most refugees, however, continued to live in the city, mainly in old tenements and shacks, a demoralized people.[36] The tatters, ignorance, and squalor of many of the poor creatures made them seem like beings from another world, their poverty expressing itself in pilfering, and their lack of proper food,

36. Leech, Margaret, *Reveille in Washington*, New York, 1941, 246-247, 250-251.

shelter, and sanitary arrangements exposing them to disease. It is not strange that fashionable women drew their skirts aside when they passed, that urchins jeered and threw stones, and that hoodlums cursed them. Yet the willingness of white soldiers to insult them because they hated the idea that black men should claim the same privileges as themselves, the readiness of white laborers to buffet them because they feared Negro competition, were actually tributes to their potentialities. They were asserting their right to a future.

The general prejudice rose to a climax on the Negro's day of jubilee—New Year's Day of 1863. Freedmen who gathered in the chapel of the Twelfth-Street camp to which many had fled when smallpox broke out in Duff Green's Row, had to mute their rejoicing, for some were afraid that any demonstration might well be the signal for a mob outbreak.[37] Conscious of injustice but too cowed to complain, proud of their freedom but humbly deferential to those who begrudged it, soft-voiced but determined to press on, their demeanor was an augury of their course for a century to come.

[III]

"Oh, you are the man who has all those darkies on his shoulders." So Grant in the autumn of 1862 addressed Chaplain John Eaton of the Twenty-seventh Ohio, a thirty-two-year-old former superintendent of schools in Toledo whom he had just appointed supervisor of the contrabands crowding into the army camps at La Grange, Tennessee.[38] The General directed Eaton to establish his first refuge at Grand Junction hard by. The cohorts of blacks might be transformed into a valuable auxiliary, said Grant, if the men were given camp duties and construction work, and the women were assigned to hospitals and camp kitchens.

As Grant's troops advanced into northern Mississippi through a region dense with Negroes, owners fled their plantations and farms, and slaves thronged into the Yankee camps. The flood of want and misery appalled all observers. It was like the oncoming of cities, wrote Eaton. Women ready to give birth, old men and toddling children, invalids in the last stages of disease, honest and hardworking hands alongside hands lazy and thievish, presented a perturbing problem. Many Northern soldiers, quite unused to color, had more bitter prejudices against it than Southerners. But even the benevolent were nonplused, fearing "the demoralization and infection of the Union soldier and the downfall of the Union cause" if dark hordes swamped the advancing columns.[39]

This Western influx presented graver problems than any encountered in the

37. *Ibid.*, 249-250.
38. The appointment was dated Nov. 11, 1862: Eaton, John, and Ethel Osgood Mason, *Grant, Lincoln, and the Freedmen, op. cit.*, 5.
39. *Ibid.*, Ch. I.

East. After Iuka and Corinth, the refugees poured in by platoons, until about 7,000 had collected in byways and purlieus of the latter town. As the Army was occupied with its wounded, they at first had to shift for themselves without tents or decent clothing, and their demands grew so desperate that (as Grant wrote later) it was impossible to advance until their needs were met. Military tasks would support only a small fraction; what should he do with the rest? He set many to collecting and ginning whatever cotton remained on the abandoned plantations, and gave others tools to erect their own shelter.[40] Citizens remaining at home were allowed to hire them at the government rate of pay. Some refugees had brought teams, farm implements, and cooking utensils with them; others needed everything. Grant might have been held liable for the hundreds of thousands of dollars' worth of Army property distributed among them, but he never hesitated to accept the responsibility. His resourceful confrontation of the situation was characteristic.

And in John Eaton, Grant found so efficient a lieutenant that, as we have noted, just before Christmas in 1862 the General appointed him superintendent of contrabands for the Department of the Tennessee. "In no case will Negroes be forced into the service of the Government," wrote Grant, "or be enticed away from their homes except when it becomes a military necessity."[41] Eaton found most troops reluctant to serve the Negro in any manner, and even parties detailed to guard the contrabands did their work unwillingly. Once Eaton was roughly arrested by a colonel as he gave directions to some wandering Negroes; once his horse, used by a sergeant in foraging for contrabands, was shot by somebody who hoped to kill Eaton himself. But his talent for organization slowly brought order out of chaos.

In Grant's retreat from Grand Junction to Memphis the refugees, though carried by rail, fared badly. In the city, where no quarters had been provided, they met new hardships. Eaton saw shivering groups around campfires on every corner. As soon as possible a refuge was prepared just below town, and large numbers were transferred thither. A Minnesota chaplain named A. S. Fiske had already done much for black fugitives, and Eaton lost no time in enlisting him as superintendent in the Memphis area. At Camp Fiske he created a model town of log huts and gardens, clean, well-drained, well-policed, and comfortable. General Grenville M. Dodge meanwhile organized another camp at Corinth.[42] New settlements of Negroes sprang up steadily all over the Department.[43]

40. Halleck authorized this; Eaton, *op. cit.*, 12.
41. General Order No. 13, Dec. 17, 1862; Eaton, *op. cit.*, 26-27.
42. During 1863 Dodge officered and mustered in two Negro regiments; Personal Records, 56, National Archives.
43. Eaton, *op. cit.*, 30-33.

The fact that two chaplains took charge of the Mississippi Valley refugees gave a strong moral imprint to their care. Strict regulations respecting marriage were enforced, for Eaton and Fiske, determined to allow "no promiscuous inter-mingling," made the family a unit of community life. Many former slaves were eager for legal weddings, and Fiske once married 119 couples in a single mass service. Since the chaplains encouraged religious activities, preachers flourished. One night, Eaton heard a black exhorter addressing the Almighty with emotion: "Oh Lord, shake Jeff Davis over the mouth of hell, but Oh Lord, doan' drop him in!" The superintendents required freedmen to labor or give a good excuse, and reduced the number dependent on the government to the lowest level. Many Negroes, drifting north to Cairo, found it a gateway to larger opportunities in the North. And many, living in Northern communities long enough to acquire new skills and ideas, returned to their old homes fully equipped to make a living.

Like Wadsworth in the East, Eaton became impressed by the capacity of many former slaves. In a report to Grant during the siege of Vicksburg, which the General sent on to Lincoln, he asserted that they were much brighter than their friends had originally supposed, that house servants were more intelligent than field-hands, proving the influence of environment, and that "all learn rap-idly". He pronounced them quite fit to bear arms if only good officers were placed over them. Among the many mulattoes, some were as indistinguishable from whites in mental traits as in complexion. "Van Dorn paroled a servant at Holly Springs," he noted, "not suspecting his African descent."[44]

From an early period Grant had foreseen the desirability of arming Negro recruits, and he told Eaton at the outset that when the contrabands demonstrated they could perform Army labor well, it would be easy to put weapons into their hands. As soon as Halleck wrote Grant that all hope of reconciliation was gone and peace must be forced by the sword, Grant was quite ready to support the enlistment of black men. When Lorenzo Thomas arrived on his Western tour for organizing Negro contingents, Eaton accompanied him to the principal Army camps. He recorded that Thomas had a peremptory way of dealing with men reluctant to accept the new policy. After calling a command before him and reading the new War Department order, he would ask those opposed to it to move one step from the ranks. A few would do so—and Thomas would order them to the guardhouse to revise their opinions. The enlistment of Negroes, as we have noted, was a conspicuous success. Probably 70,000 all told were placed under arms in the Mississippi Valley, or nearly one-third of the total of 186,000[45] in all areas taken into the Union service. They often fought bravely in numerous

44. *Ibid.,* 65-68.
45. *O.R.* III, Vol V. 661.

engagements, though, like all soldiers, they at times fell short of the highest soldierly standards.[46]

As Thomas and spring arrived together in 1863, more systematic measures had to be taken to employ those Negroes who could not enlist. After the fall work of harvesting corn and cotton, Eaton had used many in cutting wood. For the new crop season, the cultivation of abandoned lands inside or near the Union lines offered larger opportunities. Thomas instituted a plan for the leasing of plantations, and appointed a commission of three to supervise it. Calls upon Northern benevolence brought in seed and implements—a hundred ploughs at one time. Under his plan, white tenants were to get Negro hands from the government, engaging to feed, clothe, and kindly supervise them until February 1, 1864, and to pay them modest wages according to a stated scale—$7 a month for able-bodied men. Nobody knew as yet how much free Negro labor was really worth, for it was uncertain how efficient the former slave would prove, and still more uncertain how much former masters or Northern speculators could be induced to pay for him. These tenants were to pay the government a rent of $2 for every 400-pound bale of cotton they produced, and five cents for every bushel of corn or potatoes.[47]

By midsummer of 1863, an elaborate if clumsy mechanism had been created to help freedmen in the Mississippi Valley to their feet. Part of it was the leasing system under Lorenzo Thomas's three-man commission. Another part was Eaton's section of the Army administration (sometimes called the Freedmen's Department) which Thomas strengthened by ordering all the generals to appoint provost-marshals who would look after the Negroes scattered over the Army-controlled plantations. A third part was supplied by philanthropic organizations of the North, particularly the various freedmen's aid societies or commissions. Eaton specially praised the helpful activities of H. B. Spelman as head of a Cleveland agency for assisting freedmen, and the generosity of H. B. Claflin & Co. of New York, for the Cleveland group assisted small tenant farmers to sell odd lots of cotton, and Claflin's firm outfitted stores for freedmen at various points with goods at no cost.

As the Army of the Cumberland under Rosecrans advanced upon Chattanooga, tens of thousands of former slaves, men, women, and children, were liberated. Almost without exception they turned to the military for support. The men found employment as servants to officers, cooks to soldiers, teamsters, and work-hands for the Commissary's and Quartermaster's departments. They chopped wood, built roads, and repaired railway lines, while the women cooked and washed. Although destitution was common, a correspondent of the New

46. Randall, James G., *Civil War and Reconstruction*, Boston, 1953, 505.
47. Eaton, *op. cit.*, 60.

York *Tribune* thought they were in better estate than the contrabands about Washington; for while they received less help from charitable societies, they showed more self-reliance and took better care of what they earned. The Army gave them wages, food, and medicine, but no clothing, and little training or discipline.[48]

What the situation most demanded, declared the correspondent, was one man of heart and intelligence as authoritative head of a Freedmen's Department. William Whiting, Solicitor of the War Department (as previously noted) was one of those who vigorously urged a Cabinet post to deal with the many problems of emancipation. When the Freedmen's Bureau was finally created on March 3, 1865, it was not a Cabinet post, but did have wide powers, becoming a political organ as well. A wartime Department would have been effective even though the danger of political meddling in the general wartime government was great. Much would have depended upon the tact and prudence of the head of such a powerful and sensitive new governmental agency. Such a department head, with a proper staff, could have systematized and coordinated the multitudinous activities of a hundred philanthropic organizations, many of them limited in funds, skills, and persistence. He could have met the peculiar difficulties of Negro enlistments in the Border States. In Missouri, General John Schofield, after wrestling with the objections raised by legal masters, and with the governor's stipulation that State laws of Missouri must never be violated, helped see to the mustering-in of all Negroes fit for duty, who had gathered at the army posts, and were clearly entitled to their freedom under the Confiscation Act. Two regiments were thus obtained by the end of the summer of 1863, and another was authorized, although public excitement was generated in the process.

"I believe the able-bodied negroes in Missouri will be worth more to the government than they are to their masters as laborers, and that this is the general opinion among slave owners in the state," Schofield wrote E. D. Townsend, Acting Adjutant-General.[49] "I respectfully suggest that it might be wise policy to enlist all able-bodied negroes in Mo. who may be willing to enter the service, giving to their masters receipts upon which those who established their loyalty may base a claim upon the Government for the value of the services lost." A Freedmen's Department could have decided such questions of policy all the way from Missouri and Kentucky to Maryland.

The farther south the armies penetrated, the greater was the care needed by the released slaves. In the spring of 1863, those reaching Memphis impressed a Chicago journalist as pitiable victims of American heedlessness, greed, and class prejudice. They seemed indeed the mudsills of society described by Dew,

---

48. Spec. Corr., N.Y. *Tribune*, Murfreesboro, Tenn., May 30, 1863, June 8, 1863.
49. Sept. 29, 1863; Dept. of Missouri Letter-Book No. 14, 260-261 National Archives.

Harper, and other slavery apologists. The field-hands, little above animals in appearance, dirty, wretched, and half-naked, shambled along with awkward gait. "Some wear a piece of carpet or matting. A child is perhaps encased in an inverted salt or meal sack, with a hole in the top. . . . Many of the younger girls are arrayed in a single thin article of clothing, too flimsy for a real cover."[50]

When the occupation of Vicksburg and the towns south of it threw upon the government some 30,000 contrabands, their situation became appalling. They were crowded together in utter destitution, two-thirds of them in or near the half-wrecked city, and the remainder on the west bank; hardly one family properly fed, clothed, or sheltered, and many in utter despair. Some died miserably in the streets, without medical or hospital care. Debility, excitement, and confusion unfitted many for sustained labor. Men and women alike, unable to do anything but field work, would take a job and leave it in a few hours. "Housekeepers," Eaton wrote Levi Coffin, the Quaker philanthropist famous for his management of the Underground Railroad, "often had a new cook for each meal in the day."[51] For some time all efforts to establish order in the camps broke down; the sea of misery burst the dykes. Another Quaker, representing Philadelphia philanthropy, reported that the squalor of one camp gave him a feeling that approached despair, and he was told that another close by was even worse.[52]

Yet gradually, as some Negroes enlisted, and others found places on leased plantations, or gathered wood for government steamboats, the skies brightened. The Sanitary Commission supplied medicines in all large refugee camps, and soon a capable Army surgeon was appointed medical director of freedmen, with power to outfit sick-camps and hospitals, and to employ surgeons.[53]

The enlightened attitude of General Grant, manifest as long as he commanded in the West, was as creditable to his humanity as his wisdom. He gave Eaton's measures unwavering support, encouraged the enlistment of capable Negroes, and approved the hiring out of others on leased plantations. "At least three of my Army Corps commanders," he wrote Halleck in the spring of 1863, "take hold of the new policy of arming the Negroes and using them against the rebels with a will. . . ."[54] How different was this attitude from McClellan's hostility to any inroads upon slavery! It was Grant's idea in the autumn of 1862 to use refugees to harvest crops on abandoned plantations; it was he who, while employing freedmen to cut wood for the government, had the surplus sold at higher prices to independent steamboats, which yielded funds for giving housing, hospi-

50. Memphis letters, Chicago *Morning Post*, Feb. 4, 1863.
51. Eaton, *op. cit.*, 105.
52. *Report of F.R. Shipley of Friends Assn. for Relief of Colored Freedmen*, submitted Jan. 12, 1864, pamphlet in New York Hist. Soc.
53. Eaton, *op. cit.*, 130-139.
54. Grant to Halleck, Milliken's Bend, April 19, 1863, Eldredge Papers, HEH.

tals, and various comforts to the Negroes;[55] and it was he who promised these former slaves that, if they fought well, he would give them the right to vote.[56]

He could act the more freely because he did not face the monstrous problems which smouldering hatreds presented in places such as New Orleans. When Secretary Chase urged Ben Butler to treat the Negro in that city with understanding, Butler replied that he would, but added: "I assure you it is quite impossible to free him here and now without a Santo Domingo. A single whistle from me would cause every white man's throat to be cut in this city. Hate has piled up here between master and servant until it is fearful."[57] Although slavemasters in Mississippi quaked over Negro restlessness and took what precautions they could against any uprisings in the Natchez district, in 1861-62, apprehension ran so high that forty Negroes were hanged, and as many more jailed. But the slaves were in general more docile than might have been anticipated, even on plantations left without masters.[58]

[IV]

Permanent policies for the freedmen could not be determined until full evidence was accumulated upon their capacities. Late in 1862, prominent antislavery men, including Moncure D. Conway of Virginia and Washington, and Samuel Gridley Howe of Boston, addressed carefully phrased questions to a number of officers superintending the former slaves.[59] How many could read and write? Were they willing to work hard? What was their record as to honesty, chastity, and temperance? Did they show vengefulness? Two important questions ran: Do they desire to migrate to the North? and, Can they at once take their place in society as a free laboring class, able to support themselves, or do they need preparation?

Witnesses agreed that few could read on arrival at the refugee camps; scarcely one, wrote the superintendent at Fortress Monroe. Officers also agreed that, except to gain freedom, few wished to go North. If emancipated in the South, they would remain there. Their obedience, cheerfulness, and good nature won general praise. So did their desire to learn, their interest in religion (although this was emotional rather than thoughtful), and their industry. They are more pious than moral, wrote one officer; while another declared that they were somewhat given to lying and stealing, as might be expected of any enslaved people. The

55. Eaton, *op. cit.*, 12.

56. Grant, Ulysses S., *Personal Memoirs of U.S. Grant*, New York, 1885, I, 424-426; Eaton, *op. cit.*, 15.

57. Butler to Chase, New Orleans, July 10, 1862; Salmon P. Chase Papers, Pennsylvania Hist. Soc.

58. Bettersworth, John Knox, *Confederate Mississippi*, Baton Route, La., 1943, 159-173.

59. Members of the Emancipation League were responsible for the questionnaire. See Conway, Moncure, *Addresses and Reprints*, New York, 1908, 117-123, on his idea of Negro traits.

head of the contraband depot in Washington declared that they were the most religious people he had ever known, but their religion was entirely divorced from morality.[60]

The superintendents agreed, in general, that contrabands needed education and supervision before they could take a proper place in society. They were "irresponsible", wrote the East Arkansas chaplains. An aide to General Rufus Saxton at Beaufort, S.C., believed that the lack of opportunities for employment would make Union guardianship indispensable until the South was reconstructed and could furnish a healthy demand for free agricultural labor. The head of the Craney Island camp near Norfolk declared, "We can only judge of the capacity of the colored race when a generation shall arise that has had the opportunity of being fitted by education to care for themselves."

Bacon's remark that "a man that studieth revenge keeps his own wounds green" had little application to the Negroes. All witnesses agreed that they showed singularly little ill-will for their former masters. They often manifested an independent spirit, like the Negro girl who told her mistress, "The time for answering bells is gone by," but they seldom showed malice. They were often as harshly treated by Army men as by their oldtime masters. The two chaplains in East Arkansas declared that many of lower rank were "hard, unjust, and cruel," while the ordinary privates treated freedmen "as savages and brutes." General Saxton's aide reported that the generosity of many officers and privates was counterbalanced by the "abuse and injustice" of others. Scanty as the government wage of $10 a month for labor was, callous officers often withheld all or part of it. Fortress Monroe reported more than $30,000 due the black people for work, to say nothing of a great amount of night and Sunday service for which promised payment was never given.[61]

The conclusions of the field superintendents were corroborated by a new Freedmen's Inquiry Commission which shortly afterwards made its first report to Congress, a body organized primarily by three friends of the released slaves, James McKaye of Pennsylvania, Robert Dale Owen of Indiana, and S. G. Howe of Massachusetts. Stanton gave it the necessary authority, appointed Owen chairman, and asked McKaye and others to draw up its instructions.[62] After much investigation, it presented an optimistic view, reiterating the old familiar state-

60. This correspondence, originally published in the *Boston Commonwealth*, an emancipationist journal, was reprinted in the New York *Tribune*, January 27, 1863.

61. The men reporting to the Emancipation League of Boston included E.W. Hooper, aide to General Saxton; C.B. Wilder at Fort Monroe; O. Brown at Craney Island; Samuel Sawyer at Helena; George D. Wise at St. Louis; and Charles Fitch and J.G. Ferman in East Arkansas. Saxton estimated the number of contrabands in the Department of the South at about 18,000; Fort Monroe reported "several thousand" in the "several counties" it controlled; Helena reported about 4,000; St. Louis gave no numbers; the District of East Arkansas reported "about 3,000"; and the Washington Contraband Depot stated that 3,381 had passed through its camp in the previous six months. New York *Tribune*, January 27, 1863.

62. McKaye to Andrew, March 21, 1863, Andrew Papers, Mass. Hist. Soc.

ments upon Negro industry, appetite for knowledge, and piety. It assured Congress that strong local attachments and a preference for the Southern climate would keep most liberated slaves in their home communities. Admitting certain weaknesses of the race, the Commission entered a plea for the defense. Negroes evinced little regard for truth because lies had been a shield against unjust punishment. Yet, the Commission declared, even the most retarded could be quickly elevated by military discipline, regular payment for work done, and access to land —for they longed above all to own a few acres.[63]

Sympathetic Army officers were equally hopeful, as were those who studied the coastal Negroes of the Carolinas. James M. McKim of Philadelphia, who had founded a relief committee for the thousand slaves in the Port Royal (S.C.) area, brought back from the Sea Islands in the summer of 1862 a mass of facts to prove that, in spite of many handicaps, the experiment of hiring freedmen to cultivate the land had been a success. He had found some 3,800 laborers growing good crops of corn, potatoes, and cotton upon 14,000 acres.[64] General Banks wrote from Alexandria, La., early in 1864: "I entertain no doubt whatever of the capabilities of the emancipated colored people . . . I have seen them in all situations, in the last year and a half, and . . . they seem to me to have a clearer comprehension of their position and the duties which rest upon them than any other class of our people."[65]

That destitute white refugees often needed assistance as acutely as the black people was obvious, for many were too young or too old for self-support. Nevertheless, the two grim problems of the white and the black refugees were quite different. Many white folks, fallen into poverty, lacked the ingenuity to find employment and not a few showed that their initiative and industry were dulled by long ease.[66] Their numbers became appalling. "Half the world is refugeeing," wrote one plantation girl late in the war.[67] Many whites, conscious of dignity, were more reluctant than Negroes to ask help, which was given grudgingly. The sufferings of uprooted and impoverished families caught behind the Union lines were often heartrending, for they could not count on community support as could displaced wanderers farther south. John M. Palmer wrote his wife from Nashville in the autumn of 1862 that if she could see the eager competition between refugee white women and Negro women to gain a few dollars by

63. 38th Cong., 1st Sess., *Senate Exec. Doc. 53;* Governor John A. Andrew had encouraged the formation of the Commission.

64. McKim's address in Philadelphia, New York *Tribune,* July 18, 1862; see also his book, *The Freedman of South Carolina,* Philadelphia, 1862; Rose, Willie Lee, *Rehearsal for Reconstruction,* Indianapolis, 1964, *passim.*

65. Banks to James McKaye, March 28, 1864, Banks Papers, Essex Institute, now in LC.

66. Massey, Mary Elizabeth, *Refugee Life in the Confederacy,* Baton Route, 1964, 160ff., on shortcomings inside the Confederacy.

67. See Andrews, Eliza Francis, *The Wartime Journal of a Georgia Girl,* New York, 1908, 19-174, for a vivid account of wartime travels.

washing for the soldiers, selling them pies and cakes, or sewing for them, she would find the spectacle harrowing. "Indeed, in this struggle the Negro woman has an advantage over the modest white woman, as she permits the indecent liberties of coarse men, and thus gains employment. It is not uncommon for the colored wench, by a vulgar joke or licentious allusion, to drive her white competitor from the field."[68]

[V]

Dissatisfaction with government fumbling in the care of freedmen steadily rose in 1863-64. Northerners who asked for more effective measures to keep contrabands inside the South were dissatisfied; so were those who wished fuller provision made for all who migrated to the North. President Lincoln did not help matters by clinging to the impracticable idea that many former slaves might be colonized in Central America, the West Indies, or even Africa. This plan offended large numbers, including free Negroes of long standing, the new freedmen, all American idealists, and employers who wished to use Negro labor. The Freedmen's Inquiry Commission, in its second report in May, 1864, emphasized the fact that demand for Negro help both inside and outside the armed forces exceeded supply. Somehow the government was not siphoning such help to the quarters where it was needed most. Meanwhile, the equivocal status of many Negroes in Missouri, Kentucky, and other Border States—not quite slaves and not quite free—might have been corrected by a competent general administration.

Month after month, the cry of anguish rising from helpless refugees wrung the hearts of humane citizens. "You must pardon me again," a friend wrote Elihu Washburne from Cairo early in 1863. "Five hundred contrabands, men, women, and children, have been suddenly thrown in here, since three days ago, and just at this time a severe change in the weather has taken place. A severe snowstorm is raging here at this time, and these poor people are suffering terribly for the lack of fire and even food—and the few who have money are being imposed upon in all kinds of shapes by the money grabbers here . . . There are at this moment, while the snow is falling thick and fast, quite a number of women and little children crowded together in the second story of the Upper Barracks; in these apartments there are no fireplaces, nor stoves."[69]

Radical opinion in the North in 1863 levelled two heavy charges against governmental management of the freedmen. One was that no thoughtful, coherent plan had been studied and applied. The Lincoln Administration, which at first

68. To Mrs. Palmer, Nashville, October 2, 1862, Palmer Papers, Illinois State Hist. Libr.
69. H.O. Wagoner, to Washburne, Jan. 15, 1863, Washburne Papers, LC.

expected gradual emancipation, had been caught unprepared when the events of 1862 made it necessary to decree the immediate emancipation of most of the slaves. It had resorted to a series of stopgap expedients. Only in the Sea Islands area and in part of the Mississippi Valley had government made serious efforts to organize a labor system for the South, based upon a full recognition of Negro rights. Only on the islands and the coast between Charleston and Savannah, where General David Hunter had made his premature and dictatorial effort at emancipation, had an important experiment been carried through in the sweeping reconstruction of social and economic relations between the races, and the permanent establishment of the freedmen on a well-planned basis. This undertaking alone attracted national attention.[70]

More important was the charge that the makeshift expedients carelessly adopted looked toward the wrong goals. Their objects were merely policing the masses of refugees, reducing government expenses in dealing with them, and providing wood, corn, and cotton for government use. The government should have adopted a larger program, which included a new pattern of land ownership and a higher code of race relations.

General Lorenzo Thomas's plan of leasing abandoned plantations to returned owners or Northern speculators, who could employ Negroes at government-controlled wages, brought these complaints to a head. To Northern emancipationists this looked like a timid halfway house, so far as the Negroes were concerned, between slavery and independence. Behind the Union lines in the Mississippi Valley, the tracts abandoned by Confederates exceeded in area the tracts still held by loyal citizens. Why not divide the confiscated estates among those who had done so much, by the unpaid toil of half a lifetime, to make them productive? At least why not give a small homestead to every family of liberated slaves? In many areas the old slate had been sponged half-clean; why not sponge it completely? It was a half-step to raise the Negroes to the wage level; a full step would mean raising them to land-ownership. "I am informed by the planters generally," wrote Thomas W. Carter, head of the bureau of free labor in the Department of the Gulf, reviewing the year 1864-65, that planters "cannot survive the shock which has come upon them with the war, the abolition of slavery, and the . . . loss of their fortunes, their sons, and their hopes . . . They are now preparing to give way to new capital and new proprietorship."[71] Why not give way in part to Negro smallholdings?

70. Hunter from March, 1862, until June, 1863, commanded the Department of the South, including the South Carolina islands and coast mentioned, and the towns of Hilton Head, Port Royal, and Beaufort. For national interest, see "The Freedmen at Port Royal," *North American Review*, Vol. 101, July, 1865, 1-28.

71. Carter, Thomas W., *Annual Report for 1864-65*, New Orleans, 1865. In this Department plantations were being cultivated under military administration, with 50,000 freedmen on them.

This was the position taken by the New York *Tribune.* Thomas's system of leasing plantations to white men, it argued, was doubtless good for the government and the lessees, but promised no beneficial results to the Negroes. Like the system instituted by N. P. Banks in Louisiana, it overlooked the fact that the helpless freedmen, as well as the Treasury and occupants of plantations, should be consulted. Was the prospect of a cotton crop in the fall of 1863 of more importance than justice to a half-emancipated people? The Negroes should have secure homes, a permanent footing, and hope for the future.[72] In Rosecrans's army, Brigadier-General Oliver H. Payne (the resourceful officer who later became Rockefeller's partner, and a great capitalist and philanthropist), prided himself on his success in changing slave-labor to wage-labor. "We are hiring the black people to their own masters," he wrote Rosecrans. "We say to the servant that he is to have $8 per month, and is to be faithful and good, and work hard . . . We make written contracts, in which the slave is only known as a hired man."[73] This was a step forward, but men like Greeley believed that a much stronger move was needed.

The government, moreover, failed to protect many of the freedmen from abuse and exploitation by plantation lessees. James E. Yeatman, the eminent civic leader in St. Louis who became head of the Western Sanitary Commission, found in a tour down the Mississippi Valley late in 1863 that many Negroes were resentful and discouraged. He questioned thousands. Large numbers had not been paid real money for months; their employers had given them tickets for their days of actual work, presumably to be redeemed in cash when the crop was sold. Their families sometimes went without bread for days. "They all testify that if they were only paid their little wages as they earned, they could stand it; but to work and get poorly paid, poorly fed, and not doctored when sick is more than they can endure."[74] It was hard for Army men to reproach planters for dilatory payment when the Army itself paid its Negro hands but a tardy pittance.

Many planters who leased land from the government treated the freedmen badly, and were abetted in this by local police officers. "If the freedmen were left to the mercy of those who formerly owned them as slaves, or to the officers of their selection," wrote Thomas Conway of the Department of the Gulf, "we might with one count of the fingers of our hands number the years which the race would spend with us." Conway found that the fairest employers in matters of pay were the Northerners who came to the Gulf States with money and the intention of staying. Long-settled Southern masters were almost as fair; but the get-rich-

72. New York *Tribune,* May 27, 1863.
73. Payne, Gallatin, Tenn., June 1, 1863, in New York *Tribune,* June 8, 1863.
74. Yeatman, James E., *Report on the Condition of the Freedmen of the Mississippi to Western Sanitary Commission, 1863,* St. Louis, 1864; Forman, Jacob Gilbert, *The Western Sanitary Commission,* St. Louis, 1864, *passim.;* Hodges, W.R., *The Western Sanitary Commission,* St. Louis, 1906.

quick newcomers were most dishonest. The basic rate of pay was inadequate, even below the level earned by independent Negroes in slavery days. Under Federal regulations, freedmen were hired to lessees for $7 (in some places $8) a month—$84 or $96 a year, less $2 for medical attendance. The $7-hand earned 27 cents a day, and if he worked only ten days a month, his income was $2.70! Yet in antebellum years an able-bodied Negro was often hired out at from $200 to $240 a year, and a woman at from $150 to $180, with food, shelter, and clothing—and this when cotton brought only ten cents a pound! Representative Thomas D. Eliot of Massachusetts commented sharply on Lincoln's recommendation that the freedmen should labor faithfully for reasonable wages.

"So they will, if allowed," he said. "But who is to allow them? Will you let harpies go among them, or white bloodhounds whose scent is keen for prey, whose fangs are remorseless, whose pursuit is for gold at any cost of human life? Such men have been there; they are there now, under cover of government authority; and the abuses practised by them sadden and depress the freedmen."[75]

The situation was complicated in 1863 by the increasing conflict of jurisdiction between the War and Treasury Departments to which we have previously alluded. Much abandoned property everywhere was stolen by Army officers, and they or their accomplices enriched themselves, in the Mississippi Valley in particular, by trade in contraband cotton. Since this seized cotton properly belonged to the Treasury, Congress passed a much-needed law in March, 1863, for the protection of relinquished assets, enabling Treasury agents to take charge of lands and crops left by fleeing Confederates. By a subsequent order of the War Department, Army officers were required to give these agents any assistance they might require in collecting and holding. That is, the Treasury gained very nearly paramount authority, but Army men were often reluctant to recognize it. Such supervisors of the freedmen as Eaton complained that Treasury agents were excessively interested in Negroes and crops as sources of revenue, and lacked a just perception of the position of the former slaves as human beings and citizens, sharing Justice Taney's view of them as potentially profitable chattels.

Nobody could accuse Secretary Chase of indifference to the Negro. When he read Yeatman's report exposing the faults of the leasing system, he gladly agreed to have the Treasury's supervisor of special agents, William P. Mellen, work with Yeatman in drawing up better regulations for the management of abandoned lands.[76] From the beginning of 1864, no lessee was allowed more than one plantation; preference was given to men desiring small tracts; wages were lifted to $25 a month for the best men, $20 for the second-best, and $14-18 for women; and

75. *Congressional Globe*, 38th Cong., 1st Sess., 568.
76. Eaton, *op. cit.*, 145.

payment was made a first lien on crops. Every lessee was now required to pay the full monthly total whether he employed his help every working day or not, and he could not withhold more than half of their wages until the crop was sold. All laborers had to be obtained through the authorized superintendents, and given clothing and food at low prices.[77]

Although in theory the Yeatman-Mellen regulations marked a happy advance, difficulties continued. The Treasury was so anxious to encourage cotton-growing that it rented out lands exposed to guerrilla incursions. Even worse than these, were the predatory men eager to make money at the expense of both Negroes and the Treasury. The glittering prices paid for cotton attracted to the Mississippi Valley a cohort of adventurers utterly without scruples. Some recklessly traded across the lines, sending quantities of drugs, ammunition, clothing, and other contraband goods into the Confederacy, bringing out cotton in exchange. Others used every contrivance to cheat the Negroes of their crops. Many Treasury agents and Army officers conspired to seize corrupt gains. Although the planters, whether Northern dollar-hunters or Southerners professing loyalty, included many honest men, they also included many rogues. Thus, a thick fog of thievery and chicanery enveloped much of the Valley during 1864.[78]

The regulations, moreover, were so strict that they frightened prudent applicants from the field. A good many Northerners and Border men who had bid for plantations took one look at the contracts and rules, and fled. The new wage scale would have been a heartening improvement over the old rates had it been economically sound, but as Eaton and others saw, it proved impossibly high for any district where Confederate raids, poor soil, undependable hands, or other difficulties, made the return precarious. Before the end of February, 1864, Eaton and Mellen were exchanging protests, Eaton regarding the Negroes as still under his control, and Mellen assuming they were now his wards to whom he issued orders. In this dispute between the Army and the Treasury, Lorenzo Thomas took a vigorous hand, sending Stanton urgent appeals that "The military authorities must have command of the Negroes to avoid endless confusion," and declaring that, if the Treasury insisted on its plan, the Negroes would get no rations.[79] Lincoln acted instantly:

"I wish you would go to the Mississippi river at once," he wrote Lorenzo Thomas at Nashville, "and take hold of, and be master in, the contraband and leasing business." He feared that Mellen's well-intended system would be strangled by its details. "Go there and be the judge."[80]

Unfortunately, administrative confusion persisted throughout 1863 and 1864,

77. *Ibid.*, 146, 147.
78. *Ibid.*, 147-150.
79. *Ibid.*, 152, 153; Feb. 20, Feb. 27, 1864.
80. Feb. 28, 1864: Lincoln, *Collected Works*, VII, 212.

with Lincoln still too much harassed by other problems or too indifferent to give adequate attention to the problem of the freedmen. The Treasury could not legally relinquish its authority over plantations; the Army had full authority over freedmen, but was preoccupied with its military task; and semi-independent workers like Eaton and Fiske sometimes disapproved of the acts of both. Guerrilla forays continued destructive, especially in the districts about Helena, Vicksburg, and Natchez, where Confederate raiders carried off great droves of livestock in the crop season of 1864, and took nearly a thousand Negroes into the interior to be resold as slaves. Agricultural activities in much of the region were demoralized by these hit-and-run tactics. Many Negroes and loyal whites were killed, and many planters escaped ruin only by paying tribute. One investigator found late in 1864 that people in Arkansas and Mississippi were terrorized, that most planters had not made expenses, and that freedmen had flocked into camps again seeking Federal protection and care.[81] Many Negroes toiled hard, and even after repeated guerrilla raids, returned to work in places where no loyal white man dared enter. But in areas without Union safeguards, they suffered from increasing neglect. Wasting the money they earned on foolish trifles, and soon losing interest in the novelty of lawful marriages, they slumped into ignorance and lassitude.

The lack of system became glaringly evident in the vital area of education. Eaton, a professional educator, took a strong interest in schooling the refugees. His Freedmen's Department tried to obtain the services of Army chaplains and specially-trained soldiers for part-time work, welcoming qualified teachers from the North, whether individual volunteers, or agents of philanthropic organizations. The government, beginning in the autumn of 1863, offered such workers transportation, quarters, and rations.[82] Eaton had no authority, however, to superintend the schools, enforce discipline, prescribe uniform texts, or regulate the conduct of teachers, and he could contribute no money to buy books or rent schoolhouses. Inside the camps he had to use wretched quarters, and outside of them usually had none at all, for few planters cared to help educate their workers. Friction and jealousy sprang up among the independent agents working side by side, each anxious to promote the interests of a particular organization, and some eager for the easiest or showiest places.

Belatedly, Lorenzo Thomas issued an order placing Eaton as General Superintendent of Freedmen in effective charge of the schools, with power to appoint heads for his various districts from Vicksburg and Helena to Columbus, Ky., and to use them in directing all details of instruction.[83] Later, Eaton named Dr. Joseph Warren superintendent of Negro schools throughout his jurisdiction. More sys-

81. "Report of A.S. Fiske," late in 1865, as in Eaton, *op. cit.*, 157-159.
82. Lorenzo Thomas, Special Order 63, Sept. 29, 1863; Eaton, *op. cit.*, 194.
83. Sept. 26, 1864. Eaton, *op. cit.*, 196.

tematic work was then undertaken, and some women teachers exhibited a heroic devotion worthy of highest praise. Warren nevertheless had to bring home to Northern friends a sad truth when he reported: "This unfortunate class of people is so unsettled that any permanent plan for the instruction of the children is impracticable."[84] Refugees generally hoped to return to their old homes, and the best that could be done was to seize fleeting opportunities to awaken a desire for education.

It was plain by 1864, East and West, that the conflicts of authority in managing the freedmen should be ended, that their welfare must be made the paramount consideration, that a more practical wage system must be devised, and that a larger force of provost-marshals to supervise them must be put into the field. Meditating on the folly of a divided administration, N.P. Banks made an emphatic statement: "The assignment of the abandoned and forfeited plantations to one department of the government, and the protection and support of the emancipated people to another, is a fundamental error productive of incalculable evils, and cannot be too soon and too thoroughly corrected."[85] It seemed plain to progressive men that the government would do well to seize the opportunity of endowing Negroes of intelligence and industry with small parcels of land. Many of the large plantations seized from Confederates could and should have been broken up, with compensation to the owners to be determined later. Mississippi in 1860 had more than 6,460,000 acres of improved land in farms and plantations, and nearly 12,670,000 of unimproved land, with only 354,000 white inhabitants. Much of the land should have been apportioned to former slaves. Alabama had approximately 6,400,000 acres of improved land, and 12,690,000 unimproved, with only 526,500 white people. The Negro families, who longed for forty acres and a mule, might at least have been allowed twenty acres.

The brightest ray in the dark situation was the fact that freedmen, if given half a chance, prospered as small independent cultivators. They loved the land, proving themselves as expert as most masters in methods of tillage. Having small means, they leased limited tracts and farmed them carefully, and once settled, they clung to these tracts with passion throughout all the storms of war. Grant had been anxious to settle part of the black population in and about Vicksburg on a rich peninsula below the city called Davis or Palmyra Bend, where John A. Quitman, Joseph Davis (the President's brother), and other prominent Southerners had owned plantations. The freedmen who took tracts of five to a hundred acres here did make it something of an Eden. Near Helena, too, a number of Negroes who leased land from the Treasury did well, gathering stock and farm

84. *Ibid.*, 208.
85. Banks, Alexandria, La., to James McKaye, March 28, 1864, in *The Mastership and Its Fruits; The Emancipated Slave Face to Face with His Old Master,* New York, 1864, *passim.*

implements from abandoned plantations, and working alongside their hired hands in the fields. "They make more money than the white lessees when they are placed on the same footing," reported Colonel Samuel Thomas of Ohio, who looked after them.[86]

Largely because of these displays of Negro enterprise, many observers concluded that government wage-fixing should give way as soon as possible to free economic forces. An investigator in the Helena-Natchez-Vicksburg districts, early in 1864, expressed a hope that labor might soon compete in the open market, with payments fixed by supply and demand. Careful supervision, however, would be required, for neither Northern speculators nor quasi-loyal Southerners could be trusted to treat Negroes fairly. "I have no doubt," wrote N. P. Banks, "that many of the planters within our lines, who are protected by the Government in the enjoyment of their property, honestly accept the new situation, and enter into the idea of free labor with sincerity; but this attitude is coupled with an incredulity as to the success of the experiment, natural to . . . the ideas in which they have been educated. This is fostered more by the intractability and brutality of the overseers—the middle class between the laborer and the employer—than it is by an innate disposition of the planter himself."[87] Much evidence was shortly presented by J. T. Trowbridge of the willingness of some Southerners in the Carolinas to deal justly with the freedmen, along with many instances of injustice. A newspaper traveller in the South in 1863-1864 and later, Charles Carleton Coffin, correspondent of the Boston *Journal,* emphasized the strong class divisions among Southern whites. He found that many of the wealthy planter class were less likely to express social and political antagonism toward the liberated Negroes and the Unionists than the poor whites.[88]

[VI]

But a new era in the relationship between the Negro and the government was shortly to be foreshadowed: the era associated with the name of the Freedmen's Bureau. Grant later thought that the idea of the Bureau could be traced to Eaton's work at Grand Junction,[89] but in reality the innovation had many precursors. When Congress met in the closing days of 1863 to listen to Lincoln's plan of general emancipation, the provision of a bureau (which most men thought should be in the War Department) had occurred to many. The first effective bill for the purpose came from Representative Thomas D. Eliot of New Bedford, Massachu-

---

86. Eaton, *op. cit.,* 164; *National Almanac,* 1863, 309, 316.
87. Banks, March 28, 1864, in James McKaye, *The Mastership and Its Fruits, op. cit.*
88. Trowbridge, J.T., *A Picture of the Desolated States,* Hartford, 1868, Chs. LXX & LXXI; Coffin, C.C., *Marching to Victory,* New York, 1889. See especially 342, 365-450.
89. Grant, *Personal Memoirs, op. cit.,* I, 424-426.

setts, whose measure for a Bureau of Emancipation was immediately given two readings, and referred to a committee.[90] He acted for the freedmen's societies of Boston, New York, Philadelphia, and Cincinnati, which had petitioned Lincoln on the subject, and found it easy to demonstrate the need for such legislation, without which the powers of the President himself were limited. In a long February speech, Eliot read statements by Lorenzo Thomas, Yeatman, and others, describing the prevalent abuses and miseries,[91] and in another speech Representative W. D. Kelley of Pennsylvania expanded on the subject. Meanwhile a number of Democrats, including S. S. Cox of Ohio, had criticized the bill, primarily on the ground that it would invade the rights of the States.[92] It barely passed the House on March 1, 1864, by a vote of 69 to 67, with Francis P. Blair, Jr., of Missouri, among those voting in the negative. But it still had to pass the Senate, which was occupied with other matters, and disposed to take its time. The history of this agency was, therefore, to belong to the era of Reconstruction, not to the Civil War.

Few chapters upon the war years are as unhappy as that which deals with the slaves to whom the nation owed so great a debt, and for whom it did so little, both tardily and grudgingly. Years later, the Czar of Russia declared that his nation had treated its serfs with far more generosity than the United States had dealt with its slaves; and although the Russian problem was much simpler, and did not have to be attacked in the midst of a bloody and exhausting war, his statement had a certain amount of truth. If the Union Government had faced its responsibility promptly and squarely, it would have devoted far more planning, effort and money to the helpless people who had been forced to come to America unwillingly, whose labor in clearing and developing the country had been exploited for generations without recompense, who had suffered so many cruelties, and whose temper to the end had remained so patient and tractable. No really valid excuses can be accepted for the shortcomings of the nation's leaders in this field.

90. *Congressional Globe,* 38th Cong., 1st Sess., 19, 21.
91. *Ibid.,* 566-573.
92. *Ibid.,* 708-713, 772-775.

11.

IN THE FALL of 1863, the President went north out of Washington to dedicate a national cemetery at Gettysburg where so many had fallen less than six months before. On November 19 Lincoln did more than formally dedicate a final resting place; he "dedicated the nation to the defense and invigoration of free institutions wherever the influence of the republic extended; he had written one of the noblest prose-poems of the language." [1]

Popular opinion supported Lincoln that fall, as more and more people had come to comprehend that the President was the nation's greatest single asset. Not everyone was pleased, however.

Lincoln could look back on "high constructive achievements"—land to the landless, college endowments, launching the Pacific railroad, important financial measures—but now he would have to face the challenge of the Radical Republicans, conservative Republicans, War Democrats, Lincoln men, anti-Lincoln men, and men of various shades of opinion. The extremists, such as the vindictive Radicals, were becoming more powerful, as were those who feared the advocates of severity. There was increasing talk about restoration and Reconstruction. The President had taken steps in Louisiana, Tennessee, and Arkansas, but every step had been disputed. Lincoln was "plainly anxious to make it easy for any considerable body of loyal citizens to create a civil government, and to send men knocking at the door of the House." He was also clearly determined to use the powers of the Presidency as fully as possible in Reconstruction. Congress was a partner and alone could admit members, but "he was insistent that while rebellion might destroy the old structure of society in a State, and its old Constitution, it could not destroy membership in the Union, which was perdurable." [2] The great debate on Reconstruction intensified rapidly in the fall of 1863.

Adding problems for the North in 1863 was the foreign situation. The depredations of Southern cruisers such as the *Alabama* had been a continual worry to the Union, and, when it was learned that two Laird rams were being built in England for the Confederate ships, a major diplomatic crisis arose. British leaders seized the rams, but the "escape from hostilities had been by too thin a margin for comfort. . . ." [3]

As 1864 opened, the war was dragging along on numerous fronts. By early spring the future of the country lay with "two Mid-Westerners, Lincoln and Grant." The victor of Vicksburg, promoted to General-in-Chief, moved east to stay with Meade's Army of the Potomac, as W. T. Sherman took over in the West. Grant "enjoyed three blessings: the opportunity to rise gradually from low rank; the capacity to learn rapidly from his errors; and the assistance of loyal and discerning men who divined his potentialities." His principal gift was strength of character, although intellectually he must rank below other major strategists of the war. "For the work of the fighter, however, he had ·better qualities than those of the cerebral gymnast. One was logical vision. He was a clear, simple thinker, with the power of sorting out from many facts the few that were vitally important, of seeing in a complex situation the basic outline." Further, he was decisively prompt, he moved, he did not wait for perfection in training and equipment, and for the most part "he had an instinctive ability to distinguish between true and false humanitarianism." A gentle man, "he saw that the truest economy in lives was often a temporary ruthlessness in expending them." He believed in obedience to the civil authority, was generous in most cases, and modest. Nevins does not think that Grant's drinking interfered with his duties. Very occasionally there were lapses in candor toward other generals, but he had "elemental strength when the republic needed precisely that, and needed it above all else." [4]

In May of 1864 Grant and Meade moved against Lee in those vicious, searing battles of the Wilderness and Spotsylvania in Virginia, all the while edging toward Richmond. Sherman moved down the slope of Georgia toward Atlanta, against Joseph E. Johnston. Nevins describes Sherman as a "bundle of contradictions. . . . He was the most remarkable combination of virtues and deficiencies produced in the high direction of the Union armies." [5]

"As Grant and Sherman launched their simultaneous attacks upon Lee's Army of Northern Virginia and Johnston's Army of Tennessee, the anxiety of the Northern people was perhaps more intense and anguished than any they had ever before endured." [6] As Sherman pushed on relentlessly, capturing Atlanta in early September, Grant and Meade continued on beyond the Wilderness and Spotsylvania, through the reckless failure of the tragic charge at Cold Harbor, across the James, and to the siege of Petersburg, south of Richmond. "A war of greater organization, ingenuity and strategic skill had now commenced in Virginia, but its results could not be immediately registered." [7] The public did not at first understand that Lee would never again be able to swing out on his own.

NOTES

1. Nevins, *The War for the Union*, Vol. III, *The Organized War, 1863–1864*, p. 449.
2. *Ibid.*, p. 461.
3. *Ibid.*, p. 503.
4. Nevins, *The War for the Union*, Vol. IV, *The Organized War to Victory, 1864–1865*, pp. 15–17.
5. *Ibid.*, p. 27.
6. *Ibid.*, p. 29.
7. *Ibid.*, p. 51.

Cement of the Union

AS A war becomes rougher, internal politics get rougher too. Throughout the spring and summer of 1864, Lincoln's most anxious efforts, aside from military affairs, were devoted to holding a majority of Northern voters in sufficient harmony to maintain his prestige and moral power. Unity and patience!— these were his fundamental demands. If impatience grew, if men gave way to fear and anger, party disruption would open the gate to national destruction. In June he urged the Yankee journalist Noah Brooks, who sent Washington correspondence to various journals East and West, to do all he could to correct the optimistic delusion that "the war will end right off victoriously." It would not, and people must steel themselves for a cruel endurance of stubborn exertion. Although the North was further ahead than he had anticipated, he stated: "as God is my judge, I shall be satisfied if we are over with the fight in Virginia within a year." As the strain of war increased, he had to meet one domestic crisis after another. Subjected to constant vicissitudes in his relations with the Cabinet, Congressional leaders, editors, governors, and political adventurers, he fought always a central battle for balance, compromise, and an overriding insistence upon unity. If he struck a hard blow here, it was for harmony; if he yielded there, it was for harmony.

[I]

Nobody knew better than Lincoln that the prospect for his reëlection that fall was anxiously uncertain. A democracy always feels the failures of a leader more sharply than his successes. In political sagacity, adherence to principle, and vision of the national future, Lincoln rose superior to his contemporaries. The people of Civil War days, however, saw incomplete lineaments of his wisdom, generosity, and eloquence. What they did see clearly were his deficiencies in executive energy and skill. Some agreed with George Bancroft that he was self-willed and ignorant—ignorant of finance, economic forces, foreign governments, and military necessities. Others thought with Lyman Trumbull that he had drifted when decision was needed. Still others held with Charles

(*The War for the Union*, Vol. IV, *The Organized War to Victory, 1864-1865*, Chapter 3.)

Francis Adams, Sr., that in the storm then raging a stronger hand was needed on the tiller.

Lincoln's prestige had sunk to its nadir after the failure of the Peninsular Campaign and Pope's defeat just outside Washington at Second Manassas. The Democrats were embittered by his decisive removal of McClellan, and Radical Republicans had fallen into the deep depression that inspired fierce demands after Fredericksburg for a reorganization of the Cabinet. Had the United States possessed a government of British type, its Ministry might have fallen. Antietam and the Emancipation Proclamation had lifted the President's standing; Chancellorsville unquestionably depressed it again. Gettysburg and Vicksburg raised it anew; the drama of Missionary Ridge lifted men's hearts like a sudden burst of martial music. Chickamauga hurt Lincoln's prestige but Chattanooga restored it; the first bloody checks of May and June, 1864, sank it once more, and even though Grant was at the gates of the Confederate capital, many in the North did not consider that a victory.

Lincoln and the Administration, knowing the value politically of war news, kept the Baltimore Union Party convention delegates well posted, so that when the news of Hunter's victory at Piedmont (June 5, 1864) came in, there was great cheering. Stanton is credited with having sent these dispatches. Such oscillations of elation and despair were natural and understandable, but they struck many observers as unworthy of a great people with the traditions of the Seven Years' War, the long Revolutionary struggle, and of Valley Forge in its past. Surely Americans had the Spartan valor of their ancestors who had crossed the stormy seas and had subdued a rocky continent to found a nation. It was confidence that he could appeal to the deep, latent tenacity of the American people, complete faith in their chilled-steel devotion to ancient principles, which had inspired Edward Everett Hale to publish in the *Atlantic Monthly* for December, 1863, his unexpected yet clearly inspired tale "The Man Without a Country," which was more than a short story, soon soaring to a mass circulation—which was a trumpet peal lifting the national heart. It was in the same faith that the deep national fealties and convictions of the American people rose superior to the fluctuations of victories and defeats, that another gifted author, the economist and veteran journalist David A. Wells, published *Our Burden and Our Strength* (1864), which was worth as much to the Union cause as a resounding battlefield victory. This book, like Hale's imperishable story, represented the true devotion and tenacity of the Northern people, and helped nerve their arms to strike. So did another telling book of 1864, Charles J. Stillé's *How a Free People Conduct a Long War*, a study of British resolution in combating Napoleon, that helped fortify countless readers. Was this really the spirit of the majority of Northerners?

Lincoln's military missteps, beginning with War Order No. 1 for a general advance on Washington's Birthday in 1862, and his occasionally maladroit interferences with generals, were more evident than the soundness of his basic strategic ideas. Suspension of the habeas corpus, military arrests, and spasms of press censorship offended multitudes who revered the Bill of Rights. As the conflict lengthened, it was saddening to think of the battlefield agonies of tens of thousands of young men, the myriad of bereaved homes, and the coarsening of the national character which were among its effects. Little stories illuminated the popular tension—the story, for example, of a speculator who said exultantly in a crowded car, "Well, I hope the war may last six months longer; in the last six months I've made a hundred thousand dollars." Instantly a woman slapped him, crying "Sir, I had two sons—one was killed at Fredericksburg, the other at Murfreesboro!"; and the indignant spectators hustled him out the door.[1]

Few events of the war aroused such a feeling of mingled anger and anguish in the North as the April "massacre" at Fort Pillow already mentioned. The facts of this occurrence, in which 231 Union soldiers, largely Negroes, were killed while only 14 Confederates fell, have provoked some disputation. Northerners, however, saw only one side. They read headlines announcing "Attack on Fort Pillow—Indiscriminate Slaughter of the Prisoners—Shocking Scenes of Savagery"; dispatches from Sherman's army declaring "there is a general gritting of teeth here"; reports from the Missouri *Democrat* detailing the "fiendishness" of rebel behavior; and editorials like that in the Chicago *Tribune* condemning the "murder" and "butchery." Senator Henry Wilson published in the New York *Tribune* a letter from a lieutenant-colonel in the Army of the Tennessee giving gory particulars, while others poured in from survivors in the Mound City (Ill.) hospital. All this made a heavier impression because of the unquestionable facts that Confederates had previously killed some Negro soldiers after capture, and had exchanged not a single Negro private of the many captured at Battery Wagner, Port Hudson, and Olustee. Was Lincoln doing enough, men asked, to prevent such ebullitions of the barbarism of slavery and to punish them when they took place?[2]

People were now aware that the fast-lengthening casualty-rolls confronted the nation with one of the saddest tragedies of modern history. They had taken

---

1. Nevins, Allan, *The New York Evening Post*, New York, 1922, 320-321.
2. For Fort Pillow, see files of newspapers April 16-30, 1864; Castel, Albert, "The Fort Pillow Massacre: a Frank Examination of the Evidence," *Civil War History*, IV, No. 1, March, 1958, 37-50, a careful examination which reaches the conclusion that a massacre did occur; and the papers in the Chicago Historical Society of Gen. Mason Brayman, commanding this summer at Natchez, which support the charge of an inhuman massacre. Brooks, Noah, *Washington in Lincoln's Time*, ed. Herbert Mitgang, New York, 1958, 138. There is great conflict between various Confederate reports and the *Report of the Joint Committee on the War*, "Fort Pillow Massacre," Washington, 1964, 39th Cong., 1st Sess., House Report No. 65.

deaths hard when Elmer Ellsworth and Theodore Winthrop fell in the first weeks; they took them still harder as the graves of young men numbered hundreds of thousands. And at last the moral costs were all too evident. The war had so many heroic aspects that at first it had been easy to ignore the moral erosion. But now men comprehended that the conflict was accentuating some of the baser features of a society too full of frontier crudities, too casually addicted to neighborhood violence, and too often ready to let the dollar prove or excuse wrong acts. Civil wars often have a Cain-Abel savagery, and this one had sent large armies trampling across defenseless communities. Guerrilla warfare on both sides sometimes became mass-murder, as in Quantrill's raid on Lawrence, Kansas. All along the indefinite warring fronts, and in tenuously-held Federally-occupied areas, bands of outlaws, often irrespective of North or South, were busy ambushing sentries, slaying householders, and perpetrating outrages that made the blood run cold.

The treatment of prisoners of war on both sides was often a story of neglect. Financial corruption spread like some valley fog along ill-cleared waterways —graft in illicit cotton traffic, contracts, appointments to office, bounty-jumping, and tax-evasion. It was small wonder that, while the nation's sacrifices were sullied by so much rascality, sensitive men, anxious to protect the nation's character, sometimes lost heart. Some criticism of Lincoln was healthy, but the danger was that licentious criticism might lead a majority to falter in the war. "Jefferson Davis is perhaps in some respects superior to our President," Charles Francis Adams wrote from the London legation in the spring of 1863. When a perceptive man, snobbishly class-conscious, could write this, public sentiment might take any turn. James Gordon Bennett, who had little education or insight, but a good deal of hard Scotch common sense, was arguing in the *Herald* that Lincoln's vacillations had already gravely prolonged the war, and "will cause it to be interminable if another sort of man, independent of political factions and true to the Constitution, is not soon placed in the President's chair."[3]

A majority of Republicans not only saw that the party must stand or fall with Lincoln, as governors like Andrew, Morton, Curtin, and Yates of Illinois did, but admired his record and personality. Yet a powerful body of the Radicals, who had supported Frémont's emancipationist ideas, were so dissatisfied with Lincoln's conciliation of Border settlement and ten-percent plan for Reconstruction, that they were ready to revolt.[4] Among the War Demo-

---

3. New York *Herald*, quoted in Detroit *Free Press*, Jan. 7, 1864, C.F. Adams to R.H. Dana, Jr., Apr. 8, 1863, R.H. Dana Papers, Mass. Hist. Soc.
4. Welles, Gideon, "The Opposition to Lincoln in 1864," *Atlantic Monthly*, March, 1878, No. CCXLV, Vol. XLI, 366-376.

crats, indispensable to a Union Party, a large number adhered to Lincoln. They shrank from the Copperheads, respected the President's abilities, and rejoiced over his charitable attitude toward conquered Southerners. Yet here, too, some would prefer another man. They parroted the cry: "The Constitution as it is and the Union as it was," which sounded patriotic and was actually defeatist. They accepted the argument, pleasing to Lincoln-haters, that the principle of one-term Presidencies ought to be firmly established. Nobody since Andrew Jackson had served two terms, and eight men in succession had held the White House four years or less.

The Radical opposition to Lincoln might have been less formidable if he had treated members of Congress, who now included more than the usual proportion of vain, jealous, and fanatical men, with greater tact. He never concealed his contempt for "politicians" and their "sophisms." In conversation he sometimes gave the names, with biting comment, of men he thought foolish or rascally. He took pains, to be sure, to maintain his friendship with Charles Sumner, Thaddeus Stevens, Henry Wilson, Lot M. Morrill, James W. Grimes, Galusha Grow, and other influential figures. He tried to handle a few men he really despised, such as coarse Ben Wade and serpentine Henry Winter Davis, with gloves. He was ready to give Congressional leaders the patronage they wanted. But he could be as hostile to enemies like the New York Peace Democrat Ben Wood as they were to him; and, having sat in Congress himself, he had no awe of it. He was no more disposed to let Congress manage the war than when he had refused to call a special session after Fort Sumter, and he was still less willing to let it manage the peace.

He had been aloof in his relations with some of his Cabinet. To the two principal departments, State and War, he gave close attention, but Welles, Chase, Montgomery Blair, Caleb Smith, and Bates were expected to run their machines to suit themselves. His Administration remained a loose coalition, never unified, seldom harmonious. Chase still complained to friends that no coordination of the departments existed, and so little consultation that when he wished to know how the war was getting on he had to consult newspapermen. While the Cabinet is not historically a consultative body, Lincoln might have made fuller use of it for the exchange of information; it was important for Welles to know what moneys Chase could provide for ships, and for Blair to know what naval vessels might carry mail. Lincoln visited Stanton every day, saw Seward frequently, and sometimes consulted Montgomery Blair, but neglected the others. The fact was that the country did not wish a highly centralized government, and he could make no greater error than to strive to give it one.

Gideon Welles, grumbling that he had little of Lincoln's confidence, thought that Seward and Stanton got too much of it. He suspected that Seward, by his devious ways and loose talk, risked pushing some States into the Democratic column. He was equally distrustful of acid-tongued Senators like Lyman Trumbull and William Pitt Fessenden, who seemed trying to destroy confidence in the President. Their criticisms too often reached critical editors like Greeley, Medill, and Bennett. "If, therefore, the reëlection of Mr. Lincoln is not defeated, it will not be owing to them."[5] When Welles wrote this, Greeley believed that Rosecrans might be a more popular Presidential candidate than Lincoln.[6]

Secretary Chase held no stronger position in the Administration than that of financial specialist. Yet he was not only an able fiscal administrator, the creator of the national banking system and a military organizer of some limited experience within his State, but also the ambitious head of one fairly numerous wing or faction of the Republican Party in the Middle West. Chase believed that Lincoln's conception of the Executive was too constricted, but Lincoln's instinct in this matter was sound. Nevertheless, some careful enlargement of the Administration to include a bureau of transportation and supplies, the partial equivalent of the War Industries Board in the the first World War, and a bureau for the freedmen, might have strengthened it immediately, and helped it cope with the grave problems of 1864-1866. Other men agreed with Chase that Lincoln's gifts simply did not include distinction as an administrator.[7] In political acumen he was unexcelled; his sense of timing—his patient instinct for the occasion, or as Nicolay and Hay put it, his *opportunism*—was remarkable; his breadth of view was statesmanlike. But his haphazard, unsystematic ways were sometimes the despair of associates.

All spring, visitors found Lincoln painfully altered in looks and manner; as April ended, the Ohio Congressman A.G. Riddle found him worn and harassed.[8] The almost endless war, the grief and anxiety were proving an intolerable burden. Others in and outside Congress were equally worried, and nerves were growing taut. Washington, no longer close enough to battlefields to hear the guns, was still a huge receiving-station for the wounded. As boatloads of casualties steadily arrived on the Potomac waterfront, and trainloads rumbled in by rail, cohorts of ambulances jolted through the streets to the twenty-one hospitals. People from the North and West, betraying hurry, anxiety, and grief, thronged through the city on their way to hospitals in Freder-

5. Welles, *Diary*, II, 130-131.

6. Gilmore, James Robert, *Personal Recollections of Abraham Lincoln and the Civil War*, London, 1899, Chs. X-XII, especially 103, 145-46.

7. See Maurice, Sir Frederick, *Statesmen and Soldiers of the Civil War*, Boston, 1926, Ch.V, on the penalties Great Britain and the United States have both paid for lack of system in war.

8. Riddle, Albert G., *Recollections of War Times*, New York, 1895, 266-267.

icksburg or Culpeper. Details of clerks from government departments who had volunteered for half-month duty as nurses and orderlies came back with tales of the suffering they had seen. Night after night, men with anguished faces, and women who wilted at the sight of bloody forms, viewed the changing procession. Those watchers in the May or June moonlight who saw two or three thousand casualties landed at a time on the Sixth-Street Wharf never forgot the ghastly lines of shattered men, the clumps of tearful spectators, and the rigid shapes of those who had died in transit, outlined against the flowing river and distinct shores. Meanwhile, letters written in the midst of amputations, hemorrhages, and death were scattered far and wide across the country.

"There are many very bad now in hospital," ran one letter signed Walt Whitman, "so many of our soldiers are getting broke down after two years, or two and a half, exposure and bad diet, pork, hard biscuit, bad water or none at all, etc., etc., so we have them brought up here. Oh, it is terrible, and getting worse, worse, worse. I thought it was bad; to see these I sometimes think is more pitiful still."[9]

[II]

The cement of the nation had been furnished since Federalist-Republican allegiances by its political parties; what if the cement began to crumble? In the spring of 1864, it seemed to be disintegrating, for the two main parties were both more deeply riven than ever. Peace Democrats were willing to end the war even without saving the Union; War Democrats were determined to end the war on a full restoration of the Union and on no other fixed condition whatever. In opposition to them the Moderate Republicans stood for the Union, Emancipation, and a rapid Reconstruction on mild terms; the Radical Republicans demanded Union, Emancipation, and a delayed Reconstruction on steel-hard terms or rather penalties. A variety of shades of opinion might be distinguished under these four areas, but they suffice for a broad classification. If the Peace Democrats ever gained overwhelming strength in the North and Northwest, the Union was lost. If the Radical Republicans conquered majority opinion, they would insist upon nominal union in spiritual disunion.

Lincoln, the chieftain and animating spirit of the Moderate Republicans, provided by his moral leadership the truest national cement of all. He stood for a party of the Center, uniting the War Democrats and Moderate Republicans in the new Union Party. Clearly, he had two battles to fight. In the first,

9. Walt Whitman to his mother, Washington, Apr. 5, 1864; *The Wound Dresser*, New York, 1949, 160-161.

he must enforce sufficient harmony within this Union Party to gain and hold the nomination with a strong chance of election. This did not appear easy in April, and looked still harder in August, when many discontented members clamored for a new convention. In his second battle he must defeat the Democrats, who were expected to nominate McClellan. All the while the war would be a mighty tide bearing the ship of state and the several parties in unpredictable directions. Waves of hope would lift the vessel forward. Waves of dejection would stop it, spin it into eddies, or throw it upon the rocks. Was shipwreck a real danger? Very real, indeed, for a few more defeats in late summer might possibly have swept the country into an irrational demand for peace at almost any price. All spring, all summer, Lincoln and his adherents had to confront ever fluctuating difficulties and perils, while the dragging, wearisome war itself, with its inevitable drain upon national morale, was a far more important factor than the changing ideologies of the stormy time.

The Administration, though numbering old Jacksonian leaders like Welles and Blair, could do little for the Democratic rank-and-file. It offered a haven in the Union Party for staunchly individualistic War Democrats like John A. Dix and Andrew Johnson, and that was about all. To Peace Democrats it could only assert a defiant, unremitting opposition. Lincoln expressed this defiance in an April address at the Sanitary Fair in Baltimore, drawing a line between liberty as defined by wolves and defined by sheep, and coupling his use of colored troops with the general advance of emancipation.[10] On the Republican side the Moderate Republicans presented no problems of grave perplexity, but the Radical Republicans offered Lincoln nearly as much hostility as the Peace Democrats, and were as refractory and treacherous.

These Radicals showed no lack of resolution. Initially their movement had possessed four principal objects. They meant, first, to insist on a more energetic prosecution of the war; second, to require that no great army be entrusted to a general who did not believe in complete victory and emancipation; third, to persuade the President to get rid of lukewarm Cabinet members like Montgomery Blair; and fourth, to induce him to make more efficient use of his Cabinet. Later, they added another object, governmental adoption of a Reconstruction policy that would keep the South subjugated until all roots of rebellion were dead, and this they soon regarded as the most important of all. Radical critics made some mistaken assumptions. They thought that Seward and the Blairs led while Lincoln followed, when the opposite was the fact. They believed that Ben Butler would make a better military adviser than Halleck or Stanton. Nevertheless, they held a few correct ideas upon the need

10. Lincoln, *Works*, VII, 301-303.

for such firm war leadership as Grant and Sherman and Farragut were soon to supply.[11]

Lincoln never lacked humility, and this spring gave it emphatic expression. His political difficulties were brought home to him when Governor Thomas E. Bramlette of Kentucky faced a tempest over the compulsory enrollment of male slaves of twenty to forty-five for military draft. As Border State slaveholders saw Federal officers take down names, they trembled for their property. The governor hurried to Washington to talk with Lincoln, and the President thereupon explained in a letter to the Frankfort *Commonwealth* why he believed that Negro enlistments were a necessity. These enlistments, he wrote, had cost the government nothing in foreign embarrassments or in popular strength at home; they had helped the freedmen; and they had given the nation fully 130,000 soldiers, seamen and laborers. To this he added a characteristic comment. "I claim not to have controlled events, but confess plainly that events have controlled me. Now, at the end of three years struggle the nation's condition is not what either party, or any man devised, or expected. God alone can claim it. Whither it is tending seems plain. If God now wills the removal of a great wrong, and wills also that we of the North, as well as you of the South, shall pay fairly for our complicity in that wrong, impartial history will find therein new cause to attest and revere the justice and goodness of God."[12]

Feeling in Kentucky nevertheless remained so inimical to a slave-arming Administration that the self-styled Unionists there shortly took action which made it certain that the State in the fall would cast her electoral vote against Lincoln. Provost Marshals meanwhile enlisted Negroes in large numbers, for Kentuckians, seething with discontent and hatred, refused to fill the State quotas with volunteers.[13]

Beyond doubt, the astute young Maine politician, James G. Blaine, was right in believing that the prevailing judgment of the Union-Republican Party pointed to Lincoln's renomination. The party would fatally cripple itself if it repudiated the Administration. Moreover, the President's faith had fortified the national heart, for he saw as nobody else the American Idea. But would the party battle for him in a fervent or a lukewarm spirit?

Among the men whose jealous ambition impaired party harmony, the able, self-righteous Salmon P. Chase held a conspicuous place. Although he maintained with Chadband rhetoric that he never used the Treasury to build a personal machine, its staff supplied active workers on his behalf. Friendly with

---

11. See the exchange of opinion among Stanton, Chase, and Welles in Oct. 1862, on Lincoln's deficiencies, Welles, *Diary*, I, 160-169.
12. Lincoln, *Works*, 281-283; to Albert G. Hodges.
13. Coulter, E.M., *The Civil War and Readjustment in Kentucky*, Chapel Hill, 1926, 198-207.

all Radicals, he had given them energetic assistance in the State elections of 1862 in the hope of winning their support. In his financial labors he had taken pains to conciliate such leaders of industry and banking as Erastus Corning, George S. Coe, W. M. Vermilye, and George Opdyke, at the same time wooing the principal Republican editors and officers of the Union League. While pretending throughout 1863 that he was not anxious for the Presidency, he was actually burning for the office.[14]

When Lincoln at the close of 1863 announced his liberal plan of Reconstruction, Chase did not need to warn his friends that the hour for action had struck. His diary tells us nothing. But an impetuous Kansas politician of erratic judgment, Senator Samuel Clarke Pomeroy, a former Amherst student full of New England Radicalism, helped form a "national committee". Pomeroy and his Radical associates dealt just one blow—but it proved a fatal blow to Chase's aspirations. They issued a pamphlet entitled "The Next Presidential Election", and a shorter statement soon known as the Pomeroy Circular. These were at once summarized by the press and franked widely over the country by Radical Congressmen, so that Washington's Birthday in 1864 found the entire North acquainted with them. They offered an offensively phrased argument that aroused widespread irritation and derision. The reëlection of Lincoln, they declared, would be a national calamity; only an advanced thinker, versed in political and economic science, could guide the ship of state through the rapids ahead; and fortunately this advanced thinker was at hand—nobody needed to be told that Secretary Chase was the man; he even was named. Chase assured Lincoln on February 22 that he had known nothing about the circular or a formal committee, although he admitted he had consented to the use of his name to "several gentlemen" who had called on him. Ten years later, his statement that he had no prior knowledge of the circular was contradicted by its author, James M. Winchell, who declared flatly that Chase had been informed of the proposed action and approved it fully.[15]

---

14. Lincoln, *Works*, VII, 200-201; Schuckers, J.W., *The Life and Public Services of Salmon P. Chase*, New York, 1874, 356-489; Donald, David, ed. *Inside Lincoln's Cabinet*, New York, 1954, 179, 190, 208-209. Chase esteemed Lincoln, but personal uneasiness tinged his attitude, for he suspected that the virulent attack that Frank Blair made upon him in the House at the end of April might have had Lincoln's sanction. It did not; Lincoln was distressed to learn that Blair had kicked over another beëhive. But the circumstances of the attack, made as Blair departed to resume his commission as major-general with the 17th Corps in the Atlanta campaign, were highly irritating; and Blair's charges, impugning Chase's honesty, were so outrageous that the Secretary's Radical friends had advised an immediate and abrupt resignation. Much annoyed, Lincoln considered cancelling his orders restoring Blair to the army. Chase accepted the President's disclaimer of any connection with the attacks, brought to him by two Ohio politicians (Riddle, *Recollections of War Times*, Chs. XXXVII, XXXVIII), but he and his friends resented more than ever Lincoln's friendliness to the Blair clan. Congressional Globe, 38th Cong., 1st Session, Appendix, 50, 51, and Pt. II, 1829.

15. New York *Times*, Sept. 15, 1874; Schuckers, *Chase, op.cit.*, 497, 499-501.

This movement was so premature and ill-supported that John Sherman, one of Pomeroy's helpers, instantly retreated.[16] The country, in fact, received the circular with general hostility. Moderate Republicans, War Democrats, and most uncommitted voters, however critical of Lincoln, regarded him as decidedly preferable to Chase. "The Pomeroy Circular has helped Lincoln more than all other things together," wrote one of John Sherman's friends.[17] As Welles put it, the Chase gun had been far more dangerous in its recoil than its discharge. Lincoln kept a dignified silence.[18] How little strength Chase possessed was demonstrated when the Ohio legislature passed a resolution in favor of Lincoln's reëlection.

But although this first Radical foray against Lincoln quickly collapsed, an alarming amount of ill-humor was evident in the country. The New York *Times*, declaring the House had done nothing for nineteen weeks but dawdle over empty speechmaking with an utter neglect of urgent financial legislation, accused Congress of "flagrant unfaithfulness."[19] Sensible men were aghast at the Senate's passage of a bill against speculation in gold, a measure certain to defeat its object by raising the price of gold. When it did rise on June 23 to 208 in greenbacks, Congress saw that the new law must be repealed. Publication of the President's letter to Montgomery Blair, suggesting that his brother Frank let his commission as major-general lie dormant while he returned to the House, and have it revived when he wished to rejoin the army, seemed to many a flagrant evasion of the Constitutional provision that "no person holding any office under the United States shall be a member of either House of Congress during his continuance in office," and repugnant to a sentiment that in English-speaking lands went back to the "Self-Denying Ordinance" of Puritan Commonwealth days.[20]

In May, Henry Winter Davis carried through the House a Reconstruction Bill that was designed to make mincemeat out of Lincoln's policy as laid down in his annual message. Much talk was meanwhile heard about the "rotten boroughs" that might figure in Lincoln's reëlection—Arkansas, Delaware, Louisiana, Maryland, West Virginia, statehood for Nevada, and so on—and the possible perversion of democracy by manipulation of their votes.

At the same time, a sinister interpretation was placed on the government's impetuous suppression of two New York newspapers, the *World* and *Journal*

16. Details in Schuckers' *Chase*, 497-500; Zornow, W.F., "The Kansas Senators and the Reëlection of Lincoln," *Kansas Historical Quarterly*, May, 1951; letters of Philip Speed and J. Gibson to Lincoln, Feb. 22, 1864, Lincoln Mss., LC.

17. Zornow, *op.cit.*, 137.

18. Welles, *Diary*, I, 525, 533.

19. As cited in New York *World*, May 5, 1864.

20. Lincoln, *Works*, VI, 554-555; New York *World*, May 5, 1864.

of Commerce, on what turned out to be no grounds at all. In mid-May they had
been hoaxed into publication of a fictitious Presidential proclamation appoint-
ing a day of national fasting, humiliation, and prayer, and announcing an
imminent draft of 400,000 more men. This was the work of a would-be stock-
market manipulator, whose forged proclamation, foisted upon the two newspapers in the dead of night, was quickly repudiated. Sales of papers were
stopped, and bulletins announcing the imposture were posted. A dispatch boat
that was hurried down New York Bay caught the *Scotia* before she cleared the
Narrows for Europe with the forgery. Although in the temporary excitement
gold shot up ten percent, little real harm was done. The suppression was
indefensibly abrupt and harsh. Democratic spokesmen wildly asserted that
civil liberties were dead, and lamented that the United States had no Thiers
who dared denounce its despot. The editors of the two injured newspapers,
when these dailies were restored to their owners on May 22, were left boiling
with anger, and denouncing the Administration for both its arbitrary action
and its tardiness of release. Gideon Welles agreed that the suppression, for
which he correctly blamed Seward and Stanton, had been "hasty, rash, inconsiderate, and wrong."

This suppression gave Horatio Seymour an opportunity to attack the Administration afresh, and to instigate legal proceedings in the local courts
against General Dix and his subordinates, all of which only deepened the
general conviction that Seward lacked judgment. Worst of all, it reminded the
country of numerous other instances in which editors had been disciplined and
their papers stopped on charges that they were interfering with enlistments
or otherwise hampering the war effort. And the fact that three of the ablest
newspapermen of the country, Henry Villard, Adam Hill, and Horace White,
were needlessly harassed—Villard ordered under arrest by Stanton, and White
sharply questioned—added to the general feeling of uneasiness.[21]

John G. Nicolay, talking with Thurlow Weed at the end of March, had
found him gloomy. "His only solicitude," Nicolay wrote the President, "was
for yourself. He thought if you were not strong enough to hold the Union men
together through the next Presidential election . . . the country was in the
utmost danger of going to ruin." Actually, Weed doubted that Lincoln *could*
hold the Union men together. The Cabinet, he pointed out, was so notoriously
discordant and jangling that it gave the President little support and set the

21. The New York *World, Herald, Tribune,* offer full accounts in late May issues. For general
studies, see Randall, James G., *Constitutional Problems under Lincoln,* Urbana, 1951 pp. 396-499;
Nicolay and Hay, *Lincoln,* IX, 47-50; Rosewater, Victor, *History of Cooperative News-Gathering in the
United States,* New York, 1930, pp.104-105. The man guilty of the forgery, Joseph Howard, then city
editor of the Brooklyn *Eagle,* was quickly run down, but Henry Ward Beecher pleaded for him
with Lincoln, and he escaped lightly. Welles, *Diary,* II, 37-38.

nation a bad example. "Welles is a cipher, Bates a fogy, and Blair at best a dangerous friend."[22] This lack of harmony was all too obvious. Seward and Stanton were openly gleeful over Chase's discomfiture, laughing about it in a corner chat at a Cabinet meeting, while Montgomery Blair frankly delighted in every buffet that Stanton took. Judicious men feared that even though Chase and Frémont were weak candidates, their fractious followers might disrupt the party and cripple the national war effort.[23]

Everybody knew, as spring advanced, that Lincoln would be renominated by the national Convention to meet in Baltimore on June 7. Decisive majorities in both houses of the Maryland, Minnesota, Kansas, and California legislatures had called for him; so had most Union and Republican members of the New Jersey, New York, Connecticut, and New Hampshire legislatures. Republicans of diverse views knew that, all in all, he was the best candidate available.[24] But this was not the important point: the danger was that he would be named without deep conviction, and that factional quarrels would then defeat him and weaken the battle power of the North. Greeley had offered a fresh demonstration of folly in a rumbling editorial declaring that Chase, Frémont, Butler, or Grant would be better.[25] Chase made it plain in letters to friends that, while he was ready to withdraw his own name, he was far from ready to advocate the reëlection of an indecisive President subject to the influence of such political schemers as Thurlow Weed and Montgomery Blair, and leaning toward a soft Reconstruction policy.[26]

Factionalism rode higher and higher in the party. It was astonishing how much sordid greed and personal malice pervaded the organization that had seemed so happily idealistic four years earlier. Gideon Welles, resentful of stinging attacks on the Navy Department that he ascribed to contractors, claim agents, corrupt newspapermen, and such unprincipled members of Congress as John P. Hale, thought that Chase abetted his harassment. They exchanged blistering letters, and glared at each other in Cabinet meetings.[27] Blair, Chase, and Stanton, indeed, hardly concealed their mutual detestation. When Montgomery Blair wrote later that he believed Chase was the only man Lincoln ever really hated, he spoke for himself; it was Blair who nursed the hatred, for Lincoln based hatreds only on principle, not on personal feeling.[28] As for Frémont, few people except his wife Jessie and the extreme Abolitionists

22. Nicolay to Lincoln, Mar. 30, 1864, Nicolay Papers, LC.
23. Welles, *Diary*, I, 536.
24. New York *Tribune*, Feb. 23, 1864.
25. *Ibid.*, Feb. 2, 1864; he used the one-term argument.
26. Chase, Feb. 29, 1864, to James A. Hamilton, *Chase Papers*, New York Public Library.
27. Welles, *Diary*, I, Chs. XV, XVI.
28. Blair to Samuel J. Tilden, June 5, 1868; *Letters and Literary Memorials of Samuel J. Tilden*, ed. John Bigelow, New York, 1908, I, 232-233.

thought him really fit for the presidency. Yet when the Missouri House rejected 46 to 33 a resolution endorsing the Administration, the St. Louis press
explained that most Republicans of German blood favored the election of
Frémont.[29]

"Stanton has a cabinet and is a power in his own Department," growled
Welles. "He deceives the President and Seward, makes confidants of certain
leading men, and is content to have matters move on without being compelled
to show his exact position. He is not on good terms with Blair, nor is Chase,
which is partly attributable to that want of concert which frequent assemblages and mutual counselling on public measures would secure. At such a
time the country should have the combined wisdom of all." In May, 1864, R.H.
Dana, Jr., wrote his wife, "The cabinet is disjointed. There is more hate, more
censure uttered by members of the cabinet against each other than I supposed
possible. I speak for what is said directly to me." In another letter, to Motley,
Dana said: "The cabinet is at sixes and sevens . . . They say dreadful things
about one another. . . ." Blair was quite critical of Welles, for example, but not
of Seward.[30]

While the Union Leagues rallied to Lincoln's side, and Henry J. Raymond
brought the New York *Times* into a supporting position, two of the most
powerful Republican editors, Bryant and Greeley, refused to endorse him;
independent-spirited governors like John A. Andrew and Oliver P. Morton,
and critical-tempered Senators like Sumner and Fessenden stood coldly aloof.
Wisely, Lincoln refused to antagonize the doubtful ones by aggressive measures in his own behalf. He was receptive, but avoided any grasping eagerness.
He discouraged Carl Schurz from leaving the army to work for him,[31] and
evinced no anxious uneasiness lest Grant might seek the White House. Though
glad to hear from Rufus Jones that Grant spurned politics, he remarked with
philosophic magnanimity that, if Grant took Richmond, we should let him
have the office.[32] Whatever men talked about in politics interested Lincoln
keenly, but he lifted himself above appetite or animosity. As Noah Brooks told
California readers, he took almost no thought of his own future. "But, patient,
patriotic, persevering, and single-hearted, he goes right on with his duty,
pegging away just as though, as he has said to me, his own life was to end with

29. Among Frémont's supporters were some Radical Republicans, some Abolitionists, some
Germans, and some War Democrats; 350 to 400 all told.
30. Welles, *Diary*, II, 17-18; Dana to his wife, May 3, 1864 and to Motley, May 7, 1864, Dana Papers,
Mass. Hist. Soc.
31. Nicolay and Hay, *Abraham Lincoln*, IX, 56, 59, 60.
32. Grant was simply not interested. He wrote from Nashville, Jan. 20, 1864, to a politician who
tried to tempt him (I.N. Morris) that election as the next President was the last thing in the world
he desired. "I would regard such a consummation as being highly unfortunate for myself, if not
for the country." Grant Papers, Illinois State Hist. Library.

his official life, content to leave his earnest labors and conscientious discharge of duty to the disposal of God and country." To which Brooks added: "A nobler and purer nature than his never animated man."[33]

Frémont was the first possible nominee pushed into the arena. A "people's provisional committee" of Radical origin invited like-minded lovers of freedom to gather in Cleveland on May 31, and about 350 self-chosen men from fifteen states and the District of Columbia met that day in Cosmopolitan Hall.[34] Since the really important Radicals like Henry Winter Davis, Zach Chandler, and Ben Wade had stood coldly aloof, the calls were signed by such relatively obscure Missouri politicians as B. Gratz Brown, Emil Preetorius, Friedrich Kapp, and James Redpath. Although some observers believed the movement had the covert sympathy of John A. Andrew, Schuyler Colfax, and David Dudley Field, they had sense enough to keep quiet.[35] Wendell Phillips, Frederick Douglass, and Elizabeth Cady Stanton were the principal personages of some national renown to stand up for the Pathfinder, or to support the call for a convention. The proceedings were short and businesslike, for everyone present agreed that Frémont should be nominated, and everyone believed that more emphasis should be thrown upon repudiation of Administration policies than upon condemnation of the rebellion.

The brief platform, Radical from beginning to end, promised a sweeping reversal of Lincoln's policies, and an acceleration of government action against slavery. One resolution, insinuating Administration indifference to governmental integrity and economy, promised strict regard to both. It contained a forcible assertion that as the war had destroyed slavery, the Federal Constitution should now be amended to prohibit its reëstablishment, and "to secure to all men absolute equality before the law." Another plank demanded that civil liberties be protected against infringement outside of areas under martial law. A third called for a constitutional amendment restricting Presidents to a single term. The most important resolutions declared that control of Reconstruction

33. Letter dated Oct. 6, 1863, in Sacramento *Daily News.*

34. Blaine, James G., *Twenty Years of Congress,* Norwich, Conn., 1886, I, 516, says *150. American Annual Cyclopaedia,* 1864, 786, says *500.*

35. Nevins, Allan, *Frémont,* New York, 1955, 574-575. Frémont later wrote: "The Cleveland Convention was to have been the open avowal of that condemnation which men had been freely expressing to each other for the past two years, and which had been fully made known to the President. But in the uncertain condition of affairs, leading men were not found willing to make public a dissatisfaction and condemnation which could have rendered Mr. Lincoln's nomination impossible; and their continued silence and support established for him a character among the people which leaves now no choice." The New York *World* commented Sept. 20: "Frémont alone of all the recognized leaders of the Republican Party dared to stand forth as the public opponent of a man who has been for two years the object of their freely expressed private scorn. . . ." McPherson, Edward, *The Political History of the United States of America During the Great Rebellion,* Washington, 1865, 410-415.

belonged to the people through their representatives in Congress, not the Executive, and asked that the lands of rebels be confiscated and distributed among soldiers and actual settlers. Clearly, the document was not a practical program of action, but an extremist manifesto. This tiny splinter-party hoped not to elect any man, but to ally itself with malcontent Republicans in defeating Lincoln and his moderate aims. The vital question to most members was the adoption of a Radical plan of Reconstruction. Others were actuated by devotion to the Pathfinder, memories of Administration hesitancy in Kentucky and Missouri, sympathy for the freedmen, and disgust with the protracted war effort.

Frémont, now fifty-one, restless, ambitious, and erratic as ever, had neither liking nor aptitude for politics. Living in New York surrounded by Radical antislavery men who had bitterly resented his removal from command in Missouri, influenced by his impatient wife, and bruised by what that judicious corps-commander Jacob D. Cox believed to be the Administration's negligent treatment of himself and his soldiers in the West Virginia campaign, he had longed for restoration to military authority. If nearly everybody mistrusted the calculating Blairs, he had special reason for dislike in their enmity and the malicious stories they had circulated about him; if the Wades, Sumners, and Chandlers criticized Lincoln, Frémont was still more critical when he heard that Lincoln had called him a "bespattered hero." When nominated for President by acclamation, he felt reluctance, for he knew he was a mere figurehead. To his discredit, his letter of acceptance on June 4 betrayed personal animus toward the Administration, being full of shopworn Radical phrases about military dictation, usurpation, executive feebleness, incapacity, and imminent bankruptcy. But to his credit, he repudiated the platform declaration upon the confiscation of Confederate lands, and with more promptness than McClellan showed this summer, resigned his army commission.

John Cochrane, chosen for Vice-President, was neither stronger nor weaker than most such nominees. A graduate of Hamilton College, a hardworking Congressman in Buchanan's time, a former State-Rights Democrat, a patriotic brigadier-general who had himself raised a regiment, he had been elected Attorney-General of New York State on the Union-Republican platform in 1863. He had been an early advocate of the enlistment and arming of Negro troops. So astute an observer as Gideon Welles pronounced him a leader of ability and principle.

The Cleveland nominations utterly failed to impress the country. While most Moderate Republicans thought the convention a motley assemblage of weak and erratic political vagrants, the War Democrats and Peace Democrats for quite divergent reasons disdained it and its choice. Lincoln packed his condemnation into a neat quotation from the Old Testament (II Samuel, 22) about the four hundred Adullamites who withdrew from Gath into a cave. Lincoln is said to have read these words; "And every one that was in distress, and every one that was in debt, and every one that was discontented, gathered themselves unto him, and he became a captain over them; and there were with him about four hundred men."[36] Yet the Convention could not be lightly dismissed. Although in May nobody would have given a copper cent for Frémont's chances of a substantial presidential vote, in a close contest even a small poll might prove as important as James G. Birney's Liberty Party vote had been in 1844; and the full story of his rôle in the election was yet to be written.

[III]

So certain was it that Lincoln would be nominated at Baltimore and control the platform that David Davis, the President's closest Illinois friend, did not deem it worthwhile to leave his Bloomington home for the Convention. The opposition was utterly routed, he assured Lincoln, and if a spokesman for their State was needed, Leonard Swett would suffice.[37] Most of the party, indeed, demanded the renomination. As Bryant wrote, the plain people believed Lincoln honest, the rich people believed him safe, the soldiers believed him their friend, the religious people believed him God's choice, and even the scoundrels believed it profitable to use his cloak.[38] When the Convention opened on June 7 with ex-Governor William Dennison of Ohio as permanent chairman (tactfully selected as a prominent friend of Chase), more than 500 delegates were present. Louisiana, Tennessee, and Arkansas had sent representatives who were unconditionally admitted, while Virginia and Florida men were seated without a right to vote, and South Carolina was rejected.[39]

The gathering met in the Front Street Theatre, festooned with flags and soon densely packed. At the outset, a rugged Kentucky parson, Dr. Robert J. Breckenridge of a ruling border-family, made a speech awesomely Radical in temper. Fortunately, few took him seriously when he said that the government must use all its powers to "exterminate" the rebellion, and that the cement of free institutions was "the blood of traitors." Former Governor Morgan of New York called for a constitutional amendment abolishing slavery. The platform, which received perhaps less note or discussion than usual, called upon citizens

36. Nicolay and Hay, *Abraham Lincoln*, IX, 40.
37. Davis to Lincoln, June 2, 1864, David Davis Papers, Chicago Hist. Soc. (photocopies).
38. New York *Evening Post*, June 3, 1864.
39. *American Annual Cyclopaedia*, 1864, 788.

to discard political differences and center their attention upon "quelling by force of arms the Rebellion now raging." No compromise must be made with Rebels and the demand was laid down for unconditional surrender of "their hostility and a return to their just allegiance . . ." Slavery was the cause of the rebellion and thus there should be an amendment to the Constitution ending slavery. In addition to usual platitudes, harmony in national councils was called for. Discrimination in the armies was to be ended; there was to be speedy construction of the Pacific Railroad; and, of course, there was to be economy and responsibility by the Administration. Then came the ballot for President. Only Missouri voted for General Grant, and Lincoln received a renomination on the first ballot by a vote of 506 to 22. A Missourian moved that the nomination be made unanimous. Then, suffering fearfully from heat, humidity, and overcrowded hotels, the politicians concentrated their attention upon the one undetermined question—the Vice-Presidency.[40]

"Things are going off in the best possible style," Nicolay had written John Hay from Baltimore on the 6th. With only a shadow of opposition to Lincoln visible except for the Missouri Radicals, the Convention seemed too docile under Administration leadership to be exciting. When Nicolay added that Hannibal Hamlin would in all probability be renominated, he might be forgiven his bad guess, for there were as many opinions about the proper selection as factions.[41] Hannibal Hamlin, Joseph Holt, Ben Butler, Simon Cameron, John A. Dix, W.S. Hancock, Edwin D. Morgan, Andrew Curtin, and William S. Rosecrans all had advocates. Even the sixty-three-year-old War Democrat, Daniel S. Dickinson, who had done so much to rally New York after Sumter, was lustily supported by Middle State Radicals, and more slyly by Sumner and some New Englanders who saw that, if Dickinson were elected, Lincoln would

40. McPherson, *op.cit.*, 406-407. Talk about the Vice-Presidency had been going on all spring. Ben Butler later asserted that he had been approached by emissaries professing to speak for Chase and Lincoln, as they inquired whether he would accept a vice-presidential nomination. "Vice Presidential Politics in '64," *North American Review*, Vol. CXLI, No.3, Oct. 1885. He doubtless heard random questions from slandering busybodies, but his story concerning Lincoln is certainly untrue.

41. A.K. McClure says in *Abraham Lincoln and Men of War Times*, Philadelphia, 1892, 444, that Lincoln discreetly but earnestly favored Andrew Johnson's nomination. George Jones, owner of the *Times* and one of Raymond's closest friends, says Raymond was influenced by Lincoln, as McClure was. Nicolay states that, on the contrary, Lincoln's personal feelings were for the renomination of Hamlin, but he persistently withheld any opinion calculated to influence the convention. Nicolay and Hay declare: (*Abraham Lincoln, op.cit.*, Vol. IX, 72-73): "It was with minds absolutely untrammeled by even any knowledge of the President's wishes that the convention went about its work of selecting his associate on the ticket."

Out of these statements grew a controversy to which McClure gives an appendix of nearly fifty pages in his *Lincoln and Men of War Times*. It offers much personal vituperation on both sides; a few statements of historical significance; and, on the whole, a substantiation of Nicolay. McClure's recollections in 1891 of what happened in 1863 are not impressive. Nicolay, Helen, *Lincoln's Secretary, a Biography of John G. Nicolay*, New York, 1949, 207-208.

have to drop Seward from the Cabinet. Sumner was in fact suspected of being a general marplot. He would rejoice if he could get Seward out of the Cabinet by the election of Andrew Johnson. At the same time, Seward, consistently filled with a desire to protect the rights of the freedmen, and in favor of a reorganization of parties that would attract the support of both Southerners and Northern Democrats, also showed a leaning toward Johnson.[42] If the shelving of Hamlin resulted in his running against Fessenden for the Senate in Maine's next Senatorial contest, Sumner would rejoice again, for he hated Fessenden. Seeing a plain threat to Seward, the latter's friends vehemently opposed Dickinson.[43] Hence, the situation became highly confused.

Many men who would really have preferred Hamlin conceded that, as the Republican Party, a sectional organization in 1860, now claimed to possess a national character, a Southern man would better befit it than a Maine downeaster.

Hamlin deserved renomination, for he had been a dignified, salty, right-minded Vice-President, and if he had given little impression of force or stature, his office made it almost impossible to make any impression at all. The son of a poor farmer, deprived of a college education, he had steadily grown as he rose from a law office through legislature, House, and Senate. A gentleman of the old school, a six-footer of blandly courteous manners, he had clung to a stock and black swallow-tailed coat after most men abandoned them. He was punctilious in the discharge of duty; his speech had terse Yankee pungency, but also judgment and tact; and he held some firm convictions—one that amnesty ought to be granted all Southerners sincerely converted to loyalty, and another that the Negro could be developed into a useful citizen just as surely as he had been developed into a soldier.[44]

Lincoln, declared Welles, would have liked Hamlin renominated, despite his personal fondness for Andrew Johnson. But he kept his hands off, and a curious combination of circumstances gave Johnson the victory. For one, Sumner rallied most of New England against Hamlin.[45] For another, the day before

---

42. Cox, Lawanda and John H., *Politics, Principle and Prejudice, 1865-1866*, London, 1963, 220-223.

43. Glonek, James F., "Lincoln, Johnson and the Baltimore Ticket," *Abraham Lincoln Quarterly*, Vol.VI, No.5, Mar., 1951, 261 and *passim*; Hamlin, Charles E., *The Life and Times of Hannibal Hamlin*, Cambridge, 1899, 462-466.

44. Hamlin, *Hamlin, ut supra*, 461ff., and Jellison, Charles A., *Fessenden of Maine*, Syracuse, N.Y., 1962, 178ff., offer full materials.

45. Simon Cameron wrote Senator Fessenden after the convention: "I strove hard to renominate Hamlin, as well for his own sake as yours, but failed only because New England, especially Massachusetts, did not adhere to him." Lot M. Morrill bore the same testimony that the hostility of Massachusetts (i.e. Sumner) had crushed his own efforts for Hamlin. See Hamlin, *Hamlin, op.cit.*, 461-488; Noah Brooks, letter of June 7 from Baltimore in Sacramento *Union*; Charles A. Dana, Jr., in his Journal of a Trip to Washington in January, 1862, has a good characterization of Hamlin, Dana Papers, Mass. Hist. Soc.

the Convention met, the Illinois delegates conferred in Barnum's Hotel upon the attitude they should take toward two rival Missouri groups that were asking admission—a body of Radicals hotly opposed to the Blairs and hence to Lincoln, and some Conservative Republicans who would join everybody else in making the nomination of Lincoln unanimous. The Illinois men were about to vote to debar the anti-Blair contestants, an action which other States would reluctantly ratify, when suddenly a slight, thin-visaged young man arose, and announced that he wished to say a word for himself alone. In his opinion, he went on, Illinois had better favor the admission of the Missouri Radicals. He was John G. Nicolay, Lincoln's secretary! He gave no argument; it was not necessary. Next day Illinois voted as Nicolay suggested. Delegations hostile to the Blair faction joyously took their seats and, as we have noted, the 22 votes of Missouri went on the first ballot to Grant.[46]

This action reflected Lincoln's sagacity, for if the Radicals had been excluded they would have raised a damaging cry of tyranny. But the admission of Missouri Radicals had to be balanced by letting in Lincoln Moderates from Louisiana, Tennessee, and Arkansas. When Tennessee was admitted, Johnson became available. Henry J. Raymond, head of the national committee, had for months argued that a War Democrat should be nominated, and had come to Baltimore convinced that Johnson, with his record as a hot opponent of secession, an effective military governor, and a Radical with some Lincolnian ideas, was the right man. When men whispered that Lincoln must have told Raymond to take this position, the editor said nothing to dispel the idea. It was in such clever management of political movements and manoeuvres that Lincoln excelled.[47]

The Grand National Council of the Union League held a meeting on June 8, and adopted a declaration of principles or quasi-platform, pledging the Union League to vigorous prosecution of the war, to the backing of an anti-slavery amendment, support of the Monroe Doctrine, and championship of the principle that every person bearing arms in defense of the flag is "entitled, without distinction of color or nationality, to the protection of the government . . ." But the Union League's statement of principles differed from the Union platform in declaring "that the confiscation acts of Congress should be promptly and vigorously enforced, and that homesteads on the lands confiscated under it should be granted to our soldiers and others who have been made indigent by the acts of traitors and rebels."[48]

46. Carr, Clark E., *My Day and Generation*, Chicago, 1908, 133-144; Hume, John F., *The Abolitionists*, New York, 1905, Ch. XXI, tells how he cast the votes.
47. Brown, Francis E., *Raymond of the Times*, New York, 1951, 252-253. Cf. George H. Mayer, *The Republican Party, 1854-1964*, New York, 1964, 518, 519.
48. McPherson, Edward, *The Political History of the United States*, Washington, 1864, 410.

The first ballot showed Johnson, Hamlin, and Dickinson far in the lead—Johnson 200, Hamlin 150, Dickinson 108. Instantly Iowa shifted its vote to Johnson, and the avalanche began. For the credit or discredit of this decision we must turn primarily to honest Raymond, who some thought at the time had read Lincoln's mind, but more probably had just followed his own. Hamlin accepted the result with good humor, ready to work hard for both candidates.

The day after the Convention, a committee under Dennison called on Lincoln to inform him of what had been done, and hand him the first copy of the resolutions that he had seen. "I know no reason to doubt that I shall accept the nomination tendered," he replied, "and yet, perhaps, I should not declare definitely before reading and considering what is called the platform." This definite answer he delivered in writing on June 27, sounding a note of warning to the French Emperor in the remark that he would sustain the positions of the State Department and the Republican Convention respecting Mexican affairs. Andrew Johnson's acceptance carried some foolish rhetoric to the effect that treason was "worthy of the punishment of death." [49] . . .

49. Seward, Frederick W., *Seward at Washington, 1861-1872*, New York, 1891, III, 226; Stryker, Lloyd Paul, *Andrew Johnson, a Study in Courage*, New York, 1929, XI; Hamlin, *Hamlin*, op.cit., XXXVI; Lincoln, *Works*, VII, 380-382.

12.

On July 4, 1864, as Congress adjourned, the President pocket-vetoed the Wade-Davis bill, a Radical-sponsored measure designed to impose a more stringent Reconstruction policy on the South than Lincoln approved. It was a direct confrontation between the President and the Radicals. "Reconstruction was now a subject for national debate in which the Radical Republicans were outnumbered and outgunned by the combined forces of the Moderate Republicans and War Democrats." [1] The Radicals fought back against Lincoln's policy, and the battle became heated in the election year of 1864.

The Democratic nominee was George B. McClellan, the unsuccessful general, but even he could not endorse the entire "peace" plank, written in part by some of the Copperheads. The Union party coalition of Republicans and War Democrats worried for a time, and Lincoln was discouraged about prospects of victory. Then Frémont withdrew, and by the end of September and early October the campaign was really finished. Disgust with the Democratic platform and military victories at Atlanta, Mobile, and Cedar Creek in the Shenandoah Valley brought thousands of Republicans back to Lincoln's side. "Seldom has so swift a change occurred in the political situation of the great republic." [2]

By election day there was a new spirit in the air. "On nearly every front the conditions . . . as precedent to victory were now being fulfilled." [3] Grant and Meade had pinned Lee down, Sherman was advancing, the superior power of the Union was being used everywhere. The question of the retention of slavery grew more and more unreal. Reconstruction, however, "was too prickly a subject to be gripped. . . . The fact was that the country could not debate Reconstruction intensively until it made perfectly certain of defeating the Confederacy; until it knew more about the Negroes, their masters, and economic prospects North and South; until the temper of the people and the new Thirty-ninth Congress was more clearly defined; and until certain Cabinet changes now being adumbrated took reality." [4]

Lincoln remained apprehensive until the votes were counted. His majority exceeded half a million votes and he garnered 212 electoral votes to 21 for McClellan. "The election of 1864 was not so great and refreshing but that it left the country many lessons to ponder, and some to take deeply to heart." There had been a free election during a civil conflict; it had been "demonstrated that a people's government could sustain and renew itself. . . ." [5] On the other hand, there had been substantial opposition to Lincoln and to his policies.

Union armies were now definitely in a winning strategic position, and they were exploiting the situation. The Army of the Potomac doggedly threatened Lee around Petersburg and Richmond throughout the fall and winter. The Federals under Sheridan had finally cleaned up the Shenandoah Valley. Sherman moved on from Atlanta to the ocean at Savannah, Georgia, in his famous "March to the Sea" that further disrupted the South, an achievement that was "primarily moral, not physical." Confederate John Bell Hood carried out his daring campaign from Atlanta back to the heart of Tennessee, only to fail at Franklin and then to have his army virtually destroyed at Nashville in mid-December by George H. Thomas. "While dismemberment of the Confederacy had been a part of the Federal strategy since near the beginning of the war, the cardinal questions were always *where, when,* and *how* to invade the inner fortress of the South." [6] These problems had now been solved. "Leadership had shown growing proficiency under Sherman, Thomas, Grant, Schofield, Porter, and Terry. . . . The leadership had profited more and more from the experienced and vigorously supplied body of troops with which it could operate. The North could take the initiative freely now while the Confederacy had to respond. And it was even growing late for any vigorous response. By February it was plain on every front that the springtide would bring more than mild showers and lilacs and breezes." [7]

"In Northern homes the majority of the war-worn people could glimpse more and more tokens of hope. The wistful longing that had throbbed in the bars of 'When This Cruel War is Over,' seemed ever closer to fulfillment. More and more confidently the press, politicians, and people began discussing the great practical questions of the future. What new course would public and private life follow after the silencing of the guns and bugles? Might the war possibly go beyond the summer of 1865? Mr. Lincoln, now elected for four more years, had been the patient, sagacious leader in war. What would he do to meet the even more perplexing problems of peace?" [8]

Heated debate over the Thirteenth Amendment—constitutionally freeing the slaves—led to several delays, but finally the House completed passage January 31, 1865, and the states began to take action.

March 4, 1865, was inaugural day. Vice-President Andrew Johnson made a near disaster of his inaugural, when he appeared somewhat intoxicated from drinking whisky as a remedy for his illness. Then Lincoln, with a single sheet of paper in hand, advanced to the podium and was greeted by a roar of applause. His words have become familiar: "With malice toward none; with charity for all; with firmness in the right, as God gives us to see the right, let us strive on to finish the work we are in; to bind up the nation's wounds; to care for him who shall have borne the battle, and for his widow, and his orphan—to do all which may achieve and cherish a just and a lasting peace, among ourselves, and with all nations."

" 'The Last Inaugural' was at once seen to breathe an elevation of soul worthy of a great people in a climactic moment of its history. Its influence upon the events in 1865 which closely followed it was slight. But this immortal admonition was designed for the decades and the ages, not for the immediate moment, for many men were still far from ready to forget their hot malice or adopt the golden maxim of charity for all in a land so long rent by resentments and hatreds. The nobility of Lincoln's words, however, gripped the national consciousness with a force that moulded thought and action as nothing had done since Washington's Farewell Address—a force that still lifts and shapes the American purpose." [9]

Meanwhile, the "Southern will to resist was heroic; it had such iron strength that well into the last year of the war it still seemed almost unconquerable. The hardships of the Southern people, taken alone, would perhaps never have fatally sapped it. Whatever their sufferings, they might well have fought on. It was the interaction of three principal forces that brought Southerners to the point where they began to accept the idea of defeat. These forces were the heavier and heavier loss of life—the drawing of an ever-deeper stream of blood from veins that could not be replenished; the ever-sharper bite of a hundred steel teeth of internal privation; and the growing conviction that all the Southern losses would be in vain, that no matter what the struggles of the people or the feats of the armies, superior Northern strength and organization would ultimately win." [10]

Inflation, losses, the inevitable end of slavery, and a spasmodic impulse toward desertion from the army increased Southern discouragement and desperation and led to some demands for peace. "Countless Southerners felt, during this last year of the war, as if they were walking in a nightmare." [11] "The woes of displacement, the gloom of hopelessness, the friction of exile, were a cancer that ate into not merely the endurance of Southerners, but their very soul. Hundreds of thousands were never the same afterward. By the final winter of their struggle they felt the price they were paying for its maintenance almost unendurable, and knew that it would leave marks they would carry to the grave." [12] In Nevins's view, "Much was being destroyed in the South, but much had to be destroyed if a better land, with better institutions and ideas, was to be born." [13]

A million men under Northern arms could not be resisted. Sherman was moving north from Savannah through the Carolinas. The pressure on Richmond and Petersburg was increasing. Everywhere Union arms were successful in the early months of 1865. "The hammer, the anvil, and strangulation had done their work! . . . The outer fortress walls of the Confederacy had been breached before 1864, and now the inner works were being carried. To the east and south on the Atlantic and Gulf coasts the blockade had stiffened until near the end it was perhaps the major element in garroting the South." [14]

NOTES

1. Nevins, *The War for the Union*, Vol. IV, *The Organized War to Victory, 1864–1865,* p. 87.
2. *Ibid.,* p. 103.
3. *Ibid.,* p. 120.
4. *Ibid.,* pp. 126–127.
5. *Ibid.,* p. 140.
6. *Ibid.,* pp. 163–164.
7. *Ibid.,* p. 195.
8. *Ibid.,* p. 201.
9. *Ibid.,* p. 217.
10. *Ibid.,* pp. 224–225.
11. *Ibid.,* pp. 227–228.
12. *Ibid.,* p. 241.
13. *Ibid.,* p. 253.
14. *Ibid.,* p. 272.

Victory

THE EXULTATION of victory filled all loyal breasts as April covered the land with blossoms in 1865. The end that all believers in the Union regarded as inevitable had come. It could be no other way! The question among all men was still, "When would the South lay down its arms?" The dragging conflict had long since dissipated the optimistic dreams held by many Northerners in the fever after Sumter. The conflict they had hoped would be short, quick, and glorious had turned into nearly four years of agony and grief, but the endurance of harrowing anxiety and defeat had taught the people grim lessons in fortitude and intellectual realism. They knew that the Confederacy could endure but a few months longer. Mangled and suffering by the sword thrusts of Sherman in the Carolinas, lightning invasions on the Atlantic and Gulf coasts, and Union marches in the West, the Confederacy, manacled by the ever-tighter grip of the blockade, was stumbling to its doom. Cardinal attention was still fastened upon Richmond and Petersburg, where the growing strength of the blue ranks under Grant and Meade held an increasingly clear mastery of the area where the last real army of the South, feebler and more discouraged day by day, struggled to hold its ground.

In the wide domain once so proudly ruled by the Confederacy, the economic and social erosion had become ruinously destructive. Much land had been conquered or depleted. Many people were dead or in exile. Large districts had been lost or rendered unproductive, and what remained was insufficient and often could not be utilized. Yet the South largely retained its old principles and its fealty to its special concepts of sectional liberty and State rights. As so often in the history of English-speaking peoples, some long-embattled men and women had made the sad period of desperation and defeat their finest hour of spiritual renewal and philosophic resolution; so, now, they exhibited a spirit that their descendants could remember with respect and even an alloyed admiration. Their doctrines might be subject to question, to much revision, and even to condemnation, but the spirit of Dixieland had aspects and qualities that would be cherished along with the memory of Robert E. Lee.

(*The War for the Union*, Vol. IV, *The Organized War to Victory, 1864–1865*, Chapter 10.)

Many at the North had, during the dark months and years, broadened their view of both the war and the peace. The President had been re-elected, re-inaugurated, and, without disturbance, would have four years to deal with the imminent tasks of pacification and reconstruction. For the moment, however, as blossom and leaf unfolded and showers began to ease, most eyes and ears were tuned to the sound of the guns southward. This was the spring of 1865.

[I]

By March, the Administration could distract its attention from the war and its multitudinous labors and prepare to resume the long-postponed tasks required by national recovery and growth, and by governmental and social reorganization. All too many responsibilities demanded action by the President, Congress, and the States.

Lincoln once more faced a cohort of office-seekers, including many Republican politicians clamorous for favors ever since the November election. As more and more of the South came under partial or full Northern control, traders, both honest and dishonest, lifted noisy demands for commercial permits. Important Cabinet positions, including the Secretaryships of State, of the Treasury, and of the Interior, had to be filled with circumspect care. Happily, the care-worn President had a brief interval—all too brief, as it soon appeared —to concentrate upon the most exigent labors. Fortunately for him and the country, Congress was not in session, and he was free from the criticisms, denunciations, exhibitions of jealous spleen, and ebullitions of malicious plotting that would otherwise have come from Capitol Hill. In his last Cabinet meeting, on April 14, Lincoln frankly remarked that he "thought it providential that this great rebellion was crushed just as the Congress had adjourned, and there were none of the disturbing elements of that body here to hinder and embarrass us. . . ."[1] The war had begun without the benefit or interference of Congress in the administration of the government, and now it was to end the same way.

Although the pressure of office-seekers was still almost intolerable, Lincoln now seemed a little more resigned to it, and more hopeful of the government's future than he had been before, with most Northerners sharing his sanguine outlook. While many citizens, and especially politicians, were pondering the future with concern, national confidence was growing steadily, giving rise to expressions of relief and to a certain exuberance. As historians of the war have said, it is impossible to determine just when the people realized that a trium-

1. Welles, Gideon, typescript of article, "Lincoln and Reconstruction in April, 1865," John Hay Library, Brown Univ., Providence, R.I.,

phant close was inevitable. The belief in imminent victory had been spreading since the fall of 1864, which had brought victories in Georgia, Tennessee, and the Shenandoah.

On Washington's birthday, 1865, the North had thrilled to the headlines, "Charleston evacuated!" The city where the rebellion started was once more in Union hands![2] The New York *Tribune* correspondent on the scene described the fires, explosions, and the destruction of stores, bridges, and warships. The national colors once more floated over Sumter, a shapeless mass of rubble in the harbor. No American heard the news without emotion.[3] At the same time dispatches from Admiral Porter's flagship, the *Malvern*, in Cape Fear River, confirmed that Fort Anderson had fallen. The way to Wilmington at last lay open; the public, however, did not know as they read the news on February 22 that the city had been evacuated that day.

New York, like other parts of the North, was in a festive, holiday mood under sunny skies, the air soft and springlike. "We never saw Broadway so utterly jammed with human beings," reported the *Tribune*. The shipping in the harbor was gaily dressed, and at noon, guns began firing from all the forts, while the chimes of Trinity deepened the clamor. Veterans of the War of 1812 paraded, and the armories turned out the proudest militia regiments to join in the procession. The Seventh led the way, its band playing patriotic airs while the crowd cheered. At night the most elaborate fireworks the city had yet seen lighted up the skies. A huge audience pressed into the Brooklyn Academy of Music to hear Wendell Phillips speak on "Our Country, Our Whole Country." Greeley had declared in a *Tribune* editorial that the fate of the rebellion hung by a thread which a single decisive Union victory could sever. Next day, February 23, another headline, "Fall of Wilmington," blazed in the New York press over Navy Department dispatches announcing that national forces had entered the last Confederate port of importance left open.[4] Then, day by day, the newspapers offered fresh tidings of Union advances. Dispatches from Sherman in the Carolinas, Terry outside Wilmington, and Sheridan in his last victories over the remnants of Early in the Shenandoah, were especially gratifying, for they were popular heroes.

But even with the thrill of victory abounding, some faint-hearts still strove for a negotiated peace. Horace Greeley would not forsake his dream of fashioning an end to bloodshed. He wrote S.L.M. Barlow, March 15, that he was willing to go to Richmond and talk with the Confederates if Lincoln "will indicate in confidence the most favorable terms" which he was prepared "to accord to the insurgents, stating what he must require and what he is ready

2. For description of the fall of Charleston, see Chap. 9, "The Final Triumph of Union Arms."
3. New York *Tribune*, Feb. 22, 1865.
4. *Ibid.*, Feb. 23, 1865.

to concede with regard to the Union, Emancipation, confiscation, amnesty, restoration to political equality in Congress, etc. . . ."[5]

But cheering crowds, parading troops, and pounding bands did not express the deep earnestness of the people. In Washington departments and bureaus the grim work of conducting the war kept desk-lamps burning from midnight until dawn. Countless details required attention. For example, Grant had objected to the President's liberation of prisoners after merely taking the oath of allegiance. Lincoln responded that he had freed about fifty men a day recently. This was a greater number than he liked, but they were names brought to him mainly by Border State Congressmen, and vouched for by various sponsors. The President argued that in only one or two instances had his trust been betrayed.[6] As if he intended continuing this policy of calculated leniency, on March 11 he issued a proclamation giving deserters sixty days within which they might be pardoned if they came back and reported. Wilful absentees might incur severe penalties.[7]

It was often Lincoln's habit to make a memorable statement on what was ostensibly some merely perfunctory occasion. Addressing the 14th Indiana Regiment, he pithily remarked: "I have always thought that all men should be free; but if any should be slaves, it should be first those who desire it for *themselves*, and secondly, those who *desire* it for *others*. Whenever [I] hear anyone arguing for slavery, I feel a strong impulse to see it tried on him personally." He went on to remind his listeners that if the Negro fought for the rebels, he could not at the same time "stay at home and make bread for them."[8] In fact, he tolerantly held the view that, as he quaintly put it, "We have to reach the bottom of the insurgent resources; and that they employ, or seriously think of employing, the slaves as soldiers, gives us glimpses of the bottom." Lincoln, of course, was more correct than he thought, as to the glimpse of the bottom —not merely the bottom of the immediate Southern resources of white man-power, but the bottom of the age-old Southern exploitation of black manpower in all departments of life and activity.[9]

On the surface, March appeared to offer the President a quiet month, but it actually proved busy and harassing. All the old problems remained, and were growing more urgent and complex, while the President's minor tasks also made increasing demands on his time and strength. On March 20, Grant telegraphed that he wished to see the President, and thought a rest would do him good. Lincoln replied that he had been thinking of such a visit.[10] In

5. Greeley to Barlow, Mar. 15, 1865, Barlow Papers, HEH.
6. Lincoln, *Collected Works*, VIII, 347-348, Mar. 9, 1865.
7. *Ibid.*, 349-350.
8. *Ibid.*, 361.
9. *Ibid.*, 362, March 17, 1865.
10. Lincoln, *Works*, VIII, 367.

consequence, on the afternoon of March 23, Lincoln, Mrs. Lincoln, Tad, a maid, and two bodyguards left on the *River Queen* for City Point, arriving at that vital Virginia base at nine on the evening of the next day. The President had been slightly ill on the trip. He did not even have a secretary with him, and Stanton for the interim seemed to be the unofficial Washington substitute for Lincoln, the two keeping in communication by wire.

One of Lincoln's motives for the trip was apparently to escape the hectic atmosphere of the capital and the pressure of trivial details, so that he might better concentrate his attention on the military climax soon to come in Virginia. Earlier Sherman had repelled Johnston's desperate attacks at Bentonville in North Carolina with ease, and on March 22, the able young cavalry commander, James Harrison Wilson, had led his Union forces into Alabama to threaten Selma and defeat Forrest's worn troopers. On the Gulf Coast, meanwhile, Union pressure entered upon a bolder phase as Canby began an energetic movement against Mobile.

All could see that great events impended on the Virginia battlefront, and, in fact, they began to disclose themselves on March 25, the morning after Lincoln's arrival. The weary President, looking unwell, boarded a special train from City Point to the Petersburg line. He toured the field of the recent engagement at Fort Stedman, viewing the burial of men slain in that abortive Confederate attack. The cars returning to City Point bore wounded soldiers.[11]

A few miles away from the point where Lincoln had surveyed the smoke-wreathed lines, but in the grip of a mood much darker and more perturbed, President Davis, Lee, and their Confederate associates faced an ominous future. No attempts to muster a transitory optimism could conceal the ugly realities of their plight. The most exhausting efforts had proved unavailing to check the steady decline in Southern strength and spirit during 1864; instead, almost everything had grown worse.[12]

There were ardent Southerners who held, or pretended to hold, a belief that some hope of success still remained. But shrewder or more practical men could not blind themselves to the harsh fact that not even a miracle could now save the sinking cause.

In January, 1865, Lee had written letters urging the use of Negroes as soldiers. Much as he disliked this measure, it now seemed unavoidable to him if he was not to overtax the white population.[13] Lee, therefore, after describing the Northern preponderance of strength, continued with a suggestion which many people considered ghastly: "I think, therefore, we must decide whether

11. *Lincoln Day by Day: A Chronology, 1809-1865*, Lincoln Sesquicentennial Commission, Washington, 1960, 322.
12. See the previous Chapter.
13. Lee to Andrew Hunter, "Lee's View on Enlisting the Negroes," Memoranda of the Civil War, *Harper's Monthly*, Vol. XXXVI, No. 4, Aug. 1888, 600-601.

slavery shall be extinguished by our enemies and the slaves used against us, or use them ourselves at the risk of the effects which may be produced upon our social institutions. . . ."[14] As early as February 20, one of Lee's staff-officers wrote: "Our people must make up their minds to see Richmond go. . . ."[15] And in Richmond itself, the laggard Confederate Congress, on March 13, finally completed passage of a measure approving the enrollment of Negroes for army service on a voluntary basis, involving the free action both of slaveholders and slaves. Davis signed this measure immediately after Lee had pressed him hard to give his assent. Lee was now more anxiously urging prompt action upon it. Negroes might not be made available in season for the spring campaign, but "no time should be lost in trying to collect all we can."[16]

Under the law of March 13, the Confederate Congress authorized the President to call upon slaveowners to seek volunteers of 18 to 45 in age among their Negroes. However, the new legislation did not require owners to volunteer the slaves, nor did it specifically give those slaves who volunteered to serve their freedom. It was nevertheless tacitly understood that the States would emancipate such slaves. Negro troops were to be willing to go as volunteers, and would receive the same pay, rations, and clothing as other troops. Recruiting thus began in the Richmond area amid considerable early excitement, and in the last weeks of the war a few Negro troops were seen parading in Richmond.[17]

A number of officers, all white, saw the opportunity for gaining a higher rank. By March 24, the Richmond *Sentinel* reported that enlistments were continuing.[18] On March 22, the Richmond *Dispatch* had begged Virginians to give the call their support, and reported that a devoted group of farmers in Roanoke County had offered to liberate any of their slaves who volunteered.[19]

Davis, however, later recorded that insufficient time remained to obtain any result from the enactment.[20] This was not the true explanation, for the underlying problem was lack of support by any considerable number of slaveholders. Davis frankly wrote Lee on April 1 that, "I have been laboring, without much progress, to advance the raising of negro troops . . . ,"[21] to which Lee replied that he had been willing to detach recruiting officers.[22]

In the War Department, on March 23, Robert Kean wrote the following

---

14. *Ibid.*
15. Taylor, Walter H., *Four Years with General Lee*, New York, 1878, 143.
16. Lee to Davis, Mar. 10, 1865, Lee Papers, Duke Univ. Libr.
17. *American Annual Cyclopaedia*, 1865, 194.
18. Richmond *Sentinel*, Mar. 24, 1865.
19. Richmond *Dispatch*, Mar. 22, 1865.
20. Davis, *The Rise and Fall of the Confederate Government*, New York, 1881, I, 518.
21. *O.R.*, I, xlvi, pt. 3, 1370.
22. Lee to Davis, Apr. 2, 1865, Lee Headquarters Papers, Virginia State Hist. Soc.

illuminating paragraph: "This measure was passed by a panic in the Congress and the Virginia Legislature, under all the pressure of the President indirectly, and General Lee directly, could bring to bear. My own judgment of the whole thing is that it is a colossal blunder, a dislocation of the foundations of society from which no practical results will be reaped by us. The enemy probably got four recruits under it to our one. . . ."[23]

The fact is that slaveowners simply did not respond. Robert Toombs, even stronger in disapproval, felt the Negro unfit to be a soldier or at least a Confederate soldier. He believed they would rapidly "abandon their flag. . . . In my opinion the worst calamity that could befall us would be to gain our independence by the valor of our slaves . . . instead of our own. . . . The day that the army of Virginia allows a negro regiment to enter their lines as soldiers they will be degraded, ruined, and disgraced."[24]

One of Lee's officers wrote General Ewell that Lee "directs me to . . . say that he regrets very much to learn that owners refuse to allow their slaves to enlist. He deems it of great moment that some of this force should be put in the field as soon as possible, believing that they will remove all doubts as to the expediency of this measure. He regrets it the more in the case of the owners about Richmond, inasmuch as the example would be extremely valuable, and the present posture of military affairs renders it almost certain that if we do not get these men, they will soon be in arms against us, and perhaps relieving white Federal soldiers from guard-duty in Richmond."[25]

Though of small consequence in the actual life of the Confederacy, this legislative admission that Negro troops were needed and the approving actions of some in recruiting them, revealed that powerful social stresses were at work in the Confederacy, operating under duress but nonetheless important.

By March 6 it had become evident in the War Department that plans were being made to evacuate Richmond.[26] Conditions in Richmond for the average citizen had declined from bad to worse. In addition to worrying about the future of the armies and his country, the ordinary citizen had many daily hardships to encounter. Prices had risen steadily. One Richmond minister, on March 27, reported beef at $15 a pound, bacon $20, meal $100 a bushel; potatoes were $100 a bushel, and even turnip greens $10 a peck. There was another problem—what to do when the Yankees arrived—a problem which became daily more anguishing. "If we should evacuate Richmond," wrote the Reverend Mr. Alexander Gustavus Brown, "I do not know what is to become of us.

23. Kean, Robert G.H., *Inside the Confederate Government*, New York, 1957, 204.
24. Robert Toombs, Washington, Ga., to "Dear Dudley," March 24, 1865 (probably Dudley Mann), Charles A. Dana Papers, LC.
25. Lt.-Col. Charles Marshall to Ewell, Mar. 30, 1865, George Washington Campbell Papers, LC.
26. Jones, John B., *A Rebel War Clerk's Diary*, Philadelphia, 1866, 512, Mar. 6, 1865.

I have made up my mind to stay here, and take the chances."[27]

It was evident to all that the fall of Richmond must herald the beginning of the end. Some had tried to pretend otherwise. Lee, for instance, in January, in testimony to the Joint Committee on the Condition of the Army, is said to have replied to the question, "Will the Fall of Richmond end the war?": "By no means, sir, by no means. In a military point of view I should be stronger after than before such an event, because it would enable me to make my plan of campaign and battle. From a moral and political point of view the abandonment or loss of Richmond would be a serious calamity, but when it has fallen I believe I can prolong the war for two years upon Virginia soil. Ever since the conflict began, I have been obliged to permit the enemy to make my plans for me, because compelled to defend the capital. . . ."[28]

But even Lee's ideas had apparently changed. Reporting to Davis March 26 on the failure at Fort Stedman, he wrote, "I fear now it will be impossible to prevent a junction between Grant and Sherman, nor do I deem it prudent that this army should maintain its position until the latter shall approach too near."[29]

The Richmond *Sentinel* printed, as late as April 1, 1865, the statement of one unconquerable Southerner who proclaimed gallantly, if unwisely: "We are very hopeful of the campaign which is opening, and trust that we are to reap a large advantage from the operations evidently near at hand. . . . As for ourselves, *nothing* could equal, in its horror, the dreadful calamity of Yankee domination of our land. Awful as have been the four years of conflict through which we have passed, they have been four years of joy compared with what they would have been with the heel of Lincoln on our necks."[30]

But far sooner than that writer was willing to admit, the tramp of Lincoln's soldiers would make the campaign of which he was so hopeful nothing more than the last stand of the few fanatical rebels who remained staunch in spirit though weak in strength.

[II]

With Grant's two huge armies, those of the Potomac and the James, stationed around Richmond and Petersburg, Lee could really do nothing except await the now almost certain end. At the same time, Grant, impatient as he really was, had good reasons for waiting. He believed, as did most everyone,

27. Letters of the Rev. Alexander Gustavus Brown, Virginia State Hist. Soc.
28. Clipping from the New Orleans *Democrat*, July 5, 1881, interview with former Confederate Senator Benjamin Hill, Alfred Roman Papers, LC.
29. Lee, *Wartime Papers*, op.cit., 916-918.
30. Richmond *Sentinel*, April 1, 1865.

that the spring campaigning would close the war. It had been a severe winter, making roads impassable in the early Virginia spring. As Grant put it in his *Memoirs*, "It was necessary to wait until they had dried sufficiently to enable us to move the wagon trains and artillery necessary to the efficiency of any army operating in the enemy's country." Sheridan, with the cavalry in the Shenandoah, had to move his force down to Petersburg by a long circuitous route. As early as March first, Grant issued orders to keep a sharp lookout for any move by Lee.[31]

On March 3, Grant outlined his ideas to Meade,[32] proposing an attack, when rumor came that Lee was moving, but Lee was *not* moving. Therefore, Grant decided: "It is better for us to hold the enemy where he is than to force him South. . . . To drive the enemy from Richmond now would be to endanger the success of Sherman and Schofield." At the same time he warned, "It is well to have it understood where and how to attack suddenly if it should be found at any future time that the enemy are detaching heavily. My notion is that Petersburg will be evacuated simultaneously with such detaching as would justify an attack. . . ."[33]

To the west and north of the Petersburg-Richmond position in the Shenandoah, major warfare, army against army, had almost ceased. Sheridan's cavalry had a free hand in the Valley now, except for isolated local opposition. Jubal Early in the Waynesboro-Staunton area had what was called a division, though by March the infantry was well under 3,000 men. He had a few cavalry units left, but they had much too wide an area to watch. The hard winter had not helped. Morale was low, and Early himself came under severe criticism.

By March 27, Lee became convinced from all reports available that Grant was about to move. Furthermore, he was sure that Grant would move westward from his existing line now extended to the area of Five Forks and Dinwiddie Court House. No possibility of deception existed. If the Confederate lines were lengthened by the four miles that seemed required, they would be overstrained. The only troops that Lee could possibly find to move were Pickett's division of about 5,000, suffering as all were from exhaustion.[34] Upon learning of Federal troop movements westward on the 28th, Lee prepared to shift Pickett from his position north of the James to the Five Forks area. No real attempt would be made to cover the whole new extension of the lines, but

31. Grant, *Memoirs*, II, 427, 430.
32. Grant had secondary problems on his hands as well, such as attempting to have Meade confirmed as major-general in the regulars, and the continuing problem of both legal and illegal trade with the enemy. Grant to Henry Wilson, Jan. 23, 1865, and Grant to Elihu Washburne, Jan. 23, 1865, Meade Papers, Hist. Soc. of Pennsylvania.
33. Grant to Meade, City Point, Mar. 3, 1865, Meade Papers, *ut supra*.
34. Freeman, *Lee*, *op.cit.*, IV, 24-27; an excellent analysis of Lee's troop problem.

rather one to provide a movable force to meet the enemy thrust. Orders were sent out on the 29th for Pickett to move forward, collect his isolated units and join the cavalry on the extreme Confederate right. Fitzhugh Lee was in command of the hastily convoked cavalry units, numbering about 4,200. Lee next gave Pickett some help from the force on the far Confederate right, bringing his infantry to 6,400.[35]

As Pickett and the cavalry moved toward Five Forks on the night of March 29 and the morning of the 30th, the rain fell in blinding sheets.[36] Forces of both armies marched in the rain through the broken country with its narrow roads, the terrain broken in places by swamps studded with alder thickets, briars and stunted pines.[37] Despite the rain and the rough terrain Lee at this critical time kept fairly good intelligence. On March 28 he learned that Sheridan had reached Grant's left, and on the 29th that both Union infantry and cavalry were in motion.[38]

On the night of March 27, E.O.C. Ord's Army of the James, three divisions strong taken from two corps, began to march westward, reaching their position near Hatcher's Run on the morning of March 29. That morning Warren's Fifth Corps began its march. Other troops shifted position, and Sheridan's cavalry now reached Dinwiddie Court House.[39] Grant felt, "Everything looked favorable to the defeat of the enemy and the capture of Petersburg and Richmond, if the proper effort was made." And despite the rain, delays, and other impediments, great exertions were pressed, showing that the troops that had fought from the Rapidan to the James and Petersburg, and then engaged in a siege, now remained sufficiently resilient to mount another offensive drive. In fact, another move spurted on the left flank, resembling the movement Grant had carried out in the campaign of the preceding May and June.

At the same time, many shifts had been made in the corps and division commanders, and two armies were operating together. On the 31st, Sheridan pushed out from Dinwiddie Court House, while Pickett and the Confederates were moving toward Dinwiddie. In the restricted fighting that ensued Sheridan suffered a tactical defeat, and the Confederates drove to a point near the Court House. Pickett asserts that with a half hour of daylight they would have reached Dinwiddie; others declare that Pickett failed to push the drive and presently halted.[40] Grant had decided to extend his lines no farther, but to turn north toward the enemy, believing Southern lines were now thin enough to

35. See also reports of Confederate generals in *Lee Headquarters Papers*, Virginia State Hist. Soc.
36. Munford, Thomas T., "Five Forks," mss. article, Virginia State Hist. Soc.
37. *Ibid.*
38. *O.R.*, I, xlvi, pt. 3, 1363, Lee to Early, March 28, 1865, and Lee to Breckinridge, March 29.
39. *Ibid.*, pt.1, 52-53.
40. *Lee Headquarters Papers*, Virginia Hist. Soc.

permit his general offensive to succeed. Warren, with the Fifth Corps, was impeded by bad roads, darkness, rain, and mud, while an enemy attack had thrown him back severely. Later, Grant and others charged Warren with slowness, faulty alignment and failure to keep his troops together.[41] But now, every assertion relating to Warren is subject to so much controversy that historians conclude their examination with opposite opinions upon him and his actions. Details of the events of these days on the Petersburg front may be left to the specialist, for they require detailed explanations which render full narratives unwieldy.

By the night of March 31, Lee had on his right 10,600 cavalry and infantry to oppose more than 10,000 Union cavalry and as many as 43,000 infantry that could be called upon. On April 1, Lee told Davis, "The movement of Genl. Grant to Dinwiddie Court House seriously threatens our position, and diminishes our ability to maintain our present lines in front of Richmond and Petersburg. . . . It also renders it more difficult to withdraw from our position, cuts us off from the White Oak Road, and gives the enemy an advantageous point on our right and rear. . . ."[42] He feared the South Side and the Danville railroads would be cut, and therefore preparations should be made if it became necessary to evacuate positions on the James. Some critics feel that Lee should have retreated while he still had time, after the failure at Fort Stedman, near Petersburg.[43]

After hearing of the action at Dinwiddie Court House and the withdrawal of Pickett's men to Five Forks, he issued firm orders. To Pickett he wrote, April 1: "Hold Five Forks at all hazards. Protect road to Ford's Depot and prevent Union forces from striking the South-side Railroad. Regret exceedingly your forced withdrawal, and your inability to hold the advantage you had gained."[44]

At about 4 p.m. on April 1, Sheridan's attack, delivered by both cavalry and infantry, came later than he had intended, but through considerable confusion in orders, bridges being out, and difficulties over roads and numerous other impediments, Warren's Fifth Corps had been delayed. After some brief, ill-directed moves, with the cavalry striking on the left toward Five Forks and the infantry on the right, the attack finally succeeded in forcing the Confederates to fall back in confusion.

The Union actions, or lack of them, at Five Forks were no better nor worse than those of many others in battle, and can even be justified by the facts of

41. *O.R.*, I, xlvi, pt. 1, 53-54.
42. *Wartime Papers of R.E. Lee, op.cit.*, 922-923.
43. Livermore, Col. Thomas L., "The Generalship of the Appomattox Campaign," *Military Hist. Soc. of Mass. Papers*, VI, 474.
44. Pickett, La Salle Corbell, *Pickett and His Men*, Philadelphia, 1913, 386.

the situation and the orders Warren received. Grant and others later suggested that Warren's difficulty stemmed from peculiarities of temperament, or defects of personality.[45] At any rate, the sacrifice of one corps commander could not minimize the striking importance of the Union victory at Five Forks, won by both the cavalry and infantry. On April 1, a Union witness wrote: "Sheridan is a tiger, up with the front line always, and in the heat of battle. . . . All of us fought on our own hook. . . . I never saw a fight before where the victory was so well followed up. Indeed, I think I never saw a perfect victory before. . . ."[46]

One cavalry officer, Thomas J. Munford, in his lengthy analysis of Five Forks from the Confederate side, was critical in the extreme of Pickett, Rosser, and Fitzhugh Lee "talking" two miles back of the line of battle. He claimed his 1,200 "carbines" faced 12,000 infantry and 2,000 cavalry. "It was indeed a glorious target. But what could we do? A handful to a houseful! We could do nothing but shoot and run. At their first fire the smoke enveloped them completely and as soon as it drifted so that we could see them advancing again we poured into them our salute of death—then turned and scooted through the woods like a flock of wild turkeys. . . . Shells went shrieking and screeching through the air or dropped with a long, mellifluous *wh-o-o-o-m!* into the tops of the mourning pines. Soon came the great bursting fusilade of Pickett's whole line; then the roar of gallant Pegram's thunderous guns and the crashing of Torbert's ten thousand carbines gave volume to the tumultuous voice of battle. The earth trembled under the shocks of the thundering guns; rolling volumes of sulphurous smoke wreathed the trees in ghostly, trailing garments. The low sun showed faintly through the smoke-clouds like a pale moon and the woods were stifled in their sulphurous draperies. No enemy was in sight, because of the smoke, but the hellish din of war arose on every hand, the deadly balls spat against the boughs or whined like pettish voices above our heads. Occasionally a man crumbled down in his place and a little rivulet of blood trickled away on the ground. . . ."[47] The battle did not last long. In the rough, broken, boggy country, cut up by creeks, and covered with a heavy growth of briars and brambles, the Confederates were breaking up. Finally Pickett came

---

45. An immense secondary and primary literature exists on the Warren case. Among them are: Higginson, T.W., "Five Forks: The Case of General Warren," *Contemporaries,* Boston, 1899, 317-321; Catton, Bruce, "Sheridan at Five Forks," *The Journal of Southern History,* Vol.XXI, No.3, Aug. 1955, reprint; Stern, Philip Van Doren, *An End to Valor,* Boston, 1958, 129-152. The Warren Papers in the N.Y. State Library, Albany, contain countless important documents. Grant, *Memoirs,* II, 213-215, 313, 445. The Sheridan Papers in LC are limited in value due to the destruction by fire of most of his papers. *O.R.,* I, xlvi, pt. 1, has numerous reports pertaining to this.
46. Fowler, William, *Memorials of William Fowler,* New York, 1875, 129-131.
47. Munford, Thomas T., "Five Forks—The Waterloo of the Confederacy," mss., Virginia State Hist. Soc., Richmond.

galloping up. Everything was in confusion among his retreating men and the General had to stave off "utter rout."[48]

Lee told Breckinridge late on April 1 that Pickett's present position was not known, but painted a gloomy picture.[49] On April 2, Lee told Breckinridge, "I see no prospect of doing more than holding our position here till night. I am not certain that I can do that. If I can I shall withdraw to-night north of the Appomattox, and, if possible, it will be better to withdraw the whole line to-night from James River. . . . Our only chance, then, of concentrating our forces, is to do so near Danville railroad, which I shall endeavor to do at once. I advise that all preparation be made for leaving Richmond to-night. . . ."[50] The move to Dinwiddie Court House and the Battle of Five Forks disrupted all the Confederate plans.

Sheridan's pursuit of the Confederates continued well into the evening of April 1, before he took up secure positions. That night from the well-placed Federal guns in the Petersburg siege lines, shells pounded the Confederate trenches and forts, landing within the city itself. Grant had constantly alerted his forces to be ready when the crisis came—and here it was at Five Forks.

Even before the success was fully known, orders had been issued for an attack at 4 A.M. on April 2 by the Sixth, Ninth and Twenty-fourth Federal Corps, clearing the way for the Second Corps. Troops were not sanguine; they had been in the trenches too long, facing abattis, chevaux-de-frise, tangled telegraph wire, stakes driven in the ground at a forty-five degree angle, and other defensive gadgets in front of the formidable Confederate earth works. Enemy guns clearly swept the front, along which attack must come. Curt remarks were common, such as, "Well, good-bye, boys, that means death."[51]

Early morning fog shrouded the land, hiding the slight rises that supported Confederate entrenchments. It took some prodding and urging, and smothered oaths to launch the attack when the signal gun was finally heard. For a time the Federals advanced in the sil ence of the fog until the shots of the enemy pickets rapped out, followed immediately by the rolling surge of full musket fire. Enemy guns roared; but with mighty cheers the Yankees rushed ahead. Formations were lost, a few men shrank from the task, but in the main they rolled ahead. Tearing away the obstacles, leaping over some and smashing into others, the Federals vaulted over one parapet after another, scattering the thinned ranks of Confederate defenders. The Sixth Corps did not even stop there, some plowing on in pursuit of the fleeing Southerners.[52]

48. *Ibid.*
49. *O.R.*, I, xlvi, pt. 1, 1263-1264.
50. *Ibid.*
51. Stevens, Hazard, "The Storming of the Lines of Petersburg," MHSM, VI, 422.
52. *Ibid.*, 423-424.

Grant knew that Lee had now been forced to the breaking point, and that the risk had become materially slighter than it had been only a few days before.[53] Grant kept close control over activities at Petersburg on April 2, making sure that Lincoln was fully informed at City Point. The President in turn wired Stanton in Washington the results as their news reached headquarters. At 11 A.M. Lincoln informed Stanton: "Dispatches frequently coming in. All going fine. Parks, Wright, and Ord, extending from the Appomattox to Hatcher's Run, have all broken through the enemy's intrenched lines. . . ." At 2 P.M. the President relayed Grant's message of 10:45 A.M. to Washington: "Everything has been carried from the left of the Ninth Corps. The Sixth Corps alone captured more than 3,000 prisoners. The Second and Twenty-fourth Corps both captured forts, guns, and prisoners from the enemy. . . . We are now closing the works of the line immediately enveloping Petersburg. All looks remarkably well. . . ."[54]

By 4:30 Grant telegraphed Lincoln: "We are now up, and have a continuous line of troops, and in a few hours will be intrenched from the Appomattox, below Petersburg, to the river above. . . . All seems well with us, and everything quiet just now." Lincoln, grasping the magnitude of the day's operations, sent Grant the following message: "Allow me to tender to you and all with you the nation's grateful thanks for this additional and magnificent success."[55] Grant, however, was not going to be rash at such a time, but ordered a heavy bombardment early on April 3 to be followed by a 6 A.M. assault, "only if there is a good reason for believing the enemy is leaving."[56] But at 8:30 on the morning of April 3, Lincoln telegraphed Stanton: "This morning General Grant reports Petersburg evacuated, and he is confident Richmond also is. He is pushing forward to cut off, if possible, the retreating army. I start to him in a few minutes. . . ."[57]

While the message carried the essential news, the situation was not quite as simple as it seemed to indicate. The Sixth Corps under Wright penetrated the lines *en masse*, on the morning of April 2, as did two Twenty-fourth Corps divisions of Ord's command. Another division of Ord had forced the lines near Hatcher's Run. Ord and Wright moved to the right toward Petersburg to try to hold the enemy in. Parke with the Ninth and Humphreys with the Second moved ahead as well. Parke penetrated the main line but failed to carry the inner defenses. After considerable fighting, Gibbon seized two strong enclosed works, thus shortening the Federal attack line considerably, while other Fed-

53. *O.R.*, I, xlvi, pt. 3, 422.
54. *Ibid.*, 447, 466.
55. *Ibid.*, 447-449.
56. *Ibid.*, 458, Grant to Meade, Apr. 2, 1865, 7:40 P.M.
57. *Ibid.*, 508.

eral troops harassed and harried the broken Confederate units. Grant later learned that Lee had evacuated Petersburg on the night of April 2,[58] being fortunate to have kept the Federals out of town until darkness covered his retreat.[59]

From the news of the defeat at Five Forks onward, it was clear that the only course the Confederates could take was to delay at Petersburg until they could evacuate the city and salvage whatever supplies and guns they could. In one of several messages to the Secretary of War, Breckinridge, Lee wrote on April 2: "It is absolutely necessary that we should abandon our position tonight, or run the risk of being cut off in the morning. . . . It will be a difficult operation, but I hope not impracticable. . . . The troops will all be directed to Amelia Court House."[60] This would not be an orderly, organized withdrawal. Under such heavy Federal pressure, the Confederate units were too widely disposed on the long defense lines to be brought together. Lee recognized this, ordaining that Amelia Court House be the concentration point. It was then that he sent to President Davis a similar message: "I think it is absolutely necessary that we should abandon our position to-night. I have given all the necessary orders on the subject to the troops, and the operation, though difficult, I hope will be performed successfully. I have directed General Stevens to send an officer to Your Excellency to explain the routes to you by which the troops will be moved to Amelia Court House, and furnish you with a guide and any assistance that you may require for yourself."[61] Lee issued rather specific orders to his various commanders regarding routes to Amelia Court House, but in spite of his well-laid plans, the withdrawal did not go as smoothly as expected. As transportation was rapidly falling into chaos, the already long-standing supply problem became steadily worse.[62] In order to secure needed forage, for months Lee had been obliged to separate cavalry and artillery units at points too distant from the lines. In this crisis of supplies, arms orders became confused, or were not properly issued.

Reports of Lee's principal generals, forwarded later to their commander, including many not appearing in the *Official Records*, told the same doleful story of the breakdown of their positions at Petersburg and Richmond.[63]

On the morning of April 3, it was uncertain whether Lee's retreating army,

58. *O.R.*, I, xlvi, pt. 1, Grant's report, 54-55.

59. Meade, George G., *Life and Letters of General Meade*, II, 269, to his wife, Apr. 3.

60. *O.R.*, I, xlvi, pt. 1, 1265.

61. *Ibid.*, pt. 3, 1378.

62. For a good summation, see Vandiver, Frank, "The Food Supply of the Confederate Armies," *Tyler's Quarterly Historical and Genealogical Magazine*, Vol. XXVI, 77ff.

63. Taylor, Walter H., *Four Years with General Lee*, op.cit., 150; Gordon, John B., *Reminiscences of the Civil War*, New York, 1903, 418-419.

which crossed the Appomattox River at Goode's Bridge during the night, or his Union pursuers, would be first to reach the Danville Road. Early on the morning of the 6th, Lee reached Amelia Court House, where he found not a morsel of food, and had to halt and scour the surrounding area for supplies— a fatal delay, for Sheridan's cavalry pushed ahead of him, and reached the railroad at Jetersville, where the Army of the Potomac began to concentrate. The avenue for the retreat of Lee's hungry and exhausted army lay on the narrow line between the Appomattox and James Rivers. When night was falling, the head of Lee's columns reached Appomattox Station, where, as the tired veterans lay down to rest, Custer's cavalry burst like a thunderbolt upon them. The scene was set for the last act in the great drama.[64]

[III]

The strains of "Dixie" echoed from the seven hills of Richmond as marching columns climbed the streets toward the capitol. But, alas, the oncoming troops wore blue, and the regimental band pouring forth the familiar notes preceded a Negro regiment. Cavalry thundered past at a furious gallop. Worn army horses labored up the incline, dragging heavy cannon. Through the smoke of the burning city, men caught glimpses of flaming walls. Now and then they heard the report of repeated explosions. They forced their way through an hysterical crowd of dancing, shouting Negroes, some of whom were busy plundering the rapidly burning shops of ham, shoes, flour, dry-goods, bolts of cloth, chairs, and even sofas. Some of the gratefully exalted freedmen called out "Saviors, our Saviors!" to the Yankee troops. As blue-clad horsemen dashed up to the City Hall, an officer threw open the doors. Above the capitol dome two soldiers had unfurled a tiny flag. One Richmond lady sank to her knees, and, as she wrote later, "the bitter, bitter tears came in a torrent."[65]

The heart of a nation and a people was being deeply torn that April Monday in 1865. The burning of the city and scenes of anguish might have been anticipated for months; perhaps for four years. But, however it might have been foreseen, the surrender was a shock to all. For some days, great events had been occurring, and more were anticipated. Since President Lincoln had arrived in City Point, he had been indulging in the role of military tourist, or observer, combining long postponed vacation hours with a half-anxious, half-

---

64. Dowdey & Manarin, eds., *The Wartime Papers of R.E. Lee*, Boston, 1961, 901.

65. Letters of Mrs. Mary A. Fontaine to Marie Burrows Sayre, Confederate Memorial Literary Society, Richmond; and others felt equally stricken. See Letters of Emmie Sublett (age 13), Confederate Memorial Literary Soc., Richmond.

relieved watch over the death throes of the Confederacy from his *River Queen* headquarters.[66] On March 26, he saw Sheridan's troopers from the Shenandoah cross the James to add dash and strength to the irresistible panoply under Grant, Meade, and Ord, about to hew through Lee's army and advance upon Richmond. That afternoon, he attended a review of Ord's Army of the James, an occasion marked by Mrs. Lincoln's disclosure of open pique over the President's courteous attention to Mrs. Ord—a minor incident that had unfortunate social sequels.

However, national leaders were dealing with serious problems. For two days an earnest conference occupied an able group on the *River Queen*. Lincoln, Grant, and Admiral Porter conferred with Sherman, newly arrived from the Carolinas. Their decisions were expected to influence the future of the nation, but no one can be certain just what was concluded.

Sources are limited on what was said at this conference (unlike Hampton Roads) for we must depend primarily on memoirs, and on Sherman's accounts which may be colored and exaggerated. Much later, Grant was to write carefully in his own *Memoirs* that Sherman "had met Mr. Lincoln at City Point while visiting there to confer with me about our final movement, and knew what Mr. Lincoln had said to the peace commissioners when he met them at Hampton Roads, to wit: that before he could enter into negotiations with them [the Confederate agents] they would have to agree to two points: one being that the Union should be preserved, and the other that slavery should be abolished; and if they were ready to concede these two points, he was almost ready to sign his name to a blank piece of paper and permit them to fill out the balance of the terms upon which we would live together . . ."[67] The subject was to come up a few weeks afterward in the dispute over Johnston's terms of surrender to Sherman, upon which Grant wrote that Sherman doubtless thought he was following the President's wishes. It should be noted, however, that Grant stated Sherman came to the conference primarily to discuss military movements with him.

Lincoln's secretaries also dismissed the President's action as "a hasty trip to confer with Grant."[68] Yet, informal discussions in the cabin of the *River Queen* gave Lincoln, Grant, Sherman, and Porter an opportunity for a frank exchange about the prospects of early and final victory. Porter and Sherman reported that the President expressed some liberal views on the restoration of State governments in the conquered South which did not seem altogether

66. George Merryweather to his parents in England, March 26, 1865, George Merryweather Letters, property of grandson, John Merryweather, now in Chicago Hist. Soc.
67. Grant, *Memoirs, op.cit.,* II, 514-515.
68. Nicolay and Hay, *Abraham Lincoln, op.cit.,* X, 215.

compatible with the guarded language which Lincoln used elsewhere. We may presume that their private opinions sometimes colored their recollections, though we may well believe that he repeated his willingness to be generous to the verge of prudence, and let them understand that he would not be displeased by the escape from the country of Davis and other rebel leaders.[69] After the conference Sherman hurried back to North Carolina, where Schofield had been left in charge.

Sherman modestly assured his father-in-law as March closed: "It is perfectly impossible for me in case of failure to divest myself of responsibility, as all from the President, Secretary-of-War, General Grant, etc. seem to vie with each other in contributing to my success," adding that Ewing need not fear he would commit a political mistake, for he well realized that he would imperil the government by any unwise concessions. He had repelled all political advances made, and would continue to do so.[70] He thought he had "a clear view of another step in the game," a statement as dubious as it was cloudy.[71]

Sherman's *Memoirs* give a full and naturally somewhat defensive account of the meeting with Lincoln. He recalled that he was received by Grant "most heartily" and that they discussed the situation fully. When he went aboard the *River Queen* with Grant, he found the President highly curious about the incidents of the great march, and quick to enjoy its more ludicrous aspects, such as the activities of the bummers, and their eager devices to collect food and forage when many Americans supposed the invaders to be starving. At the same time he expressed anxiety lest some misfortune should befall the army in North Carolina during Sherman's absence. Sherman assured him Schofield could handle anything that came up. Clearly the assemblage on March 27 had its cheerful social moments.

The next day, after talks with Meade and others, Grant, Sherman, and Porter returned to the *River Queen*, where a more discursive conversation was held on such military topics as Federal operations, and Lee's possible activities. Many expected a bloody battle, and Lincoln inquired anxiously if it could not be avoided. "During this interview," relates Sherman, "I inquired of the President if he was all ready for the end of the war. What was to be done with the rebel armies when defeated? And what should be done with the political leaders? . . . He said he was all ready; all he wanted of us was to defeat the opposing armies, and to get the men composing the Confederate armies back to their homes, at work on their farms and in their shops. As to Jeff. Davis, he was hardly at liberty to speak his mind fully, but intimated that he ought to

69. *Ibid.*, X, 215-216.
70. Howe, M.A. DeWolfe, ed., *Home Letters of General Sherman*, New York, 1909, 337-338.
71. *Ibid.*

clear out, 'escape the country,' only it would not do for him to say so openly. . . ."
After Lincoln told an apropos story, Sherman remarked that he ". . . inferred
that Mr. Lincoln wanted Davis to escape, 'unbeknown' to him."

Sherman made no notes, later using those of Admiral Porter, and with
some confusion over the dates. He continued: "Mr. Lincoln was full and frank
in his conversation, assuring me that in his mind he was all ready for the civil
reorganization of affairs at the South as soon as the war was over; and he
distinctly authorized me to assure Governor Vance and the people of North
Carolina that, as soon as the rebel armies laid down their arms, and resumed
their civil pursuits, they would at once be guaranteed all their rights as citizens
of a common country; and that to avoid anarchy the State governments then
in existence, with their civil functionaries, would be recognized by him as the
government *de facto* till Congress could provide others . . . ." Grant does not
mention this, nor does Porter; and Porter has no record of the last vital clause
respecting final Congressional provision as an important part of the utterance
thus somewhat hazily attributed to Lincoln.

Sherman also tells us: "I was more than ever impressed by his kindly
nature, his deep and earnest sympathy with the afflictions of the whole people
resulting from the war. . . . His earnest desire seemed to be to end the war
speedily, without more bloodshed or devastation, and to restore all the men of
both sections to their homes. . . ."[72]

The recollections written by Admiral Porter[73] in 1866, despite their gossipy
and often inaccurate character, may also merit brief quotation. His statement
that Lincoln visited City Point "with the most liberal views toward the rebels,"
partially confirms Sherman's account. He seems less clearly credible when he
writes: "Mr. Lincoln did, in fact, arrange the (so-considered) liberal terms
offered General Jos. Johnston, and, whatever may have been General Sherman's private views, I feel sure that he yielded to the wishes of the President
in every respect. . . ."[74]

In another account, written to Isaac N. Arnold of Chicago, Sherman expressed himself cautiously upon this meeting with Lincoln, and his talk with
him of the experience of the campaign. He also says that General Grant and
himself explained their next moves to Lincoln, though various leaders often
said that Grant never told Lincoln of his plans in advance. Lincoln is said to
have deprecated the probable necessity of one more bloody battle. Of the
second visit Sherman wrote: "I ought not and must not attempt to recall the
words of that conversation. . . . Though I cannot attempt to recall the words

72. Sherman, *Memoirs, op.cit.*, II, 324-328.
73. *Ibid.*, 328-331, written in 1866.
74. *Ibid.*

spoken by any one of the persons present, on that occasion, I know we talked generally about what was to be done when Lee and Johnsons [*sic.*] armies were beaten and dispersed. . . ." Sherman recalls that Lincoln remarked that he hoped there would be no more bloodshed, that the men of the Rebel armies would be disarmed and sent back home, and "that he contemplated no revenge —no harsh measures—but quite the contrary, and trusted that their suffering and hardships in the war would make them now submissive to law—I cannot say that Mr. Lincoln or any body else used this language at the time, but I know I left his presence with the conviction that he had in his mind, or that his cabinet had, some plan of settlement, ready for application the moment Lee and Johnston were defeated. . . ."[75]

The conference of the President and his generals was the last quiet moment in national events. That same day, Lee wrote his daughter: "Genl. Grant is evidently preparing for something. . . ."[76] He was correct in a conjecture that sprang naturally from the expectation (which he had held all spring) of an advance by Grant.

On March 29 Lincoln asked Grant, as he had asked other generals for four years: "How do things look now?" And on the 30th the President told Stanton he felt he should be back in Washington, but disliked to leave without seeing nearer to the end of Grant's movement. Stanton did not object, and Seward came down for a day or two. But most of the time Lincoln was without his official family. By March 31, as the battle news from Petersburg came in, Lincoln seemed depressed, and on April 1 he walked the deck of the *River Queen* most of the night. One of his bodyguards wrote: "I have never seen suffering on the face of any man as was on his that night."[77]

Indeed, the last campaign against the Army of Northern Virginia had begun. For twelve days, as we have seen, Grant extended his lines to the westward, stretching Lee's to the breaking-point and beyond. Union troops moved in rainy weather against Lee's far right, tearing away one of the last mobile forces in the Confederate defenses. On April 2, observers of the Petersburg line watched the Federal masses break the enemy.

Perhaps twenty miles distant from Lincoln, the scene was quite different. In Richmond a congregation quietly gathered in Lee's church to hear the service, a scene that is indelibly imprinted in Civil War history.

Lee had told Breckinridge on April 2 that he despaired of doing more than hold his position at Petersburg until night, and that preparations should be

75. Sherman to Arnold, Nov. 28, 1872, Isaac N. Arnold Papers, Chicago Hist. Soc. Cf. Naroll, Raoul S., "Lincoln and the Sherman Peace Fiasco Another Fable?" *Journal of Southern History*, Vol.XX, No.4, Nov. 1954, 459-483.
76. *Wartime Papers of R.E. Lee, op.cit.,* 919.
77. Lincoln, *Works*, VIII, 376-377; *Lincoln Day by Day*, III, 323-324; Crook, William H., "Lincoln's Last Day," compiled by Margarite S. Gerry, *Harper's Monthly*, Vol. CXV, Sept., 1907, 520.

made to quit the capital. Life in the city during the most recent days had gone on much as before, with the clouds of war ever darker, but not yet oppressive. Southerners were familiar with St. Paul's Episcopal Church, where the Reverend Dr. Charles Minnigerode now lifted his last prayer for the President of the Confederacy.[78] The waiting concourse watched in awed suspense as a messenger from the War Department slipped down the aisle, and the President quietly walked out of the church.

As Davis himself said, "the congregation of St. Paul's was too refined to make a scene at anticipated danger."[79] Hastening to his office, Davis summoned the heads of departments and bureaus, and gave instructions for removing the government. The news spread rapidly and, as Davis proceeded from his office to his house, many personal friends ventured questions. "The affection and confidence of this noble people in the hour of disaster," he declared, "were more distressing to me than complacent and unjust censure would have been. . . ." Mrs. Davis had already left.[80]

One resident later recalled: "The hours I remained in Richmond on that melancholy Sunday, after leaving St. Paul's, were among the saddest of my life. I felt that our cause was the Lost Cause. Many of the scenes . . . were heartrending. The bad news had spread with lightning speed all over town. . . . The men, generally, were on the street, and large numbers of the ladies stood in the doors and on the steps of their houses, many bathed in tears, making inquiries and giving utterance to woeful disappointment and anguish. . . ."[81]

It was a lovely spring Sunday "when delicate silks that look too fine at other times seem just to suit . . ." wrote one woman. "I have never seen a calmer or more peaceful Sabbath morning, and alas! never a more confused evening. . . ."[82] "Then Mr. Davis, oh, so bowed, and anxious, came. When he told us he feared Richmond must be evacuated by midnight, the truth was forced upon us. . . ."[83]

By afternoon of April 2, officials started leaving on the Richmond & Danville Railroad. Sixty midshipmen under Captain William H. Parker escorted what remained of the Confederate treasury.[84]

Secretary Mallory wrote of the final scene in Richmond: "As usual the

---

78. Note the minister's name is often misspelled Minnegerode. St. Paul's and the Richmond Civil War Centennial Committee confirm the correct spelling.

79. Davis, Varina, *Jefferson Davis, a Memoir by His Wife,* New York, 1890, II, 582-584.

80. *Ibid.* For other accounts of the scene in St. Paul's, see Longstreet, *From Manassas to Appomattox,* Philadelphia, 1896, 607, his wife's account; Bruce, H.W., "Some Reminiscences of the Second of April, 1865," Southern Historical Society Papers, IX, No.5, May 1881, 206-207.

81. Bruce, *op.cit.,* 206-207.

82. Letters of Mrs. Mary A. Fontaine to Mrs. Marie Burrows Sayre, Confederate Mem'l. Literary Society, Richmond, Apr. 30, 1865.

83. *Ibid.*

84. Hanna, A.J., *Flight into Oblivion,* Richmond, 1938, contains secondary account of the flight of the Confederate government.

President's face was closely scrutinized as he entered St. Paul's alone . . . but its expression varied not from the cold, stern sadness which four years of harrassing mental labour had stamped upon it. . . . the cold, calm eye, the sunken cheek, the compressed lip, were all . . . impenetrable. . . ." Dull, booming sounds of the distant guns could be heard.[85]

At the President's office, Davis explained to his Cabinet the necessity for evacuation, and each pursued his duties, including the transfer of important papers to the depot. Mallory saw Secretary Benjamin, impeccably dressed and calmly carrying his habitual cigar, walking to his office, and caught sight of Mayor Mayo, spotless in white cravat, ruffles, and waistcoat, busy with plans to protect the people. "The African church had, at an early hour, poured its crowded congregation into the streets; and American citizens of African descent were shaking hands and exchanging congratulations upon all sides. Many passed through the confused streets," writes Mallory, "with eager faces, parted lips, and nervous strides, gazing about for friends and helpers."[86]

The government train finally got under way about 11 P.M. Hundreds sought to leave on it, but only those whose services were essential to the government were allowed, some women excepted. The train moved off "in gloomy silence over the James River," continues Mallory. "A commanding view of the riverfront of the city caught their sad and wistful gaze; and as the last flickering lights died away, many spoke with sad and philosophic frankness upon the hopes, achievements, errors, and tragic final collapse of the Confederate Cause, until all relapsed into silence."[87] But one man retained a sense of cheerful detachment. Even at the end, Benjamin's epicurean philosophy and inexhaustible good humor cropped out in well-informed discussion of other lost causes, and he munched his sandwich and puffed his cigar with unconquerable poise.[88]

Slowed by the bad roadbed, the train did not make the 140 miles to Danville, Virginia, until mid-afternoon April 3. Government operations were reorganized, and continued in Danville until the evening of April 10. No substantial evidence supports the assertions made later that the movement of the official train prevented the collection of supplies at Amelia Court House for Lee's retiring army. Davis denied that he or the president of the railroad, who was with him, knew anything about supply plans.[89]

85. Mallory, S.R., *Diary*, Southern Historical Collection, Univ. of N.C. Library. His story of the last days of the Confederacy is one of the best records, though apparently written sometime afterward.
86. *Ibid.*
87. *Ibid.*
88. *Ibid.*
89. Davis, Jefferson, *op.cit.*, II, 675-676.

A large crowd met the party at the Danville station as the train came in, "and the President was cordially greeted. There was none of the old, wild, Southern enthusiasm, however, and there was that in the cheers which told almost as much of sorrow as of joy. . . ."[90]

Elsewhere the scene was different. One Confederate soldier, moving through the falling city of Richmond, said: "the men, as usual, light-hearted and cheerful round the fire, though an empire was passing away around them. . . ."[91] As they renewed their march, a tremendous explosion took place toward the James, probably a gunboat going up; others followed which "told, in anything but a whisper, the desperate condition of things. . . ." Passing through the Richmond suburb of Rockets, the soldier found a different atmosphere. "The peculiar population of that suburb were gathered on the sidewalk; bold, dirty-looking women, who had evidently not been improved by four years' military association, dirtier-looking (if possible) children, and here and there skulking, scoundrelly looking men, who in the general ruin were sneaking from the holes they had been hiding in. . . ." The rebel soldier continued: "The great crowd, as we soon saw, were . . . pillaging the burning city. . . . The roaring and crackling of the burning houses, the trampling and snorting of our horses over the paved streets . . . wild sounds . . . through the cloud of smoke that hung like a pall around him, made a scene that beggars description. . . . the saddest of many of the sad sights of war—a city undergoing pillage at the hands of its own mob, while the standards of an empire were being taken from its capitol, and the tramp of a victorious enemy could be heard at its gates. . . ."[92]

War refugees, particularly in recent months, had gathered in Richmond, which, it was believed, held about 5,000 deserters. The passage of Confederate troops westward April 3 was hindered by the flames. "As we sat upon our horses on the high hill on which Manchester stood, . . . a suburb south of the James," wrote one observer, "we looked down upon the City of Richmond. By this time the fire appeared to be general. Some magazine or depot for the manufacture of ordnance stores was on fire about the centre of the city; it was marked by the peculiar blackness of smoke; from the middle of it would come the roar of bursting shells and boxes of . . . ammunition. . . . On our right was the navy yard at which were several steamers and gunboats . . . burning in the river, from which the cannon were thundering as the fire reached them. . . ."[93]

90. Mallory, *Diary*, *op.cit.*
91. Boykin, Edward M., *The Falling Flag, Evacuation of Richmond, Retreat, and Surrender at Appomattox*, New York, 1874, 9.
92. *Ibid.*, 11-12.
93. *Ibid.*, 15.

Most of the residents of Ricnmond remained in the city, along with many refugees from Petersburg and nearby towns. General Alexander wrote that on April 3, Irish, Germans, and Negroes—men, women and children—crowded the city, "carrying off bacon, corn, bedding, saddles, harness, and every variety of army stores . . ." Nearly every shop on Main Street was plundered.[94]

A Richmond lady, describing the night of April 2-3, relates: "All through that long, long night we worked and wept, and bade farewell, never thinking of sleep; in the distance we heard the shouts of the soldiers and mob as they ransacked stores; the rumblings of wagons, and beating of drums all mixed in a confused medley. Just before dawn explosions of gunboats and magazines shook the city, and glass was shattered, and new houses crumbled beneath the shocks. Involuntarily I closed the shutters, and then everything had become still as death, while immense fires stretched their arms on high all around me. I shuddered at the dreadful silence. Richmond burning and no alarm. . . . I watched those silent, awful fires; I felt that there was no effort to stop them, but all like myself were watching them, paralyzed and breathless. After a while the sun rose as you may have seen it, a great red ball veiled in a mist."[95]

Among the refugees who did leave Richmond were men in broadcloth—politicians, members of Congress, and prominent citizens, nearly all on foot, but a few in carriages. One observer thought the ladies generally calmer than the men.[96]

Another resident of Richmond was struck by the burning of government offices, all the major newspapers, and other business establishments. Most of the windows were broken in her house and a shell from an exploding ordnance depot entered the library.[97]

The first major fires had been set by order of Confederate authorities, though some officers opposed this needless loss. Mrs. LaSalle Corbell Pickett described the scene as a saturnalia, saying that some law-officers fled from the frenzied mob. Liquor added to the excitement.[98] General Ewell, commanding in Richmond, admitted destroying military stores, but maintained that in many instances the mobs set fire to business and other buildings.[99]

One family feared their large, convenient house would be taken over by the Yankees, but their free colored man, Peter, said: "Don't you be scared, Miss

94. Letter of April 3, 1865, E.P. Alexander Papers, Southern Hist. Coll., Univ. of N.C.
95. Letters of Mrs. Mary A. Fontaine, Confederate Mem'l. Literary Soc., Richmond, April 30, 1865.
96. Blackford, Lieut.-Col. W.W., *War Years With Jeb Stuart*, New York, 1945, 283.
97. *Diary of Miss Lelian M. Cook*, Virginia State Historical Society, Richmond.
98. Johnson, Rossiter, ed., *Campfire and Battlefield*, New York, 1896, containing article by Mrs. LaSalle Corbell Pickett, "The First United States Flag Raised in Richmond after the War," 453-454.
99. *O.R.*, I, xlvi, pt. 1, 1292-1295.

May. I done tell 'em you is a good Union woman." This of course aroused indignation, and the young girls could hardly be restrained from hanging out a Confederate flag.[100]

Thirteen-year-old Emmie Sublett told of Confederate troops passing through the city the night of April 2-3, with friends in the army dropping by to say farewell. The family hid their jewelry, even covering ten gold pieces with green to make them buttons. In the murky red light of the next morning the Yankees came, "and first of all placed the *horrible stars and stripes* (which seemed to be to me so many slashes) over our beloved capitol. O, the horrible wretches! I can't think of a name horrible enough to call them. It makes us fifty times more southern in our feelings to have them here; . . ." But the fiery teenager did admit that the Yankees "have behaved very well indeed. No private property has been touched, and no insults have been offered to any of the citizens. . . ." Emmie noted that the Richmond girls went around the streets coolly, thickly veiled and without noticing the Yankees. "It seems a dreary life for one who is just setting out in life. . . ."[101]

Youthful Emma Mordecai, who lived just outside the city, came in April 4 and wrote that Richmond "could no longer be recognized. Yankee officers on fine horses dashing down Broad St., and the sidewalks thronged with people I never saw before, and negro soldiers, drunk and sober. The Screamersville population looked truly joyous, and seemed to be delighted at the new order of things. . . ." She spoke of general rubble and streets strewn with fragments of paper. To her the city was "desecrated, desolate and defiled."[102]

While it was obvious most of the white population were proudly sensitive, all evidence indicates that the Union forces occupied Richmond in an orderly manner, and without giving offense. One woman reported shortly after the occupation that they could no longer afford to keep Negro servants. "We now see what idle lives they must have led. We love the colored people and shall always love them, yet believe they have kept many families poor. We all prefer German servants. . . ."[103]

Two small Federal cavalry guidons were raised over the Confederate capitol by Major Atherton H. Stevens, Jr., Fourth Massachusetts Volunteer Cavalry, and Lieut. Johnston S. de Peyster of New York raised a larger flag.[104]

General Godfrey Weitzel with troops of the Army of the James promptly

100. Papers of Emmie Crump Lightfoot, Confederate Memorial Literary Society, Richmond.
101. Letter of April 29, 1865, Letters of Emmie Sublett, Confederate Mem'l. Lit. Soc.
102. Letters of Emma Mordecai, Confed. Mem'l. Lit. Soc., Richmond, April 5, 1865.
103. Benetta Valentine to her brother, E.V. Valentine, April 21, 1865, Valentine Family Letters, Valentine Museum, Richmond.
104. Maj.-Gen. G. Weitzel to the Governor of New York, Nov. 5, 1865, *Battles and Leaders*, extra-illustrated ed., HEH; Langdon, Loomis L., "The Stars and Stripes in Richmond," *Century*, May-October, 1890, 308-309.

took charge, extinguishing fires and partially restoring order. However, by April 14, War Clerk Jones thought that Weitzel's rule became "more and more despotic daily. . . ."[105]

The brigade under Edward H. Ripley was ordered to lead the way in for the infantry. "The bands had arranged a succession of Union airs which had not been heard for years in the streets of the Confederate capital," wrote Ripley.[106] He described the "surging mob of Confederate stragglers, negroes, and released convicts" that seemed in full control from the moment Ewell crossed the James, burning bridges behind him. "The air was darkened by the thick tempest of black smoke and cinders which swept the streets, and, as we penetrated deeper into the city, the bands were nearly drowned by the crashing of the falling walls, the roar of the flames, and the terrific explosions of shells in the burning warehouses. Densely packed on either side of the street were thousands upon thousands of blacks, . . . They fell upon their knees, throwing their hands wildly in the air and shouted 'Glory to God! Glory to God! Massa Linkum am here! Massa Linkum am here!' while floods of tears poured down their wild faces. . . ." Ripley's brigade had immediate command of the city. Other troops were cleared out although there was some disorder from the Negro troops. Regiments went to work fighting the fires, primarily by blowing up and pulling down buildings in the flames' path. Prisoners were released, Confederates rounded up, streets were patrolled and order brought from chaos. "This was done well, as even Confederates admitted."[107]

Charles A. Dana arrived shortly to preserve as many Confederate records as he could. He wrote Stanton that, "The malignity of the thorough rebel here is humbled and silenced, but only seems the more intense on that account. . . . there is a great throng of people after victuals. Confederate money is useless and they have no other."[108]

Reporters came in with the troops, for the public at the North was avid for news from this strange capital of rebeldom. One leading journalist wrote: "There were swaying chimneys, tottering walls, streets impassable from piles of brick, stones, and rubbish. Capitol Square was filled with furniture, beds, clothing, crockery, chairs, tables, looking-glasses. Women were weeping, children crying. Men stood speechless, haggard, woebegone, gazing at the desolation. . . ."[109] The capitol several times caught fire from cinders. "If it had not been for the soldiers the whole city would have gone. . . ." Another reported:

105. Jones, *A Rebel War Clerk's Diary*, op.cit., 357.
106. Eisenschiml, Otto, ed., *Vermont General; The Unusual War Experiences of Edward Hastings Ripley, 1862-1865*, New York, 1960, 301.
107. *Ibid.*, 296-306.
108. Dana to Stanton, April 6, 1865, Stanton Papers, LC.
109. Coffin, Charles Carleton, *The Boys of '61*, Boston, 1881, 508.

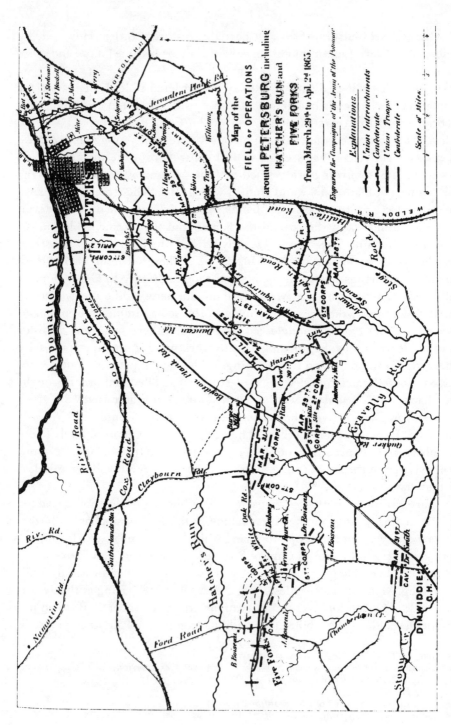

Map of Operations around Petersburg, March 29–April 2, 1865

"This town is the Rebellion; it is all that we have directly striven for; quitting it, the Confederate leaders have quitted their sheet-anchor, their roof-tree, their abiding hope. Its history is the epitome of the whole contest, and to us, shivering our thunderbolts against it for more than four years, Richmond is still a mystery. . . ."[110] However, "no people in their subjugation wear a better front than these brave old spirits, whose lives are not their own. Fire has ravaged their beautiful city, soldiers of the color of their servants guard the crossings and pace the pavement with bayoneted muskets. But gentlemen they are still, in every pace, and inch, and syllable,—such men as we were wont to call brothers and countrymen. . . ."[111]

Another Northern reporter was struck by the number of Negroes abroad and their exultant bearing. Not less than a thousand were promenading the State House grounds which they had never before been allowed to enter. One colored man was heard to exclaim, "We-uns kin go anywhar, jist anywhar we wanter. No passes!" A white citizen reported that three of his former slaves had told him they were a committee to inform him that the twenty-seven he had owned were free, but would continue to work for him on condition that they were *paid in greenbacks!* He took the news hard. Not a Negro in the city, it was reported, had failed to learn that he was free, and to count on the fact.[112]

In Washington there was the expected rejoicing. "Today is one long to be remembered in the annals of our country, for today we have occupied Richmond, the boasted stronghold of rebellion. . . ."[113] A large crowd assembled at the War Department and there were speeches by Stanton, Seward, Vice-President Johnson and others. News came in of rejoicing throughout the country, and on the night of April 3, there was a "grand illumination" all over Washington.[114] The news had come in about 10 A.M., April 3, with newspaper extras being sold throughout the city. "From one end of Pennsylvania Avenue to the other the air seemed to burn with the bright hues of the flag. The sky was shaken by a grand salute of eight hundred guns, fired by order of the Secretary of War—three hundred for Petersburg and five hundred for Richmond. Almost by magic the streets were crowded with hosts of people, talking, laughing, hurrahing, and shouting in the fullness of their joy. Men embraced one another, 'treated' one another, made up old quarrels, renewed old friendships, marched through the streets arm in arm, singing and chatting in that happy sort of abandon which characterizes our people when under the influ-

---

110. Townsend, George Alfred, *Campaigns of a Non-Combatant*, New York, 1866, 330.

111. *Ibid.*, 331.

112. New York *Tribune*, April 10, 1865.

113. Ms. Diary and Journal, David Homer Bates Collection, Stern Collection, Rare Book Room, LC.

114. *Ibid.*

ence of a great and universal happiness. The atmosphere was full of the intoxication of joy. . . ."[115]

Stanton read to the throng Grant's despatch telling of the capture of Richmond, and the fact that the city was burning. The War Secretary asked the
crowd what they could reply. Some shouted "Let her burn!" "Burn it!" "Burn
it!" and another, "Hold Richmond for the Northern mudsills!"[116] In fact,
reporter Noah Brooks, said: "a more liquorish crowd was never seen in Washington than on that night."

In a remarkably few days, the Orange & Alexandria Railroad was opened
and steamers were plying from Washington to Richmond. The Richmond
post-office was opened by Federal authorities almost at once. These were
outward tokens of restoration, though some deep scars of the war would
remain for decades.

On April 2, Lincoln had spent the day inspecting lines and entrenchments.
He also telegraphed to Stanton in Washington, Mrs. Lincoln, and Grant, and
relayed messages from the General-in-Chief.

Monday, April 3, as Lee's disorganized and scattered troops were straggling
toward Amelia Court House, as President Davis was traveling to Danville, and
as Richmond was being occupied, President Lincoln went into Petersburg. He
reviewed the passing troops, and conferred for an hour-and-a-half with Grant
in a house vacated by a fleeing resident,[117] Grant having requested the meeting.
The town was nearly deserted when the general and the President met. The
correspondent of the New York *Tribune*, riding through Union lines at Petersburg on the morning of April 3, found the troops all astir, with knapsacks being
slung, blankets rolled, and every preparation made for an immediate advance.
Some units had occupied the town a few hours earlier, and a general fusillade
was resounding, with bands playing "Hail, Columbia," "Yankee Doodle,"
"Kingdom's Coming," "We'll All Drink Stone Blind," and one striking up
"Old Hundred." Although the enemy had removed his dead and wounded,
many evidences of his heavy casualties were visible. The correspondent saw
one dying Confederate, emaciated, half-clad, and pallid, with a wound in the
side of his head red with clotted gore. Doors were closed and window-blinds
shut in parts of the city not wrecked by the siege. But its whole eastern half
showed how much shot and shell had been poured into it. Chimneys were
smashed, windows splintered, walls toppled, porches knocked to bits, and even
whole buildings obliterated. Before the war, Petersburg had been one of the
neatest, most attractive Southern centers. Now it was an expanse of ruin.[118]

115. Brooks, Noah, *Washington in Lincoln's Time*, New York, 1895, 219.
116. *Ibid.*, 220.
117. Nicolay and Hay, *op.cit.*, X, 216.
118. New York *Tribune*, April 10, 1865.

It was here that Lincoln was said to have congratulated Grant, saying, "Do you know, General, that I have had a sort of sneaking idea for some days that you intended to do something like this?"[119] Grant was anxious that the Eastern armies should get the credit for vanquishing their long-time enemies. He wanted no bickering over the laurels and Lincoln agreed. The General is quoted as saying: "I had a feeling that it would be better to let Lee's old antagonists give his army the final blow and finish up the job. The Western armies have been very successful in their campaigns, and it is due to the Eastern armies to let them vanquish their old enemy single-handed. . . ."[120] Lincoln had informed Stanton of his plans to visit Grant. The Secretary expressed concern for the President's safety. Lincoln then told him of plans to go to Richmond, adding: "I will take care of myself. . . ."[121]

However, the truth is that Lincoln did not seem to take adequate good care of himself in his visits to Richmond on April 4 and 5. On the morning of April 4, the President started up the James on the *River Queen*, escorted by Admiral Porter's flagship, a transport, another small vessel and a tug. But, because of the obstructions in the river, the President went on in the twelve-oared barge of the Admiral. They landed, with no one to meet them, about a block above Libby Prison.

We still may wonder why Lincoln made such a hazardous trip so soon to the former enemy capital. Its propagandist value was no longer important. It is true he held some vital political talks, but was it necessary to go into Richmond to do this? Possibly the President was chiefly curious to see the now lifeless heart of the Confederacy. Perhaps he wished to demonstrate the restoration of a united country in which people could move about freely. His secretaries correctly wrote: "Never in the history of the world did the head of a mighty nation and the conqueror of a great rebellion enter the captured chief city of the insurgents in such humbleness and simplicity."[122]

Up the streets of Richmond the small party of ten armed sailors, a contraband guide, Admiral Porter, three officers and Lincoln, walked toward the capitol. The newly-freed Negroes crowded around, and continual risk was evident. The streets abounded with drunken rebels, liberated Negroes and onlookers. Confusion reigned and fires still blazed.[123]

Lincoln and his escort proceeded to the White House of the Confederacy, now used as General Weitzel's headquarters, which Davis had quitted less than forty-eight hours earlier. In the afternoon, the President took a drive about the

---

119. Grant, *Memoirs*, II, 459-460.
120. Coolidge, Louis A., *Ulysses S. Grant*, 2 vols., Boston, 1924, Vol.I, 193.
121. Lincoln, Works, VIII, *op.cit.*, 384-385.
122. Nicolay and Hay, *op.cit.*, X, 216-218.
123. Penrose, Major Charles B., "Lincoln's Visit to Richmond," *Century*, June, 1890, Vol. XL, No.2, 307.

city. A youthful Confederate girl, who wrote vividly of the fall of the city, stated: "You know Lincoln came to Richmond Tuesday the 4th and was paraded through the streets in a vehicle very much like an ambulance, only a little nicer, but *very common indeed,* attended by a bodyguard of about one hundred horsemen and dashing through the streets like the horses were wild. The 'monkey show' came right by here, but we wouldn't let them see us looking at them, so we ran in the parlor and peeped at them. . . ."[124]

During this first visit to Richmond Lincoln did see, upon his own request, John A. Campbell. Thus, for the third time during the Civil War, the former Associate Justice of the Supreme Court of the United States was to play a prominent, though controversial, part in national affairs. Twice before, as the intermediary between the Confederate commissioners and Seward during the crisis immediately preceding Sumter, and again at Hampton Roads in February, 1865, this highly-respected jurist had been involved. Even though he had been Assistant Secretary of War of the Confederacy, he had not fled Richmond.[125]

At their first meeting in Richmond, Campbell told the President that he was no official spokesman for Confederate leaders, but that obviously the war was over, "and all that remained to be done was to compose the country." Campbell said later: "I spoke to him particularly for Virginia, and urged him to consult and counsel with her public men and her citizens as to the restoration of peace, civil order, and the renewal of her relations as a member of the Union. . . ." Campbell informed Lincoln that prominent men in the state were ready to work for pacification. It must be remembered that at Hampton Road: Campbell had not been adamant in refusing Lincoln's terms for settlement. Of this new meeting he later made a brief record. Campbell declared that ir referring to his remarks on Virginia, Lincoln "answered that my general principles were right; the trouble was how to apply them. . . ." The President wanted another talk with Campbell, and would stay in Richmond overnight.[126]

124. Letters of Emmie Sublett, *op.cit.*

125. As in so many events, controversy surrounds the identity of the men who attended two Lincoln-Campbell conferences, and the question of precisely what was said or meant. The following account is primarily based on Nicolay and Hay, *op.cit.,* X, 219-228; Connor, Henry G., *John Archibald Campbell,* Boston, 1920, 174-182; Letter of John A. Campbell to Horace Greeley, April 26, 1865, unsent, Southern Historical Collection, Univ, of N.C., Campbell-Colston Collection; Campbell, John A., "A View of the Confederacy from the Inside; a Letter from Judge John A. Campbell, July 20, 1865," *Century,* October, 1889, 952; Welles, *Diary,* II, 279; Lincoln, *Collected Works,* VIII, April 5, 1865, 386-387 (to Campbell); Lincoln to Grant, April 6, 1865, 388; Lincoln to Weitzel, April 6, 1865, 389; Lincoln telegram to Weitzel, April 12, 1865, 405; Lincoln to Weitzel, April 12, 405-408; *O.R.,* I, xlvi, pt.3, 655, 656, 657, 724. For worthy secondary accounts, see Randall-Current, *Last Full Measure,* New York, 1955, 346-347, 353-356; Hesseltine, William B., *Lincoln's Plan of Reconstruction,* 137-139.

126. Connor, *op.cit.,* 174-176.

Lincoln spent the night on the *Malvern* in the James; he saw Campbell again the morning of April 5. Again, the details and even the substance of who said what, and what was understood and not understood, is confused and debatable. Campbell and a lawyer, Gustavus Myers, saw the President and Weitzel. The President, now prepared, read and commented on a paper or memorandum. In this, as he had so often done, Lincoln called for restoration of national authority, and promised no retreat by the executive on the slavery question, and no cessation of hostilities short of an end to the war, plus the disbanding of all hostile forces. He stated that other propositions not inconsistent with the major points would be considered by the North. Lincoln said that confiscated property would be returned to the people of a State which should immediately withdraw its troops and halt its support of the rebels. Of course, that did not refer to slaves.[127]

Campbell said he did not believe there would be any opposition to the terms, and further stated: "Mr. Lincoln told me that he had been meditating a plan, but that he had not fixed upon it, and if he adopted it, would write to General Weitzel from City Point. This was to call the Virginia Legislature together, 'the very Legislature which has been sitting up yonder,' pointing to the Capitol, 'to vote the restoration of Virginia to the Union.' He said he had a government in Virginia—the Pierpont Government—but it 'had a very small margin,' and he was not 'disposed to increase it.' " There are many accounts, all of them after the event, as to what Lincoln said, or Campbell thought he said, and the nuances are important, though too lengthy to chronicle here.

Campbell later wrote to Greeley in an unsent letter: "My intercourse with President Lincoln both here and at Hampton Roads impressed me favorably and kindly to him. I believe that he felt a genuine sympathy for the bereavement, destitution, impoverishment, waste, and overturn that war had occasioned at the South. . . . "[128]

Campbell went on that Lincoln, in the conversation regarding the Virginia Legislature, "had expressed his object in desiring them to meet and to vote. . . ." Is this what Lincoln really said? Or did he, in exacting, carefully-chosen words, qualify the rôle of the Virginia Legislature? Certainly, at any rate, it was a departure in policy to suggest making use of the Virginia Legislature in any form.

Back at City Point on April 6, Lincoln wrote Weitzel the well-known statement: "It has been intimated to me that the gentlemen who have acted as the Legislature of Virginia, in support of the rebellion, may . . . now desire

127. Lincoln, *Collected Works*, VIII, 386-387.
128. John A. Campbell to Horace Greeley, April 26, 1865, Campbell-Colston Papers, Southern Historical Collection, Univ. of N.C.

to assemble at Richmond, and take measures to withdraw the Virginia troops, and other support from resistance to the general government. If they attempt it, give them permission and protection, until, if at all, they attempt some action hostile to the United States, in which case you will notify them and give them reasonable time to leave; and at the end of which time, arrest any who may remain. Allow Judge Campbell to see this, but do not make it public. . . ."[129]

Campbell gathered together a group of the legislators in Richmond, along with others, and issued a call for the legislature to meet. Lee surrendered April 9. On April 12, Lincoln wrote Weitzel calling the whole thing off. On April 14, Campbell and R.M.T. Hunter wired for permission to visit Lincoln. Thus, we have the second incident within a few days—the first involving Lincoln and Sherman, the second involving Lincoln and Campbell—in which confusion and misunderstanding abound.

Lincoln may not have placed high expectations upon the Virginia legislature, for the same day that he wrote Weitzel, April 6, he told Grant, "I do not think it very probable that anything will come of this; but I have thought best to notify you, so that if you should see signs, you may understand them. From our recent dispatches it seems that you are pretty effectually withdrawing the Virginia troops from opposition to the government . . ."[130]

In his letter of April 12 to Weitzel, Lincoln seems to take a tortuous dialectical approach in order to end the possibility that the Virginia Legislature would meet. He stated that Campbell "assumes, as appears to me, that I have called the insurgent Legislature of Virginia together, as the rightful Legislature of the State, to settle all differences with the United States. I have done no such thing. I spoke of them not as a Legislature, but as 'the gentlemen who have *acted* as the Legislature of Virginia in support of the rebellion.' I did this on purpose to exclude the assumption that I was recognizing them as a *rightful* body. I dealt with them as men who have power *de facto* to do a specific thing, to wit, 'to withdraw the Virginia troops, and other support from resistance to the General Government,' for which in the paper handed Judge Campbell I promised a specific equivalent, to wit, a remission to the people of the State, except in certain cases, of the confiscation of their property. I meant this and no more. Inasmuch, however, as Judge Campbell misconstrues this, and is still pressing for an armistice, contrary to the explicit statement of the paper I gave him; and particularly as Gen. Grant has since captured the Virginia troops, so that giving a consideration for their withdrawal is no longer applicable, let my letter to you, and the paper to Judge Campbell both be withdrawn or counter-

129. Lincoln, *Collected Works*, VIII, 389.
130. *Ibid.*, VIII, 388.

manded, and he be notified of it. Do not now allow them to assemble; but if any have come, allow them safe return to their homes. . . ."[131]

It may or may not be true that Campbell misconstrued Lincoln's full meaning, and it certainly was true that the surrender at Appomattox had taken the Virginia troops out of the war. But it also appears from his language and action that, after consultation with his Cabinet and its disapproval, Lincoln manoeuvered his course out of what had become an embarrassing situation.

It has long been assumed, and probably with a correct interpretation of the limited evidence available, that the Cabinet on April 11 was unanimous against the proposal of Lincoln to use the Virginia Legislature. Two days later, Welles had a talk with Lincoln in which the President said that as all Cabinet members had taken a view differing from his own, "he concluded he had perhaps made a mistake, and was ready to correct it if he had. . . ."[132] Stanton and Speed were the men most determined against the plan, while Dennison also was quite firm. Lincoln possibly said, as Welles reported, that "Their decisive opposition . . . was annoying him greatly . . ."[133] Welles pointed out to the President that the North had never recognized any of the Confederate "organizations."

Despite some intervals of anxiety, these days at the end of the war constituted a fairly happy interlude in the melancholy life of Lincoln, with plenty of good news, particularly from the military fronts. According to the New York *Tribune* correspondent, he returned to the capital much stronger "in body and soul" than he had left.[134] How could he fail to feel joyful on entering Richmond to behold Negroes, wild with delight, shouting, "Glory to God! Glory! Glory!"

On the other hand, the Campbell meeting had been a disappointment. Lincoln was indignant over accounts of it in the Richmond *Whig*, repeated in the Washington *Chronicle*. A paragraph appeared in Greeley's *Tribune*, on April 10, headed "Peace Rumors," which said: "R.M.T. Hunter and Judge Campbell were the leading spirits in the recent Richmond conference on peace." It added that they had admitted the hopelessness of their cause, the wickedness of a further waste of life in a fruitless struggle for independence, and were primarily anxious that such generous terms should be conceded by the government that continuance of the struggle would be impossible. "This and many other statements are afloat tonight, but beyond the fact that the President has returned with the deliberate purpose of issuing some sort of an address to the common masses of the South, all is sheer conjecture." Yet

131. *Ibid.*, VIII, 406-407.
132. Welles, *Diary, op.cit.*, II, 279-280.
133. Welles, Gideon, Typed Mss. of article, "Lincoln and Reconstruction," John Hay Library, Brown University.
134. New York *Tribune*, April 10, 1865.

Greeley, one of the foremost advocates of what he termed "magnanimity in victory," continued hopeful. On his editorial page of April 11, he declared: "We had hoped to print herewith the President's proclamation of amnesty and oblivion to the partisans of the baffled rebellion, and we do not yet despair of receiving it before we go to press." He went on to present a forcible argument against the indulgence of passion, and in behalf of a prompt restoration of the Union. In an editorial April 14 he wrote: "We entreat the President promptly to do and dare in the cause of magnanimity! The Southern mind is now open to kindness, and may be majestically affected by generosity." Thus, Lincoln's meeting with Campbell aroused the hopes of those who advocated generosity toward the South.

At 11 P.M. on April 8, the Lincoln party had left City Point for Washington. He had heard late on the 5th, after returning from Richmond, that Secretary Seward had fallen from his carriage and had suffered serious injuries. Mrs. Lincoln, Senator Sumner and others had come down from Washington for a visit to Richmond. Haunting the headquarters offices, Lincoln was keeping as close touch as possible on the progress of the Union armies as they sought to bring Lee to bay. He was intensely interested in the skirmishing near Amelia Court House, Sheridan's movements to cut Lee off from North Carolina, the engagement at Sayler's Creek April 6, and, of course, the question of how soon and in what way the war in Virginia would end.

On the 7th, Lincoln sent his well-known telegram to Grant: "Gen. Sheridan says 'If the thing is pressed I think that Lee will surrender.' Let the *thing* be pressed."[135]

Concerned over Seward's condition, Lincoln then turned back for the capitol and should have been content in knowing that his generals were pressing the "thing", indeed.

[IV]

"We have Lee's army pressed hard, his men scattering and going to their homes by thousands. He is endeavoring to reach Danville, where Jeff Davis and his Cabinet have gone. I shall press the pursuit to the end. Push Johnson [sic] at the same time and let us finish up this job at once." Thus, Grant wrote Sherman from Burkeville, Va., April 6, 1865.[136] Grant had been pressing since May of the previous year, and he was not about to stop.[137]

Now, however, had come the time to combine personal messages to Lee

---

135. Lincoln, *Collected Works*, VIII, 392.
136. *The History of America in Documents*, Rosenbach Company Catalogue, 1951, pt.1, 69-70.
137. For military events of the campaign from Richmond to Appomattox, see Chap.IX.

along with the use of military force against him. Appraising the losses to Lee's army at Sayler's Creek, in other fighting and in general attrition, Grant believed the situation of the Army of Northern Virginia utterly hopeless, and on April 7, opened correspondence with the Confederate general. From Farmville he wrote Lee that he regarded it his duty "to shift from myself the responsibility of any further effusion of blood, by asking of you the surrender of that portion of the C. S. Army known as the Army of Northern Virginia. . . ."[138]

Lee, in the field, read the communiqué, handed it to Longstreet, who read it and returned it, saying, "Not yet."[139] Lee formally replied to Grant: "Though not entertaining the opinion you express on the hopelessness of further resistance on the part of the Army of Northern Virginia, I reciprocate your desire to avoid useless effusion of blood, and therefore, before considering your proposition, ask the terms you will offer, on condition of its surrender. . . ."[140]

Grant had already received Lincoln's instructions of March 3 not to treat of anything but surrender, even if his tendency had been otherwise. He, therefore, sent Lee a firm and careful response on April 8 from Farmville: "I would say that, peace being my great desire, there is but one condition I would insist upon, namely that the men and officers surrendered shall be disqualified for taking up arms again against the Government of the United States until properly exchanged. . . ." He reiterated that any meeting would be for surrender. About midnight the same day, Grant received the reply, also carefully worded. Lee did not think the emergency was great enough for surrender, but he was interested in "restoration of peace." For this purpose he would be glad to talk with Grant.[141]

The verbal sparring of the two military leaders was worthy of diplomatic usage. Grant, on the morning of April 9, as his army nearly ringed Appomattox Court House, replied that he had no authority to treat on the subject of peace, but that he and the entire North desired peace. "By the South laying down their arms they will hasten that most desirable event, save thousands of human lives, and hundreds of millions of property not yet destroyed. . . ."[142]

After the war, Grant declared that "I saw clearly, especially after Sheridan had cut off the escape to Danville, that Lee must surrender or break and run into the mountains—break in all directions and leave us a dozen guerrilla bands to fight. My campaign was not Richmond, not the defeat of Lee in actual

138. *O.R.*, I, xlvi, pt.1, 56.
139. Longstreet, James, *From Manassas to Appomattox*, Philadelphia, 1896, 619.
140. *O.R.*, I, xlvi, pt.1, 56.
141. *Ibid.*, 56-57.
142. *Ibid.*

fight, but to remove him and his army out of the contest, and if possible, to have him use his influence in inducing the surrender of Johnston and the other isolated armies. . . ."[143]

Grant's staff secretary, Badeau, wrote a friend that, after the assault at Petersburg, "there was no pause, no hesitancy, no doubt what to do. He commanded Lee's army as much as he did ours; caused and knew beforehand every movement that Lee made, up to the actual surrender. . . . There was no let up; fighting and marching, and negotiating all at once. This accounts for the change in Lee's views; at the beginning of the correspondence you remember, he said he didn't agree with Grant that a surrender was inevitable, and he didn't think so till the very morning it occurred."[144]

The night of April 8 from Appomattox General Pickett wrote his wife: "It is finished. Oh, my beloved division! Thousands of them have gone to their eternal home, having given up their lives for the cause they knew to be just. The others, alas, heart-broken, crushed in spirit, are left to mourn its loss. Well, it is practically all over now. We have poured out our blood, and suffered untold hardships and privations, all in vain. And now, well—I must not forget, either, that God reigns. . . ."[145]

Learning of the condition of his army and the Union positions on the morning of April 9 in the Appomattox area, Lee requested a suspension of hostilities until terms of surrender could be arranged.[146] Later, Lee wrote Davis that "The apprehensions I expressed during the winter, of the moral condition of the Army of Northern Virginia, have been realized. . . ."[147] The disintegration of the rebel army had reached such a point that, on the 9th, Lee had only 7,892 effective infantry, and how truly effective even these were is dubious.

Many accounts exist of the last days of Lee's army and of what the General did and said.[148] A staff officer close to Lee related that on the morning of April 9 the General asked him, "Well, Colonel, what are we to do?" The officer replied that if they could abandon the trains, the army might escape. "Yes," said the General, "perhaps we could; but I have had a conference with these gentlemen around me, and they agree that the time has come for capitulation."

---

143. "Grant as a Critic," New York *Herald*, July 24, 1878, interview with Grant by John Russell Young.

144. Adam Badeau to James H. Wilson, May 27, 1865, J.H. Wilson Papers, LC.

145. Pickett, George E., *Soldier of the South: General Pickett's War Letters to His Wife*, ed. Arthur Inman, Boston, 1928, 128-133, letter of April 8, 1865.

146. *O.R.*, I, xlvi, pt.i, 1266, Lee's report; Ibid., 57, Grant's report.

147. Lee to Davis, April 20, 1865, *Wartime Papers of R.E. Lee*, 938-939.

148. Freeman, D.S., *R.E. Lee*, New York, 1935, IV, *passim*, for details and analysis.

"Well, sir," said the officer, "I can only speak for myself; to me any other fact is preferable. . . ." "Such is my individual way of thinking," interrupted the General. "But," added the officer, "of course, General, it is different with you. You have to think of these brave men and decide not only for yourself but for them." "Yes," he replied; "it would be useless and therefore cruel to provoke the further effusion of blood, and I have arranged to meet General Grant with a view to surrender, and wish you to accompany me."[149]

That morning of April 9, Lee was described "as calm and cool as at any time since he took command of the army, just as if the army was to pass in review before him. His face denoted great self-command and his dignity was conspicuously grand. He spoke out in his usual tone of voice, nor did it portray in the slightest the fierce conflict going on within. . . ."[150] The same soldier depicted Lee as clad in his best and newest uniform, with elegant cavalry boots, gold spurs, shining sword and accoutrements.

As for the army, another officer described the men as gathering as usual, on clear, cool, fresh mornings, around fires for breakfast. Noises from the distance of the approaching enemy seemed not to bother them. The responsibility lay with the officers.[151]

The final council-of-war held the night of the 8th, with what top officers were left, had come to the only conclusion possible. The absence of so many familiar names and faces was proof of the exhaustion of the Army of Northern Virginia. The discussion included the fate of the Southern people after surrender. There in the woods around the small fire, some spoke of the possibility of forcing a way through Grant's lines and saving a fragment of the army which would continue "a desultory warfare until the government at Washington should grow weary and grant to our people peace, and the safeguards of local self-government. . . ." But that was just chatter. As General Gordon later wrote: "If all that was said and felt at that meeting could be given, it would make a volume of measureless pathos. In no hour of the great war did General Lee's masterful characteristics appear to me so conspicuous as they did in that last council. . . ."[152] The conference did decide that they might attempt on the 9th to break through the Federals and ultimately join Joseph E. Johnston in North Carolina, but this was a forlorn hope and came to naught. General Gordon had a staff officer ask Lee where he should camp, to which Lee replied, "Yes, tell General Gordon that I should be glad for him to halt just beyond

149. Taylor, Walter H., *Four Years with General Lee*, New York, 1877, 151-152.
150. Transcript narrative of J.H. Sharp, 13th Virginia Artillery Battalion, Henry T. Sharp Papers, Southern Hist. Collection, Univ. of N.C.
151. Boykin, Edward M., *The Falling Flag*, 55-56.
152. Gordon, John B., *Reminiscences of the Civil War*, New York, 1904, 433-436.

the Tennessee line." Of course, that was 200 miles away, so Lee had had his grim joke.[153]

As General Grant's messenger was seen bringing news of the arrangement for the surrender, Longstreet is quoted by Gen. E.P. Alexander as saying to Lee: "General, unless he offers us honorable terms, come back and let us fight it out."[154] Alexander, admittedly overwrought, wanted to attempt to break out. He reported that Lee answered: "I appreciate that the surrender of this army is, indeed, the end of the Confederacy. But that result is now inevitable, and must be faced. And, as Christian men, we have no right to choose a course from pride or personal feelings. We have simply to see what we can do best for our country and people. Now, if I should adopt your suggestion and order this army to disperse, the men going homeward would be under no control, and moreover, would be without food. They are already demoralized by four years of war, and would supply their wants by violence and plunder. They would soon become little better than bands of robbers. A state of society would result, throughout the South, from which it would require years to recover. The enemy's cavalry, too, would pursue to catch at least the general officers, and would harass and devastate sections that otherwise they will never visit. Moreover, as to myself, I am too old to go to bushwhacking, and even if it were right to order the army to disperse, the only course for me to pursue would be to surrender myself to General Grant. . . ."[155]

The scene at the house of Wilbur McLean in Appomattox Court House on April 9, 1865, has been depicted many times in words, and often, though less accurately, in paintings, on the screen, and by television. No matter how familiar the scene, it will always conjure in the minds of millions of Americans historic memories and profound reflections. It will always inspire the imaginations of these millions to recreate a vivid vision of the impeccable Lee in his new uniform and the somewhat shoddy figure of Grant, who had been suffering from a severe headache for several days, and who looked half-sick in his shabby, field-worn private's uniform.

Many were to describe the physical and moral statuesqueness with which Lee loomed through these stormy hours. George Cary Eggleston wrote of the General at Amelia Court House as bearing a "heart-broken expression" on his face, and with "still sadder tones of voice."[156] "Lee's carriage no longer is erect; the troubles of those last days had already plowed great furrows in his forehead. His eyes were red as if with weeping; his cheeks sunken and haggard;

153. *Ibid.*, 436.
154. Alexander, E.P., *Military Memoirs of a Confederate*, New York, 1907, 609.
155. Alexander, E.P., "Lee at Appomattox," *Century*, April, 1902, 921-926.
156. Eggleston, George Cary, *A Rebel's Recollections*, with Introduction by David Donald, Bloomington, Ind., 1959, 130.

his face colorless. No one who looked upon him then, as he stood there in full view of the disastrous end, can ever forget the intense agony written upon his features. And yet he was calm, self-possessed, and deliberate. Failure and the sufferings of his men grieved him sorely, but they could not daunt him, and his moral greatness was never more manifest than during those last terrible days. . . ."[157]

It is well remembered that Grant and Lee chatted for a while, probably a bit awkwardly, about the weather, their Mexican War experiences, and several minor matters. Finally, Lee brought up the subject of their meeting. Grant wrote out the terms on field paper, on a little knobbed-legged table. Presently, Lee, sitting at the side of the room at a marble-topped table, rose and went over to read Grant's paper, which was addressed to General Lee:

"In accordance with the substance of my letter to you of the 8th instant, I propose to receive the surrender of the Army of Northern Virginia on the following terms, to wit: Rolls of all the officers and men to be made in duplicate, one copy to be given to an officer to be designated by me, the other to be retained by such officer or officers as you may designate. The officers to give their individual paroles not to take up arms against the Government of the United States until properly exchanged; and each company or regimental commander sign a like parole for the men of their commands. The arms, artillery, and public property to be parked and stacked, and turned over to the officers appointed by me to receive them. This will not embrace the side-arms of the officers, nor their private horses or baggage. This done, each officer and man will be allowed to return to his home, not to be disturbed by U. S. authority so long as they observe their paroles and the laws in force where they may reside. . . ." Lee accepted in writing.[158]

It all sounded so simple—just surrender and few details. Lee seemed satisfied with the terms that officers were to retain side arms and baggage. Turning to Grant, he explained that Confederate cavalrymen owned their own horses, which would be needed for plowing and planting, to which Grant replied that he would give orders to allow every man who claimed to own his horse or mule to take the animal with him. This was not put into the final terms, but Grant did carry out his word. During the copying of the documents,

---

157. *Ibid.*, 130-131.
158. *O.R.*, I, xlvi, pt.1, 57-58. Many and repetitious are the accounts of the scene of Lee's surrender. Among the more important original accounts are: Marshall, Charles, *An Aide-de-Camp of Lee*, ed., Sir Frederick Maurice, Boston, 1927, 268-275; Adam Badeau to Wilson, May 27, 1865 (typescript), J.B. Wilson Papers, LC; Pamphlet, "General Ely S. Parker's Narrative of Appomattox," Benjamin Harrison Papers, LC; "Lee's Surrender," endorsed by Grant as being accurate, Orville E. Babcock Papers, Chicago Hist. Soc.; "Grant as Critic," New York *Herald*, July 24, 1878; Grant, *Memoirs*, II, 483-496. For excellent secondary sources, see Freeman, *Lee*, IV, 117-148; Stern, Philip Van Doren, *An End to Valor*, Boston, 1958, 257-270; Catton, Bruce, *Grant Takes Command*, Boston, 1968, 404ff.

he arranged for supplying Lee with 25,000 rations. Grant signed his letter to Lee, stating the terms, and Lee signed a letter of acceptance to Grant. Thus, simply and briefly, without emotion or display, the war was ended.

General Lee, no longer in command of the Army of Northern Virginia or the remaining scattered remnants of other Confederate armies, stepped into the front yard of the McLean House. Union officers saluted by raising the hat; Lee returned the salute in like manner. Then, looking into the distance toward the encamped Confederates, he "smote the palms of his hands together three times, his arms extended to their full length. . . ."[159]

General Grant rode away toward his headquarters. Staff Officer Horace Porter asked the General if he did not think he should notify Washington of what had taken place. Grant exclaimed that he had forgotten it momentarily, and asking for note-paper, he wrote out a telegram while sitting on a roadside stone.[160]

As one Confederate artilleryman noted, many pathetic incidents occurred. Some men were crying, overcome by grief over the crushing defeat and their dread uncertainties, whether they should return home or try to join the effort to reach Johnston.[161] Others ran down the hillsides, wildly cheering, to express their relief.[162] Breaking ranks, many tearfully bade Lee goodbye.[163]

Staff-Officer Walter Taylor writes that no description could do the scene justice, as Lee returned to his army. "Cheeks bronzed by exposure in many campaigns, and withal begrimed with powder and dust, now blanched with deep emotion and suffered the silent tear; tongues that had so often carried dismay to the hearts of the enemy in that indescribable cheer which accompanied the charge, or that had so often made the air to resound with the paean of victory, refused utterance now; brave hearts failed that had never quailed in the presence of an enemy; but the firm and silent pressure of the hand told most eloquently of souls filled with admiration, love, and tender sympathy, for their beloved chief."[164]

One officer was seen to break his sword over his knee, others to rip their insignia from their collars.[165] "Men, we have fought through the war together;

159. Merritt, Maj.-Gen. Wesley, "Note on the Surrender of Lee," *Century*, April, 1902, 944.

160. Badeau, Adam, Letter to the Editors of Century Magazine, Sept. 2, 1885, Western Reserve Hist. Soc., Cleveland; Grant notebook with letter of W.D. Thomas, June 5, 1902, Rosenbach Foundation, Philadelphia.

161. Reminiscences of George W. Shreve, Virginia State Library, Richmond.

162. Boykin, *The Falling Flag, op.cit.*, 63.

163. Stinson, Thomas A., "War Reminiscences from 1862 to 1865," in *The War of the Sixties*, compiled by E.R. Hutchins, New York, 1912, 341.

164. Taylor, Walter, *Four Years . . .* , *op.cit.*, 153.

165. A Private, *Reminiscences of Lee and Gordon at Appomattox Courthouse*, Southern Hist. Soc. Papers, Vol.VIII, No.1, January 1880, 38-39.

I have done my best for you; my heart is too full to say more," Lee told Gordon's men.[166]

Federal soldiers, for the most part, treated the Confederates considerately. "Success had made them good-natured," said one Southerner. "Those we came in contact with were soldiers—fighting men—and, as is always the case, such appreciate their position and are too proud to bear themselves in any other way. . . . The effect of such conduct upon our men was of the best kind; the unexpected consideration shown by the officers and men of the United States army toward us; the heartiness with which a Yankee soldier would come up to a Confederate officer and say, 'We have been fighting one another for four years; give me a Confederate five dollar bill to remember you by,' had nothing in it offensive. . . ."[167] General Alexander wrote later, "In common with all of Grant's army, the officers and soldiers of our escort and company treated the paroled Confederates with a marked kindness which indicated a universal desire to replace our former hostility with special friendships. . . ."[168] Another soldier testified that the Union troops were very friendly, "in fact almost oppressively so. . . ."[169]

A Union veteran from the West drew the final scene in memorable paragraphs:

"Out of the dark pine woods, down the rock-strewn road, like a regiment of whirlwinds they come; Meade, bareheaded, leading them, his grave scholarly face flushed with radiance, both arms in the air and shouting with all his voice: 'It's all over, boys! Lee's surrendered! It's all over now! . . .' The men listen for a moment to the words of their leaders, and then up to the heavens goes such a shout as none of them will ever hear again. . . . The air is black with hats and boots, coats, knapsacks, shirts and cartridge-boxes, blankets and shelter tents, canteens and haver-sacks. They fall on each others' necks and laugh and cry by turns. Huge, lumbering, bearded men embrace and kiss like schoolgirls, then dance and sing and shout, stand on their heads and play at leapfrog with each other. . . . The standard bearers bring their war-worn colors to the center of the mass and unfurl their tattered beauties amid the redoubled shouts of the maddened crowd. The bands and drum corps seek the same center, and not a stone's throw apart, each for itself, a dozen bands and a hundred drums make discordant concert. . . . All the time from the hills around the deep-mouthed cannon give their harmless thunders, and at each hollow boom the vast concourse rings out its joy anew that murderous shot and shell

166. Lee, Fitzhugh, *General Lee*, New York, 1894, 377.
167. Boykin, *The Falling Flag . .* , *op.cit.*, 65.
168. Alexander, *Military Memoirs*, *op.cit.*, 614.
169. Haskell, John, *The Haskell Memoirs*, ed. Gilbert Govan and James W. Livingood, New York, 1960, 100.

no longer follow close the accustomed sound. But soon from the edges of the surging mass, here and there, with bowed heads and downcast eyes men walk slowly to the neighboring woods. Some sit down among the spreading roots and, with their heads buried in their hands, drink in the full cup of joy till their whole being feels the subtle influence of the sweet intoxication. Others in due and ancient form, on bended knees, breathe forth their gratitude and praise, while others still lie stretched among the little pines, and cry and sob and moan because their natures cannot contain the crowding joy. . . . For a brief moment, now and then, the clamor rounds itself into the grand swelling strains of 'Old Hundredth,' 'The Star-Spangled Banner' or 'Marching Along.' And the waving banners keep time to the solemn movement. . . ."[170]

In Chattanooga an artilleryman, destined to become one of the most eloquent church leaders of Chicago, recorded in his diary how he heard the news from a telegraph bulletin. Two hundred guns fired in rapid succession. There were the huzzahs of troops. "How the thought of peace and tranquility throbs in each soldier's breast when he thinks of the home and associates he left so reluctantly to follow the path of duty, soon to be restored to him. No wonder his spirits should be exuberant, aye, even intoxicated with delight. . . ."[171]

On Monday, April 10, Grant and Lee met again. Lee's aide relates that Grant wanted Lee to go and meet President Lincoln. He quotes Grant as saying, "If you and Mr. Lincoln will agree upon terms, your influence in the South will make the Southern people accept what you accept, and Mr. Lincoln's influence in the North will make reasonable people of the North accept what he accepts, and all my influence will be added to Mr. Lincoln's." Lee was apparently pleased, but said that as a Confederate soldier he could not meet Lincoln. He did not know what President Davis was going to do, so could not make terms.[172]

At this meeting, Lee held a friendly conversation with Meade and others. He told Meade that the years were telling on him, to which Meade replied: "Not years, but General Lee himself has made me gray."[173]

Meanwhile, Lee's aide, Charles Marshall, was composing the General Orders, No. 9. This, Lee's farewell to his men, was brief, stating that they had been compelled to yield. "You will take with you the satisfaction that proceeds from the consciousness of duty faithfully performed; and I earnestly pray that

170. Lee, Major Henry, "The Last Campaign of the Army of the Potomac from a Mud-Crusher's Point of View," California Commander Mollus, War Paper No.10, San Francisco, 1893, 8-10.
171. Jones, Jenkin Lloyd, *An Artilleryman's Diary*, Wisconsin History Commission, Madison, Wis., 1914, 321.
172. Marshall, *An Aide-de-Camp of Lee, op.cit.*, 274-275.
173. Gordon, *Reminiscences . . . , op.cit.*, 443.

a merciful God will extend to you his blessing and protection. With an increasing admiration of your constancy and devotion to your country, and a grateful remembrance of your kind and generous considerations for myself, I bid you all an affectionate farewell."[174]

On the morning of April 12 came the stacking of arms and colors. Rarely has there been such a scene! "Great memories arose," wrote Joshua L. Chamberlain, a Maine veteran. "Great thoughts went forward. We formed along the principal street . . . to face the last line of battle, and receive the last remnant of the arms and colors of that great army which ours had been created to confront for all that death can do for life. We were remnants also: Massachusetts, Maine, Michigan, Maryland, Pennsylvania, New York; veterans, and replaced veterans, cut to pieces, cut down, consolidated, divisions into brigades, regiments into one. . . ."[175]

General Gordon gathered the pitiful remains of his command, "wholly unfit for duty." "As my command, in worn-out shoes and ragged uniforms, but with proud mien, moved to the designated point to stack their arms and surrender their cherished battle-flags, they challenged the admiration of the brave victors." Gordon relates that the Union troops marshalled in line to salute their late foes, and that "when the proud and sensitive sons of Dixie came to a full realization of the truth, that the Confederacy was overthrown and their leader had been compelled to surrender his once invincible army, they could no longer control their emotions, and tears ran like water down their shrunken faces. The flags which they still carried were objects of undisguised affection. . . . Yielding to overpowering sentiment, these high-mettled men began to tear the flags from the staffs and hide them in their bosoms, as they wet them with burning tears . . . some of the Confederates . . . so depressed, so fearful as to the policy to be adopted by the civil authorities at Washington, that the future seemed to them shrouded in gloom. They knew that burnt homes, . . . poverty and ashes, would greet them on their return from the war. . . ."[176]

General Chamberlain, who ordered the final salute to the Confederates, wrote later that the moment affected him deeply. "Before us in proud humiliation stood the embodiment of manhood; men whom neither toils and sufferings, nor the fact of death, nor disaster, nor hopelessness could bend from their resolve; standing before us now, thin, worn, and famished, but erect and with eyes looking level into ours, waking memories that bound us together as no

174. Marshall, *An Aide-de-Camp of Lee, op.cit.*, 275-278; *O.R.* I, xlvi, pt. 1, 1267.
175. Chamberlain, Joshua L., *The Passing of the Armies*, New York, 1918, 258.
176. *Ibid.*, 447-448.

other bond . . . was not such manhood to be welcomed back into a Union so tested and assured?"[177]

"What visions thronged as we looked into each other's eyes! Here pass the men of Antietam, the Bloody Lane, the Sunken Road, the Cornfield, the Burnside Bridge. . . . The men who left six thousand companions around the bases of Culp's and Cemetery Hills at Gettysburg; the survivors of the terrible Wilderness, the Bloody Angle at Spotsylvania, the slaughter-pen of Cold Harbor, the whirlpool of Bethesda Church! . . . Here are the men of McGowan, Hunton, and Scales, who broke the Fifth Corps lines on the White Oak Road, and were so desperately driven back on that forlorn night of March 31st by my thrice-decimated brigade. . . ."

Lincoln spent the whole of April 9 aboard the *River Queen.* As the vessel steamed up the Potomac, the President diverted himself by reading, chiefly from Shakespeare, and by conversation on literary subjects. Some of his companions long remembered the feeling with which he recited the immortal lines from *Macbeth:*

> Duncan is in his grave;
> After life's fitful fever he sleeps well;
> Treason has done his worst: nor steel, nor poison,
> Malice domestic, foreign levy, nothing,
> Can touch him further.

He seemed in excellent health, though tired, with an outlook both philosophic and cheerful.[178] Passing Mount Vernon as the *River Queen* neared Washington, the President, probably inspired by a companion's remark, mused, "Springfield! How happy, four years hence, will I be to return there in peace and tranquility!"[179] Upon arrival in Washington, he visited the injured Secretary Seward, and received the news from Appomattox. Crowds in front of the White House called for Lincoln, and he briefly responded.

On the rainy morning of April 10, 1865, great booming noises shook the city, breaking windows in Lafayette Square. Five hundred guns fired in all. Quickly the crowds, as on a few days before when Richmond fell, formed again. Actually, a few newsmen and others up late had already heard the news, and sent it over the wires to the nation. The enthusiasm was not quite as great over the news from Appomattox as that of Richmond. Perhaps the mud dampened things, but slowly the implications of what had happened grew on the people.

177. Chamberlain, *op.cit.,* 260-261.
178. Chambrun, Marquis de, "Personal Recollections of Mr. Lincoln," *Scribner's,* XIII, No.1, January 1913, 34-35.
179. *Ibid.*

The Federal departments had the day off. Treasury employees gathered in the hall of their building singing "Old Hundredth" before marching across to the White House to serenade the breakfasting President with the "Star Spangled Banner." Impromptu processions sprang up everywhere, the whole converging on the White House, where the President, serenaded repeatedly, responded with brief sentences. When one of the larger processions appeared, young Tad Lincoln was seen waving a captured flag from a White House window. At this point, the President spoke briefly and promised them remarks at more length the next day, then asking the band to play that "captured" tune —"Dixie."[180]

Across the land the rejoicing was the same everywhere. In Chicago the people manifested a characteristic exuberance. On the stroke of midnight, one hundred guns were fired by the Dearborn Light Artillery, their echoes arousing the sleepers who had not left their beds at the stroke of the bell. Throughout the night the popular jubilation reigned unchecked, bonfires burned brightly, and cheers and laughter rose higher. At early dawn the streets were still crowded, and grew fuller and more joyously animated as the day wore on, with people giving no thought to business or meals in their abandonment to relief and exultation. Thousands of guns were fired, and a huge surge of fireworks poured upward in broad daylight, the more splendid pyrotechnical displays being reserved for evening. The people realized that the "four years of failure" had at last closed triumphantly, and felt that the menacing coils and fangs of the secession serpent had been crushed into dust. Thus the Chicago *Tribune*, on April 11, 1865, so often uncertain in the past but now so completely exultant, proclaimed.

New York diarist George Templeton Strong was aroused by the ringing of his doorbell on the night of April 9. A friend gave him the glad tidings of Appomattox. Unable to hold his hand steady, with wet eyes, he wrote the epitaph of the Army of Northern Virginia. "There is no such army any more. God be praised!" A hard rain dampened the celebration, but the guns kept firing all day.[181]

For at least three days after April 9, Washington was said to be "a little delirious," as it really had been since the fall of Richmond. Everyone celebrated and "The kind of celebration depended on the kind of person. . . ."[182]

Richmond, on Sunday night, heard volley after volley of artillery, as Federal troops celebrated the surrender of Lee. Emma Mordecai pathetically re-

180. Lincoln, *Works*, VIII, 393-394; Brooks, *Washington in Lincoln's Time, op.cit.*, 222-224.
181. Strong, George Templeton, *Diary of the Civil War*, ed. Allan Nevins, New York, 1962, 578-579.
182. Crook, William H., "Lincoln's Last Day," compiled and written down by Margaret Spalding Gerry, *Harper's Monthly*, Vol. CXV, Sept. 1907, 525.

corded that, for her circle, "this was agony piled on agony—Rose sat on the floor before the fire, weeping bitterly. . . . When Richmond fell I had given up all hope, so this was scarcely a new blow to me."[183]

Then a lightning bolt struck, and once more it was demonstrated that the unexpected, irrational, and fortuitous event has a larger place in history than the planned, expected, and rational occurrence.

183. Mordecai, Emma, *Diary*, Southern Hist. Coll., Univ. of N.C. Library.

Epilogue

"AMERICANS may reflect that it was perhaps fortunate for the future psychology of the nation, and for its national memories during long decades to come, that the war, which had filled four years with sullen rumblings and confused clamor, should end with a clap of thunder in the sudden murder of the Chief Magistrate, an event which caught the horrified attention of the civilized world, writing 'finis' to America's agonizing years of violence and bloodshed, and lifting the dead President to a position where he would be apotheosized by later generations, the influence of his deeds and words deepened by the tragedy. . . . A fitting climax of the years of anger and butchery, it would help impress upon the American mind the terrible nature of the conflict. Although in its immediate results it was a long-felt disaster, its larger consequences were not so unhappy, for it seemed to give fuller meaning to the long contest, and enabled people to view their fallen Chief in a more heroic light, as William Cullen Bryant realized when he wrote in his elegiac poem that the assassination had placed Lincoln 'among the sons of light.' " [1]

Lincoln's task, these early April days, was that of Reconstruction. In his last public address on April 11, the President said, "We simply must begin with, and mould from, disorganized and discordant elements." He still advocated the plan by which Louisiana was being reorganized, but he was fully aware of the growing opposition to his relatively mild policies.

The events of Good Friday, April 14, 1865, and the following days of horror have been recorded, but to Nevins it is the meaning of that dreadful act that bears attention. "The assassination of Lincoln needs to be regarded more closely as part of the fabric of its time. It is not an isolated episode, or a set eruption of violence upon a detached stage as in a melodrama. The psychological tensions of that spring of 1865 should properly be measured and weighed—the force of the interrelated series of blows upon emotions North and South produced by Sherman's great march, Appomattox, the fall of the Confederacy, and the disbandment of armies. These formed the background of the irresponsible crime—all contributing together to test the country's moral fortitude and inner faith in itself." Assassination imposed a fourfold test on the American government and people, "all the more gruelling because it came on the very heels of victory, when men were feeling the first sense of true relief and relaxation in years." The first question confronting the nation was whether the government could be transferred from one fully tested, admired, and beloved leader to a new, untried national leader, Andrew Johnson. Secondly, would the assassination deepen the hatred between North and South? Thirdly, and most crucial, would the murder "divert national thought upon the problem of Reconstruction into sinister channels, and perhaps poison the politics of the country for years to come"? Lastly, important to the dignity of the nation, how would the judicial aspects of the case be carried out? Could there be a fair trial for the participants? [2] In this latter problem the nation did not emerge in so happy a light. The conspirators were captured, tried, and four were hanged, others imprisoned. Historians and legal scholars have harshly criticized many aspects of the trial and its punishments.

"The wave of sorrow that overspread the North, universal and heartfelt, was heightened by the sense of contrast with the jubilant victory cries which resounded only a few days before. . . . The Southern response to Lincoln's assassination was naturally less emotional than that of the North. It ran a wide gamut of emotions, from deep mourning and regret at one extremity, through callous indifference, to relief and rejoicing at the other extreme." [3] Fortunately, the "transfer of national authority to a new Administration headed by Andrew Johnson was effected quietly, decorously, and with an elevated dignity creditable to the republic." [4] Prompt action on Reconstruction was now clearly needed, and Johnson faced an angry crisis.

First he had to deal with the surrender to General Sherman of Joseph E. Johnston and his army in North Carolina. Sherman had tentatively granted terms to the Confederates that amounted almost to political reconstruction rather than the surrender of an army. Johnson had to disavow these terms and he did so, but the scars of the argument between the two Federal leaders remained. Other surrenders of smaller bodies continued until the gray hosts had melted away. On May 10 at Irwinville, Georgia, President Jefferson Davis was captured and imprisoned. The same day, Johnson proclaimed the insurrection virtually at an end.

Quickly, almost immediately after Appomattox, the great armies of the United States disbanded. There was a grand review in May in Washington, and then most of the soldiers of the Union went home in a remarkable display of government efficiency and with a minimum of confusion and disruption. Most of them made the transition to civilian life with surprisingly little difficulty, but with a full store of memories. Now the great war machine in its many facets had to be disbanded and mobilized for peace. "The sudden surplus of manpower and energy released by the end of the war found an outlet apart from the normal life of the nation—in a great Westward surge. . . . Without it, the absorption of thousands into the normal stream of life would have been much more difficult, or perhaps even impossible without severe economic dislocation." [5]

The country now developed into "a Mature Nation." "From the flame and ashes of the Civil War emerged, not instantaneously as in the Oriental fable, but slowly and gradually, a phoenix-like apparition—a new country, in the main a creation of evolution rather than revolution, its golden wings and feathers mingled with more familiar and time-tested adjuncts of flight and splendor." The shock of war had obscured old sentiments about the irresistible destiny of the nation. "Now succeeded a sense of release and relief. It was tinged with less exultation than men had anticipated; rather, it expressed simply a deep sense of happiness that the American people had regained their former sense of grandeur and beauty in their country. . . ." The changes of this momentous period "spring largely from internal forces that were not directly connected with the war itself." These included the westward movement, invention and technology, the diffusion of population, the increased productivity of agriculture, mining, and industry, and the accumulation of capital. They "had a purgative value, clearing the mind of the nation, as it cleansed the bosom of the people of old prejudices, misunderstandings, and passions which would have yielded to no less powerful and painful a medicine." [6]

Nevins does not believe that the question of the inevitability of the war can ever be settled; it is essentially a useless question beset with too many imponderable factors. The war had, however, been a spiritual necessity, even if a cruel one, "an integral incident of growth and reorientation." The nation could face the future "with a lightened heart and fuller sense of freedom. . . . The republic emerged from the struggle . . . in the grip of some heady new impulses of vast extent and irresistible force." [7] There was the impulse that the railroad and telegraph gave to all enterprise; the discovery of incalculable natural wealth; the greater confidence of the rest of the world in American institutions; the increased availability of capital for development; the demand for labor. "Probably the greatest single change in American civilization in the war period, directly connected with the conflict, was the replacement of an unorganized nation by a highly organized society—organized, that is, on a national scale. . . . Most important of all, the prolonged duration of the conflict produced results in the thought, feeling and practices of the people proportionate to its length and multi-faceted force. At its end, Americans who looked about for its consequences, good and bad, found plenty of both. Some were elementary and superficial, such as the firm knotting of the Union tie, and the shattering of the many myths which had marked Southern thought and conduct. And some of the most striking and obvious of the elementary consequences were written into the new Thirteenth, Fourteenth, and Fifteenth Amendments to the Constitution, which in effect constituted the terms of a treaty of peace between North and South, and had all the effect of a far-reaching and adamantine compact. One prime result was a better understanding by the people of the nation of the true character of the huge American continent, so variegated, so radiantly beautiful, so well-stored with aesthetic as well as economic wealth." [8]

"Another profoundly important moral sequel of the Civil War, which originated during the conflict, was the enlargement and liberalization of attitudes toward the Negro, both North and South. No reflective American could doubt that, as Reconstruction began, the problem of race relations was not only still one of the greatest, but the most urgent, that the country faced. . . . The Civil War had brought the country emancipation from slavery, an institution deeply harmful to the white and the black alike, and the Fourteenth Amendment had brought the beginnings of a too-long-deferred acceptance of the principle of equality." [9] The war did not end the idea of black inferiority. On the other hand, it exploded the myth that abolition would mean destruction or confiscation of a great deal of Southern wealth.

"The war more or less directly affected every one of the 35,000,000 men, women, and children in the two sections, Northern and Southern, of the United States. It happily exploded many suppositions that Americans had long held and dreaded as probable results of a stubborn conflict." It did not "militarize" the people and failed to lead to adventures in foreign conquest. There was no intense subjugation of the South despite the beliefs of many. "The spirit of the republic in the year of victory was good. It was not boastful or arrogant, for repeated checks and defeats had taught lessons of humility." [10]

"America had long been a nation of dauntless explorers, and inventive pragmatists. Much of distinction in American life now logically found varied practical expressions, and the mechanical field admitted as high endeavors as any area of the arts and letters. . . . For all the general poverty of the American cultural scene by the end of the war, it had some aspects of undeniable distinction. . . . Another heartening fact was that, with the triumphant close of the war, the American people began to realize that they had larger destinies than those of a purely national character. . . . Now she faced a larger body of duties, for the republic must turn from responsibilities that were merely American to purposes of a cosmopolitan and international character. . . ." It was hoped by some that America "would now assume the leadership in the stern battle rising in all lands between tyranny and liberty, between privilege and equality, furnishing sympathy, moral encouragement, and the support of a successful, enduring, republican society, consistent in all its aims." [11]

"The sense of Americans in 1865 that they stood at the close of one era and the beginning of another, a sense which gave millions a new hopefulness and a more convinced belief in the national destiny, was confirmed and strengthened by the evident fact that the perspective of all mankind had been sharply and decisively revolutionized by Union victory in the war. To multitudes the world lost its constricted and limited appearance and wore a new freshness. It was suddenly evident to the American people that the United States had swiftly and unexpectedly, but undeniably, become one of the principal world powers, with a new set of responsibilities, challenges, and opportunities." [12]

NOTES

1. Nevins, *The War for the Union*, Vol. IV, *The Organized War to Victory, 1864–1865,* p. 319.
2. *Ibid.*, pp. 327–328.
3. *Ibid.*, p. 335.
4. *Ibid.*, p. 338.
5. *Ibid.*, pp. 390–391.
6. *Ibid.*, p. 392.
7. *Ibid.*, pp. 392–393.
8. *Ibid.*, pp. 395–396.
9. *Ibid.*, pp. 397–398.
10. *Ibid.*, pp. 400–401.
11. *Ibid.*, pp. 402–404.
12. *Ibid.*, p. 404.

Index